The Illustrated Encyclopedia of the World's

TANKS
AND
FIGHTING VEHICLES

The Illustrated Encyclopedia of the World's
TANKS
AND
FIGHTING VEHICLES

A technical directory of major combat vehicles from World War 1
to the present day

Chief author and consultant: Christopher F Foss

a Salamander book

Published by Salamander Books Limited
LONDON

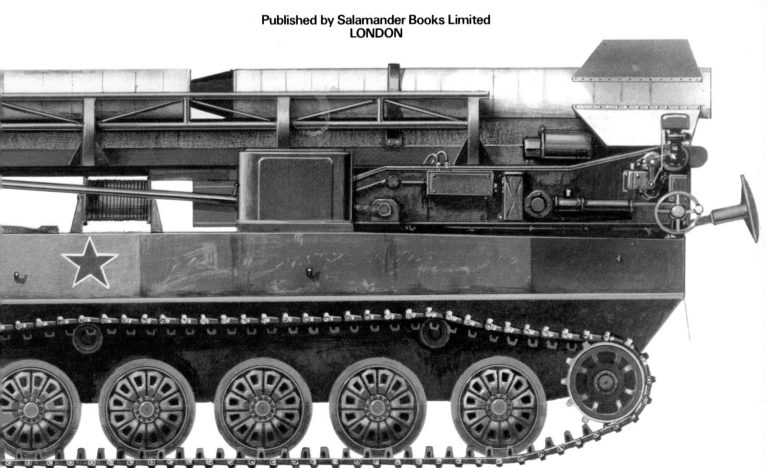

A Salamander Book

Published by Salamander Books Ltd.,
Salamander House,
27 Old Gloucester Street,
London WC1N 3AF
United Kingdom

© Salamander Books Ltd. 1977

ISBN 0 86101 003 5

Distributed in Australia/New Zealand by
Summit Books, a division of Paul Hamlyn Pty Ltd.,
Sydney, Australia

Credits

Editor: Ray Bonds

Designers: Ian Reeve, Rod and Andrew Sutterby, C. Steer

Colour drawings: Profile Publications Ltd.,
Terry Hadler, Tom Brittain, Mike Roffe, David Palmer, John W. Wood

Line drawings: Terry Hadler

Filmset by SX Composing, Leigh-on-Sea, Essex, England

Colour reproduction by Paramount Litho, Basildon, Essex, England

Tritone colour reproduction by Web Offset Reproductions,
32 Paul Street, London EC2, and
Adtype Ltd., 29 Clerkenwell Road, London EC1, England

Printed in Belgium by Henri Proost et Cie, Turnhout

The Authors

**Consultant and Chief Author:
Christopher F. Foss**
Christopher Foss has made a study of the
world's armoured fighting vehicles over
several years and is recognised as a leading
authority on this and allied subjects. He is
currently Weapons Correspondent for
Defence magazine and has written hundreds of technical articles and commen-
taries on military equipment for publications
throughout the world, including *Armies
and Weapons, Armor, Battle, Defence
Africa, Defence Latin America* and *Defence
Materiel Great Britain.* He also wrote some
of the Profile Publications series of booklets
AFV/Weapons Profiles. He has several
authoritative books to his credit already,
including *Jane's World Armoured Fighting
Vehicles, Jane's Pocketbook of Modern
AFVs, Jane's Pocketbook of Towed Artillery,* besides contributing annually to *Jane's
Infantry Weapons* and *Jane's Weapon
Systems.* He is also author of four books in
an Ian Allan series: *Armoured Fighting
Vehicles of the World, Infantry Weapons of
the World* (with T. J. Gander), *Artillery of
the World* and *Military Vehicles of the
World.* He also contributed to Salamander's
*The Encyclopedia of Land Warfare in the
20th Century.*

John F. Milsom
Having been educated at a military public school and at the Portsmouth College of Technology, John Milsom served with the Scientific Civil Service of the British Ministry of Defence, where he was concerned with several military studies associated with armoured warfare and the tactical and scientific development of weapon systems. This involved long terms of employment in war games and field trials. In the meantime he also began his career as a military historian and left the Civil Service to carry out this work full-time in 1972. Following a series of articles in various technical military publications, his first book was published in 1970, entitled *Russian Tanks 1900-1970*. He has since written several other books, including *German Half-Tracks of World War II, German Armoured Cars of World War II, German Military Transport of World War II, Russian Tanks of World War II, Armoured Fighting Vehicles,* and *The Crusader,* besides a series of weapons handbooks, several of the Profile Publications *AFV/ Weapons Profile* series and numerous other booklets. His main specialist interest is the development of the mechanisation of Soviet ground forces.

Colonel John Stafford Weeks
Colonel John Weeks is currently Project Manager, Infantry Weapons, British Ministry of Defence, and he is also a lecturer in infantry weapons at RMCS Shrivenham, England. Commissioned in July 1948, he has served with the British Army in many parts of the world, including the Middle East, Far East, Mediterranean, Scandinavia, USA and Western Europe. He is a military adviser to the authoritative annual publications, *Jane's Weapon Systems, Jane's Infantry Weapons* and *Brassey's Infantry Weapons,* and he has written several books himself, including *Men Against Tanks, Airborne Equipment, Infantry Weapons of World War II* and *Military Small Arms of the Twentieth Century.* He is also the author of numerous articles on military equipment in various publications, including *Ordnance, American Rifleman, British Army Review, War Monthly* and *Guns Review.*

Captain Geoffrey Tillotson, RAOC
Geoffrey Tillotson, BSc(Hons) Applied Science, is currently an Ammunition Technical Officer, British Army, responsible for antitank guided missiles. His Army service has included duty in Germany, Denmark, Norway, and Kenya, and his avid interest in ordnance dates back more than 12 years.

Richard M. Ogorkiewicz, MSc(Eng), ACGI, DIC, CEng, FIMechE
Richard M. Ogorkiewicz is a mechanical engineer with an international reputation in the field of the technology of armoured fighting vehicles. During the past twenty-eight years he has written extensively on the subject in professional journals throughout the world and is the author of two widely recognised text books—*Armour* and *Design and Development of Fighting Vehicles.* He has also lectured on the subject at the invitation of the military authorities of several countries, as far apart as the United States, Sweden and Brazil, and has been widely consulted on the design and development of tanks and other armoured fighting vehicles.

Editor's Acknowledgements

A great many people have helped us to produce this book. They include manufacturers of tanks and other armoured fighting vehicles, defence organisations of many different countries, military archives all over the world, and individuals who have scoured their photographic collections on our behalf. We sincerely thank them all.

The book is sectionalised into the nations in which the armoured fighting vehicles were manufactured, and the nations are arranged alphabetically. Within the sections the vehicles are dealt with chronologically by year of entry into service, although where it was not possible, within this strict order, to give the vehicle the space it deserved, the order has been slightly modified.

Ray Bonds

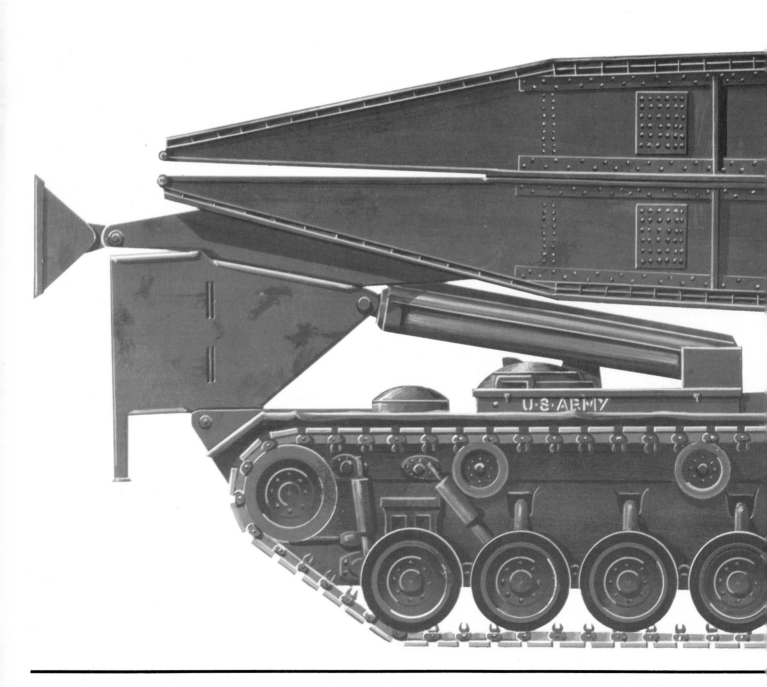

Contents

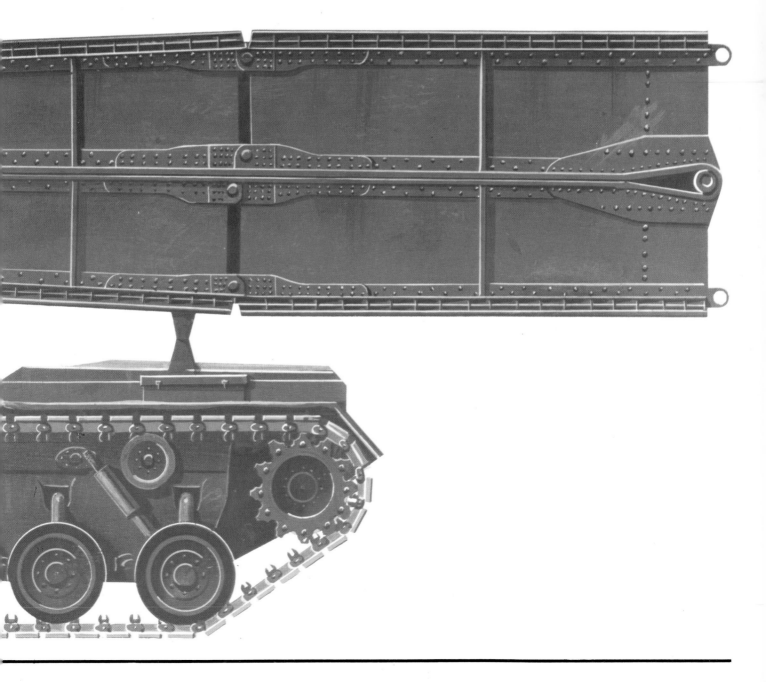

Foreword

by Richard M. Orgorkiewicz,
MSc(Eng), ACGI, DIC, CEng, FIMechE.

The entry of armoured fighting vehicles on the world scene is generally associated with the appearance of tanks in the middle of World War I. In fact, the first use of tanks on the Western Front in 1916 was preceded by the development of armoured cars, which started in 1900. Moreover, the broad concept of fighting vehicles may be traced as far back as the war-chariots, which were widely used in the Near East in the second millenium BC, or to the siege vehicles used by the Assyrians in the 9th century BC.

Nevertheless, the importance of armoured fighting vehicles dates from the middle of World War I, when the first tanks were built in Britain and in France in response to the contemporary tactical problem of attacking enemy trench lines. They proved very successful in this, as the British tanks first showed at the battle of Cambrai in 1917, and thus provided a means of breaking the deadlock of trench warfare.

Once tanks were built, it was soon realised that they were also capable of performing other roles, such as close support of the infantry and the exploitation of breakthroughs, which horse cavalry was no longer able to perform. A few far-sighted military thinkers, like General Fuller and Captain Liddell Hart in Britain and General Estienne in France, perceived that the potentialities of tanks extended even further — to being the principal equipment of future ground forces. They advocated, therefore, that armies be reorganised around tanks. But tanks needed to be developed further before such radical ideas could be put into effect.

Considerable progress in the development of tanks did, in fact, take place during the 1920s and early 1930s, as was shown by the much greater speed of tanks built by the Vickers-Armstrong company in Britain and by Christie in the United States. Progress was also made towards new types of formations which would make more effective use of tanks. A major step in this direction was the Experimental Mechanised Force which the British Army formed in 1927 and within 10 years several armies created new formations based on tanks.

The most successful of the new formations proved to be the *Panzer* divisions of the German Army, which played a decisive

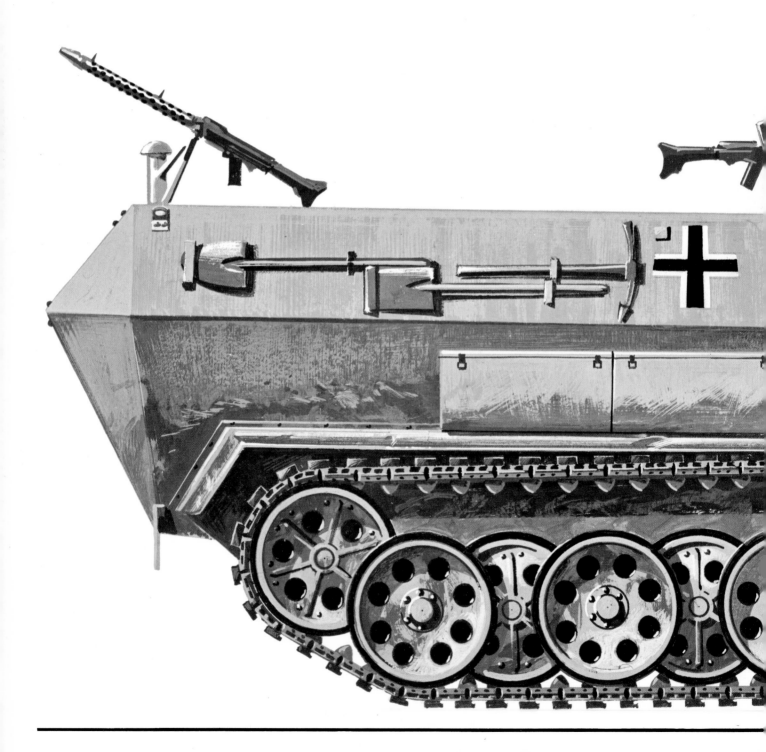

role in the *Blitzkrieg* campaigns against Poland in 1939 and France in 1940. In these and subsequent campaigns of World War II *Panzer* and other armoured divisions demonstrated that they had both greater striking power and greater mobility than the infantry divisions on which armies had been based. They became, therefore, the decisive element in ground warfare and their number grew in all armies. Thus, the German Army expanded its *Panzer* divisions from six to more than 30 and the Soviet Army ended the war in 1945 with about as many armoured formations, as did the Western Allies.

The growth in the number of armoured formations went hand in hand with greatly increased production of tanks and other armoured vehicles. The United States alone built 88,000 tanks and the Soviet Union produced about as many. The design of tanks had also made great progress. In particular, their gun power rose from that of guns of 37mm to 47mm to the 88mm gun of the German Tiger or even the 122mm gun of the Russian Stalin tanks.

Yet, in spite of the decisive role played by tanks in World War II, their future has been questioned frequently. The principal reason for this has been the development of new anti-tank weapons, such as the 'bazooka' rocket-launchers and, most recently, anti-tank guided missiles. However, none of these weapons has affected the fundamental value of tanks, which is their ability to make weapons mounted in them more mobile and, therefore, more effective. In consequence, tanks have lost none of their importance, even though their armour can be perforated. Instead, they have become the primary equipment of the ground forces which consist more and more of formations based on tanks and other armoured vehicles.

The fact that tanks have lost none of their importance since World War II was vividly demonstrated during the Korean War in the early 1950s and, more recently, during the Arab-Israeli wars of 1967 and 1973. It is also demonstrated by the continuing development of tanks, which has produced in recent years a number of greatly improved new models, and by their large scale deployment in critical areas like Western Europe where NATO has a total of 7,000 tanks to face some 19,000 Russian and other Warsaw Pact tanks. Such large scale deployment of tanks shows clearly that they are a major element of military strength and, consequently, an important instrument of political power.

AUSTRO-DAIMLER ARMOURED CAR

Crew: 4–5.
Armament: One (later two) 7.92mm machine-guns.
Armour: 0.16in (4mm) maximum.
Dimensions: Length 15ft 11in (4.6m); width 5ft 9in (1.76m); height 9ft (2.743m).
Weight: 6614lbs (3,000kg).
Engine: Four-cylinder petrol engine developing 40hp.
Performance: Road speed 28mph (45km/h); range 155 miles (250km).
History: Prototype built in 1904 but not placed in production.

The Austro-Daimler armoured car (or Daimler *Panzerwagen*) had the distinction of being the first armoured car to be fitted with a turret which could be traversed through 360°, and the first armoured car to be provided with all-wheel (4×4) drive. The vehicle was designed by an officer of the Austro-Hungarian Army with the assistance of Paul Daimler, who was the son of Gottleib Daimler, one of the pioneers of the automotive industry. The prototype was completed at the Daimler factory at Wiener-Neustadt in 1904. It consisted basically of a 4×4 armoured body with the engine at the front, driver and commander behind the engine and the dome-shaped turret at the rear. When first built, the vehicle was armed with a single water-cooled Maxim machine-gun, but in 1905 a new turret was installed which was open at the rear and fitted with twin water-cooled machine-guns. An interesting feature of this vehicle was that the driver and co-driver's seats could be raised when the vehicle was not in action to give them improved visibility. The Austro-Hungarian armoured car was demonstrated to both

the German and Austro-Hungarian armies but attracted little real interest and was never placed in production. Its main features were copied in most subsequent armoured cars. Emperor Franz Josef was not impressed with the armoured car as it is said that it made too much noise and scared his horses!

Above: The Austro-Daimler armoured car of 1904 was the first to have a fully-rotating turret and all-wheel (4x4) drive. The innate conservatism of the German and Austro-Hungarian army staffs meant that the vehicle was never put into production.

SAURER ARMOURED PERSONNEL CARRIER

Crew: 2 plus 8.
Armament: One 20mm Oerlikon 204 GK cannon.
Armour: 8mm–12mm (0.32–0.47in).
Dimensions: Length 17ft 8in (5.4m); width 8ft 2in (2.5m); height (with turret) 7ft 1in (2.17m).
Weight: Combat 29,762lbs (13,500kg).
Ground pressure: 7.25lb/in² (0.51kg/cm²).
Engine: Model 4FA six-cylinder diesel developing 250hp at 2,400rpm.
Performance: Road speed 40mph (65km/h); range 186 miles (300km); vertical obstacle 2ft 8in (0.8m); trench 7ft 3in (2.2m); gradient 75 per cent.
History: Entered service with the Austrian Army in 1961. Production complete, not exported.
(Note: data relate to the Saurer 4K 4FA-G APC.)

After the end of World War II, Austria was governed by the four major powers (United States, Britain, France and the Soviet Union). In 1955 the four powers withdrew and Austria became a neutral country. When the

Austrian Army was formed, much of its initial equipment came from Russia and the United States. One of the Austrian Army's urgent requirements was for a fully-tracked armoured personnel carrier. The Saurer company started design work in 1956 and the first prototype was completed in 1958, and after further development work the first production models, known as 4K 4F, were completed in 1961. The first model was armed with an American 0.5in (12.7mm) Browning machine-gun and provision was made for mounting up to four 7.62mm MG42 machine-guns around the top of the troop compartment. The last production model was the 4K 4FA-G. This is armed with a turret-mounted 20mm Oerlikon 204 GK cannon in a GAD AOA turret. This gun has an elevation of +70° and a depression of −12°, and traverse is a full 360°. A total of 425 rounds of 20mm ammunition is carried, of which 100 are for ready use. The Saurer APC can ford to a depth of 3ft 3in (1m). It is not, however, provided with an NBC system. There are a number of variants

of the basic vehicle including an ambulance, artillery fire-control vehicle, anti-aircraft fire-control vehicle, radio vehicle and 81mm mortar carrier. In addition there have been numerous trials vehicles. Further development by Saurer (taken over by Steyr–Daimler–Puch in 1970) has resulted in the *Panzerjäger* K tank-destroyer, armed with a turret-mounted 105mm gun, and the 4KH 7FA-B armoured recovery vehicle, both of these being in service with the Austrian Army.

Below: The Saurer 4K 4FA-G—last production model of the Saurer series of APCs in Austrian Army service since 1961. It is armed with a turret-mounted 20mm Oerlikon cannon. Variants include ambulance, fire-control and radio vehicles and an 81mm mortar carrier. The 105mm Panzerjäger K tank-destroyer and the 4KH 7FA-B ARV, developed from the Saurer series since 1970, are both currently in service.

MINERVA, SAVA AND MORS ARMOURED CARS

Belgium was the first country to be invaded by the Germans during World War I. At first the Belgians used a variety of standard cars fitted with machine-guns to harass the advancing Germans. Some of these were soon provided with simple armoured shields for their weapons, and by mid-August 1914 the Belgians had started to armour the complete vehicle. The Minerva armoured car had a hull of 5mm (0.2in) armour, this being provided with a vision port for the driver and in the front, with single ports in each side of the hull and in the rear. The top of the crew compartment was open, and as no doors were provided this provided the normal means of entry and exit. The engine was provided with armour protection and there were two doors in front of the radiator. Armament consisted of a single machine-gun, this being provided with a semi-circular shield. There were numerous different models of the Minerva armoured car, and late production vehicles had a turret similar to that fitted to the SAVA armoured car. The chassis of the Minerva was similar to the civilian car but its rear wheels were dual to compensate for some of the additional weight. The Minerva remained in service until the 1930s, and was then followed by improved armoured cars such as the SAVA and Mors. The former had a chassis supplied by the *Société Anversoise pour Fabrication de Voitures Automobiles*, with the armoured hull supplied by the Cockerill company. This had better armour protection than the earlier vehicle and the driver's armour was well sloped in an effort to deflect bullets. A hull door was also provided. Armament consisted of a turret-mounted 8mm Hotchkiss machine-gun, mounted in a turret unusual in that it was dome shaped and open at the rear. When Antwerp fell to the advancing Germans in October 1914, the Minerva factory was also lost. The Belgian Army already had some Mors armoured cars fitted with machine-guns and some armour, so it was decided to bring these up to armoured car standard. Armament consisted of a turret-mounted 37mm gun, provided with a shield; if required a Hotchkiss machine-gun could be mounted above the 37mm gun. This armoured car had a drawback similar to that of the Minerva, in that the only means of entering and leaving the vehicle was by climbing over the side of the hull. Some of these Mors armoured cars, together with some Peugeot armoured cars, served in Russia between 1915 and 1917 before returning to Belgium. Armoured cars played a vital role in the early days of World War I, but once trench warfare became established they were of virtually no use as their cross-country capabilities were very limited.

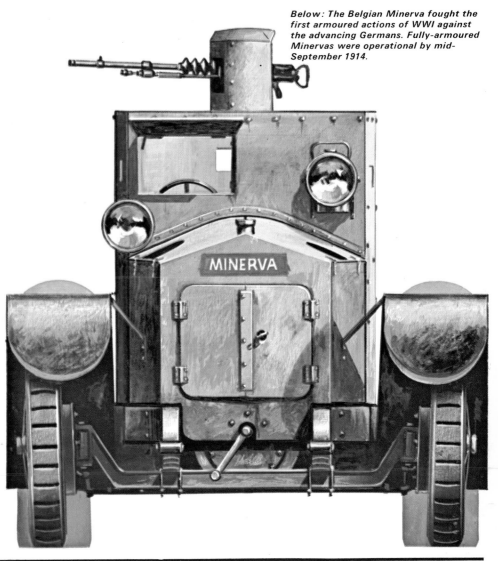

Below: The Belgian Minerva fought the first armoured actions of WWI against the advancing Germans. Fully-armoured Minervas were operational by mid-September 1914.

EE-9 ARMOURED CAR

Crew: 3.
Armament: One 90mm gun; one 7.62mm machine-gun co-axial with main armament; four smoke dischargers.
Armour: 6mm–20mm (0.23–0.79in).
Dimensions: Length (hull) 17ft (5.18m); width 8ft 9in (2.63m); height 7ft 9in (2.36m).
Weight: Combat 26,500lbs (12,020kg).
Engine: Mercedes-Benz (built in Brazil) Model OM 352 six-cylinder diesel developing 172hp at 2,800rpm.
Performance: Road speed 62mph (100km/h); range 497 miles (800km); vertical obstacle 2ft (0.6m); gradient 60 per cent.
History: Entered service in 1973. In service in Brazil and Qatar. Still in production.

Some South American armies acquired armoured vehicles as early as the 1920s, but it was not until 1942–43 that the first armoured vehicle was designed and built in South America. This was the Argentinian Nahuel tank, of which less than 20 were built. After World War II there were so many surplus vehicles on the market that no further design work took place. Then in the mid-1960s Brazil designed and built two AFVs. The VBB was a 4×4 vehicle which did not progress beyond the prototype stage, whilst the tracked Cutia-Vete TI AI was built in some numbers. In 1970 the Engesa company, well known for its range of tactical trucks, built the prototype of a 6×6 amphibious armoured personnel carrier known as the EE-11 Urutu, which was placed in production in 1972. The EE-11 was followed late in 1970 by the EE-9 Cascavel 6×6 armoured car, or CCR (*Carro de Reconhecimento sobre Rodas*). This uses a number of EE-11 components. The Cascavel has a hull of all-welded steel construction with the driver at the front, turret with the commander

and gunner in the centre, and engine and transmission at the rear. Prototypes were armed with a 37mm gun as used on the American M8 Greyhound armoured car, but production vehicles have the same turret as fitted to the French AML 90 armoured car. This has a 90mm gun and a 7.62mm co-axial machine-gun, these having an elevation of +15° and a depression of −8°, and a traverse of 360°. Two smoke dischargers are mounted on each side of the turret. Twenty rounds of 90mm

and 2,400 rounds of 7.62mm machine-gun ammunition are carried. Standard equipment includes bullet-proof tyres and powered steering. An air-conditioning system can be installed if required. The EE-9 has no amphibious capability but can ford streams to a depth of 3ft 3in (1m). It is interesting to note that Qatar, which has the pick of military equipment, placed an order for the Cascavel armoured car at a very early stage.

Right: The EE-9 Cascavel armoured car in service with the Brazilian Army since 1973 was developed by the Engesa Company from the EE-11 Urutu APC. It mounts a 90mm gun and 7.62mm mg in the French AML-90 turret.

Britain

Having started the whole idea of armoured warfare, Britain proved to be remarkably slow to develop it to its logical conclusion. Conservatism in tactical thinking was probably more evident in Britain between the wars than in any other country. It has always been said that the British, like the French too, were supremely well equipped in 1939 to fight the battles of 1919, and to a great extent the British were equally well equipped mentally. The general approach to the use of tanks reflected the trench warfare attitude which hampered all other arms, and this despite the highly successful and innovative trials which had been carried out during the twenties and early thirties.

The trials with the Experimental Mechanised Force had fairly clearly shown the way to use armoured formations, and the strident voice of Liddell Hart had broadcast the lessons loudly enough for anyone to

hear, yet the British insisted on maintaining three different types of tank, as if there was to be some curious form of social class in armoured warfare. Light tanks were used for reconnaissance, their armour and weapons too light for anything else. They had grown up from the one-man tank idea of the 1920s, an idea that was fundamentally wrong, but which in the end led to the useful and successful infantry carrier. The light tank was soon shown to be little better than cannon-fodder, particularly in the desert where it could not easily hide from hostile gunfire.

The next class was the cruiser, derived from the Whippet of 1918 and meant as a fast, wide-ranging armoured cavalry horse. It was the most promising idea of all, but to get the required performance armour had to be sacrificed to keep the weight

down. As with all British tanks, the cruisers were under-engined. They were also under-gunned, and this told heavily against them in the long-range battles in the desert where the German tanks could out-shoot them with ease. But the cruisers were meant to engage other tanks, and that was right. The tragedy was that they were never given the equipment to do it properly.

The third class of tank was the 'I' or Infantry tank. This was World War I with a vengeance. It was a slow-moving, heavily armoured vehicle armed mainly, or even solely, with machine-guns, and intended to move with a walking infantry advance and engage enemy machine-gun nests or strongpoints. The heavy armour was to keep out

light anti-tank fire and the vehicle was never meant to get into actual combat with another tank. The result was a whole series of tanks which were more or less invulnerable to small guns, but which were so pitifully armed that they were all but incapable of inflicting any damage on their opponent. The requirement to move at little more than walking pace led to gross under-powering and the almost total inability to manoeuvre against the more agile Germans. The small turrets could only accept small guns, and were difficult if not impossible to up-gun successfully. Although many of these tanks were left behind at Dunkirk, the idea persisted and indeed it has not been entirely eradicated to this day, for British tanks are still the slowest and lowest powered among those of the major nations.

Despite the lessons of the pre-war experiments, the British never learned to use their armoured formations as separate shock troops, though the desert battles showed some signs of the idea developing, and in this may lie the whole failing of the philosophy. Modern British tanks such as the Chieftain are the best protected of any, but their use in war is still very much that of mobile gun platforms in support of infantry, despite the introduction of integrated battle groups of all arms in the BAOR.

It is not a happy history, and one would have wished it otherwise. Timidity and lack of tactical enterprise hampered the designer and builder and the user, throwing away the incomparable lead gained in World War I.

Column of British Crusader and Sherman tanks moving forward in North Africa. The tank in the foreground is a Crusader I (CS).

13

ROLLS-ROYCE ARMOURED CAR

Crew: 3.
Armament: One 0.303in Vickers machine gun.
Armour: 8mm or 9mm (0.31in or 0.35in).
Dimensions: Length 16ft 2in (4.92m); width 6ft 4in (1.93m); height 8ft 4in (2.53m).
Weight: 7,840lbs (3,556kg) — 1914 Pattern; 8,512lbs (3,861kg) — 1920 Pattern Mark I; 9,296lbs (4,217kg) — 1924 Pattern Mark I.
Engine: Rolls-Royce six-cylinder inline water-cooled petrol engine developing 45-50hp.
Performance: Speed 45mph (72.5km/h); range 180 miles (288km).
History: Produced by the Admiralty for RNAS armoured car squadrons in 1914, and modified by the War Office in 1920 for service with the Army and RAF. Supplied to Eire and various colonies and still in service for internal security duties in India in 1945.

The Rolls-Royce was the most successful of the rash of armoured cars built on to existing commercial chassis in the first days of World War I. A simple body of thin sheet steel was built on to a Silver Ghost car chassis, and a light round turret placed above the crew compartment. At the back was a short platform for carrying external loads. Twin rear wheels were fitted, and two spare wheels were carried. There were no episcopes or vision blocks, the crew using slits in the armour to see out. The single Vickers gun was mounted on a yoke in the turret and projected through a hole in the armour plate. Some protection for the gunner was provided by a moving plate on the turret face. In this guise the Rolls-Royce became the most widely used armoured car in the entire war. It saw action in France, Egypt, the Dardanelles, East Africa, Russia and the guerilla warfare in Arabia. It survived to be used in police work throughout the Empire in the inter-war years. In 1920 the War Office built a batch of armoured cars based on the 1914 Pattern, but improving on it: the wheels were disc type, in place of the original spoked pattern, the turret was built up slightly and louvres were put into the armoured doors over the radiator. In 1924 another pattern emerged, with slight variations to the body and turret: a cupola for the commander was added to the turret top, the extra weight requiring larger wheels and wider tyres. The Vickers was given a ball mounting in the front of the turret. In 1940 there were roughly 75 of these cars still in service with the British Army, and at least as many in the colonies and dominions. Those in Britain were used for local defence but never saw action. At Habbaniyah in Iraq a small number of RAF cars fought against Rashid Ali's uprising in 1941 and the 11th Hussars used them in the early desert campaigns in 1941. These Egyptian cars were basically 1924 Pattern, but had been further modified for desert use by the fitting of an open-topped turret and the changing of the armament to a Boys anti-tank rifle on the right of the turret and a large-bore smoke discharger on the left. A Bren light machine-gun was on a pintle mount at the rear of the turret. Sand channels were carried along the running boards, water and petrol cans were strapped on both sides, and the platform at the back was loaded with camouflage nets and bed rolls. By this time the old Rolls was quite unsuited for modern war, and as soon as some modern cars were delivered the Rolls cars were quietly withdrawn and scrapped.

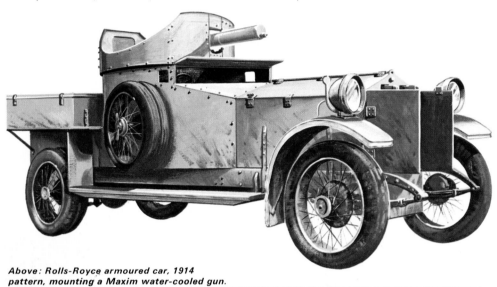

Above: Rolls-Royce armoured car, 1914
pattern, mounting a Maxim water-cooled gun.

LITTLE WILLIE LANDSHIP

Crew: 2 plus 2 or 4 gunners.
Armament: As first built, one 2pounder automatic gun in a fixed, dummy turret; one .303in (7.7mm) Maxim machine-gun; a varying number of .303in (7.7mm) Lewis light machine-guns.
Armour: 6mm (0.23in).
Dimensions (as first built): Length (less steering tail) 18ft 2in (5.45m); width 9ft 4in (2.8m); height 10ft 2in (3.05m).
(After rebuild and removal of turret): as above, except height 8ft 0½in (2.41m).
Weight: 40,320lbs (18,289kg) as first built.
Ground pressure: unknown.
Engine: Daimler six-cylinder inline water-cooled petrol engine developing 105hp at 1,000rpm.
Performance: Road speed 2mph (3.2km/h); cross-country speed ¾mph (1km/h); vertical obstacle 1ft (0.3m) on Bullock tracks; vertical obstacle 2ft (0.6m) on later tracks; trench 4ft (1.2m), later increased to 5ft (1.5m); gradient 30 per cent.
History: Built by William Foster & Co Ltd in August 1915, and first tested on September 6, 1915. Rebuilt with new tracks during October and November. The vehicle is still in existence at the Royal Armoured Corps Museum at Bovington in Dorset.

'Little Willie', the immediate predecessor of the 'tank', was the first successful project of the Landship Committee, set up in February 1915 by Mr Winston Churchill, then First Lord of the Admiralty. This committee, largely composed of Admiralty personnel, was charged with designing and producing a number of armed and armoured 'landships' with a view to breaking the deadlock of trench warfare that had set in in France. Army interest at this stage was minimal. The Royal Navy had by now amassed considerable experience in the operation of armoured cars in France, but knowledge of cross-country mobility was very limited, so the Committee, aided by such experts as Colonel E. O. Swinton and that venerable exponent of mechanisation Colonel Crompton, initiated a number of projects using vehicles or track systems available at that time. By the summer of 1915, Commander Hetherington was tackling 'Big Wheeled' landships at the William Foster works, the experimental Armoured Car Squadron (RN) at Wormwood Scrubbs was testing a three-tracked Killen Strait tractor, and Colonel Crompton was designing a range of tracked landships based on the British Pedrail tracks and the American Bullock Creeping Grip tractor. Progress with these experiments was slow, and so on July 29 the Committee instructed Mr Tritton of Fosters to construct a landship using a pair of lengthened Bullock tracks recently ordered from America. To assist him with this project, Lieutenant W. G. Wilson joined him from the Royal Naval Air Service. The 'Bullock Track machine' bore a striking resemblance to one of Crompton's designs, although Crompton was not directly involved. In essence the vehicle was a rectangular box of boiler plate, riveted to an angle-iron frame, mounted on a pair of lengthened Bullock Creeping Grip tracks, and balanced at the rear by a pair of 4ft 6in (1.37m) wheels on a steerable axle. A fixed dummy turret was fitted on top, and for the initial trials full armament was carried. Internally, the 105hp Daimler engine was located at the rear, facing aft. The drive from the clutch ran forward to a two-speed gearbox, worm and differential (inherited from the Foster wheeled tractor) located just behind the driving seats. Roller chains took the drive back from each end of the differential shaft to sprockets on the central bogie pivot, and further roller chains inside the track frames took the drive back to the rear track sprockets. The two 'drivers' sat on a full width bench seat at the front of the vehicle. The right-hand man controlled the engine through foot pedals and a central gear lever, and could initiate gentle turns by means of a steering wheel acting through cables to the rear axle. For tight turns the left-hand man could apply band brakes to either end of the differential shaft, thus locking either track. This machine was tried out over a set of obstacles near Lincoln, and several short-comings were revealed, notably in the tracks, which were made up of cast components. They tended to sag away from the frames, and then lay themselves in a curve while the rest of the machine continued in a straight line! After a couple of false starts, Tritton designed a completely new track system, using pressed-steel track plates fixed to separate links which 'locked' into guideways on the bottom of the track frames. Included in the suspension were laterally-sprung rollers to take up the side forces. These tracks were fitted to the machine during November, and when tried out in December proved an immediate success, as well as increasing the vehicle's obstacle-crossing ability. After this Little Willie fell out of the limelight as new vehicles were built. Its essential features were carried on into 'Mother', the first of the rhomboidal tanks, however.

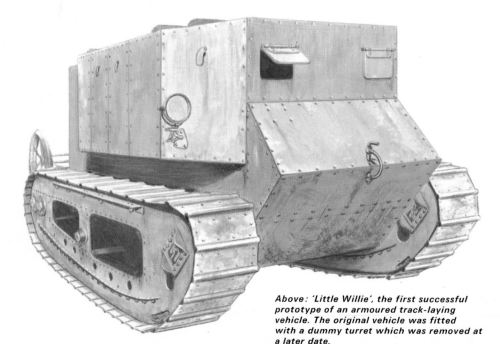

Above: 'Little Willie', the first successful
prototype of an armoured track-laying
vehicle. The original vehicle was fitted
with a dummy turret which was removed at
a later date.

MARK I TANK

Mk 1 (male), Mk 1 (female)
Crew: 8.
Armament: (Male) two 6pounder QF guns; four 8mm Hotchkiss machine-guns. (Female) four .303in (7.7mm) Vickers machine-guns; one 8mm Hotchkiss machine-gun.
Armour: 6mm–12mm (0.23–0.47in).
Dimensions: Length 32ft 6in (9.75m); male width 13ft 9in (4.12m); female width 14ft 4in (4.3m); height 8ft 0½in (2.41m).
Weight: Combat 62,720lbs (28,450kg) for male; 60,480lbs (27,434kg) for female.
Ground pressure: 26lb/in^2 (1.8kg/cm^2) at 1in (25.4mm) sinkage.
Power/weight ratio: 3.75hp/t.
Engine: Daimler six-cylinder inline water-cooled petrol engine developing 105hp at 1,000rpm.
Performance: Speed 3.7mph (5.95km/h); range 23½ miles (37.8km); vertical obstacle 4ft 6in (1.35m); trench 11ft 6in (3.45m); gradient 24 per cent.
History: A total of 150 Mk.I tanks was built in 1916 by William Foster of Lincoln and the Metropolitan Carriage, Wagon and Finance Company of Wednesbury. Some 49 of these vehicles, the first tanks to see action, took part in the Battle of Flers-Courcelette in September 1916, and Mk.I vehicles were in use for various purposes right to the end of the war.

During the building of 'Little Willie' at Fosters in 1915, Lieutenant Wilson produced a second design to meet the revised War Office requirement of crossing an 8ft (2.44m) trench and surmounting a 4ft 6in (1.37m) parapet. The high prow that this requirement dictated resulted in the characteristic rhomboidal shape that remained virtually unaltered to the end of the war. The Landship Committee authorised Fosters to proceed with this machine, and on January 16, 1916 the prototype, known as 'Mother' (also as the Wilson Machine or Big Willie) ran for the first time. It lived up to every expectation and dealt with a specimen 'battle-field obstacle course' with ease. As a result of the success of Mother, a firm order was placed for 100 Mk.I 'tanks', split between Fosters and the Metropolitan Carriage, Wagon and Finance Co. The order was later increased to 150. In May 1916 a new unit, known

for security as the Heavy Section, Machine Gun Corps, was formed to man these vehicles. Its commanding officer was Colonel Swinton, one of the earliest exponents of the 'landship' concept. The hull of the Mk.I tank was basically the rectangular box structure used on Little Willie, though made of armour plate this time. In place of pivoting track frames, the Mk.I Tank (and all subsequent heavy tanks of the war) had two large track frames, rhomboidal in outline, fixed to the sides of the hull. These frames had the high prows and large radius curves along their bottom edges that contributed to the machine's incredible performance over obstacles. The return of the track was carried up inclines at the rear and then ran forward along skidways on either side of the hull roof. Internally, the Daimler engine and Foster transmission were the same as those used in Little Willie, though in this case the engine was at the front, driving back to the gearbox and differential. Secondary gearboxes were built into the side of each track frame, and through these different ratios could be selected for each track, producing a form of geared turn. Steerable wheels were once more included at the rear, but proved such a liability in action that they were soon removed. The high top run of the track precluded the use of a turret for the main armament, and so, naval experience was drawn on in the fitting of 'sponsons' outside each track frame to carry one 6pounder gun (also provided from naval sources) and one machine-

gun on each side. These sponsons could, with considerable effort, be removed completely for the tank's rail movement. Some doubt was expressed, during the design stage, of a gun-armed tank's ability to hold off massed infantry, so half the production Mk.I tanks were completed as 'females', armed with two Vickers MGs in each sponson in place of the 6pounder guns. Conditions for the crews of these early tanks were incredible. The commander and driver sat high up at the front in a cupola, from which forward vision was very limited by the track horns, the two 'gearsmen' crouched on either side of the gearbox, and the gun crews knelt or squatted on tiny seats in the gun sponsons. Right in the middle sat the bellowing, unsilenced six-cylinder engine, and right around the crew compartment ran the unsprung tracks! Normal conversation was impossible, and simple instructions were passed by banging on the engine casing, together with hand signals! Much against the wishes of those who were campaigning for the first mass tank attack to be a surprise action on good ground, the Mk.I tanks were thrown in to action at Flers-Courcelette on September 15, 1916. The ill-fated Somme offensive had bogged down, the going was awful, and many crews were inexperienced. Forty-nine tanks started off, but very few reached their objectives. Those that did keep going, however, swept all opposition before them. Army staffs took note and orders for further tanks quickly followed.

Above right: Front and rear views of Tank Mk I, developed from the experimental 'Mother'. It was built in two basic types, 'male' and 'female', differing only in armament. A 'male' is shown here.

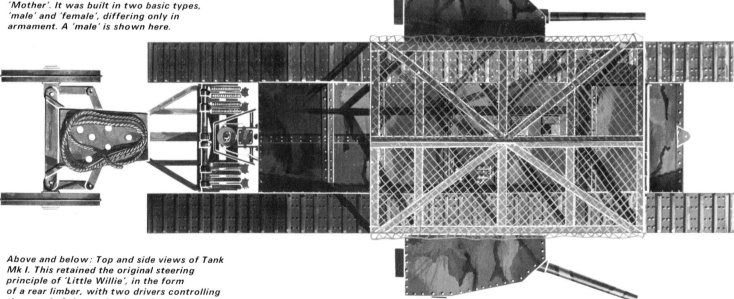

Above and below: Top and side views of Tank Mk I. This retained the original steering principle of 'Little Willie', in the form of a rear limber, with two drivers controlling the speed of the tracks through rods and cables to the rear gearbox. This tank is a 'male', with two 6-pounder QF guns mounted in side sponsons and a secondary armament of four 8mm Hotchkiss machine-guns.

MARK IV TANK

Mks IV (male and female).
Crew: 8.
Armament: Two 6pounder guns and four .303in Lewis machine-guns (Male); six .303in Lewis machine-guns (Female).
Armour: 12mm (0.47in) maximum; 6mm (0.25in) minimum.
Dimensions: Length 26ft 5in (8.05m); width 13ft 9in (4.19m); height 8ft 2in (2.48m).
Weight: Combat 62,720lbs (28,450kg) for the Male; 60,480lbs (27,434kg) for the Female.
Engine: Daimler six-cylinder water-cooled inline petrol engine developing 100hp or 125hp.
Performance: Speed 3.7mph (5.92km/h); range 35 miles (56km); vertical obstacle 4ft 6in (1.371m); trench 10ft (3.048m).
History: Entered service with the British Army in June 1917 and continued in use until the end of the war. Also used by Eire (one Mark V), Latvia (Mark V), Japan (one Mark IV), Russia, Canada, France and the United States (Mark V).

The Mark IV was the workhorse of the Tank Corps in World War I. It was derived from the Mark I and incorporated the improvements introduced in the Marks II and III, though all three of these early models were built only in comparatively small numbers. The Mark IV was the classic rhomboidal shape, and outwardly little different from its predecessors. There were many detailed changes, however: the crew compartment was better ventilated and escape hatches were located in the roof as well as the sides; a fan drew cooling air for the engine from inside the tank and blew it out through the radiator, which was at the back between the rear horns; and a silencer was fitted to the exhaust to reduce some of the deafening noise inside (on the earlier models silencers had been made by the crew from oil drums). The engine was improved, though the tank was still underpowered. Aluminium pistons allowed the revolutions to be increased, and so more power was developed. Twin carburettors improved the induction flow and a vacuum fuel system ensured that petrol reached the engine at all times. With the previous gravity arrangement, it was not uncommon for the engine to be starved of fuel while plunging into deep trenches or on steep slopes. The armour was the improved type fitted to the Marks II and III, and kept out the German tungsten-cored anti-tank bullets. Closer attention to riveting the joints reduced much of the bullet splash which had been a hazard on the Mark I. Splash was still a danger, however, and crews were issued with

leather face masks and goggles, though few could tolerate wearing them. The track-rollers were strengthened and so were the drive-chains from the gear-shafts. A plain idler wheel was fitted on the front, and wider tracks were tried. The second gear-shaft, which took a great deal of strain in action, had been found to twist, and in the Mark IV it was made from nickel steel. The sponsons were hinged to allow them to be swung in for rail travel. With the earlier marks the sponsons had to be unbolted and stowed inside the tank for shipment, and their removal and replacement was a long and tiring business. An unditching beam was fitted as standard and carried on top of the hull at the rear. Rails carried the beam clear of the cupola when it was used. Chains were provided to attach it to the tracks at each side, and once clear of the obstacle the beam could be recovered and restowed by the crew. The armament was not a happy story. Because of a shortage of Hotchkiss machine-guns Lewis guns were substituted, and this proved to be a mistake. The Lewis had a large round cooling-jacket and a larger hole had to be made in the armour for it. This allowed splinters and bullet splash to come inside, and the jacket itself was vulnerable to the intense small arms fire which a tank attracted. Later Mark IVs reverted to the Hotchkiss, much to the relief of the crews. The 6pounders were reduced in length from the original 40 calibres to 23 calibres. This had been done on some of the later Mark IIIs, which were virtually identical with the Mark IV. The shorter barrel meant that there was no danger of the muzzle being dug into the ground when the tank was crossing wide trenches. This had happened with the Mark Is, and the shortening also made the gun easier for the crew to handle when stowing the sponsons. The eight-man crew was distributed in the same way as in the Mark I. The driver sat in the cupola in front and controlled the speed and direction of the vehicle. Beside him was the commander, who also operated the brakes and fired the front machine-gun. At the rear, seated alongisde the engine, were the two gearsmen: they changed the secondary gears to each track, and so steered the tank in wide curves; sharp turns were by brakes to each side. These gearsmen were almost totally deafened all the time, and they changed their gears in response to hand signals from the driver. They also acted as gunners mates to the 6pounders. Two men fired the 6pounders, and the last two men fired the machine-guns in the rear of each sponson and generally assisted the 6pounder gunners if necessary. One of them would also be detailed to fire the rear machine-gun, which pointed out between the rear horns. There were no lights inside the tank,

and the only illumination came from daylight filtering through the vision slits and hatch covers. The gearsmen would have had to peer hard through the gloom and smoke from the engine to see their signals, and when the guns fired more smoke was added to the inside. In general, a Mark IV on the move was sheer hell for its crew. The temperature rapidly rose to almost 90° and in summer was well over that. The naked engine and gearbox screamed and shrieked and smoked, the radiator fan roared, the tracks clanged and banged round the hull, and the whole unsprung mass rolled and pitched over the ground, occasionally dropping suddenly into holes or trenches. A speed of 3mph 4.8km/h) was the maximum that any hull and crew could possibly stand, and in battle the noise and danger from bullets striking the sides, or shells exploding alongside, were enough to drive men almost witless. Few could tolerate the protective helmets or masks provided, and many crewmen were injured by being thrown around inside on rough ground, or falling against the hot engine and gearbox. For the gunners, targets appeared fleetingly in the restricted view of their vision slits, and most shooting was done 'on the fly' as the tank rolled on. Few shots were carefully aimed unless the vehicle was stationary. Nevertheless, the armament was formidable, especially that of the Male, and when the first German tanks appeared in April 1918 some Females were given a male sponson on the right-hand side so that they could protect themselves, the resulting marriage being called an 'Hermophrodite'. Altogether 420 Male and 595 Female Mark IVs were produced, and the type was used from the Battle of Flers in September 1917, through Cambrai, to the end of the war. Although there were five later marks of rhomboidal tank, only the Mark V was made in any quantity and by 1919 these large, slow moving, vulnerable vehicles were obsolete and were replaced by lighter, faster models.

Below left: The standard Mk IV tank of World War I. This was one of the most widely-used and most successful British tanks of the 1914-1918 war.

Below and bottom: Some British Mk IV tanks were captured by the Germans. Designated 'Beutepanzerwagen' (captured armoured vehicles), they were used by the Germans against the Allies.

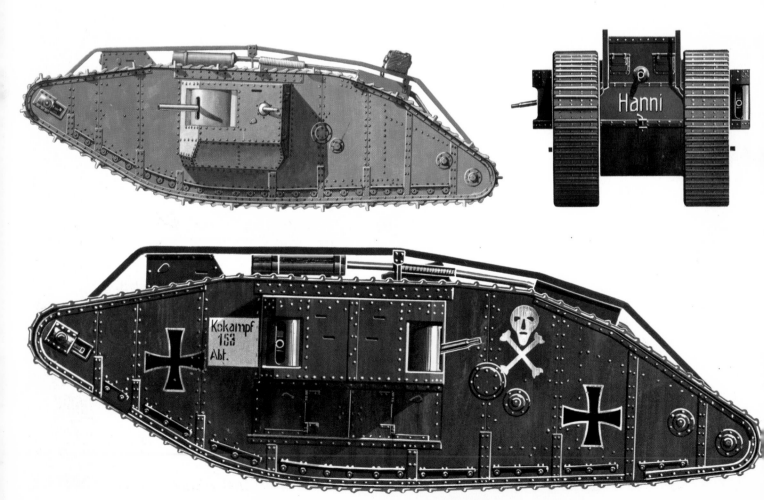

MEDIUM C TANK

Crew: 4.
Armament: Four .303in Hotchkiss machine-guns.
Armour: 14mm (0.55in) maximum; 6mm (0.25in) minimum.
Dimensions: Length 25ft 10in (7.856m); width 8ft 11in (2.71m); height 9ft 8in (2.94m).
Weight: Combat 43,680lbs (19,813kg).
Engine: Ricardo six-cylinder water-cooled inline petrol engine developing 150bhp at 1,200rpm.
Performance: Speed 7.9mph (12.64km/h); range 75 miles (120km); vertical obstacle 4ft 6in (1.371m); trench 10ft (3.352m); gradient unknown.
History: Designed in December 1917 and intended for the campaigns of 1919. The war ended before more than a small number were built, and these continued in service with the Tank Corps until the Vickers mediums came into service in 1923.

The Medium C would have been the main fighting tank in the proposed breakthrough of the German lines in 1919. It combined the experience of the Mark IV and the Medium A (Whippet) into one machine. The great improvement lay in the conditions for the crew, which was now grouped together in one compartment with voice tubes connecting each position. One man could control the tank, which had been impossible in the Mark IV, and the commander was placed in a small rotating cupola at the back of the turret where he had a good view. The engine was isolated in a compartment at the rear, which to some extent lowered the noise level and reduced the amount of smoke inside the vehicle. Ventilation was also improved, and the post-war Medium C tanks had extra armoured ventilators in the back of the turret. The suspension was uninspired, and reflected the designers' involvement with the earlier rhomboidal machines. The tracks ran all round the hull, and the bogies were unsprung. The Medium C was the last tank to be so designed, and the speed was low as a result. In fact 7.9mph (12.64km/h) could only be achieved on smooth, flat grassland or a good road. Track life was also very short. A good point was the provision of long mud chutes, which kept the bogies clean, and a Wilson gearbox and transmission. The turret had mountings for five guns, though only four were fitted. Guns could be shifted from one port to another, but this cannot have been easy to do when the tank was moving. Only female tanks were built, but it had originally been intended that there should be a male version with one 6pounder gun. Apparently one was actually made, but never put into service. The 6pounder was mounted in the front of the turret, presumably on a vertical mantlet as in the sponsons of the rhomboidals, and this gun must have cut down space in the fighting compartment even further. A hatch in the roof could be opened and one of the Hotchkiss guns mounted on a pintle for AA fire, though this naturally exposed the gunner completely. Extravagant plans were made for the production of the Medium C. After the pilot model had been demonstrated 200 were ordered. In October 1918 a further 4,000 females and 2,000 males were ordered, but immediately cancelled. By February 1919 36 of the original 200 had been completed, and all further work stopped, the remaining half-completed hulls being scrapped. One feature of the Medium C design which was in advance of its time was that assemblies and sub-assemblies were intended to be manufactured in different factories, coming together only for final construction. All other tanks had been built wholly under one roof, which was slower and more expensive. Although so few Medium Cs were ever made, the design was a significant step in tank history. It was the truly interim design between the war-time rhomboidals and the later fully-sprung fast models. The Vickers mediums took the next logical step and laid the basis for all modern tanks.

Above: The Medium C was the final British tank of World War I. It was armed only with four .303in Hotchkiss machine guns.

Below: The Medium C's design represented a great improvement over earlier tanks. It had a greatly-improved transmission, much higher speed, and excellent cross-country capability for its time. It was intended to operate in conjunction with the new Medium D design in the projected advance designated 'Plan 1919'.

MARK A WHIPPET MEDIUM TANK

Crew: 3.
Armament: Four .303in Hotchkiss machine-guns
Armour: 14mm (0.55in) maximum; 5mm (0.2in) minimum.
Dimensions: Length 20ft (6.09m); width 8ft 7in (2.61m); height 9ft (2.74m).
Weight: Combat 31,360lbs (14,225kg).
Engine: Two Tylor six-cylinder water-cooled inline petrol tractor engines, each developing 45hp.

Performance: Speed 8mph (12.8km/h); range 40 miles (64km).
History: In service with the British Army early in 1918, first saw action in March 1918 and then in continuous use until the end of the war. Not used in peace-time. Approximately 200 were produced. Also used by Japan and Russia.

No sooner had the early rhomboidal Mark Is shown their capabilities than the War Office called for a lighter, faster tank capable of carrying out the traditional cavalry task of exploiting a breakthrough and following up a retreating enemy. The idea was for an armoured substitute for the horse and Sir William Tritton, the designer of the Mark I and the managing director of William Foster & Co of Lincoln, set about designing what he called the 'Tritton Chaser', a self-explanatory name. It was decided that trench-crossing was less important than with the battle tanks, since it was

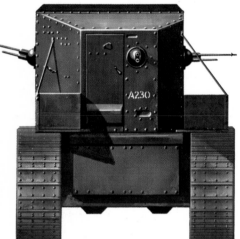

Above: Whippet tanks of 3rd Battalion at Maillet Mailly, France, 30 March 1918, accompany infantry of the New Zealand Division. Unlike the heavier British tanks of WWI, Whippets could operate independently and effectively because of their fairly high speed and maneouvrability.

Left and right: Front and rear views of a medium tank Mark A (Whippet) of 17th Battalion, based in Dublin, June 1919. The tank shown is No. A230, christened 'Gofasta' by its crew. About 200 Whippets were built, entering service in 1918.

Below: Side view of a Whippet tank. Notable features include a fixed turret mounted towards the rear and special mudchutes along the tank's side. The crew entered the tank from the rear, through a specially-provided armoured door.

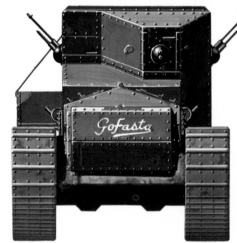

MARK II MEDIUM TANK

reasonable to assume that the latter would have done the job of dropping fascines into the wider holes, and so the length of the 'Chaser' could be reduced, which would ensure a reduced weight and a generally smaller size. The layout resembled that of the then-current armoured cars, in that the engine compartment was at the front, the driver looking out over a long bonnet. Behind him was to be a rotating turret containing the commander and gunner. In the production models the rotating turret was unfortunately dropped to simplify manufacture, but this brought about a sharp increase in the crew difficulties since the commander and his gunner now found themselves having to handle no less than four machine-guns within the confines of a fighting compartment never intended for such a task. Sir William Tritton was well aware of the power losses caused through steering by brakes on the final drive-shafts, and in an effort to overcome this, yet not introduce more manufacturing complications, he used an engine for each track. Theoretically this is straightforward, in practice anything but that. In the Whippet, as the new type was officially named, the driver had a steering wheel connected to the two throttles, and movement of the wheel was translated into differential movement of the throttles. For straight ahead driving he could lock both output shafts by a splined sleeve, thus effectively destroying any steering at all. The whole process was fiendishly difficult to manage, and it was common practice for drivers to stall one engine and spin the tank on one track. On soft ground the stalled track was then shed, and the tank was immobile. The idea was revived in a wheeled amphibian of the US Navy in World War II with predictably similar results. The layout of the tracks was the first indication of a break away from the idea of running them all round the hull, and the concept was quite modern in appearance. The mud chutes were a substantial step forward, helping considerably in clearing the tracks and bogies and so reducing the maintenance load. Unfortunately the bogies were unsprung and high speed was out of the question; in fact the quoted top speed could only be achieved on smooth ground, and on the battlefields of Flanders the Whippet was nowhere near as fast as a horse. The range was too short for a vehicle intended to follow up a breakthrough: 40 miles (64km) were just too few and crews carried extra petrol in tins strapped on the outside of the hull, a suicidal habit in action. The normal petrol tank was in front of the engine, between the front horns, in the best position to receive anti-tank fire, although it was armoured. Despite the shortcomings, and it is easy to find more, the Whippet was considered a great success and the Germans set about copying it almost exactly, though they wisely tried to mount a 57mm gun in the turret. The Armistice overtook the German design, although it was further developed in Sweden as the m-21 by Bofors (one still exists) to become a much more useful tank. The British abandoned the design in 1919 and scrapped the 200 that had been made. As an experiment the Tank Corps' Central Workshops in France took a Whippet and gave it sprung bogies. This improved the ride considerably and when a 360hp Rolls-Royce Eagle aero engine was taken from a Handley Page bomber and fitted instead of the two Tylors, 30mph (48km/h) was easily obtained. The implications were ignored, however, and British tank thinking turned to the Medium C and its derivatives.

Crew 5.
Armament: One 3pounder gun; one .303in Vickers machine-gun mounted co-axially; two .303in Vickers machine-guns mounted in hull.
Armour: 12mm (0.47in) maximum; 8mm (0.31in) minimum.
Dimensions: Length 17ft 6in (5.33m); width 9ft 1½in (2.78m); height 9ft 10½in (3.01m).
Weight: Combat 30,128lbs (13,666kg).
Engine: Armstrong Siddeley eight-cylinder air-cooled inline developing 90bhp.
Performance: Speed 16mph (25.6km/h); range 120 miles (192km); vertical obstacle unknown; trench 6ft 6in (1.981m); gradient unknown.
History: Entered service with the British Army in 1926 and continued in use as a training vehicle until 1941. Also used by Australia.

The Vickers medium tanks were the first truly post-war models to go into service with the Royal Tank Corps, and they showed a number of advances over war-time designs. The Vickers mediums were also the first fast tanks in British service (the top speed was officially 16mph or 26km/h, but it was actually nearer 30mph or 48km/h), and they were the first with revolving turrets. In other respects their war-time ancestry still showed they still mounted machine-guns in the hull, and were the last tanks so to do. The entrance hatches were in the sides of the hull above the track guards, and although there was plenty of room inside for the crew, these small hatches were apparently difficult to use when evacuating a wounded man. The hull was built up from flat plates with as few curves as possible, and was very box-like in shape. The turret was large and square and much narrower than the hull. The engine was in front, on the left with the driver alongside on the right. The driver's view was excellent, if a little vulnerable: he had a large vertical plate in front of him, and could open a large hatch for road driving. The commander had no cupola, and had to rely on vision blocks in the turret, or put his head out of the top. Of the four men in the turret, one fired the 3pounder; the second loaded for him and handled the co-axial machine-gun; the third was the radio operator, when a radio was fitted, and a machine-gunner for one of the hull guns; and the fourth was the commander, who handled the other gun if necessary, although there was sufficient room for the men to move about and change from one station to another. Ventilation was reasonable, and the great heat of the old rhomboidals was gone. There were some crew comforts such as a fireless cooker, some cooking utensils and rations for three days. The suspension was multi-roller, and by no means intended for speed. The road wheels were small and sprung by short coils on vertical rods, giving a few inches of movement. The tracks were of steel plates, with a distinctive H-shaped grip indented in each of them. These tanks, and there were about 160 of them in all, served in the Tank Corps throughout the difficult inter-war years and on mobilisation in 1939 they were used for training gun crews and drivers. A few were used in North Africa in the early months of the war, and several ended their days dug into the ground as anti-invasion pill-boxes around Britain.

Above: The Vickers medium tank was the first standardized tank to enter British service after WWI. It was a very successful design, remaining in service until shortly before World War II.

*Below: While the vehicle shown above is a Vickers medium tank Mk II, the one below is a normal medium Mk II**. The Vickers medium tank was the first to be adopted with a fully-rotating turret.*

CARDEN-LOYD TANKETTE MARK VI

Crew: 2.
Dimensions: (Mark VI) Length 8ft 1in (2.46m); width 5ft 9in (1.75m); height 4ft 4in (1.22m).
Armament: One 0.303in Vickers machine-gun.
Armour: 5mm (0.2in) minimum; 9mm (0.35in) maximum.
Weight: 3,360lbs (1,524kg).
Engine: Ford Model T four-cylinder watercooled inline developing 40bhp at 2,500rpm.
Performance: Speed 25mph (40km/h); range 90 miles (144km); vertical obstacle 1ft 4in (0.41m); trench 4ft (1.22m).
History: Developed from a line of private-venture designs of the 1920s. First issued in 1927 and a total of 270 delivered by 1930. Supplied to India and Canada, with commercial sales to more than 11 foreign countries and licensed building in 5 others.

The Carden-Loyd Mark VI was directly descended from the 'one-man tank' idea of 1925. Colonel Gifford Martel built a one-man tank incorporating ideas of his own, and Messrs-Carden and Loyd did the same thing independently at the same time. In the event the Carden-Loyd variants proved to be more successful, largely because the two men had more time to develop their ideas. They concentrated on a small tracked carrier, rather than a tank, though they were plagued throughout by the prevailing military view that anything with tracks and a little armour was a tank and should be used as such.

The first five marks of Carden-Lloyd were rather crude and very simple little machines driven by a variety of engines, but settling on the Ford Model T motor because of its availability and simplicity. The hulls were all straight forward boxes of one shape or another with the engine in or near the middle, the two crew members side-by-side in front, and light tracked running gear. The Carden-Loyd tracks were the secret of the success of the entire series and merit some examination.

The engine drove to the front sprocket, via a Model T gearbox and a differential which protruded through the front armour. The other wheels were mounted on a horizontal steel beam bolted to brackets on the hull. Below the beam were the road wheels, all quite small and in later models sprung by short leaf springs also below the beam. The vertical movement on these wheels was very small, but it was sufficient for the moderate speeds employed. At the rear of the beam was the idler wheel, with a track tensioner. This arrangement proved to work very well and to give little trouble. The early marks found that track life was distressingly short and there were several arrangements for attaching pneumatic tired wheels for road running, and also ideas for carrying the wheels permanently attached and jacking them up and down as required. By the time the Mark VI appeared the tracks would last for upwards of 600 miles (965km) and the extra wheels could be abandoned.

The Mark VI of 1927 had a shallow hull from which the driver's and gunner's heads protruded. A small deck sloped down in front of them, and on this the Vickers gun was mounted. It was completely exposed, and could only be traversed through a small arc of fire, but the main use of the carrier was to move the gun from one place to another over ground which was under small-arms fire, and this it could do quite well. The Vickers' tripod was stowed on the front deck in front of the driver, who sat on the left. There were several attempts to improve the armour protection by raising it and giving the crew vision slits or blocks. The Mark VIB

of 1931 had raised and sloped sides, with a housing for the gun so that only the barrel was exposed.

Carden-Loyds were supplied direct to the army who then modified them for the role in which they were to be used. The most usual one was as carriers of support weapons, namely Vickers machine-guns and Stokes mortars. Two versions towed 3.7in howitzers or 20mm Oerlikon anti-tank guns. For these tasks there was a specially built tracked limber in which rode the gun crew, no doubt in some discomfort. The guns were towed on their wheels or on tracks also. There was also a GS trailer meant to be used mainly for ammunition re-supply and an artillery observation trailer fitted with wireless.

As the uses expanded and the loads grew heavier several different engines were tried, including the four-cylinder and six-cylinder Meadows and the air-cooled Armstrong-Siddeley.

Vickers sold several hundred Mark VIs abroad, many of them intended as light tanks. In this role the crew

were given overhead cover by fitting two pyramid-like covers over their seats, although the gun was still left out on the front deck. A 'Patrol Tank' had extra space behind the driver for an extra man, but this involved a larger and heavier hull and was not entirely successful.

Despite its small size, the Carden-Loyd was an excellent vehicle and gained much affection from its users. It proved the case for infantry carriers, exploded the myth of the 'tankette', and at very low cost gave the impoverished postwar army a taste of mobile warfare which was to be invaluable from 1940 onwards.

Right: A Carden-Loyd tankette without the Vickers .303in water-cooled machine-gun. More than 300 Mk VI carriers entered British service in a wide variety of roles.

Below: A Carden-Loyd Mk VI with spring suspension, Vickers machine-gun, and sponson stowage boxes over its tracks.

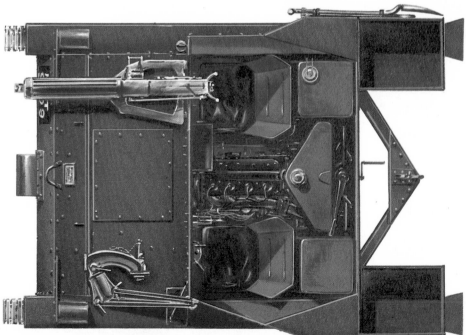

Right and facing page: Top, front, rear and side views of a Carden-Loyd Mk VI machine gun carrier, No. T612, built in 1929 and issued to the 2nd Bttn, Lincolnshire Regt. This vehicle is the only known survivor of the Carden-Loyd series of the inter-war period and is preserved at the Royal Armoured Corps Tank Museum, Bovington Camp, Dorset, England. The little carrier spread its influence throughout the world and derivatives or copies saw service in the Italian-Abyssinian War, the Spanish Civil War and even in World War II. The Carden-Loyd itself saw action only with the Bolivian Army, against Paraguay, in the Gran Chaco War of 1932-35. The Bolivians used Carden-Loyd Mk VIb tankettes together with Vickers-Armstrong 6-ton tanks of the 47mm gun and twin-turreted machine-gun type. The lightly-armoured tankettes proved very vulnerable to artillery and armour-piercing machine-gun fire. In British service, the Carden-Loyd was of considerable importance as a training vehicle for mobile warfare, at a time when military expenditure was rigorously controlled.

VICKERS MARK VI LIGHT TANK

Marks I-VI, VIA, VIB and VIC.
Crew: Marks II, III, & IV,2; Marks V & VI, 3.
Armament: One 0·303in Vickers machine-gun in turret (Marks II-IV); and one 0·5in Vickers and one 0·303in Vickers in turret (Mark V & VI).
Armour: Mark II 4mm (0·16in) minimum, 10mm (0·39in) maximum; Marks III-V 12mm (0·47in); and Mark VI 14mm (0·55in).
Dimensions: Length 11ft 9in (3·58m) – Mark II, 12ft 11in (3·99m) – Mark VI; width 6ft 3½in (1·91m) – Mark II, 6ft 9in (2·05m) – Mark VI; and height 6ft 7½in (2·02m) – Mark II, 7ft 4in (2·23m) – Mark VI.
Weight: 11,648lbs (5,283kg) Mark VI, 9,520lbs (4,318kg) Mark II.
Engine: Marks II & III, Rolls-Royce six-cylinder water-cooled inline petrol engine developing 60hp; Marks IV, V & VI, Meadows six-cylinder water-cooled in line petrol engine developing 88bhp.
Performance: Marks II & III speed 30mph (48km/h), range 150 miles (240km); Mark VI speed 35mph (56km/h), range 130 miles (208km); vertical obstacle 2ft (0·61m) trench 5ft (1·52m); gradient 60 per cent.
History: Developed from the Carden-Loyd series of light tanks and carriers, the Mark I came into service in 1929. Progressive marks were produced through out the 1930s until the Mark VI of 1936, which was itself improved and went up to the Mark VIC. Mark VIs remained in service until 1941 and saw service in France, Egypt, Malta and Persia. They were supplied to Australia, Canada, South Africa and India.

The various marks of Light Tank derived directly from the miscellany of Carden-Loyds which had appeared during the 1920s. In 1928 Vickers took over the Carden-Loyd firm and concentrated on one design for both the British Army and for export. The Mark I was the first light tank with a rotating turret that the firm had made, and it went into British service in 1929. This set the pattern for the rest, though there was to be considerable change and modification before the final model was accepted. All the light tank series featured the Horstmann coil-spring suspension with twin and single bogies and one or more return rollers. All had the engine at the front of the hull, beside the driver.

The Mark VI was heavier, faster and harder-hitting than its forerunners, though still lightly armoured by 1940 standards and lacking in effective cross-country performance. For the most part they were used for reconnaissance, although a few in Egypt were converted to mobile artillery observation posts. The Indian Army sent some Mark VIs to Persia when that country was occupied in 1941.

The Mark I (1929 Model) was very similar to the Carden-Loyd Mark VIII. The suspension was by leaf springs and the turret was cylindrical in shape. A Mark IA came in 1930 and had coil springs and the turret off-set from the centre-line.

The Mark II appeared in 1931 and was the first to fit the Rolls engine. The turret was rectangular with sloping sides and mantlet and an armoured sleeve over the gun. There was a square hatch for the commander and another in front for the driver. Vision was through slits and glass blocks. Mark IIs had two sets of twin bogies on each side and a raised rear idler. This was peculiar to that mark and was not repeated on others. The Mark IIA was an improved Mark II with few external differences, and entered service in 1933.

The Mark III came out in 1934, but few were built. The turret was lower and narrower than that of the Mark II and there was a front grille for the radiator.

The Mark IV also appeared in 1934 and was a distinct improvement over the previous models. It was one of the first British tanks to have the hull built out over tracks to give more internal volume, and the turret was circular once again. The rear idler of the Mark II was dropped, and the suspension reverted to a set of twin bogies and one single one on each side. It was slightly smaller than the Marks II

Below and right: Side, rear and front views of the Mk VIB, the standard British light tank at the beginning of World War II. It remained in service until 1941.

and III and could mount either a 0·5in or 0·303in Vickers.

The Mark V (1935) was the first light tank with a 3-man crew. The hull was lengthened and the track extended by adding a rear idler behind the single road wheel and springing it in the same way. The turret was larger and the sides sloped sharply. Two machine-guns were mounted in the turret, which was cramped for the two men in it, but the commander was given a small cylindrical cupola. A smoke discharger, fired by a bowden cable, was mounted on the right hand side of the turret. The driver's hatch became smaller, and the deck in front of the turret was larger than previously. Only 22 Mark Vs were built, but they formed the basis for the Mark VI, and

LANCHESTER ARMOURED CAR

Mks I, IA, II and IIA
Crew: 4.
Armament: One .5in Vickers machine-gun and one .303in Vickers machine-gun in turret; one .303in Vickers machine-gun in hull (not all models).
Armour: 10mm (0.39in).
Dimensions: Length 20ft (6.1m); width 6ft 7½in (2.01m); height 9ft 3in (2.82m).
Weight: 16,000lb (7,620kg) – Marks I & IA; 15,568lb (7,062kg) – Marks II & IIA.
Engine: Lanchester six-cylinder water-cooled in-line petrol engine developing 88bhp at 2,200rpm.
Performance: Speed 45mph (72km/h); range 200 miles (320km).
History: First delivered in 1928 and declared obsolete in 1939. Some 39 were built: 4 prototypes, 18 Mk Is, 4 Mk IAs, 7 Mk IIs & 6 Mk IIAs. None were supplied to foreign countries, though a few went to Malaya in 1940.

The Lanchester was the first armoured car in British service to have been specifically designed as such. All previous ones had used a commercial chassis with an armoured body built on. The Lanchester was intended from the first to be for the cavalry, and it was given a rigid six-wheeled chassis with the drive to four rear wheels in the expectation of improving the cross-

several ideas tried out on the Mark Vs later became standard.

The Mark VI (1936 onwards) was the last in the series and the largest and heaviest. The turret was enlarged to accommodate a No 7 wireless set and cupola was hexagonal. The Mark VIA changed the position of the return rollers and the VIB reverted to a cylindrical cupola. Many carried an external mounting for a Bren gun for AA defence. The Mark VIC mounted a BESA 15mm heavy machine-gun and a coaxial 7·92mm BESA. The cupola was abandoned and two domed hatches gave a little more head-room for the crew, though at the expense of the commander's view. The Mark VI had a Wilson pre-selector gearbox and there were steady improvements to the Meadows engine. The twin radiator inlet louvres on the front of the engine cover were reduced to one on this mark and most versions had deflector plates in front of the driver's vision block to reduce bullet splash.

The great majority of the light tanks were used for training after 1940, when it was realised that none of them were a match for the German *Panzers*; there was no hope of mounting a larger gun in the tiny turret, and in any case the armour protection was quite inadequate for modern war. As they wore out they were scrapped and armoured cars took over the reconnaissance role.

Above right: A Mk VI light tank; note the mainly circular turret extended at rear for a No 7 wireless set.

Right: Side view of the Mk VIB light tank. This was the final development of the Carden-Loyd series, mounting one .50in and one .303in Vickers machine-guns.

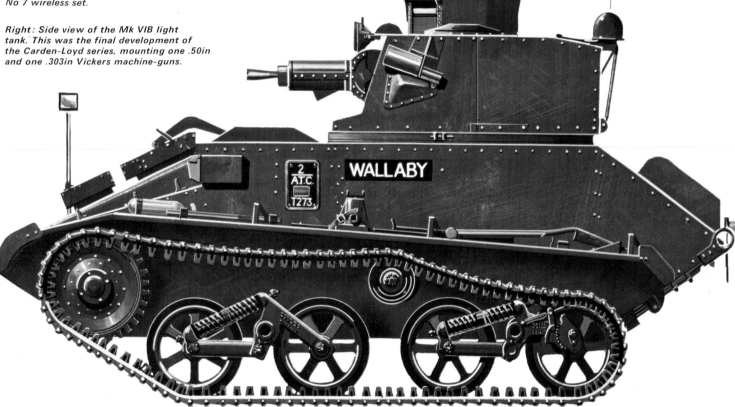
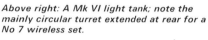

country performance over the then current 4 × 2 vehicles. Nevertheless, the layout was very similar to that of the Rolls-Royce, with a small square crew compartment with a round turret above it and a flat load platform at the rear. The commander had a cupola and the armament was considerably increased. The 0.5in Vickers was a powerful gun with a reasonable performance against lightly armoured vehicles and considerable destructive power against trucks and lorries. The cooling jackets of all three guns were protected with armoured sleeves.

An interesting feature of the Lanchester was that a duplicate steering wheel and linkage was fitted at the rear of the crew compartment facing backwards.

The Marks I and IA had twin rear wheels and a circular, flat-topped cupola. The Mark IA had the hull machine-gun removed and a No 9 wireless set installed instead. This was a bulky, heavy set which cannot have responded well to being bumped across rough ground and which needed a large aerial for good reception.

The Mark II vehicles used single rear wheels and a cupola with sloping sides. Again, the Mark IIA fitted a wireless set and only the two turret guns.

Left: Lanchester Mk I armoured car—the 39 built saw service largely in the colonies.

Right: A later version of the Lanchester armoured car—with improved armour, larger turret and twin machine-guns— adopted by the British Army in 1931.

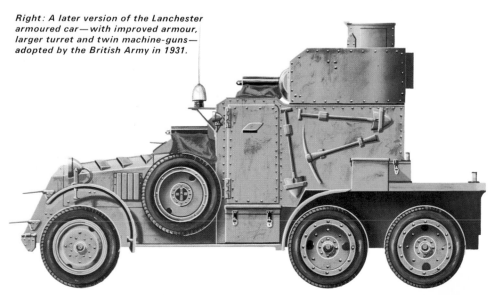

A11 MATILDA I INFANTRY TANK

Crew: 2.

Armament: One .3in or .5in Vickers machine-gun.

Armour: 60mm (2.36in) maximum; 10mm (0.39in) minimum.

Dimensions: Length 15ft 11in (4.85m); width 7ft 6in (2.28m); height 6ft 1½in (1.86m).

Weight: Combat 24,640lbs (11,161kg).

Engine: Ford eight-cylinder petrol engine developing 70bhp at 3,500rpm.

Performance: Road speed 8mph (12.8kp/h); range 80 miles (128km); vertical obstacle 2ft 1in (0.635m); trench 7ft (2.133m).

History: Served with the British Army only between 1938 and 1940.

The origin of the Matilda I lay in a request from General Sir Hugh Elles to Vickers for a tank to be built down to a price. Sir John Carden led the design team and the result was probably the most unfortunate one of his career. The concept of the infantry tank called for good protection, low speed to keep pace with infantry assaulting on foot, and only limited offensive power. It was thought to be sufficient to give the tank an armament of machine-guns and no more. These limits were bad enough, but the price limit was equally daunting at £6,000 for the complete vehicle. Not surprisingly the Matilda I was reduced to the barest essentials, and perpetuated a number of mistakes which had already been well aired. The first was the crew. Two-man tanks had been shown to be scarcely workable in the 1920s and early 30s, but Carden was forced to return to a one-man turret because he could not afford the space for two. One machine-gun made a mock of the whole idea of fire-power, and to have a complete tank to carry one gun was a great waste of manufacturing effort and money. Finally, to give the vehicle a top speed scarcely better than that of a running man was quite ludicrous. Those were the limitations, however, and the General Staff accepted the design and the first production order was placed in April 1937. The first models were delivered in 1938 and issued to the 1st Army Tank Brigade, who took them to France in 1939. By 1940 139 had been built and they formed the greater part of the vehicle strength of the 1st Brigade. Their severe limitations showed up with frightening clarity in the *Blitzkrieg*, and all were finally lost on the way to, or at, Dunkirk. Their crews fought valiantly, and they had one small success, but the tank was hopeless in battle. Carden had built the smallest vehicle that he reasonably could and used as many existing components as possible. Since protection was important he put thick armour on the front and used a cast turret. The armour was more than satisfactory and was comfortably invulnerable to the German anti-tank guns in France. The suspension was a less happy story. It was the same as had been fitted to the Vickers 6ton (6,096kg) tank of 1928, and it could only cope with low speeds and moderate power outputs when carrying twice the weight it was designed for. The final drawback lay in the engine, which was the well-proved but low-powered Ford V-8. In order to drive the Matilda it had to be well geared down and the power was taken through a simple transmission to

a rear sprocket. When the armament limitations became clear the turret was up-gunned by fitting the Vickers 0.5in machine-gun. This was some improvement, but it took more space in the small turret, and was tiring to use.

Above: Recruits to the British Royal Tank Corps "somewhere in England" in 1940 carrying out maintenance training to an Infantry tank Mk I, Matilda. The tank saw action only for a limited period, due to suspension and engine problems.

Above: The Matilda Mk I, armed with a .303in Vickers machine-gun. This tank was originally conceived as a heavily-armoured, slow-moving infantry support tank, designed by a team led by Sir John Carden to a specification laid down by General Sir Hugh Elles. Its frontal armour was almost inpenetrable by any contemporary anti-tank gun, but the vehicle proved both ineffective and expensive.

Left: Side view of the Matilda Mk I. A single smoke-bomb discharger is fitted to the turret. 139 of these tanks were delivered to BEF units in France, taking part in the battles against the Wehrmacht until the Dunkirk evacuation. Experience showed that more powerful armament was needed—leading to the development of the Matilda Mk II. Vehicles which were recovered from Dunkirk were retained for training purposes.

CRUISER TANK MARK IV

Mks IV, IVA and .VC; A13 MkII
Crew: 4.
Armament: One 2pdr gun and one Vickers 0·303 machine-gun (Mark IVA mounted a 7·92mm Besa).
Armour: 6mm (0·24in) minimum; 38mm (1·5in) maximum.
Dimensions: Length 19ft 9in (6·02m); width 8ft 4in (2·54m); height 8ft 6in (2·59m).
Weight: 33,040lbs (14,987kg).
Engine: Nuffield Liberty V-12 water-cooled petrol engine developing 340bhp.
Performance: Speed 30mph (48km/h); range 90 miles (144km); vertical obstacle 2ft (0·61m); trench 7ft 6in (2·29in); gradient 60 per cent.
History: Deliveries began in December 1938 and were completed in late 1939. Some 335 tanks were made and were issued to units of 1st Armoured Division' in France in 1939/40. Some also went to the Western Desert where they were used by the 7th Armoured Division. Withdrawn from service during 1942.

The Cruiser Mark IV derived directly from a Christie tank bought in the USA in 1936. Morris Motors were given the task of redesigning the Christie to make it battle-worthy, and to do this they had to build a new hull and a better turret. The Christie could reach 50mph (80km/h) on roads, and very high speeds across country, but these had to be reduced since it was quickly found that the crew were injured by being thrown about.

The only engine available which gave the necessary power was the American Liberty aero-engine of World War I, and this was de-rated to 340hp to improve torque and reliability. The later Mark IVA had a Wilson combined speed change and steering gear-box and a BESA rather than Vickers coaxial machine-gun. The Mk IV CS was the close support model. The Christie suspension was a great success and gave the Cruiser a very good performance in the desert. It was retained on all British cruiser tanks for the rest of the war.

Above: Cruiser Tank Mk IV of 1st Armoured Division, 1940. This tank has additional armour plating over the mantlet.

Right: A Cruiser Mk IVA. Officially designated A13 Mk II, this tank was developed from an American Christie tank purchased from the USA in 1936.

The turret had undercut sides and sloped upper plates, but the hull was still much of a box and had many sharp angles in which shot could lodge. Some extra plates were added to the desert Cruisers, but they were always under-armoured and after a short while in service various mechanical weaknesses became apparent and reliability was not as good as it should have been. Despite the shortcomings of the Cruiser it was a stepforward for British tank design and it set the pattern for the wartime cruisers which followed.

CARDEN–LOYD UNIVERSAL CARRIER

Carden-Loyd series, Bren Carrier, T16 (in US).
Crew: 4–5.
Armament: One Bren light machine-gun or one Boys anti-tank rifle.
Armour: 12mm (0.47in).
Dimensions: Length 12ft 4in (3.75m); width 6ft 11in (2.10m); height 5ft 3in (1.60m).
Weight: Combat 8,848lbs (4,013kg).
Engine: Ford eight-cylinder water-cooled inline petrol engine developing 85bhp at 2,800rpm.
Performance: Speed 32mph (51km/h); range 160 miles (256km); vertical obstacle 2ft 4in (0.711m); trench 5ft 3in (1.6m); gradient 60 per cent.
History: Developed in 1939 from a long line of infantry carriers of similar size. About 35,000 were built in UK during World War II, 5,600 in Australia, 520 in New Zealand, and over 29,000 in Canada. It was also built in the United States as the T16, of which almost 14,000 were produced. Production ceased in 1945 and the vehicle remained in service until the early 1950s. Many variants were built and the identification and classification of the many types is a complex subject.

Memories of the carrier are fading in the infantry now, but in its day it was one of the best-loved of any special vehicle. It was derived from the Carden-Loyd series of the 1930s, but the original idea was formed in the Ammunition Carrier of 1921, an armoured, tracked vehicle intended to convey 18pounder ammunition across bullet-swept ground impassable to Army Service Corps horse-drawn wagons. The first Universal Carrier had a roughly similar mission on a smaller scale, namely the carriage ·of infantry across ground denied by small-arms fire, and specifically — hence the popular name of Bren Gun Carrier — the carriage of a Bren light machine-gun and its team. In fact there was only one model of the carrier actually named the Bren Carrier, but whatever the task the whole family was known to its users as Bren Carriers. The hull was a simple steel box with a Ford V-8 engine in the middle. In front sat the driver with a gunner alongside him. The radiator was in the bulkhead between them and the fan noise effectively prevented conversation when the engine was running. Behind were two coffin-shaped compartments, one on each side of the engine and gearbox, in which the main load was carried. This could be either men, or men and a weapon and its ammunition. In some cases the weapon would be mounted on the top of the engine and available for action without dismounting. Most of the carriers in service were used for the infantry support weapons such as mortars, medium machine-

guns and anti-tank guns. Mortars and Vickers guns could be carried inside, anti-tank guns were towed. Extra carriers were usually needed for the ammunition. The running gear was developed from the Vickers and Loyd series and was a set of three road wheels on each side, two paired and one single. All were suspended by coil springs in a way introduced by the Horstmann company. The set of twin wheels in one bogie was on a shaft running through the body, and this shaft could be moved from side to side, bowing the track and giving gentle turns without altering track speed. The drive sprocket was at the rear, connected to a normal Ford differential. Sharp turns were made using simple

brakes. Steering was by a wheel: small movements bowed the track, and more turning motion brought the steering brakes into play. Driving controls were identical with those of a lorry and the specialised training needed was minimal. The multitude of different roles for the carrier meant that there was no uniform way of carrying equipment, nor a standard way of loading. By 1945 most carriers were carrying far more than they were designed to do, without apparent difficulty. It was usual to have a spare road wheel on the front glacis plate and a large camouflage net tied on behind. Some units fitted removable canvas tops for winter weather.

Left: A Universal Carrier operating in Italy. There were many variants of this type of vehicle, evolved from the Carden-Loyd gun carrier of the early 1930s. It saw service in all theatres of operation and was the forerunner of the modern APC, remaining in service until the early 1950s.
Below: A typical example of a late model Universal Carrier. The Bren is mounted next to the driver.

A9 MARK I CRUISER TANK

Crew: 6.
Armament: One 2pounder gun; three .303in Vickers machine-guns. (CS version had one 3.7in howitzer in place of the 2pounder.)
Armour: 14mm (0.55in) maximum; 6mm (0.25in) minimum.
Dimensions: Length 19ft (5.79m); width 8ft 2in (2.49m) height 8ft 8in (2.64m).
Weight: Combat 28,728lbs (13,013kg).
Engine: AEC Type 179 six-cylinder water-cooled inline petrol engine developing 150bhp.
Performance: Road speed 25mph (40km/h); cross-country speed 15mph (24km/h); range 150 miles (240km); vertical obstacle 3ft (0.92m); trench 8ft (2.43m).
History: Used by the British Army between 1938 and 1941.

The main British tank strength throughout the 1920s and the first half of the 1930s was made from the Vickers Medium Mark II, with the scouting (or reconnaissance) role being undertaken by light tanks of various kinds, ultimately types coming after the Carden-Loyd models. This combination was becoming out of date by 1934, quite plainly, and new designs were needed. In particular, it was becoming apparent to the General Staff that better medium tanks were required for the tank-to-tank confrontations which it was foreseen might occur on future battlefields. 1934 was not a good time to be planning major expenditure on military equipment, however; the depression was at its height, and money was almost unobtainable. Several replacements were suggested for the Vickers mediums, and the best was perhaps the Vickers A6, the '16 tonner' of 1928. But the A6 came too soon, and it would also have needed a good deal of development. It had good cross-country performance, but lacked an effective gun (a 3pounder of low velocity) and had thin armour. Despite this it showed the way with a central turret, diesel engine and Wilson epicyclic gearbox. However, in 1934–35 the ruling constraint on designers of military equipment was cost: the A6 was estimated at £16,000, and that meant its demise despite its virtues. Sir John Carden set to work in 1934 to design a tank to meet a General Staff specification for a successor to the Vickers mediums, but with a slightly different role to fulfil. The difficulty with the tank specifications of the 1930s was that nobody had any clear idea what they wanted the vehicles to do in the next war. The old ideas of crossing trenches had not entirely died out, yet it was realised that tanks would be required to act on their own, much in the way that cavalry had done, and also there was a need for armoured reconnaissance. The result of this somewhat baffled thinking was to stipulate a family of three types: cruisers, which were meant to be the cavalry type of machine, yet able to fight it out with other

tanks if called upon to do so; infantry tanks which moved at slow speed with the assaulting infantry, and only had to knock out machine-gun nests (a throwback to 1918); and light tanks for the reconnaissance role. Nobody thought out the armament requirement to cope with these different tasks, and the cruisers were particularly badly served since they were given either the 3pounder, which was feeble, or the later 2pounder, which had good armour penetration for its day, but could not fire HE shell. All medium tanks were well supplied with machine-guns, which were quite useless against other armoured vehicles. With these crippling restrictions around him Sir John Carden produced the first A9 early in 1936. It epitomised all that had served to restrict the design. It was lighter than the mediums so that it could be powered by a commercial engine. At the same time it tried to incorporate all the best features of the Medium Mark III, and to a great extent succeeded, but only by making everything so much lighter that the armour protection was largely negated. The overall weight was only two-thirds that of the Medium Mark III, and the design weight had even less than this. The general layout was reasonable for its day, with a central turret, engine at the rear and acceptable cross-country performance from the suspension. One of the features which spoiled the A9 was the vertical armour, all of it too thin, and the multitude of angles and corners in which armour-piercing shot could lodge, instead of being glanced off. A point in the A9's favour, however, was the fact that it was the first British tank to have power (hydraulic) traverse for the turret. This was a substantial step forward, and was to be followed on all succeeding designs. Another notable first was the carriage of an

auxiliary engine for starting, battery charging, and driving a fan for the fighting compartment. These were sensible innovations, and went some way to offsetting the failings of the A9 as a fighting tank. The crew was a generous allowance of six men, split into a commander, gunner, loader, driver and two hull machine-gunners. The driving and fighting compartments were combined into one, hence the need for a fan to clear the fumes from three machine-guns and a 3pounder. The two hull machine-guns were mounted in small sub-turrets in front, one on each side of the driver. The gunners were cramped, and so was the driver, and the whole concept was strongly reminiscent of World War I. The arcs of fire of the machine-guns were limited, and their use doubtful. They were the last relic of World War I, and only appeared again for a brief time on the Crusader I. The engine was originally meant to be the Rolls-Royce car engine from the Phantom series. The pilot model, however, showed that the vehicle was under-powered and an AEC bus engine was substituted. This just managed to give the tank a speed of 25mph (40km/h) on the road, but had to be geared down considerably to do it. The suspension could manage the cross-country speed of 15mph (24km/h) but the pilot model at first shed its tracks at these speeds. Trials started in 1936 and at the same time the War Office was changing its policy on tanks generally. The A9 had begun as a medium tank replacement, but now the cruiser idea was born, and the vehicle became the Cruiser Tank Mark I. The first contract for a limited number was placed in August 1937 with Vickers, which was to build 50. Another contract with Harland and Wolff of Belfast specified a further 75, and these constituted the total production.

Left: The A9 tank, officially called Tank, Cruiser A9 Mk I. A total of 125 were built by two contractors and saw service in France, Libya and Greece in 1939-41. They differed from the A10 in having two auxiliary machine gun turrets mounted on the hull front and in the type of engine louvres, which can be seen on the side of the hull, just behind the turret, in this photograph.

BEAVERETTE MARK II LIGHT RECONNAISSANCE CAR

Crew: 3.
Armament: One .303in Bren light machine-gun or one Boys anti-tank rifle.
Armour: 9mm (0.35in) maximum.
Dimensions: Length 13ft 6in (4.114m); width 5ft 3in (1.6m); height 5ft (1.524m).
Weight: 4,480lbs (2,032kg).
Engine: Standard petrol engine developing 45bhp.
Performance: Road speed 40mph (64.37km/h).
History: Entered service with the British Army in 1940. Also used by the Royal Air Force and Home Guard.

When France fell in the summer of 1940, it was expected that the Germans' next move would be the invasion of Great Britain by both sea and air. As no army vehicles could be spared for the protection of airfields and aircraft factories, Lord Beaverbrook, in charge of aircraft protection, set about obtaining his own vehicles. The Beaverette was essentially a Standard or Humber Super Snipe car chassis fitted with a body of mild steel to a maximum thickness of 0.35in (9mm). The front armour was reinforced by a layer of 3in (76mm) oak planking. Some 2,800 Beaverettes were built in four different marks. The Mk I and Mk II had an open roof and were normally armed with a Bren light machine-gun or a .55in (14mm) Boys anti-tank rifle. (Although the rifle was at first known as the Stanchion, it was renamed the Boys after the death of its designer, Captain Boys.) The Mk III had a fully enclosed fighting compartment with a small turret on top, armed with a light machine-gun. This model weighed almost 3 tons (3,048kg) and had a road speed of 24mph (39km/h). The last model was the Mk IV, which had a slightly different hull top. Most of the British armoured units lost all of their equipment in France and some of them were re-formed with Beaverettes as their initial

equipment. Many locally produced vehicles were pressed into service in 1940, and some of these, had they been used in action, would have been deathtraps for their crews. Railway and bus depots did build some quite good armoured vehicles at this time. One of the more interesting vehicles was the Bison, designed by the Concrete Company Limited. This consisted of a 6×4 or 4×2 truck chassis with its cab protected by concrete, and a concrete pillbox mounted on the flatbed to the rear of the cab. The vehicle was claimed to be immune from attack from machine gun fire. These were used for airfield defence, and one still exists to this day at the Royal Air Force Regiment headquarters at Catterick Camp. Another vehicle was the Armadillo.

Above: A considerably modified Beaverette, the Mk IV, used by the Irish Army.
Right: Beaverette Mk II light reconnaissance cars, used by a mechanised cavalry unit in the summer of 1940.

This was a standard truck with a wooden box mounted on the flatbed, with another box mounted inside the first one, with the space between filled with small pebbles, which were said to give protection against small arms fire. The Armadillo was normally armed with a Lewis machine-gun, and firing slits were provided in the sides, front and rear. The driver's cab was armoured with mild steel.

The limitations of the design were soon obvious and the A13 was put in hand as the next model. The intrinsic limitations of the 2pounder meant that tanks could not deal with strongpoints or pillboxes, and this brought about the concept of the Close Support tank. CS tanks carried large-calibre guns for firing HE and other types of ammunition, and a few CS models of the A9, mounting a short-barrelled 3.7in howitzer, were built. The three machine-guns remained. The suspension was a Vickers refinement of the popular multi-bogie system, and it was successful enough to be incorporated into the later Valentine almost without alteration. The steering brakes were mounted externally on the rear sprockets, where they cooled easily, but were perhaps a little exposed to damage. The tracks were narrow, and none too strong, but the low power output of the engine and the relatively gentle gearbox gave them a reasonably long life. A9s were issued to 1st Armoured Division, which took them to France in 1939 and 1940, and left practically all of them at Dunkirk. The 2nd and 7th Armoured Divisions took the type to Egypt and used it until 1941, by when it was clearly well out of date and out-gunned. No attempt was made to use the hulls for other tasks, and those that remained in service were scrapped. It was not the fault of the tank or the designer that it was inadequate, for the specification and the financial stringency of the times forced the A9 to be less than satisfactory.

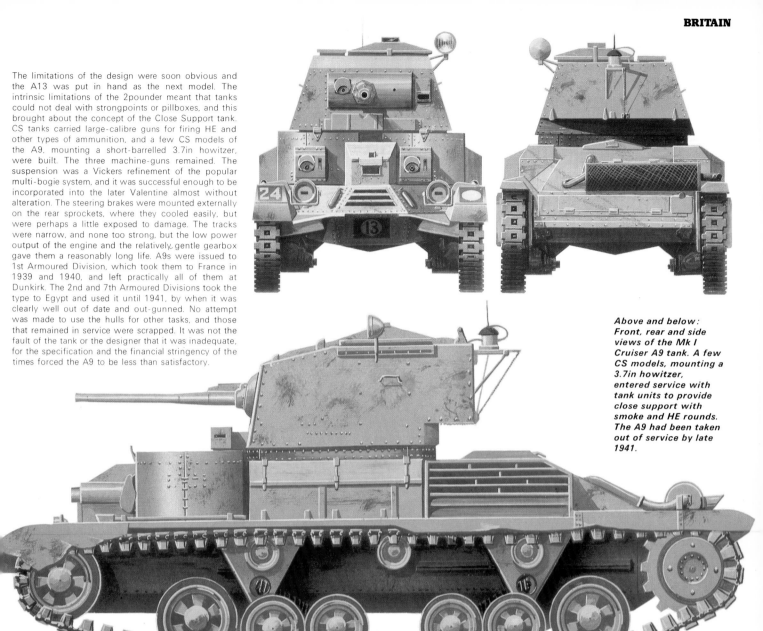

Above and below: Front, rear and side views of the Mk I Cruiser A9 tank. A few CS models, mounting a 3.7in howitzer, entered service with tank units to provide close support with smoke and HE rounds. The A9 had been taken out of service by late 1941.

A12 MATILDA II INFANTRY TANK

Matilda II Marks I to V.
Crew: 4.
Armament: One 2pounder gun; one .303in Vickers machine-gun (Mark I); one 2pounder gun; one 7.92mm BESA machine-gun (Mark II); one 3in howitzer; one 7.92mm BESA machine-gun (Mark II CS).
Armour: 0.55in (14mm) minimum; 3in (78mm) maximum.
Dimensions: Length 18ft 5in (5.61m); width 8ft 6in (2.59m); height 8ft 3in (2.51m).
Weight: 59,360lbs (26,926kg).
Power to weight ratio: 7.17hp/ton (Mark III).
Engine: Two AEC six-cylinder inline diesels developing a total of 174bhp (Marks I and II); two Leyland six-cylinder inline diesels developing a total of 190bhp (Mark III).
Performance: Road speed 15mph (24km/h); cross-country speed 8mph (12.8km/h); range 160 miles (256km); vertical obstacle 2ft (0.61m); trench 7ft (2.13m); fording depth 3ft (0.91m).
History: Served with the British Army from 1939 to 1945. Also used by Australia and Russia.

When the Matilda I was still in the prototype stage the War Office was already debating whether it could be up-armoured and up-gunned to meet a revised General Staff specification which said in effect that if tanks were to survive while supporting infantry on foot, they must be able to withstand the fire of anti-tank guns, yet carry sufficiently heavy armament to cope with enemy infantry, gun positions and tanks. This brought about a fundamental change in approach to the design of infantry tanks. Previously it had been considered that machine-guns were sufficient armament, but the new specification required some sort of shell-firing gun, and a large enough turret in which to put it. At first it was thought that Matilda I (A11) could be given a two-man turret and a 2pounder gun, but it was soon apparent that there was no hope of this within the narrow hull limits, and in any case the weight of the turret would have defeated the already overloaded Ford engine and another would have to be fitted. The weight of the tank was intended to be kept down to 14 tons (14,225kg), and the A11 could not possibly meet it with the changes already mentioned, so a new design was called for. This new tank was entrusted to the Design Department at Woolwich Arsenal and was largely based on the prototype A7 of 1932. The same

suspension was used, suitably strengthened, and the same powerplant of twin commercial diesels was put in. The requirement for thick armour meant that a cast turret and bow plate would be the most satisfactory solution, but British industry in the mid-1930s had only a very limited capacity for large castings, and this severely restricted the firms who could be given contracts for this work. It also meant that riveted and welded. hulls and turrets were retained on British tanks long after other countries had gone over to castings. However, the contract for Matilda II was given to the Vulcan Foundry of Warrington in November 1936 and they produced a wooden mock-up by April 1937. Another year elapsed before the pilot model (made in mild steel) was ready, the delay mainly being occasioned by difficulties in the supply of the Wilson gearbox. Trials with this model were carried out during 1938, but an initial order for 65 tanks was given even before the pilot model appeared, and shortly afterwards this was increased by a further 100. Luckily the trials showed the design to be satisfactory, the only changes being minor ones to the suspension and engine cooling. Rearmament started in earnest during 1938 and tanks were in desperately short supply, so further orders were given, which were more than Vulcan could manage. Other firms were called in, and contracts were let to Fowler, Ruston & Hornsby, LMS Railway Works, Harland & Wolff and North British Locomotive Works. Vulcan were the main contractor, and undertook most of the casting work. The Matilda was not easy to put into mass production, mainly because of the castings and certain features of the design were quite difficult. For some reason the side skirts were in one piece, involving another large casting, and an immediate easement to production was to reduce the number of

mud chutes from six to five. By September 1939 only two Matildas were in service, but by the spring of 1940 at least one battalion (7th Royal Tank Regiment) was equipped and the tank gave a good account of itself in the retreat to Dunkirk and the subsequent fighting around the port. At the same time several units in Egypt had received it, and used it in the early campaigns against the Italians. After Dunkirk the Matilda I was dropped altogether and the Matilda II became simply the Matilda, by which it was known for the rest of the war. In Libya in 1940 and 1941 Matilda was virtually immune to any anti-tank gun or tank that the Italians could deploy. This happy state of affairs continued until about mid-1941 when the first units of the *Afrika Korps* appeared and brought their 8.8cm *Flak* guns into action in the ground role against tanks. This gun could knock out the Matilda at ranges far beyond the 2pounder's ability to reply, and the Matilda began to fade from the battle. Attempts to up-gun it to carry a 6pounder were failures because the turret ring was too small to take a larger gun, and the last action when Matilda was used as a gun tank was the first battle of El Alamein in July 1942. The Matilda was a conventional British tank with the usual three compartments in the hull, the driver sitting centrally behind the nose plate. There was no hull gun, an unusual departure for the time, but sensible, for they were rarely effective in battle. The heavy cast turret was small, and the three men in it were cramped. In the CS version with a 3in howitzer, space was even scarcer. The commander had a circular cupola, but it gave him only limited vision and this lack of good vision was the worst feature of the vehicle, though it was no worse than many other designs of that time. The turret was rotated by hydraulic power, and was one of the first to use this system

Right: The Matilda II was one of the most famous British tanks of WWII. It formed a major part of the British armoured forces during the 8th Army's battles in the Western Desert.

Below: Front and rear views of the Matilda II tank. Although noted for its very heavy armour, the tank was very slow, with a maximum road speed of 24km/h, and was also poorly armed.

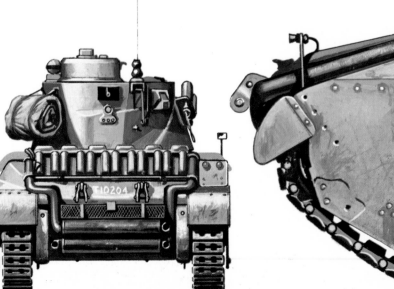

Left: The BA-3 armoured car, from which the BA-6, BA-9 and BA-10 were developed. It mounted a 37mm gun and a 7.62mm machine-gun in a revolving turret, with another 7.62mm gun forward.

developed by the Frazer Nash Company, who also developed the turret controls for aircraft. Some 67 rounds of 2pounder and 4,000 of .303in ammunition were carried. The twin AEC diesels were coupled together and drove to a Wilson epicyclic gearbox and a rear sprocket. The suspension was derived from the A7 and was either known as the 'scissors' or 'Japanese' type. It originated with the Vickers Medium C, though a similar type also appeared on the French tanks of the 1920s and 1930s. It consisted of sets of bogies linked together and working against horizontal compression springs. Each bogie had four rollers, arranged in pairs, so that to each suspension point there were four pairs of rollers, two link units, and two springs; the whole was supported by one vertical bracket attached to the

hull. On each side there were two of these complete units, one four-roller unit and one large road wheel at the front. The track ran back along return rollers at the top of the side skirt. This apparently complicated arrangement worked well, though it inevitably limited the top speed. Mark III Matildas, and later marks, were fitted with Leyland diesels which gave slightly more power and were made in larger numbers than the AECs. The Mark V fitted an air servo on top of the gearbox to ease gear changing, but apart from these minor modifications, the Matilda stayed very much as it had been designed. Up to the first battle of El Alamein the Matilda had gained the somewhat high-flown title of 'Queen of the Battlefield', or at least some people called it that. After El Alamein it was apparent that the

type was well past its best, and was replaced with the increasing quantities of Grants and Shermans. The problem was to know what to do with the Matildas, most of which were still in good running order. The thick armour and reasonable protection made it an attractive vehicle for special applications, and it was the first British tank to be equipped as a flail mine-clearer, some of which were used at El Alamein. The flail was followed by a host of other devices, including anti-mine rollers, large demolition charges, bridge-layers, dozer blades, Canal Defence Lights (CDL) to illuminate the battlefield at night, gap-crossing devices and flamethrowers. One was even used as an experimental radio-controlled vehicle. Matildas were supplied to the Australian Army, which used them in the Pacific campaign and still had it in service for driver training as late as 1953. The Australians paid particular attention to developing flamethrowing variants which were useful against Japanese infantry positions in the jungle, and a dozer version was also frequently used in that theatre, mainly to improve tracks for wheeled vehicles to follow the tanks. Some Matildas went to Russia, where the thickness of armour was admired, but as in the Churchill later on, the 2pounder gun was politely dismissed as near useless. There are also some reports that the suspension clogged in the winter snow, though the Russians were not particularly communicative about the equipment provided to them. By 1945 the Matilda was being replaced even in the specialist applications with Grant and Sherman hulls. The supply of spares and components was geared to the tanks that existed in the largest numbers, and these were the American models, the heavy cruisers and the Churchill. After four or five years continuous use the Matildas were worn out, and it was not worth rebuilding them. A few were still in service at the end of the war, though not as gun tanks. However, the Matilda can claim to be the only British tank which served right through World War II and there are very few others which can approach that record, whatever their nationality.

Left: This illustration emphasises many notable features of the Matilda tank. Note the special anti-aircraft mounting on the turret for a Bren light machine gun. The apertures along the hull sides were to allow mud that had caked in the tracks to be expelled while moving. Certain standard features of most British tanks of the period are also to be seen, particularly the smoke-bomb projectors. The turret was rotated by hydraulic power.

CRUSADER CRUISER TANK

Crusaders I to III

Crew: 5 in the Mark I; 4 or 5 in the Mark II; 3 in the Mark III.

Armament: Crusader I one 2pounder gun and two 7.92mm BESA machine-guns; Crusader II one 2pounder gun and one or two 7.92mm BESA machine-guns; Crusader III one 6pounder gun and one 7.92mm BESA machine-gun.

Armour: Crusader I 40mm (1.57in) maximum and 7mm (0.28in) minimum; Crusader II 49mm (1.93in) maximum and 7mm (0.28in) minimum; Crusader III 51mm (2in) maximum and 7mm (0.28in) minimum.

Dimensions: Length 19ft 8in (5.99m); width 8ft 8in (2.64m); height 7ft 4in (2.23m).

Weight: Combat Crusader I and II 42,560lbs (19,279kg); Crusader III 44,240lbs (20,040kg).

Ground Pressure: 14.7lb/in² (1.04kg/cm²).

Engine: Nuffield Liberty 12-cylinder water-cooled inline petrol engine developing 340bhp

Performance: Road speed 27mph (43.2km/h); range 100 miles (160km); vertical obstacle 2ft 3in (0.685m); trench 8ft 6in (2.59m); gradient 60 per cent.

History: In service with the British Army from 1939 to 1943.

The Crusader was to a great extent developed from the Covenanter, which it outwardly resembled. The Covenanter was a pre-war design which started in 1937 and was similar to the Cruiser Mark IV, or A13. The Crusader followed in the design pattern of these cruisers, but was designated to be a heavy cruiser, which was a difficult specification to fulfil within the weight and size limitations. It was equally difficult to fulfil when the main armament was only a 2pounder gun. The specification did show, however, that the limitations of the previous models had been appreciated. They were too lightly armoured, but were also too lightly armed, and nothing could be done about this in 1939. The Crusader was built by a consortium of firms under the leadership of Nuffield Mechanisations Ltd, and 5,300 were made before production ceased. The hull was similar to that of the Covenanter, with a long flat deck and a well raked glacis plate. The Christie suspension was very similar, except for an extra wheel station and the spring units, which were contained inside the hull. This suspension was the strong point of the Crusader and enabled it to move much faster than the official top speed of 27mph (43.2km/h). In the Western Desert Crusader drivers and fitters opened up the engine governors to let the Liberty engine go as fast as it could, and the result was sometimes a speed as high as 40mph (64km/h). The Christie wheels could cope with this quite well and still give the crew a tolerable ride, the casualty usually being the engine. The hull was divided into the usual three compartments, with the driver sharing the front one with a hull machine-gunner in the previous marks. The Crusader I had the hull machine-gun in a small sub-turret on the front deck, but this was changed to a ball-mounting in the front plate, and abandoned altogether in the Mark III because the space was needed for storage, particularly of ammunition. The fighting compartment had the turret above it, and was none too large. It was not ideal for the commander either since he had to combine the tasks of commanding, gun loading, and often wireless operating as well: the usual drawbacks to a two-man turret. The engine was the elderly but well tried Nuffield Liberty, basically an aero-engine from World War I de-rated from 400 to 340hp. The early Crusaders had considerable trouble with their engines, mainly from the cooling arrangements. The large fan often broke its drive shafts, and the air-cleaners were difficult to keep clean, but after some experience and modification the engine went very well. Undoubtedly the tank was rushed into service before all its development troubles had been ironed out, and in its first engagement in June 1941, Operation 'Battleaxe' more Crusaders fell into enemy hands through mechanical failure than through battle damage. Nevertheless the tank went on to fight in all the major actions throughout the Desert Campaign, and by Alamein the Crusader III with a 6pounder gun had arrived. The 6pounder required a larger mantlet, which was flatter than that for the 2pounder and rather ugly. The same mantlet could also be fitted with a 3in Close Support howitzer, though not many were so modified. The Crusader was outdated by the end of the North African campaign. A few went to Italy and some hulls fought in North-West Europe adapted to such uses as AA vehicles and gun-towers. In the desert the Crusader became popular, and its speed was liked, but the armour was too thin, and the armament always too weak.

Above: Crusader I (Cruiser Mk VI) in North Africa. Basically an enlarged A13 Mk III Covenanter, Crusaders used the A13's Nuffield Liberty engine. The Crusader I mounted a 2-pounder gun and two 7.92mm machine guns.

Below: Front and rear views of a Crusader II (Cruiser Mk VIA). The auxiliary sub-turret appeared only on early models. Insignia is that of the 9th (Queen's Royal) Lancers, 1st Armoured Division.

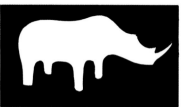

Above: The formation sign of the 1st Armoured Division.

Above: The formation sign of the 6th Armoured Division.

Above: 'Desert Rat' sign of the 7th Armoured Division.

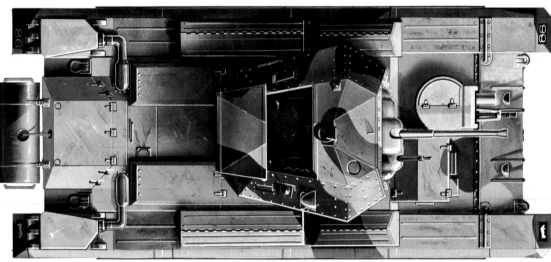

Top: A Crusader in desert disguise. The 'Sun Shield' of hessian-covered tubing was intended to make the tank resemble a large truck when seen from a distance, or from the air.

Above and below: Top and side views of a Crusader II. 5,300 Crusaders were built; plagued by mechanical failure and weak armour, they nevertheless fought in all the major North African campaigns. Outdated by 1943, a few served on in Italy.

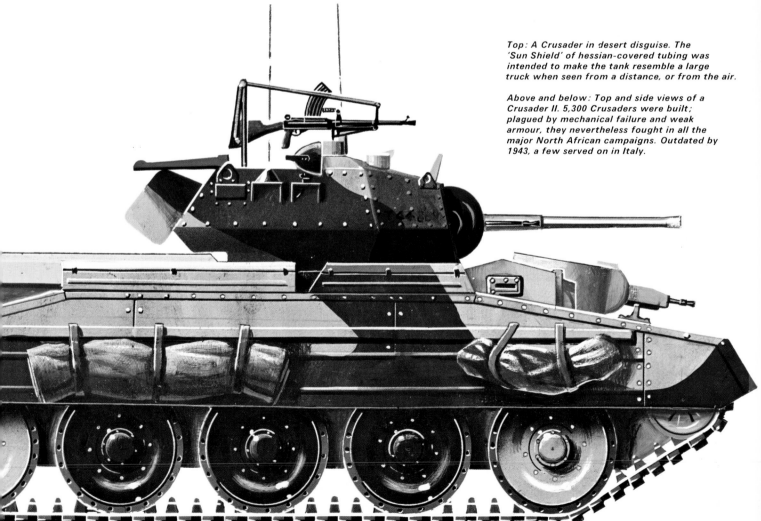

DAIMLER DINGO SCOUT CAR

Marks I, IA, IB, II and III.
Crew: 2.
Armament: One ·303in Bren light machine gun.
Armour: 30mm (1.18in) maximum.
Dimensions: Length 10ft 5in (3.175); width 5ft 7½in (1.714m); height 4ft 11in (1.498m).
Weight: Combat 6,720lbs (3,048kg).
Engine: Six-cylinder petrol engine developing 60bhp.
Performance: Maximum road speed 55mph (88.5 km/h); range 200 miles (322km).
History: Entered service with the British Army in 1940 and phased out of front line service in 1950s, when it was replaced by Ferret. Used post-war by many armies. Still used by Cyprus and Portugal.

In the late 1930s the Alvis company of Coventry built the prototype of a 4×4 scout car called the Dingo, to meet a Mechanisation Board specification. This had a crew of two and was armed with a standard .303in Bren light machine-gun. In 1937 the BSA company also designed a scout car with a crew of two. This was armed with a Bren but was slightly heavier than the Alvis vehicle. Morris Commercial Cars Ltd also built a model, and this had a number of interesting features. In general terms, though, it was inferior to the Alvis and BSA scout cars and so was not developed further. Comparative trials between these vehicles were carried out in 1938 and the BSA vehicle was accepted for service with some modifications. In fact there was not a great deal to choose between these vehicles as far as performance was concerned. By this time Daimler had taken over BSA and the vehicle entered production in 1939 as the Car, Scout, Daimler, Mark I, but it was commonly known as the Dingo. Production of all marks amounted to 6,626. The Mark I was followed by the Mark IA, which had a folding rather than a sliding roof. The Mark IB had the fan draught reversed. All Mark I vehicles had steering on all four wheels, but this feature was dropped from the Mark II onwards. The Mark II had different radiator grills.

whilst the Mark III had no overhead armour at all. (In service most of the earlier vehicles had their overhead armour removed.) For operations in the desert two sand channels were normally carried on the front of the hull. Communications equipment consisted of Numbers 11 and 19 sets. Daimler could not meet the requirements of the British Army, so from 1942 the Humber company also built scout cars, producing almost 4,300 vehicles by the end of the war. The Daimler Dingo was also manufactured in Canada. The chassis was supplied by the Canadian Ford Motor Company, whilst the hulls were supplied by the International Harvester Company. The Canadians built two models, the Scout Car Marks III and IV (Lynx I) and the Scout Car Mark II (Lynx II). These

were heavier than the British vehicles but fitted by more powerful engines, however. Total production in Canada amounted to 3,255 vehicles of all types. By 1945 the Canadians had built the prototype of the Universal Scout Car, which weighed 5 tons (5,080kg) and was powered by a 120hp engine. This vehicle did not enter production.

Right: A Daimler scout car, typically mounting a .303in Bren light machine gun, shows its cross-country capability.

Below: Daimler scout car, known as the 'Dingo'; a name 'appropriated' from Alvis.

DAIMLER MARK I ARMOURED CAR

Crew: 3.
Armament: One 2pounder gun; one 7.92mm BESA machine-gun co-axial with main armament.
Armour: 16mm (0.63in) maximum.
Dimensions: Length 13ft (3.96m); width 8ft (2.44m); height 7ft 4in (2.23m).
Weight: Combat 16,800lbs (7,610kg).
Engine: Daimler six-cylinder inline petrol engine developing 95bhp.
Performance: Road speed 50mph (80kp/h); range 205 miles (328km) with auxiliary tanks.
History: In service with the British Army from 1941 to 1960. Also used after World War II by a number of other countries.

The Daimler armoured car was one of the more advanced wheeled AFVs of World War II and owed its inception very largely to the BSA-Daimler scout car of 1939. The armoured car was very much an enlarged version of the scout car, and the family likeness is apparent when the two are seen side-by-side. Both were short, stubby vehicles with an almost square

wheel plan, and polygonal-shaped bodies. The Daimler had no chassis, all the running gear being attached to strongpoints in the hull. The engine compartment was at the rear, covered by a sloping armoured decking. The driver sat in the front of the hull, between the front wheels, and had a reasonable view forward, though the view was fairly restricted when he was closed down. In the centre of the hull was the fighting compartment, with the commander and gunner. The original intention had been to arm the turret with two .303in machine-guns, or any other combination such as a 0.5in and a .303in gun, but all production vehicles were given a turret almost exactly similar to that of the Tetrarch tank, and carrying a 2pounder gun with co-axial BESA 7.92mm machine-gun. This was an entirely sensible move and it enabled the Daimler to look after itself on the battlefield. The turret was also fitted for wireless from the beginning, and the vehicle's electrical system was designed to cope with charging radio batteries, a feature not found on every AFV at that time. Towards the end of World War II the 2pounder was more than outclassed by the

latest anti-tank guns and the larger guns on German armoured cars. In an attempt to step up its performance the gun was fitted with the Littlejohn 'squeeze-bore' attachment, which was also used on the Tetrarch's gun. This was not a complete success since it restricted the gun to using armour-piercing ammunition only, and so the vehicle lost some of the flexibility possible with different types of ammunition. One or two cars in North-West Europe in 1944 and 1945 had the turrets removed completely and were used as regimental command vehicles, though they were a little cramped. The driver had power steering, a rare luxury in World War II, and the well-known Daimler pre-selector gearbox. The power was taken forwards from the engine to a main transfer box which contained the differential, and from there it went outwards to four driving shafts, which led to each wheel, via universal joints. This apparently complicated system originated with the BSA scout car and was entirely successful. It gave excellent traction and allowed a large measure of independent movement at each wheel, which were sprung on long coil springs. The gearbox had five forward speeds, and the driver could use all of them in reverse if need be. There was a second steering wheel in the back of the turret which the commander could use in an emergency, the driver doing the gear-changing and accelerating. Another modern feature, most uncommon at the time, was disc brakes on all four wheels. The Daimler first came into service in 1941, being issued to units in the UK first of all. The type was then sent to North Africa, and thereafter to practically every theatre of war, including the South-East Asia Command. Some 2,700 were built in all, a figure which includes the Mark II, though the differences were slight. After the war the Daimler continued as the standard armoured car in British service, and was used in practically every peace-keeping action all over the world until replaced in the early 1960s by the Saladin.

Left: Front view of a Daimler Mk I armoured car, used in reconnaissance troops of armoured car regiments in the ratio of 2:2. In spite of its agility and armament, 2-pounder and co-axial 7.92mm machine-gun, the vehicle was very vulnerable in combat.

Right: Rear view of a Daimler Mk II armoured car, showing the improved armoured radiator grille. Other major differences from the Mk I included a more bulbous gun mantlet and the incorporation of an escape-hatch for the driver.

Left: Rear view of a Daimler Mk I of the 11th Hussars, part of the 7th Armoured Division, Berlin, 1945. Note tools at rear of the vehicle.

Above and below: Side and front views of a Daimler Mk I of the 11th Hussars. Note the unusually high angle of elevation of the gun—particularly useful for engaging targets on a higher level, when in a built-up area or travelling on a road overlooked by high ground.

VALENTINE INFANTRY TANK MARK III

Marks I-XI.

Crew: 3 (4 in Mks III and IV).

Armament: One 2pdr and one 7·92mm BESA machine-gun (Mks I-VII); one 6pdr and one 7·92mm BESA machine-gun (Mks VIII-X); and one 75mm gun and one 7.92mm BESA machine-gun (Mk XI).

Armour: 8mm (0·31in) minimum; 65mm (2·56in) maximum.

Dimensions: Length (overall) 17ft 9in (5·41m); width 8ft 7½in (2·63m): height 7ft 5½in (2·27m).

Weight: 35,840lb (16,257kg).

Engine: AEC petrol engine developing 135hp (Mk I); AEC diesel developing 131hp (Mks II, III, VIII); GM diesel developing 138hp (Mks IV, IX); and GM diesel developing 165hp (Mks X, XI).

Performance: Road speed 15mph (24kph): range 90miles (144km); vertical obstacle 3ft (0·91m); trench 7ft 9in (2·36in); gradient 60 per cent.

History: Entered service with the British Army in May 1940; obsolete by May 1945. Also used by Canada, France and the Soviet Union. Also built in Canada.

The Valentine tank was a private venture by Vickers-Armstrong Ltd and built to the prewar concept of the British Army that there should be two types of tank, a cruiser for the open warfare as practised by cavalry, and a heavy support tank for the infantry. These latter were needed to be heavily armoured and performance was a secondary consideration. In designing the Valentine, however, Vickers took several mechanical components from existing cruisers which they were building for the War Office, and so saved both time and effort in trials and production. In fact, the Valentine was more of a well armoured cruiser than a pure infantry tank, but its low speed was always a handicap to its use in open warfare.

The name of Valentine derived from the date when the design was submitted to the War Office, 14 February 1938. An order was not placed until July 1939, when 275 were demanded in the shortest possible time. The first ones were issued to service in May 1940 and several were given to the cavalry to make up for the losses of the Dunkirk evacuation and only later found their way to the tank brigades for their proper role of infantry support. By the time production ceased in early 1944 8,275 Valentines of all marks had been built. Some 1,420 were made in Canada and 1,390 of these, together with 1,300 from UK, were sent to Soviet Russia. The Russians put them into action straight away and admired the simplicity and reliability of the engine and transmission, but they disliked the small gun which was of little use on the Eastern Front. In some cases they replaced it with their own 76·2mm tank gun.

In British service the Valentine first saw action in the Western Desert in 1941 and successive marks of it continued in the desert right through until the end of the campaign. Some were also landed with the 1st Army in Tunisia. These desert Valentines gained a great reputation for reliability and it is reported that after El Alamein some motored over 3,000 miles (4,830km) on their own tracks following the 8th Army. A squadron was landed with the assault force on Madagascar in 1942 and the 3rd New Zealand Division had Valentines in the Pacific campaign. Some of these tanks had their 2pdr guns replaced by 3in howitzers for close support work. A very small number went to Burma and were used in the Arakan, and a few were put into Gibraltar. By 1944, when the invasion of north-west Europe was mounted, the Valentine had been superseded as a gun tank, but the hull and chassis had already been utilised in a wide variety of different roles, and in these guises many Valentines were taken to France.

Probably no other tank has had so many changes built on to the basic structure. In addition to going through 11 marks as a gun tank, the Valentine was converted for DD drive (amphibious), bridgelaying, flamethrowing and more than one type of minefield clearing. It was an invaluable experimental vehicle for all manner of strange ideas: in one case a stripped chassis was fitted with rockets in an attempt to create that Jules Verne concept — the flying tank. It failed spectacularly.

As with most tanks the hull was divided into three compartments, driving, fighting and engine. The driver sat on the centre line of the vehicle and was rather cramped. He got in and out by a hatch above his head, and when closed down his vision was restricted to a small visor and two episcopes.

The fighting compartment had the turret mounted on it, and the turret was the worst feature of the whole tank. It was always too small, no matter which mark is considered, and no amount of redesign ever cured this trouble. In the marks which had a three-man crew the two in the turret were overworked, or at least the commander was. He had to load the main armament, command the vehicle, select targets for the gunner, and operate the wireless. His vision was extremely restricted because there was no cupola for him and he had to rely on a single episcope when closed down. This naturally meant that he rarely did close down properly, and left his hatch open so that he could bob up to get a view. This led to casualties as soon as the fighting started. In the back of the turret was the No 19 radio set, which also had a short range set built into it for infantry co-operation. The commander operated these two sets, and also gave instructions to his crew through an RT set. Not surprisingly the Marks III and V, with a four-man crew, were popular with commanders, though the space in the turret was no better and the vision just as bad.

The gun was as poor as the turret. The 2pdr was an accurate little weapon but it was already outdated in 1938 though it survived in the early desert battles because it could just defeat the Italian and lighter German tanks at its maximum range. However, 1,000 yards (915m) was the most that it could do and another drawback was the lack of an HE shell for general targets. Some 79 rounds were carried, and about 2,000 rounds for the coaxial BESA. The Marks VIII, IX and X were fitted with a 6pdr though even that was nearly out of date by the time it appeared and, incredibly, the Marks VIII and IX had no coaxial machine-gun with their 6pdr, so the crew were quite incapable of engaging infantry except with the main armament. The Mark X had the BESA installed, but this cut down the space left for the crew. Most marks carried a Bren LMG inside the turret and this gun could be mounted on the roof, though of course it could only be fired by the commander fully exposing himself through his hatch. The Canadian-built Valentines were equipped with Browning 0·3in machine-guns in place of the BESA and some, but not all, of the later marks were fitted with smoke dischargers on the turret sides.

The turret was traversed with a hydraulic motor controlled by a spade grip. This gave a good lay, but the final touches were done by handwheel. With the 2pdr the gun's elevation was laid by the gunner's shoulder-piece, there being no gearing involved at all. The later guns were laid in elevation by a hand gear wheel.

In contrast with the fighting compartment, the engine was well housed and easy to get at. Maintenance was easy for a tank, and the entire unit was most reliable. The Mark I had the AEC petrol engine, but all successive marks used diesels, which appear to have given little trouble. The power went through a five-speed Meadows gearbox to steering clutches and steering brakes, the latter being prominently

Right: Side view of a Valentine Mk II of No. 1 Troop, A Squadron 50th RTR, 23rd Armoured Brigade. This shows the tank as it appeared in Tunisia at the time of the Mareth battle of March 1943. The original yellow desert camouflage of the 8th Army has been modified to blend in with the Tunisian landscape. The tank is armed with the 2-pounder gun, for which 60 rounds of ammunition were carried.

mounted on the outside of the drive sprockets.

One of the first conversions of the Valentine was to a self-propelled gun, the Bishop. This was a 25pdr in a thin armoured box on top of a Valentine chassis, and was intended for desert work. It was slow, cramped and carried too little ammunition. It was phased out by the time of the Sicilian invasion. At the same time a 17pdr conversion was made, and this was more successful. A fixed gun mount was built over the driving and fighting compartments and the gun pointed over the rear decking. It worked well and was christened Archer. Archer was built in some numbers and remained in service until the early 1950s with the British Army. One difficulty was that the driver had to leave his seat before the gun could be fired as it recoiled directly into his position; another trouble was that there was no overhead cover for the crew. It served well at a time when anti-tank defence was

sparse, however, and when a heavy punch was needed to keep the Panthers and Tigers at bay. Some 39 rounds of ammunition were carried, but there was once again little space for the gun crew and almost none for their kit. In winter a canvas tilt could be erected over the open roof, but in bad weather an Archer was a miserable vehicle and it could be bitterly cold.

All the marks were built with riveted plate armour and virtually no curves anywhere. Canadian Valentines and some of the British-built Marks X and XI were given cast nose plates which were both stronger and cheaper than the built-up versions, but in general the armour layout was uninspired. The maximum thickness of 65mm (2·56in) was naturally in front, but at the rear and on top it was down to 8mm (0·31in) and by 1944 this was very thin indeed.

The suspension was typical of its period and is

usually described as being a slow-motion type. It consisted of two three-wheeled bogies on each side, the wheels being sprung by horizontal coils in linked bogies. The front and rear wheels were bigger than the others, giving a distinctive appearance to the side view, and the hull was carried well above ground level. The track was returned on three top rollers and was built up from cast track links. These worked very well in all conditions except the Russian winter, when apparently they collected packed snow and stopped the tank altogether.

The Valentine DD version was used mainly for training, but a few were landed during the Italian campaign. None went to Normandy. The basic Valentine was carefully waterproofed and fitted with a collapsible screen which suspended the hull below water level. An external screw was fitted and this had to be hinged up when the vehicle beached.

Above: Side view of Valentine Bishop self-propelled gun. 100 were built on the Valentine II chassis.

Right: A Valentine captured by the Germans in North Africa and subsequently used by the Afrika Korps, only to be knocked out by its original owners in a later battle. The Afrika Korps was forced to supplement its weapon and supply requirements with a large amount of captured material, because Allied aircraft and naval units were able effectively to prevent its trans-Mediterranean supply by sea or air from the European mainland.

Right: Front and rear views of a Valentine II of 50th Royal Tank Regiment.

Below right: Front views of (left) Valentine I of A Squadron, 17/21st Lancers, 6th Armoured Division, in October 1941, and (right) a Valentine XI used as a command vehicle in 30th Corps Anti-Tank Regiment, Royal Artillery, in North-West Europe during the campaigns of 1944-1945.

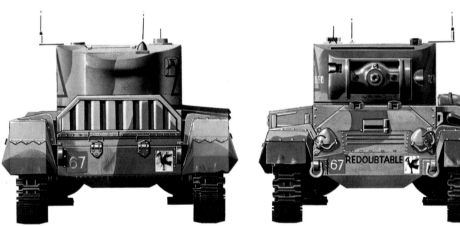

LIGHT TANK MARK VII (TETRARCH)

Crew: 3.

Armament: One 2pounder gun and one 7.92mm Besa machine-gun coaxially mounted in the turret; the Tetrarch I CS mounted a 3in howitzer in place of the 2pounder.

Armour: 16mm (0.63in) maximum; 4mm (0.16in) minimum.

Dimensions: Length 13ft 3in (4.04m); width 7ft 7in (2.31m); height 6ft 11in (2.10m).

Weight: Combat 16,800lbs (7,620kg).

Engine: Meadows MAT 12-cylinder horizontally opposed petrol engine developing 165bhp at 2,700 rpm.

Performance: Speed 40mph (64km/h); range 140 miles (224km); vertical obstacle 1ft 8in (0.508m); trench 5ft (1.524m); gradient 60 per cent.

History: Designed in 1937 and first prototype completed December 1937. Production not ordered until 1940. By 1942 171 completed and manufacture ceased. Intended as a fast light tank, but used by Airborne Forces as a gliderborne support vehicle. Half-squadron took part in Madagascar landings, one squadron in Normandy airborne assault, and a few in the Rhine crossing. In service until 1950. Some 20 sent to Soviet Russia in 1941.

The Light Tank Mark VII was a marked change from the previous Vickers models and incorporated several interesting and radical ideas. The inadequate armament of the Mark VI light tanks had been appreciated, and the Mark VII was given a 2pounder (40mm), the same type as that being carried by the British medium tanks of the time. The Tetrarch's armour was too light, but the chief intention was speed, and much thought had been put into the suspension. The four large road wheels on each side represented a reversion to one of Walter Christie's earliest ideas, that of the fast dual-purpose armoured vehicle. The tracks were meant to be removable so that the Tetrarch could run on roads like an armoured car if it chose so to do, and thick solid rubber tires, together with soft Christie springing, gave a tolerable ride. Maximum speed was very high for its day, and the Tetrarch was meant to be a fast-moving, hard-hitting reconnaissance tank, capable of dashing over the battlefield and fighting for its information when it had to. The War Office was having second thoughts about this idea just as the prototype appeared, for the Spanish Civil War had not shown light tanks to be as effective as everyone had hoped, and it was not until 1940, when tanks of all kinds were desperately short, that a production order was given. Production was slow, partly because of difficulties with the unusual suspension, and partly because the factory was bombed. Some of the first production models went to Russia, and others took part in the Madagascar operations; the remainder were put in reserve straight from the factory to be kept as airborne tanks. The Hamilcar glider was specifically designed to carry the Tetrarch, but only one squadron flew to Normandy in 1944. One Hamilcar broke up while crossing the English Channel as a result of flying into the slipstream of the towing plane, and its Tetrarch and crew plunged into the sea. A few more Tetrarchs were used in the Rhine crossing in May 1945, but after that they were never used again, although a dwindling number remained on strength until the gliders disappeared in 1950. The hull was a light box, with vertical sides and within the track width (not built out over the tracks, that is). In front was a large sloping glacis plate marred by a central square box which covered the driver's head and shoulders. The entire front of this box could be swung open to allow the driver to see, but when it was closed down the driver had only a small vision block in the middle of it. The glacis plate was 0.63in (16mm) thick, as was the front of the turret. The turret was reasonably roomy, but the view was poor and there was no cupola for the commander. He was in any case very busy since he acted as loader for the 2pounder. It may be no accident that on the few occasions when the Tetrarch was in action it was generally used as a static gun, where the commander would have been able to give all his attention to controlling his gunner. There was a smoke discharger on each side of the turret, and most Tetrarchs had a spare petrol tank in a frighteningly vulnerable position on the rear decking. The Meadows engine drove to a gearbox which gave five forward speeds and drove through the rear road wheel. The two centre wheels could be moved out or in, to bow the track for steering gentle curves. The idea was derived from the Bren Carrier, but was greatly improved on the Tetrarch and worked very well. Track bowing was controlled by a steering wheel, but sharper turns required the driver to use two levers and apply brakes to the final drive-shafts. By the time the Tetrarch was ready for service, the 2pounder was already well outclassed, and in an attempt to improve its performance a Littlejohn adaptor was fitted. This gave a higher muzzle velocity, but it could not be used with HE shell, and so was only a marginal improvement. It seems

Left: A Mk ICS (Close-Support) version of the Tetrarch light airborne tank is driven from a Hamilcar glider. Unlike the conventional model, this Tetrarch mounts a 3-inch howitzer firing either smoke or HE rounds. The vehicle seen here, on trials, is debarking with the aid of sand-bags. Under operational conditions, a special ramp would be used. The Tetrarch remained in British service until 1950.

Below: Rear, front and side views of a typical service-used Tetrarch light airborne tank Mk ICS, with detailed enlargements of its unit markings. This tank was used by Headquarters Squadron, 6th Airborne Reconnaissance Regiment, 6th Airborne Division, which was flown into Normandy on the evening of the D-Day landings, 6 June 1944, to help secure the River Orne crossings.

extraordinary that with the known failings of the Tetrarch the War Office should have ordered a successor on the same pattern, but they did and 102 were built by 1944. This tank was the Mark VIII, or Harry Hopkins as it was felicitously named. Mechanically it was very similar to the Tetrarch, but the hull was simplified in outline and had a long flat top deck with a steeply sloping glacis plate. This last was in one piece and 1.5in (38mm) thick. The turret was lower and had sloped sides, though the front plate was still flat, but a better mantlet was fitted. The armament was unchanged, and the weight went up to 19,040lbs (8,636kg). This tank was never used in action (few were even issued for service use), and it could be described as a waste of factory effort at a time when such effort was badly needed for other things. A derivation of the Harry Hopkins was the Alecto self-propelled gun, developed in response to a General Staff requirement of April 1942 for a light self-propelled gun for infantry support, using the 95mm Howitzer. The Alecto used a totally redesigned hull from the Harry Hopkins, with the gun mounted low down in the front. The crew was four, the height reduced by nearly 9in (227mm) and the speed reduced to 30mph (48km/h). In order to keep the weight down as much as possible, the armour was only 0.4in (10mm) at its thickest, but it was all-welded, a new technique at that time. Had the Alecto gone into action it seems quite likely that it would not have survived for long, for all SP guns were the target for the heaviest retaliation that could be fired at them, and 10mm of armour would not have kept out any AP projectiles. As it happened, few were built and none saw action. After the war a very small number were tried as reconnaissance vehicles, with limited success.

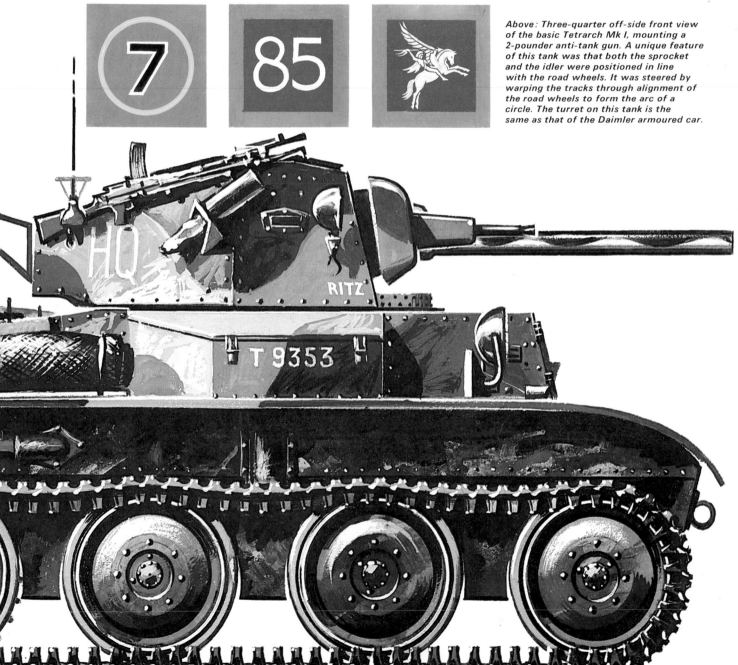

Above: Three-quarter off-side front view of the basic Tetrarch Mk I, mounting a 2-pounder anti-tank gun. A unique feature of this tank was that both the sprocket and the idler were positioned in line with the road wheels. It was steered by warping the tracks through alignment of the road wheels to form the arc of a circle. The turret on this tank is the same as that of the Daimler armoured car.

HUMBER MARK I ARMOURED CAR

Crew: 3.
Armament: One 15mm BESA machine-gun; one 7.92mm BESA machine-gun.
Armour: 15mm (0.59in) maximum.
Dimensions: Length 15ft (4.572m); width 7ft 2in (2.184m); height 7ft 10in (2.387m).
Weight: 15,094lbs (6,846kg).
Engine: Rootes six-cylinder petrol engine developing 90hp at 3,200rpm.
Performance: Maximum road speed 45mph (72.4km/h); range 250 miles (402km).
History: Entered service with British Army in 1941. Phased out of service shortly after end of World War II. Still used by a number of countries including Burma, Ceylon, Cyprus, India and Mexico.

In 1938 Guy Motors built prototypes of a vehicle called the Tank, Light, Wheeled, Mk 1, based on

components of the Guy Quad-Ant artillery tractor. After trials, a production order was given to Guy Motors and production started in 1939. The Guy has the distinction of being the first British armoured vehicle to enter production with a hull of all-welded construction, which was both quicker and cheaper than the previous riveted construction. Some 101 were built, the first 50 as Mk Is (these had Vickers .5in and .303in machine-guns), and the other 51 as Mk IAs (these had 15mm and 7.92mm BESA machine-guns). In service, the light tank designation was dropped, and the type became the Guy Armoured Car. Production stopped as Guy already had large orders for military vehicles. The Humber Mk I armoured car, which was to have been known as the Tank, Light, Wheeled, Mk III, did in fact have a hull built by Guy Motors, somewhat modified, but mounted on a Rootes Karrier artillery tractor. The driver was seated at the front of the hull, the two-man

turret with the commander and gunner was located in the centre, and the engine was at the rear. The Mk I was followed by the Mk II, which had a redesigned hull. The Mk III had a larger, three-man turret whilst the Mk IV had a three-man turret and was armed with a 37mm gun and a BESA 7.92mm machine-gun. Most Humbers also had .303in Bren light machine guns for anti-aircraft defence and smoke dischargers. An anti-aircraft model with four 7.92mm BESA machine-guns was also developed and placed in service in 1943–44, but by the time this entered service the threat from German aircraft had passed and it was withdrawn from service. The Humber was also built in Canada as the Armoured Car, General Motors, Mk I (Fox I). These were slightly heavier than the British vehicles and had a more powerful engine. Total production of the Humber in both Britain and Canada amounted to about 5,600 vehicles of all marks.

Left: The Humber armoured car—one of the standard British armoured cars of WWII.

Below: The Humber Mk III armoured car. Generally, British armoured cars of World War II were far more advanced than those of other nations—and the Humber was no exception. It was well-armoured and armed and had excellent road and cross-country performance. Its maximum speed was 72.4km/h.

AEC ARMOURED CAR MARK I

Mk I, Mk II, Mk III.
Crew: 3.
Armament: One 2pounder (40mm) gun; one 7.92mm BESA machine-gun co-axial with main armament; one .303in Bren anti-aircraft light machine-gun; one 2in (51mm) bomb-thrower.
Armour: 2.25in (57mm) maximum; 0.25in (6.35mm) minimum.
Dimensions: Length 17ft (5.181m); width 9ft (2.743m); height 8ft 4½in (2.552m).
Weight: Combat 24,640lbs (11,176kg).
Engine: AEC A195 six-cylinder water-cooled diesel developing 105bhp at 2,000rpm.
Performance: Road speed 35mph (56.3km/h); range 250 miles (402km).
History: Entered service with British Army in 1942 and some also used by Yugoslavia in 1944–45. A few AEC armoured cars were in service in Lebanon as late as 1976.

The AEC armoured car was a private venture by the Associated Equipment Company (AEC). A mock up was completed but no official interest was shown by the British Army; in 1941 the mock up was shown unofficially at a military parade held in Horse Guards Parade in London attended by the Prime Minister, Mr Churchill. As a result Churchill suggested that the vehicle be placed in production and the first production order was placed with AEC in June 1941. The AEC armoured car used automotive components of the Matador 4×4 artillery tractor also built by AEC and the Mark I, of which 122 were built, had the turret of the Valentine tank, armed with a 2pounder (40mm) gun and a co-axial 7.92mm BESA machine-gun. These had an elevation of +15° and a depression of −15°. The turret was powered in traverse but the guns had to be elevated by the gunner's shoulder! A 2in (51mm) smoke discharger was provided and there was also a Bren .303in light machine-gun on a special anti-aircraft mount. Some 58 rounds of 2pounder am-

munition, 2,925 rounds of BESA and 600 rounds of .303in ammunition were carried. The hull had a minimum thickness of 0.25in (6.35mm) and a maximum thickness of 2.25in (57mm). The driver was seated at the front of the hull, the turret was located in the centre with the commander on the right and the gunner on the left, and the engine was at the rear of the hull. The Mark I was followed by the Mark II, which had a redesigned hull, a more powerful engine and a new turret fitted with a 6pounder (57mm) gun and a

co-axial 7.92mm BESA machine-gun. The AEC Mark III was similar to the Mark II but had a 75mm gun, rather than the 6pounder, and other modifications. The crews of the Marks II and III were increased from three to four men. Production of all marks of the AEC armoured car totalled 629 vehicles. The Mark I entered service from 1942 and was normally used to give fire support to the lighter Humber armoured cars. Although rather large, the AEC had good armour protection and was well armed.

Right: The AEC armoured car Mk III. Based on a lorry chassis, mounting a 75mm gun, this vehicle gave good service from 1942 onward. Several other versions were brought into service.

Right: Top view of the AEC armoured car showing layout of vehicle with driver at front, turret in centre and engine at rear.

AEC COMMAND VEHICLE

AEC HP, AEC LP
Crew: 8.
Armament: None.
Armour: 9mm (0.35in) maximum.
Dimensions: Length 26ft 1in (7.949m); width 7ft 11in (2.413m); height 8ft 10in (2.692m).
Weight: 40,320lbs (18,289kg).
Engine: AEC Model A198 six-cylinder diesel developing 150bhp at 1,900rpm.
Performance: Maximum road speed 30mph (48.5km/h).
History: Entered service with the British Army in 1944 and remained in service for some years after the war.

From the earliest days of armoured warfare, one of the problems has been the effective command and control of the armoured forces. In World War I and in the period immediately after it, tanks were modified for use in the command role, but these did not prove a success as there was insufficient room for all of the equipment required. The British Army had a rather simple Armoured Command Vehicle (ACV) before World War II. The first proper ACV entered service in late 1940. This was the Guy Lizard, which was not built in large numbers. The Lizard was followed by the AEC 4×4 ACV. This was based on the Matador chassis, used by the Royal Artillery to tow its 5.5in guns. A total of 416 of these was built, but it was soon discovered than an even larger vehicle was required. AEC then built a 6×6 ACV, 151 of these were built in 1944–45. Two basic models were built, the HP and LP. The HP was the High Power model, and this had a No 19 set, a No 53 set and an R107 set. The LP (Low Power) model had a No 19 set, a No 19 (HP) set and an R107. A cypher machine was also carried quite frequently. The hull provided the crew with protection from small arms fire; there was a door in each side of the hull, another door in the rear of the hull and a roof hatch. The ACV was divided into the engine compartment, the driver's compartment, and the staff section, with the wireless compartment at the rear of the hull. The staff compartment was provided with desks and mapboards. When the ACV was being used in the static role radio aerials could be erected. The AEC had 6×6 drive with 6×4 being used for normal road work and 6×6 for cross-country work. The tires were of the runflat type. To cope with the additional power required for the radios and ventilation system, an auxiliary engine was mounted at the rear of the hull. The ventilation system provided air for the staff and wireless sections, as well as air to cool the No 53 radio set. Today most armies have special models of their basic APC for the command role: the British, for example, use a modified version of the FV432, the Americans a modified version (M577A1) of the M113A1, whilst the Russians have a BTR152 with a higher roof.

Above: The AEC 6x6 command vehicle entered British service in 1944.

Below: Rear of AEC command vehicle which was developed for use by senior command staff in the field, incorporating such equipment as map-boards and radio. Heavy armour protected it from attack by aircraft.

A22 CHURCHILL INFANTRY TANK

Churchills I to VIII

Crew: 5.

Armament: Churchill I one 2pounder gun, one 7.92mm BESA machine-gun and one 3in howitzer in the hull; Churchill II one 2pounder gun and two 7.92mm BESA machine-guns; Churchill III-IV one 6pounder gun and two 7.92mm BESA machine-guns; Churchill IV NA 75 one 75mm gun, one .3in Browning machine gun and one 7.92mm BESA machine-gun; Churchill V and VIII one 95mm howitzer and two 7.92mm BESA machine-guns; Churchill VI and VII one 75mm gun and two 7.92mm BESA machine-guns; Churchill I CS two 3in howitzers and one 7.92mm BESA machine-gun.

Armour: Crusader I-VI 102mm (4in) maximum and 16mm (0.63in) minimum; Crusader VII and VIII 152mm (6in) maximum and 25mm (1in) minimum.

Dimensions: Length 24ft 5in (7.44m); width 10ft 8in (3.25m); height 8ft 2in (2.49m).

Weight: Combat Churchill III 87,360lbs (39,574kg).

Engine: Bedford 12-cylinder water-cooled inline developing 350bhp.

Performance: Road speed 15.5mph (24.8km/h); cross-country speed 8mph (12.8km/h); range 90 miles (144km); vertical obstacle 2ft 6in (0.812m); trench 10ft (3.048m).

History: In service with the British Army from 1941 to 1952. Also used by Eire, India and Jordan.

The Churchill was the replacement for the Matilda II, the specification having been drawn up with that in mind. It was to the project number A20 that the new tank was first assigned, and design work started in September 1939 by Harland and Wolff of Belfast. The diversity of manufacturers was a deliberate policy of the War Office before World War II, the intention being not only to spread the workload among factories who were feeling the pinch after the Depression, but also to extend the knowledge and expertise of building AFVs to the widest possible extent. The A20 went as far as four prototypes in June 1940, but no farther. It was to have been rather like a World War I rhomboidal, with side sponsons mounting 2pounder guns. Vauxhall Motors took over the contract for the next infantry tank, the A22, and were able to use the A20 as a starting base. The beginnings were not auspicious with Dunkirk just over, and virtually no armour force

in the UK at all. Vauxhall were given one year in which to design, test and produce the tank, the stipulation being that the production lines had to be assembling the type within 12 months. With this extraordinary time limit to constrain them, the design team set to work and the first pilot model was actually running within seven months. The first 14 production tanks were off the line by June 1941, within 11 months of design starting, and volume production followed on quickly after that. Such a rush was bound to bring its problems, and the early marks of Churchill had no lack of them. The engine was special design, a 'flat twelve' not unlike two Bedford lorry engines laid on their sides and joined to a common crankcase. The idea was to make an engine that was both compact and accessible. Compact it certainly was, but it was scarcely accessible. The petrol pump was driven by a flexible shaft underneath the engine, and had an unfortunate habit of snapping. The hydraulic tappets, copied from American engines, were meant to run without adjustment, but frequently broke, necessitating a change of engine. The carburettor controls were also hydraulic, and also got out of adjustment. The power output was low for the weight of the hull, and the overall response sluggish. In fact the tank was rushed into service before it was ready. After a year of use most of the troubles were ironed out and it became quite reliable, but the first 12 months saw it gain a reputation for fragility and unreliability which it never completely lived down. The A22 specification was more modern than any that had gone before, and it called for a low silhouette and thick armour, both requirements for survival on the battlefield. Unfortunately the first Vauxhall design perpetuated the worst features of the armament stagnation that had blighted British tanks since 1918. The turret carred only a 2pounder gun, and by 1940 it was becoming clear that this size was a complete anachronism. The difficulty was that there was none other. The 6pounder design was in being, but the Ordnance Factories were tooled up for 2pounders, and in the desperate days after Dunkirk there was no time to change over, so 2pounders it had to be for another year or more. A 3in Close Support howitzer was mounted low down in the front of the hull, alongside the driver. This was much like the arrangement in the French Char B, and there was little enough faith in that idea; but again, the designers had little option but to use the weapons available to them.

Above: Front and rear views of a Churchill III armed with a 6-pounder gun, for which a total of 84 rounds of armour-piercing and high-explosive ammunition were carried.

A very few Close Support Churchills I were built, and these had the unusual armament of two 3in howitzers, the second one replacing the 2pounder gun in the turret, but the idea was not pursued further. The Churchill II and later marks dropped the hull gun in favour of a BESA machine-gun. By March 1942 the 6pounder was available and was fitted to the turret of the Churchill III in that month. Improvement followed and the Mark VII had a 75mm gun, the Mark VIII a 95mm Close Support howitzer, and some North African Mark IVs were re-worked in Egypt to accommodate a 75mm gun and 0.3in Browning machine-gun in the turret, both these weapons being taken from Shermans and perhaps Grants. The armour of the Churchill was probably the best part of the vehicle, and was very heavy for the time. The thickness of the frontal plates went up with successive marks, and most of the earlier marks were re-worked, as time and supplies permitted, to be given extra 'appliqué' plates welded on. Turrets increased in size and complexity and the Mark VII was given the first commander's cupola in a British tank to have all-round vision when closed down — a great step forward, though it was

Far left: One of many Churchill variants, the AVRE with SBG (Standard Box Girder) bridge attachment, during the D-Day landings. Note the Sherman flail tank to the left.

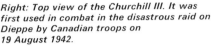

Right: Top view of the Churchill III. It was first used in combat in the disastrous raid on Dieppe by Canadian troops on 19 August 1942.

common enough in German tanks by that time. The hull was roomy, which was fortunate in view of the amount of development which was done on it, and the ammunition stowage was particularly generous. The Mark I was able to carry 150 rounds of 2pounder and 58 of 3in howitzer ammunition, still leaving room for five men. The hull was sufficiently wide to allow the Mark III's 6pounder turret to be fitted without too much trouble, though the 75mm and 95mm weapons caused a little difficulty and had a rather smaller turret-ring than was ideal. These latter turrets looked a little slab-sided, as a result of the fact that some were built up with welding, rather than cast as complete units. The Churchill was the first British tank with the Merritt-Brown regenerative steering, which had been tried out in the A6 10 years before. This system not only saved a great deal of power when turning, but also enabled the driver to make much sharper turns, until in neutral he could turn the tank on its own axis. This system, or some variant of it, is now universally used by all tank designers. Another innovation, for British AFVs at least, was the use of hydraulics in the steering and clutch controls, so that driving was far less tiring than it

had been on previous designs, and the driver could exercise finer judgement in his use of the controls. The suspension was by 11 small road wheels on each side. Each of these wheels, or more properly bogies, was sprung separately on vertical coil springs, and the amount of movement was limited so that the ride was fairly harsh. However, such a system had the merits of simplicity, cheapness, and relative invulnerability to damage; each side could tolerate the loss of several bogies and still support the chassis, and the manufacture and fitting of bogies was not too difficult. Churchills were used on most of the European battlefronts. The first time they were in action was the Dieppe raid of August 1942, in which several Mark Is and IIs took part, together with a few Mark IIIs. Few got over the harbour wall, and most were either drowned when disembarking, or captured. A number of Mark I, II and III examples were sent to Russia, and a few Mark IIIs were tried at Alamein. Thereafter they were used in Tunisia and Italy in ever-increasing numbers until the end of the war. Several brigades of Churchills were deployed in North-West Europe, where their thick armour proved very useful, but throughout the cam-

paign the Churchill was hampered by being outgunned by German armour. There were many variants on the Churchill chassis as it was quickly found that it was well suited to such tasks as bridging, mineclearing, armoured recovery, and (probably best of all) flame-throwing. The Churchill was also a particularly successful Armoured Vehicle Royal Engineers (AVRE) and fulfilled several different RE roles until replaced by the Centurion AVRE in the early 1960s. Altogether 5,460 Churchills were produced, and they remained in service in varying numbers until the 1950s. The lack of adequate gun power was realised quite early in the Churchill's life, however, and in 1943 Vauxhall developed an improved version carrying a 17 pounder in the turret. The turret-ring had to be enlarged, and so the hull was widened. The armour remained the same thickness, and weight went up to 50 tons – 112,000lbs (50,736kg). To support this extra load the tracks were widened, new bogies fitted, and the Bedford engine geared down. Top speed was only 11mph (17.6km/h) and although the prototypes were still being tried in 1945, the idea came to nothing, and the Black Prince, as it was to have been called, was scrapped.

Right: A post-war view of a Churchill AVRE Mk VIII (FV3903). This was a standard Churchill Mk VII with a modified turret mounting a 165mm BL Mk I low-velocity gun, for which 31 rounds were carried. It was also fitted with a cradle which held a 10-ton fascine, some 2.438m in diameter and 3.962m in length.

Above, top line: Insignia of Churchill Mk III 'Bert' of the Calgary Regiment at Dieppe. Bottom line: Insignia of 51st Royal Tank Regiment's Churchill Mk III 'Cyclops'.

Left: Side view of a Churchill Mk III of the 51st Royal Tank Regiment, which took part in the tank's first notable success, the action fought at Steamroller Farm, Tunisia, on 28 February 1943.

A27M CROMWELL CRUISER TANK

Cromwell Marks I to VIII.
Crew: 5.
Armament: One 6pounder gun; one 7.92mm BESA machine-gun co-axial with main armament; one 7.92mm BESA machine-gun in hull (Marks I to III); one 75mm QF Mark V or VA gun; two 7.92mm machine-guns (Marks IV, V and VII); one 95mm howitzer; two 7.92mm BESA machine-guns (Marks VI and VIII).
Armour: 0.31in (8mm) minimum; 3in (76mm) maximum; 0.4 (10mm) minimum; 3in (76mm) maximum in welded variants; 4in (102mm) appliqué armour.
Dimensions: Length 20ft 10in (6.35m); width 10ft (3.04m); height 9ft 3¾in (2.84m).
Weight: 61,600lbs (27,942kg).
Ground pressure: 14.7lb/in² (1kg/cm²).
Power to weight ratio: 21.8hp/ton.
Engine: Rolls-Royce Meteor V-12 water-cooled petrol engine developing 600bhp at 2,250rpm.
Performance: Road speed 40mph (64km/h); cross-country speed 18mph (29km/h); range 173 miles (277km); vertical obstacle 3ft (0.92m); trench 7ft 6in (2.28m).
History: Served with the British Army from 1942 to 1950.

The Cromwell emerged from a General Staff specification drawn up in late 1940 and early 1941 for a 'heavy cruiser'. The cruisers built to the traditional ideas of a light fast vehicle capable of fulfilling the cavalry role of pursuit and exploitation had proved to be unequal to the modern battlefield in two vital areas, protection and gun power. The 1941 specification called for cruiser tanks with an all-up weight of around 25 tons (25,401kg), front armour of 2.75in (70mm) thickness, and a 6pounder gun on a 60in (1.52m) turret ring. Nuffield produced the first model, designated the A24 and originally called the Cromwell. This was an improved Crusader and used several of its components, among which was the Liberty engine which quickly proved itself incapable of performing satisfactorily in a tank weighing nearly 60,000lbs (27,216kg). The name was soon changed to Cavalier, and the unsuccessful vehicle was used only for training and a few specialist roles. However, it served one purpose, for never again were British tanks ordered 'off the drawing board' without trials, although it must be said that this proved to be a mixed blessing, since the trial process became inordinately long. Early in 1941 Leyland had collaborated with Rolls-Royce in looking for a satisfactory tank engine, and hit upon the Meteor, a derated Merlin aircraft engine. With 600hp this gave more than enough power for the heavy cruiser tanks, and since the main components were already well developed it seemed likely that it would be both robust and reliable. Leyland therefore began work on a tank which came to be called the Centaur, but this was really a Cromwell with a Liberty engine. There were no

Meteors to be had when the Centaur was first produced, so it was fitted with the available Liberty engines, and was a bit more successful than the unfortunate Cavalier. A particular feature was the fact that the engine compartment could accept the Meteor when it became available, and many of the production run were so converted after 1943. Meanwhile the Birmingham Railway Carriage and Wagon Company had taken on the design of the final version of Cromwell and produced the first pilot version in January 1942. At this date the name was still causing confusion, and it was variously known as the A27M, (M for Meteor) Cromwell M, or Cromwell III. The nomenclature was only finally cleared up when Cavalier and Centaur were confirmed as names. Because of the failures from too few trials, the Cromwell was exhaustively tested, a luxury at that time of the war, and the first production models did not appear until January 1943; which was far too long. The Meteor engine gave little trouble, and amply demonstrated that power was a necessary feature of tank design. The first engines were built by Rolls-Royce themselves in order to get the design right, but production was switched away from them as soon as possible, to leave them free to concentrate on aircraft engines, and the Meteor was put out to contract. Just as the first Cromwells appeared, the General Staff changed its policy towards tank armament. Up till then the main armament gun had been required to be used in an anti-tank role, but experience in the desert and North Africa showed that after a breakthrough the main targets were not tanks at all, but dug-in infantry and anti-tank guns. What was needed was not an AP-firing gun but one that could fire a substantial HE shell against these softer targets. The Shermans and Grants carried a 75mm gun with such a performance and there was a demand for these to be mounted on British vehicles. The new General Staff specification reflected this approach, though it was also agreed that the need for a Close Support (CS) tank had not yet vanished. The fitting of a 75mm gun inserted some further delay into the programme, and there was also a need to retrofit 75mm guns into tanks that had been produced with the 6pounder. The first 75mm guns were delivered in late 1943, and by this time they were probably already close to the end of their time, though they had to be used until the end of the war. The 75mm was a new gun, developed from the 6pounder and using several components from that gun. The barrel was the same, bored out and shortened and fitted with a muzzle brake. The breech and mechanism was also similar, and not surprisingly there were several initial defects, not fully overcome until May 1944. The ammunition was American, taken from Lease-Lend supplies without modification, and gave no trouble. The American gun was interesting in that it had been directly derived from the French 75mm (*soixante-quinze*) of World War I. In 1933 these 75s were adapted for tank use by fitting a sliding breech and different buffer and recuperator, but the

ammunition was still the same original French design, and indeed French ammunition could be fired. After Syria was taken from the Vichy French in late 1941, a quantity of French field gun ammunition was shipped to the Western Desert and used in Grant tanks. The gunner used a normal telescope for sighting the 75mm, but he could also use a range drum and clinometer for long range shooting. The two BESA machine-guns were mounted in the turret and hull, the latter displaying the last surviving remnant of the idea of mounting machine-guns all round the hull, which went back to the first tanks of World War I. Later on in the war many Cromwell crews were sceptical of the value of the hull gun, and it was frequently left out on the variants. The hull conformed to the standard British design of three compartments, and was built of single armour plate, either welded or riveted. In the front compartment were the driver and hull gunner, separated from the turret by a bulkhead with an access hole in it. The commander, gunner and loader were in the turret in the centre compartment, contained in a rotating basket, the gunner on the left with the commander behind him and the loader on the right. The turret traversed by hydraulic power and was extremely accurate in fine laying. The turret could be fully rotated through 360 degrees in 15 seconds. The commander had a cupola, the early models having only two episcopes, the later ones with eight, thereby providing all-round vision. Twenty-three rounds of 75mm ammunition were stowed ready for use in the turret and the balance of a full load of 64 rounds was stowed around the walls of the compartment. Some 4,950 rounds of BESA ammunition were carried. The No 19 wireless set was in the back of the turret behind the loader, who listened in on the net. In the rear compartment the engine was placed between two fuel tanks and two large air cleaners. The radiators were right at the back, mounted upright. Transmission was through a Merritt-Brown regenerative gearbox, which had proved successful in the Churchill tank in 1941. It was used in a cruiser for the first time in the Cromwell, but the combination of Meteor and Merritt-Brown was to be the mainstay of British tank designers for years to come. The suspension was Christie-type, adapted from the A13 and strengthened. Even so it could not tolerate the top speed of 40mph (64km/h) and after the Mark IV the maximum speed was reduced to 32mph (52km/h) by gearing down the final drive. The track was wider than that of the A13, and the ride that it gave was remarkably good. The Cromwell proved itself to be both fast and agile, and was popular with its crews. Maintenance was not too difficult, and the reliability of the Meteor was a blessing to those who had had to cope with the vagaries of overstrained Liberty engines in other designs. A possible drawback for the crew was the difficulty of getting out in a hurry, especially for the driver and hull gunner. Later marks were given side doors to the front compartment so that the two men could climb

Right: Cromwell Mk IV cruiser tank of the 2nd Battalion, Welsh Guards, which formed part of the Guards Armoured Division Reconnaissance Regiment throughout the campaign in Western Europe. The white square enclosing an 'A' indicates that the vehicle belongs to the 2nd Squadron and that it is the commander's tank.

Above: A Cromwell Mk III, formerly known as a Centaur or Cromwell X, fitted with a Rolls-Royce Meteor engine. An auxiliary fuel tank could be carried at the rear to extend its radius of action. The gun mounted is the 6-pounder (57mm), for which 64 rounds of ammunition were carried.

out whatever the position of the turret and gun. In allowing for these doors some stowage space was lost on the track guards, and there was only a small bin behind the turret. Local enterprise often fitted extra bins, for space was tight for five men. Cromwells were used for training throughout 1943 and early 1944, and the opportunity for action did not come until the Normandy invasion. It was then the main equipment of the 7th Armoured Division and a number of armoured reconnaissance regiments. After the breakout from Caen, the Cromwell was able to do the job it was designed for, and exploit the assault. Supported by 95mm Howitzer CS versions the Cromwell squadrons out manoeuvred and outran the heavier German tanks, but they were always outgunned, even by the comparatively light Panthers. Attempts to fit the 17pounder gun were a failure, and the Cromwell crews relied for their success on superior training and manoeuvrability when in action. The attempt to fit the 17pounder gun resulted in a tank called the Challenger, built to specification A30. The first model appeared in August 1942, based on a lengthened Cromwell with an extra wheel station. Performance was poor because the hull was too narrow for the large turret, and the extra weight and longer track base reduced speed and agility. Nevertheless it was approved for service early in 1943 and 260 were built. A later attempt to improve on the Challenger produced the Avenger, a Challenger

with a better turret, but only thin sheet steel on the roof. The final step in trying to make Cromwell into an SP gun was in 1950, when the Centurion 20pounder was put into a two-man turret on the normal Cromwell hull. This just about worked, and it was issued to the Territorial Army and sold in small numbers to Austria and Jordan. As a gun tank Cromwell was numerically the most important British cruiser of the war, and though never the main battle tank of the army, it supplemented the Shermans in all British tank formations by 1945. Its speed and power were the best ever seen in British tanks till that time, and there was plenty of scope for development in the basic design. It must always be a matter for regret that valuable time was lost in the early stages with the prototypes, for had the Cromwell been in action in the desert and Italian campaigns, it would have been a winner from the start.

Above: Canadian-crewed Cromwell tanks in action in France. In armoured regiments the Cromwells were usually employed with Sherman Fireflies, in the troop ratio of three Cromwells to one Firefly.

Below: Cut-away side view of a Cromwell IV. Note the turret armament of a 75mm QF Mk V gun and a co-axial 7.92mm BESA machine gun. The 75mm gun fired fixed HE, APC, AP and smoke rounds.

Bottom: Front and rear views of the Cromwell IV cruiser. The frontal insignia are, from left to right, the unit number, the squadron number, and the sign of the Guards Armoured Division.

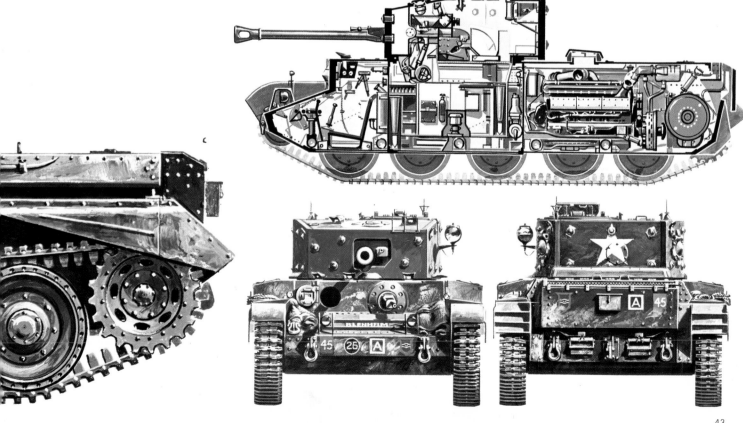

A34 COMET CRUISER TANK

Crew: 5.
Armament: One 77mm gun; one 7.92mm BESA machine-gun co-axial with main armament; one 7.92mm BESA machine-gun.
Armour: 102mm (4in) maximum; 14mm (0.55in) minimum.
Dimensions: Length 25ft 1½in (7.66m); width 10ft (3.04m); height 8ft 9½in (2.98m).
Weight: Combat 78,800lbs (35,696kg).
Ground pressure: 13.85lb/in² (0.88kg/cm²).
Engine: Rolls-Royce Meteor Mark 3 12-cylinder water-cooled inline petrol engine developing 600bhp at 2,550rpm.
Performance: Road speed 32mph (51km/h); range 123 miles (196km); vertical obstacle 3ft (0.92m); trench 8ft (2.43m); gradient 35 per cent.
History: In service with the British Army from 1944 to 1958. Still used by Burma, Eire, Finland and South Africa.

The requirement for the Comet was first seen during the tank battles in the Western Desert in late 1941 and early 1942, when it was apparent that British tanks had no gun capable of defeating the Germans. The response was a long time coming, almost too long, since the Comet only appeared at the last moment for useful service in the war. The Cromwell, whilst an excellent tank, had been given too small a gun, which could not fire HE. Nor was its 6pounder very powerful against armour. An attempt to upgun it to carry the 17pounder met with little success, (the Challenger), and by late 1943 there was an urgent need for a fast cruiser with reasonable protection and a gun capable of taking on the later marks of German tank. Leyland was given the task of developing the new tank early in 1943, the first priority being to decide upon a suitable gun. The criterion chosen was to look for the most powerful gun that could be mounted on Cromwell, and then a tank would be built using as many Cromwell components as possible. After much searching and deliberation Vickers-Armstrong designed a lighter and more compact version of the 17pounder, the Vickers HV 75mm. This gun fired the same shell as the 17pounder but used a shorter and wider cartridge case which was easier to handle in a turret. It was slightly less powerful, and had a shorter barrel and lower muzzle velocity, but it was still far ahead of any gun carried on Allied AFVs at that time, except the SP tank destroyers. To avoid confusion in names and ammunition supply, the new gun was called the 77mm. The first mock-up of the Comet was ready in late September 1943, and production was planned to be under way in mid-1944. The need for the Comet had become pressing. The first prototypes were delivered early in 1944, but there was a good deal of redesign to be done, and what had started as an up-gunned Cromwell soon reached the point where 60 per cent of the vehicle was a complete redesign, albeit a similar design. The hull was largely untouched, and there was criticism of the retention of the hull gun and the vertical front plate it required. The Cromwell's belly armour was also kept, although this had been shown to be too light. But there was no time to do more, and despite front line pressures continual changes and modifications meant that the first production models were not delivered until September 1944, and did not reach the first units until just before Christmas. The 11th Armoured Division was re-equipped with Comets in the first months of 1945, and was the only division to have a complete stock by the end of the war. Other divisions were issued with Comets as the year went by, though more slowly. In early 1949 the Centurion replaced the Comet, although Comets were still in Berlin and Hong-Kong until the late 1950s. Although practically a new tank, the Comet was easily recognisable as a Cromwell sucessor, and it was in essence an up-gunned and up-armoured version. The hull was welded, with side doors at the front for the driver and hull gunner. The turret was also welded, with a cast mantlet and front armour. The space inside was good, and access was fairly easy. The commander was given all-round vision with the same cupola as the Cromwell, and ammunition was stowed in armoured bins, a distinct step forward. The turret was electrically traversed, a development of the excellent system tried out in the Churchill, and to provide adequate electricity a generator was driven by the main engine. As with the later marks of the Cromwell, there were only two stowage bins over the tracks, and there was a prominent bin at the back of the turret. This to some extent counter-balanced the overhang of the gun. The suspension was meant to be identical with that of the Cromwell, but it was quickly found that this was not adequate for the extra weight and so it was strengthened and given return rollers. With this suspension the Comet was remarkably agile and tough, and its cross-country speed could often be more than the crew could tolerate with comfort. The Meteor engine had adequate power for all needs and on a cross-country training course a good driver could handle a Comet like a sports car – and frequently did. It was sufficiently strong to stand up impressively to high jumps at full speed. The Comet only went to one variant on its solitary mark, surely a record for any British tank: the main feature of the variant was a change in the exhaust cowls, a modification found necessary after the Normandy fighting. These helped to hide the tank at night, and as also at that time it was usual to lift infantry into battle on the decks and track guards, the cowls protected them from the exhaust. The Comet was the last of the cruisers, and also the last properly developed British tank to take part in the war. It was not universally popular, and met strong criticism at first, mainly because its detractors believed that it perpetuated the faults of the Cromwell, which in some minor respects it did. This was particularly so in the case of the nose plates and the hull gun. However, to remove them would have involved an extensive redesign and the building of new jigs for the factory. This was out of the question in 1943. The disappointment at the lack of effective belly armour is less easy to refute, since it should have been foreseen, but it was only appreciated too late. Perhaps most of the exasperation of the users sprang from the fact that it was such a good tank and came so late that it was never given a chance to prove itself properly. Certainly it would have given British tank crews the edge over the Germans could it but have been delivered in 1942. Two years later it was already dropping behind.

Left- Side view of the Comet of the C.O., 1st RTR, 7th Armoured Div., Berlin, 1945.

IRON DUKE IV

T335104

Below: A Comet, still in service with the Finnish Army, fires its co-axial gun.

Left: Front and rear views of a Comet of the 1st Royal Tank Regiment. The Comet was essentially an up-gunned, up-armoured version of the Cromwell, with the same overall layout but with enough improvement to be classed for all practical purposes as a new tank. The vehicle shown carries the insignia of the 7th Armoured Division and the 22nd Armoured Brigade.

Above: A Comet in action during the closing stages of World War II. The Comet was never used in any major tank-versus-tank battle; it more often operated against small pockets of one or two tanks, supported by infantry with anti-tank weapons. Note the camouflage netting around the turret and the infantry riding on deck and track guards.

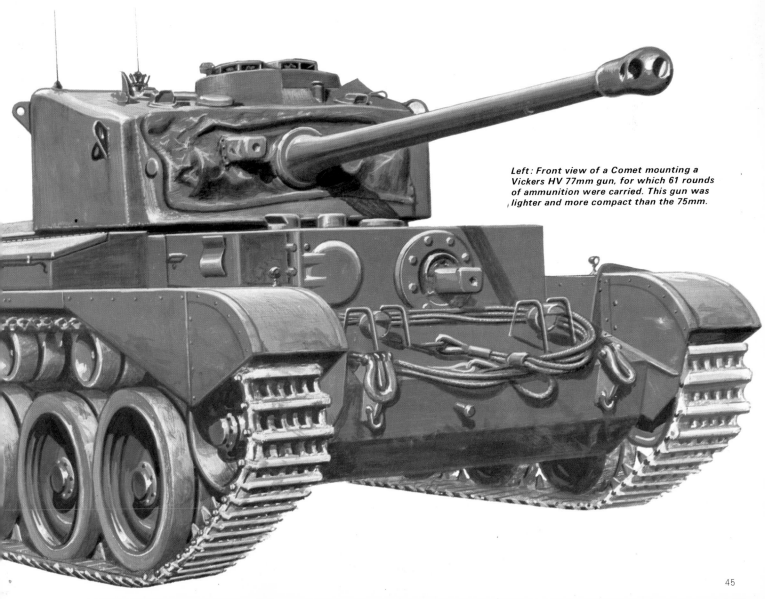

Left: Front view of a Comet mounting a Vickers HV 77mm gun, for which 61 rounds of ammunition were carried. This gun was lighter and more compact than the 75mm.

ARCHER SELF-PROPELLED ANTI-TANK GUN

Crew: 4.
Armament: One 17-pounder (76.2mm gun); one .303in Bren light machine-gun for use in anti-aircraft role.
Armour: 8mm–60mm (0.31–2.36in).
Dimensions: Length (including armament) 21ft 11in (6.679m); length (hull) 18ft 6in (5.638m); width 9ft 0½in (2.755m); height 7ft 4½in (2.247m).
Weight: Combat 35,840lbs (16,257kg).
Engine: General Motors six-cylinder inline diesel developing 192bhp at 1,900rpm.
Performance: Road speed 20mph (32km/h); road range 140 miles (225km); vertical obstacle 2ft 9in (0.838m); trench 7ft 9in (2.362m); gradient 60 per cent.
History: Entered service with the British Army in 1944. Also used postwar. Some were supplied to the Egyptian Army after 1945.

The towed 17-pounder anti-tank gun was capable of defeating most German tanks of World War II, but lacked mobility. So from an early stage it was decided to develop a self-propelled version of the 17-pounder. The end results were the Challenger, which entered service in 1944, and the Avenger, which arrived too late to see action. Before these vehicles were ready, it was suggested that a model be developed on an existing tank chassis. In July 1942 Vickers started design work on this vehicle which was based on the Valentine tank chassis, which was by that time becoming obsolete. The first prototypes were completed early in 1943, with the first production Archers following early in 1944. The type saw action in Europe from October 1944 until the end of the war. Some 800 Archers were ordered, but only 665 had been completed by the end of the war. The Archer continued in service with the Royal Artillery until the early 1950s, when it was finally withdrawn from service. The Archer had the 17-pounder gun at the front of the vehicle with the barrel pointing to the rear, over the engine compartment. This had two advantages: first, there was no barrel overhanging at the front of the hull;

and second, the vehicle was in the right direction for a quick retreat should this become necessary. The gun compartment had an open roof, and its sides were only 0.8in (20mm) thick. The 17-pounder gun had an elevation of +15° and a depression of −7½°, traverse being 22½° left and right. Some 52 rounds of 17-pounder and 24 magazines (each holding 30 rounds)

of Bren gun ammunition were carried. The crew of four consisted of the commander, gunner, loader and driver. Without doubt the 17-pounder was the most successful British anti-tank gun of World War II, and was mounted in some models of the Sherman, known as Fireflies, and in the American M10 Gun Motor Carriage, known as the Achilles.

Above: The Archer self-propelled anti-tank gun entered service in 1944.

A39 TORTOISE HEAVY ASSAULT TANK

Crew: 7.
Armament: One 32pounder gun; three 7.92mm Besa machine-guns.
Armour: 225mm (8.86in) maximum; 35mm (1.38in) minimum.
Dimensions: Length (hull) 23ft 9in (7.24m); length (over gun) 33ft (10.1m); width 12ft 10in (3.91m); height 10ft (3.05m).
Weight: Combat 174,720lbs (79,252kg).
Engine: Rolls-Royce Meteor 12-cylinder liquid-cooled petrol engine developing 600hp.
Performance: Speed 12mph (19.2km/h).
History: Designed in 1942, the project was not pushed hard, and the first six prototypes were not completed until 1947, whereupon the idea was abandoned.

This monster tank epitomises the triumph of armour protection over all other considerations. It was really an assault gun, but the very restricted traverse, 20 degrees to each side, would have severely limited it even in that role. It could never have been a battle tank in any sense of the word, and how it was meant to be moved to and from the battlefield is problematical, since it was incapable of being carried on the tank transporters known in 1942. The 32pounder was another name for the 3.7in AA gun, and it was a powerful weapon, well able to penetrate all known armour of World War II. Could it have been put into a proper tank chassis, and there is no reason why it should not have been, it would have been a world-

beater. In the Tortoise it never stood a chance. The three secondary Besa machine-guns were mounted one in front of the hull and the other two in a small turret on top of the hull roof. The only other weapons were 12 smoke dischargers. The tracks were massive, as they needed to be, and were carried on multi-wheeled

bogies with heavy skirting plates which also acted as carriers for the outward ends of the axles. The geared-down Meteor could offer a top speed of only 12mph (19.2km/h), which was virtually useless. The entire exercise was a great waste of effort and talent, but did not detract greatly from the British war effort.

Above: The Tortoise was developed from 1942 as an assault tank, but never saw action. Weighing 78 tons, it would have been very difficult to deploy on the battlefield.

Left: Side view of the Tortoise. The 32-pounder gun, with a limited traverse of 20° left and right, was the largest fitted to any British AFV during World War II.

FERRET MARK 2/3 SCOUT CAR

Mk 1/1, Mk 1/2, Mk 2/3, Mk 2/6, Mk 3, Mk 4, Mk 5
Crew: 2.
Armament: One .3in machine-gun; three smoke dischargers on each side of hull.
Armour: 16mm (0.63in).
Dimensions: Length 11ft 1in (3.385m); width 6ft 3in (1.905m); height 6ft 2in (1.879m).
Weight: Combat 7,680lbs (4,395kg).
Engine: Rolls-Royce B.60 Mk 6A six-cylinder in-line-water-cooled petrol engine developing 129bhp at 3,750rpm.
Performance: Road speed 58mph (93km/h); range 186 miles (300km); vertical obstacle 1ft 4in (0.406m); gradient 60 per cent.
History: Entered service with the British Army in 1953. Also used by Bahrein, Brunei, Burma, Cameroon, Canada, Ceylon, France, Gambia, Ghana, Iran, Indonesia, Iraq, Jamaica, Jordan, Kenya, Kuwait, Libya, Malagasy, Malaysia, Malawi, Oman, New Zealand, Nigeria, Qatar, Rhodesia, Sierra Leone, Somalia, South Africa, South and North Yemen, Sudan, United Arab Emirates, Uganda, Upper Volta, Zaïre and Zambia.

The Ferret was developed by the Daimler company of Coventry to meet a British Army requirement for a fast and light 4×4 scout car. The first prototype was completed in 1949, with production getting under way in 1952. Production continued until 1971, by which time 4,409 vehicles had been built. The Ferret has seen action in most parts of the world and has proved to be a tough and reliable vehicle. The hull of the Ferret is of all-welded steel construction with a maximum armour thickness of .6in (16mm). The driver is seated at the front of the hull with the commander in the centre and the engine and transmission at the rear. One of the reasons why the Ferret has proved so popular is that it is very easy to maintain under combat conditions. The Ferret Mk 1/1 has an open top and is normally armed with a .3in or Bren light machine-gun on a simple pintle mount. The Mk 1/2 is almost identical but has a small flat turret with a .3in machine-gun mounted on top. The Mk 2/3 is similar to the Mk 1 but has a turret-mounted .3in machine-gun, with an elevation of +45° and a depression of −15°, and a hand-operated traverse of 360°. Some 2,500 rounds of ammunition are carried. The Mk 2/6 is a Mk 2/3 with a British Aircraft Corporation Vigilant wire-guided anti-tank missile mounted on each side of the turret, which still retains its .3in machine-gun. The Vigilant can be launched by the commander from within the turret, or away from the vehicle with the aid of a separation cable and controller. Two spare missiles are carried. The Mk 3 is a Mk 1/1 with larger wheels, modified suspension and a flotation screen. The last is carried in a collapsed position in a trough around the top of the hull. With the screen erected, the vehicle propels itself in the water with its wheels. The Mk 4 is a Mk 2/3 with

larger wheels, modified suspension and a flotation screen. The last model to enter service was the Mk 5, or FV712. This model is used only by the British Army. It has a modified suspension, larger wheels and a new turret of all-welded aluminium construction. This has four launcher-boxes, two on each side, for the British Aircraft Corporation Swingfire long-range anti-tank missile; a further two missiles are carried in reserve. These missiles can be launched from within the vehicle, or away from the vehicle by means of a controller and separation cable. A 7.62mm machine-gun is mounted in the front of the turret, which is traversed by hand. The Mk 5 has a crew of two men. The standard Ferret can ford streams to a maximum depth of 3ft (0.914m) without preparation. It is not fitted with an NBC system and does not have any night-vision equipment. There have been many trials versions of the Ferret at various times, including one with a 20mm Oerlikon cannon, a special recovery vehicle complete with hand-operated winches, another with a turret-mounted recoilless rifle and one with a built-out hull of reinforced plastic and polyurethane foam to give it amphibious capability. It could be argued that more effort should have been made in the early 1960s to give the Ferret a new lease of life, especially as by that time the French Panhard AML 4×4 armoured car had appeared on the world market. The Panhard vehicle is not a lot heavier than the Ferret, but is armed with a wide variety of armament installa-

tions, including a 90mm gun. A number of armies have replaced or supplemented the Ferret with the Panhard AML. In 1966 Daimler was awarded a contract to develop a new wheeled vehicle called the Combat Vehicle Reconnaissance (Wheeled), or FV721 Fox. Fifteen prototypes were built by Daimler for the army. The production contract was awarded to the Royal Ordnance Factory at Leeds, however, and Daimler then had to close down their armoured vehicle production lines when the last Ferret was completed in 1971. The Fox is now in service with the British Army and has also been ordered by Iran, Kenya, Nigeria and Saudi Arabia. The Fox has a hull and turret of all-welded aluminium construction and is powered by the same Jaguar engine as the Alvis Scorpion CVR(T). It is armed with a turret-mounted Rarden 30mm gun, with an elevation of +41° and a depression of −14°, and a traverse of 360°. A 7.62mm machine-gun is mounted co-axially with the main armament. The Fox has a crew of three: driver, gunner and commander. A flotation screen is fitted and a full range of night-vision equipment is provided, including an image-intensifier sight to the right of the main armament. A further development of the Fox was the FV722 or Vixen, a Combat Vehicle Reconnaissance (Wheeled) Liaison, and was to have replaced the Ferret. This was cancelled in the 1974 defence cuts, and the Ferret will therefore have to remain in service with the British Army for some years yet.

Above: A Ferret Mk 2/6 launches a BAC Vigilant ATGW. The missiles can be launched from within the vehicle or, if required, away from it by using a separation cable and controller.

Left: The Ferret Mk 4 is basically the early Mk 2/3 with larger wheels and a flotation screen carried in a collapsed position around the top of the hull. The Mk 4 is used only by Britain.

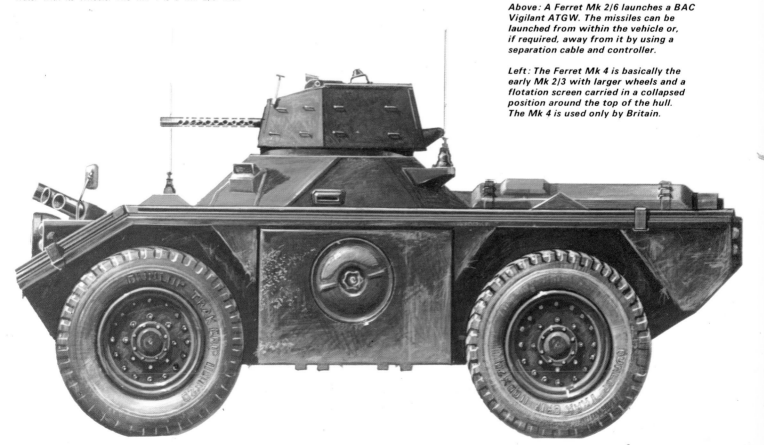

A41 CENTURION MARK 13 MAIN BATTLE TANK

Crew: 4.
Armament: One 105mm L7 series gun; .3in machine-gun co-axial with main armament; one .5in ranging machine-gun; one .3in machine-gun on commander's cupola; six smoke dischargers on each side of the turret.
Armour: 17–152mm (0.67–6.08in).
Dimensions: Length (gun forward) 32ft 4in (9.854m); length (hull) 25ft 8in (7.823m); width (including skirts) 11ft 1½in (3.39m); height 9ft 10½in (3.009m).
Weight: Combat 114,250lbs (51,820kg).
Ground pressure: 13.5lb/in² (0.95kg/cm²).
Engine: Rolls-Royce Meteor Mk IVB 12-cylinder liquid-cooled petrol engine developing 650bhp at 2,550rpm.
Performance: Road speed 21.5mph (34.6km/h); range 118 miles (190km); vertical obstacle 3ft (0.914m); trench 11ft (3.352m); gradient 60 per cent.
History: Entered service with the British Army in 1949. The Centurion is still used by Australia (being replaced by the Leopard), Canada (being replaced by the Leopard), Denmark, India, Iraq, Israel, Jordan, Lebanon, the Netherlands, Kuwait, South Africa, Sweden and Switzerland. Centurion MBTs are no longer used by Britain, Egypt or Libya.

The Centurion was developed from 1944 by the AEC company of Southall, Middlesex, under the designation A41 cruiser. Six prototypes were completed by the end of the war but arrived in Germany too late to see any combat. Centurion production was undertaken by the Royal Ordnance Factory at Leeds, Vickers Limited at Elswick and Leyland Motors of Leyland. Total production amounted to some 4,000 tanks and late production models cost about £50,000. The Centurion has seen combat in Korea, India, South Arabia, Vietnam, the Middle East and Suez and has proved to be one of the outstanding vehicles developed since World War II. Although designed over 30 years ago, the Centurion is still an effective fighting vehicle. One of the reasons why it has been so successful is that it has proved capable of being upgunned and uparmoured to meet the latest requirements. The only drawback of the Centurion has been its slow speed and its poor operational range. Early models had a range of only 65 miles (104km) and various methods of increasing this were tried, including the fitting of fuel drums on the rear of the hull, but these were prone to damage when the tank was travelling across country, and were also a fire hazard. The Mk 5 could tow a jettisonable mono-wheel armoured trailer which carried another 200 gallons (909 litres) of fuel. Later models had additional fuel which increased operating range to 118 miles (190km). The Centurion was replaced in the British Army from 1967 by the Chieftain MBT, and a modified Centurion (the FV4202) had been used in the development of the Chieftain. The Centurion was to have been replaced by the so-called Universal Tank in the early 1950s, but this programme was dropped, the only thing to come out of it being the FV214 Conqueror. The Centurion has a hull of all-welded steel construction, with a turret of cast armour with the top welded into position. The driver is seated at the front of the hull on the right, with the other three crew members in the turret, the commander and gunner on the right and the loader on the left. The engine and transmission are at the rear of the hull. The engine is a development of the Rolls-Royce Merlin aircraft engine which was used to power the World War II Spitfire and Hurricane fighters. The suspension is of the Horstmann type, and each side has three units, each of these having two road wheels. The drive sprocket is at the rear and the idler at the front, and there are six track-return rollers. The top half of the tracks and suspension are covered by armoured track skirts, providing some measure of protection against HEAT attack. The last model of the Centurion was the Mk 13, a modified Mk 10. In all there have been no less than 25 marks of the Centurion gun tank. The Mk 13 is armed with the famous L7 series 105mm gun, which has an elevation of +20° and a depression of −10°, in a turret with 360° traverse. The gun is fully stabilised in both elevation and traverse. A .3in machine-gun is mounted co-axially with the main armament, and there is a similar weapon on the commander's cupola. A .5in ranging machine-gun is provided and there are six smoke dischargers on each side of the turret. Some 64 rounds of 105mm, 600 rounds of .5in and 4,750 rounds of .3in ammunition are carried. When first introduced into service the Centurion had no night-vision equipment, but later marks have infra-red driving lights and an infra-red searchlight mounted to the left of the main armament. The Centurion can ford to a depth of 4ft 6in (1.45m) without preparation, and although many amphibious kits were developed, none of these was adopted. The Centurion has also served as the basis for a whole range of vehicles. Two bridgelayers are currently in service, both of them based on the Mk 5 hull. The FV4002 has a bridge which is kept in the horizontal position when travelling; this is swung vertically through 180° to be laid into position. The ARK (FV4016) bridgelayer itself enters the gap, whereupon ramps are opened out at each end. The ARK can be used to span gaps of up to 75ft (22.86m) in width. The Mk 2 ARV (FV4006) is still the standard Armoured Recovery Vehicle of the British Army as it has not yet been fully replaced by the Chieftain ARV. The FV4006 has a winch with a maximum capacity of 90 tons (91,445kg) and spades are provided at the rear of the hull. The type has a crew of four and is armed with a .3in machine-gun. The Beach Armoured Recovery Vehicle (BARV) is capable of operations in water up to 9ft 6in (2.895m) in depth. The Armoured Vehicle Royal Engineers (AVRE) or FV4003 is armed with a 165mm demolition gun and also has a dozer blade at the front of the hull; if required it can tow a trailer with the Giant Viper mine-clearance equipment. There have also been many trials models, including a 25-pounder self-propelled gun (this had a Centurion chassis with five road wheels, a 5.5in self-propelled gun, the Conway 120mm tank-destroyer, and a 180/183mm tank-destroyer. Many armies have modified the tank to meet their own specific requirements. The Israelis have fitted a Centurion with a new turret mounting a 155mm gun, but this has not yet entered service. Israel has also rebuilt many of its Centurions with 105mm guns, new American Continental diesel engines, new transmissions and many other modifications. Vickers are offering a refit kit for the Centurion, including a new diesel, semi-automatic transmission, a new cupola and a modified gun-control equipment. Switzerland has already ordered two of these for trials purposes.

Above left: A Centurion FV4002 armoured vehicle launched bridge begins to swing its bridge into position. The bridge takes two minutes to lay and four minutes to recover and can span up to 13.716m. It is based on a Mk 5 hull.

Left: Mounting 105mm guns, British-built Centurions of the Israeli Armoured Corps advance on the Golan heights during the 1973 Yom Kippur War. Developed in 1944-45, the Centurion has proved one of the most successful tanks of all time, and more than 4,000 have been built.

Right: A Centurion AVRE (Armoured Vehicle Royal Engineers) armed with a 165mm demolition gun for destroying fortifications. An hydraulically-operated dozer blade is mounted on the hull front and a fascine can be carried to fill an anti-tank ditch.

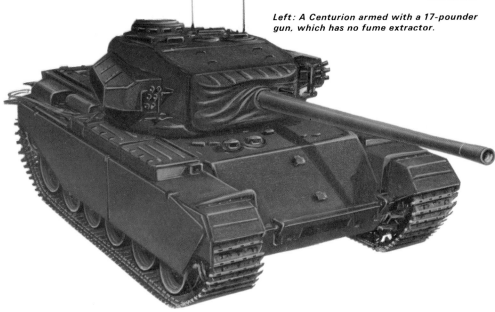

Left: A Centurion armed with a 17-pounder gun, which has no fume extractor.

Left: A Centurion of the Royal Australian Armoured Corps acting in an infantry support role in South Vietnam.

Below: A Swedish Army Centurion mounting a 105mm gun. The Swedish Army has 350 Centurions of three basic marks.

FV603 SARACEN ARMOURED PERSONNEL CARRIER

FV603, FV604, FV610 and variants
Crew: 2 plus 10.
Armament: One 0.3in turret-mounted machine-gun; one 7.62mm Bren light machine-gun; six smoke dischargers.
Armour: 8mm–16mm (0.32–0.63in).
Dimensions: Length 17ft 2in (5.233m); width 8ft 4in (2.539m); height 8ft 1in (2.463m).
Weight: Combat 22,420lbs (10,170kg).
Ground pressure: 13.93lb/in² (0.98kg/cm²).
Engine: Rolls-Royce B.80 Mk.6A eight-cylinder petrol engine developing 160hp at 3,750rpm.
Performance: Road speed 45mph (72km/h); range 250 miles (400km); vertical obstacle 1ft 6in (0.46m), trench 5ft (1.52m); gradient 42 per cent.
History: Entered service in 1953. Still in service with Brunei, Great Britain, Hong-Kong, Indonesia, Jordan, Kuwait, Libya, Nigeria, Qatar, South Africa, Sudan,

Thailand, United Arab Emirates and Uganda. No longer used by Australia and no longer in production.

After the end of World War II, the British Army issued a requirement for a new armoured car to replace a variety of wartime vehicles. This was designated the FV601 and design work was carried out by the Fighting Vehicles Design Department (later the Fighting Vehicles Research and Development Establishment, and now the Military Vehicle and Engineering Establishment). The design parents were the Alvis company of Coventry. With the beginning in 1948 of the guerrilla campaign in Malaya, design of the FV603, or Saracen as it became known, was pushed ahead while that on the FV601 (Saladin) was held back. The first prototypes of the Saracen were completed in 1952, with production vehicles following very soon afterwards – so soon in fact that there were many problems

with the early vehicles as the prototypes could not be fully tested and developed in the time allowed. Production of the Saracen continued at the Alvis factory at Coventry until 1972. Until the introduction of the FV432 tracked APC, the Saracen was the only real APC available to the British Army. It was used in the British Army by infantry battalions and armoured car regiments, whilst the FV610 was used by the Royal Artillery as a command post. Although replaced in infantry regiments by the FV432, the Saracen is still being used in large numbers in Northern Ireland, where it has proved very useful in the internal security role. The hull of the Saracen is of all-welded steel construction varying in thickness from 0.315in (8mm) to 0.63in (16mm). The engine is at the front of the hull with the personnel compartment at the rear. The driver is seated to the rear of the engine with the radio operator and commander farther to his rear. The Saracen has full 6×6 drive with the steering on the front four wheels. The steering is power-assisted to reduce driver fatigue. The eight infantry are seated on individual seats down each side of the hull, which they enter and leave via twin doors in the rear of the hull. There is also an emergency escape hatch in each side of the hull. A total of eight firing-ports are provided, three in each side of the hull and one in each of the rear doors. The main armament consists of a 0.3in machine-gun mounted in a turret (with a traverse of 360° and an elevation of −15° to +45°); a 7.62mm Bren light machine-gun is mounted on a hatch to the rear of the gun turret; and a total of 3,000 rounds of machine-gun ammunition is carried. Three smoke dischargers are mounted on each side of the front of the vehicle. The Saracen does not have an NBC system or night-vision equipment. A ventilation system, however, is provided as standard. The Saracen can ford to a depth of 3ft 6in (1.07m) without preparation, and although a deep fording kit was developed, this is no longer in use. The Saracen has proved to be very popular with armies in the Middle East as it has excellent cross-country capabilities in the desert. Two variants were developed to meet the special requirements of the Middle East. The first was a standard Saracen with its roof and turret removed to improve ventilation for the infantry. The second model had a reverse-flow cooling system. Some of these were also used by the British Army – indeed some Saracens in Northern Ireland have this system as these vehicles were destined for Libya before the contract was ended. These were stored at Coventry airport and when the troubles in Northern Ireland flared up they were rushed

Above: The Alvis FV603 Saracen APC entered service with the British Army in 1953 but has now been replaced in most units by the tracked FV432. The Saracen is still used for internal security duties in Northern Ireland and by other armies.

FV200 CONQUEROR HEAVY TANK

Crew: 4.
Armament: One 120mm gun; one .3in machine-gun co-axial with the main armament; one .3in machine-gun on commander's cupola; six smoke dischargers on each side of the turret.
Armour: 178mm (7.12in) maximum.
Dimensions: Length (overall) 38ft (11.58m);

Below: Side view of a Conqueror heavy tank, in British service from 1956 to 1966.

length (hull) 25ft 4in (7.721m); width 13ft 1in (3.987m); height (overall) 11ft (3.352m).
Weight: Combat 145,600lb (66,044kg).
Ground pressure: 12lb/in² (0.84kg/cm²).
Engine: M.120 No.2 Mk.1A 12-cylinder petrol engine with fuel injection system developing 810bhp at 2,800rpm.
Performance: Road speed 21.3mph (34km/h); range 95 miles (153km); vertical obstacle 3ft (0.914m); trench 11ft (3.352m); gradient 60 per cent.
History: Entered service with the British Army in 1956 and phased out of service in 1966. At least five are still in existence, four in Britain and one in France.

In 1944 development of a new tank, designated the A45, was started. The vehicle was to have been an infantry support tank and would have worked with the A41 heavy cruiser (later known as the Centurion). After the war this became known as the FV200 Series or Universal Tank. The basic idea was to build a tank which could be quickly adopted to carry out the roles of flamethrower tank, dozer tank and amphibious tank. The first prototype was completed in 1948; this had a remote-controlled machine-gun on the left track guard and a Centurion turret with a 17pounder gun. The following year the project was cancelled as it was found that the Centurion tank could undertake many of the roles projected for the FV200 series. The FV201 chassis was then used as the basis for a new heavy tank to compete with the Russian IS-3 which appeared in 1945, and this became known as the FV214 or Conqueror. For trials purposes a model known as the Caernarvon (FV221) was built, this being a Conqueror chassis with a Centurion turret. The first prototype of the FV214 was completed in 1950, with

production being carried out from 1956 to 1959. A total of 180 Conqueror Mk.1s and Mk.2s was built, plus some armoured recovery vehicles designated FV219. The FV200 series included the following projected variants: Armoured Vehicle Royal Engineers (AVRE) in two different models, flail tank for clearing mines, self-propelled anti-tank gun (medium), self-propelled anti-tank gun (heavy), self-propelled artillery (medium), self-propelled artillery (heavy), bridgelayer and ARK bridgelayer, Beach Armoured Recovery Vehicle (BARV), artillery tractor and assault personnel carrier. It was lucky for the British Army that these were not built as some of them would have proved a liability on the battlefield! The Conqueror was issued to armoured regiments in Germany on a maximum scale of nine per regiment, with the task of providing long-range anti-tank support for the Centurion. The Conqueror proved difficult to maintain and its electrical system was always giving trouble. It had a very small range of action and was difficult to move about the battlefield because of its weight of

65 tons (66,044kg). By the time it was phased out of service in 1966 the Centurion with the 105mm gun was in service in large numbers. The hull of the Conqueror is of all-welded construction. The driver is seated at the front of the hull on the right, with some ammunition stowed to his left. The cast turret is in the centre of the hull with the gunner on the right and the loader on the left, both these crew members having their own hatches. The commander has his own cupola, which can be traversed through 360°. The engine, a modified version of the Meteor used in the Centurion, and transmission (five forward and two reverse gears) are mounted at the rear of the hull and separated from the fighting compartment by a fire-proof bulkhead. The suspension, of the Horstmann type, consists of four units each side, each of these having two road wheels, these in turn being supported by three concentric springs. The drive sprocket is at the rear and the idler at the front, and there are four track-return rollers. The main armament of the Conqueror is a 120mm gun. This has an elevation of +15° and a

FV1609 HUMBER PIG APC

over by sea, some still in their desert camouflage. The FV604 is a command vehicle with additional radios, mapboards and a tent which can be erected at the rear of the hull if required. The FV610 is also a command vehicle, but has a much higher roof so that the command staff can work standing. This FV610 also has radios, mapboards and auxiliary charging equipment, and a tent can be erected at the rear of the vehicle to increase the working area. No armament is fitted. Over the years there have been many experimental projects based on this basic chassis. Some never reached the prototype stage, including a Saracen derivative with a 25pounder gun. Other projects were built as prototypes: the FV610 with Robert surveillance radar and the Saracen mine-clearance vehicle (not used operationally). The latter was developed for the Middle East, and for mine-clearance was driven backwards, roller-type mine-clearance equipment being mounted to the rear of the troop compartment.

FV1611, FV1612, FV1613, FV1620
Crew: 2 plus 8.
Armament: None.
Armour: 10mm (0.39in) maximum.
Dimensions: Length 16ft 2in (4.926m); width 6ft 8½in (2.044m); height 7ft (2.13m).
Weight: Combat 12,764lbs (5,790kg).
Engine: Rolls-Royce B.60 Mk.5A six-cylinder petrol engine developing 120hp at 3,750rpm.
Performance: Road speed 40mph (64km/h); range 260 miles (402km), no trench crossing capability.
History: Entered service with the British Army in 1955. Still used by the British Army in Ireland and also used by Portugal.

After the end of World War II the British Army issued a requirement for a 1-ton 4×4 cargo truck, and this was built by the Humber company. As there were insufficient Saracen APCs available later, it was decided to develop an armoured personnel carrier based on the 1-ton 4×4 truck chassis, and this became the FV1609. The chassis were built by Humber and the bodies by GKN Sankey (who later built the FV432 APC) and the Royal Ordnance Factory at Woolwich. The most common were the FV1611 APC, the FV1612 radio

vehicle and the FV1613 ambulance. Most of these were withdrawn from service with the British Army by the early 1960s, some being stored and others scrapped. When the troubles in Ireland started up again the Humbers were quickly returned to service as internal security vehicles, and recently they have been given additional armour protection as it has been found that AP bullets will penetrate the original hull of the vehicle. The most common name for the Humber APC is the Pig. The most interesting model of the series to enter service was the FV1620, or Hornet as it is known. This has a twin launcher at the rear of the hull for two Malkara wire-guided missiles, another two missiles being carried in reserve. The Malkara was developed in Australia and has a maximum range of 2,500 yards (2,286m) and a maximum flight speed of 400mph (644km/h). The missile itself weighs 206lbs (93.4kg) and is 6ft 5½in (1.967m) in length. Perhaps the heaviest anti-tank missile ever to enter service, it was capable of destroying any tank on the battlefield, including the IS-3. At one time the Hornet was to have been issued on a wide scale, but in the end it was used only by the Parachute Squadron, Royal Armoured Corps, and was replaced by the Ferret Mk.5 with Swingfire missiles in the 1960s.

Above: An Alvis FV610 command vehicle moving at speed. The FV610 has a higher roof than the standard FV603 Saracen, so that its occupants can work standing, with mapboards and additional communication equipment. A large penthouse tent can be erected at the rear of the vehicle if required.

Above: The Conqueror was developed as a counter to the Russian IS-3 tank, but was replaced by the 105mm-gunned Centurion.

Above: The Humber Pig APC entered service in 1955. It is now extensively used for internal security duty in Northern Ireland.

Below: The FV1620 Hornet, mounting two Malkara missiles. The Australian-developed Malkara had a range of 2,286m.

depression of −7° (not over the rear part of the hull), traverse being a full 360°. Elevation and traverse are powered. The ammunition is of the separate-loading type (that is, separate projectile and cartridge case). A total of 35 rounds of HESH and APDS is carried. An interesting cartridge-case ejection system was developed for the Conqueror: this ejects the empty cartridge cases through a door in the side of the turret. It would appear that this is not a reliable system, however. A .3in machine-gun is mounted coaxially to the left of the main armament and there is a similar weapon on the commander's cupola which can be laid and fired from within the turret. Six smoke dischargers are mounted on each side of the turret. The Conqueror can ford streams to a maximum depth of 4ft 9in (1.45m). The only other version to enter service was the FV219 ARV.

FV601 SALADIN ARMOURED CAR

Crew: 3.
Armament: One 76mm gun; one .3in machine-gun co-axial with main armament; one .3in anti-aircraft machine-gun; 12 smoke dischargers.
Armour: 10mm–32mm (0.39–1.27in).
Dimensions: Length (with gun forward) 17ft 4in (5.284m); length (hull only) 16ft 2in (4.93m); width 8ft 4in (2.54m); height 9ft 7in (2.93m).
Weight: Combat 25,550lbs (11,590kg).
Engine: Rolls-Royce B.80 Mk.6A eight-cylinder petrol engine developing 160bhp at 3,750rpm.
Performance: Road speed 45mph (72km/h); range 250 miles (400km); vertical obstacle 1ft 6in (0.46m); trench 5ft (1.52m); gradient 60 per cent.
History: Entered service with the British Army in 1959. In service with Bahrain, Great Britain, Germany (Border Police), Ghana, Indonesia, Jordan, Kenya, Kuwait, Libya, Oman, Nigeria, Portugal, Qatar, Sudan, Tunisia, Uganda, United Arab Emirates and Yemen. No longer in production in and not now used by Australia.

The British Army used armoured cars extensively during World War II, and after the war it issued a requirement for a new armoured car with better cross-country mobility than wartime vehicles. This emerged as the FV601 and its design parents were Alvis of Coventry. At first it was to have had a 2pounder gun and a crew of four. In many respects the FV601 was very similar to the American M38 6×6 armoured car, which was standardised in 1945 but did not enter service with the US Army. The FV601, or Saladin as it became known, should have entered service with the British Army in the early 1950s, but its introduction into service was delayed, not only because its new

76mm gun was not ready, but mainly because it was decided to give priority to the FV603 Saracen armoured personnel carrier. The latter uses many Saladin components, and at that time the Saracen was urgently required in the Far East. The prototypes of the Saladin were completed in 1952–53, but it was not until 1959 that the first production vehicles were completed. The Saladin was issued to armoured car regiments of the Royal Armoured Corps. It has been used in action in many parts of the world including Jordan, Aden and the Far East, and its ability to get back to base after

Left: The Alvis FV-601 Saladin armoured car. Now replaced in most British Army units by the Scorpion CVR(T), it is still in TAVR use.

losing a wheel to a mine has proved useful on more than one occasion. The vehicle is capable of undertaking a variety of roles including reconnaissance, border patrol and internal security, and it is still used by the British Army in Ireland in the last role. Production of the Saladin continued until 1972. It has been replaced in most front-line British units by the Alvis Scorpion CVR(T), but is still used by TAVR units. The hull of the Saladin is of all-welded steel construction varying in thickness from 0.3in (8mm) on the hull floor to a maximum of 1.26in (32mm) on the turret

FV432 ARMOURED PERSONNEL CARRIER

FV432, FV434, FV438, FV439 and variants.
Crew: 2 plus 10.
Armament: One 7.62mm general purpose machine-gun.
Armour: 6mm–12mm (0.24–0.47in).
Dimensions: Length 17ft 3in (5.251m); width 9ft 2in (2.8m); height (with machine-gun 7ft 6in) (2.286m).
Weight: Combat 33,130lbs (15,280kg).
Ground pressure: 11.09lb/in² (0.78kg/cm²).
Engine: Rolls-Royce K.60 No.4 Mk.4F six-cylinder multi-fuel engine developing 240bhp at 3,750rpm.
Performance: Road speed 32mph (52km/h); water speed 4.1mph (6.6km/h); range 360 miles (580km); vertical obstacle 2ft (0.609m); trench 6ft 9in (2.05m); gradient 60 per cent.
History: Entered service with the British Army in 1963.

It is still in service, but no longer in production. During World War II the British Army did not have any armoured personnel carriers as such, although it did use Bren and Loyd carriers as well as the Kangaroo (Ram tank) for this role. Many prototypes of tracked armoured personnel carriers were developed in the late 1940s and early 1950s, but it was not until the late 1950s that a suitable design was ready for production. This was the FV432, the first production model of which was completed by GKN Sankey of Wellington, Shropshire in 1963. Production continued until 1971. In appearance the FV432 is very similar to the American M113 armoured personnel carrier of the same period. There is one major difference between them, however: the hull of the M113 is of all-welded aluminium construction whilst the hull of the FV432 is of welded

steel. This means that the FV432 is not an inherent amphibian, so before entering the water the crew must erect a flotation screen which is carried in a collapsed position around the top of the hull. This takes about 10 minutes, and the vehicle is then propelled in the water by its tracks. Although offered for export, no foreign country purchased the FV432 as the American M113 was considerably cheaper. The driver is seated at the front of the hull on the right, with the commander to his rear and the engine to his left. The personnel compartment is at the rear of the hull and the infantry enter and leave via a single door in the hull rear. There is also a four-part circular roof hatch. The infantry are seated on individual seats down each side of the hull; these can be folded up so that stores can be carried. Initially the FV432 was simply armed with a standard

Below: The FV434 is the repair member of the FV432 family, used by the Royal Electrical and Mechanical Engineers for making repairs on the battlefield. An hydraulic crane is mounted to the right of the hull and is used to transfer engines. Like other vehicles of the FV432 family, the FV434 can 'swim', propelled by its tracks, with the aid of a flotation screen.

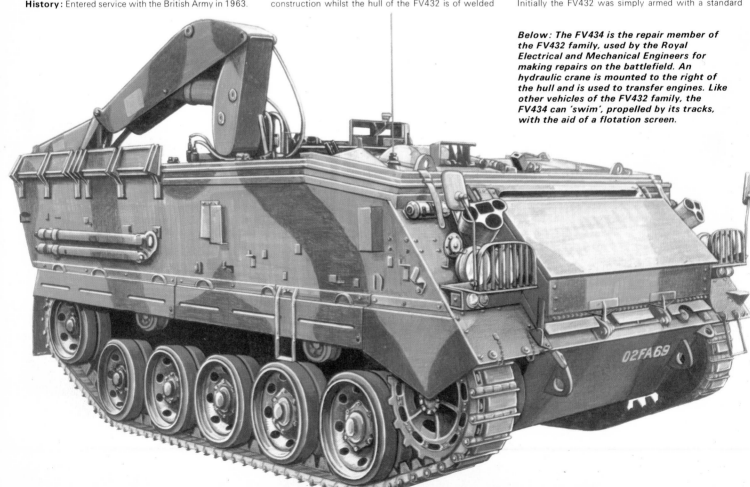

front. The driver is seated at the front of the hull with the other two crew members in the turret, the gunner on the left and the commander on the right. All three crew members are provided with their own hatch for entry and exit. The turret is in the centre and the engine, with the transmission and fuel tanks at the rear of the hull, separated from the fighting compartment by a fireproof bulkhead. There is a crew escape-hatch in each side of the hull above the centre wheel. The Saladin has 6×6 drive with power-assisted steering on the front four wheels. The main armament of the Saladin consists of a 76mm gun with an elevation of +20° and a depression of −10°, traverse being a full 360°. A .3in machine-gun is mounted co-axially with the main armament and there is a similar weapon on the commander's side of the turret for use in the anti-aircraft role. Six smoke dischargers are mounted either side at the front of the turret. The 76mm gun can fire a variety of ammunition, including HE, HESH, Smoke and Canister, the last for use against massed infantry attacks. A total of 43 rounds of 76mm and 2,750 rounds of machine-gun ammunition is carried. The Saladin can ford to a maximum depth of 3ft 6in (1.07m) without preparation. A flotation screen was developed and tested, but this was not adopted by the British Army. The Saladin has no NBC system or night-vision equipment. Saracens and Saladins were used in some numbers by the Australian Army, but when the M113 APCs were introduced the Saladins were withdrawn from service. Some of the Saladin turrets were then fitted to the M113s, and the variant became known as the M113 (Fire Support).

Right: Cutaway of the Alvis Saladin. In action, the commander would load the 76mm gun.

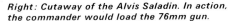

7.62mm GPMG on the commander's cupola, with no armour protection. Recently some FV432s have been provided with a fully enclosed turret armed with a 7.62mm GPMG. Smoke dischargers are mounted on each side of the front of the hull. Standard equipment in the FV432 includes night vision equipment and a complete NBC system. The FV433 Abbot self-propelled gun uses many components of the FV432 APC. The basic FV432 has been adopted for some 30 different roles. These include a command vehicle with additional radios and mapboards, ambulance, 81mm mortar carrier, artillery fire-control vehicle with the Field Artillery Computer Equipment, radar vehicle with the ZB298 ground-surveillance radar system mounted on the roof, fitted with the Green Archer mortar-locating radar system (this is now being replaced with

the lighter Cymbeline radar system), sonic detection vehicle, minelaying vehicle towing the Bar minelaying system, fitted with the Swedish Carl Gustav anti-tank launcher, mounting a 120mm Wombat recoilless rifle, to name just a few. The FV434 is a special fitters' vehicle used by the Royal Electrical and Mechanical Engineers, and as such is provided with an hydraulic crane to carry out engine changes in the field. The FV438 is an anti-tank missile vehicle and has two launcher bins for the British Aircraft Corporation Swingfire missile, with another 14 missiles carried inside the hull; a 7.62mm GPMG is also fitted for close defence. The Swingfire is wire-guided and has a maximum range of 4,374 yards (4,000m). Unlike other missiles such as the TOW and HOT, the Swingfire can be launched from within the vehicle or, if the tactical situation

demands, away from the vehicle with the aid of a separation sight and cable. This means that the FV432 can be out of sight behind a hill with the missile controller in a well camouflaged position, making detection almost impossible. The FV439 is a special signals vehicle used by the Royal Signals. Recently some FV432s have been fitted with a new cupola mounting twin 7.62mm GPMGs for use against low-flying aircraft. There was a project to fit some of the FV432s in the mechanised battalions with the complete turret of the Fox armoured car, but this has recently been cancelled. Although perhaps obsolete by today's standards, the FV432 has served the British Army well and will remain in service until the 1980s. By that time it should be supplemented by a British-designed mechanised infantry combat vehicle.

Above and above left: Rear and side views of an FV432, the standard APC of the British Army, in service since 1963. Production—by GKN Sankey of Wellington, Shropshire—was completed in 1971. The basic model mounts a 7.62mm GP machine-gun, but recently some have been fitted with cupola-mounted twin 7.62mm GP machine-guns for anti-aircraft use.

Left: An FV438 launches a BAC Swingfire ATGW, which has a range of 4,000m and can disable any known tank. The advantage of the Swingfire over some other missiles is that it may be launched away from the FV438, using a separation sight and cable. Two missiles are carried in the ready-to-launch position, with 14 stored within the FV438.

FV433 ABBOT SELF-PROPELLED GUN

Abbot SPG, Falcon SPAAG
Armament: One 105mm gun; one 7.62mm light machine-gun for anti-aircraft defence; two three-barrelled smoke dischargers.
Armour: 6mm–12mm (0.24–0.47in).
Dimensions: Length overall 19ft 2in (5.84m); width 8ft 8in (2.641m); height 8ft 2in (2.489m).
Weight: Combat 36,500lbs (16,556kg).
Ground pressure: 12.65lb/in² (0.89kg/cm²).
Engine: Rolls-Royce K.60 Mk.4G six-cylinder multi-fuel engine developing 240bhp at 2,750rpm.
Performance: Road speed 30mph (48km/h); water speed 3.1mph (5km/h); range 242 miles (390km); vertical obstacle 2ft (0.609m); trench 6ft 9in (2.057m); gradient 60 per cent.
History: Entered service with British Army in 1964. No longer in production. Value Engineered Abbot is in service with Indian Army.

Self-propelled artillery was first used by the British Army as far back as 1927, and during World War II the advantages of SP artillery became even more apparent. During the war the British Army used a variety of self-propelled guns (SPGs), including the Bishop (25-pounder on a Valentine chassis), the Sexton (25-pounder on a Ram chassis) and the American Priest (105mm on a Sherman chassis). After the war various experimental self-propelled guns were built. In the 1950s it was decided to use the FV430 chassis as the basis for both an APC and an SPG. The first prototype of the SPG, designated FV433, was completed in 1961. Production was undertaken at the Vickers works at Elswick, Newcastle-upon-Tyne, between 1964 and 1967. The FV433, called the Abbot, is in service with medium regiments of the Royal Artillery in Britain, and in Germany with the British Army of the Rhine. Each regiment normally has three batteries each with six Abbots, usually supported in action by the 6×6 Alvis Stalwart load carrier to supply additional ammunition. The Abbot has a crew of four. The driver is seated at the front of the hull and the other three crew members are seated in the turret. The turret is mounted at the rear of the hull and has full power traverse through 360°. The 105mm gun has an elevation of from −5° to +70°. The gun fires separate-loading ammunition of the following types: High Explosive, Smoke Base Ejection, Target Indicating, Illuminating, Squash Head Practice and High Explosive Squash Head, the last being for use against tanks. The gun has a maximum range of 15,550 yards (17,000m). A 7.62mm Bren light machine-gun is mounted on the roof for anti-aircraft defence, and in addition smoke dischargers are mounted each side of the turret. Forty rounds of 105mm and 1,200 rounds of 7.62mm ammunition are carried. A flotation screen is carried collapsed around the top of the hull. This can be erected in 10 to 15 minutes, and the Abbot can then propel itself across rivers with its tracks at a maximum speed of 3mph (5km/h). The Abbot is provided with an NBC system and infra-red driving lights for night driving. There are two variants of the Abbot. The first is the Value Engineered Abbot, in service with the Indian Army. This is essentially a standard Abbot with such things as the NBC system and flotation screen removed. The second is the Falcon (prototype) anti-aircraft vehicle. This has a new turret armed with twin 30mm Oerlikon cannon; these have a maximum effective range in the anti-aircraft role of 2,743 yards (3,000m). A total of 620 rounds of 30mm anti-aircraft ammunition is carried.

Above: Abbot self-propelled guns at firing practice. The Abbot serves with the Royal Artillery in Britain and with B.A.O.R. in Germany in regiments of 18 guns. The 105mm gun has a range of 17,000m and fires 12rpm.

Right: The Falcon anti-aircraft vehicle is a joint development by Vickers and the British Manufacturing & Research Company. A new turret on an Abbot hull mounts twin 30mm cannon with effective range of 3,000m.

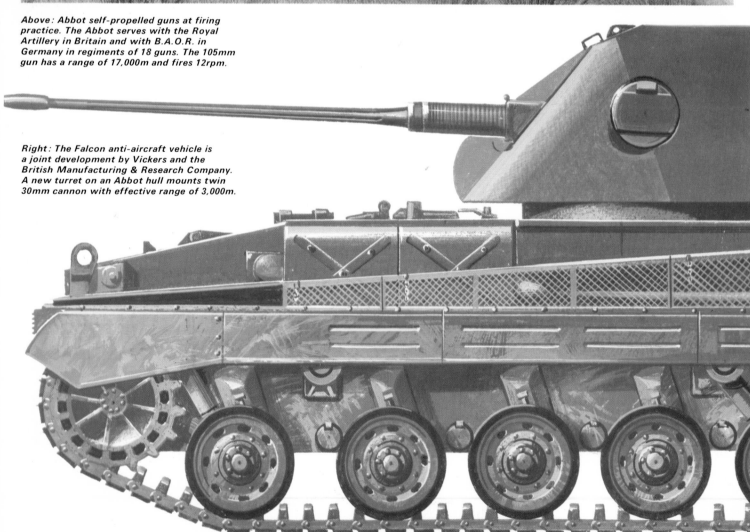

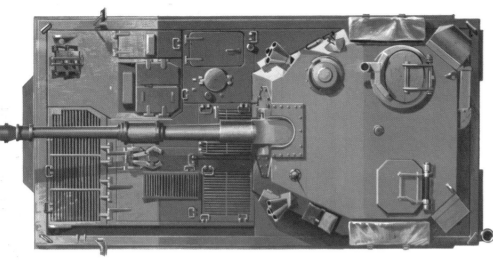

Above and above right: Top and rear views of the FV433 Abbot SPG. The driver's position is on the right of the hull with the engine on his left. The three other crewmen—commander, gunner and loader—are housed in the turret.

Right: Abbot SPG with its 105mm gun locked in travelling position. The flotation screen, in the stowed position around the top of the hull, can be erected in 10 to 15 minutes. The Abbot is propelled through the water by its tracks at a maximum 5km/h.

Above: An Abbot with its 105mm gun at the maximum elevation of +70°. The gun can be depressed to −5° and the turret has full power traverse through 360°.

VICKERS MAIN BATTLE TANK

Mk 1, Mk 2, Mk 3
Crew: 4.
Armament: One 105mm gun; one .3in machine-gun co-axial with main armament; one .3in anti-aircraft machine-gun; one .5in ranging machine-gun; 12 smoke dischargers.
Armour: 80mm (3.16in) maximum.
Dimensions: Length (including main armament) 31ft 11in (9.728m); length (hull) 26ft (7.92m); width 10ft 5in (3.168m); height (to commander's cupola) 8ft 8in (2.64m).
Weight: Combat 85,098lbs (38,600kg).
Ground pressure: 12.37lb/in² (0.87kg/cm²).
Engine: Leyland L.60 Mk.4B six-cylinder multi-fuel engine developing 650bhp at 2,670rpm.
Performance: Road speed 35mph (56km/h); range 300 miles (480km); vertical obstacle 3ft (0.914m); trench 8ft (2.438m); gradient 60 per cent.
History: Entered service with the Indian Army in 1965 and with Kuwait in 1971. Still being built in India.

In the 1950s the Indian Army was equipped with a variety of tanks including the French AMX-13, American M4 Sherman and British Centurion. In the late 1950s a decision was made to set up a tank plant in India and teams were sent abroad to select a design

which would meet the requirements of the Indian Army. The Vickers design was successful and in August 1961 a licensing contract was signed. Two prototypes were completed in 1963, one being retained by Vickers and the other being sent to India in 1964. Meanwhile plans were being drawn up for a factory to be built near Madras. Vickers delivered some complete tanks to India before the first Indian tank was completed early in 1969. These first tanks had many components from England, but over the years the Indian content of the tank has steadily increased and today the Indians build over 90 per cent of the tank themselves. Production has now passed the thousand mark, and the tank gave a good account of itself in the last Indian-Pakistani conflict. The Indians call the tank *Vijayanta* (Victorious). In designing the tank, Vickers sought to strike the best balance between armour, mobility and firepower within the limits of a tank weighing 38 tons (38,610kg). The layout of the tank is conventional. The driver is seated at the front of the hull on the right with ammunition stowage to his left, and the other three crew members are located in the turret: the commander and gunner to the right and the loader to the left. The engine and transmission are at the rear of the hull. The engine and transmission are the same as those used in the Chieftain MBT. The

suspension is of the torsion-bar type and consists of six road wheels with the drive sprocket at the rear and the idler at the front, there being three track-return rollers. The Vickers MBT is armed with the standard 105mm L7 series rifled tank gun, this having an elevation of +20° and a depression of −7°, traverse being 360°. A .3in machine-gun is mounted co-axially with the main armament and a similar weapon is mounted on the commander's cupola. Six smoke dischargers are mounted each side of the turret. Some 44 rounds of 105mm and 3,000 rounds of .3in machine-gun ammunition are carried. The main armament is aimed with the aid of the ranging machine-gun method, which has been used so successfully in the Centurion tank with the 105mm gun. The gunner lines up the gun with the target and fires a burst from the .5in ranging machine-gun, and can follow the burst as the rounds are all tracer. If they hit the target he knows that the gun is correctly aimed and he can then fire the main armament. Some 600 rounds of ranging machine-gun ammunition are carried. Two types of main calibre ammunition are used: HESH (High Explosive Squash Head) and APDS (Armour-Piercing Discarding Sabot). A GEC-Marconi stabilisation system is fitted, and this enables the gun to be aimed and fired whilst the vehicle is moving. The

Below: The Vickers MBT Mk I, in service in India and Kuwait. More than 1,000 have been built in India by the Avadi Company of Madras. At first the tanks were assembled from British-supplied components, but the Indians now build some 95 per cent of the tank themselves.
Bottom: One of the prototypes of the Vickers MBT. It has a flotation screen in the stored position around the hull top; this has not been fitted to production tanks.

model of the tank used by India and Kuwait is the Vickers MBT Mk.1. There was to have been a Mk.2, with four launchers for the British Aircraft Corporation Swingfire ATGW. The latest model is the Mk.3, which has already been built in prototype form. This model has a laser rangefinder, new commander's cupola (he can now load, aim and fire his machine-gun from within the turret) and a General Motors diesel which develops 800bhp at 2,500rpm. Optional equipment for the Vickers MBT includes an NBC system, night-vision equipment for the driver, commander and gunner, an air-conditioning system for use in hot climates and a flotation screen. The latter is carried in a trough around the top of the hull and can be erected by the crew in 15 minutes. The tank can then propel itself across rivers with its tracks. The standard Vickers MBT can ford streams to a maximum depth of 4ft 8in.

Right: The prototype Vickers MBT Mk 3, now in production, with a new General Motors engine, new commander's cupola, laser rangefinder, and a thermal sleeve for the main armament.

Below: A Vickers MBT demonstrating its 105mm gun—the famous L7 rifle mounted in many other contemporary tanks.

FV4201 CHIEFTAIN MAIN BATTLE TANK

FV4201 MBT, FV4204 ARV, FV4205 AVLB. Shir Iran

Crew: 4.

Armament: One 120mm L11 series gun; one 7.62mm machine-gun co-axial with main armament; one 7.62mm machine-gun in commander's cupola; one .5in ranging machine-gun; six smoke dischargers on each side of turret.

Armour: Classified.

Dimensions: Length (gun forward) 35ft 5in (10.795m); length (hull) 24ft 8in (7.518m); width overall (including searchlight) 12ft (3.657m); height overall 9ft 6in (2.895m).

Weight: Combat 121,250lbs (55,000kg).

Ground pressure: 14.22lb/in² (0.9kg/cm²).

Engine: Leyland L.60 No 4 Mk 8A 12-cylinder multi-fuel engine developing 750bhp at 2,100rpm.

Performance: Road speed 30mph (48km/h); road range 280 miles (450km); vertical obstacle 3ft (0.914m); trench 10ft 4in' (3.149m); gradient 60 per cent.

History: Entered service with the British Army in 1967 and also used by Iran. On order for Kuwait.

In the 1950s the British Army issued a requirement for a new tank to replace the Centurion tank then in service. The army required a tank with improved firepower, armour and mobility. The chieftain was designed by the Fighting Vehicles Research and Development Establishment (now the Military Vehicles and Engineering Establishment), and the first prototype was completed in 1959. The Chieftain (FV4201) was

preceded by a tank known as the FV4202, however. This was designed by Leyland, and two of them were built and used to test a number of features later adopted for the Chieftain. The FV4202 used some Centurion automotive components. The Chieftain prototype was followed by a further six prototypes in 1961–62, and after more development work the Chieftain was accepted for army use in 1963. The Chieftain finally entered service with the British Army only in 1967 as there were problems with the engine, transmission and suspension. The Chieftain has now replaced the Centurion gun tank in the British Army. There are two production lines for the Chieftain, one at the Royal Ordnance Factory at Leeds and the other at Vickers' Elswick works. Total production for the British Army amounted to 700 or 800 tanks. In 1971 the Iranian Army placed an order for 700 Chieftains, this order being followed by a further order for a new model called the 'Shir Iran'. In 1976 Kuwait placed an order for about 130 Chieftains. The current price of a fully equipped Chieftain tank is just over £300,000. The Chieftain has a hull front of cast construction, with the rest of the hull of welded construction, and the turret is of all cast construction. The driver is seated in the front of the hull in the semi-reclined position, a feature which has enabled the overall height of the hull to be kept to a minimum. The commander and gunner are on the right of the turret, with the loader on the left. The commander's cupola can be traversed independently of the main turret by hand. The engine and transmission are at the rear of the hull. Suspension is of the Horstmann type, and consists of six road

wheels, with the idler at the front and the drive sprocket at the rear, and there are three track-return rollers. The main armament consists of a 120mm gun with an elevation of +20° and a depression of −10°, traverse being 360°. A GEC-Marconi stabilisation system is fitted, enabling the gun to be fired whilst the tank is moving across country with a good chance of a first-round hit. A 7.62mm machine-gun is mounted co-axially with the main armament and there is a similar weapon in the commander's cupola, aimed and fired from within the cupola. The gunner aims the 120mm gun by using a .5in ranging machine-gun, although many Chieftains now have a Barr and Stroud laser rangefinder fitted. A six-barrelled smoke discharger is mounted on each side of the turret. Some 64 rounds of 120mm, 300 rounds of .5in and 6,000 rounds of 7.62mm ammunition are carried (Chieftain Mk 5 only). The 120mm gun fires a variety of ammunition, of the separate-loading type, including High-Explosive Squash Head (HESH), Armour-Piercing Discarding Sabot (APDS), Smoke, Canister and Practice. The separate-loading ammunition (separate projectile and charge) makes the job of loader a lot easier, and also enables the projectiles and charges to be stowed separately, which is considerably safer. When the HESH round hits the target, it is compressed onto the armour, so that when the charge explodes shock waves cause the inner surface of the armour to fracture and break up, pieces of the armour then flaking off and flying round the fighting compartment. The APDS round consists of a sub-calibre projectile with a sabot (a light, sectioned 'sleeve' that fits round

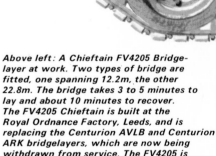

Above left: A Chieftain FV4205 Bridge-layer at work. Two types of bridge are fitted, one spanning 12.2m, the other 22.8m. The bridge takes 3 to 5 minutes to lay and about 10 minutes to recover. The FV4205 Chieftain is built at the Royal Ordnance Factory, Leeds, and is replacing the Centurion AVLB and Centurion ARK bridgelayers, which are now being withdrawn from service. The FV4205 is armed with two 7.62mm machine guns.

Left: A Chieftain MBT of the Royal Armoured Corps moves up. The 120mm is the most powerful mounted in any western tank and fires a wide range of separate-loading ammunition. It is fully stabilized and can fire effectively while the tank moves across rough country. More than 700 Chieftains have been built for the British Army. A model with new Chobham armour and a Rolls-Royce 12-cylinder diesel engine is built for the Iranian Army.

Right: A Chieftain fires its 120mm gun at night on the ranges at Suffield in Canada. The Chieftain's night vision equipment includes an infra-red search-light mounted on the left side of the turret, with a maximum range of 1,000m infra-red or 1,500m as a conventional searchlight. The Chieftain MBT has now replaced all Centurion battle tanks in the British Army and is also used by the forces of Iran and Kuwait.

the projectile and fills the full bore of the gun) around it: when the round leaves the barrel of the gun the sabot splits up and falls off, the projectile then travelling at a very high velocity until it strikes the target and pushes its way through the armour. The Chieftain is fitted with a full range of night-vision equipment including an infra-red searchlight, mounted on the left side of the turret. An NBC pack is fitted in the rear of the turret. This takes in contaminated air, which is then passed through filters before it enters the fighting compartment as clean air. The Chieftain can ford streams to a depth of 3ft 6in (1.066m) without preparation. Deep fording kits have been developed but are not standard issue. The Chieftain can be fitted with an hydraulically operated dozer blade if required. There are two special variants of the Chieftain, the FV4204 Armoured Recovery Vehicle and the FV4205 Bridgelayer. The latter was the first model to enter service and is built at the Royal Ordnance Factory at Leeds. This has a crew of three and weighs just over 53 tons (53,851kg). Two types of bridge can be fitted: the No 8 bridge to span ditches up to 74ft 10in (22.8m) in width, and the No 9 bridge to span gaps of

up to 40ft (12.2m). The bridgelayer takes three to five minutes to lay the bridge and 10 minutes to recover it. The Chieftain ARV has now started to replace the Centurion ARV. The vehicle has a crew of four and a combat weight of 52 tons (52,835kg). Two winches are fitted, one with a capacity of 30 tons (30,482kg) and the other with a capacity of 3 tons (3,048kg). When the spade at the front of the vehicle is lowered, the main winch has a maximum capacity of 90 tons (91,445kg). Armament consists of a cupola-mounted 7.62mm machine-gun and smoke dischargers. The Shir Iran is really a new tank. This will have a hull and turret of the new Chobham Armour and its 120mm gun will fire a range of improved 120mm ammunition. The Chieftain's main weakness has always been its Leyland engine, but the Shir Iran will have a new Rolls-Royce CV12TCA 12-cylinder diesel, which will develop 1,200hp at 2,300rpm. This will be coupled to a new David Brown TN 37 transmission with four forward and three reverse gears. These improvements will give the Iranians one of the most effective main battle tanks in the world. The first production Shir Iran tanks should be completed in 1977–78.

Above: The gunner's position in a Chieftain. On many British models the .50in ranging machine gun has been supplemented by a Barr & Stroud laser rangefinder.

Below: Side view of Chieftain showing the thermal sleeve on the 120mm barrel. The 7.62mm machine gun in the commander's cupola can be aimed and fired from within the tank. Smoke dischargers are mounted on turret.

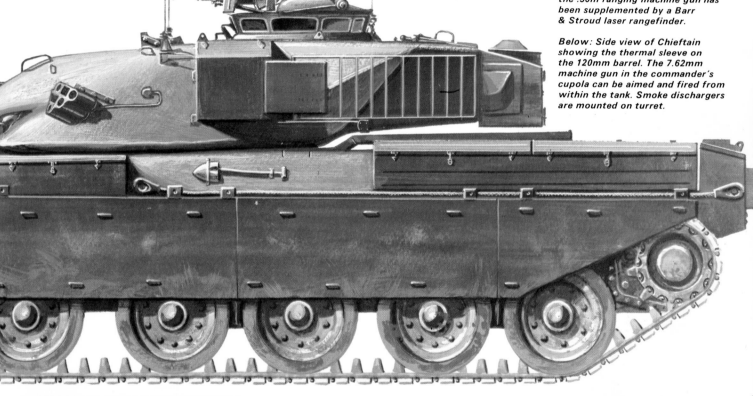

FV101 SCORPION RECONNAISSANCE VEHICLE

FV101, FV102, FV103, FV104, FV105, FV106, FV107
Crew: 3.
Armament: One 76mm gun; one 7.62mm machine-gun co-axial with main armament; three smoke dischargers on each side of turret.
Armour: Classified.
Dimensions: Length 14ft 5in (4.388m); width 7ft 2in (2.184m); height 6ft 10in (2.096m).
Weight: Combat 17,548lbs (7,960kg).
Ground pressure: 4.9lb/in² (0.345kg/cm²).
Engine: Jaguar six-cylinder inline petrol engine developing 195bhp at 4,750rpm.
Performance: Road speed 54mph (87km/h); water speed 4mph (6.5km/h); range 400 miles (644km); vertical obstacle 1ft 8in (0.508m); trench 6ft 9in (2.057m); gradient 70 per cent.
History: Entered service with the British Army in 1973.

Below: Side view of the Scorpion Combat Vehicle Reconnaissance (Tracked), now in service with the British and Belgian armies and in several Middle East countries. The Scorpion has an all-welded aluminium hull and is manufactured by Alvis of Coventry. It mounts a 76mm gun and 7.62mm co-axial machine gun, with six smoke dischargers. It incorporates an NBC system.

Also used by Belgium (there is a co-production agreement between Belgium and Britain for the Scorpion), Iran, Nigeria, Saudi Arabia and the United Arab Emirates.

In the late 1950s the standard reconnaissance vehicles of the British Army were the 4×4 Ferret and the 6×6 Saladin, the latter of which had only recently entered service. In the early 1960s a requirement was issued for a new reconnaissance vehicle, and it was eventually decided to build two vehicles for the role. These became the CVR(Tracked) Scorpion and the CVR (Wheeled) Fox. The first prototype of the Scorpion was completed by the Alvis company of Coventry in 1969, although test rigs were running some time before this. Production started late in 1971 and first production vehicles were completed in 1972. The Scorpion has a hull of all-welded construction and is the first vehicle

of all aluminium construction to be accepted into service with the British Army. The driver is seated at the front of the vehicle on the left, with the transmission to his front and the engine to his right. The engine is the same as that used in the Fox 4×4 vehicle. The turret is towards the rear of the hull with the commander on the left and the gunner on the right. Suspension is of the torsion-bar type and consists of five road wheels with the drive sprocket at the front and the idler at the rear. A flotation screen is carried collapsed around the top of the hull and when erected the Scorpion can be propelled in the water by its tracks. The main armament consists of a 76mm gun with an elevation of +35° and a depression of −10°, and a traverse of 360°, both elevation and traverse being manual. A 7.62mm machine-gun is mounted co-axially with the main armament. Forty rounds of 76mm and 3,000 rounds of 7.62mm ammunition are carried. Three smoke dis-

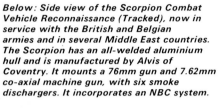

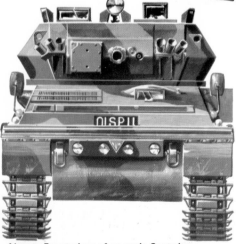

Above: Front view of an early Scorpion. The Scorpion CVR(T) replaced the Saladin armoured car, also Alvis-built, from 1973.

Right: Scorpion reconnaissance vehicles of the 14th/20th King's Hussars take part in their first major exercise with B.A.O.R., in the Harz region of Germany, late 1973.

chargers are mounted on each side of the turret. Standard equipment includes an NBC pack and night-vision equipment for both the driver and gunner. From an early stage it was decided that the basic Scorpion chassis would be used for a whole series of roles. The FV102 Striker is the anti-tank member of the family and has a hull similar to the FV103 Spartan APC. On the top of the hull at the rear is a launcher box for five BAC Swingfire long-range ATGWs, and there are a further five missiles carried inside of the hull, although the reserve missiles cannot be loaded into the launchers from inside the hull. The FV102 has a crew of three and is also armed with a 7.62mm machine-gun and smoke dischargers. The FV103 Spartan APC has a crew of three and can carry four fully equipped infantry. The latter enter and leave the vehicle via a door in the rear of the hull. The troop compartment is provided with roof hatches and periscopes, although there is

no provision for the crew to fight from within the vehicle. The Spartan will not replace the FV432 but be used for special roles such as carrying Blowpipe SAM teams and carrying spare missiles for the FV102 Striker. The ambulance version of the family is the FV104 Samaritan. This has a crew of two and can carry four stretcher patients or two stretchers and three sitting patients. This model is unarmed. The FV105 Sultan is the command vehicle and has a higher roof, and can carry a maximum of six men including the driver. This model has additional radios and mapboards, and to increase the working area a penthouse can be erected at the rear of the hull. Armament consists of a 7.62mm machine-gun. To recover disabled members of the family, the FV106 Samson armoured recovery vehicle has been developed. This is based on the Spartan APC hull and has a winch mounted in the rear of the hull. Maximum pull is 12 tons (12,193kg),

and two spades can be let down at the rear of the hull to stabilise the vehicle when the winch is being used. The final member of the family is the FV107 Scimitar. This has the same hull and turret as the Scorpion but is armed with a 30mm Rarden cannon and a co-axial 7.62mm machine-gun. The Rarden cannon has been designed specifically for defeating the armour of light armoured vehicles such as personnel carriers. It has an elevation of +40° and a depression of −10°, and 165 rounds of 30mm and 3,000 rounds of 7.62mm ammunition are carried. The Rarden fires a variety of ammunition, including High Explosive, Armour-Piercing, Armour-Piercing Discarding Sabot, and Armour-Piercing Special Explosive Tracer. The Rarden cannon is also mounted in the Combat Vehicle Reconnaissance (Wheeled) Fox. The Scorpion is one of the most versatile vehicles used by the British Army and has attracted large orders from the Middle East and Europe.

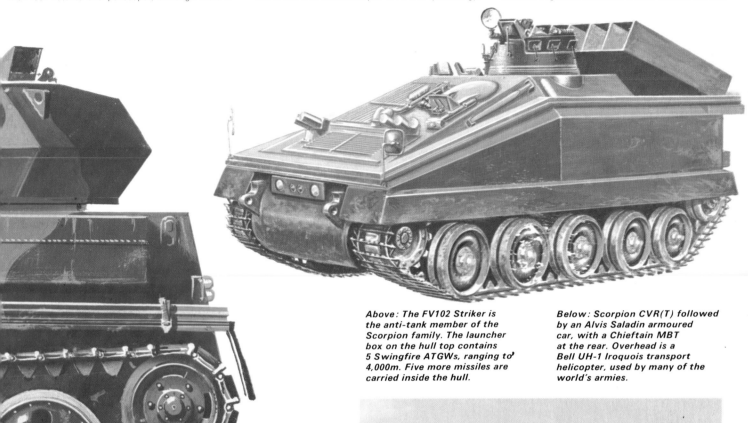

Above: The FV102 Striker is the anti-tank member of the Scorpion family. The launcher box on the hull top contains 5 Swingfire ATGWs, ranging to 4,000m. Five more missiles are carried inside the hull.

Below: Scorpion CVR(T) followed by an Alvis Saladin armoured car, with a Chieftain MBT at the rear. Overhead is a Bell UH-1 Iroquois transport helicopter, used by many of the world's armies.

Below: The FV103 Spartan is the APC member of the Scorpion family. With a 3-man crew, it can carry 4 fully-equipped infantrymen.

RAM I AND II CRUISER TANK

Crew: 5.
Armament: One 2pounder gun; one .3in machine-gun co-axial with main armament; one .3in machine-gun in cupola on hull top; one .3in machine-gun for anti-aircraft use.
Armour: 90mm (3.56in) maximum.
Dimensions: Length 19ft (5.791m); width 9ft 5in (2.87m); height 8ft 9in (2.667m).
Weight: Combat 64,000lbs (29,030kg).
Ground pressure: 13.3lb/in² (0.94kg/cm²).
Engine: Continental R975-EC2 nine-cylinder radial developing 400bhp at 2,400rpm.
Performance: Road speed 25mph (40.2km/h); road range 144 miles (232km); vertical obstacle 2ft (0.609m); trench 7ft 5in (2.26m); gradient 60 per cent.
History: Used only for training.

In 1940 the Canadian armoured forces consisted of two Vickers tanks, 12 Carden-Loyd carriers and 14 new Mk VI light tanks. Further tanks were not available as Britain did not have enough tanks to meet even her own requirements. The Canadians were able to purchase 219 American M1917 two-man tanks and a few Mk VIII tanks from the United States as scrap. These fulfilled a valuable training role until further and more modern tanks were available. Canada's first venture into tank construction was to build the British Valentine tank, 1,420 being built between 1941 and 1943. Of these 30 were kept in Canada for training and the remaining 1,390 were supplied to the Russians. Manufacture of the Valentine was undertaken at the Canadian Pacific Railway workshops at Angus, Montreal, and was a result of a British rather than a Canadian order. In 1940 the Canadians started looking for a cruiser tank to meet the requirements of the Canadian Armoured Corps, and finally decided to take the chassis of the American M3 Grant tank and redesign the hull to accept a turret with a traverse of 360°, rather than have a gun mounted in the side of the hull with limited traverse. The first prototype was completed by the Montreal Locomotive Works in June 1941, production starting late in 1941. The first vehicles were known as the Ram I, but only 50 of these were built before production switched to the Ram II, which had a 6pounder gun. Some 1,899 Ram IIs had been built by the time

production was completed in July 1943. The Ram I had a hull of all-cast construction. The driver was seated at the front of the hull on the right with the small machine-gun turret to his left. This latter was armed with a .3in machine-gun and had a traverse of 120° left and 50° right. The other three crew members were in the turret in the centre of the hull, the turret being a casting with the front part bolted into position. The main armament consisted of a 2pounder gun with an elevation of +20° and a depression of −10° and a .3in M1919A4 machine-gun was mounted co-axially with the main armament. A similar weapon could be mounted on the commander's cupola for use in the anti-aircraft role. Some 171 rounds of 2pounder and 4,275 rounds of .3in machine-gun ammunition

were carried. The Ram II was armed with a 6pounder gun, and the small turret on the hull was replaced by a more conventional ball-type mounting. A total of 92 rounds of 6pounder and 4,000 rounds of .3in machine-gun ammunition was carried. Other modifications of the Ram II over the earlier vehicle included the elimination of the side doors in the hull, a modified suspension, a modified clutch, new air cleaners and so on. Most Rams were shipped to Britain where they were used by the 4th and 5th Canadian Armoured Divisions, although these formations were re-equipped with Shermans before the invasion of Europe in June 1944, so the Ram did not see combat. There were a number of variants of the Ram tank, and some of these did see combat. The Ram Command and

Above right: The Canadian Ram I tank, a redesigned hull on a US M3 Grant chassis, was developed in WWII. Its main armament was a 2-pounder gun.

Below: The Canadian Ram II tank, armed with the more powerful 6-pounder gun. Produced in large numbers, the Ram II saw extensive service with Canadian forces.

SEXTON SELF-PROPELLED GUN

Observation Post Vehicle had a crew of six, and in appearance was almost identical to the normal tank, although it had only a dummy gun and the turret could be traversed through a mere 90° by hand wheel. Internally, additional communication equipment was provided. Eighty-four Ram COPVs were built. A Ram Armoured Vehicle Royal Engineers was developed, but this did not enter service. The Ram was also used as an ammunition carrier and as a towing vehicle for the 17pounder anti-tank gun. Perhaps the most famous version of the vehicle was the Ram Kangaroo. In 1944 the Canadian II Corps had to carry out an assault in Falaise in Normandy, and as there were not sufficient half-tracks available, they used as APCs some American M7 105mm Priest SPGs with their guns removed. Later it was decided to do the same with the Rams, as there were plenty of these in England. By the end of 1944 special battalions, equipped with Kangaroos, had been formed by both the British and Canadians. The conversion of the Ram was simple, and carried out at REME workshops. Basically, the turret was removed and benches were provided for 10 to 12 troops. The Kangaroo remained in service with the British and Canadian Armies for some years after the war. There was also a Ram Armoured Recovery Vehicle. Finally there was the Ram flamethrower, known as the Badger, which was used operationally in Holland early in 1945. The flame-gun was mounted in place of the bow machine-gun. The Ram was followed in production by the Grizzly tank, this being the Canadian version of the Sherman M4A1. Production started at the Montreal Locomotive Works in August 1943, and 118 were built before production stopped in late 1943. By that time the Americans were producing sufficient tanks to meet the Allied requirements. The Canadians also developed an anti-aircraft tank based on the Grizzly chassis, the Skink: this was armed with four 20mm Polsten cannon in a turret with a traverse of 360°, the guns having an elevation of +80° and a depression of −5°. Some 1,920 rounds of 20mm ammunition, in magazines of 30 rounds, were carried. Only three of these Skinks were built. One at least was tested operationally in Germany in 1945, although not in the anti-aircraft but in the ground-ground role. The Canadians also built large numbers of Bren gun and Windsor carriers, the latter being widely used for towing 6pounder anti-tank guns and 4.2in mortars.

Sexton SPG, Sexton GPO
Crew: 6.
Armament: One 25pounder (88mm) gun; two 303in Bren anti-aircraft light machine-guns.
Armour: 26mm (1.03in).
Dimensions: Length 20ft 1in (6.121m); width 8ft 11in (2.717m); height (to top of superstructure) 8ft (2.438m).
Weight: Combat 57,000lbs (25,855kg).
Ground pressure: 11.5lb/in² (0.81kg/cm²).
Engine: Continental R975-4 nine-cylinder air-cooled radial developing 484bhp at 2,400rpm.
Performance: Maximum road speed 25mph (40km/h); range 180 miles (290km); vertical obstacle 2ft (0.609m); trench 8ft 3in (2.514m); gradient 60 per cent.
History: Entered service with British and Canadian Armies in 1944 and still used today by India, Italy, Portugal and South Africa.

Following the success of the American 105mm M7 Priest self-propelled gun in the North African campaign, the British Army issued a requirement for a similar vehicle armed with the 25pounder gun rather than the American 105mm weapon. To meet this requirement the Americans built a vehicle called the T51, essentially an M7 Priest with its 105mm gun replaced by a 25pounder. At that time the Americans could not undertake production, so the Canadians developed a similar vehicle based on the Grizzly I tank (this being the Canadian version of the Sherman M4A1). The first prototype was completed in 1942 and production started the following year at the Montreal Locomotive Works. Production continued until late 1945, by when 2,150 Sextons had been built. The Sexton was used from 1944 and proved to be a first class vehicle. It served with the British Army until the mid-1950s, and is still used by a few armies today. The Sexton has a crew of six, consisting of the commander, driver, gunner, gun-layer, loader and wireless operator. The superstructure is of all-welded construction, giving the crew protection from mortar, artillery and small arms splinters. The top of the fighting compartment is open, however, although a tarpaulin can be fitted in bad weather. The driver is seated at the front of the vehicle on the right, with the other five crew members in the fighting compartment. The engine is at the rear of the hull. The armament

consists of a 25pounder with an elevation of +40° and a depression of −9°, traverse being 25° left and 15° right. Recoil is limited to 20in (508mm) compared with the normal 36in (914mm). Standard 25pounder sights for both direct and indirect laying are provided. The barrel is identical to that of the standard 25pounder, but the saddle and pintle were redesigned to increase their strength, to compensate for the lack of the standard gun's trail. The calibre of the weapon is 88mm, but British guns were normally called after the weight of their projectile. Some 112 rounds of ammunition (mostly HE or Smoke, but 18 AP) are carried. Also carried are two .303in Brens for use in the anti-aircraft role, two .303in rifles, two 9mm Sten sub-machine guns, a signal pistol and 12 hand grenades. The Bren guns, together with other stores, are normally stowed on the rear decking. Whilst in production the Sexton underwent a number of changes: first models had a nose which consisted of three sections bolted together, whilst later models had a nose cast in one piece. There was only one variant of the Sexton, the Gun Position Officer (GPO) vehicle. This has no armament and internally is provided with an additional radio (No 19) and battery, a Tannoy Control Unit and battery and a mapboard. Apart from tanks and self-propelled guns, the Canadians built a variety of other armoured vehicles during World War II, some of British design and some of Canadian design. These included the Bren gun carrier, Windsor carrier, Lynx scout car, Fox armoured car, light reconnaissance car and a whole series of vehicles based on the 4×4 ¾-ton armoured truck. Under development at the end of the war were the Universal Scout Car and the CAPLAD multi-purpose 4×4 armoured vehicle.

Below: The Sexton self-propelled gun was a conversion of the Ram tank to mount the British 25-pounder field gun/howitzer and was, in effect, a Canadian sequel to the US M7 Priest. The crew compartment was often covered by a tarpaulin.

Bottom: A Sexton in firing position during the offensive in Germany, early 1945. Sometimes these SPGs were accompanied by specially-converted Ram tanks as ammunition carriers.

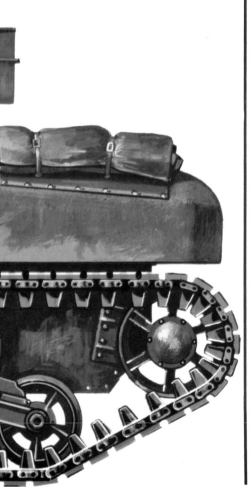

LT-35 (LTM-35) S-IIa LIGHT TANK

Crew: 4.

Armament: One 37.2mm gun; one 7.92mm Type 37 machine-gun co-axial with main armament; one 7.92mm Type 32 machine-gun in hull front.

Armour: 35mm (1.38in) maximum; 12mm (0.47in) minimum.

Dimensions: Length 16ft 1in (4.9m); width 7ft 1in 2.159m); height 7ft 3in (2.209m).

Weight: Combat 23,148lbs (10,500kg).

Ground pressure: 7.6lb/in² (0.6kg/cm²).

Engine: Skoda six-cylinder water-cooled inline petrol engine developing 120hp at 1,800rpm.

Performance: Road speed 25mph (40km/h); range 120 miles (193km); vertical obstacle 2ft 7in (0.787m); trench 6ft 6in (1.981m); gradient 60 per cent.

History: Used by Czech Army from 1937–39, German Army from 1940–45, Hungarian Army (see text) and Romanian Army.

The LT-35 was developed by Skoda in the 1930s and was officially designated the Skoda 10.5ton tank Model T-11 or LT-35 (LTM-35) S-IIa. After trials it went into production in 1936 and entered service with the Czech Army the following year. When the Germans invaded Czechoslovakia they took over all remaining LT-35s and also continued production for the German Army. The Germans called the tank the PzKpfw 35(t) and issued the type to the 6th *Panzer* Division in time for the invasion of France in 1940. The tank remained in front-line service until at least 1942, when most were withdrawn and converted to tow mortars and artillery. Some were also used in the recovery role. Main armament of the LT-35 was a Skoda Type A3 37.2mm gun, with an elevation of +25° and a depression of −10°, and a co-axial 7.92mm CZ Type 37 machine-gun. There was a similar machine-gun in the hull front, on the left. Some 90 rounds of 37mm (AP and HE) and 2,550 rounds of 7.92mm ammunition were carried. The hull and turret of the tank were of riveted and bolted armour plate with a maximum thickness of 35mm (1.38in) and a minimum thickness of 12mm (0.47in). The driver and bow machine-gunner were in the front of the hull, and the commander and loader/radio-operator in the turret. The tank was rather complex, however, and was very prone to mechanical breakdowns. After their experiences in Russia with the tank, the Germans carried out some redesign work on the tank's engine and steering system. Further development resulted in the Skoda S-IIb medium tank, one of which was tested in 1938 but not placed in production. Another Skoda medium was the S-IIr/T-21. Once again this was tested by the Czech Army but not placed in production. The Hungarians obtained a licence to build the latter tank in 1940, and they carried out a major redesign of the vehicle. This included a new three-man turret and a more powerful 260hp engine. This entered service as the 40M *Turan* I and was armed with a 40mm gun and two 8mm machine-guns, combat weight being 15.75 tons (16,000kg). The Turan II had a 75mm gun but did not enter service, and there was also a 105mm self-propelled gun on a Turan chassis.

Below: An LT-35—the PzKpfw 35(t) in German service—operates with a panzer division in Russia. Many LT-35s were taken over by the German Army after the occupation of Czechoslovakia.

OT-64 SKOT ARMOURED PERSONNEL CARRIER

OT-64A, OT-64B, OT-64C, OT-64D

Crew: 2 plus 15.

Armament: One 14.5mm KPVT machine-gun; one 7.62mm PKT machine-gun co-axial with KPVT weapon.

Armour: 10mm (0.39in) maximum.

Dimensions: Length 24ft 5in (7.44m); width 8ft 2in (2.5m); height 8ft 10in (2.68m).

Weight: Combat 31,967lbs (14,500kg).

Engine: Tatra T 928-18 eight-cylinder multi-fuel engine developing 180hp.

Performance: Road speed 59mph (94.4km/h); water speed 5.6mph (9km/h); range 442 miles (710km); vertical obstacle 1ft 8in (0.5m); trench 6ft 7in (2m); gradient 60 per cent.

History: Entered service in 1963. In service with Czechoslovakia, Egypt, Hungary, India, Libya, Morocco, Poland, Sudan, Syria and Uganda. (Note: data relate to OT-64 Model C).

The vast majority of the equipment used by the Warsaw Pact forces is of Soviet design and construction, although in some cases the satellite countries have been allowed to build slightly modified versions in their own countries: the Czechs, for example, have built a version of the Russian BTR-50P APC under the designation OT-62. Rather than adopt the BTR-60P which the Russians were developing in the late 1950s, the Czechs and the Poles went ahead and designed the OT-64 APC which entered service in 1963. The Czechs call the vehicle the OT-64 or SKOT (*Středni Kolovy Obojživelny Transporter*). These vehicles are normally used in Polish and Czech motor rifle divisions, whilst the tank divisions used the BMP-1 MICV. In many respects the vehicle is superior to the Russian BTR-60P. The OT-64 uses many components of the Tatra 813 heavy truck which is noted for its excellent cross-country capabilities. The hull is of all-welded steel construction with a maximum thickness of 0.4in (10mm). The driver and commander are seated at the front of the hull with the engine to their rear, and both are provided with a roof hatch and a side door. The troop compartment is at the rear of the hull, and entry to this is via twin doors in the hull rear. Firing-ports are provided in the hull sides and rear, and hatches are provided in the roof of the compartment. The infantry sit facing each other, and their seats can be folded upwards so that stores can be carried. The OT-64 is fully amphibious, being propelled in the water by two propellers at the rear of the hull, and steered by two rudders. Before entering the water a trim vane is erected at the front of the hull. Standard equipment includes a front-mounted winch, night-vision equipment, a tyre pressure-regulation system and an NBC system. The first model to enter service was known as the OT-64A: these were often unarmed, although some were provided with a 7.62mm machine-gun on a simple mounting without a shield. These were followed by the OT-64B, armed with either a 7.62mm or a 12.7mm machine-gun with a shield to protect the gunner from small arms fire. The third model to enter service was the OT-64C: this has a multi-fuel engine rather than the diesel fitted to the earlier vehicles, and also has the complete turret of the Russian BRDM-2 reconnaissance vehicle. This turret has a 14.5mm KPVT machine-gun with a co-axial 7.62mm PKT machine-gun, both guns being capable of an elevation of +29° and a depression of −4°. A total of 500 rounds of 14.5mm and 2,000 rounds of 7.62mm ammunition is carried. The most recent model to enter service is the OT-64 Model D. This has a new turret with the same weapons as the earlier OT-64C, but the guns can be elevated to +89.5°, enabling them to be used against low-flying aircraft and helicopters. To give the OT-64 some anti-tank capability some early vehicles have been fitted with two launchers for the Russian 'Sagger' anti-tank missile system over the rear of the troop compartment; more recently some OT-64 Model Cs have been fitted with a similar missile on each side of the turret.

Right: An early model of the Czech OT-64 8-wheeled armoured personnel carrier emerges from a water obstacle. Later models were fitted with varying types of turrets and armament.

Below: Latest version of the OT-64, with standard 14·5mm KPVT machine-gun.

LT-38 (TNHP) LIGHT TANK

Crew: 4.
Armament: One 37.2mm gun; one 7.92mm Type 37 machine-gun co-axial with main armament; one 7.92mm Type 37 machine-gun in hull.
Armour: 30mm (1.18in) maximum; 8mm (0.3in) minimum.
Dimensions: Length 14ft 11in (4.546m); width 7ft (2.133m); height 7ft 7in (2.311m).
Weight: Combat 21,385lbs (9,700kg).
Engine: Six-cylinder water-cooled inline petrol engine developing 150hp at 2,600rpm.
Performance: Road speed 26mph (42km/h); road range 125 miles (201km); vertical obstacle 2ft 7in (0.787m); trench 6ft 2in (1.879m); gradient 60 per cent.
History: Entered service with Czech Army in 1938 and later used by German Army until 1942. Variants remained in service with German Army until 1945. (Note: Data relate to late production LT-38.)

There were two main tank manufacturers in Czechoslovakia before World War II, Skoda of Pilsen and CKD (*Ceskomoravska Kolben Danek*), the latter being an amalgamation of four companies. In addition, the Tatra company did some development work, mainly on wheel-cum-track vehicles. The two major companies built a variety of AFVs for the Czech Army and for export before World War II started. The CKD LTLH (or TNHB) was developed in the early 1930s and aimed at the export market, where it was known as the LT-34. Further development of this resulted in the LTL-P (TNHS). This was entered in trials organised by the Czech Army in 1937 to find a new light tank for the army. The TNHS was found to meet the army requirement and a modified version was placed in production the following year as the TNHP (or LT-38). Other countries which purchased CKD vehicles in the 1930s included Afghanistan, Latvia, Peru, Sweden (which also built the vehicle as the Strv.m/41), Switzerland, and Yugoslavia. One even went to Great Britain for trials purposes. The LT-38 served with the Czech Army until the German invasion. The Germans then took over these tanks and also continued production for themselves. The Germans designated the tank the PzKpfw 38(t), which continued in production in Czechoslovakia until 1942. The tank was used in action by the 7th and 8th *Panzer* Divisions during the

invasion of France in 1940. The main armament consisted of a Skoda A7 37.2mm gun which fired AP and HE rounds. The gun had an elevation of +12° and a depression of −6°. A 7.92mm 7165 CZ Type 37 machine-gun was mounted co-axial with the main armament, and there was a similar weapon in the front of the hull. Ninety rounds of 37mm and 2,550 rounds of 7.92mm machine-gun ammunition were carried. The hull was mainly of riveted construction, although the top of the superstructure was bolted in place. The suspension was of the semi-elliptic leaf-spring type, with one spring controlling a pair of road wheels. There were four road wheels, with the idler at the rear and the drive sprocket at the front. Two return rollers were fitted, although these supported the inside of the track only. The LT-38 was renowned for its reliability and ease of maintenance. The hull was also adopted for a wide range of other roles, including a smokelayer, reconnaissance vehicle, ammunition carrier and artillery prime mover. Its chassis was most widely used to mount artillery, anti-tank and anti-aircraft weapons. The Bison was in production from 1942 to 1944, and was armed with a 15cm gun. The *Marder* III, or SkKfz 139, was armed with a captured Russian

Above: A German 'Marder' type SPG, converted from a captured Czech LT-38 light tank and mounting a captured Russian 76.2mm anti-tank gun. Other German conversions of the LT-38 included the 'Bison' of 1942-44, mounting a 150mm gun; other 'Marder' types mounting 75mm PaK 40 or PaK 40/3 guns; the 20mm Flak 30 or Flak 38 anti-aircraft model, and, most famous of all, the Jagdpanzer 38(t) Hetzer (see separate entry in German section).

76.2mm anti-tank gun with a limited traverse of 21° left and 21° right, 28 rounds of HE and APC ammunition being carried. There were two other *Marder* III types, one armed with a 7.5cm Pak 40 and the other with a Pak 40/3. The anti-aircraft model was known as the 2cm Flak 30 or Flak 38, this being armed with a 20mm gun with an elevation of 90° and full traverse through 360°, 1,040 rounds of 20mm ammunition being carried. The most famous model was the *Jagdpanzer* 38(t) *Hetzer*, for which there is a separate entry in the Germany section of this book.

France

France ended World War I with a small but effective tank force and a successful light tank in the Renault M-17. The Renault formed the basis for many variants in other countries and its speed could be considerably increased with better suspension. In France the general staff was mesmerised by the trench-warfare concept, and the Maginot Line was conceived not long after the Versailles Treaty was signed. Victory brought complacency and short-sightedness and in France more than in any other country the next war was seen in terms of the campaign of 1919.

Infantry was to be the supreme force on the battlefield, and the tank force must act in concert with the infantry, and strictly under their control. Immediately this restricted the tank designer to vehicles that travelled at walking pace and, with no need to improve mobility, the designers turned to protection and firepower. The infantry needed to be supported by a mass of machine-guns moving forward with them, helped on occasions by a few light guns. Armour needed to be thick enough to keep out the known anti-tank guns of the enemy infantry defence, but little more, and there was no apparent need to consider having to fight other tanks. Incredibly, horsed cavalry was brought back for reconnaissance, backed up by a few light tanks.

Faced with these constraints, the French designers did well. The heavy tank, which was the infantry support tank, was the *Char* B, big, heavy, slow and well-armed. First designed in the early 1920s, it was still the standard infantry tank in 1940. The armour was excellent and could survive direct hits from German 50mm guns, but the short-barrelled 75mm gun was fixed on the centre-line of the hull, and could only be traversed if the vehicle was swung. In almost every aspect the *Char* B showed its World War I ancestry, and it is hardly surprising that it failed to carry out its primary task of supporting when called upon to do so in earnest.

The French light tanks were no better and no worse than any others, but the formation of the Mechanised Division in 1934, the *Division Legère Mecanique,* or

DLM brought out the fact that the reconnaissance role demanded something better than an AFV armed with a machine-gun or two. The Renault was finally replaced by the R-35a and the H-35, both good tanks for their day, and both carrying reasonably effective armour-defeating guns. They had cast turrets and hulls, and a modern system of steering. With proper tactical training and good command and control these tanks could have been very effective in 1940. As it was they were frittered away in small local actions as the *Blitzkreig* rolled over the country, and they never had a chance to show their worth. If the *DLM* had been allowed to operate on its own, if it had had a proper system of supply, and if many other things too . . . then the French armoured troops could have shown their true ability, but they never had an opportunity.

Post-war France has shown that she has assimilated all the lessons of World War II and has built up an independent armoured force based on the highly successful AMX series of tanks. The latest version, the AMX-30 can now be considered a powerful and flexible main battle tank which rates as well as the others in NATO. There is a full supporting range of armoured vehicles for the modern division, including self-propelled artillery, and armoured cars. In fact, the emphasis seems to be more on mobility and speed than in other armies, with tactics designed to take full advantage of this.

The Renault FT-17 was the most widely used French tank of World War I and many were still in service in 1940.

CHARRON ARMOURED CAR

In 1901–1902 the French company of Charron, Girardot et Voigt (or CGV) modified a car by removing the rear seats and installing a circular body of steel plate, inside which was mounted a machine-gun protected by a shield. This attracted little interest and was followed in 1903–1904 by the first French armoured car. The Austro-Daimler armoured car was built at about the same time, as both have at times been claimed as the first armoured car as we know it today. The Charron had full armour protection for the engine and crew and was armed with a turret-mounted Hotchkiss machine-gun in a turret with a traverse of 360°. Two large observation windows were provided in each side of the hull and these could be covered up by plates when required. For increased observation the driver's armour plate could be raised into the horizontal position. Steel channels were carried on each side of the hull, and these were laid across ditches when required. Similar channels are still carried on such vehicles as the French Panhard AML and British Ferret scout cars. The tyres were of the self-cleaning type and the tops of the rear wheels were armoured. Two of these armoured cars were built, one of which was used by the French Army and the other sold to the Russians. The latter was used to subdue the riots in Saint Petersburg in 1905, and the Russians later ordered additional vehicles, although some of these appear to have been 'borrowed' by the Germans for use in one of their exercises en route to Russia! Panhard also built a vehicle similar to the first CGV car and Hotchkiss produced four similar vehicles for the Turks, although these ended up by being taken over by a dissident faction and being used to overthrow the people who ordered them in the first place. The French Schneider company, which later built the famous Schneider tanks, also built some armoured vehicles for the Spanish Army. These were very heavy vehicles and were really pillboxes on wheels as they had so many

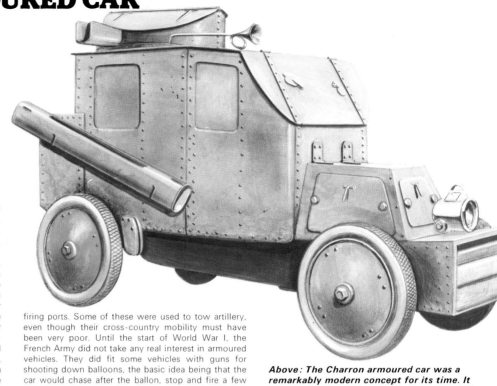

firing ports. Some of these were used to tow artillery, even though their cross-country mobility must have been very poor. Until the start of World War I, the French Army did not take any real interest in armoured vehicles. They did fit some vehicles with guns for shooting down balloons, the basic idea being that the car would chase after the ballon, stop and fire a few rounds, and resume the chase once again. During World War I, the Allies fitted a number of vehicles with anti-aircraft guns up to 75mm in calibre for use in the anti-aircraft role and some of these survived until after the war.

Above: The Charron armoured car was a remarkably modern concept for its time. It mounted a Hotchkiss machine-gun in a fully rotating turret and had rubber tyres and electric lighting. Several Charrons were bought by the Imperial Russian government. A few served as mobile A/A mounts in WWI.

SCHNEIDER ASSAULT TANK

Crew: 6.
Armament: One 75mm howitzer in nose; one 8mm machine-gun in each side of the hull.
Armour: 0.45in (11.5mm) maximum.
Dimensions: Length 20ft 9in (6.32m); width 6ft 9in (2.05m); height 7ft 7in (2.3m).
Weight: Combat 32,187lbs (14,600kg).
Ground pressure: 11.3lb/in² (0.72kg/cm²).
Power to weight ratio: 3.83hp/ton.
Engine: Schneider four-cylinder water-cooled petrol engine developing 55hp.
Performance: Road speed 4.6mph (7.5km/h); range 30 miles (48km); vertical obstacle 2ft 9in (0.787m); trench 5ft 9in (1.752m); gradient 57 per cent.
History: Entered service with French Army in 1916 and phased out of service after end of World War I.

In 1915, the French company of Schneider was acting as agent for the American Holt tractor, which had already been adopted by the British Army for towing heavy artillery. In May 1915 Schneider purchased two Holt crawler tractors, one of 45hp and the other of 75hp, for trials. As a result of these trials the French Army placed an order for 15 of the 45hp model, or

Baby Holt as the type became known, for delivery in 1916. Late in 1915 the Baby Holt was fitted with mock-up armour to the engine and driver's position and demonstrated to General Pétain. For some time a French officer named Colonel Estienne had been pressing for a tank-like vehicle to cross trenches and barbed wire, and in December 1916, he and Brillié (of the Schneider company) designed a vehicle whose chassis owed a lot to the American Holt tractor. The hull was of armour plate only 0.45in (11.5mm) thick the front was shaped like a boat and a barbed-wire cutter was mounted at the front of the hull. The rear of the hull was square cut and two doors were provided in the rear of the hull for entry and exit. The engine was at the front of the hull, offset to the left. The driver was located to the right of the engine. On later production models an additional layer of armour 0.31in (8mm) thick was added to give protection against the armour-piercing bullet which the Germans introduced. This was known as the 'K' bullet and had a tungsten-carbide core. Armament consisted of a 75mm Schneider gun (it was to have been a 37mm gun in the original design) mounted in the front of the hull on the right, and a single Hotchkiss Model 1914 machine-gun mounted in each side of the hull. Some 90 rounds of

75mm and 4,000 rounds of machine-gun ammunition were carried. The first production Schneiders were delivered for training purposes late in 1916 and they were first used in action on 16 April 1917, at Chemin des Dames. Of the 132 Schneider tanks used in this battle some 57 were destroyed, with many more damaged beyond repair. Most of the losses were attributable to the petrol tanks catching fire and the tank blowing up. These fuel tanks were right next to the hull machine-gun positions. Just over 400 Schneider tanks were built, the last being delivered in August 1918. Some were disarmed and used as supply carriers during the later stages of the war. Schneider also built the prototype of a vehicle (CA2) which had a turret-mounted 47mm gun, but unfortunately this was not placed in production. The CA3 had numerous improvement over the original Schneider tank but this never even reached the prototype stage.

Right: The Schneider tank negotiates a steep gradient on trials. One of the most successful French tanks of World War I, the Schneider saw extensive service on the Western Front.

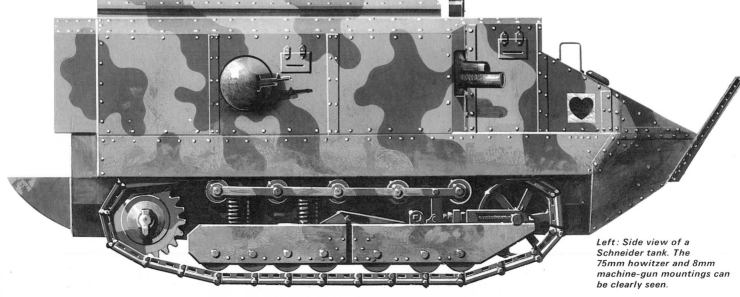

Left: Side view of a Schneider tank. The 75mm howitzer and 8mm machine-gun mountings can be clearly seen.

LAFFLY-WHITE AND RENAULT ARMOURED CARS

Before World War I, the Renault company was one of the largest manufacturers of automobiles in France. Early in 1914 it fitted some of its vehicles with additional armour, and these were used to harass the Germans, in a similar fashion to the Belgians with their armoured cars. These were followed by some cars with almost full armour protection, normally armed with an 8mm Hotchkiss machine-gun frequently provided with a shield. Later in 1914 Renault started to build cars with full armour protection, and these remained in service in diminishing numbers to the end of the war. These were armed with either a Hotchkiss machine-gun or a 37mm gun mounted in the open topped compartment at the rear of the hull; sometimes a shield was provided to protect the gun crew from small arms fire. The only means of entry and exit for the crew was by climbing over the side. From 1915 the French concentrated on Peugeot and White armoured cars, including the Laffly-White (modified M18). The latter consisted of an imported American White truck chassis with an armoured body with full overhead protection for all of the crew. The engine was at the front and the driver and co-driver were in the centre, each being provided with a vision flap which could be closed down if required. The turret was at the rear of the hull, was provided with two roof hatches and could be traversed through 360°. Armament consisted of a Hotchkiss machine-gun and a 37mm gun, these being mounted on opposite sides of the turret. Additional firing and vision ports were provided in the turret. The White armoured car was powered by a four-cylinder water-cooled petrol engine which developed 35hp, this giving the vehicle a top road speed of 28mph (45km/h). It was a 4×2 vehicle with drive to the rear wheels. The controls were duplicated at the rear so that the car could be driven backwards with some degree of safety. Fully loaded the vehicle weighed about 5.9 tons (6,000kg). These Whites were built in large numbers

Left: The Laffly-White was one of the most successful French armoured cars of World War I and remained in service with the French Army until 1940.

and some remained in service until the early days of World War II, by which time they had been modernised and fitted with pneumatic tires and an electrical system! Various Peugeot cars were armoured and in the end the French standardised two basic models of the Peugeot: the *Auto-mitrailleuse* Peugeot was armed with a Hotchkiss machine-gun, whilst the *Auto-canon* Peugeot was armed with a 37mm gun. Like the British, the French also used heavier guns mounted on lorries to provide mobile fire support to their armoured cars as well as for general duties. The *Auto-canon* 47mm Renault (or *Auto-Canon des Fusiliers Marins*) was basically a fully-armoured truck chassis with a 47mm gun mounted in its rear. This was provided with armoured protection and could be traversed through about 200°.

RENAULT FT-17 LIGHT TANK

Crew: 2.
Armament: One Hotchkiss 8mm machine-gun (see text).
Armour: 22mm (0.87in) maximum; 6mm (0.24in) minimum.
Dimensions: Length (with tail) 16ft 5in (5m); width 5ft 9in (1.74m); height 6ft 7in (2.14m).
Weight: Combat 15,432lbs (7,000kg).
Ground pressure: 8.5lb/in² (0.59kg/cm²).
Engine: Renault four-cylinder water-cooled petrol engine developing 35bhp at 1,500rpm.
Performance: Road speed 4.7mph (7.7km/h); road range 22 miles (35km); vertical obstacle 2ft (0.6m); trench crossing (with tail) 5ft 11in (1.8m), (without tail) 4ft 5in (1.35m); gradient 50 per cent.
History: Entered service with the French Army in 1918 and continued in service until 1940. Remaining vehicles taken over by the Germans in 1940. Also used by the United States (also built in the US as the 6 Ton Tank M1917), Belgium, Brazil, Canada (from the United States in 1940), China, Czechoslovakia, Finland, Greece, Great Britian (used in France in 1918 for command role), Holland, Italy (also further developed to become FIAT 3000 light tank), Japan (used as the Type 79 until 1940), Manchuria, Poland, Romania, Soviet Union (also built in Russia as the KS and with modifications as the MS-1 and MS-2), Spain and Yugoslavia.

Colonel J. E. Estienne first approached Louis Renault in 1915 to build his *Char d'Assaut*, but at that time Renault had no experience of building tracked vehicles and was heavily committed to other projects. By the following year, however, Renault had received contracts from the French Army to design tracked vehicles, mainly for the artillery. Some sources have stated that the FT-17 (*Faible Tonnage*) was designed by Estienne, others that it was designed by Renault, and some that it was a joint development! By late 1916 a mock-up had been completed with the first prototype following in February and March 1917. In the early days of the project there was a considerable amount of conflict within the various sections of the army not only on the value of the vehicle, but also on what its armament should be. The first production contract was awarded to Renault, but as subsequent orders went up in leaps and bounds to 3,500 tanks, it was apparent that Renault alone could not hope to

build these tanks by the end of 1918. Therefore other companies were brought into the programme, including Berliet, Delaunay Belleville and SOMUA (*Societé d'Outillage Mècanique et d'Usinage d'Artillerie*). In addition there were many other component manufacturers, including some in Great Britain who supplied a proportion of the armour plate. Renault completed its first production tanks in September 1917, but the whole programme was delayed by acute shortages of components. By the end of 1917, just 83 FT-17s had been built and most of these had no armament. Other manufacturers did not start delivering vehicles until mid-1918, and as a result of a shortage of turrets each manufacturer designed its own to start with. The FT-17 was essentially a narrow armoured box with the driver at the front, turret with a traverse of 360° in the centre, and the engine and transmission at the rear.

The driver entered the tank via twin doors over his compartment, whilst the commander/gunner entered via doors in the turret rear. Maximum armour thickness was 16mm (0.63in) and the hull was of riveted construction. The renault FT-17 was the first tank with a turret that could be traversed through 360° to enter service. The suspension consisted of coil and leaf springs and pivoted bogies. There were nine small road wheels on four bogies, with the drive sprocket at the rear and the large idler at the front. The latter was of laminated wood with a steel rim. There were six return rollers. Most FT-17s were fitted with a tail at the rear of the hull to increase the trench-crossing capabilities of the tank, but this could be removed for transport. From a very early stage it was decided that there would be four basic models of the FT-17. The first model to enter service was the *Char Mitrailleur*

Above: Renault FT-17 light tanks of the US 326th Bn, 311th Tank Center, move up the line near 35th Division HQ, near Boureuilles, Meuse, on 26 September 1918. In the foreground, the machine-gun version; behind, the 37mm-gunned version.

Below, left and right: Side, front and rear views of a Renault FT-17—a standard production model of 1918 with the round turret mounting a 37mm gun. This tank was built in very large numbers and served with numerous armies throughout the 1930s. Many modifications were made to the FT-17 by the countries which it served, including the US-built 6-ton Tank M1917.

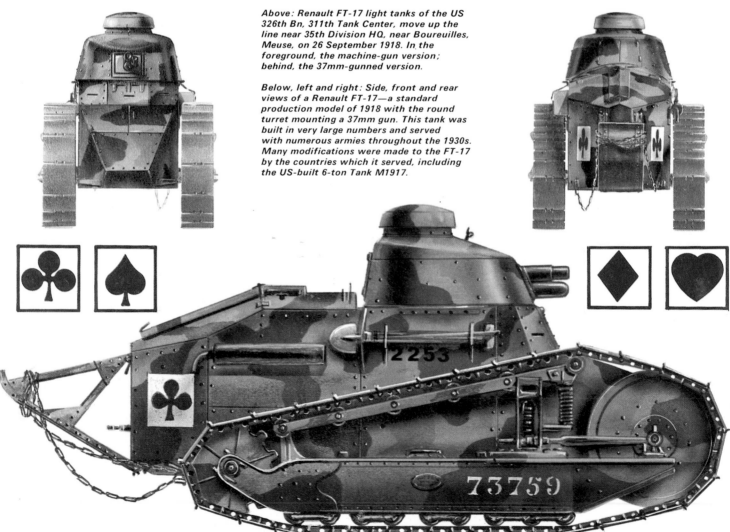

8mm, which was armed with an 8mm machine-gun with an elevation of +35° and a depression of −20°· 4,800 rounds of machine gun ammunition were carried. This was followed by the 37mm model, armed with a 37mm Puteaux gun with an elevation of +35° and a depression of −20°; 237 rounds of ammunition were carried − 200 HE, 25 AP and 12 shrapnel. The signals vehicle had no turret but was fitted with a superstructure, carrying a single radio, and had a crew of three (radio-operator, observer and driver). The self-propelled gun was called the *Char Canon* 75S and was armed with a 75mm gun in an open mount. This did not enter service, however. Subsequently many other variants were developed, including an amphibious version, bridgelayer, bulldozer, cargo carrier with redesigned hull, fascine carrier for crossing trenches (*Char Fascine*), mineclearing tank (*Char*

Demineur), searchlight carrier (this had a searchlight on a high tower and was used for internal security operations by the French police after the war) and a smoke-laying tank. Most of these were for trials purposes, although some were used in the war. The Renault FT-17 was first used in action on 31 May 1918, when 21 tanks supported infantry in the battle of the Forest of Retz. Later that day the Germans counter-attacked and most of the ground was lost again. At the end of the day only three FT-17s were still operational. Losses were heavy in many of the early engagements, but as the crews gained experience and tactics improved, losses dropped considerably. By the end of the war just over 3,000 tanks had been completed and production continued for a short time afterwards. After the war the tank was used in action in most of the French colonies including Morocco, Syria and Tunisia.

One of the advantages of the Renault was that its small size enabled it to be transported by lorry from one part of the front to another, whereas the heavier tanks had to be brought up by rail and then proceed to the front line under their own power. After the end of the war many FT-17s were exported, and in many cases these were the first armoured vehicles of some armies. Such was the demand that eventually exports were stopped as the French Army would have ended up with no Renaults at all. In the 1920s many attempts were made to modernise the FT-17, and some were fitted with Citroën-Kégresse rubber band tracks, although these were for trials only. Further development by Renault resulted in the NC1 (or NC27) light tank which had an up-armoured hull and new suspension. This was tested by the French Army but was not adopted, though some examples were sold to Japan and Yugoslavia. This was followed by the NC2 (or NC31) which had a more powerful engine and weighed 9.5tons (9,653kg). Armament consisted of turret-mounted twin 7.5mm machine-guns, and some of this model were purchased by Greece. In the 1930s those FT-17s remaining in service were rearmed with new ·7.5mm Hotchkiss machine-guns and then became known as the FT-31. These carried 3,600 rounds of standard ammunition plus a further 450 rounds of armour-piercing ammunition. There were still some 1,600 FT-17s in service when the Germans invaded France in 1940, and many of these were captured by the Germans. The Germans called them the PzKpfw 18R 730(f) and used them mainly for the internal security role and for guarding airfields and other strategic targets. Some of the tanks had their turrets removed, the turrets being installed in coastal defences. Some remain to this day in the Channel Islands.

Left: Obsolete Renault FT light tanks captured by the Germans in 1940 in use by the internal security forces of the occupying power. Many French AFVs were used by the Wehrmacht from 1940 on.

Below: Late production models of the Renault FT light tank. The special unditching tail, fitted at the rear, can be clearly seen.

SAINT CHAMOND ASSAULT TANK

Crew: 8.

Armament: One 75mm gun; four 8mm machine-guns.

Armour: 0.67in (17mm) maximum.

Dimensions: Length 28ft 6in (8.687m); width 8ft 9in (2,667m); height 7ft 9in (2.362m).

Weight: Combat 48.501lbs (22.000kg).

Ground pressure: 11.3lb/in² (0.79kg/cm²).

Engine: Panhard four-cylinder petrol engine developing 90hp.

Performance: Road speed 5mph (8km/h); range 37 miles (59.5km); vertical obstacle 1ft 3in (0.381m); trench 8ft (2.438m); gradient 57 per cent.

History: Entered service with the French Army in 1916 and phased out of service shortly after the end of the war. Also used by Russia, Italy and the United States (in France), although it was not used operationally by the latter two countries.

The Schneider was the first tank to be designed and built in France but it was nothing to do with the STA (*Service Technique Automobile*) whose job it was to supply such vehicles for the French Army. The STA therefore quickly started work on an 'official' tank without even consulting Colonel Estienne who had designed the Schneider tank. The first prototype was completed in February 1916 at the Saint Chamond works of the *Compagnie des Forges et Aciéries de la Marine et Homécourt,* and two months later it was decided to build 400 of the tank, which became known as the Saint Chamond. Like the Schneider, the Saint Chamond was also based on a Holt Tractor type chassis, although in this case the chassis was longer. The hull was of riveted construction with a maximum

thickness of 0.67in (17mm), this being a great improvement over that of the Schneider tank. The front of the hull was boat-shaped, with the driver and commander seated at the front of the hull, one on each side, each being provided with a circular cupola in the roof. On the prototypes the suspension was covered by armoured plates, but these were left off of production tanks, for when these were fitted, the tracks soon became blocked up with mud. The suspension consisted of three bogies. The front bogie had the idler and two small road wheels, the centre bogie had three small road wheels whilst the last bogie had three small road wheels and the drive sprocket; there were five small return rollers. One of the more unusual features of the Saint Chamond was that each track was powered by an electric motor, power for these being provided by a dynamo driven by the Panhard petrol engine mounted in the centre of the hull. The transmission was a Crochat-Collardeau. First production vehicles were armed with a 75mm Saint Chamond gun but these were later replaced by the standard 75mm Model 1897 gun. Four 8mm Hotchkiss machine-guns were fitted, one in the front of the hull on the right, one in each side of the hull and one in the rear. Some 106 rounds of 75mm and 7,500 rounds of machine-gun ammunition were carried. The Saint Chamond was first used in action at Laffaulx Mill on 5 May 1917. During this action all but one of the 16 Saint Chamonds used became stuck in the first line of German trenches. The main disadvantage of this tank was that the front and rear of the hull hung over the tracks, and when crossing trenches or ditches the nose just dug into the ground and the tank was immobilised. The French did modify some tanks to

overcome this problem but none of the various schemes tried was satisfactory. The inability of the French tanks to cross the German trenches stemmed from the fact that both the Schneider and the Saint Chamond were based to a large extent on a commercial crawler tractor. The British also had Holt tractors, but soon realised that something more was required to cross the German trenches. The lozenge shape of the British tanks enabled them to cross wide trenches. The Mark I, for example, could cross a trench 11ft 6in wide (3,505m) when fitted with its tail, and climb a vertical obstacle of 4ft 6in (1.372m). Several modifications were carried out on production tanks, including revised commander's and driver's cupola and the roof was angled so that grenades would roll off of the roof before they exploded. In all, 400 Saint Chamonds were built, the last of these being completed in March 1918. Some Saint Chamond tanks had their 75mm guns removed for use in the supply role. Production of the Schneider and Saint Chamond was finally stopped as it had been decided to concentrate on building larger numbers of the smaller Renault FT 17 two-man tanks.

Below: French Saint Chamond tanks on their way to the front. Better-armoured than the Schneider (France's first tank), the 23-ton Saint Chamond mounted a 75mm gun and four 8mm machine-guns. But faulty design revealed itself when the first of 400 Saint Chamonds built went into action in May 1917.
The hull overhung the tracks so much that when crossing trenches the tank's nose became embedded in the far side of the obstacle.

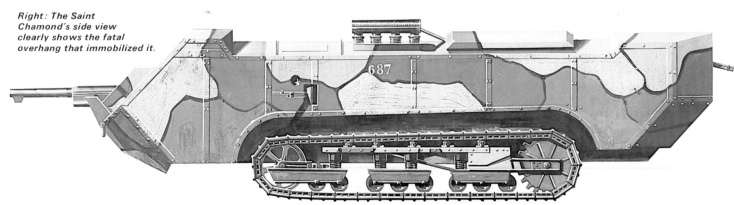

Right: The Saint Chamond's side view clearly shows the fatal overhang that immobilized it.

RENAULT UE SUPPLY CARRIER

UE and German variants.
Crew: 2.
Armament: None (see text).
Armour: 7mm (0.28in).
Dimensions: Length 8ft 10in (2.692m); width 5ft 7in (1.701m); height 3ft 5in (1.04m).
Weight: 4,409lbs (2,000kg).
Engine: Renault petrol engine developing 35hp.
Performance: Road speed 18mph (29km/h); range 60 miles (96.5km/h); vertical obstacle 1ft 4in (0.406m); trench 4ft (1.219m); gradient 40 per cent.
History: Entered service with the French Army in 1931 and used until 1940. Also used by Free French and German Army (see text).

Above: Renault carrier, usually for towing a supply trailer.

When the British Carden-Loyd Mark VI carrier appeared in the late 1920s, it attracted the interest of almost every army in the world. Many countries purchased quantities of these carriers from Britain and some built modified versions under licence — Italy, Czechoslovakia and Russia, for example. France purchased at least one model and Làtil obtained a licence to build the type in France, it being known there as the Latil *Tracteur* N. The Renault *Chenillette d'Infanterie* Type UE owed a lot to the Làtil vehicle, and entered service with the French Army as a supply carrier in 1931. It was very small and had a crew of two, driver on the left and the co-driver or commander on the right, each of these being provided with a dome-shaped cupola to cover their heads in combat. These cupolas were provided with vision slits. The engine and transmission were at the front of the hull. The suspension on each side consisted of three bogies, each of these having two wheels, with the idler at the rear and the drive sprocket at the front. There were two track-return rollers. The load area was at the rear of the hull, but as this could not carry very much a tracked trailer was normally towed, this carrying 1,102lbs (500kg) of cargo. The trailer could also be towed on its wheels if required. This carrier was to have been replaced by the *Chenillette* Lorraine but large numbers of the Renault were still in service when France fell in 1940. These vehicles were normally unarmed, although some had a Hotchkiss machine-gun in a raised position on the right of the hull. The Free French used a number of these carriers, and at least two anti-tank models were developed: one mounted a 47mm French anti-tank gun on a pedestal whilst the other mounted a British 6pounder anti-tank gun, fitted with a Galliot muzzle-brake. The basic vehicle was used by the Germans as an ammunition carrier under the designation *Gepanzerter Munitionsschlepper* UE (*f*). The Germans also adopted the vehicle for a variety of other roles. Some were fitted with a 3.7cm *Pak* (anti-tank) gun, this being provided with a shield, under the designation 3.7cm *Pak* (*Sf*) *auf Infanterie Schlepper* UE (*f*). There were also two models adapted to launch rockets, one carrying four *Wurfrahmen* 40 launching-racks, two on each side of the hull for launching 28cm or 32cm rockets, whilst the other had four similar rockets in the ready-to-launch position on top of the hull towards the rear.

Below: The Renault Chenillette d'Infanterie Type UE, here towing an anti-tank gun, entered service in 1931. One of many 'tankettes' inspired by the British Carden-Loyd Mk VI, the unarmed carrier served into WWII.

CHAR 2C HEAVY TANK

Char **1A,** *Char* **1B and** *Char* **2c.**
Armour: 45mm (1.77in) maximum.
Crew: 12–13.
Armament: One 75mm gun; four 8mm machine-guns.
Dimensions: Length 33ft 8in (10.27m); width 9ft 8in (2.95m); height 13ft 2in (4.01m).
Weight: Combat 154,320lbs (70,000kg).
Engines: See text.
Performance: Road speed 8mph (12km/h); range 100 miles (160km); vertical obstacle 4ft (1.219m); trench 13ft 6in (4.114m); gradient 50 per cent.
History: Entered service with French Army shortly after end of World War I and destroyed in 1940.

The first French tanks were the Saint Chamond and the Schneider, but these both had one major shortcoming, their inability to cross German trenches. In 1916 the FCM (*Forges et Chantiers de la Méditerranée*) at La Seyne, near Toulon, started the design of a new 'breakthrough tank', the first of two prototypes being completed late in 1917. One of the prototypes had an electrical transmission and the other a mechanical transmission. These tanks were known as the *Char* FCM 1A, weighed 39.37 tons (40,000kg) and had a crew of seven men. They were powered by Renault 12-cylinder petrol engines, giving them a top speed of just 4mph (6.4km/h). Armament consisted of a 75mm

gun and machine-guns. The 1B was similar, but the 75mm gun was replaced by a 105mm weapon. The FCM 1A was not placed in production but was followed by the *Char* 2C. Ten of these were built by 1918, but they did not enter service with the French Army until after the war. If the war had not ended, it was anticipated that 300 *Char* 2Cs would have been built for the 1919 campaigns. These 10 tanks were modified in the 1930s and were still operational with the 51st Battalion when war broke out in 1939. They took no part in the Battle of France as most of them were destroyed on their special railway wagons by the *Luftwaffe*. Main armament of the *Char* 2C consisted of a turret-mounted 75mm gun. The four 8mm machine-guns were mounted as follows: one in the hull front, one in each side of the hull in the forward part of the tank, and the last turret-mounted on the hull top towards the rear of the tank. When built the tanks were powered by German six-cylinder Mercedes engines developing 180hp each, but these were later replaced by more powerful Maybach engines developing 250hp each. The *Char* 2C had the distinction of being the first tank to have two turrets. It was very heavy and if it had been used operationally would have been more of a liability than an asset. One *Char* 2C was rebuilt as the only *Char* 2C-*bis*, which had additional armour. Sautter-Harlé engines and a 155mm howitzer.

Above, below and bottom: The French Char 2C was one of the largest AFVs built. It was developed near the end of WWI and served until 1940, supplementing the Maginot Line defences. Only 10 were built.

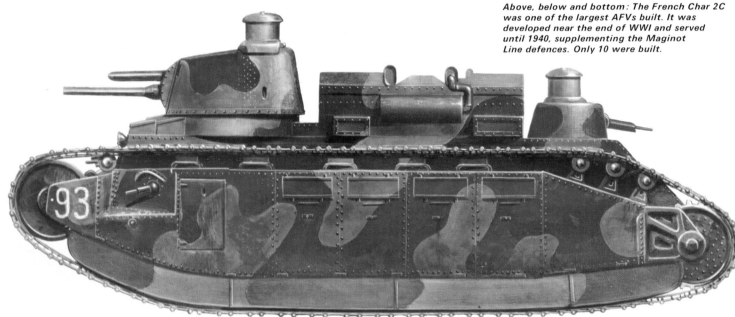

RENAULT AMC 35 LIGHT TANK

AMC 35 (ACG1), plus Belgian and German variants.
Crew: 3.
Armament: One 47mm gun; one 7.5mm machine-gun co-axial with main armament.
Armour: 25mm (1in) maximum.
Dimensions: Length 15ft (4.572m); width 7ft 4in (2.235m); height 7ft 8in (2.336m).
Weight: 31,967lbs (14,500kg).
Engine: Renault four-cylinder petrol engine developing 180hp.
Performance: Maximum road speed 25mph (40km/h); range 100 miles (161km); vertical obstacle 2ft (0.609m); trench 6ft (1.828m); gradient 60 per cent.
History: In service with the French Army from 1935 to 1940. Also used by the Belgian and German Armies (see text).

As well as building a light tank to meet the AMR requirement (the Renault AMR 33 VM), Renault also built a tank to meet the AMC (*Auto-Mitrailleuse de Reconnaissance*) requirement. The first prototype, which was completed in 1933, had a turret from the Renault light tank, featuring a 37mm gun. Trials with this prototype were not satisfactory so a further prototype was built, under the designation AMC Renault 34 YR. This was the first French light tank to have a two-man turret, at last enabling the tank commander to carry out his proper role, that is to command the tank, and not operate the armament. AMC 34 YR armament consisted

of a 25mm gun and a co-axial 7.5mm machine-gun. It was powered by a Renault four-cylinder petrol engine which developed 120hp, giving the tank a maximum road speed of 25mph (40km/h). Combat weight was 10.63 tons (10,800kg). This tank was followed by the Renault AMC 35 or ACG1, of which early models were built by Renault, but then the majority by AMX. The tank had a crew of three, with the driver at the front of the hull and the other two crew members in the turret. Armament consisted of a 47mm gun and a co-axial 7.5mm machine-gun, although some tanks had the 47mm gun replaced by a long barrelled 25mm anti-

tank gun. The suspension was of the scissors type with horizontal springing. There were five road wheels on each side, with the drive sprocket at the front and the idler at the rear, and five track-return rollers. Production of the AMC 35 amounted to about 100 tanks, of which 12 were purchased by the Belgians in 1937. The tanks were re-designated *Auto-Mitrailleuses de Corps de Cavalerie*, and had a turret of Belgian design and construction armed with a 47mm anti-tank gun and a co-axial 13.2mm machine-gun. After the fall of France some AMC 35s were taken over by the Germans, who called them the PzKfpw AMC 738 (f).

Right: The Renault AMC 35 was developed as a light armoured combat vehicle to operate with French mechanized units. The hull was of riveted construction and several types of turret were fitted. The 47mm-gunned version seen here has a cast turret. It was in French service in 1935-1940.

PANHARD AMD 178 ARMOURED CAR

Crew: 4.
Armament: One 25mm gun; one 7.5mm machine-gun.
Armour: 13mm (0.5in) to 18mm (0.71in).
Dimensions: Length 15ft 8½in (4.787m); width 6ft 7¼in (2.01m); height 7ft 7in (2.286m).
Weight: 18,740lbs (8,500kg).
Engine: Four-cylinder water-cooled petrol engine developing 105bhp at 2,000rpm.
Performance: Maximum road speed 45mph (72km/h); range 187 miles (301km); vertical obstacle 1ft (0.304m); gradient 40 per cent.
History: Entered service with French Army in 1935 and phased out in 1960. Also used by German Army (see text).

The prototype of the AMD (*Automitrailleuse*) was completed in 1933 under the Panhard designation of Model 178, and after trials the vehicle was accepted for use with the French Army. The AMD saw action in the Battle of France, and many were captured and used by the Germans. The Germans gave the vehicle the designation Sd.Kfz.178, and some German vehicles had different armament. When France fell a number of AMDs, without their turrets, were hidden by the French Army. The Germans used the AMD for the reconnaissance role and some were even fitted with railway wheels to patrol railway lines. By 1942 turrets had been built and fitted to most of these vehicles. These were then issued to Vichy French forces in the south of France, but most of these were lost when German forces took over Vichy in 1942. As soon as Paris fell in 1944, the AMD was put back in production by Panhard, and production continued until the 8×8 EBR appeared a few years later. The last AMDs were finally withdrawn from service in 1960. For its years the AMD was a first-class vehicle and had a number of advanced features. The AMD had a hull of riveted construction with the driver at the front, commander and gunner in the turret, and rear driver on the right side, looking towards the rear. The vehicle was armed with a 25mm gun, and a 7.5mm Model 31 machine-gun was mounted to the left of the main armament, elevation of which was +14° and depression −12°. Some 150 rounds of 25mm and 3,750 rounds of 7.5mm ammunition were carried. There were also two other models used by the French: one had two 7.5mm machine-guns, whilst the second was a radio vehicle which was often left unarmed. AMDs used after World War II had a new turret with two hatch covers rather than the earlier model's one, and were armed with a 47mm gun and a 7.5mm co-axial machine-gun. These were known as AMD Model Bs.

Above and right: The Panhard AMD 178 was one of the best French armoured cars. Mounting a 25mm gun, it served well with both French and Germans.

HOTCHKISS H-35 AND H-39 LIGHT TANKS

H-35, H-39 and German variants.
Crew: 2.
Armament: One 37mm SA 38 gun; one 7.5mm Model 1931 machine-gun co-axial with main armament.
Armour: 40mm (1.57in) maximum; 12mm (0.47in) minimum.
Dimensions: Length 13ft 10in (4.22m); width 6ft 1in (1.85m); height 6ft 7in (2.14m).
Weight: Combat 26,456lbs (12,000kg).
Ground pressure: 12.8lb/in² (0.90kg/cm²).
Engine: Hotchkiss six-cylinder water-cooled petrol engine developing 120bhp at 2,800rpm.
Performance: Road speed 22.5mph (36km/h); range 93 miles (150km); vertical obstacle 1ft 8in (0.5m); trench 5ft 11in (1.8m); gradient 60 per cent.
History (H-35): Entered service with the French Army in 1936 and used until fall of France. Also used by Free French, Germany and Israel (after World War II). (Note: data relate to the H-39.)

When the first *DLM* (*Division Légère Mécanique*) was formed in 1934, the French Army wanted a light tank to operate with the *SOMUA* S-35 medium tank. In 1933 the French infantry ordered a light tank, the prototype of which was completed by Hotchkiss in 1934. This was rejected by the infantry in favour of the similar Renault 35 tank. The cavalry, however, accepted the tank for service as the *Char Léger* Hotchkiss *modèle* 35H, and in the end the infantry also accepted the tank for its *DCs* (*Divisions Cuirassées*) formed shortly before war broke out. The H-35 weighed 11.22 tons (11,400 kg) and was powered by a six-cylinder petrol engine which developed 75bhp at 2,700rpm and gave the tank a top road speed of 17mph (28km/h). The H-35's maximum armour thickness was 34mm (1.34in). The H-35 was followed by the H-38 and the H-39, which had a number of modifications including thicker armour and more powerful engines, which increased their speed. Production of the H-35/H-39 family amounted to about 1,000 tanks, of which some 821 were in front-line service when World War II broke out. The hull of the H-39 was of cast sections bolted together. The driver was seated at the front of the hull, slightly offset to the right, and was provided with a two-piece hatch cover, one part of which opened upwards and the other part forwards. A hull escape hatch was provided in the floor of the tank. The turret was also of cast construction and this was built by APX and was identical to that fitted to the Renault R-35 and R-40 tanks. The turret was provided with a cupola, which could be traversed, and the commander entered via a hatch in the turret rear, which also folded down horizontally to form a seat, this being used when the tank was not in action. The engine was at the rear of the hull on the left, with the fuel tank on the right, these being separated from the fighting compartment by a fireproof bulkhead. Compared with the earlier H-35, the deck of the H-39 was almost horizontal, the earlier model's deck having been more sloped. An external fuel tank could be fitted if required, as could a detachable skid tail, the latter being designed to increase

the tank's cross-country performance. Power was transmitted to the gearbox and transmission at the front of the hull by a shaft. The suspension on each side comprised three bogies, each with two wheels. These were mounted on bellcranks with double springs between the upper arms. The drive sprocket was at the front and the idler at the rear; there were two track-return rollers. Main armament consisted of a 37mm gun with a 7.5mm machine-gun mounted co-axially to the right. Two different models of 37mm gun were fitted: the SA 38 with a long (33 calibre) barrel, giving a muzzle velocity of 2,300fps (701m/s), or the shorter SA 18 gun (21 calibre) with a muzzle velocity of 1,273fps (388m/s). The former was the more common weapon for the H-39. Some 100 rounds of 37mm and 2,400 rounds of 7.5mm machine-gun ammunition were carried. The empty cartridge cases for the latter went into a chute which deposited them outside of the tank. Like most French tanks of this period, the Hotchkiss H-35/H-39 had one major drawback, and this was that the commander also had to aim and load the gun. When France fell the Germans took over many H-35 and H-39 tanks, some being used on the Russian Front without modification apart from the installation of a German radio and a new cupola. This had a flat roof and was provided with a two-piece hatch cover which opened to the left and

right. Some were also provided with a searchlight over the main armament. The Germans also developed two self-propelled guns based on the Hotchkiss H-35 and H-39 chassis, the conversion work being carried out by Alfred Becker of Krefeld, a firm which also converted many Lorraine supply carriers into self-propelled artillery pieces. The anti-tank model was known as the 7.5cm *Pak* 40 L/48 *auf Gw* 39H (*f*), and had its turret removed and replaced by an open-topped armoured superstructure mounted at the rear of the hull. In the front of this superstructure was mounted a 7.5cm anti-tank gun. Twenty-four such conversions were produced from 1942. This version weighed 12.3 tons (12,500kg) and had a crew of five. The second model was the 10.5cm *Panzer-feldhaubitze* 18 *auf Sfh* 39H (*f*) or 10.5cm *le FH* 18 *GW* 39H (*f*), 48 of these being built from 1942. This model was armed with a 10.5cm howitzer and was provided with a similar superstructure to the anti-tank model. When the state of Israel was formed after the end of World War II, it could not obtain any modern tanks at all and had to rely on what equipment was left in the area after the war. These included some French H-39 tanks and a number of these were rearmed with British 6-pounder anti-tank guns. Israel also obtained various armoured vehicles as 'scrap' and these were also modified and pressed into service.

Above: French soldiers with an H-35 light tank. Some 821 H-35/H-39s were in front-line service with French armoured divisions at the beginning of World War II.

Left: A Hotchkiss H-39 light tank during the Battle of France, 1940. This tank, mounting the long-barrelled 37mm SA 38 gun, has its access hatches open.

Right: A German-modified H-39 fitted with radio, with the aerial mounted on the track guard. This tank has the optional rear-mounted detachable skid tail.

Left: A Hotchkiss H-35 tank mounting the short-barrelled SA 18 37mm gun. Note the size of the tank in comparison with the man

Left: Side view of a Hotchkiss H-39, which has a near-horizontal rear engine deck as compared to the downward-sloping deck of the earlier Hotchkiss H-35 tank.

Below: Front and top views of the H-39 light tank. This was used together with the H-35 in a cavalry role, or in a direct support role with infantry.

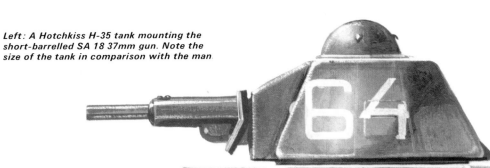

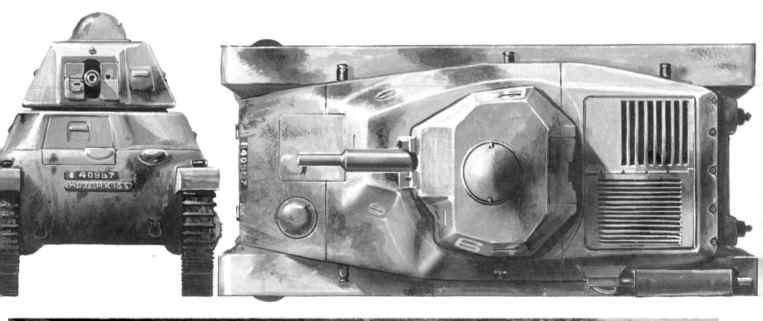

CHAR B1 HEAVY TANK

Char B1, B1-*bis*, B1-*ter* and German variants.
Crew: 4.
Armament: One 75mm gun in hull; one 7.5mm machine-gun in hull; one 47mm turret-mounted gun; one 7.5mm machine-gun co-axial with 47mm gun (see text).
Armour: 60mm (2.36in) maximum.
Dimensions: Length 21ft 5in (6.52m); width 8ft 2in (2.5m); height 9ft 2in (2.79m).
Weight: Combat 70,548lbs (32,000kg).
Ground pressure: 19.7lb/in² (1.39kg/cm²).
Engine: Six-cylinder inline water-cooled petrol engine developing 307bhp at 1,900rpm.
Performance: Road speed 17mph (28km/h); range 93 miles (150km); vertical obstacle 3ft 1in (0.93m); trench 9ft (2.75m); gradient 50 per cent.
History: Entered service with the French Army in 1936 and used until fall of France in 1940. Also used by the German Army (see text).

In France, like other countries after World War I, not only were funds for tank development in very short supply, but there were different schools of thought on what role the tank would play on the battlefield of the future. Some wanted the tank to support the infantry, others wanted the tank to have a more decisive role, whilst the cavalry wanted it for their role of reconnaissance. In 1921 the *Section Technique des Chars de Combat*, under the leadership of the famous French exponent of armour, General Estienne, requested five companies to draw up a design for a tank weighing 14.75 tons (15,000kg), to be armed with a hull-mounted 47mm or 75mm gun. In 1924 four different mockups were presented at Rueil and three years later orders were given for the construction of three tanks, one each from FAMH (*Forges et Aciéries de la Marine et d'Homécourt*), FCM (*Forges et Chantiers de la Méditerranée*) and Renault/Schneider. These were completed between 1929 and 1931 and were known as the *Char* B. These weighed 24.6 tons (25,000kg) and were armed with a hull-mounted 75mm gun, two fixed machine-guns in the front of the hull, and two turret-mounted machine-guns. They had a crew of four. With modifications the type entered production as the *Char* B1, but only 35 of these had been built before it was decided to place in production an improved model with heavier armour and a more powerful engine, to be known as the *Char*

B1-*bis*. Some 365 were built by the fall of France. Of these there were 66 *Char* B1-*bis* tanks in the 1st, 2nd, 3rd and 4th DCRs (*Division Cuirassées de Réserve*), and a further 57 in independent companies. The *Char* B1-*bis* had excellent armour which could withstand attack from any German anti-tank gun except the famous 88mm. The hull of the tank was of cast sections bolted together. The driver was seated at the front of the hull on the left and steered the tank with a conventional steering wheel which was connected in turn to a hydrostatic system. Mounted to the driver's right was the 75mm SA 35 gun, which had a very short barrel (17.1 calibres), elevation being +25° and depression −15°. The gun was fixed in traverse and was aimed by the driver, who swung the tank until the gun was lined up with the target. An unusual feature of this gun was that an air compressor was provided to blow fumes out of the barrel. A 7.5mm Chatellerault machine-gun was fixed in the front of the hull on the right, lower than the 75mm gun. This machine-gun could be aimed by the driver or commander. The APX turret was identical to that installed on the SOMUA S-35 tank and was armed with a 37mm gun with an elevation of +18° and a depression of −18°. A 7.5mm

Above, rear view of the Char B1-bis tank. The turret, with hatch opening downwards, was known as the 'command post', since its sole occupant was the commander, who had to load, aim and fire the turret guns, as well as command the tank. Only the commander and the driver, of the crew of four, were able to see out of the tank.

machine-gun was also mounted in the turret, and this had an independent traverse of 10° left and 10° right. Some 74 rounds of 75mm (HE), 50 rounds of 47mm (AP and HE) and 5,100 rounds of machine-gun ammunition were carried. The tank had a crew of four, the driver/gunner, wireless operator, loader and commander. The last had to aim, load and fire the turret guns as well as command the tank. The loader was just as busy, as he had to pass ammunition to the commander as well as load the hull-mounted 75mm gun. Normal means of entry and exit was via a large door in the right of the hull. The driver had a hatch over his position, and there was also a hatch in the turret rear on the right. There were two emergency exits, one in the floor of the tank, and another hatch in the roof of the engine compartment. The engine, transmission and fuel tanks were at the rear of the hull, and a compressed air starting system was fitted in addition to the normal electric starting system. Another interesting feature of the tank was the installation of a gyroscopic direction indicator, also driven by the compressor. The suspension on each side consisted of 16 double steel bogie wheels. Of these, three assemblies had four

wheels each and these were controlled by vertically mounted coil springs and semi-elliptical leaf springs. There were also three independent bogie wheels forward and one to the rear, with quarter-elliptic leaf springs. The drive sprocket was at the rear and the idler at the front, the latter being coil sprung to act as the tensioner. Further development of the *Char* B1-*bis* resulted in the *Char* B1-*ter*. This had additional armour, a fifth crew member (a mechanic) and the 75mm hull gun had a traverse of 5° left and 5° right. Only five of these were built and none were used in action. The tank was also used by the German Army for a variety of roles. The driver training model had the turret and hull-mounted gun removed, the latter being replaced by a machine-gun. The type was then known as the PzKpfw B1 (*f*) *Fahrschulewagen*. The Germans also modified 24 tanks in 1942–43 for use in the flame-thrower role. These had flameguns fitted in place of the hull guns and the type was known as the PzKpfw B1-*bis* (*Flamm*). The gun turret was retained to give the vehicle some anti-tank capability. Finally there was a self-propelled gun model. This had the hull gun and turret removed, and on top of the tank was mounted a standard German 105mm howitzer. The

conversion work was carried out by Rheinmetall-Borsig. Very few such conversions were effected and most of these served in France. A few *Char* B1-*bis* tanks were used by the French when they liberated the port of Royan in 1944. The *Char* B1-*bis* would have probably been followed in production by the ARL 40 but this was still at the design stage when France fell. The type was eventually placed in production as the ARL 44 in 1946. The main other French infantry tanks (medium/heavy) were the *Char* D1 and *Char* D2. The *Char* D1 was developed in the early 1930s and 160 were built for the infantry between 1932 and 1935. These weighed 12.8 tons (13,000kg) and were armed with a turret-mounted 47mm gun and a fixed machine-gun in the front of the hull, fired by the driver. Later production models had thicker armour, a more powerful engine and a machine-gun mounted co-axially with the main armament. Before production of the D1 was even completed, work started on more powerful and heavier armoured tank called the *Char* D2. This weighed 15.75 tons (16,000kg) and was powered by a six-cylinder petrol engine developing 150hp. By 1940 about 100 had been built.

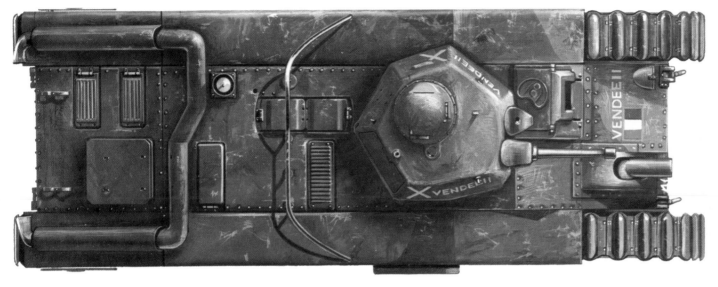

Left, a rare photograph of a 'killed' Char B1. At the start of World War II this type was one of the world's most formidable tanks.

Above, top view of Char B1-bis. The driver sat in front and to the left of the turret, which was at the rear of the fighting compartment.

Left and above, side and front views of Char B1-bis. The main 75mm gun, to the right and below the driver, was operated by the driver. It was fixed and the driver had to aim it by pointing the entire tank at the target. Ammunition for the weapons was stored on the walls and under the floor of the fighting compartment.

RENAULT AMR 33 VM LIGHT TANK

AMR 33 VM, 35 ZT and German variants.
Armament: one 7.5mm machine-gun.
Crew: 2.
Armour: 13mm (0.51).
Dimensions: Length 11ft 6in (3.504m); width 5ft 3in (1.6m); height 5ft 8in (1.727m).
Weight: 11,023lbs (5000kg).
Engine: Reinastella eight-cylinder liquid-cooled petrol engine developing 84bhp.
Performance: Maximum road speed 37mph (60km/h); vertical obstacle 2ft (0.609m); trench 5ft (1.524m); gradient 60 per cent.
History: Entered service with the French Army in 1934–35 and used until fall of France in 1940. (Note: data relate to *AMR 33 VM*.)

Right: Pilot model of the AMC 34. In the inter-war years the French did much light tank development.

During World War I the French cavalry used armoured cars for the reconnaissance role in small numbers. These lacked mobility for cross-country operations, however, and in 1922–23 specifications were issued for a new vehicle to be called the AMC, or *Auto-Mitrailleuse de Cavalerie*. Various projects were started over the next few years but little progress was made. In 1931 requirements for three different types of vehicle for the cavalry were drawn up: firstly, the AMD (*Auto-Mitrailleuse de Découverte*), a requirement eventually filled by the Panhard AMD 178 armoured car; secondly, the AMR (*Auto-Mitrailleuse de Reconnaissance*), a light tracked vehicle with a crew of two, to be armed with a single 7.5mm machine gun; and thirdly, the AMC (*Auto-Mitrailleuse de Combat*), to support the lighter AMR with heavier armour and more powerful armament. Renault built a small tracked vehicle to meet the AMR requirement,

and after trials an order for 123 production vehicles was placed in 1933. These vehicles entered service with the French Army under the designation AMR Renault 33 VM. The hull was of riveted construction, with the driver at the front, the commander/gunner in the turret, which was offset to the left of the hull, and the engine on the right side. The suspension was unusual and consisted of four road wheels: a twin-wheeled bogie in the centre, pivoted at the lower end

of a vertical coil, and single wheels, front and rear, on bell cranks. The drive sprocket was at the front and the idler at the rear, and there were four track-return rollers. Further development resulted in the Renault AMR 35 ZT, of which 200 were built. This weighed 6.4 tons (6,500kg) and was powered by a Renault four-cylinder water-cooled petrol engine which developed 85hp and gave the vehicle a top road speed of 34mph (55km/h). Armament consisted of a 7.5mm machine-

RENAULT R-35 LIGHT TANK

R-35 and German variants.
Crew: 2.
Armament: One 37mm gun; one 7.5mm machine-gun co-axial with main armament.
Armour: 45mm (1.77in) maximum.
Dimensions: Length 13ft 10in (4.2m); width 6ft 1in (1.85m); height 7ft 9in (2.37m).
Weight: 22,046lbs (10,000kg).
Ground pressure: 9.52lb/in² (0.67kg/cm²).
Engine: Renault four-cylinder petrol engine developing 82bhp at 2,200rpm.
Performance: Road speed 12.42mph (20km/h); range 87 miles (140km); vertical obstacle 1ft 10in (0.5m); trench 5ft 3in (1.6m) or 6ft 7in (2m) with tail; gradient 60 per cent.
History: Entered service with the French Army in 1936 and used until fall of France. Also used by Germany, Italy (tanks received from Germany), Poland, Romania, Turkey and Yugoslavia.

In 1934 the French infantry issued a requirement for a new light tank to replace the large number of World War I Renault FT-17 two-man tanks which were still in service (these in fact remained in service with French Army until 1940, and with the German Army for some years later still). This new light tank was to weigh 7.87 tons (8,000kg), have a crew of two, a maximum road speed of 12.42mph (20km/h), be armed with twin 7.5mm machine-guns or a single 37mm gun, and have a maximum armour thickness of 40mm (1.57in). Four companies submitted designs: *Compagnie Général de Construction des Locomotives*, Delaunay-Belleville, FCM and Renault. The Renault model, called the Renault ZM (or R-35) was selected for production and the first 300 were ordered in May 1935. The prototype was armed with twin turret-mounted 7.5mm machine-guns and differed in many details to the production models. The suspension was based on that used in the Renault *Auto-mitrailleuse de Reconnaissance* 1935 Type ZT (AMR) which had already been accepted for service. Production of the Renault R-35 amounted to between 1,600 and 1,900 tanks, and when war was declared this was the most numerous of all of the French tanks, and many were also exported. In May 1940 there were some 945 R-35/R-40 tanks in front line use, and of these 810 were organic to armies and another 135 were with the 4th *DCR* (*Division Cuirassée de Réserve*). Their role was the support of the infantry and their slow road speed gave them little strategic mobility. The FCM entry in the original competition was also adopted for service as the *Char Léger Modèle* 1936 FCM, but only 100 were built by 1940 and these were sufficient to equip a mere two battalions. The FCM tank was faster than the R-35 and had a much larger radius of action. It was powered by a 90hp diesel and its suspension was similar to that used on the *Char B1*. Its hull was of welded construction and in this respect was quite advanced. Combat weight was about 10.33 tons (10,500kg). Some of these FCMs were converted to

self-propelled guns after the German invasion. Like most French tanks, the hull of the R-35 was of cast sections which were then bolted together. The driver was seated at the front of the hull, slightly offset to the left, and was provided with two hatch covers, one of which opened forwards and the other upwards, the operation of the latter being assisted by a hydraulic ram. The APX turret was in the centre of the hull and was identical to that installed on the Hotchkiss H-35 and H-39 tanks. This was provided with a cupola but the commander entered the turret via a hatch in the rear of the turret, and this hatch also acted as a seat for the commander when the tank was not in action. Main armament consisted of a 37mm SA 18 gun with a 7.5mm machine-gun mounted co-axially. Some 100 rounds of 37mm and 2,400 rounds of 7.5mm ammunition were carried. The empty cartridge cases for the machine-gun were deposited into a chute which carried them out through a hole in the floor of the tank. Late production tanks were armed with the long-barrelled SA 38 37mm gun. The engine was at the rear of the hull on the right, with the fuel tank (this being of the self-sealing type) on the left. A fireproof bulkhead separated the engine and fighting compartments. The suspension on each side consisted of five rubber-tired wheels, the first being mounted inde-

pendently and the others on two bogies. These were mounted on bellcranks with springs. The drive sprocket was at the front and the idler at the rear, and there were three track-return rollers. Most tanks had a tail fitted to increase their trench-crossing capabilities. When first developed the tank was not provided with a radio, although these were fitted to late production tanks. This addition meant even more work for the commander, who already had to command the tank as well as aim, load and fire the armament. Another development of the R-35 was the AMX-40. This had a new suspension designed by AMX, consisting of 12 small road wheels, with the drive sprocket at the front and the idler at the rear, and there were four track-return rollers. This suspension was an improvement over the Renault suspension. Two battalions were equipped with the AMX-40, or R-40 as the type was sometimes called. The R-35 was also used as a fascine carrier. This model had a frame running from the front of the hull over the turret to the rear, on top of which was carried a fascine for dropping into trenches. Some tanks were also provided with FCM turrets of cast or welded construction, although these were not adopted for service. Other trials versions included a mine-detection tank and a remote-controlled tank. The Germans used the R-35 for various roles. The

gun, or a 13.2mm Hotchkiss machine-gun or a 25mm Hotchkiss anti-tank gun. Quantities of both the AMR 33 VM and the AMR 35 ZT were captured by the Germans, the former being given the designation PzSpWg VM 701 (f) and the latter PzSpWg ZTI 702

(f). Some of these had their turrets removed and replaced by a new superstructure mounting an 80mm mortar. The (f) stood for French, captured British tanks having the suffix (e), American (a), Czechoslovakian (t) and so on.

Above: One of the most widely-used French light reconnaissance tanks was the AMR 33 Renault VM, mounting a 7.5mm machine-gun. The tank served with French mechanised cavalry units until the German occupation.

Left: The Germans made wide use of captured French vehicles, converting them to various special roles. Most were adapted as self-propelled guns; others were used as ammunition carriers, tractors, and so on. Shown here is one of the best-known adaptions: a Czech 47mm anti-tank gun mounted in a specially-armoured super-structure on a Renault R-35 light tank hull and chassis. It was not traversable.

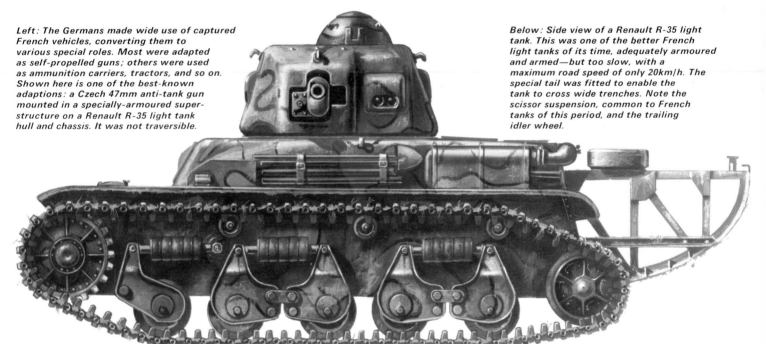

Below: Side view of a Renault R-35 light tank. This was one of the better French light tanks of its time, adequately armoured and armed—but too slow, with a maximum road speed of only 20km/h. The special tail was fitted to enable the tank to cross wide trenches. Note the scissor suspension, common to French tanks of this period, and the trailing idler wheel.

basic tank was used for the reconnaissance role on the Eastern Front from 1941 onwards under the designation PzKpfw R-35 (4.7cm). Many had their turrets removed and were used for towing artillery (*Traktor*) or for carrying ammunition, the latter version being known as the *Munitionpanzer* 35R (f). The anti-tank variant was known as the 4.7cm *Pak* (t) *auf GW* R35 (f), this consisting of an R-35 with its turret removed and replaced by a new open topped super-structure in the front of which was mounted a Czech 47mm anti-tank gun. About 100 of these were con-verted, but they were already obsolete by the time conversion work was completed. Alfred Becker fitted some with a 105mm howitzer and these were known as the 10.5cm *leFH* 18 *auf GW* 35R (f). Some examples were also fitted with an 80mm mortar, these being known as the *Mörserträger* 35R (f).

Right: Rear and front views of the R-35 light tank. Playing-card insignia were often painted on the turret for identification of sub-units. When open, the door in the turret rear provided a seat for the commander. The effectiveness of French armour was often increased by casting it in the most suitable ballistic shape.

CHAR SOMUA S-35 MEDIUM TANK

S-35 and S-40.
Crew: 3.
Armament: One 47mm gun; one 7.5mm Model 31 machine-gun co-axial with main armament.
Armour: 56mm (2.2in) maximum.
Dimensions: Length 17ft 11in (5.46m); width 6ft 11in (2.108m); height 8ft 10in (2.592m).
Weight: Combat 44,200lbs (20,048kg).
Ground pressure: 13.08lb/in² (0.92kg/cm²).
Engine: SOMUA eight-cylinder water-cooled petrol engine developing 190hp at 2,000rpm.
Performance: Maximum road speed 23mph (37km/h); road range 160 miles (257km); vertical obstacle 1ft 8in (0.508m); trench 7ft 8in (2.336m); gradient 65 per cent.
History: Entered service with the French Army in 1936 and used until fall of France in 1940. Also used by Germany and Italy (see text).

Above: A column of Hotchkiss light tanks led by a Somua S-35 medium tank. After the occupation of France in 1940, the Germans took over all available French tanks.

In the early 1930s the French cavalry issued a requirement for a tank to be called the AMC, or *Automitrailleuse de Combat*. A vehicle to this specification was built by SOMUA (*Société d'Outillage Mécanique et d'Usinage d'Artillerie*) at Saint Ouen. After trials this was accepted for service with the cavalry under the designation AMC SOMUA AC-3. Soon afterwards it was decided that the type would be adopted as the standard medium tank of the French Army, and it was redesignated the *Char* S-35, the 'S' standing for SOMUA and the '35' for the year of introduction, 1935. About 500 had been built by the fall of France. The 1st and 2nd (both with the French 7th Army) and the 3rd (with the French 1st Army) *DLM*s (*Divisions Légères Mécaniques*) each had 87 S-35s. The 6th *DLC* (*Division Légère de Cavalerie*) in Tunisia had 50 and some were also with the 4th *DCR* (*Division Cuirassée de Réserve*). Tank for tank, the S-35 was more than a match for any of the German tanks of that time, but bad tactics gave them little chance to prove their worth apart from a few isolated actions. The S-35 had good armour, mobility and firepower, but it also had the usual French weakness in that the commander was also the gunner and loader. The hull was of three cast sections bolted together. These sections were the hull floor, front superstructure and rear superstructure, which were joined by bolts just above the tops of the tracks, with the vertical join between the front and rear parts near the rear of the turret. These joints were one of the weak points of the tank as a hit on one of these was likely to split the tank wide open. The hull had a maximum thickness of 1.6in (41mm). The driver was seated at the front of the hull on the left, and was provided with a hatch to his front. This hatch was normally left open as the tank moved up to the front. The radio operator was located to the right of the driver. Normal means of entry and exit for the driver and radio operator were through a door in the left side of the hull; a floor escape hatch was also provided for use in an emergency. The turret was also of cast construction and had a maximum thickness of 2.2in (56mm). It was identical with that fitted to the *Char* B1-*bis* and D2. Main armament consisted of a 47mm SA 35 gun with an elevation of +18° and a depression of −18°, the turret being traversible through 360° by an electric motor. The 47mm gun could fire

both HE and AP rounds with a maximum muzzle-velocity of 2,200fps (670m/s). A 7.5mm Model 31 machine-gun was mounted co-axially to the right of the main armament. This machine-gun was unusual in that it had a limited traverse of 10° left and 10° right of the main armament. Some 118 rounds of 47mm and 1,250 rounds of machine-gun ammunition were normally carried. Provision was also made for mounting

another 7.5mm machine-gun on the commander's cupola for use in the anti-aircraft role. This last does not appear to have been fitted in action as no doubt the commander already had enough to do without having to cope with this weapon as well! The engine and transmission were at the rear of the hull, with the engine on the left and the self-sealing petrol tank on the right. The engine compartment was separated from

Above: The final version of the Somua medium tank, the S-40, had a more powerful 220hp engine. The tank seen here has just been captured by the French resistance.

Left: Side view of the S-40. This well-designed AFV, undoubtedly the best French tank of World War II, greatly impressed the Germans. Casting was used extensively to armour the S-40.

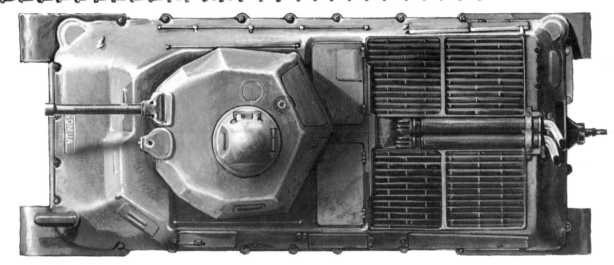

Left: Side view of the Somua S-35. Note especially the access panels and doors. The tank had the same turret as fitted to the Char B1-bis and D2, and had a 47mm SA 35 gun and a 7·5mm Model 31 machine-gun.

Left and right: Front, back and top views of a Somua S-35 tank. Of particular interest are the wide area of engine air-intake grilles at the rear, the shrouded turret machine-gun, and the twin exhaust pipes running down the centre of the rear deck. The tank was very well laid-out and ample vision devices were provided.
Below: A new Somua S-35 on its special trailer, towed by a Somua tractor, awaits delivery to the French Army. It served in 1940.

the fighting compartment by a fireproof bulkhead. The suspension on each side consisted of two assemblies, each of which had four bogie wheels mounted in pairs on articulated arms, these being controlled by semi-elliptic springs. The ninth bogie wheel at the rear was provided with its own spring. The idler was at the front and the drive sprocket at the rear, and there were two small track-return rollers. The lower part of the suspen-

sion was provided with an armoured cover which could be hinged up to allow access to the bogie assemblies. In 1940 production of an improved model, the S-40 started. This had a more powerful 220hp engine and modified suspension, but few of these had been completed by the fall of France. Another interesting vehicle was the SAu 40 self-propelled gun, although this existed only in prototype form. This had a

hull-mounted 75mm gun to the right of the driver, and a different turret was fitted. The S-35 was also used by the Germans for a variety of roles including crew training, internal security and some were even used on the Russian front. The Germans called the type the *PzKpfw* 35C 739 (*f*). Some were also fitted as command vehicles, and a few were handed over to the Italian armed forces.

CHENILLETTE LORRAINE TYPE 37L SUPPLY CARRIER

Type 37L and German variants.
Crew: 2.
Armament: None.
Armour: 6mm (0.24in) maximum.
Dimensions: Length 13ft 9½in (4.203m); width 5ft 2in (1.574m); height 4ft (1.219m).
Weight: 12,456lbs (5,650kg).
Engine: Delahaye Type 135 six-cylinder water-cooled petrol engine developing 70bhp at 2,800rpm.
Performance: Road speed 22mph (35km/h); range 85 miles (137km); vertical obstacle 1ft 8in (0.508m); trench 5ft (1.524m); gradient 50 per cent.
History: In service with the French Army from 1937 to 1940. Also used by Free French and German Army (see text).

In the 1930s the *Sociètè* Lorraine, well known builders of railway rolling stock, turned their attention to building armoured vehicles. At that time the French Army was looking for a replacement vehicle for the large number of Renault UE carriers then in service. The company built a tracked carrier known as the Chenillette Lorraine Type 37L which met the requirements of the French Army and was accepted for service in 1936. The production contract was not signed until the following year, however, and the first production vehicles started to leave the Lorraine factory at Lunéville, near the Franco-German border, late in 1937. In 1939 it was decided to transfer production to a disused Lorraine factory in the south of France at Bagnères de Bigorre, but production had hardly started here when France was invaded in the summer of 1940. Lorraine also built a smaller model of the vehicle for use in the infantry supply role. This had two rather than three bogies and was known as the *Chenillette Légère*, and carried ammunition in a box at the rear of the hull. The box could be released by the driver without leaving his position. The Lorraine was used mainly by the French armoured divisions (the *Divisions Cuirassèes*). There were two main production models: first, an ammunition carrier which also towed a

tracked ammunition carrier; and second, an ammunition carrier which towed a tracked trailer carrying fuel, this being used to refuel tanks in the field. The French were one of the first armies to recognise the requirement for the logistic support of their armoured forces. Just before France fell an armoured personnel model was built. This had the personnel compartment at the rear of the hull and was provided with front, side and rear armour protection, but no overhead armour. The hull of the Lorraine was of armoured construction with the transmission at the front and the driver and commander to the rear of this. The engine was in the centre of the hull and the cargo area at the rear. The suspension on each side consisted of three bogies, each with two wheels, the drive sprocket being at the front and the idler at the rear, and there were four track-return rollers. When France fell the Germans captured large numbers of the type and put them to good use. In fact the German models became better known than the French models. The original supply vehicle was used by the Germans under the designation of *Munition Transport Kampfwagen auf* Lorraine *Schlepper* (f), but the Germans soon realized that the Lorraine hull could be adopted to mount artillery. The first self-propelled artillery version mounted a German World War I 15cm howitzer in a lightly armoured superstructure at the rear of the hull. To cope with the recoil forces a large spade was provided at the rear of the hull and this was lowered before the weapon was fired. The 15cm howitzer had an elevation of +40° and a depression of −1½°, traverse being 7° left and 7° right. The howitzer fired an HE projectile weighing 90lbs (40.8kg) to a maximum range of 9,500 yards (8,600m). Some 102 were converted by Alfred Becker from 1942 and some were captured after the Battle of El Alamein. The German designation for this vehicle was the 15cm *sFH auf* Lorraine *Schlepper* (f). This was followed by a model carrying the 10.5cm leFH 18 howitzer, but only 24 of these were converted in 1943, and these were known as the 10.5cm *leFH* 18 *auf GW* Lorraine *Schlepper* (f).

The Germans also used the type as the basis for an anti-tank vehicle. The first such model was a standard Lorraine with a French Model 1937 or Model 1939 47mm anti-tank gun, provided with a shield, mounted at the front of the cargo area. This was known as the 4.7cm *Pak* 181 *oder* 183 (f) *auf Panzerjäger* Lorraine *Schlepper* (f). The second model was a more ambitious conversion and was known as the *Marder* (Marten) or 7.5cm *Pak* 40/1 *auf* Lorraine *Schlepper* (f) *Marder* 1 (*SdKfz* 135). This was armed with a 7.5cm anti-tank gun with an elevation of +22° and a depression of −5°, traverse being 32½° left and right. Some 48 rounds of ammunition were carried, and the vehicle had a crew of five. These conversions served the German Army until the end of the war, although the chassis was very heavily overloaded. One of the more unusual German models was a Russian 122mm gun which was captured on the Eastern Front and mounted on a Lorraine chassis, which in turn was mounted on a railway wagon and used in France until it was captured by the French resistance in Burgundy during September 1944. The Free French also used these vehicles, and at least one was fitted with the British 17pounder anti-tank gun, this being provided with a French muzzle-brake designed by Galliot. As mentioned earlier, the French had decided to transfer production of the Lorraine to the south of France. Thus when France fell the factory was

Below: The Renault UE, like the Chenillette Lorraine, was a French Army tracked carrier, employed mainly to transport supplies and ammunition. It was essentially a French replica of the British Carden-Loyd Mk VI machine-gun carrier. As with many other captured French AFVs, the Germans often equipped them as self-propelled guns; the version shown here mounts a 37mm anti-tank gun.

in unoccupied France, so production continued of a new forestry tractor. This type had two bogies and ran on gas as there was a shortage of petrol. At the same time the armour required to turn these tractors into fighting vehicles was made and hidden away. When the Germans occupied this part of France in November 1942, they inspected the factory but failed to discover any of the armoured components. Later

in the war these tractors were fitted with the armour and played their part in pushing the Germans out of the country. Some of them were modified to carry a Hotchkiss machine-gun in the front of the hull on the right. The *Chenillette* Lorraine remained in service with the French Army for a few years after the war and a self-propelled gun model of local construction turned up in Syria in the mid-1950s.

Above: Side and front views of a tracked armoured trailer used to carry supplies and ammunition and towed either by the Renault UE or the Chenillette Lorraine. A canvas tilt was provided.

Another version of the Chenillette Lorraine towed a tracked trailer containing fuel and was used to refuel tanks in the field; an example of French realization of the need for logistic support for armour.

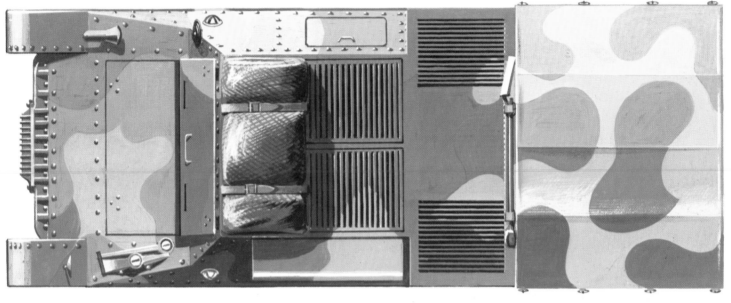

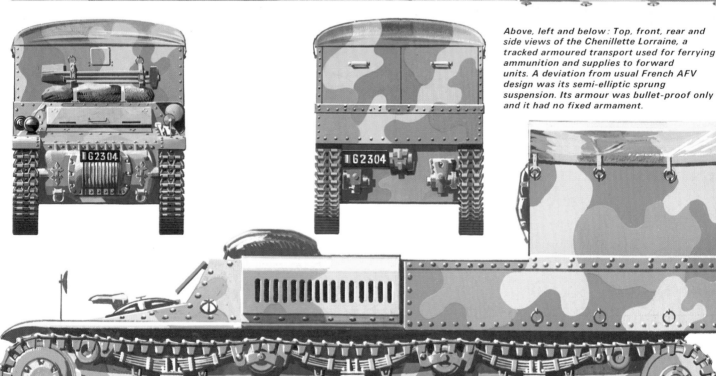

Above, left and below: Top, front, rear and side views of the Chenillette Lorraine, a tracked armoured transport used for ferrying ammunition and supplies to forward units. A deviation from usual French AFV design was its semi-elliptic sprung suspension. Its armour was bullet-proof only and it had no fixed armament.

ARL 44 HEAVY TANK

Crew: 5.

Armament: One 90mm gun; one 7.5mm machine-gun co-axial with main armament; one 7.5mm anti-aircraft machine-gun.

Armour:

Dimensions: Length 34ft 6in (10.52m); width 11ft 2in (3.4m); height 10ft 6in (3.2m).

Weight: About 105,820lbs (48,000kg).

Engine: Maybach petrol engine developing 700hp.

Performance: Road speed 23mph (37.3km/h); range 93 miles (150km); vertical obstacle 3ft (0.93m); trench 9ft (2.75m); gradient 50 per cent.

History: In service with the French Army from 1947 to 1953.

One of the drawbacks of the *Char* B1 was that the 75mm gun mounted in the front of the hull had very limited traverse. So in 1938 the *ARL* (*Atelier de Construction de Rueil*) started a project to mount a 75mm gun in a new turret on a *Char* B1 chassis. By the fall of France in 1940 this project, known as the ARL-40, was still on the drawing board. During the occupation of France design work continued in secret at Rueil, and once Paris was liberated in 1944 the new design was placed in immediate production. The first production tank was completed in 1946. This was a considerable achievement for the French at that time. The tank became known as the ARL-44 or *Char de Transition*, and at one time it was intended to build 300 of them. In the end, however, only 60 were built. These were issued to the 503rd Regiment and made only one public appearance, on 14 July 1951. Production was undertaken by Renault and the FAMH (*Forges et Aciéries de la Marine et d'Homécourt*), with the turrets being supplied by Schneider. Whilst the tracks and suspension were similar to those of the earlier *Char* B1, the hull was new, as was the turret and engine. The driver and co-driver were seated at the front of the hull with the other three crew members in the turret.

The engine was at the rear of the hull. The ARL-44 was to have been followed by the AMX-50, but although various prototypes of this later tank were built and tested, the type was not placed in production as large quantities of M47 tanks were available from the United States.

EBR-75 ARMOURED CAR

EBR-75, EBR VTT and variants

Crew: 4.

Armament: One 90mm gun; one 7.5mm machine-gun co-axial with main armament; one 7.5mm machine-gun in each driver's position.

Armour: 8mm–15mm (0.32–0.59in).

Dimensions: Length (overall) 20ft 2in (6.15m); length (hull) 18ft 3in (5.56m); width 7ft 11in (2.42m); height (on eight wheels) 7ft 7in (2.32m).

Weight: Combat 29,760lbs (13,500kg).

Engine: Panhard 12-cylinder air-cooled petrol engine developing 200hp at 3,700rpm.

Performance: Road speed 65mph (105km/h); range 404 miles (650km); vertical obstacle 1ft 4in (0.4m); trench 6ft 7in (2m); gradient over 70 per cent.

History: Entered service with the French Army in 1951. Also in service with Algeria, Morocco and Portugal (VTT Model only). No longer in production. (Note: data relates to EBR with FL-11 turret.)

In the late 1930s the Panhard company designed for the French Army an 8×8 armoured car called the AMR 201, the first prototype of which was completed in December 1939. This was sent to North Africa when the war started, and its subsequent fate is still uncertain. After the war one of the French Army's immediate requirements was for an 8×8 armoured car. Panhard designed a slightly larger model of the earlier AMR 201, with the designation Model 212, the first prototype of which was completed in 1948. This was a considerable achievement for Panhard. The type entered production in 1950 and production continued until 1960, by which time 1,200 had been built. The French Army call it the EBR, or *Engin Blindé de Reconnaissance*. It is still the standard heavy armoured car of the French Army, although it will be replaced from 1979 by the new 6×6 AMX-10RC vehicle. The EBR has a number of interest-ing features. It has eight wheels: the front and rear pairs are conventional tyred wheels and are used for steering (the EBR has two drivers, one at the front and one at the rear, the latter also acting as the radio operator), and centre four wheels have steel grousers. When travelling across country these four central wheels are lowered until they are in contact with the ground and so improve the cross-country ability of the EBR. When first built the EBR was armed with a 75mm gun in an FL-11 oscillating turret. This turret has full 360° traverse and the gun has an elevation of from −6° to +13°. A 7.5mm machine-gun is mounted co-axially with the 75mm gun, and a single 7.5mm machine gun is mounted in each of the drivers' positions. These latter machine-guns are fixed and operated by the drivers. Two smoke dischargers are mounted each side of the turret, and a total of 56 rounds of ammunition is carried. Some years ago most of the EBRs were rearmed with a new 90mm gun which fires fin-stabilised HEAT and HE rounds. The HEAT round will penetrate 12.6in (320mm) of armour at 0° (ie vertical). Some EBRs, however, were fitted with the complete FL-10 turret of the AMX-13 light tank, although this increased vehicle weight to 15 tons and also added to the overall height of the vehicle. Two variants of the EBR were developed. The first of these was an anti-aircraft model with twin 30mm cannon, which was not placed in production. The second was the armoured personnel carrier designated the EBR ETT or VTT, 30 of which were built by Panhard for service in North Africa. Some were subsequently exported to Portugal, where they are still in service.

Below and right: Panhard EBR armoured cars with the FL-II turret mounting a 75mm gun. The vehicles on the right have their four central wheels lowered for rough going.

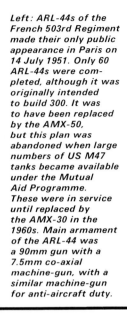

Left: ARL-44s of the French 503rd Regiment made their only public appearance in Paris on 14 July 1951. Only 60 ARL-44s were completed, although it was originally intended to build 300. It was to have been replaced by the AMX-50, but this plan was abandoned when large numbers of US M47 tanks became available under the Mutual Aid Programme. These were in service until replaced by the AMX-30 in the 1960s. Main armament of the ARL-44 was a 90mm gun with a 7.5mm co-axial machine-gun, with a similar machine-gun for anti-aircraft duty.

Below: The ARL-44 heavy tank was the first French-designed AFV to enter service with the French Army after World War II. Its design dated back to the ARL-40 of 1940; the ARL-44 was designed by the Atelier de Construction de Rueil (ARL) during the German occupation. The first production model of the ARL-44 was completed in 1946 —a remarkable achievement when the condition of the French engineering industry after five years of German occupation is taken into account.

AMX-13 LIGHT TANK

AMX-13, ARV, AVLB and variants
Crew: 3.
Armament: One 75mm gun; one 7.5mm or 7.62mm machine-gun co-axial with main armament; two smoke dischargers on each side of the turret.
Armour: 10 to 40mm.
Dimensions: Length (gun forward) 20ft 10in (6.36m); length (hull) 15ft (4.88m); width 8ft 2in (2.5m); height 7ft 7in (2.3m).
Weight: Combat 33,069lbs (15,000kg).
Ground pressure: 10.81lb/in² (0.76kg/cm²).
Engine: SOFAM Model 8 GXb eight-cylinder water-cooled petrol engine developing 250hp at 3,200rpm.
Performance: Road speed 37mph (60km/h); range 218 miles (350km); vertical obstacle 2ft 2in (0.65m); trench 5ft 3in (1.6m); gradient 60 per cent.
History: Entered service with the French Army in 1953–54. Also used by Algeria, Argentina, Chile, Dominican Republic, Ecuador, El Salvador, India, Indonesia, Ivory Coast, Kenya, Lebanon, Morocco, the Netherlands, Nepal, Peru, Salvador, Saudi-Arabia, Singapore, Switzerland, Tunisia and Venezuela. No longer used by Austria, Cambodia, Egypt or Israel.

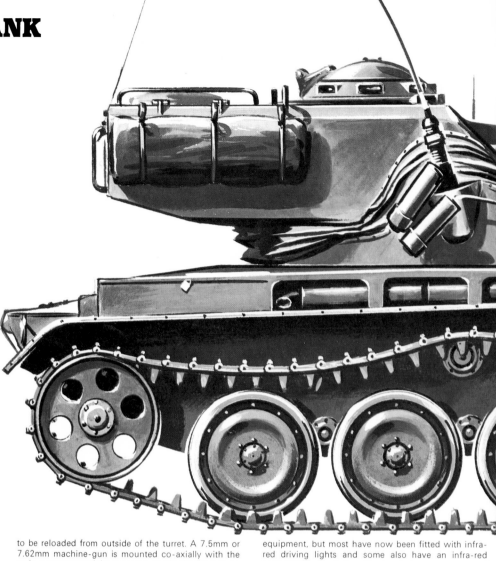

The AMX-13 was one of the three armoured vehicles developed by the French after the end of World War II, the others being the Panhard EBR-75 and AMX-50 heavy tank. The AMX-13 was designed by the *Atelier de Construction* d'Issy-les-Moulineaux near Paris and the first prototype was completed in 1948–49, which in itself was quite an achievement. The type entered production at the *Atelier de Construction* Roanne in 1952 and production continued at this plant until the early 1960s, when production was transferred to the Creusot-Loire plant at Chalon-sur-Saône. The move was necessary because the Roanne plant was tooling up for the production of the AMX-30 MBT. The AMX-13 is still available, and it is estimated that some 4,500 AMX-13 type vehicles, including tanks, self-propelled guns and artillery, have so far been built. The AMX-13 was designed for use as a tank destroyer or reconnaissance vehicle and is still the standard light tank of the French Army. The hull is of all-welded steel construction and has a maximum thickness of 1.575in (40mm). The driver is seated at the front of the hull on the left, with the engine to his right. The turret is towards the rear of the hull, with the commander on the left and the gunner on the right. The suspension is of the torsion-bar type and there are five road wheels, with the idler at the rear and the drive sprocket at the front. There are two or three track-return rollers. To keep the height of the tank as low as possible the French designed the tank for crew members with a maximum height of 5ft 8in (1.727m). The turret is of the French-designed oscillating type and has two parts. The lower part is mounted on the turret ring and has two trunnions on which upper part, the top of the turret (together with the gun) is mounted. On this type of installation the top of the turret is elevated or depressed complete with the gun, which is fixed. The fitting of a turret of this type enabled the French to install an automatic loader, and this in turn reduced the crew to three as a crew member was not required for loading purposes. The gun is fed from two revolver-type magazines, each of which holds six rounds of ammunition, giving a total of 12 rounds for ready use. The empty cartridge cases are ejected automatically through a hole in the rear of the turret. Once the 12 ready rounds have been expended, the magazines have

to be reloaded from outside of the turret. A 7.5mm or 7.62mm machine-gun is mounted co-axially with the main armament and there are two smoke dischargers on each side of the turret. The oscillating turret is also fitted to the Panhard 8×8 EBR heavy armoured car and the Austrian *Panzerjäger* tank destroyer. The first AMX-13s to enter service were armed with a 75mm gun which fired either HE or HEAT rounds. The latter would penetrate 6.7in (170mm) of armour at a range of 2,187 yards (2,000m). The next model had a slightly different oscillating turret and was armed with a 105mm gun, firing a HEAT round which would penetrate 14.17in (360mm) of armour. This model was not adopted by the French Army, but was purchased by the Netherlands. Some fatigue problems were encountered when the type first entered service. All AMX-13s in use with the French Army today have been refitted with a new 90mm gun firing fin-stabilised rounds, 34 rounds of 90mm and 3,600 rounds of machine-gun ammunition being carried. The AMX-13 can ford to a depth of 2ft (0.6m) without preparation, but has no amphibious capability. When it first entered service the AMX-13 did not have any night-vision

equipment, but most have now been fitted with infra-red driving lights and some also have an infra-red searchlight mounted on the turret. France was one of the first countries to make use of wire-guided anti-tank missiles, and many AMX-13s have been fitted with two SS-11 missiles on each side of the main armament to give them long-range anti-tank capability. Some years ago an AMX-13 was fitted with the HOT missile system, three missiles being mounted in their launcher boxes on each side of the turret. This model was not adopted, however, and the French Army is now developing a special version of the AMX-10P MICV armed with the HOT system. The basic AMX-13 tank was followed by the AMX VCI armoured personnel carrier and the 105mm Mk.61 self-propelled howitzer. Both of these have their own entries, and so are not described here. The bridgelayer version, or *Char Poseur de Pont*, is provided with a scissors type bridge which can be laid over the rear of the hull. When in position this allows tanks weighing up to 23.62 tons (24,000kg) to cross ditches and other obstacles; two of these bridges can be laid side by side so that an AMX-30 MBT can use them. The *Char de Depannage* is the armoured

Left: An AMX-13 light tank of the French Army is refuelled. The AMX-13 has been in service since 1953-54 and is still produced for export by Creusot-Loire, builders of the other members of the AMX-13 series.

Left and right: The first AMX-13s to enter service mounted a 75mm gun in an oscillating turret. Later models had a 90mm or 105mm gun. An automatic loader enables a high rate of fire for a short time, before the two 6-round magazines have to be reloaded.

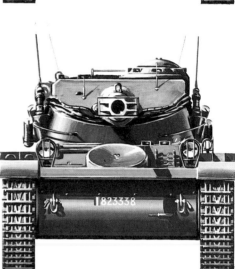

recovery version. This is fitted with an 'A' frame pivoted at the front of the hull and swinging back onto the rear of the hull when not required. It can be used to change engines and transmissions. When this 'A' frame is being used, the front suspension can be locked to provide a more stable platform. Two winches are provided, the main one having a capacity of 15.75 tons (16,000kg). Four spades are mounted at the rear of the hull. The ARV has a crew of three. Armament consists of a 7.5mm or 7.62mm machine-gun and smoke dischargers. Without doubt the AMX-13 has been one of the most successful tank designs since World War II and has given birth to a whole range of vehicles which can only be equalled by the Russian PT-76 light tank and the American M113 families.

Right: Top view of the first model of the AMX-13 light tank to enter French Army service. It has a crew of three: the driver is at the front left with the SOFAM petrol engine to his right; the commander and gunner travel in the tank's turret.

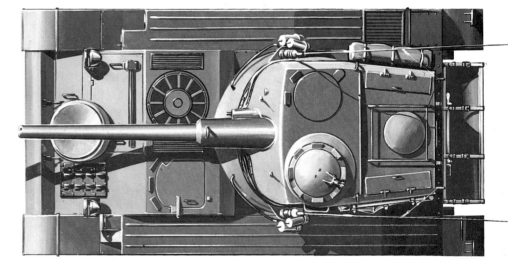

Left: An AMX combat engineer vehicle using its hydraulically-operated dozer blade. Known as the Véhicle de Combat du Génue (VCG), it also has an 'A' frame pivoted at the front of the hull. An hydraulic winch with a capacity of 4 tons and 60m of cable is also fitted. Armament consists of a turret-mounted 7.62mm or 12.7mm machine-gun, with four smoke dischargers mounted on either side of the hull. The VCG carries a six-man crew.

Right: An AMX-13 with four Aéro-spatiale Harpon ATGWs mounted over its main armament. This model was built for trials but was not adopted by the French Army. The Harpon is a development of the SS-11 ATGW with an improved guidance system. All the operator need do is keep his optical sight on the target while a separate infra-red tracker follows flares fitted to the missile. Like the SS-II, Harpon has a maximum range of 3,000m.

AMX 105mm SELF-PROPELLED GUN

Mk.61 (Obusier de 105 Model 1950 sur Affût Automoteur) fixed and turretted models

Crew: 5.

Armament: One 105mm howitzer; one 7.5mm anti-aircraft machine-gun.

Armour: 12mm–20mm (0.47–0.79in).

Dimensions: Length 21ft (6.4m); width 8ft 8in (2.65m); height (with cupola) 8ft 10in (2.7m).

Weight: Combat 36,376lbs (16,500kg).

Ground pressure: 11.38lb/in² (0.8kg/cm²).

Engine: SOFAM 8 GXb eight-cylinder water-cooled petrol engine developing 250hp at 3,200rpm.

Performance: Road speed 37.28mph (60km/h); range 218 miles (350km); vertical obstacle 2ft (0.65m); trench 6ft 3in (1.9m); gradient 60 per cent.

History: Entered service with the French Army in 1952. Still in service with France, Israel, Morocco and the Netherlands. No longer in production.

This self-propelled 105mm gun was the first vehicle to be developed from the AMX-13 light tank chassis. The initial prototype was completed in 1950, with production vehicles following in 1952. The type remains in service with the French Army, although both this and the 155mm Mk.F3 self-propelled weapon are to be replaced by the 155mm GCT self-propelled gun in the next five years. In the 1950s most armies had both 105mm and 155mm self-propelled weapons, but over the past 10 years the 105mm self-propelled gun has been dropped as the 155mm round is much more effective. The Mk.61's chassis is similar to that of the AMX-13 light tank, although it is higher at the back. The driver is seated at the front of the hull on the left with the engine to his right. The other four crew members are the commander, gunner and two loaders, located in the gun compartment at the rear of the hull, which is of all-welded construction with a maximum armour thickness of 0.8in (20mm). The gun has an elevation of +70° and a depression of −4.5°, traverse being limited to 20° left and 20° right. Both elevation and traverse are manual. One of the drawbacks of this weapon is that it cannot be quickly laid onto a new target, as would a gun mounted in a turret with a traverse of 360°. Two barrels were developed for the weapon, one of 23 calibres and the other of 30 calibres. (The term calibre in this context indicates the length of the gun barrel from the breech ring to the muzzle measured in terms of the gun's bore: for example the 105mm gun has a 23 calibre barrel, so its length is 23 times the calibre of 105mm, which equals 7ft 11in or 2,415m.) Both barrels are provided with a double-baffle muzzle-brake, whose primary purpose is to retard the force of recoil: as the projectile leaves the muzzle, the gases driving it strike the baffles of the muzzle-brake and are deflected to the sides and rear; the gases exert a forward force on the baffle that partially counteracts the rearward force of recoil. Fifty-six rounds of ammunition are normally carried, including six anti-tank rounds. The HE projectile weighs 35.27lbs (16kg) and has a maximum range of 16,404 yards (15,000m), muzzle velocity being from 772 to 2,198fps (220 to 670m/s). The fire control equipment consists of a ×6 telescope for anti-tank operations and a goniometer with a magnification of ×4. Most vehicles have a 7.5mm anti-aircraft machine-gun on the roof for anti-aircraft defence. Some vehicles are fitted with a turret-mounted 7.5mm machine-gun with a traverse of 360°. The vehicle's suspension is similar to that of the AMX-13 light tank and consists of five road wheels, with the drive sprocket at the front and the idler at the rear; there are three track-return rollers. Shock absorbers are provided for the first and fifth road wheels. This model does not have an NBC system and has no amphibious capability, although it can ford streams to a depth of 2ft 8in (0.8m). The Mk.61 was followed in the late 1950s by a model with a similar gun in a turret with a traverse of 360°, the gun having an elevation of +70° and a depression of −7°. Eighty rounds of ammunition were carried, including six for anti-tank use. A 7.5mm anti-aircraft machine-gun was mounted in a cupola on the roof of the turret. This had full traverse through 360° and could be elevated from −15° to +45°. Total combat weight was 17 tons and crew of five. The type was tested by the French and Swiss armies but was not adopted. Other self-propelled weapons on AMX-13 chassis include the AMX-13 DCA with twin 30mm anti-aircraft guns and the 155mm Mk.F3 self-propelled gun both of which are in service with the French Army.

Below: The AMX 105mm SP howitzer, with an AMX VCI command vehicle in the background. This SPG has been in French service since 1952 and is now being replaced by the 155mm GCT self-propelled gun.

Bottom: The AMX 105mm self-propelled howitzer with turret-mounted main armament was developed in the 1950s, on the AMX-13 light tank chassis.

HOTCHKISS CARRIERS

Spz. 11-2, Spz. 51-2, Spz. 22-2, Spz. 2-2, Spz. Kurz. and variants
Crew: 5.
Armament: One 20mm cannon.
Armour: 8mm–15mm (0.32–0.59in).
Dimensions: Length 14ft 10in (4.51m); width 7ft 6in (2.28); height 6ft 6in (1.97m).
Weight: Combat 18,078lbs (8,200kg).
Ground pressure: 8.24lb/in² (0.58kg/cm²).
Engine: Hotchkiss six-cylinder inline petrol engine developing 164hp at 3,900rpm.
Performance: Road speed 36mph (58km/h); range 242 miles (390km); vertical obstacle 2ft (0.6m); trench 4ft 11in (1.5m); gradient 60 per cent.
History: Entered service with the German Army in 1958. Will be phased out of service in 1977–78.

As soon as World War II ended, the Hotchkiss company quickly resumed its military activities, especially in the field of armoured vehicles. Hotchkiss built a series of light tracked vehicles, designated TT 6-52 and CC 2-52, for the French Army. Although improved models were built and tested, they were not adopted by the army. In the mid-1950s the German Army was re-formed and one of its main requirements was for a light armoured reconnaissance vehicle. Late in 1955 the Germans tested some of these Hotchkiss carriers, as a result of which they suggested certain modifications, carried out by Hotchkiss. The Germans subsequently adopted the vehicle and production started at the Hotchkiss plant in Paris in 1958, production continuing until

1962: just under 2,400 were built for the German Army. In addition some were assembled in Germany by Klöckner-Humboldt-Duetz. All of the Hotchkiss vehicles share many common components such as engine, transmission, steering gear, cooling system, tracks and suspension, optical equipment and much of their hulls. The reconnaissance model is known as the Spz.11-2 and has a crew of five: commander, gunner, radio-operator, driver and rifleman. The driver is seated at the front of the hull on the left side with the engine to his right, a fireproof bulkhead separating the engine and driver's compartments. The turret is in the centre of the hull. Main armament comprises a 20mm Hispano-Suiza cannon. This has an elevation of +75° and a depression of −20°, traverse being 360°, and both traverse and elevation are manual. Some 500 rounds of 20mm ammunition are carried. The hull is of all-welded steel construction varying in thickness from 0.3in (8mm) to 0.6in (15mm). A hull escape-hatch is provided in the floor of the vehicle. The normal method of entry and exit is via twin doors in the rear of the hull. The suspension is of the torsion-bar type and consists of five road wheels, with the idler at the rear and the drive sprocket at the front; there are three track-return rollers. None of the Hotchkiss carriers is provided with an NBC system, although they do have an air-conditioning system. Other equipment includes a Graviner automatic fire extinguishing system. The vehicle can ford to a maximum depth of 3ft 3in (1m) without preparation. The reconnaissance model is now being replaced by the 8×8 *Luchs* reconnaissance

ammunition and anti-tank weapons, a sad end for a company which had developed so many armoured vehicle. A number of other models was also adopted by the German Army. The mortar-carrier was known as the *Panzermörser* 81mm Spz.51-2: the 81mm mortar fires over the forward part of the hull, with a traverse of 30° left and 30° right, elevation limits being from +45° to +90°. Fifty 81mm mortar bombs are carried, and most vehicles also have a 7.62mm MG3 machine-gun on the roof for local protection. The command model is the Spz.22-2 (*Artilleriebeobachter*): this had three radios and a crew of five, and is normally armed with a 7.62mm MG3 machine-gun. The ambulance model, the Spz.2-2 (*Kr.Kw.Krankenwagen*), is unarmed and has a crew of three: a driver and two medical orderlies. It normally carries two stretchers and one sitting patient, although provision is made for carrying a further two stretcher patients on the roof, although it would appear that this has not proved too popular with the patients concerned! Finally the German Army has a cargo version called the *Spz.Kurz. Nachschubpanzer*. This has a different hull and only the driver's position is armoured. This last vehicle can easily be recognised from the other members of the family as it has an open (and lower) rear hull and only four road wheels. Hotchkiss also built other versions, but these were not adopted. The anti-tank model was fitted with a turret-mounted 90mm gun firing a HEAT round which could penetrate 14in (350mm) of armour. A 120mm mortar-carrier was built in prototype form, as was an armoured personnel carrier. Other variants projected by Hotchkiss included an anti-tank missile vehicle, a radar carrier and a recovery vehicle. In the early 1960s Hotchkiss built the prototype of a fully amphibious armoured personnel carrier known as the TT A 12. This was tested by the French Army but was not adopted. Hotchkiss also built the hulls for the prototypes of the Crotale SAM system. In the 1960s Hotchkiss closed down both their armoured vehicle and truck facilities, and now concentrate on mortars, ammunition and anti-tank weapons, and no longer any armoured vehicles.

Left: The French-designed Hotchkiss Spz. II-2 was the standard reconnaissance vehicle of the German Army from 1958. It is now being replaced by the Spähpanzer Luchs. The Spz.II-2 mounts a 20mm Hispano-Suiza cannon with an elevation of +75° and a depression of −20°; 500 rounds of 20mm ammunition are carried.

Below: The Hotchkiss Spz.22-2 command reconnaissance vehicle mounts a single 7.62mm MG3 machine gun. The primary role of this vehicle is artillery observation and control and three radios are carried. The Spz.22-2 has a crew of five: commander, observer, radio operator, driver and one rifleman.

AMX VCI ARMOURED PERSONNEL CARRIER

Crew: 1 plus 12.
Armament: One 7.5mm or 12.7mm machine-gun.
Armour: 10mm–30mm (0.39–1.18in).
Dimensions: Length 18ft 2in (5.544m); width 8ft 3in (2.51m); height 7ft 7in (2.32m).
Weight: 30,865lbs (14,000kg).
Ground pressure: 9.9lb/in² (0.7kg/cm²).
Engine: SOFAM 8 GXb eight-cylinder water-cooled petrol engine developing 250hp at 3,000rpm.
Performance: Road speed 40mph (65km/h); range 249 miles (400km); vertical obstacle 2ft 2in (0.65m); trench 5ft 3in (1.6m); gradient 60 per cent.
History: Entered service with the French Army in 1956. In service with Argentina, Belgium, Ecuador, France, Indonesia, Italy, Netherlands, United Arab Emirates and Venezuela. In production (see text).

Once the AMX-13 light tank was firmly established in production, the French turned their attention to other vehicles which could be developed on the same basic chassis. The prototype of the APC variant was completed in 1954, with production vehicles following two years later. The current name for the vehicle is the AMX VCI, the latter standing for *Véhicule de Combat d'Infanterie*. It was first built at the French government arsenal at Roanne, but when production of the AMX-30 MBT began there in the 1960s, the manufacture of all members of the AMX-13 light tank family, including the VCI, was taken over by Creusot-Loire, who still market and manufacture the whole family. In many respects the VCI was many years ahead of its time when it first entered service with the French Army, and it is still one of the best vehicles of its type. The front part of the hull is almost identical to that of the AMX-13 tank, with the driver located on the left side and the engine to his right. The commander and gunner are in the centre and the personnel compartment is at the rear of the hull. The infantry enter and leave the vehicle via twin doors in the rear of the hull, each of these being provided with a firing-port. The infantry are seated on seats in the centre of the compartment facing outwards. On each side of the personnel

compartment are two sets of hatches, and each of these has two parts. The top part folds upwards whilst the lower part, which has integral firing-ports, folds downwards. When the vehicle first entered service it was armed with a standard French 7.5mm machine-gun on a simple pintle mount. Since then a variety of armament installations has been fitted, including a 12.7mm machine-gun which can be loaded and fired from within the vehicle, a turret-mounted 7.5mm machine-gun with an elevation of +45° and a depression of −15°, and more recently a turret-mounted 20mm cannon similar to that installed on the AMX-10P MICV. The VCI is normally provided with both an NBC system and night-vision equipment. Its only drawback is that it has no amphibious capability, although it can ford streams to a maximum depth of 2ft (0.6m). It is now being replaced by the AMX-10P MICV in the French Army. The basic VCI has been adapted to undertake a wide variety of roles, including battery command vehicle for use with artillery units, 81mm and

120mm mortar carriers to provide fire support for the infantry, command vehicle, ambulance, VCA support vehicle for the 155mm AMX Mk.F3 self-propelled gun, ENTAC missile-launching vehicles and the Combat Engineer Vehicle or *Véhicule de Combat du Génie* as the French call it. The last carries a wide range of equipment, including an hydraulically operated dozer blade at the front of the hull, a winch and a cable, and an 'A' frame. The 'A' frame is hinged at the front of the hull and is used for lifting heavy objects. When not required it is swung back over the rear of the hull. This model has a crew of 11 and retains its machine-gun for local protection. The ENTAC vehicle is provided with two launchers for the French ENTAC missile, each launcher having two missiles in the ready-to-launch position. These are raised from within the hull when required. The missile has a minimum range of 438 yards (400m) and a maximum range of 2,187 yards (2,000m). The AMX VCI chassis has also been used for a wide variety of trials purposes.

Right and below: The AMX-VCI APC, reckoned one of the best vehicles of its type, has been in service with the French Army since 1956. Currently being replaced by the AMX-10P MICV, it is still built for export.

PANHARD AML-90 LIGHT ARMOURED CAR

Crew: 3.

Armament: One 90mm gun; one 7.62mm machine-gun co-axial with main armament; one 7.62mm machine-gun on turret roof (optional); two smoke dischargers each side of turret.

Armour: 8mm–12mm (0.32–0.47in).

Dimensions: Length (overall) 16ft 9in (5.11m); length (hull) 12ft 5in (3.79m); width 6ft 6in (1.97m); height (with A/A MG) 6ft 10in (2.07m).

Weight: Combat 12,125lbs (5,500kg).

Engine: Panhard Model 4 HD four-cylinder petrol engine developing 90hp at 4,700rpm.

Performance: Road speed 62mph (100km/h); range 372 miles (600km); vertical obstacle 1ft (0.3m); trench (using one channel) 2ft 8in (0.8m); gradient 60 per cent.

History: Entered service in 1961. In service with Algeria, Angola, Burundi, Chad, Congo, Ecuador, Eire, Ethiopia, France, Iraq, Ivory Coast, Kenya, Kampuchea, Libya, Malaysia, Mauritania, Morocco, Nigeria, Portugal, Rhodesia, Rwanda, Saudi-Arabia, Senegal, South Africa, Spain, Tunisia, United Arab Emirates, Venezuela, Volta and Zaire. Still in production.

The standard armoured car in the French Army in the 1950s was the heavy Panhard EBR-75. It was found during the conflict in North Africa that this vehicle was too heavy for many of the roles it was undertaking. As an interim measure the French purchased 200 British Ferret scout cars. They soon started to design a similar vehicle, and the first prototype of the AML (*Automitrailleuse Légère*) was completed by Panhard and Levassor of Paris in 1959. Two years later it was in service with the French Army. Since then over 3,400 have been built by Panhard, and a further 1,000 have been built under licence in South Africa, where the type is known as the Eland. One of the most common models is the AML 90. This is armed with a turret-mounted 90mm gun, with an elevation of +15° and a depression of −8°, firing two basic types of ammunition: HEAT (muzzle velocity 2,493ft/s or 760m/s) and HE. HEAT rounds will penetrate 12.6in (320mm) of armour at an angle of 0° (ie vertical) or 5.5in (140mm) of armour at an angle of 60°; effective range is 1,640 yards (1,500m). Both Israel and South Africa have knocked out numerous Russian T-54 tanks with their AML 90s. The HE round has a muzzle velocity of 2,133ft/s (650m/s). Both the HEAT and HE rounds are fin-stabilised. A 7.62mm machine-gun is mounted co-axially with the main armament and an additional machine-gun can be mounted on the roof for anti-aircraft defence, although this last applies to most members of the AML family. The AML 90 carries 20 rounds of 90mm and 2,400 rounds of 7.62mm ammunition. The basic AML can ford rivers and streams to a maximum depth of 3ft 7in (1.1m) but a flotation kit has been developed which can be fitted to any of the AML family as a permanent fixture. The vehicle is propelled in the water by its wheels, although to increase water speed a propeller kit is also available. One of the disadvantages of vehicles such as the AML, compared with tracked vehicles, is that they cannot easily cross ditches. AMLs do, however, carry steel channels bolted on the front of the hull. Bolted end to end, these form a bridge so that the AML can cross ditches and similar obstacles. There are many variants of the AML, and the following are in service: an anti-aircraft vehicle with twin 20mm cannon and a total of 600 rounds of ammunition; AML 60-7 with a 60mm mortar and twin 7.62mm machine-guns; AML 60-12 with a 60mm mortar and 12.7mm machine-gun; AML 60-20 with a 60mm mortar and a 20mm cannon; and the more recent AML 30. This has a 30mm HS 831 cannon and a 7.62mm co-axial machine-gun. Some AMLs have been fitted with anti-tank missiles such as the SS-11 in addition to their normal armament. Components of the AML series are also used in the Panhard M-3 armoured personnel carrier, which is often used in conjunction with the AML by some armies.

Left: Among the many variants of the Panhard AML series of light armoured cars are models equipped to fire four SS-II ATGWs, seen here, or two of the heavier SS-12s.

Below: The Panhard AML-90 with its standard armament of a turret-mounted 90mm gun and co-axial 7.62mm machine gun. More than 3,400 AML types have been built by Panhard since 1961, and around 1,000 have been licence-built in South Africa.

AMX-30 MAIN BATTLE TANK

AMX-30, ARV, AVLB, SPAAG and variants.
Crew: 4.
Armament: One 105mm gun; one 20mm cannon or one 12.7mm machine-gun co-axial with main armament (see text); one 7.62mm machine-gun on commander's cupola; two smoke dischargers on each side of turret.
Armour: 50mm (1.96in) maximum, estimated.
Dimensions: Length (including main armament) 31ft 1in (9.48m); length (hull) 21ft 8in (6.59m); width 10ft 2in (3.1m); height (overall) 9ft 4in (2.85m).
Weight: Combat 79,366lbs (36,000kg).
Ground pressure: 10.95lb/in² (0.77kg/cm²).
Engine: HS-110 12-cylinder water-cooled multi-fuel engine developing 700hp at 2,400rpm.
Performance: Speed 40mph (65km/h); range 400 miles (650km); vertical obstacle 3ft 1in (0.93m); trench 9ft 6in (2.9m); gradient 60 per cent.
History: Entered service with the French Army in 1967. Also in service with Greece, Iraq, Libya, Morocco, Peru, Saudi-Arabia, Spain and Venezuela, and on order for Qatar. It was ordered by Chile but these have not been delivered. Still in production.

After the end of World War II France quickly developed three vehicles, the AMX-13 light tank, the Panhard EBR 8×8 heavy armoured car and the AMX-50 heavy tank. The last was a very interesting vehicle with a hull and suspension very similar to the German PzKpfw V Panther tank used in some numbers by the French Army in the immediate postwar period. The AMX-50 had an oscillating turret, a feature that was also adopted for the AMX-13 tank. The first AMX-50s had a 90mm gun, this being followed by a 100mm and finally a 120mm weapon. At one time it was intended to place the AMX-50 in production, but as large numbers of American M47s were available under the US Military Aid Program (MAP) the whole programme was cancelled. In 1956 France, Germany and Italy drew up their requirements for a new MBT for the 1960s. The basic idea was good: the French and Germans were each to design a tank to the same general specifications; these would then be evaluated together; and the best tank would then enter production in both countries, for use in all three. But like many international tank programmes which were to follow, this came to nothing: France placed her AMX-30 in production and Germany placed her Leopard 1 in production. The AMX-30 is built at the *Atelier de Construction* at Roanne, which is a government establishment and the only major tank plant in France. The first production AMX-30s were completed in 1966 and entered service with the French Army the following year. The type has now replaced the American M47 in the French Army and has also been exported to a number of countries. No total production figures have had been released but it is estimated that about 2,000 AMX-30s have been built so far. The hull of the AMX-30 is of cast and welded construction, whilst the turret is cast in one piece. The driver is seated at the front of the hull on the left, with the other three crew members in the turret. The commander and gunner are on the right of the turret with the loader on the left. The engine and transmission are at the rear of the hull, and can be removed as a complete unit in under an hour. Suspension is of the torsion-bar type and consists of five road wheels, with the drive sprocket at the rear and the idler at the front, and there are five track-return rollers. These support the inner part of the track. The main armament of the AMX-30 is a 105mm gun of French design and manufacture, with an elevation of +20° and a depression of −8°, and a traverse of 360°, both elevation and traverse being powered. A 12.7mm machine-gun or a 20mm cannon is mounted to the left of the main armament. This installation is unusual in that it can be elevated independently of the main

Different anti-aircraft weapons can be mounted on the same basic AMX-30 chassis. Left, AMX-30 fitted with Roland 2 A/A missile system. Right, the AMX-30S 401A with twin 30mm cannon.

Left, front view of the AMX-30 MBT. On the commander's cupola are no less than ten periscopes for all-round vision, and a single-piece hatch that opens to the rear. The commander uses a x10 sight for aiming his 7.62mm machine-gun, which is laid and fired from within the tank. The cupola is contrarotating, therefore the commander can keep the machine-gun trained on the target while lining up the turret with the target. The machine-gun can be used against both ground and airborne targets. The driver sits at the front of the hull on the left and the other three crew members are in the turret.

armament to a maximum of 45°, enabling it to be used against slow flying aircraft and helicopters. There is a 7.62mm machine-gun mounted on the commander's cupola and this can be aimed and fired from within the turret. Two smoke dischargers are mounted each side of the turret. Fifty rounds of 105mm, 600 rounds of 12.7mm and 1,600 rounds of 7.62mm ammunition are carried. There are five types of ammunition available for the 105mm gun: HEAT, HE, Smoke, Illuminating and Practice. The HEAT round is the only anti-tank round carried. This weighs 48.5lbs (22kg) complete, has a muzzle velocity of 3,281 feet per second (1,000m/s) and will penetrate 14.17in (360mm) of armour at an angle of 0°. Most other tanks carry at least two, and often three, different types of anti-tank ammunition, for example HESH, APDS and HEAT. The French HEAT round is of a different design to other HEAT rounds and the French claim that it is sufficient to deal for any type of tank it is likely to encounter on the battlefield. Other HEAT projectiles spin rapidly in flight as they are fired from a rifled tank gun, but the French HEAT round has its shaped charge mounted in ball bearings, so as the outer body of the projectile spins rapidly, the charge itself rotates much more slowly. The AMX-30 can ford streams to a maximum depth of 6ft 7in (2m) without preparation. A schnorkel can be fitted over the loader's hatch, and this enables the AMX-30 to ford to a depth of 13ft 2in (4m). Infra-red driving equipment is fitted, as is an infra-red searchlight on the commander's cupola and another such searchlight to the left of the main armament. An NBC system is fitted as standard equipment. For export the AMX-30 can be delivered without NBC or night-vision equipment and with a much simpler cupola. A special model has been developed for use by Saudi-Arabia, this being known as the AMX-30S. It has a laser rangefinder, sand shields and a modified transmission. There are a number of experimental models of the AMX-30, and the following models are already in production or in service. The AMX-30D is the armoured recovery vehicle and has a crew of four (commander, driver and two mechanics). Equipment

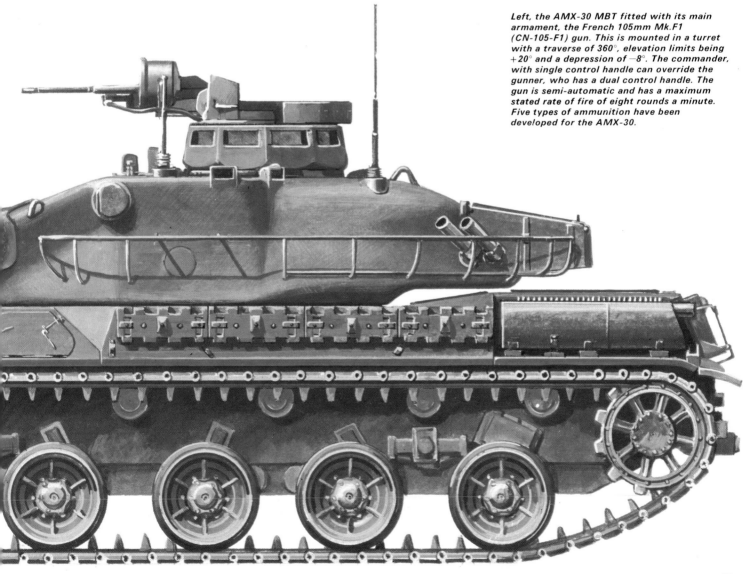

Right, the AMX-30D armoured recovery vehicle, which has a hydraulically-operated dozer blade mounted at the front. A spare tank engine can be carried at the rear

fitted includes a dozer blade at the front of the hull, a crane (hydraulically operated) and two winches, one with a capacity of 34.45 tons (35,000kg) and the other with a capacity of 3.94 tons (4,000kg). Armament consists of a cupola-mounted 7.62mm machine-gun and smoke dischargers. The bridgelayer version carries a scissor type bridge which, opened out, can span a gap of up to 65ft 7in (20m); this model has a crew of three (commander, bridge operator and driver). The AMX-30 has also been modified to carry and launch the French-developed Pluton tactical nuclear missile. The missile is elevated for launching and has a maximum range of 62 miles (100km). This model is now in service with the French Army and has replaced the American-supplied Honest John missiles. An anti-aircraft gun tank is now in production for Saudi-Arabia, armed with twin 30mm cannon and fitted with an

all-weather fire-control system. This has not been adopted by the French Army as it already uses the AMX-13 anti-aircraft tank with a similar turret. Saudi-Arabia has also ordered an anti-aircraft missile system called the Shahine, a development of the Crotale missile system which is now in service with the French Air Force and a number of other armies. One AMX-30 vehicle carries six missiles in the ready-to-launch position, as well as the launch radar, whilst another tank has the search and surveillance radar. The French Army has modified the AMX-30 to carry the Roland SAM system: two missiles are carried in the ready-to-launch position with a further eight missiles inside the hull. Roland 1 is a clear-weather system and Roland 2 is the all-weather system. Roland has also been adopted by the United States and Norway, and has been developed with Germany.

Left, the AMX-30 MBT fitted with its main armament, the French 105mm Mk.F1 (CN-105-F1) gun. This is mounted in a turret with a traverse of 360°, elevation limits being +20° and a depression of −8°. The commander, with single control handle can override the gunner, who has a dual control handle. The gun is semi-automatic and has a maximum stated rate of fire of eight rounds a minute. Five types of ammunition have been developed for the AMX-30.

AMX-10P MECHANISED INFANTRY COMBAT VEHICLE

AMX-10P, AMX-10TM, AMX-10PC, AMX-10ECH, AMX-10HOT and variants
Crew: 2 plus 9.
Armament: One 20mm M693 cannon; one 7.62mm machine-gun co-axial with main armament; four smoke dischargers.
Armour: 30mm (1.18in) maximum, estimated.
Dimensions: Length 19ft 1in (5.778m); width 9ft 1in (2.78m); height overall 8ft 4in (2.54m).
Weight: Combat 30,423lbs (13,800kg).
Ground pressure: 7.53lb/in² (0.53kg/cm²).
Engine: Hispano-Suiza HS 115-2 V-8 water-cooled diesel developing 276hp at 3,000rpm.
Performance: Road speed 40mph (65km/h); water speed 4.9mph (7.92km/h); range 373 miles (600km); vertical obstacle 2ft 4in (0.7m); trench 5ft 3in (1.6m); gradient 60 per cent.
History: Entered service with the French Army in 1973. Also in service in Greece and Saudi-Arabia, and on order for Qatar. In production.

The AMX-10P has been developed to replace the AMX VCI which has been in service with the French Army since 1956. The first prototype was completed in 1968 with deliveries to the French Army commencing in 1973. The vehicle has been designed to operate with the AMX-30 MBT as part of the tank/infantry team. The hull is of all-welded construction, with the driver seated at the front on the left side with the engine to his right. The power-operated turret is in the centre of the vehicle and has seats for both the gunner and vehicle commander. The main armament consists of a 20mm M693 cannon, capable of a full 360° traverse, with an elevation of +50° and a depression of −8°. A 7.62mm machine-gun is mounted co-axially with the main armament. A total of 800 rounds of 20mm and 2,000 rounds of 7.62mm ammunition is carried. One of the features of the 20mm cannon is that it has a dual feed ammunition system, which allows the gunner to select the type of ammunition (eg, armour-piercing or high explosive) according to the target that he is engaging. For example, if he is engaging APCs he will select the AP round, but if he is engaging enemy troops he will select the HE round. The personnel compartment is in the rear portion of the hull, and the infantry enter and leave via a large power-operated ramp right at the rear. The ramp, when up, is provided with two firing-ports. Over the top of the troop compartment are two roof hatches, which are pivoted in the centre. Six periscopes are provided in the roof of the troop compartment, two on each side and two in the rear, enabling the infantry to observe the terrain so that when they leave the vehicle they are familiar with the surrounding area. Two smoke dischargers are mounted on each side of the vehicle at the rear of the hull. The AMX-10P is fully amphibious and is propelled in the water by two water-jets, one in each side of the hull. Before the vehicle enters the water a trim vane has to be erected at the front of the hull. Other standard equipment includes an NBC system and night-vision equipment for both the driver and gunner. Although called a MICV by the French, to many other observers the AMX-10P is not a true MICV as apart from the two rather primitive firing-ports in the rear of the hull, there is no provision for the crew to fire their small arms from within the vehicle. The basic AMX-10P can be quickly adapted to carry cargo, and it is also being developed to undertake a wide variety of other roles. The AMX-10 TM tows the 120mm Brandt mortar; 60 mortar bombs are carried inside the hull. The AMX-10 PC is a special command vehicle and has additional radios, a generator and a tent which can be erected when required to give additional working space for the command staff. A special model has been developed to mount the RATAC radar system for the control of artillery fire. There is also an ambulance model, whilst the ECH variant is a repair vehicle for supporting the whole AMX-10 family. Currently under development is the AMX-10P HOT, a basic vehicle with the turret removed and replaced by a new turret mounting four HOT anti-tank missiles in the ready-to-launch position (additional missiles being carried internally). The AMX-10P HOT is also armed with a 7.62mm machine-gun. The latest model, which is still being developed, is the AMX-10C. This has a new chassis but uses the same suspension and many other components of the AMX-10P. It has the complete turret of the AMX-10RC with its 105mm gun. It is thought that the AMX-10C is being developed as the replacement for the AMX-13 light tank. Not being content with this complete family of tracked vehicles, the French have also developed some wheeled 6×6 vehicles which use many components from the AMX-10P MICV. The first of these to enter production is the AMX-10RC 6×6 armoured reconnaissance vehicle, intended as the replacement for the 8×8 Panhard EBR armoured cars which have now been used by the French Army since the 1950s. The AMX-10RC has a turret-mounted 105mm gun with a co-axial 7.62mm machine-gun, the 105mm weapon firing fin-stabilised HEAT-T and HE rounds. It has a comprehensive fire-control system including a laser rangefinder and a night TV system. The suspension of the vehicle can be adjusted to suit the type of ground being crossed, as on the AMX-10P, and the type is also fully amphibious.

Left: An AMX-10P mechanized infantry combat vehicle is put through its paces in a demonstration at Satory, near Paris, in 1975. The AMX-10P is fully amphibious, propelled by two water-jets. It mounts a 20mm M693 cannon and co-axial 7.62mm machine-gun.

PANHARD M-3 ARMOURED PERSONNEL CARRIER

M-3, and VPM, VTS, VAT, VPC and VDA versions.
Crew: 2 plus 10.
Armament: Varies according to role (see text below).
Armour: 8mm–12mm (0.32–0.47in).
Dimensions: Length 14ft 7in (4.45m); width 7ft 10in (2.4m); height (without armament) 6ft 7in (2m).
Weight: Combat 13,448lbs (6,100kg).
Engine: Panhard Model 4 HD four-cylinder petrol engine developing 90hp at 4,700rpm.
Performance: Road speed 62mph (100km/h); water speed 2.5mph (4km/h); range 373 miles (600km); vertical obstacle 1ft (0.3m); trench (using one channel) 2ft 8in (0.8m); gradient 60 per cent.
History: Entered service in 1971. In service with Angola, Eire, France, Iraq, Kenya, Lebanon, Malaysia, Portugal, Saudi-Arabia, Spain, United Arab Emirates and Zaire. Still in production.

Following its success with the AML armoured car, the Panhard company realised that there was a requirement for a 4×4 armoured personnel carrier to operate with the AML. The first prototype of the new APC was completed in 1969, production models following two years later. Since then a whole range of vehicles has been developed and large numbers have been exported, especially to the Middle East and Africa. The M-3 is not used by the French Army, although the French Police use it as a riot control vehicle. According to Panhard, 95 per cent of the automotive components of the AML are common to the M-3, which makes the spares problem relatively simple. The basic vehicle is fully amphibious and is propelled in the water by its wheels. The hull of the M-3 is of all-welded steel construction which gives the crew protection from small arms fire and shell splinters. The driver is seated at the front of the vehicle, with the engine and transmission to his rear. The latter has six forward and one reverse gears. The M-3 is fully amphibious, being propelled in the water by its wheels. For use in hot climates an air-conditioning system can be installed. The basic M-3 has been designed for use as an APC. Doors are provided in the hull sides and rear so that the personnel can leave the vehicle quickly when required. The crew can use their small arms through three hatches in each side of the hull and there is also a firing-port in each of the rear doors. The M-3 can be fitted with a wide range of armament installations: a typical vehicle would have a turret mounting twin 7.62mm machine-guns at the front and a single 7.62mm machine-gun on a simple mount at the rear. Special versions include the VPM, which has an 81mm breech-loaded mortar, VAT repair vehicle, VTS ambulance, VPC command/cargo vehicle and the new VDA anti-aircraft vehicle. The last has a power-operated turret mounting twin 20mm rapid-fire cannon with an elevation of +85° and a depression of −5°. A radar scanner is mounted on the turret rear to provide early warning. The latest model in the family is the M-3 HOT. This has four HOT (High-subsonic Optically-guided Tube-launched) missiles in the ready-to-launch position, with a further 10 missiles in reserve inside the hull. This model has a crew of three: driver, commander and missile controller. The HOT missile has a minimum range of 68 yards (75m) and a maximum of 3,658 yards (4,000m).

Right: A Panhard M-3 armoured personnel carrier shows its cross-country capability. The M-3 is fully amphibious, propelled at 4km/h by all four wheels.

AMX GCT SELF-PROPELLED GUN

Crew: 4.
Armament: One 155mm gun; one 7.62mm anti-aircraft machine-gun; four smoke dischargers.
Armour: 50mm (1.96in) maximum, estimated.
Dimensions: Length (with gun forward) 33ft 3in (10.4m); length (hull) 21ft 3in (6.485m); width 10ft 4in (3.15m); height (without anti-aircraft MG) 10ft 10in (3.3m).
Weight: 88,185lbs (41,000kg).
Ground pressure: 12.8lb/in² (0.9kg/cm²).
Engine: Hispano-Suiza HS-110 12-cylinder multi-fuel engine developing 700hp at 2,400rpm.
Performance: Road speed 37mph (60km/h); range 280 miles (450km); vertical obstacle 3ft 3in (0.93m); trench 9ft 6in (2.9m); gradient 60 per cent.
History: Entering service with French Army in 1977–8.

At the present time the standard self-propelled artillery of the French Army consists of 105mm and 155mm weapons on modified AMX-13 type chassis. It was decided some years ago that both of these weapons would be replaced by a new 155mm weapon as the current weapon of this calibre, the Mk.F3, has a number of drawbacks: the gun cannot be traversed through a full 360°, the gun is on an open mount with no protection for the crew against small arms fire and NBC attack, and it has to be supported in action by a modified AMX armoured personnel carrier for the rest of the crew and the ammunition for the gun. The four main requirements laid down by the French Army were: mobility similar to that of a main battle tank, ability to engage targets quickly through a full 360° at all ranges, high rate of fire with effective ammunition, and full protection for the crew from both NBC attack and small arms fire. The first prototype of the GCT (*Grande Cadence de Tir*) was completed in 1973; further models followed two years later, and the type is now in production for the French Army. No export orders have been received so far. The GCT consists of a slightly modified AMX-30 main battle tank chassis with a new turret of all-welded steel construction. The crew of four consists of the commander, driver and two gunners (one of the gunners is in charge of the fire-control system and elevation and traverse of the main armament, whilst the other prepares the charges and controls the loading of the gun). The main armament consists of a 155mm gun with a double baffle muzzle-brake, capable of an elevation of +66° and a depression of −5°, traverse being a full 360°. Elevation and traverse are hydraulic, with manual controls in case of hydraulic failure. The gun is fully automatic and can fire eight rounds in one minute. A total of 42 projectiles and their separate bagged charges is carried in the rear of the turret,

arranged in seven racks of six for both projectiles and bags. The propelling charges are contained in combustible cases so that the crew does not have to worry about empty cases littering the floor of the turret. A typical ammunition load would consist of 36 High Explosive and six Smoke rounds. Large doors are provided in the rear of the turret for reloading purposes, and it takes three men about 30 minutes to reload the ammunition. Types of ammunition fired include High Explosive, Smoke and Illuminating, of both French and American manufacture. The HE round has a maximum range of 25,700 yards (23,500m), although a rocket-assisted round with a range of 32,808 yards (30,000m) is now being developed. A 7.62mm anti-aircraft machine-gun is mounted on top of the turret, with traverse through a full 360° and elevation limits from −20° to +50°. Some 2,000 rounds of 7.62mm ammunition are carried. In addition there are two smoke dischargers on each side of the turret. The GCT is

provided with an NBC system, and night-vision equipment can be fitted if required. The vehicle can ford to a depth of 7ft 3in (2.2m) without preparation. As the crew may well have to remain in the vehicle for up to 24 hours at a time, a bunk has been installed in the turret to allow one member of the crew to rest. Whilst the introduction of the GCT will increase the effectiveness of the French artillery arm, it is considered by some to be too expensive and too heavy when compared with other self-propelled guns such as the American M109. On the credit side, the ability to fire a large number of rounds in a short space of time is of vital importance on the battlefield of the 1970s. This is because once an SP gun has fired one round, enemy gun-locating radars will start to pinpoint its exact position, and within a few minutes the enemy will be returning fire. The role of the GCT will be to fire a burst of eight rounds and then quickly move off to a new firing position before the enemy counter-fire arrives.

Above: AMX 155mm GCT self-propelled gun with its turret traversed to the left. This weapon consists of a modified AMX-30 MBT chassis with a new turret mounting a 155mm gun which can fire an HE round to a maximum range of some 30,000m; rate of fire is 8 rpm.

Below: An AMX 155mm GCT with its turret traversed to the rear to reduce the overhang of the weapon when travelling over rough country. The GCT is fully sealed and can operate in an NBC zone. A 7.62mm machine-gun is roof-mounted for anti-aircraft use.

Above: Rear view of the AMX 155mm GCT self-propelled gun, now entering service with the French Army to replace the 155mm Mk.F3 SPG. The doors at the turret rear are open and the ammunition racks can be clearly seen. Normally 36 rounds of HE and six smoke rounds of separate-loading ammunition are carried. A maximum eight rounds per minute can be fired. Reloading takes three men about 30 minutes.

Germany

The remarkable thing about the German use of tanks is that they ever managed to do it at all. Germany never built a successful tank in World War I, and ended it with the crippling restrictions of the Versailles Treaty preventing any manufacture at all. Although there was no lack of good thinkers among the few serving soldiers in postwar Germany, they had no opportunity to try their ideas in practice, though a few vehicles were built in great secrecy in Russia, and some tactics were tried in conjunction with the Soviet Army – to the advantage of both.

The great difference between the Germans on the one hand and the British and French on the other was that the former were quite determined not to repeat the stalemate of the trenches in any future war, and in the tank they saw the way to avoid it. The writings of Liddell Hart were assimilated and digested, and when rearmament started in 1933 tanks were high on the priority list.

Having no experience of their own to go on, the German general staff largely copied the British mechanised formations with separate tank and infantry brigades, but spurred on by Hitler's insistence on high-quality manpower and equipment

in the armoured forces, the first *Panzer* division was formed in 1935. This very quickly expanded far beyond the British ideas to become a completely separate and powerful force with all arms integrated into it and capable of carrying out any operation of war entirely on its own without external help. Unlike the British, the German Army looked upon the *Panzer* divisions as needing to be self-sufficient formations, and the only external aid they needed to call for was aircraft, though after the Polish campaign each division had *Luftwaffe* units affiliated to it together with liaison officers in radio contact with the squadrons. The *Panzer* units were very much

a small separate army and they were used as such. Without such a philosophy the invasion of Russia would never have got much farther than the Polish frontier and the *Blitzkrieg* would never have been born at all. *Panzers* were the spearhead of the marching army, well able to clear the ground ahead of them, and to crush all but the heaviest resistance by their own efforts.

In the beginning the equipment was not able to keep up with this philosophy, and there were frequent improvements and changes of detailed design during the mid-1930s, but the basic requirements led to tanks which were fast and well armed. Protection often came lower down the list, and experience in Russia brought about changes in that respect, but the general idea that tanks should be mobile and hard-hitting persisted and is still the rule today. The aberrations

such as Royal Tiger and Mouse which appeared at the end of the war were not true reflections of the German *Panzer* aims. They were desperate expedients to try to correct a lost position.

The disadvantage to the *Panzer* idea is that of cost. Germany soon found that to keep these expensive armoured formations in being meant that other arms often suffered from serious shortages of their own equipment, and to the end of the war most of the German army depended on horses for its supplies and basic transport because there were neither sufficient lorries nor sufficient fuel. Maintenance areas were heavily loaded with armoured repair and renovation tasks, and the lines of communication were largely devoted to keeping the *Panzers* supplied. In the end it was worth it, and from the German experience have come the present-day integrated armoured formations and wide enveloping tactical battle tactics practised by all modern armies.

The post-war account of German armoured forces has to some extent been a repeat of that of the 1920s. When West Germany re-armed in 1956 the army was given mainly US equipment, and much of that is still in service; but a steady growth of national wealth brought with it a greater expenditure on the armed forces and a resurgence of interest in armoured troops. Germany has now the largest and best equipped army in Europe, though it is one which is intended for defence of the Homeland rather than offensive action far from the frontiers. Once again there are armoured formations with a full range of vehicles and supporting arms and services full integrated. Germany now designs excellent tanks, and the Leopard series has sold in large numbers around the world. In fact, it is perhaps not too much of an exaggeration to say that the country is very nearly back to the same position as she held, in respect of armoured warfare, in 1940.

A German PzKpfw IV tank, with infantry support, moves slowly forward during the German advance in the Caucasus in December 1942.

EHRHARDT BAK ARMOURED CAR

Crew: 5.
Armament: 50mm gun.
Armour: 3mm to 5mm (0.12in to 0.2in).
Dimensions: Not know.
Weight: 7,055lbs (3,200kg).
Ground pressure: Not known.
Power to weight ratio: 19hp/ton.
Engine: One Ehrhardt four-cylinder water-cooled petrol engine developing 60hp.
Performance: Road speed 28mph (45km/h); range 100 miles (160km); verticle obstacle negligible; trench negligible; gradient negligible.
History: Prototype completed in 1906, but not placed in production.

Right: The final model of the Ehrhardt BAK armoured anti-balloon vehicle. The 50mm gun had limited traverse but high elevation. For its time, this was an exceptionally advanced vehicle.

The *BAK* was the very first purely German armoured motor vehicle, and also the first of a series of this type of weapon. The first Ehrhardt *BAK* (the acronym BAK stands for *Ballon-Abwehr Kanone*, or Anti-Balloon Gun), and was produced by the Ehrhardt firm in Zella St Blasii during 1906. It mounted a quick-firing 5cm gun and was intended primarily for use against enemy observation balloons which had then begun to cause concern among European high commands. This first model, of which only one example was built, was based on a commercial Ehrhardt light lorry chassis powered by a 60hp four-cylinder engine. The power was taken to the rear wheels only by chain drive. A very novel feature for that time was the use of pneumatic tires, although these would have proved vulnerable had the vehicle ever participated in actual combat operations. The 5cm gun was produced by the German Rheinmetall firm, renowned for its high-class artillery productions. The gun was 30 calibres long and was mounted in a partly-armoured/partly-open turret mounted on the roof of the vehicle hull. The mounting allowed elevations up to 70 degrees for the engagement of aerial targets, but the weapon could also be used against ground targets. The turret could only traverse through 30 degrees each side of centre. One hundred rounds of ammunition were carried in special containers on each side of the vehicle. The hull and turret fronts were 5mm (0.2in) thick. The vehicle was exhibited for the first time publicly at the 7th International Automobile Exhibition in Berlin, during 1906. During 1908 an open (unarmoured) version of this car appeared, and in 1910 the Ehrhardt firm developed a similar gun mounting for the Rheinmetall 6.5cm anti-aircraft gun (35 calibres long). This time the vehicle had four-wheel drive. About the same time the Daimler firm began to develop the *BAK* vehicle. The first was a 7.7cm Krupp gun mounting, also having four-wheel drive, but completely unarmoured. In 1909 Daimler produced a self-propelled 5.7cm Krupp gun (30 calibres) based on a four-wheel drive chassis. The gun was mounted in an open-topped, armoured, rotating turret and could elevate to fire at balloons. Partial armour was provided around the crew and ammunition compartments. One of the most successful designs turned out by Daimler was the *K-Klak*, and this was used during World War I. It was powered by a four-cylinder 60/80hp engine, had four forward and two reverse gears, and weighed 7.87 tons (8,000kg). Ehrhardt produced a similar model based on the same chassis as the 1915 armoured car, the E V/4. In 1911 Daimler modified the *BAK* vehicle to have more extensive armour.

Kfz 13 ARMOURED CAR

Kfz 13 and *Kfz* 14.
Crew: 2.
Armament: One 7.92mm MG 13 or MG 34 machine-gun.
Armour: 5 to 8mm (0.2in to 0.31in).
Dimensions: Length (overall) 13ft 9in (4.2m); width 5ft 7in (1.7m); height 4ft 11in (1.5m).
Weight: 4,189lbs (1,900kg).
Power to weight ratio: 32hp/ton.
Engine: Adler 65 six-cylinder water-cooled inline petrol engine developing 60hp at 3,200rpm.
Performance: Road speed 38mph (60km/h); range 200 miles (320km); verticle obstacle negligible; trench 3ft 3in (1m); gradient 15 degrees.
History: Entered service with German Army in 1934 and still in use in early part of World War II. Later used for training.

The *Kfz* 13 was a medium armoured car based on the chassis of the Adler Standard six-passenger car. It was built to a military specification issued by the German high command during 1932. From 1934 onwards it appeared in relatively large numbers under the designation Medium Armoured Passenger Car *Kfz* 13. The basic vehicle had no radio and a companion communications vehicle was introduced under the designation *Kfz* 14. It was distinguishable by the large square frame aerial which protruded above the vehicle. Both models served with German cavalry regiments until the appearance of new four-wheeled armoured cars during 1937. Daimler-Benz in Berlin-Marienfelde acted as parent firm for the cars, the armoured hulls being produced by Deutschen Edelstahl in Hanover. The *Kfz* 13 had a two-man crew and a light machine-gun mounted on a pintle, protected by an armoured shield and provided with 2,000 rounds of ammunition. The *Kfz* 14 radio version had a three-man crew. The frame aerial could be folded down around the hull. Because of the bulk of the radio equipment, consisting of a long-range wireless telegraphy and radio-telegraphy transmitter and receiver, with an operational range of about 20 miles (32km), the *Kfz* 14 mounted no armament. Both models were open-topped and protected all around by 8mm (0.31in) welded armour, apart from the floor which was 5mm (0.2in) thick. These vehicles were popularly known by the troops as 'Bathtubs' (*Badewannen*). During the early combat operations by the German Army in World War II, it was found that their armour was inadequate against contemporary machine-gun fire, their cross-country performance was poor, and that they were unstable. Although classified as obsolete at the outbreak of World War II, these vehicles were used extensively during the Polish campaign, during the invasion of the Low Countries and France, and even during the initial phase of the campaign in Russia. They were eventually relegated to a training role, and were replaced by a new series of four-wheeled armoured cars based on the standard military passenger car chassis.

Left: The Kfz 13 light armoured reconnaissance car was the first armoured vehicle to be standardized by the German Wehrmacht. Although based on a commercial chassis it was a well-designed vehicle and served in the early campaigns of WWII. Its armour was very light and it mounted only one machine-gun.

Right: The Kfz 13 in service with the Wehrmacht. The 7.92mm gun was mounted in an armoured shield and had limited traverse. A special radio version existed, with a collapsible rectangular frame aerial that circumscribed the hull. Designated Kfz 14, the radio version seldom mounted any armament.

EHRHARDT E-V/4 ARMOURED CAR

Panzerkraftwagen E-V/4, Daimler M1915, Panzerkraftwagen A5P and *Panzerkraftwagen Ehrhardt 17.*
Crew: 8.
Armament: Three 7.92mm MG 08 machine-guns.
Armour: 6mm to 9mm (0.24in to 0.35in).
Dimensions: Length (overall) 17ft 5in (5.3m); width 6ft 7in (2m); height 9ft 6in (2.9m).
Weight: 20,944lbs (9,500kg).
Power to weight ratio: 9.1hp/ton.
Engine: One four-cylinder water-cooled engine developing 85hp.
Performance: Road speed 38mph (60km/h); range 156 miles (250km); vertical obstacle negligible; trench negligible; gradient 25 degrees.
History: Prototype completed in 1915 and remained in service after World War I.

Right: The Ehrhardt was one of the standard German armoured cars of WW1. It was less advanced than Allied armoured cars, but gave good service on the Ukraine Front in 1918.

Early in World War I the Germans experienced successful operations against them by Belgian and British armoured car units. As a result, on 22 October 1914 the German high command issued a specification for an armoured car. During 1915 special designs were requested from Büssing, Daimler and Ehrhardt. The basic requirements were: four-wheel drive, reverse control facilities at full speed, a top speed of at least 40km/h (25mph) and a fighting compartment for three machine-guns (to be fired through loop-holes) with 3,000 rounds. The three firms each delivered one prototype vehicle by July, and the vehicles were assembled into a unit and despatched to the Western Front, in upper Alsace. The Daimler model, designated *Panzerkraftwagen Daimler M1915*, had a conventional layout with the engine at the front and, in conformity with the original specification, had four-wheel drive and additional rear steering controls (operating on the front wheels). The engine was a four-cylinder 80hp Daimler M1464 with a transmission giving four forward and four reverse speeds. The wheels were cast and spoked, and had solid rubber tires. Double wheels were used at the rear and the front wheels were fitted with flanges to reduce the ground pressure in cross-country operations. A fixed cylindrical turret was attached, having four machine-gun ports. Six further machine-gun ports were located in the hull, two on each side and one at front and rear. The armament which could be moved from one loop-hole to another, comprised three Maxim 08 machine-guns. The Ehrhardt model, designated *Panzerkraftwagen A5P*,

differed significantly from the other two, it being over 30 feet (9.14m) long. It was powered by a 90hp six-cylinder Büssing engine and was automotively similar to the other two except that the gearbox provided five speeds in both directions instead of four, and both front and rear wheels were steered. Shortly after taking part in operations on the Western Front, these cars were transferred to the Schmettow Cavalry Corps in Romania, where they played a vital part during the Battle of Kronstadt. In December 1916 these armoured cars were returned to Germany, where it was decided to assign the Erhardt firm the final development contract. During 1917 Ehrhardt delivered a series of a further 12 cars, which were designated *Panzerkraftwagen Ehrhardt 17*. These were formed into the Armoured Machine-Gun Platoons Nos 2 to 6 (*PzKw MG Zuge* 2-6), each having two vehicles. Twenty

more Ehrhardt cars were ordered later in 1917, and these were completed in 1918. The Model 17 was basically the same as the E-V/4, but had refinements added as a result of combat experience. The weight was reduced to 7.14 tons (7,250kg) through improved armour application. The floor was armoured and a rotating turret replaced the original fixed type. The radiator armour could now be opened or closed by a lever from within the driving compartment, and the lights were provided with armoured covers. Some vehicles were fitted with two-way wireless equipment, which could only be used when the vehicle was stationary. This model was used successfully on the Ukrainian Front in 1918. The further 20 cars ordered in 1917 were not completed in time to take part in operations, but after the war they were delivered to the new German Army (*Reichsheer*).

LK II CAVALRY TANK

Leichte Kampfwagen II
Crew: 3.
Armament: One 5.7cm gun or two 7.92mm Maxim machine-guns.
Armour: 0.24in (6mm) minimum; 0.43in (11mm) maximum.
Dimensions: Length 16ft 7in (5.06m); width 6ft 4in (1.95m); height 8ft 2in (2.5m).
Weight: 18,739lbs (8,500kg).
Power to weight ratio: 6.6hp/ton.
Engine: Daimler four-cylinder water-cooled inline petrol engine developing 55bhp.
Performance: Road speed 10mph (16km/h); range 40 miles (65km); trench 6ft 6in (2.04m); gradient 45 degrees, for short climbs only.
History: Prototypes only built.

The Germans awoke late to the possibility of the tank and by 1918, realising that they were behind, were prepared to copy anything that the British used. When the Whippet appeared it was duly captured and copied, but some of the faults of that unhappy vehicle were corrected. The same general layout was copied, but this may have been for another reason. In their haste to get the design going, the Germans took an armoured car and replaced the wheels with tracks. This immediately gave them the front engine layout, the central driver, rear turret and rear final drive. A rotating turret was too difficult to make in quantity and an alternative fixed

box with a front-mounted gun was fitted. It was intended to use the rotating turret for the machine-gun version. By more careful designing and perhaps good fortune, the *LK* II came out considerably lighter than the Whippet, yet had roughly the same protection. It was thus able to make better use of its power and was both faster and more agile. From the driver's point of view, it was far easier to control than the British tank and the commander could give more time to controlling the tank, since he did not have the responsibility for firing a gun as did the Whippet's commander. Unfortunately this vehicle never came into service and it seems that no more than two were actually completed. When the war ended the design was sold to Sweden, which took it into service as the m/21. Krupp, who had designed the *LK* II, lent their experience to the Swedes and the m/21 incorporated what would have been built into the *LK* III. One change was to fit a small rotating turret on top of the fixed one and mount a 3.7cm gun in it. Another was to increase the crew to four and fit a small radio to a proportion of the fleet. Later, in 1926, another *LK* II appeared, though this one was far more advanced than the previous model and was really an amalgam of the *LK* and the Vickers Medium. It had a sprung track, using coupled bogies, a lower silhouette, a fully rotating turret carrying the 3.7cm gun, and reasonably sloped armour. The weight increased by 0.98 ton (1,000kg) but the speed and agility improved markedly.

Below and bottom: The German LK II cavalry tank, mounting a 57mm gun. Designed by Krupp, it incorporated features of captured British Whippet tanks on a modified armoured car chassis. Only prototypes had been built by the end of WWI.

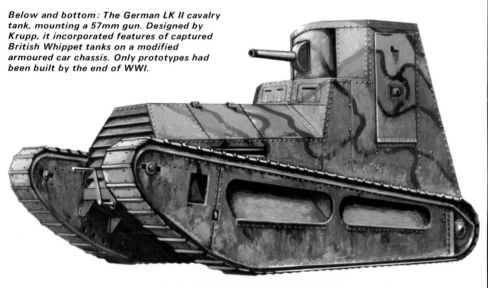

A7V BATTLE TANK

A7V *Sturmpanzerwagen.*
Crew: 18.
Armament: One 5.7cm gun; six or seven 7.92mm Maxim machine-guns.
Armour: 0.59in (15mm) minimum; 1.18in (30mm) maximum.
Dimensions: Length 24ft 1in (7.34m); width 10ft 0½in (3.07m); height 10ft 10in (3.3m).
Weight: 65,918lbs (29,900kg).
Power to weight ratio: 6.8hp/ton.
Engines: Two Daimler four-cylinder water-cooled inline engines each developing 100bhp at 1,600rpm.
Performance: Road speed 5mph (8km/h); range 25 miles (40km); trench 7ft (2.13m).
History: Used in limited numbers by the German Army during 1918.

Badly shaken by the British success with their first tanks, the German general staff cast around for a quick answer, and late in 1916 decided to build their own, and better, type of tank. Design contracts were hurriedly let in November of that year and finalised on 22 December. Having no background of tracked vehicles to call upon, the resident representative of Holt tractors, a Mr. Steiner, was brought in to produce the chassis. Throughout the summer of 1917 the prototypes underwent their trials, revealing many weaknesses, particularly in the engine cooling and tracks. On 1 December 1917 the general staff could wait no longer, and 100 tanks were ordered to be ready in time for the great spring offensives. Since nobody could think of a suitable name, it was decided to call the machine the A7V, from the initial letters of the committee that first called for it – the *Allgemeine Kriegsdepartment 7 Abteilung Vehkerwesen.* The design was uninspired and showed every sign of weakness. All that had been done was in effect to take a large Holt tractor chassis and suspension, put on it a large rectangular steel box and then to fit in as many weapons as possible: a 5.7cm gun with 250 or 500 rounds and six or seven machine-guns with 36,000 rounds. The result was thoroughly unwieldy and sharply lacking in any ability to move on any surface other than a flat and hard road. The thinking behind the design had been to produce a mobile fortress for the support of the infantry, and the concentration had been on the fortress aspect to the virtual exclusion of anything which gave suitable mobility on the battlefields

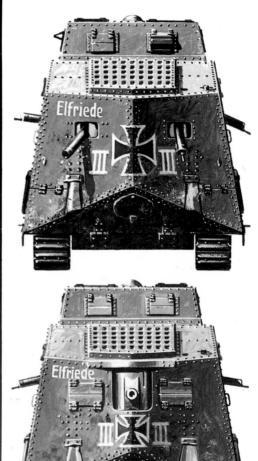

of the Western Front. The very limited ground clearance of 15.75in (40cm) ensured that rough and muddy ground caused the tank to belly down and stick. The absence of any 'lift' at the front idler meant that there was barely any ability to climb a step, or to pull out from a hole or trench, since all that happened was that the nose dug in. The one advantage to the track arrangement was that it was protected by armour, and perhaps the Germans had seen enough Mark IVs with shattered tracks to feel that their system was worthwhile. The interior of the hull was in the form of one large compartment, with the engines standing on the floor in the front half, just behind the driver. These were linked to a common transmission shaft which drove through a gearbox to the final drive at the rear of the body. From there the drive went by shafts to the sprockets, passing through steering brakes on the way. It was an easier arrangement than on the British tanks. The tracks ran on 24 sprung bogies and allowed a top speed of 8mph (13km/h) under ideal conditions. However, the tank's weight was far too much for the engine and transmission, despite gearing down, and engine reliability suffered. The driver's task was easier than on the Mark IV, and two engineers were carried for running repairs, and played no part in the actual driving. The commander sat in the square cupola above the fighting compartment, but he could only give his instructions by shouting, and in the infernal din of the engines and tracks this must have been difficult. The driver and engineers came from the engineer corps, but the two men who manned the 5.7cm gun were artillerymen. Their gun was a low velocity version, from captured Belgian stock. The machine-gunners worked in pairs to each gun, and were infantrymen. The crew was thus drawn from three different military disciplines, and this led to a lack of cohesion in their performance — a fact which several German commentators touch upon. Vision for the crew was poor, as with all World War I tanks, and comfort was negligible. The thickness of armour was good, but this was nullified by the fact that most of it had to be supplied in an unhardened state. However, on the one occasion when a British Mark IV male met an A7V in action, there is good reason to think that the

three hits scored with the British 6pounder guns did not penetrate the German armour. Actual battle use of the A7V was very limited. The 100 ordered in 1917 were never delivered, and perhaps no more than 35 were completed. These were grouped into battalions of five vehicles, and were invariably used unimaginatively, to their detriment. Their first operation seems to have been on 29 March 1918 and the last was on 8 October. Despite the poor showing of their first tank, the German general staff were not discouraged, and quietly set about learning where they had gone wrong, with results clear to everyone when the *Blitzkrieg* was launched some 20 years later.

Above: Top and side views of the A7V 'Elfriede': identified at the time of her loss as belonging to Abteilung III, Imperial German Army Tank Force. An Abteilung comprised a total of five tanks, with six officers and 170 other ranks. By 1918, Germany had eight tank units, most of which used captured tanks.
Below: A7V moving forward with crew riding outside of the vehicle for comfort, when in action all of the 18-man crew were inside of the hull and conditions in side of the tank were unbearable: they were often overcome by heat and fumes.

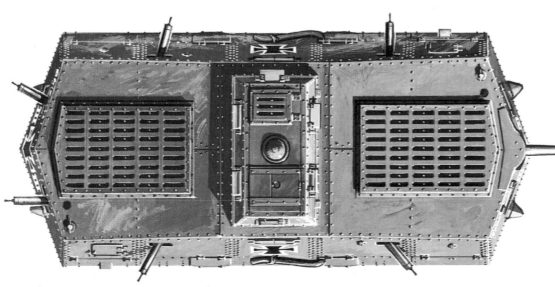

Left: Top, front and rear views of the A7V tank 'Elfriede', the first enemy tank to be engaged and captured by British tank units in WWI. She was hit by four 6-pounder shells fired by a male Mk IV tank of A Coy, 1st Bttn, Tank Corps, and immobilized. After her capture she was taken for detailed examination by Allied intelligence. Known names of other A7Vs include 'Wotan', 'Hagen' and 'Schnuck'.

PzKpfw V EXPERIMENTAL MEDIUM TANK

Crew: 7.
Armament: One 7.5cm *KwK* L/24 gun; one 3.7cm gun co-axial with main armament; four 7.92mm MG 13 machine-guns in pairs in two sub-turrets.
Armour: 0.57in (14.5mm).
Dimensions: Length about 21ft 4in (6m); width 9ft 6in (2.9m); height 8ft 6in (2.65m).
Weight: 47,950lbs (21,750kg).
Power to weight ratio: 16.8hp/ton.
Engine: Maybach V-12 water-cooled inline petrol engine developing 360bhp.
Performance: Road speed 19mph (30km/h); trench 7ft 2in (2.2m); gradient 30 degrees.
History: In service with the German Army from 1936 to 1940.

The Versailles Treaty forbade Germany to possess any tanks, and various devices were resorted to in order that the restrictions might be overcome. One was to produce tanks and call them by innocuous names. Heavy tanks were known as Heavy Tractors, and light tanks as Light Tractors. In January 1934 there was a conference to decide on the specifications for medium tanks (or tractors) which would equip the medium tank companies in the new *Werhmacht*. These tanks would carry a large-calibre gun to give effective HE fire to support the smaller high-velocity guns of the more numerous battle tanks. The 7.5cm gun was chosen for the main armament. This was a Krupp gun, whose performance was well known and approved. In addition there was a requirement for the new tank to carry machine-guns. Three firms undertook the design study: Krupp, Rheinmetall-Borsig and MAN. Rheinmetall's solution used the existing suspension from their commercial tractor, and the tank was designed round this as it stood, merely one more set of bogies being added on each side. The resulting vehicle was an amalgam of existing French, British and Russian designs, though it showed some features of its own which were laudable. In broad outline the *PzKpfw V* was one of the multi-turreted tanks of the early 1930s, of which there were many examples, but it had its special points. The turret was a better design than most of the uninspired box shapes of the day, there was a reasonable cupola for the commander, and the suspension bogies had a good range of travel. About six were built, and there is reason to believe that none

may have actually carried armour plate. They were made in steel, as were most prototypes at that time. The hull shape was derived directly from the *Grosstraktor* (large tractor) of 1929, and may well have been almost unchanged. The suspension was greatly improved by using the commercial bogies, and at the top the track returned over four rollers. The driver and the front gunner sat in the bows; behind was the fighting compartment; and the engine was in the rear, driving a rear sprocket. The turret was mounted on a small

pedestal and to its right front was a small machine-gun turret. There was another such turret behind and to the left of the main turret, a layout which both Vickers and the Japanese had tried. In the event the *PzKpfw V* was no more than a test bed for the gun and mounting. It never saw service as a production tank, but there is a well known propaganda photograph of two of them driving through Oslo in 1940, which shows that the German Army was prepared to make intelligent use of its surplus experimental vehicles.

Below: When Germany re-armed in the 1930s many experimental tanks were built. The multi-turreted PzKpfw V (NbFz) was one of the most famous.

Right: Factory assembly of an NbFz tank, along with a number of other German AFVs including several experimental vehicles. The small machine-gun turret on the right-hand side of the PzKpfw V was the same as that fitted to the PzKpfw I light tank and mounted two 7.92mm machine-guns. The tank never went into full-scale production; only about six were built.

SdKfz 232 ARMOURED CAR

Schwerer Panzerspähwagen **(8 *Rad*), or *SdKfz* 232, and variants.**
Crew: 4.
Armament: One 2cm gun.
Armour: 0.2in (5mm) minimum; 1.18in (30mm) maximum.
Dimensions: Length 19ft 2in (5.85m); width 7ft 3in (2.2m); height 9ft 6in (2.9m).
Weight: 19,400lbs (8,800kg).
Power to weight ratio: 17.32hp/ton.
Engine: Büssing-NAG L8V-GS eight-cylinder water-cooled petrol engine developing 150hp at 3,000rpm.
Performance: Road speed 53mph (85km/h); range 170 miles (270km); vertical obstacle 1ft 7in (0.5m); trench 4ft 1in (1.25m); gradient 30 degrees.
History: In service with the German Army from 1937 to 1945.
(Note: Data relate to eight-wheeled versions.)

As mentioned under the history of the *SdKfz* 231 armoured car, there were two basic types — a six-wheeler and an eight-wheeler. The six-wheeled vehicles have already been described under the *SdKfz* 231. The eight-wheeled armoured car was the most powerful and best-known model to be used by the German Army throughout World War II. During 1934 the German high command issued the Büssing-NAG firm of Leipzig with a development contract for a new eight-wheeled chassis with all-wheel drive and steering. As the result, the Büssing-NAG 8×8 GS chassis, with a new armoured body, took over the functions of the original six-wheeled *SdKfz* 231 series. For this reason, all armoured cars on the GS chassis received the same designations as their six-wheeled predecessors but with the suffix '8 *Rad*' (eight-

wheeled) as a distinguishing mark. The car was the most advanced cross-country wheeled vehicle that could be built at that time, utilising the latest technological knowledge. Its excellent cross-country ability and high road speed were achieved only by virtue of a relatively complex chassis layout. The first production batch was delivered to the German Army during 1937. In 1938 an improved hull design was introduced together with minor automotive changes. Full replace-

ment of the six-wheeled model had not been completed by the beginning of the war, hence its use during early operations. With varying superstructures the car fulfilled a number of roles (as listed under the *SdKfz* 231). Some 1,235 were produced before eventual replacement by the *SdKfz* 234 series.

Below: The 8-wheeled SdKfz 232 was one of the most successful German armoured cars.

SdKfz 231 ARMOURED CAR

SdKfz 231 6Rad, SdKfz 231 8Rad and other versions.
Crew: 4.
Armament: One 7.92mm MG34 machine-gun.
Armour: 5mm to 15mm (0.2in to 0.6in).
Dimensions: Length (overall) 18ft 3in (5.57m); width 6ft (1.82m); height 7ft 5in (2.25m).
Weight: 10,692lbs (4,850kg).
Ground pressure: Not known.
Power to weight ratio: 13.6hp/ton.
Engine: Daimler-Benz M 09 six-cylinder water-cooled inline petrol engine developing 65hp at 2,900rpm.
Performance: Road speed 40mph (65km/h); range 155 miles (250km); vertical obstacle negligible; trench 6ft (1.83m); gradient 13 degrees.
History: In service with German Army from 1938 to 1945.

When the German Army began to introduce their standard range of armoured reconnaissance vehicles during the mid-1930s, as for all other specially-developed military vehicles, they attributed to them 'Special Vehicle' or *Sonderkraftfahrzeuge* numbers (*SdKfz* for short). These numbers did not refer at that time to a particular vehicle, but to a particular class of vehicle. As the result, the anomaly occurred where certain radically different vehicles had the same

SdKfz numbers. A prime example of this is the *SdKfz* 231 heavy armoured car. The first models were based on 6-wheeled chassis, but later vehicles utilised a specially-developed 8-wheel chassis. As a result certain suffixes were added to distinguish between the various models: the six-wheeled version became referred to as *SdKfz* 231 (*6Rad*), and the eight-wheeled version as *SdKfz* 231 (*8Rad*), the word *Rad* standing for wheel. The following models existed:
  SdKfz 231 (*6Rad*)—models by Daimler-Benz, Büssing-NAG and Magirus. This was a weapons vehicle for the heavy platoons of the motorised units.
  SdKfz 232 (*Fu*) (*6Rad*)—a special radio version of above.
  SdKfz 263 (*6Rad*)—a special radio/command version of *SdKfz* 231 (*6Rad*) with fixed turret.
  SdKfz 231 (*8Rad*)—an eight-wheeled heavy weapons vehicle produced by Büssing-NAG.
  SdKfz 232 (*Fu*) (*8Rad*)—a special radio version of *SdKfz* 231 (*8Rad*).
  SdKfz 233—a self-propelled 7.5cm howitzer.
  SdKfz 263 (*8Rad*)—a special radio/command version of *SdKfz* 231 (*8Rad*).
During 1944 a new version of the eight-wheeled armoured car was developed by Büssing-NAG, designated *SdKfz* 234. This is covered under another section. The *SdKfz* 231 (*6Rad*) was the first tactical

armoured car series to be adopted by the German Army. Development began during the late 1920s. Three firms – Daimler-Benz, Büssing-NAG and Magirus were issued with contracts for the development of armoured cars based on their commercial six-wheeled lorry chassis. The specifications were for a model six-wheeled armoured car employing a 1.48 ton (1,500kg) 6×4 cross-country lorry chassis. Daimler-Benz were the first to develop the armoured car, their model appearing during 1932. In 1933 Büssing-NAG delivered their first model of the six-wheeled armoured car. The final version of the six-wheeled armoured car was produced by Magirus during 1934. The six-wheeled armoured car, like the other German models, was built as a reconnaissance model (weapons vehicle) and as a radio vehicle. There was also an additional heavy radio vehicle with a fixed turret. All three firms produced versions of the weapons vehicle - those by Daimler-Benz being armed with only a single 7.92mm MG 34 with 1,500 rounds, and those by Büssing-NAG and Magirus having co-axial mounting for a 20mm cannon and a 7.92mm MG 34 machine-gun. Due to the fact that the armoured bodies were manufactured by two companies there were slight differences to the armour shape, particularly to the front radiator grills. Some 1,000 of all models of the six-wheeled armoured car were produced up until 1936, when the various roles were taken over by the superior eight-wheeled chassis. Even so, some of these vehicles were used in France and Poland and after for training.

Left: The original German heavy armoured car was a 6-wheeler based on a commercial lorry chassis, built by several firms. Soon after the beginning of World War II it was replaced by the 8-wheeler.

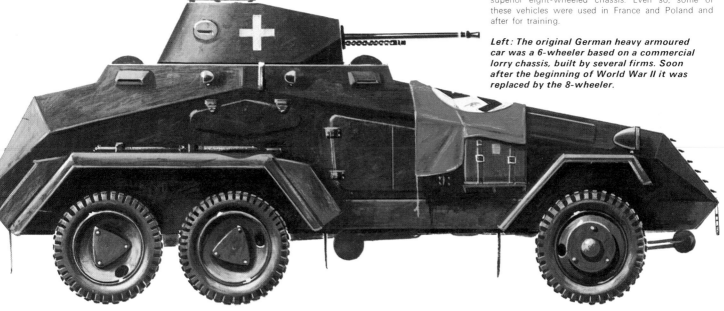

Below: The 8-wheeled armoured car was one of the Wermacht's most popular vehicles of World War II and was extensively used in the Western Desert.

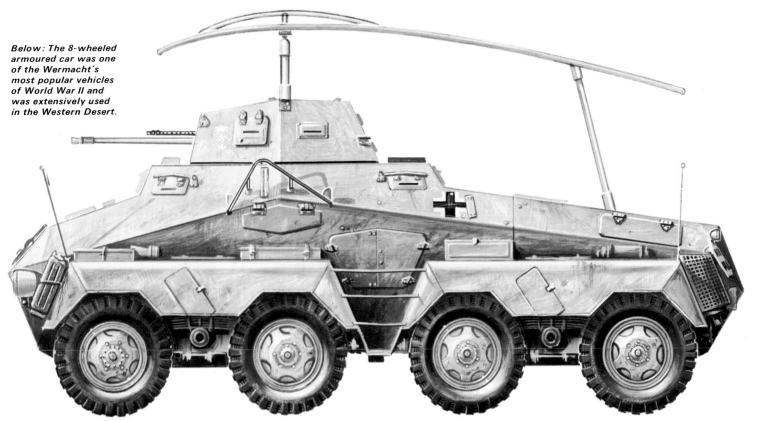

SdKfz 251 ARMOURED PERSONNEL CARRIER

Mittlerer Schützenpanzerwagen, or *SdKfz 251,* and many variants.
Crew: 2+10.
Armament: A large variety of weapon installations was available.
Armour: 0.28in (7mm) minimum; 0.47in (12mm) maximum.
Dimensions: Length 19ft (5.8m); width 6ft 10in (2.1m); height 5ft 9in (1.75m).
Weight: 20,393lbs (9,250kg).
Power to weight ratio: 11hp/ton.
Engine: Maybach HL 42 TKRM six-cylinder water-cooled inline petrol engine developing 100hp at 2,800rpm.
Performance: Road speed 34mph (55km/h); range 200 miles (320km); vertical obstacle 1ft (0.3m); trench 6ft 7in (2m); gradient 24 degrees.
History: In service with the German Army from 1939 to 1945.
The *SdKfz 251* was an armoured halftracked vehicle

employed by the German Army during World War II in a great variety of roles. It was used for anything from an armoured personnel carrier, to ground or anti-tank weapons platform, as well as rocket-launcher, flamethrower, bridging, engineer, chemical vehicles etc. Development of the vehicle was initially carried out in 1934 by the Hanomag firm, which was requested to produce a 2.95ton (3,000kg) halftrack for army use. The vehicle finally evolved was the Hanomag HL KL 6, which was an unarmoured half-tracked tractor standardised in the German Army as the *SdKfz II.* The German high command requested that an armoured version be developed, and the same firm produced the HL KL 6P. This was standardised as the *SdKfz 251.* The *SdKfz 251* entered service just in time to take part in the German invasion of Poland in September 1939, and saw extensive action in all war theatres thereafter. The basic troop-carrier vehicle received the designation *SdKfz 251/1* and seated 10 men as well as the driver and commander. Altogether, there were more than 20 other variants, all distinguished by an 'oblique-stroke number' following the *SdKfz 251*

designation. Strictly speaking, the *SdKfz 251* was a 'three-quartertracked' vehicle, since the track system occupied more than three-quarters the total vehicle length. The track system employed the overlapping (Famo) road wheel layout later utilised for the Panther medium tank. To maximise the carrying capacity within the vehicle, the armoured hull used the hexagonal cross-section used on armoured cars, and the engine was placed at the front to enable doors to be attached at the rear. To provide the driver with maximum vision, the bonnet had to be kept low, and for this reason an almost-horizontal arrangement of the steering wheel was adopted. A novel feature employed on this, and all other German halftracks of the period, was the method of steering. For normal road travel the steering wheel moved the front wheels only (up to angles of about 15°), but across country, where greater deviations from the straight and level were required, the Cletrac system took over. The only disadvantage of this type of vehicle was its excessive cost in comparison with purely wheeled or tracked types.

Left and right: Side and front views of the SdKfz 251 APC. The Germans made extensive use of half-track vehicles and this was one of the most successful. In a multiplicity of roles, it took part in almost every operation conducted by the German Army during World War II.

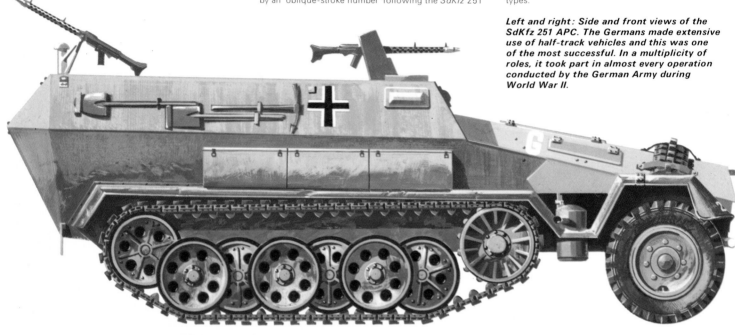

SdKfz 222 ARMOURED CAR

SdKfz 221, 222, 223, 260 and 261.
Crew: 3.
Armament: One 20mm cannon; one 7.92mm machine-gun.
Armour: 5mm to 30mm (0.2in to 1.18in).
Dimensions: Length (overall) 17ft 9in (4.8m); width 6ft 5in (1.95m); height 6ft 7in (2m).
Weight: 9,480lbs (4,300kg).
Power to weight ratio: 17.7hp/ton with 75hp engine.
Engine: Horch/Auto-Union V8-108 eight-cylinder water-cooled petrol engine developing 75 or 81hp at 3,600rpm.
Performance: Road speed 50mph (80km/h); range 187 miles (300km); vertical obstacle 10in (0.25m); trench 4ft (1.31m); gradient 22 degrees.
History: In service with German Army from 1938 to 1945.

This light armoured reconnaissance car was one of a whole series of light 4-wheeled armoured cars developed on the standard heavy passenger car chassis. There were five models. The *SdKfz* 221 was issued to motorised reconnaissance units as a replacement for the *Kfz* 13 armoured car from 1936. It was classed as a weapons vehicle, and had an open-topped, seven-sided, two-man turret. The armament comprised one 7.92mm machine-gun only. The *SdKfz* 222 was the standard armoured car introduced during 1938 as a weapons vehicle for divisional reconnaissance units. This model was built in much larger numbers than the *SdKfz* 221. It had an open-topped, 10-sided two-man turret. The armament comprised both a 20mm cannon with 220 rounds and a 7.92mm light machine-gun with 2,000 rounds. The *SdKfz* 223 was a wireless car model of the *SdKfz* 222, and was introduced during 1938. It carried long-range radio equipment and was similar to the *SdKfz* 222 apart from a smaller turret mounting only a 7.92mm machine-gun. It also had a frame aerial around the hull. The turret was nine-sided. The

SdKfz 260 was a small armoured wirless car employed by headquarters units, for which a much greater range was required from the wireless set. It was similar to the *SdKfz* 223 except that the turret was set further to the rear to make room for the bulky radio equipment. It very rarely mounted any armament. A rod-type aerial was employed. The *SdKfz* 261 was externally identical to the *SdKfz* 260 except that the earlier models had a folding frame aerial. The *SdKfz* 222 armoured car was initially built on the Standard Chassis Model A, but after 1938 the Model B chassis was employed. The main advantages of the Model B were a more powerful engine (81hp as opposed to 75hp) and better brakes (hydraulic as opposed to mechanical). Remaining in service until the end of World War II, the *SdKfz* 222 proved very useful in North Africa and Western Europe. But it was found to be greatly restricted in Russia and was gradually replaced there by the *SdKfz* 250/9 light

armoured halftrack which mounted the same turret. A hinged wire-mesh anti-grenade was attached to the open-topped turret. This divided along the centreline of the vehicle and could be folded outwards to facilitate firing the armament. The armament itself could be elevated almost to the vertical position to allow the engagement of aircraft. On later models the thickness of the nose-plate on the hull was increased from 14.5mm to 30mm (0.57in to 1.18in).

Right: The SdKfz 222 was the standard German light armoured reconnaissance car of WWII. A characteristic feature was the wire-mesh anti-grenade screen attached to the turret top.

Below: Faceted armour was a standard feature of German armoured cars.

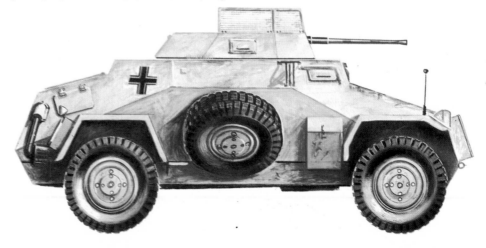

Above and right: The rocket-firing version of the SdKfz 251. The vehicle above has the rocket projectors removed; that on the right is firing.

PzKpfw I LIGHT TANK

SdKfz 101.
Crew: 2.
Armament: Two 7.92mm MG 34 machine-guns.
Armour: 0.28in (7mm) minimum; 0.51in (13mm) maximum.
Dimensions: Length 13ft 3in (4.03m); width 6ft 9in (2.05m); height 5ft 8in (1.72m).
Weight: 11,905lbs (5,400kg).
Ground pressure: 5.71lb/in² (0.4kg/cm²).
Power to weight ratio: 11.32hp/ton.
Engine: Krupp M305 four-cylinder horizontally-opposed air-cooled petrol engine developing 60hp at 2,500rpm.
Performance: Road speed 23mph (37km/h); range 125 miles (200km); vertical obstacle 1ft 2in (0.355m); trench 4ft 7in (1.4m); gradient 58 per cent.
History: Served with the German Army from 1934 to 1941 as a tank, and to 1945 in other roles. Also used by Spain.
(Note: Data relate to *PzKpfw* I A.)

In 1933, when Germany began openly to rearm, it was realised that the development of a full family of armoured vehicles would take several years. In the meantime it was decided to build light vehicles which the new armoured formations could use for training and experience. Contracts were therefore laid for a series of armoured vehicles between 3.9 and 6.9 tons (4,000 and 7,000kg) overall weight, and Krupp's design was the one chosen. The *PzKpfw* I A was a small two-man tank which was inadequate in most respects even by the modest standards of the day. The hull was lightly armoured and had many openings, crevices and joints, all which generally weakened it and made it vulnerable to attack. The engine was low powered and as a result performance was poor. The gearbox was a standard commercial crash type, with five forward speeds and one reverse. Fittings were minimal, and there was little evidence of designing for crew comfort. The suspension showed evidence of plagiarisation of some of the features of the Carden-Loyd light tanks of the 1920s, in that an external beam carried the outer ends of the bogie axles and the rear idler. The drive-sprocket was at the front, which meant that the transmission train ran along the floor of the hull to a differential besides the driver's feet. Both driver and commander shared the same compartment, the driver climbing in through a hull door on the side, the commander using a large hatch in the turret roof. Since his vision was very restricted when the vehicle was closed down, the commander generally spent his time standing up with the upper half of his body well exposed. The little turret was traversed by hand, and the commander fired the two machine-guns, for which there were 1,525 rounds of ammunition. The inadequacies of the Krupp engine became quickly apparent, and it was superseded by a more powerful one of 100bhp. This was a six-cylinder water-cooled inline Maybach, and to fit it in the chassis an extra 1ft 5in (43cm) of length had to be added to the hull. This brought about changes in the suspension, and an extra wheel station was added. In turn this lengthened the track in contact with the ground, and so the rear idler was lifted up. This was designated the *PzKpfw* IB, which was altogether a better vehicle, although it suffered from the same failings in armour and armament as did the IA. These two models were the mainstay of the German armoured formations during the prewar years, and they trained many thousands of crews in the tasks of driving tracklaying vehicles, and introduced them to the requirements of team work, maintenance and small unit tactics. Over 2,000 IBs were built, reflecting the greater use that could be made of the more powerful model, and although only meant as interim vehicles until the proper battle tanks could be introduced, they were in action as early as 1936 in the Spanish Civil War, and after that in Poland, the Low Countries in 1940, Africa, Greece, the Balkans and even in Russia during 1941, though by then they were well out-dated and inadequate for anything except very minor tasks. In their early days these little tanks had survived very largely by virtue of the fact that there was no effective anti-tank armament in service with any army, and tanks were virtually immune to infantry weapons. However, as soon as any light guns could be brought to bear the *PzKpfw* I was doomed, and many were destroyed by British 2pounder fire in the retreat to Dunkirk. Several experiments were tried on the type, one such being the introduction of radio. This was only fitted to the IB version, and judging from photographs there was a sizeable proportion of each

unit which could communicate by this means. The other vehicles watched for hand signals from their sub-unit leader. A successful variant to the basic tank was the conversion to a small command vehicle, an idea which started in 1936. By 1938 200 had been completed. The turret was replaced by a square full-width superstructure with a low square cupola on top. A single machine-gun was fitted for self-defence, and could be removed and set up on its ground mount. The crew was increased to three, and two radio sets were fitted. These vehicles were allotted to armoured units of all kinds, and altogether 96 of them saw action in France. Many others went to Russia in the following year, though they must have been terribly vulnerable

Above: A PzKpfw I light tank in France, 1940. The first standardized tank of the Wehrmacht, it saw wide use in the initial campaigns. It mounted two 7.92mm machine-guns in a rotating turret.

to any form of effective fire. A very small number of redundant *PzKpfw* Is were converted to other roles. A few were made into repair tractors, and others became ammunition carriers. About 200 were fitted with a 4.7cm gun and became light SP anti-tank guns; a very few others were fitted with 15cm guns, but in both cases the chassis was overloaded and the idea was dropped after limited use.

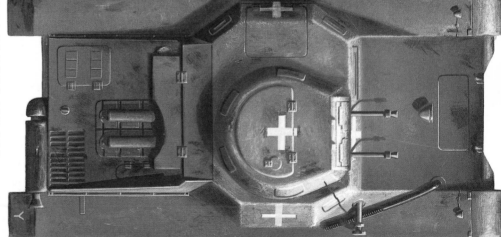

Right: Rear, front and top views of the PzKpfw I light tank. An unusual, but not unique, feature of this tank was that the turret with its twin 7.92mm MG 34 machine-guns was offset to the right. It entered service with the German Army in 1934.

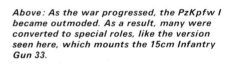

Above: As the war progressed, the PzKpfw I became outmoded. As a result, many were converted to special roles, like the version seen here, which mounts the 15cm Infantry Gun 33.

Left: The PzKpfw Model A.
Below: The PzKpfw Model B.
The main difference lay in the location of the rear idler wheel.

PzKpfw II LIGHT TANK

PzKpfw II, or **SdKfz** 121 *Ausf* A to F.
Crew: 3.
Armament: One 2cm *KwK* 30 or 38 gun; one 7.92mm MG 34 machine-gun co-axial with main armament.
Armour: 0.39in (10mm) minimum; 1.18in (30mm) maximum in the *Ausf* A, B and C; 0.57in (14.5mm) minimum; 1.38in (35mm) maximum in the *Ausf* F.
Weight: 20,944lbs (9,500kg).
Ground pressure: 11.3lb/in² (0.8kg/cm²).
Power to weight ratio: 13.9hp/ton.
Engine: Maybach HL 62 TR six-cylinder water-cooled inline petrol engine developing 130hp at 2,600rpm.
Performance: Road speed 25mph (40km/h); range 120 miles (192km); vertical obstacle 1ft 5in (0.43m); trench 5ft 8in (1.72m); fording depth 3ft (0.91m); gradient 50 per cent.
History: In service with the German Army from 1936 to 1943. Also used by Spain.

The *PzKpfw* II was the second interim vehicle introduced into German service before the war, when it became obvious that the larger tanks were going to be delayed in their production. The German factories had trouble in making these latter vehicles, and when it was realised that it would be at least 1938 before any heavy tanks would be in service, it was decided to build a second series of interim designs, this time in the 9.84 ton (10,000kg) range. The specification was released in 1935, and the design from MAN finally selected. A number of prototypes was built, and some of them were sent to Spain for full-scale trials in action. The first production models appeared in 1935, but deliveries were slow for the next 18 months as changes were made in the design. The armour was increased in thickness, particularly in the front, and some changes were made in the suspension. The weight increased by nearly 1.95 tons (2,000kg), and experiments were made to improve the engine horse-power. An extra 10hp was found by boring out the cylinders of the Maybach engine, though the lower power motor appears to have continued to be fitted to some versions. The three variants of the *PzKpfw* II, the *Ausf* A, B and C, were all very similar, with only minor dimensional differences. The *Ausf* A had the original low power engine and weighed 16,105lbs (7,305kg). About 100 were built in 1935 and 1936. The *Ausf* B featured the higher power engine, new reduction gears and tracks, and again the weight increased. The *Ausf* C appeared in 1937 and carried thicker front armour, bringing the weight up to the final figure of 20,944lbs (9,500kg). Issues to units

began in earnest in 1937, and by 1939 there were sufficient for over 1,000 to take part in the Polish campaign. Manufacture of the general type continued up to late 1942 or early 1943, by which time the basic tank was well outdated. In the French campaign in 1940 it was already apparent that the armament and armour were insufficient, though as a reconnaissance vehicle the tank was ideal. The hull was built up from welded heat-treated steel, 1.18in (30mm) thick on the front and 0.39in (10mm) on the sides and rear. The turret was made in a similar way, again 1.18in thick on the front and 0.63in (16mm) around the sides and back. The engine was in the rear compartment, driving forward through the fighting compartment to a gearbox and final drive in front. The gearbox was a ZF crash-type with six forward speeds and one reverse, the steering being by clutches and brakes. The driver sat off-centre to the left side. The fighting compartment had the turret above it, again offset slightly to the left. The armament was an improvement on that of the

PzKpfw I, but still not very effective, the 2cm gun had a maximum range of 656 yards (600m), and only fired armour-piercing ammunition, but it had a reasonably rapid rate of fire. Some 180 2cm and 1,425 7.92mm rounds were carried. However, armour penetration of these 2cm rounds was not impressive. Once again, vision was poor from the turret, and fire-control difficult when fully closed-down. Most vehicles seem to have had radio. The suspension was distinctive. There were five road wheels hung on quarter-elliptic leaf springs, with the rear idler and front drive sprocket both clear of the ground. This suspension was quite effective, and within the limits of its engine power the *PzKpfw* II was quite manoeuvrable and agile. The tracks were narrow, but apparently quite strong. Despite the limitations of the design, the *PzKpfw* II formed the backbone of the armoured divisions of the German Army, and as late as April 1942 860 were still on strength, although they were then all but obsolete. An attempt to improve the performance was made in

Above right: A PzKpfw II Ausf B or C of the Afrika Korps advances across the desert with soft-skinned vehicles.

Right: Views of a PzKpfw II Ausf F of 6th Panzer Div. after the Polish campaign, with the new black-cross national markings.

PzKpfw III BATTLE TANK

late 1940 with the F variant. Thicker armour was fitted to the front and sides and a higher velocity gun installed, though its calibre was still only 2cm. However these changes did little to increase the battlefield value of the tank, and the extra 2,204lbs (1,000kg) of weight that they entailed put an extra strain on the engine. The basic chassis was used for several different special-purpose vehicles; and also as a test-bed for a variety of ideas, including the use of torsion-bar suspension systems. Some were turned into flame-thrower vehicles, capable of about 80 shots of 2 to 3 seconds duration at a range of 38 yards (35m). Some 55 were unsuccessfully modified as amphibians for the invasion of Britain, and there were several SP gun versions, dealt with separately. In the end the *PzKpfw* II faded quietly out of use, having shown the German Army how to train and handle armoured formations in the difficult days before the war started. With an experienced crew it could give a good account of itself, but it was always too lightly armed.

PzKpfw III, or *SdKfz* 141, *Ausf* A to N.
Crew: 5.
Armament: *Ausf* A, B, C and D one 3.7cm *KwK* L/45 gun, two 7.92mm MG 34 machine-guns co-axial with main armament; one 7.92mm MG 34 machine-gun in hull.
Ausf E, F, G and H one 5cm *KwK* 39 L/42 gun; one 7.92mm MG 34 machine-gun co-axial with main armament; one 7.92mm MG 34 machine-gun in hull.
Ausf J and L one 5cm *KwK* 39 L/60 gun; one 7.92mm MG 34 machine-gun co-axial with main armament; one 7.92mm MG 34 machine-gun in hull.
Ausf M and N one 7.5cm *KwK* L/24 gun; one 7.92mm MG 34 machine-gun co-axial with main armament; one 7.92mm MG 34 machine-gun in hull.
Armour: *Ausf* A, B and C 0.57in (14.5mm) minimum; 3.54in (90mm) maximum.
Ausf D to G 1.18in (30mm) minimum; 3.54in (90mm) maximum.
Ausf H to N 1.18in (30mm) minimum; 3.15in (80mm)

maximum, but often seen with additional plate and spaced armour.
Dimensions: Length *Ausf* A and B 18ft 6in (5.7m); *Ausf* D to G 17ft 8in (5.4m); *Ausf* H 18ft 1in (5.52m); *Ausf* J to N 21ft 1in (6.4m).
Width *Ausf* A to C 9ft 2in (2.8m); *Ausf* D to G 9ft 6in (2.9m); *Ausf* H to N 9ft 8in (2.95m).
Height *Ausf* A 7ft 7in (2.35m); *Ausf* B and C 8ft 4in (2.55m); *Ausf* D to G 8ft (2.4m); *Ausf* H to N 9ft 8in (2.5m).
Weight: *Ausf* A to C 33,069lbs (15,000kg); *Ausf* D and E 42,769lbs (19,400kg); *Ausf* F and G 44,753lbs (20,300kg); *Ausf* H 47,619lbs (21,600kg); *Ausf* J to N 49,163lbs (22,300kg).
Ground pressure: *Ausf* A to C 15.3lb/in² (0.973kg/cm²); *Ausf* D 13.2lb/in² (0.93kg/cm²); *Ausf* E and H to N 13.5lb/in² (0.95kg/cm²); *Ausf* F and G 14.1lb/in² (0.99kg/cm²).
Power to weight ratio: *Ausf* A to C 15.58hp/ton;

continued on page 112

Above: Side view of a PzKpfw III Ausf J of the 3rd Panzer Division, Russian Front, 1941. Note the spare wheels and track shoes on the rear hull deck, indicating the maintenance problems faced by the Germans in long-distance operations. The only way to ensure a supply of common spare parts was for the tanks to carry them!

Left: Rear view of a captured, disabled PzKpfw III, showing the rear decking armoured engine louvres and the turret side door which, with another door exactly opposite, provided excellent access to the interior of the turret.

Below: Supporting infantry, a PzKpfw Ausf J acts as a protection against enemy fire during the advance on Moscow in 1942. The PzKpfw III was the back-bone of Panzer Divisions in the earlier stages of the Russian campaign, until its replacement by later models of the PzKpfw IV.

▶ *Ausf* D 16.75hp/ton; *Ausf* E and H to N 15.71hp/ton;
Ausf F and G 15hp/ton.

Engine: *Ausf* A to C Maybach HL 108 TR V-12 water-
cooled inline petrol engine developing 230hp at
2,600rpm; *Ausf* D Maybach HL 120 TR developing
320hp at 3,000rpm; *Ausf* E to N Maybach HL 120
TRM developing 300hp at 3,000rpm.

Performance: Road speed *Ausf* A to C 20mph
(32km/h); *Ausf* E to N 25mph (40km/h). Cross-
country speed all models 11mph (18km/h). Range
Ausf A to C 94 miles (150km); *Ausf* D 103 miles
(165km/h); *Ausf* E to N 109 miles (175km). Vertical
obstacle all models 2ft (0.6m). Trench *Ausf* A to G
7ft 6in (2.3m). Fording depth *Ausf* A to J 2ft 7in
(0.8m); *Ausf* L to N 4ft 3in (1.3m). Gradient 30 degrees.

History: In service with the German Army from 1939
to 1945. Also used by Spain and Turkey.

In 1935, having gained some experience with the
small tanks of that time, the Germans began to draw
up specifications for their main battle tanks. The
intention, as stated by General Guderian, was to have
two basic types, the first carrying a high-velocity gun
for anti-tank work, backed up by machine-guns; and
the second, a support tank for the first, carrying a large-
calibre gun capable of firing a destructive HE shell. The
intention was to equip the tank battalions with these
in the ratio of three companies of the first type to one
company of the support vehicles. The *PzKpfw* III was
the first of these two vehicles, and originally a high-
velocity 5cm gun was called for. But the infantry were
being equipped with the 3.7cm anti-tank gun, and it
was felt that in the interest of standardisation the tanks
should carry the same. However, a large turret ring
was retained so that the vehicle could be up-gunned
later without much difficulty. This was an important
consideration and it undoubtedly enabled the *PzKpfw*
III to remain in service for at least two years longer
than would otherwise have been the case, for had the
turret been as small as that of the Matilda, for
example, it would have been impossible to put in a
larger gun, and by 1943 the tank would have disappeared. The specification called for a weight of
14.76 tons (15,000kg), which was never achieved, and
the upper limit had to be set at 23.62 tons (24,000
kg) in deference to German road bridges. The first
prototypes appeared in 1936, and Daimler-Benz was
chosen to be the main contractor. The *Ausf* A, B, C and
D all appeared during the development phase, and
were only produced in comparatively small numbers,
and all were used to try out the different aspects of the
design. The *Ausf* E became the production version,

and was accepted in September 1939 as the *Panzerkampfwagen* III (3.7cm) (*SdKfz* 141). Production was
spread among several firms, none of whom had had
any previous experience of mass-producing vehicles —
a fact which was to cause some trouble later on. The
PzKpfw III *Ausf* E now formed the basis of the armoured
divisions of the *Wehrmacht*. Some 98 were available
for the invasion of Poland, and 350 took part in the
Battle for France in May 1940. These tanks were mainly
Ausf E, but there was still a number of earlier marks in
service. All versions featured a good crew layout. There
was room for every man to do his job, and the prominent 'dustbin' cupola at the rear of the turret gave the
commander an excellent view. The driver was assisted
by a pre-selector gearbox giving him ten forward
speeds and one reverse. The gearbox was rather complicated, and maintenance was difficult, but gear
changing was easy and driving far less tiring than
in many contemporary tanks at that time. The 320hp
from the Maybach engine was adequate, if not exactly
generous, and cross-country performance reasonably
good. However, the tank was not entirely successful
in action. The 3.7cm gun was not good enough to
penetrate the armour of the British infantry tanks in
France, and the 1.18in (30mm) of frontal armour could
not keep out 2pounder shot. The same happened
in the Western Desert when the *PzKpfw* III first went
out with the *Afrika Korps*, but a new Krupp 5cm gun
was rushed into production in late 1939 and was fitted
to the *Ausf* E to H. This gun was not entirely satisfactory
either as it was a low-velocity weapon, but it fired a
useful HE shell and could outrange the British
2pounder. Some 99 rounds of 5cm ammunition and

*Above: A PzKpfw III crew member surrenders
to British infantry on 29 October 1942.
The tank has the equipment storage racks
at the hull rear mounted by many Afrika
Korps tanks.*

2,000 of 7.92mm ammunition were carried. A steady
programme of improvement and development was
now applied to the *PzKpfw* III. The *Ausf* H introduced
extra armour bolted on to the hull and turret, and the
tracks were widened to carry the extra weight. The
complicated ten-speed gearbox was replaced by
a simple six-speed manual change, and some of these
features were retrofitted to earlier marks. By 1941
there were nearly 1,500 *PzKpfw* IIIs in service, and the
type was very successful in the first stages of the
invasion of Russia. But the T-34 and KV tanks were
impervious to the 5cm low-velocity gun, and in a
crash programme a high-velocity version was introduced, though even this soon proved to be inadequate on the Eastern Front. However, it did well in
the desert. Improved versions were now being designed
fast. Production of the *PzKpfw* III had never reached
the intended numbers (indeed it never did) and the J
version, which carried 78 5cm rounds, was meant to
be easier to produce and at the same time to provide
better protection. The M went a bit further and also
cut out many minor items such as hatches and vision
ports. Some 2,600 were built in 1942, but already the
tank was being outmoded and the N version carried
a low-velocity 7.5cm gun to provide HE support to the
heavy tank battalions. Some 64 7.5cm and 3,450
7.92mm rounds of ammunition were carried.

*Above: Rear view of a PzKpfw III Ausf G
battalion HQ tank of the 15th Panzer
Division, Afrika Korps, 1942. The frame
on the rear hull deck is the aerial for
the extra radio equipment installed
in the tank to enable it to function
efficiently in the command role.*

*Above, top line: Alternative versions
of 3rd Pz Div's 'bear' emblem. Bottom
line, left: the tactical marking of 3rd
Pz Div; right: the Afrika Korps emblem.*

*Below: Side view of a PzKpfw III Ausf E
of 15th Panzer Division. The tank has the
37mm Kwk L/45 gun, replaced on later
vehicles by the harder-hitting 50mm KwK L/42
armament.*

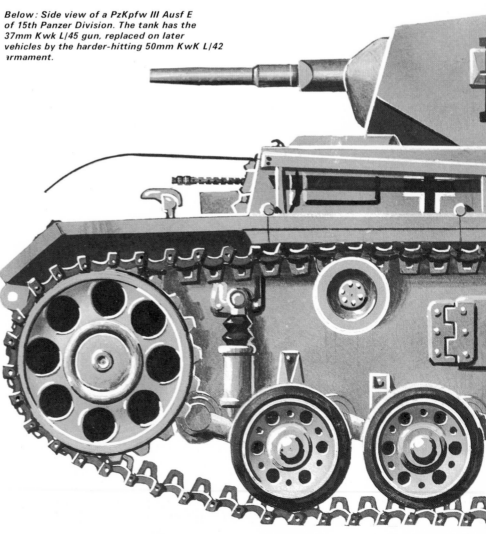

Above and below: Front and rear views of a PzKpfw JII Ausf J of 3rd Panzer Division on the Russian Front, 1941. The tank is armed with the 50mm KwK L/42 low-velocity gun.

Above: A PzKpfw III in action at Zhitomir in the Ukraine, during street fighting in the town. German armour was designed for fast-moving 'Blitzkrieg' operations in open country rather than for close-quarter fighting with infantry in towns.

PzKpfw IV MEDIUM TANK

SdKfz 161.
Crew: 5.
Armament: One 7.5cm *KwK* L/24 gun; one 7.92mm MG 34 machine-gun co-axial with main armament; one 7.92mm MG 34 machine-gun in hull.
Armour: 0.79in (20mm) minimum; 3.54in (90mm) maximum.
Dimensions: 19ft 5in (5.91m); width 9ft 7in (2.92m); height 8ft 6in (2.59m).
Weight: 43,431lbs (19,700kg).
Ground pressure: 10.6lb/in² (0.75kg/cm²).
Power to weight ratio: 15.5hp/ton.
Engine: Maybach HL 120 TRM V-12 inline diesel developing 300hp at 3,000rpm.
Performance: Road speed 25mph (40km/h); cross-country speed 12.5mph (20km/h); range 125 miles (200km); vertical obstacle 2ft (0.6m); trench 7ft 6in (2.3m); fording depth 2ft 7in (0.8m); gradient 30 degrees.
History: In service with the German Army from 1936 to 1945. Also used by Italy, Spain and Turkey. Last used by Syria in 1967.
(Note: Data relate to the *PzKpfw* IV *Ausf* D.)

The *PzKpfw* IV was the only German tank to stay in continuous production throughout World War II, and it was probably in production longer than any other tank from that war, with the exception of the T-34. It began with the German specifications of 1935 in which it was foreseen that the main battle would be fought with two types, the more numerous one carrying a high-velocity gun (the *PzKpfw* III) and a support tank carrying a large-calibre gun firing a good HE shell. This was the *PzKpfw* IV. The gun chosen from the beginning was the 7.5cm short-barrelled *KwK*, and the tank was not to exceed 23.62 tons (24,000kg) in overall weight. In fact the specification called for a very similar vehicle to the *PzKpfw* III, and

Below: Disabled PzKpfw IV Ausf H tanks on the Voronezh Front in 1943. Note the skirt armour plates on the front tank, called Schürzen; they were 5mm thick and were intended to detonate hollow-charge projectiles and anti-tank rifle rounds prematurely. The detachable hull plates were often lost in the heat of battle, but the turret plates were a permanent fixture.

the layout of both was much the same, as were their tasks. Contracts were laid with a variety of firms, and there was the same fairly extended development time while the different designs were refined. It was 1939 before deliveries could be made in any quantity, and by that time the models had progressed to the Type D. This was the model which took part in the Polish and French campaigns, finally advancing into Russia in 1941, when its deficiencies became too apparent to be ignored further. The Type D was slightly larger than the *PzKpfw* III, but had the same thin hull form and general shape. There were three compartments for the crew, the driver and radio operator occupying the front, with the hull machine-gun on the right side and set

Right: Front view of a PzKpfw IV Ausf A of 1st Panzer Division. Only 35 of this model were built, in 1936. One of its distinguishing features was the large 'dustbin-type' cupola at the rear of the turret.

slightly back from the driver. In the fighting compartment the turret contained the commander, gunner and loader. The turret itself was traversed by an electric motor, whereas that of the *PzKpfw* III was hand-operated. The commander had a prominent cupola at the rear of the turret, and good all-round vision. There were escape hatches in the turret sides. The engine was in the rear compartment, and was the same as that of the *PzKpfw* III, although the layout of the ancillaries was slightly different. The drive ran forward to a front gearbox and sprocket. Suspension was by four coupled bogies on each side, sprung by leaf springs. There was a large idler wheel at the back and four small return rollers. There was room enough in the hull for

80 rounds of ammunition for the gun, and 2,800 rounds in belts for the machine-guns. Battle experience soon showed that in this form the tank was a sound design and well laid out, but the armour was too thin for it to be able to perform its proper task of supporting the *PzKpfw* IIIs as it had scarcely any advantage over any other tank. There followed a steady programme of improvement which was to continue until the end of the war. The next model, the E, was given thicker armour on the nose and turret, and a new cupola. Older models were retrofitted, which confuses precise identification of many photographs today. The F model was intended to be the main production version, though it too was soon overtaken, and a long-barrelled

version of the 7.5cm gun was fitted. This long gun completely changed the role of the vehicle as it now became a fighting tank and began to take over that duty from the *PzKpfw* III from about mid-1941 onwards. The F was made in large numbers and fought on all fronts, as did the G which came soon after it, differing outwardly only in respect of its thicker armour and side skirting plates. In 1943 another lease of life was injected by fitting the more powerful 7.5cm *KwK* 40 L/48 which enabled the *PzKpfw* IV to take on almost any tank in the world, and to give a good account of itself against the T-34. These larger guns had of course changed the turret, which from the G onwards was protected with extra plates, making it appear much

longer at the rear. Large 0.2in (5mm) skirting plates hung over the sides and radically altered the look of the tank, making it appear deep and rather clumsy. The last model was the J, which came out in 1944. By this time many raw materials were scarce and the design had to be simplified, but it was still basically the tank which had started the war five years before. By 1945 over 8,000 had been delivered and many more were built for specialist purposes. A few were still in service with the Syrian Army in the Arab-Israeli War of 1967, and apparently went well. Whatever the drawbacks of the original design, the final versions were extremely sound and reliable tanks with an excellent battle record.

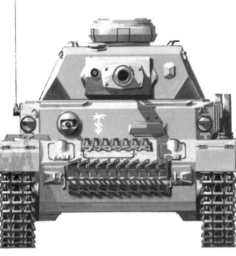

Far left: Front view of a PzKpfw IV Ausf F2 of the Afrika Korps, mounting the 75mm KwK L/43 gun.

Left: Rear view of a PzKpfw IV Ausf F2 of the Gross Deutschland Panzer Division.

Below: Two PzKpfw IVs and a PzKpfw III of the 14th Panzer Division on the Eastern Front, 1942. The tank in the foreground mounts the 7.5cm KwK L/24 gun and carries spare track shoes on the front as additional armour. This practice proved its worth in combat with the Soviet T-34/76 medium tanks: their 76.2mm guns could not quite pierce the PzKpfw IV's front armour.

PANZERJÄGER I SELF-PROPELLED ANTI-TANK GUN

4.7cm *PaK (t) (Sfl) auf PzKpfw I Ausf* B, or
SdKfz 101.
Crew: 3.
Armament: One 4.7cm *PaK (t)* L/43.3 gun.
Armour: 0.28in (7mm) minimum; 0.51in (13mm)
maximum.
Dimensions: Length 14ft 6in (4.42m); width 6ft 0½in
(1.85m); height 7ft 4½in (2.25m).
Weight: 14,109lbs (6,400kg).
Ground pressure: 6.68lb/in² (0.47kg/cm²).
Power to weight ratio: 15.87hp/ton.
Engine: Maybach NL 38 TR six-cylinder water-
cooled inline petrol engine developing 100bhp at
3,000rpm.
Performance: Road speed 25mph (40km/h); range
88 miles (140km); vertical obstacle 1ft 2in (0.355m);
trench 4ft 7in (1.4m); fording depth 1ft 10in (0.58m);
gradient 30 degrees.
History: In service with the German Army from 1940
to 1943.

One of the great inadequacies of the *PzKpfw I* series,
and for that matter the *PzKpfw II* also, was the lack of
effective fire-power. This, together with poor armour,
quickly made them obsolete on the battlefield, and
designers were quick to find uses for the chassis which
then became available. One major need was for anti-
tank guns to be more mobile, for in prewar thinking
they were moved and used in much the same way as
artillery itself. The Germans were the first to spot the
fallacy in this argument, for if the guns were not placed
where the opposing tanks were going to come, then
they were useless. As there were never enough anti-
tank guns to go round, it followed that the most useful
ones would be those which could move as fast as the
tanks which were attacking them. This line of thought
led directly to 'mounting an anti-tank gun on a tank
chassis, and the first one was constructed in 1939 by
the firm of Alkett in Berlin. The gun chosen was a
Czech 4.7cm, there being a good supply of these after
the annexation of Czechoslovakia. The gun's performance was excellent for that time. Alkett removed
the *PzKpfw I* turret and built a fixed steel box of
remarkably ungainly appearance in its place. The box
surrounded the gun mounting on three sides, the
back being open, and there was no roof. The sides

sloped inwards to allow for some degree of protection
from armour-piercing shot, but front and sides were only
0.57in (14.5mm) thick, and the sides did not even
reach back behind the breech. In fact, the protection
was really from the front only: the crew worked the
gun standing on the engine deck and the armour was
in the nature of an improved shield as fitted to ground
mounted guns. The fixed armour and the high mounting placed restrictions on the degree to which the gun
could be moved, and traverse was limited to 15° either
side of centre, while elevation was 12°, though with an
anti-tank gun this is less important. The centre of
gravity was raised, making the vehicle awkward on
cross-country runs, and the silhouette was so high
that it must have been an embarrassment to hide at
times. The 4.7cm gun was effective and useful.
Muzzle velocity was 2,543fps (775m/s), which was
good. Some 86 rounds of ammunition were carried.
There was no supporting machine-gun, and for local
protection the crew had to use their own personal

weapons. The three-man crew was divided into a
driver and two gunners, the latter being sufficient for
such a small gun. These guns were not made in large
numbers because there were not enough chassis that
could be used. They were issued to units in 1940 and
took part in the invasion of France. Others were sent
to North Africa, where they were a useful stop-gap
until the later designs came to replace them. The real
value of the 4.7cm *Panzerjäger* was that it was the first
SP anti-tank gun to be used in combat, and it was a
complete success. From it sprang the long line of
successors, which still exist today.

*Below: The Germans made great use of
obsolete AFVs as self-propelled weapons, and
the Panzerjäger I was one of the most
common. On a PzKpfw I hull and chassis, the
turret was replaced by an armoured
superstructure mounting a 47mm PaK (t)
L/43.3 gun.*

StuG III ASSAULT GUN

Sturmgeschütz 7.5cm Kanone, or *SdKfz* 142.
Crew: 4.
Armament: One 7.5cm *StuK* 37 L/24 gun.
Armour: 1.18in (30mm) minimum; 3.54in (90mm)
maximum.
Dimensions: Length 18ft (5.49m); width 9ft 8in
(2.95m); height 6ft 4in (1.94m).
Weight: 48,501lbs (22,000kg).
Ground pressure: 13.6lb/in² (0.97kg/in²).
Power to weight ratio: 13.86hp/ton.
Engine: Maybach HL 120 TRM V-12 water-cooled
petrol engine developing 300bhp at 3,000rpm.
Performance: Road speed 25mph (40km/h); cross-
country speed 15mph (24km/h); range 102 miles
(164km); vertical obstacle 2ft (0.6m); trench 7ft 6in
(2.3m); fording depth 2ft 7in (0.8m); gradient 30
degrees.
History: In service with the German Army from 1940
to 1945.

Having specified in 1935 the range of tanks required,
the German Army Weapons Department was asked
for an armoured close support vehicle. Daimler-Benz
developed the chassis, and Krupp the gun. The
specification called for a low silhouette and a large-

calibre gun. The one subsequently chosen was a short-
barrelled 7.5cm and to bring down the roof height it
had to be mounted in the hull, rather than on it. The
chassis was that of the *PzKpfw III*, and the turret was
replaced by a low fixed superstructure running up to
the driver's plate. The gun was mounted so that the
muzzle projected through this plate, and was slightly
offset to the right of the vehicle. The driver's position
remained unchanged, except that he now sat in the
front of a large fighting compartment in which were
the three members of the gun crew. Some 44 rounds
of ammunition for the gun were stowed internally
around the sides of the fighting compartment and
there was no machine-gun for local defence or for the
engagement of secondary targets. The overall silhouette was commendably low and the armoured
protection quite good by the standards of the day.
Unusually for an assault gun, there was an armoured
roof of 0.39in (10mm) thickness. Only five examples
were ready for the invasion of France, but by the end of
1940 184 had been produced, and deliveries reached
a rate of 30 per month. This continued until late 1941,
when production slowed down, but continued up to
March 1945 in later marks. In early 1942 the Model F
appeared. This was armed with a long-barrelled 7.5cm

gun and had extra bow armour. The Model G fitted
an even longer 7.5cm (48 calibres) and now carried an
externally mounted machine-gun for local defence
and AA use. From 1943 onwards all models fitted side
aprons over the suspension as a defence against
hollow charge attack. The Model G had an enlarged
superstructure to accommodate the longer gun, and
a commander's cupola was fitted at the left rear corner.
Final versions had partially cast superstructures and
large cast mantlets; in addition the bow plates were
interlocked for greater strength and smoke dischargers
were fitted to the sides of the front plate. Late in 1941
the chassis was up-gunned to carry the 10.5cm *StuH*
42 howitzer, in order to provide close support for
armoured and infantry formations. This gun was the
standard 10.5cm close-support gun of the artillery, and
had only a limited anti-armour performance. The
superstructure was virtually unchanged, but because
of lack of space, only 36 rounds could be carried, and
some chassis were converted to carry ammunition. The
StuG III assault guns gave the German Army a
relatively simple armoured and very mobile gun. They
were highly successful, if somewhat outclassed by the
end of the war, and over 10,500 had been built by
March 1945.

*Left: One of the best
German SPGs was the
Sturmgeschütz III—
a short-barrelled 75mm
gun mounted in an
armoured super-
structure on the
chassis of a PzKpfw
III medium tank.*

*Right: The Sturmgesch-
ütz III needed to be
up-gunned during the
war, so a more powerful
long-barrelled 75mm
gun, seen here in
action, was fitted.
More than 10,500 of
these were built.*

SdKfz 250 LIGHT ARMOURED PERSONNEL CARRIER

Leitchter Schützenpanzerwagen, or *SdKfz 250,* and many variants.

Crew: 2+4.
Armament: A large variety of weapon installations was available.
Armour: 0.31in (8mm) minimum; 0.59in (15mm) maximum.
Dimensions: Length 15ft (4.56m); width 6ft 4in (1.95m); height 6ft 6in (1.98m).
Weight: 11,680lbs (5,380kg).
Power to weight ratio: 18.9hp/ton.
Engine: Maybach HL 42 TRKM six-cylinder water-cooled inline petrol engine developing 100hp at 2,800rpm.
Performance: Road speed 37mph (60km/h); range 186 miles (300km); vertical obstacle 1ft 3in (0.38m); trench not known; fording depth 2ft 4in (0.71m); gradient 40 degrees.
History: In service with the German Army from 1940 to 1945.

Alongside the medium armoured halftrack (*SdKfz* 251), the German Army also had a requirement for a light armoured halftrack. The Demag 0.98ton (1,000kg) unarmoured halftrack was adopted as the basic model on which to develop this. In order to enable this vehicle to support the weight of an armoured body, it was necessary to shorten the chassis by removing the last axle from the track system. The armoured body was developed by Büssing-NAG. The resulting vehicle was tested during 1939 and accepted for the German Army as the *SdKfz* 50. It was introduced into service just in time to take part in the invasion of France in 1940, and like its companion vehicle, the *SdKfz* 251, served on all fronts throughout World War II. The vehicle served as the basis for some 13 different variants, the basic model being designated *SdKfz 250/1*. All manner of weapons were mounted on the vehicle, ranging from light machine-guns to powerful anti-tank guns, and the vehicle was adapted for many other functions for the engineer, signal, chemical and ordnance troops, and for the *Luftwaffe*. Certain modifications of this vehicle existed, and these had their own unique *SdKfz* numbers (as opposed to an oblique stroke number attached to the original *SdKfz* 250 designation). One of these was the *SdKfz* 252, which was an armoured

ammunition carrier designed to accompany the 7.5cm assault gun on the *PzKpfw* III chassis (*Sturmgeschütze*). This vehicle often towed a small two-wheeled trailer. Another such vehicle was the *SdKfz* 253 armoured artillery observation vehicle, also intended to accompany the 7.5cm assault gun. Both vehicles had a fully-enclosed armoured body with access through roof hatches and a rear door. It should be noted that most of the *SdKfz* 250 vehicles were open-topped.

Right: A unit of SdKfz 250 light APCs prepares for action in Russia. These vehicles served on all fronts from 1940.

Below: Side view of the SdKfz 250 light armoured half-track personnel carrier, as used in the Western Desert.

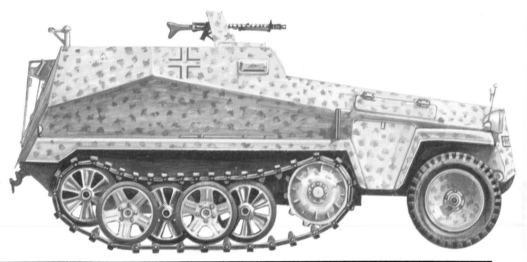

WESPE SELF-PROPELLED HOWITZER

10.5cm *leichte Feldhaubitze* 18/2 *auf FgstPzKpfw*
II *(Sf),* or *SdKfz* **124.**
Crew: 5.
Armament: One 10.5cm *le FH* 18/2 howitzer; one
7.92mm MG 34 machine-gun in hull.
Armour: 0.39in (10mm) minimum; 0.79in (20mm)
maximum.
Dimensions: Length 15ft 10in (4.8m); width 7ft 6in
(2.27m); height 7ft 7in (2.32m).
Weight: 25,728lbs (11,700kg).
Ground pressure: 11.65lb/in² (0.82kg/cm²).
Power to weight ratio: 12.18hp/ton.
Engine: Maybach HL 62 TR six-cylinder water-
cooled inline petrol engine developing 140bhp at
2,600rpm.
Performance: Road speed 25mph (40km/h); cross-
country speed 15mph (24km/h); range 88 miles
(140km); vertical obstacle 1ft 5in (0.42m); trench
5ft 7in (1.7m); fording depth 2ft 8in (0.8m); gradient
30 degrees.
History: In service with the German Army from 1942
to 1945.

This small self-propelled gun was probably the best-
known and most important of the German artillery
vehicles. It was based on the standard *PzKpfw* II chassis,
being built on these when the tank had obviously
become obsolete in its original role. The turrets were
removed and replaced by superstructures built by the
firm of Alkett. This superstructure was a simple open
box, with a vertical slot at the front to accommodate
the gun barrel, tall sloping sides, and an open back and
top. It was placed behind the mid-point of the chassis
so that the driving compartment did not have to be
altered, but this meant that the floor of the fighting
compartment was above the engine, and was very high
above ground level. Despite the height of the superstructure, it only just concealed a man from the
shoulders downwards when he stood up at the front
shield, and as he moved back in the compartment he was
progressively more exposed until the armour came
only to his waist at the rear. This was inevitable in a
vehicle which was not specially designed for the job,
but was in fact a clever and very practical adaptation of
an obsolete tank chassis. The gun was the standard
10.5cm field gun of the German artillery, and was
built by Rheinmetall-Borsig. It was given a generous
elevation of up to 45°, but the traverse was limited
to 17° either side of centre, which was probably
adequate for most shooting, but meant that the driver
had to start up and swing the vehicle when a large
correction was called for. With a five-man crew, space
was cramped in the fighting compartment, and only 32
rounds could be carried for the gun. This meant that the
Wespe (Wasp) had to be accompanied by an am-

*Above: The Wespe
(Wasp) self-propelled
10.5cm howitzer. A
novel feature, inherited
from the basic PzKpfw
II tank, is the vehicle's
quarter-elliptic
suspension.*

*Left: The Wasp ready
for action. The AFV
was an extremely
effective light self-
propelled field
howitzer, introduced
in 1942 and thereafter
seeing action in all
theatres.*

munition limber, or carrier. In many cases this was
another variant of the same chassis, one such carrier
having the same high superstructure with the gun slot
blanked off and the inside racked for ammunition. The
high silhouette of the *Wespe* made it unstable on
cross-country journeys, and some caution was called
for from the commander and driver. It must also have
been difficult to camouflage and conceal, though it
would generally have relied on its armour and mobility
to get it clear of counter-battery fire and similar sources
of trouble. There are no photographs of any sort of
roof covering for bad weather, and the *Wespe* must
have been a miserable vehicle in winter for the crew.
Altogether 683 were built at the special factory set aside
for the conversion. This was in Famo in Poland, and it

continued to convert chassis for one purpose or
another until overrun by the Red Army in 1944. It also
produced 158 of the ammunition carriers on the same
chassis. The name *Wespe* was unofficially given to the
vehicle when it first appeared in 1942, and for some
reason Hitler ordered that it should be dropped in
January 1944, and the German Army had to revert to
the more clumsy title of *SdKfz* 124. Although a conversion from a vehicle intended for other uses, the
Wespe was a reasonable success, and one of the
more numerous of the German SP guns. The suspension was probably overloaded, and the ammunition
stowage was certainly inadequate, but it was a
reliable and well-proved gun platform, and served
well for nearly four years of active war.

NASHORN SELF-PROPELLED ANTI-TANK GUN

8.8cm *PaK* **43/1** *auf PzJg* **III/IV,** or *SdKfz* **164.**
Crew: 4.
Armament: One 8.8cm *PaK* 43/1 L/71 gun.
Armour: 0.39in (10mm) minimum; 1.18in (30mm)
maximum.
Dimensions: Length 27ft 8in (8.44m); width 9ft 8in
(2.95m); height 9ft 7in (2.94m).
Weight: 52,800lbs (23,950kg).
Ground pressure: 12.1lb/in² (0.85kg/cm²)

Power to weight ratio: 12.73hp/ton.
Engine: Maybach HL 120 TRM V-12 water-cooled
inline petrol engine developing 300hp at 3,000rpm.
Performance: Road speed 25mph (40km/h); cross-
country speed 15mph (24km/h); range 125 miles
(200km); vertical obstacle 2ft (0.6m); trench 7ft 6in
(2.3m); gradient 30 degrees.
History: Served with the German Army from 1943
to 1945.

The *Nashorn* (Rhinoceros) was the first SP gun to be
fitted into a specialist chassis made up from a *PzKpfw*
IV hull and suspension with the ubiquitous Maybach
TRM engine. The engine was moved to the front,
enabling a proper fighting compartment to be laid
out at the rear, and lowering the floor level of that
compartment. The engine was now directly behind the
transmission, and made a convenient powerpack alongside the driver. One great difficulty facing the German

FLAKVIERLING SELF-PROPELLED AA VEHICLE

Flakpanzer IV (2cm) *auf FgstPzKpfw* IV, or
Vierlings flak, 2cm.
Crew: 5.
Armament: Four 2cm *Flak* 38 L/55 cannon; one
7.92mm MG 34 machine-gun in hull.
Armour: 0.63in (16mm) minimum; 1.18in (30mm)
maximum.
Dimensions: Length 19ft 5in (5.91m); width 9ft 7in
(2.92m); height 8ft 11in (2.72m).
Weight: 48,501lbs (22,000kg).
Engine: Maybach HL 112 TR V-12 water-cooled
petrol engine developing 272hp at 2,800rpm.
Performance: Road speed 25mph (40km/h); cross-
country speed 12mph (19km/h); range 120 miles
(200km); vertical obstacle 2ft (0.6m); trench 7ft 6in
(2.3cm); gradient 30 degrees.
History: Served German Army from 1943 to 1945.

*Below: The Germans made great
use of anti-aircraft tanks. Here,
the Flakpanzer IV has its four 20mm
cannon ready for action, with
sides folded down.*

From mid-1943 onwards the Germans were uncom-
fortably aware that the air war was going against them,
and the armoured formations began to demand some
mobile AA defence. Hitler called for a *Flakpanzer*
mounting twin 3.7cm AA guns and a number of
PzKpfw IV chassis were diverted from production for
them. Since there were only a few 3.7cm twin mountings, single 3.7cm guns were used and an existing
quadruple 2cm mount added also. Hitler disapproved
of the 2cm guns, but an order for 150 was placed just
the same and deliveries began in late 1943. For this
vehicle, and others built on the same chassis, the hull
was a standard *PzKpfw* IV with a flat platform in place
of the turret. On this platform was the gun mounting,
with all-round traverse and a shield which moved with
the barrels. As a result the vehicle was very high and
vulnerable to ground attack. To give the gun crew some
protection when not in action there were three
rectangular plates of 0.39in (10mm) armour along the
front and sides of the hull, standing up around the gun.
Before the guns could engage enemy aircraft, or any
other target, these screens had to be lowered over the
sides, and they were hinged along their bottom edges
to allow this. The crew than had no more protection
than their small shield offered. The tactical value of
such an arrangement was naturally questionable, but
it gave the armoured formations some measure of AA
defence, and the combined rate of fire of 3,000 rounds
per minute was formidable enough. Some 3,600 rounds
of 2cm ammunition were carried, which was enough
for several engagements. Later versions of the *Flak-
vierling* had a more sophisticated turret of 0.63in
(16mm) armour, giving all round protection when in
action, but even so their AA value was doubtful since
their traverse rate was limited and the fire-control
arrangements were crude. Each *Panzer* battalion had
three or four AA vehicles in the HQ company, and they
were often used against unarmoured ground targets.

*Above: Flakviering with side armour folded
down to provide a platform for the gun crew,
drawing shows how sides fold up for crew
protection.*

troops on the Eastern Front in 1942 was the movement
of the large 8.8cm *PaK* 43/1 anti-tank gun. On a towed
mounting this was both heavy and awkward, yet it was
a most important part of the defensive equipment of
the army, and quite large numbers of men and vehicles
were often needed to move one gun in or out of
position. This immediately limited its use and it
became imperative to put it onto an SP chassis. The
PzKpfw III/IV chassis was the one selected, but it
was already quite heavy for its tracks, and even with
the extra-wide Eastern Front links the ground pressure
would not allow more than token armour to be fitted
once the *PaK* 43 gun was installed. In any case, armour
plate was very short in Germany at that time, and most
of the *Nashorn* production had to be given unhardened
plate which made the vehicles yet more vulnerable.
A large fighting compartment was built behind the
centreline of the hull, and the 8.8cm gun mounted on
the floor. The barrel then came 7ft 4in (2.24m) above
the ground, which was high enough, and at least 2ft
(0.6m) more than when the gun was on its cruciform
ground mount. In fact the greatest drawback to the
Nashorn was its height, which necessitated large
vulnerable side plates on the fighting compartment,
and these had to be nearly vertical to allow enough
room inside, though the front plate was quite well
sloped. Another recognition feature of the *Gw* III/IV
chassis was the engine inlet louvres. These were let into
the side armour on either side of the fighting compart-

ment, and roughly half way along. They were just
above the trackguards, and intruded into the fighting

compartment to a small extent to allow the trunking to
carry the air forward. The *Nashorn* did its job in
carrying the 8.8cm gun well enough, but it was always
too vulnerable for a direct-fire gun. Some 473 were
made during 1944.

*Right: The Nashorn
(Rhinoceros) was one
of the most powerful
German self-propelled
anti-tank guns of the
war. Based on the
PzKpfw IV chassis, it
mounted an 88mm gun.*

*Left: The Nashorn entered service with the
German Army in 1943 and was based on a
modified PzKpfw III/IV chassis and armed
with the 88mm gun. The main drawback of this
vehicle was its armour and height which
made it difficult to conceal in the field.*

ELEFANT SELF-PROPELLED TANK DESTROYER

Panzerjäger Tiger (P), or *SdKfz* 184.
Crew: 6.
Armament: One 8.8cm *PaK* 43/2 L/71 gun.
Armour: 1.18in (30mm) minimum; 7.9in (200mm) maximum.
Dimensions: Length 22ft 4in (6.8m); width 11ft 1in (3.38m); height 9ft 10in (3m).
Weight: 149,913lbs (68,000kg).
Ground pressure: 17.6lb/in² (1.24kg/cm²).
Power to weight ratio: 9.56hp/ton.
Engines: Two Maybach HL 120 TR V-12 water-cooled inline petrol engines each developing 320bhp at 3,000rpm.
Performance: Road speed: 12.5mph (20km/h); cross-country speed 11mph (17km/h); range 94 miles (150km); vertical obstacle 2ft 7in (0.78m); trench 10ft 6in (3.2m); fording depth 4ft (1.22m); gradient 22 degrees.
History: In service with the German Army between 1943 and 1944.

One of the wasteful aspects of the German enthusiasm for competing designs was that the unsuccessful builder invariably had a number of completed vehicles which were not wanted. When Porsche lost the contract for the Tiger I, more than 90 chassis were already in various stages of completion. So as not to waste them, it was decided to use these for a large and powerful SP gun for tank hunting. Only two actual tanks had been built, and the remaining hulls were modified to suit the new concept. The chosen gun was the L/71 8.8cm, and it was too long to go above the tank's central fighting compartment, so a major redesign was undertaken. The two engines were moved forward to the middle of the hull, the fighting compartment was put at the back, and the electric transmission behind that. A large box-like superstructure was built over the rear half of the hull with as much slope to the armour as was possible, and the gun mounted in that. Even so it overhung the front by 4ft (1.22m). The hull was shallow and flat on top, very similar to that of the Henschel Tiger, and with the same distinctive 'snout' to the front plates. The superstructure was quite large and roomy, with a circular cupola at the right front for the commander. Crew access was through a circular hatch in the rear plate, and there were very few other holes in the armour. All joints were overlapped, and all were welded. The suspension was by three pairs of road wheels on each side, mounted on three torsion bars. The wheels were steel-rimmed and resilient to give some initial softness. There were no return rollers, and the front idler was mounted higher than the other wheels to help in obstacle climbing. The two Maybach engines were coupled to a Siemens Schuckert electric generator, and the rear sprockets were each driven by an electric motor. The steering had to be assisted by hydro-pneumatic motors, but there was no need for gear-changing which eased the driver's work. The enormous gun, with 50 rounds gave *Elefant* the ability to knock out most allied tanks and vehicles at a far greater range than they could effectively fire back but an astonishing omission was to fit no other gun at all, not even one machine-gun for local defence. In later models this was changed, and the wireless operator who sat beside the driver was given a hull gun in a ball mounting, but even so it had a limited traverse and little flexibility. The phenomenal thickness of armour rendered the *Elefant* invulnerable to any Allied attack from the front, though this was only achieved at the expense of great weight and ground pressure, and bogging was one of the great dangers with the vehicle. It was soon found that careful reconnaissance was essential before any move was made either cross-country or by road. Great things were expected of this highly specialised tank destroyer and two special battalions were rushed to Russia in time for the Battle of Kursk. Here they led the attack and broke through the Soviet defences, only to be surrounded in the rear areas and almost wiped out. When more prudently used as mobile pillboxes, they were far more successful, and made a good reputation for themselves on other Russian battlefronts and also in Italy.

Far left and left: Rear and front views of the Ferdinand/Elefant tank-destroyer. The rear view shows the plate by which the gun was inserted or removed. As these illustrations show, the vehicle had exceptionally thick armour and was thus very difficult to knock out. Its novel Porsche suspension allowed the designers to keep its height down to 3m, presenting a difficult target. It weighed no less than 68,000kg.

Right: The Ferdinand (later called the Elefant) self-propelled 88mm anti-tank gun. Based on a rejected Porsche design for the Tiger I, the Ferdinand tank-destroyer was placed in production and used on the Russian Front in 1943-44. Fifty rounds were carried for the PaK 43/2 L/71 gun.

Right: Side view of the Ferdinand/Elefant. The device at the front of the hull, attached to the 88mm gun, was to hold the gun in place when travelling cross-country—a necessity with long-barrelled guns.

Left: Enlarged side view of the Ferdinand/ Elefant stresses the massive size of the vehicle. The bolts gave added strength to the armour. Slow and unwieldy, it served best as a mobile pillbox.

Below: Top view of the Ferdinand/Elefant. The air-intake grilles, hatches and vision devices are features of particular interest. Lifting eyes can be seen at both front and rear.

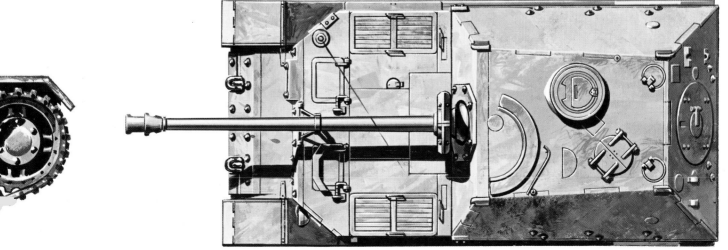

PzKpfw VI TIGER I HEAVY BATTLE TANK

***PzKfpw* VI Tiger I, or *SdKfz* 181.**
Crew: 5.
Armament: One 8.8cm *KwK* 36 L/56 gun; one 7.92 mm MG 34 machine-gun co-axial with main armament; one 7.92mm MG 34 machine-gun in hull.
Armour: 1.02in (26mm) minimum; 4.33in (110mm) maximum.
Dimensions: Length 27ft (8.25m); width 12ft 3in (3.73m); height 9ft 4in (2.85m).
Weight: 121,253lbs (55,000kg).
Ground pressure: 14.8lb/in² (1.04kg/cm²).
Power to weight ratio: 12.93hp/ton.
Engine: Maybach HL 230 P 45 V-12 water-cooled inline petrol engine developing 700bhp at 3,000rpm.
Performance: Road speed 24mph (38km/h); cross-country speed 12mph (20km/h); range 62 miles (100km); vertical obstacle 2ft 7in (0.8m); trench 5ft 11in (1.8m); fording depth 4ft (1.2m); gradient 35 degrees.
History: In service with the German Army from 1942 to 1945. (Note: Data relate to the Tiger I *Ausf* E.)

Despite the decision to mass produce the *PzKpfw* III and IV, and the fair certainty at the time that these two models would be adequate for the expected battles of the future, the German general staff also called for an even heavier tank in 1937. This was to be of 29.53 tons (30,000kg) or more and was to be a heavy 'break-through' tank to lead the armoured assaults. The design lapsed until 1941, by when it was realised that the *PzKpfw* IIIs and IVs had been less successful than had been expected against the heavily armoured French and British tanks in 1940. This view was fully endorsed when the Soviet T-34s and KV-Is were met later in 1941, and resulted in a specification for a heavy tank capable of mounting the highly successful 8.8cm high-velocity gun in a turret with full traverse and carrying sufficient armour to defeat all present and future anti-tank weapons. Two firms submitted prototypes, using some of the developments from the 1937 ideas. These were Porsche and Henschel. The turret was common to both and came from Krupp. The Porsche design was unconventional and was not accepted, although it became a self-propelled gun. The Henschel design was relatively conventional, was obviously easier to make, and was thus accepted. This was given the designation *PzKpfw* VI and the name Tiger. Production began slowly in August 1942. At the time of its introduction, and for some time afterwards, the Tiger was the most powerful tank in the

world. The 8.8cm gun, which had 92 rounds of ammunition, was enormously formidable, and the armour ensured that any frontal shot could not penetrate. So effective was it that the Allies had to evolve special tactics to cope with it, though there were occasions when the tank was used so ineffectively that it never realised its potential. Its appearance was a shock to the Allies, however, and it rapidly gained a reputation for being the greatest menace on the battlefield. The Tiger was intended to be deployed in special battalions of 30 vehicles under the control of an army or corps headquarters. In general this was done, though some armoured divisions were given their own Tiger battalions, particularly those of the *Waffen*-SS.

Hitler had taken a personal interest in the Tiger, and he pressed for its use at the earliest opportunity. They were thrown into battle near Leningrad in the late summer of 1942, well spread out and in small numbers on poor ground. The result was a fiasco, as was the Kursk battle next year. But when used in ambush, where their gun could inflict the most damage, and where the heavy armour allowed a phased withdrawal, the Tiger was supreme. Indeed, in 1944 one solitary Tiger held up an entire division in France, and knocked out 25 Allied tanks before being stalked and destroyed. The hull of the Tiger was a comparatively simple welded unit with a one-piece superstructure welded on top. The armour was not well sloped, but was

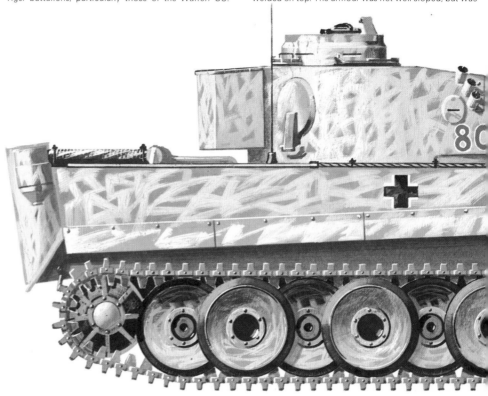

thick. At the front it was 3.94in (100mm), around the sides 3.15in (80mm) and 1.02in (26mm) on the decks. To assist production all shapes were kept simple, and a long box-like side pannier ran along the top of the tracks. The turret was also simple, and the sides were almost upright. The mantlet was very heavy, with 4.33in (110mm) of armour, and carried the long and heavy gun. The turret traverse was very low-geared and driven by a hydraulic motor which took its power from the gearbox. Thus when the main engine was stopped, the turret had to be traversed by hand. The engine was changed in late 1943 to one of slightly greater power, but in general it was reliable and powerful enough. The difficulty was that the tank's range was always too limited for operations, and top speed was low because of the need to gear down the transmission. The weight was too great for the usual German clutch and brake steering and Henschel adapted the British Merritt-Brown regenerative unit and coupled it to a pre-selector Maybach gearbox with eight forward speeds.

The result was a set of controls which were very light for the driver, but by no means easy to maintain or repair. The suspension was formed by overlapping road wheels, and was the first German tank to carry this distinctive feature, which gave a soft and stable ride. There were no less than eight torsion-bars on each side, and the floor was tightly packed with them. The difficulty with the overlapping wheels was that in the Russian winter nights they froze together and jammed the tracks, and the Russians often timed their attacks for dawn, when they could be sure of the Tigers being immobilised. The tracks were too wide for rail transport, and narrower ones were fitted for normal road and railway transport, when the outer set of road wheels were also removed. This changing of tracks was tedious and expensive in tracks, and restricted mobility to some extent. The crew were housed in four compartments in the hull, the driver and hull gunner being separated in front, with the gearbox between them. The turret was fairly normal,

though there was little room to spare when 92 rounds of 8.8cm ammunition were fully stowed. The gun was balanced by a heavy spring in a tube on the left of the turret. The 8.8cm shell could penetrate 4.4in (112mm) of armour at 492 yards (450m), which was more than enough for the armoured vehicles of the day. It was much feared by the crews of the comparatively vulnerable Shermans, the main Allied tank. The Tiger was reasonably compact, but it was very heavy. It could not cross German bridges, and the first 400 models were capable of wading through deep rivers when they came to them. The necessity of fitting and re-fitting special tracks for rail travel was tedious, and the road wheels gave trouble from overloading. More nimble Allied tanks found that they could outmanoeuvre the Tiger and attack it from the rear, and these, together with the other limitations, caused it to be phased out in 1944. By August of that year 1,300 had been made, not many in view of their reputation and effect on Allied morale.

Left, above and below: Five views of a PzKpfw VI Tiger (Model H) of the 1st SS Panzer Division 'Leibstandarte Adolf Hitler'. The camouflage scheme is a pattern used on the Russian Front. The bands around the barrel indicate 'kills'.

A characteristic feature of the Tiger tank, later applied to other German tanks, was the use of overlapping bogie wheels. Note the huge exhaust mufflers, multi-barrel smoke projectors, towing cable and spare tracks.

Left: A Tiger (Model E) captured in Tunisia. Originally developed to combat new Soviet armour on the East Front, the Tiger was also supplied to the Afrika Korps and won great fame in the desert battles. Later, the tank was deployed against the Allies in Europe. The hard-hitting 88mm gun was once an AA gun.

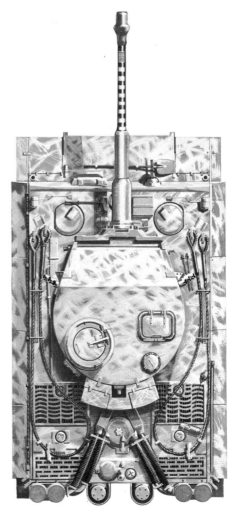

PzKpfw V PANTHER BATTLE TANK

Panzerkampfwagen V, or *SdKfz* 171.
Crew: 5.
Armament: On 7.5cm *KwK* 42 L/70 gun; two 7.92mm MG 34 machine-guns.
Armour: 0.6in (20mm) minimum; 4.72in (120mm) maximum.
Dimensions: Length 22ft 6in (6.68m); width 10ft 10in (3.3m); height 9ft 8in (2.95m). (Dimensional data relate to the *Ausf G.*)
Weight: 98,766lbs (44,800kg).
Ground pressure: 12.5lb/in² (0.88kg/cm²).
Power to weight ratio: 15.9hp/ton.
Engine: Maybach HL 230 P 30 V-12 water-cooled petrol engine developing 700bhp at 3,000rpm.
Performance: Road speed 29mph (46km/h); cross-country speed 15mph (24km/h); range 110 miles (177km); vertical obstacle 3ft (0.9m); trench 6ft 3in (1.9m); fording depth 4ft 7in (1.4m); gradient 35 degrees.
History: In service with the German Army from 1943 to 1945. Also used by the Soviet Union and France after the war.

Until the invasion of Soviet Russia, the *PzKpfw* IV had been the heaviest tank in the German Army, and had proved quite adequate. In early October 1941 the new Soviet T-34 appeared and proved the *PzKpfw* IV to be completely out of date. The sloped armour, speed and manoeuvrability of the T-34 brought about a profound change of heart on the part of the Germans, and a new requirement was hurriedly drawn up. At first, to save time, it was even considered that the T-34 should be copied directly, but national pride forbade this approach and the specification issued in January 1942 merely incorporated all the T-34 features. Designs were submitted in April 1942, and the first trial models appeared in September, the MAN design being chosen for production. There were the usual multitude of

modifications called for as a result of the prototype's performance, and spurred on by Hitler himself, MAN brought out the first production tank in January 1943, but Daimler-Benz had to be brought in to help. From then on production forged ahead, but never reached the ambitious target of 600 vehicles a month set by Hitler. There were many difficulties. The engine and transmission were overstressed to cope with the increase in weight, cooling was inadequate, engines caught fire, and the wheel rims gave trouble. When the Panther first went into action at Kursk in July 1943, it was at Hitler's insistence, and it was a failure. Most broke down on the journey from the railhead, and few survived the first day. All that were salvaged had to be sent back to the factory to be rebuilt. Later models corrected the faults, and the Panther soon became a fine tank which was superior to the T-34/76 and very popular with its crews. The hull was fairly conventional in the German fashion, with a large one-piece glacis plate in which were originally two holes, one for the gunner, and one for the driver. The G model had only the gun hole, the driver using a periscope. The turret was well sloped, although rather cramped inside, but the commander was given a good cupola. The mantlet was massive, with tiny holes for the machine-gun and the gunner's binocular sight. From the front the protection was excellent. The suspension was by inter-leaved bogies sprung on torsion bars and it gave the Panther the best arrangement of any German tank of the war. The trouble was that the bogies could freeze up when clogged with snow in Russian winters,

and so immobilise the vehicle. Maintenance was also difficult since the outer wheels had to be removed to allow access to the inner ones. Steering was by hydraulically operated disc brakes and epicyclic gears to each track, which allowed the tracks to be stopped separately when required without loss of power. It was an adaption of the Merritt-Brown system, but rather more complicated in design. The long 75mm gun (with 79 rounds) could penetrate 4.72in (120mm) of sloped plate at 1,094 yards (1000m) and this, together with the protection of the thick frontal armour, meant that the Panther could stand off from Allied tanks and knock them out without being harmed itself. The US Army reckoned that it took five Shermans to knock out one Panther and over 5,000 Panthers had been built by the end of the war. After 1943 the Germans needed numbers of tanks rather than improved designs, and the Panther was simplified to ease production. The hull sides were sloped more, the mantlet was thickened to prevent shot being deflected into the decking, and the gearbox was improved to cope with the weight problem. In 1944 and 1945 over 3,900 Panthers were built, more than any other German tank during that time. Despite its complexity and high manufacturing cost, the Panther was a successful design and many consider it to have been one of the best tanks produced during the war. Towards the end of the war its petrol engine and complications were distinct disadvantages, but it was a powerful supplement to the *PzKpfw* IVs of the armoured formations, and it was really only defeated by the overwhelming Allied air strength.

Right and below: Side, front and rear views of the PzKpfw V Panther, one of the best tanks of World War II. Designed around the general concept of the Russian T-34, it incorporated certain very advanced features. Among those apparent here are its sloping armour, inter-leaved suspension and low turret.

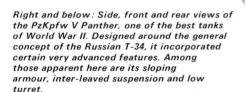

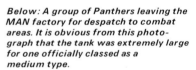

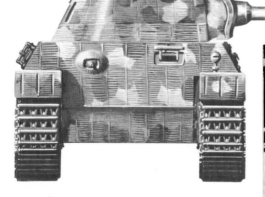

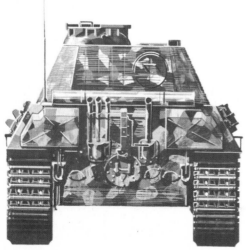

Below: A group of Panthers leaving the MAN factory for despatch to combat areas. It is obvious from this photograph that the tank was extremely large for one officially classed as a medium type.

HUMMEL SELF-PROPELLED HOWITZER

15cm *Panzerfeldhaubitze* 18M *auf Gw* III/IV, or *SdKfz* 165.
Crew: 6 (including 4 gun crew).
Armament: One 15cm *Pz FH* 18/1 howitzer.
Armour: 0.39in (10mm) minimum; 0.79in (20mm) maximum.
Dimensions: Length 19ft (5.8m); width 9ft 6in (2.92m); height 9ft 2in (2.81m).
Weight: 51,808lbs (23,500kg).
Ground pressure: 10.8lb/in² (0.76kg/cm²).
Power to weight ratio: 13hp/ton.
Engine: Maybach HL 120 TRM V-12 water-cooled petrol engine developing 300bhp at 3,000rpm.
Performance: Road speed 25mph (40km/h); range 120 miles (180km); vertical obstacle 2ft (0.6m); trench 7ft 6in (2.29m); fording depth 2ft 8in (0.8m); gradient 27 degrees.
History: In service with the German Army from 1943 to 1945.

Below: This side view clearly shows the external features of the Hummel SPG.

Bottom: The crew of a Hummel SPG prepare to open fire on the Russian Front, 1944.

The final development of the heavy tank howitzer was the 15cm gun on the *PzKpfw* III/IV chassis, developed by Alkett. As with the *Nashorn*, this chassis had the engine moved to the front so that the fighting compartment could be lowered. The mean height of the gun barrel was reduced to 2.3m (7ft 6in) above ground level, which for a makeshift SP gun was very good. This powerful weapon was the most successful, and in all 666 were built for service in the tank battalions of the *Panzer* divisions. The gun was well able to take on the heaviest and most formidable target which presented itself, and the vehicle was in great demand as a support weapon. The difficulty was that there were not enough to go round, and only the favoured battalions were able to get them. The prototypes had a muzzle brake to the gun, but production versions dispensed with it, probably because it involved extra manufacturing effort and the use of high grade casting steel. The amount of ammunition that could be carried was always a matter of concern, and in this model only 18 rounds could be stowed inside the fighting compartment. There was therefore always a need for additional armoured vehicles to bring up ammunition and in most cases these were based on a similar chassis and superstructure without the gun. Manufacturing records show that the ratio of these ammunition carriers to SP guns was roughly 1:4, which seems low, but perhaps no more chassis could be spared. The *Hummel* never quite fitted in to the general plan for an assault gun; it was neither one thing, nor completely the other. As a general support gun it needed to be in an artillery unit with all the sophisticated fire-control backing available there. In an armoured unit it needed none of this, but became another direct-fire gun used on targets which were in sight of the gunner. Whilst excellent for this latter purpose, it was really a waste of a good and powerful gun to use it so. However, Russia in 1943 was a place where fire-power counted, and the *Hummel* provided it. The name is the German word for Bumblebee, and one might think it harmless enough; but Hitler saw fit to order that it should cease to be known as such, and there is in existence a German Army order of 27 February 1944 forbidding the use of the name *Hummel* from then on.

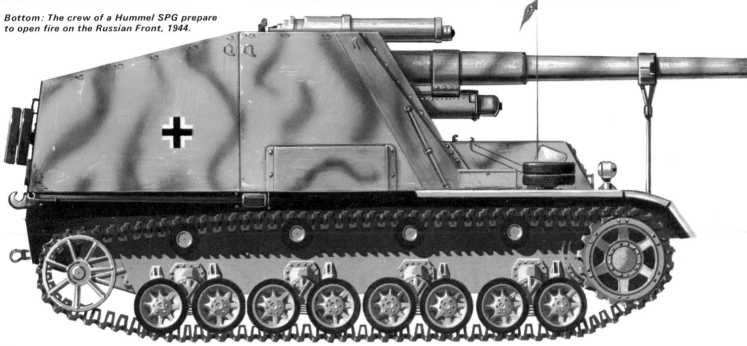

PzKpfw VI TIGER II HEAVY BATTLE TANK

PzKpfw VI Tiger II, or *SdKfz* 182.
Crew: 5.
Armament: One 8.8cm *KwK* 43 L/71 gun; two 7.92mm MG34 machine-guns.
Armour: 1.57in (40mm) minimum; 7.28in (185mm) maximum.
Dimensions: Length 23ft 9in (7.25m); width 12ft 3in (4.72m); height 10ft 1in (3.27m).
Weight: 153,000lbs (69,400kg).
Ground pressure: 15.2lb/in² (1.07kg/cm²).
Power to weight ratio: 8.78hp/ton.
Engine: Maybach HL 230 P 30 V-12 water-cooled inline petrol engine developing 600bhp at 3,000rpm.
Performance: Road speed 24mph (38km/h); cross-country speed 11mph (17km/h); range 68 miles (110km); vertical obstacle 2ft 9in (0.85m); trench

8ft 2in (2.5m); fording depth 5ft 3in (1.6m); gradient 35 degrees.
History: In service with the German Army from 1944 to 1945.

The Tiger I had hardly entered service before the German general staff requested a bigger and better successor, superior in armour and hitting power to anything that the Soviet Army was likely to produce. Once again Porsche and Henschel were asked for designs which were to incorporate the latest sloped armour and the longer 71-calibre 8.8cm gun. Porsche updated its Tiger I design and this time was so sure of an order that it started work on the turret and actually put casting in hand. Unfortunately the Porsche ideas of electric transmission were once more rejected,

supplies of copper being too small, and the contract went to Henschel for the second time. However, 50 Porsche turrets were made and fitted to the first models. Henschel then fitted its own turret, which was simpler and had better protection. Another requirement of the specification was to liaise with MAN in order to standardise as many parts as possible with the

Below: A column of Tiger IIs moving up on the Russian front during the latter part of World War II. The 'King Tigers' were deployed in the heavy tank battalions of the German Army, which were often broken up into units of five tanks or less to try to stem the advance of numerically superior Allied tanks.

JAGDTIGER TANK DESTROYER

12.8cm *PJK* 80 *auf Panzerjäger* Tiger *ausf* B, or *SdKfz* 186.
Crew: 6.
Armament: One 12.8cm *PaK* 44 L/55 gun; one 7.92mm MG 34 or MG 42 machine-gun.
Armour: 1.18in (30mm) minimum; 9.84in (250mm) maximum.
Dimensions: Length 25ft 7in (7.8m); width 12ft 3in (4.72m); height 9ft 3in (2.83m).
Weight: 158,070lbs (71,700kg).
Ground pressure: 15.2lb/in² (1.07kg/cm²).
Power to weight ratio: 9.92hp/ton.
Engine: Maybach HL 230 P 30 V-12 water-cooled petrol engine developing 700bhp at 3,000rpm.
Performance: Road speed 24mph (38km/h); cross-country speed 11mph (17km/h); range 68 miles (110km); vertical obstacle 2ft 9in (0.85m); trench 8ft 2in (2.5m); fording depth 5ft 11in (1.8m); gradient 35 degrees.

History: In service with the German Army from 1943 to 1945.

Following the normal German SP gun practice of taking the current heavy tank and giving it the next size of gun up, when the Tiger II tank appeared it was immediately considered as a possible SP gun. Since the tank mounted the 8.8cm gun, the next size up was 12.8cm, a huge gun to put on a vehicle. It was not such a high velocity weapon as the 8.8cm, but it fired an armour-piercing shell weighing no less than 62.4lbs (28.3kg) with a greater armour penetration at long range. This enormous gun made the *Jagdtiger* the most powerful German vehicle of the war, or rather the most powerful one to be introduced into service in useful numbers. Some 38 rounds of 12.8cm and 2,925 rounds of 7.92mm ammunition were carried. The chassis was almost the same as that of the Tiger II, except that it was lengthened by 9.84in (250mm). On it was mounted a large central superstructure whose

armour was sloped as best it could be within the limitations of the space needed to house and service the gun. Because of the barrel overhang it was not possible to extend the front plate upwards as in the Panther derivatives, and a separate front plate had to be fitted a few feet back along the hull top. This front plate was pierced for the gun mounting, and to protect the crew it was made of armour of the extraordinary thickness of 9.84in (250mm), the heaviest of the war. The first prototype was shown in late 1943 and immediately 150 were ordered. In the event no more than 70 were ever completed, and it seems likely that only 48 of these were in service with units when the war ended. Quite apart from the manufacturing difficulties of building vehicles of this size, and rolling armour plate of the thickness required, the great weight of the *Jagdtiger* counted against it from the beginning. The engine was always overstressed, as was the transmission. It was impossible to operate the vehicle on anything but the strongest roads and crossing bridges

Panther II, which never appeared, and the subsequent delays meant that production did not get under way until December 1943. The Tiger II, known to its own side as the *Königstiger* and to the Allies as the Royal Tiger, was a massive and formidable vehicle. It was intended to dominate the battlefield, and that it could do, providing that its crew used it sensibly. It was the heaviest, best protected and most powerfully armed tank to go into production during World War II, and its armour and gun would do justice to a main battle tank today. The price paid for all this superiority was size, weight and low performance. Manoeuvrability, ground pressure and that subtle thing 'agility' all suffered, and inevitably the reliability of the over-stressed engine and transmission decreased. None of this mattered in a defensive battle, but it counted heavily

in an offensive, and when tried in the Ardennes the Tiger II was not impressive. Several had to be destroyed on the Eastern Front when they could not be withdrawn, though that sometimes happened through fuel short-ages as much as from breakdowns. The hull was welded, as was that of the Tiger I, but the armour was better sloped, using the experience of the T-34. Hull layout was similar to that of the Panther, and the large turret was roomy although the gun came right back to the rear wall and made a complete partition longi-tudinally. Some 78 rounds of ammunition were stowed round the turret sides and floor and there were plenty of racks and shelves for the minor equipment. The com-mander's cupola allowed an excellent view, though he usually chose to have his head out of the top. The long and powerful 8.8cm gun could outrange and out-shoot the main armament of nearly all Allied tanks, and this allowed the Tiger II to stand off and engage targets as it chose. Barrel wear was a difficulty with this high-velocity gun, and the later models had a two-piece barrel which allowed the faster-wearing

part to be changed easily. Only one model was built, and altogether no more than 485 examples were completed. Production never suffered despite the heaviest Allied bombing, and Henschel always had at least 60 vehicles in construction on its shop floors at any one time. At the peak it was taking only 14 days to complete a Tiger II. Severe fuel shortages forced the factory to use bottled gas for testing, though petrol was supplied for operations. The Tiger II was introduced into service in the autumn of 1944, on the same distribution as the Tiger I, and again in small units of four or five. Its enormous size and weight made it a ponderous vehicle, often difficult to conceal; in a fast moving battle it was quickly left behind, and this fate did occur to several in Russia. But when used properly it was enormously effective and could engage many times its own numbers of enemy, and knock them all out without damage to itself. However, the Tiger II was the last sensible word in the saga of heavy German tanks. After that the trail led to the monstrosi-ties of the *Maus*, where reason had gone mad.

Right: The PzKpfw VI Tiger II ('King Tiger') with the Porsche turret —one of the first 50 production models. It proved a good heavy tank, especially suited to operating in a defensive role.

Below: The PzKpfw VI Tiger II with the more usual Henschel turret, a simpler and better-protected mounting for the heavy tank's long 88mm KwK 43 L/71 main armament.

and rivers was a nightmare. Although on paper the performance was the same as the Tiger II, in fact the fuel consumption and range were much worse. For Germany, with critically short supplies of all fuel, such excesses were hard to justify. The *Jagdtigers* were grouped into small support units and were intended to be deployed as the battle demanded, in much the same way as the Tiger II. Their lack of mobility was found to be a severe drawback, and their main use came in the final retreat into Germany, and the delaying actions fought along the Western Front.

Right: A Panzerjäger Tiger ausf B with a 128mm PaK 44 gun. Out of an order for 150, only 70 were completed by the war's end, and fewer still entered combat. Because of Allied bombing of the 128mm PaK 44's manufacturing facilities, several of these tank-destroyers had to be armed with the 88mm PaK 43/3 gun.

JAGDPANTHER TANK DESTROYER

Jaqdpanzer P V, or *SdKfz* **173**
Crew: 5.
Armament: One 8.8cm *PaK* 43/3 L/71 gun; one 7.92 m MG 34 machine-gun in hull.
Armour: 0.59in (15mm) minimum; 3.15in (80mm) maximum.
Dimensions: Length 23ft 7in (7.2m); width 10ft 10in (3.27m); height 8ft 11in (2.72m).
Weight: 100,309lbs (45,500kg).
Ground pressure: 12.79lb/in² (0.9kg/cm²).
Power to weight ratio: 15.63hp/ton.
Engine: Maybach HL 230 P 30 V-12 water-cooled petrol engine developing 700bhp at 3,000rpm.
Performance: Road speed 28.5mph (46km/h); cross-country speed 15mph (24km/h); range 100 miles (160km); vertical obstacle 3ft (0.91m); trench 8ft (2.45m); fording depth 5ft (1.55m); gradient 35 degrees.
History: In service with the German Army from 1944 to 1945.

Attempts to mount the excellent long-barrelled 8.8cm L/71 gun on a mobile chassis had not been very successful. The *Elefant* was too large and the *PzKpfw* IV too light and too lightly armoured. The Panther chassis was chosen as the best one for development, and the basic chassis, powertrain and lower hull were taken intact and a new superstructure added. The first model was shown to Hitler on 20 October 1943 and gained his immediate approval. On the chassis

was fitted a well shaped superstructure with the large gun running most of the way through the fighting compartment. It projected through the front plate with a pot mantlet protecting the opening. Traverse was limited to 11° either side of centre, and elevation restricted to 14°. Luckily the Panther's regenerative steering allowed the hull to be swung easily and lined up accurately, so that the limited traverse was less important than it might have been. In any case it was intended that in action the well-protected front should at all times be facing the enemy, and when so used the *Jagdpanther* was extremely effective. To simplify production the front glacis plate of the Panther was extended up to the top of the super-structure and this allowed the original hull to be used with minimum alteration. The original sides of the Panther were too sloped to allow enough room in the fighting compartment of the SP gun, so the plates were changed to a different angle, and the same angle incorporated in the Panther *Ausf* G, thereby offering better protection to the tank also. To take the extra weight of the vehicle a later modification of gearbox, the AK7-400, was fitted and this too was later put into the tank for the same reason. The first deliveries were made in February 1944, and although it was intended to build 150 a month, no more than 382 were made in all, by MIAG and MNH. As deliveries progressed minor alterations were made to the design. The mantlet changed at least three times, and all but the first models were given the two-piece 8.8cm gun

barrel which allowed the quicker-wearing section of the bore to be changed easily. Some 60 rounds of 8.8cm and 600 rounds of 7.92mm ammunition were carried. The vehicles were issued to special units whose sole job was tank destroying, and which were kept under command of the highest formation in the battle, usually army. A *Jagdpanther* battalion was intended to have 30 vehicles on strength, but many had to be content with less due to delivery difficulties. It was as well for the Allied armies that no more than 382 *Jagdpanthers* were ever delivered, for it was probably the best tank destroyer in use by any army during World War II, and certainly the best produced in Germany. It was fast, well armed and well armoured. On the battlefield it was extremely effective and given a wide berth whenever possible. They were popular with their crews, which led to high morale among them and a more aggressive use than might have been the case with less powerful weapons. Their weak point was the complicated suspension, and well-placed shots among the road wheels could often bring the vehicle to a halt. It was then an easy target for an Allied tank, which could approach from a flank without danger.

Below: Side view of a Jagdpanther, showing the fine lines of this AFV. Its general design— like that of the Panther tank, on which chassis it was based—was much influenced by Russian armoured development.

HETZER TANK DESTROYER

7.5cm *PaK* **39 L/48** *auf Panzerjäger* **38** *(t),* or *SdKfz* **138/2.**
Crew: 4.
Armament: One 7.5cm *PaK* 39 L/48 gun; one 7.92mm MG 34 machine-gun.
Armour: 0.31in (8mm) minimum; 2.36in (60mm) maximum.
Dimensions: Length 15ft 7in (5.1m); width 7ft 2in (2.36m); height 6ft 5in (2.1m).
Weight: 38,380lbs (17,400kg).
Ground pressure: 16lb/in² (1.13kg/cm²).
Power to weight ratio: 8.76hp/ton.
Engine: Praga six-cylinder water-cooled inline petrol engine developing 150hp at 2,600rpm.
Performance: Road speed 26mph (42km/h); range 130 miles (217km); vertical obstacle 2ft 1in (0.7m); trench 4ft 3in (1.4m); gradient 25 degrees.

History: In service with the German Army from 1944 to 1945. Used between 1945 and 1970 by the Swiss Army.

When the Germans occupied Czechoslovakia in 1938 they took over both the relatively large quantity of armoured fighting vehicles then in service with the Czechoslovakian Army and the Czech manufacturing facilities. One of the most impressive vehicles in use with the Czech Army at that time was the Skoda TNHP light tank, which was adopted in quantity by the German Army as the *PzKpfw* 38(*t*) (38 for the year of adoption, and (*t*) for the German equivalent of

'Czech'). This tank, together with its contemporary, the *PzKpfw* 35(*t*) formed a substantial proportion of the armoured forces used by the Germans to attack France and the Low Countries. By 1943 the *PzKpfw* 38(*t*) tank was approaching obsolescence, but its basic chassis was still a remarkable piece of engineering. For this reason, the Germans decided to utilise the chassis as the basis for a new series of light armoured vehicles. The only one of these actually to be completed and adopted by the German Army was the *Hetzer* light self-propelled 7.5cm anti-tank gun, although numerous makeshift conversions had been carried out by this time. In 1943 the basic tank chassis

Right: Side view of a Hetzer tank-destroyer based on the chassis of the PzKpfw 38(t)— originally the Czech LT-38 light tank. The Hetzer was to have been the basis of the German 1945 light tank and SP programme. It remained in service with the Czech and Swiss armies long after World War II.

Right and below: The side view of the Jagdpanther clearly shows its main external features. The Jagdpanther shown in the photograph below is coated with 'Zimmerit' anti-magnetic-mine paste, which was often applied to German AFVs in the closing stages of World War II. About 382 Jagdpanthers entered service.

was widened to accommodate the more powerful 7.5cm gun. This followed a request by General Heinz Guderian for a light tank destroyer. By May 1944 the first batch of these vehicles had been delivered to units of the German Army, and by the end of the war a total of 1,577 had been produced. The parent, controlling firm was BMM of Prague, while Skoda continued to produce the automotive components. The *Hetzer* was a very well-designed vehicle, it had a low and compact silhouette and the well-sloped armour provided good protection. The 7.5cm gun was placed in a limited-traverse mounting at the front of the hull. After the war the *Hetzer* continued to be used by the Czechoslovakian Army and numbers were produced after the war for the Swiss Army, which adopted it as the *PzJg* G13. The Swiss vehicles had new 160hp engines.

Above right: Camouflage scheme and markings of the Hetzer light self-propelled 75mm anti-tank gun, as used in Northern Europe in 1944-45. The 7.92mm machine-gun mounted in a shield was a standard feature of German SPGs of this period. Note especially the hooded headlamp.

Right: Front and rear views of the Hetzer. The gun is mounted on the right-hand side to allow the driver operating room; his visor is clearly visible to the left of the gun. The vehicle was armoured overall, with access through hatches in the roof. The commander could operate the roof-mounted machine-gun, which was used against both ground and air targets. The Hetzer entered service in 1944.

SdKfz 234 ARMOURED CAR

Panzerspähwagen (8 Rad), or SdKfz 234, SdKfz 234/1 and SdKfz 234/2.

Crew: 4.

Armament: One 5cm *KwK* L/60 gun; one 7.92mm MG 34 machine-gun.

Armour: 0.35in (9mm) minimum; 1.18in (30mm) maximum.

Dimensions: Length 22ft 4in (6.8m); width 7ft 7in (2.33m); height 7ft 10in (2.38m).

Weight: 25,882lbs (11,740kg).

Power to weight ratio: 18.18hp/ton.

Engine: Tatra Model 103 V-12 air-cooled diesel developing 210hp at 2,250rpm.

Performance: Road speed 53mph (85km/h); range 625 miles (1,000km); vertical obstacle 1ft 8in (0.5m); trench 4ft 5in (1.35m); gradient 30 degrees.

History: In service with the German Army from 1944 to 1945.

(Note Data relate to *SdKfz 234/2.*)

During August 1940 the German high command requested the development of a more advanced version of the heavy eight-wheeled armoured car. The new vehicle was to be similar to the original but have a monocoque hull and to be suited to operations in hot climates. As the result, the Tatra firm received an order for the development of a 12-cylinder diesel engine; hitherto all German armoured cars had been powered by petrol engines. Despite the early start this new armoured car did not enter service until 1944. The first trial vehicle was delivered to the German Army in July 1941, but the engine gave considerable problems. These were eventually solved and production began in late 1943. Several variants were produced: a basic commander's model (*SdKfz 234/1*), an armoured car with a 5cm gun with 55 rounds (*SdKfz 234/2*) called the Puma, and two 7.5cm self-propelled gun versions: a short-barrelled one (*SdKfz 234/3*) and a long-barrelled one (*SdKfz 234/4*). The most popular model

was the *SdKfz 234/2 Puma*, which had a horseshoe-shaped rotating turret. One remarkable feature of these cars was the phenomenal range of action (as demanded under desert conditions) of over 600 miles (965km). Although originally intended for service with the *Afrika Korps*, they entered service too late for this, but were used very effectively in Russia and North-West Europe. About 2,300 were built, and they were the last German armoured cars to be produced during World War II. The *SdKfz 234/1* was a commander's car with an open-topped, fully-rotating. six-sided turret mounting a 2cm cannon. The Puma was designed to combat the light and medium tanks found in Soviet reconnaissance units, and mounted the turret originally intended for the World War II project Leopard light tank (which never went into production). It was soon found that more powerful guns were required to penetrate the Russian tanks, and consequently the two self-propelled 7.5cm gun versions were developed.

Below: The SdKfz 234/2 Puma armoured car mounting the 50mm KwK L/60 gun was the most popular version in German service in Russia and NW Europe in 1944-45.
Bottom: SdKfz 234/3 8-wheeled armoured car mounting a short-barrelled 75mm gun.

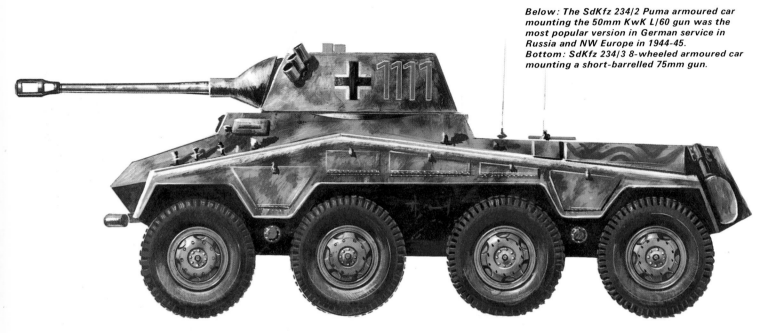

B IV FUNKLEPANZER DEMOLITION TANK

Crew: None.
Armament: None
Armour: 5.9in (150mm) maximum.
Dimensions: Length 11ft (3.35m); width 5ft 11in (1.8m); height 4ft 1in (1.25m).
Weight: 7,937lbs (3,600kg).
History: In service with the German Army from 1943 to 1945.

This little vehicle was one of the more bizarre offshoots of the German tank programme. The development of radio-controlled weapons never got far beyond the experimental stage during the war, due to the necessity to use valve sets, which were bulky and fragile. Most remote-controlled devices relied on trailing wires for the command signals, and this was generally success-

ful enough. The B IV *Funklepanzer* was a late development. It was attached to a few heavy tank battalions, all had Tiger I as the fighting vehicle, and it was intended to assist the advance of the formation by destroying field fortifications beyond the abilities of the tank guns, or demolishing obstacles, or even detecting mines. Another possible use, kept in the background and not meant for service unless circumstances called for it, was gas decontamination, though now it is hard to see exactly how effective this would have been. For carrying out the more mundane tasks the *Funklepanzer* carried a 992lb (450kg) disposable load on the front plate. This load could be dropped off by remote control, and if it was an explosive charge, it could be detonated either by a time fuze activated by the dropping or by another radio signal. Mine detection

was undertaken by a standard detector mounted in front which radioed the information continuously back to the controlling vehicle. Other means then had to be employed to remove the mine. The B IV was based on the chassis of the Borgward *VK* 301 ammunition carrier, which was too small and too lightly armoured to be of any operational use after 1943. It was both light and reasonably mobile, and made a good base for the bulky and complicated radio equipment needed for the variety of functions built into the *Funklepanzer*. The radio command range was roughly 1.24 miles (2km), depending on conditions. This was more than far enough, since the operator had to have the vehicle in full view the whole time. Operational use of the *Funklepanzer* was very limited, and there are only scanty records of its deployment in the field.

Right: The SdKfz 301 Funklepanzer radio-controlled tank, designed to deliver an explosive demolition charge.

Below: The mode of operation of the SdKfz 301, carrying a 450kg disposable HE charge on its front plate. The vehicle is guided to the target by radio, drops the charge (in black in the diagram) and withdraws. It saw restricted service in 1943-45.

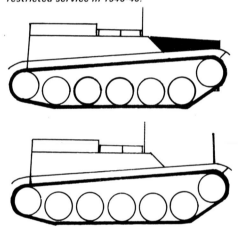

Below: The SdKfz 301 Funklepanzer with its disposable charge on the ground in front of it. Note how the load is shaped to fit the vehicle. The square, folding turret for a driver (if required) is erected.

MAUS HEAVY TANK

Crew: 6.
Armament: One 12.8cm *KwK* L/55 gun; one 7.5cm L/36.5 gun co-axial with main armament; one 2cm cannon.
Armour: 1.57in (40mm) minimum; 13.78in (350mm) maximum.
Dimensions: Length (including gun) 30ft 10in (10.1m); width 11ft 2in (3.67m); height 11ft 9in (3.63m).
Weight: 414,465lbs (188,000kg).
Ground pressure: 20.6lb/in² (1.45kg/cm²).
Power to weight ratio: 5.84hp/ton.
Engine: Daimler-Benz MB 509 V-12 water-cooled inline petrol engine developing 1,080hp at 2,400rpm.
Performance: Road speed 12.5mph (20km/h); range 116 miles (186km); vertical obstacle 2ft 2in (0.72m); trench 13ft 9in (4.5m); gradient 30 degrees.
History: Built only in prototype forms.

Left: Maus heavy tank. It was planned to build 150 of these, but by May 1945 only two had been built with nine more partially completed.

During the course of World War II the Germans directed a great amount of effort and resources to the development of super-heavy AFVs. There were two tank models under development (the *Maus* (Mouse) and the E-100) but neither of these was ever taken into service. On 8 June 1942, Dr. Ferdinand Porsche (the famous car designer) was approached concerning the possibility of producing a tank type vehicle mounting a 12.8cm or 15cm gun in a revolving turret. A co-axial 7.5cm gun was also to be incorporated. At this time Porsche was head of the German Tank Commission and had a great deal of influence with Hitler, on whom he urged the development of super-heavy tanks. The majority of German tank designers and the leading theoreticians of tank warfare, however, were opposed to the use of such super-heavy tanks. When the project was first suggested, the vehicle was referred to as the *Mammut* (Mammoth), and allocated the project Number 205. The Alkett firm began assembly of the first tank on 1 August 1943. Krupp supplied the hull in mid-September and the new tank, now referred to as the *Maus* (Mouse) made its first trial run at Alkett on 23 December 1943. On 10 January 1944 the tank was sent to Böblingen near Stuttgart for extensive trials. Apart from slight trouble with the

suspension the trials were fairly successful. At this time instructions were given to Porsche by Hitler that the completed tank, with turret and guns, was to be ready by June. By 9 June the turret had been assembled and fitted to the tank and further trials were commenced. These were very satisfactory, and at the beginning of October orders were received to send the tank to the proving ground at Kummersdorf. A second prototype (Mouse II) was sent to Kummersdorf without trials. This model had a different engine, which gave considerable trouble. By the end of the war a further nine

prototypes were in various stages of construction, and production plans had been made for 150. The vehicles at Kummersdorf were blown up by the Germans prior to the arrival of the Russians.

Right: The Maus I ('Mouse') heavy tank, complete with turret and armament. It was powered by a Daimler-Benz MB 509 petrol engine giving a road speed of 20km/h and mounted a 128mm KwK L/55 gun, co-axial 75mm L/36 and a 20mm cannon.

HS-30 SPZ 12-3 ARMOURED PERSONNEL CARRIER

Spz. 12-3, Jpz. 3-3 and variants.
Crew: 2 plus 6.
Armament: One 20mm cannon; eight smoke dischargers.
Armour: 10mm—30mm (0.39—1.53in).
Dimensions: Length (including armament) 20ft 8in (6.31m); length (hull) 18ft 3in (5.56m); width 8ft 4in (2.54m); height (with turret) 6ft 1in (1.85m).
Weight: Combat 31,967lbs (14,600kg).
Ground pressure: 10.66lb/in² (0.75kg/cm²).
Engine: Rolls-Royce B.81 Mk.80F eight-cylinder petrol engine developing 235hp at 3,800rpm.
Performance: Road speed 36mph (58km/h); range 174 miles (270km); vertical obstacle 2ft (0.6m); trench 5ft 3in (1.6m); gradient 60 per cent.
History: Entered service with the German Army in 1959 and production completed in 1962. Still in service.

When the West German Army was reformed after World War II, it was in urgent need of tanks, self-propelled artillery and armoured personnel carriers. Most of the early equipment came from the United

States, including large numbers of M47 tanks, M7 Priest self-propelled guns and various other armoured vehicles. At that time the Swiss company of Hispano-Suiza (now a part of the Oerlikon-Bührle group) had designed a self-propelled anti-aircraft gun as a private venture. To meet the German Army's APC requirement it was quickly redesigned. The Swiss did not, however, have the facilities to manufacture the vehicle, which they called the HS-30, in the large numbers required by the Germans. Subsequently production was undertaken in England by Leyland Motors and in Germany by Henschel and Hanomag. The first production vehicle was completed in 1958 and production continued until 1962. The development of the HS-30 had been rushed and once in troop service numerous faults were discovered, especially with the power pack and the suspension. It did not take long to rectify these faults, however, and since then the vehicle has given good service. Today it is still in service in some numbers with the German Army, although many units now have the *Marder* MICV. In many respects the HS-30 was one of the better vehicles developed in the 1950s. Its armour (0.3 to 1.2in, or 8 to 30mm) gives it adequate

protection from small arms fire, it is well armed even by today's standards, and its low silhouette increases its chances of survival on the battlefield. Its main armament consists of a turret-mounted 20mm Hispano-Suiza 820 cannon manufactured under licence in Germany by the Rheinmetall company. This has an elevation of +75° and a depression of −10°, with a traverse of 360°. A total of 2,000 rounds of 20mm ammunition is carried. Four smoke dischargers are normally mounted on each side of the hull at the front. The driver is seated at the front on the left side with the commander to his rear. A 7.62mm MG3 machine-gun is often mounted at the commander's station. The personnel compartment is in the centre of the hull. Although there is a door in the hull rear on the left side, the normal method of entry and exit for the infantry is by simply jumping over the side of the vehicle. When travelling, the roof of the personnel compartment is covered by two steel hatches. The engine, built by Rolls-Royce, is mounted at the rear of the hull on the right side. Some HS-30s have been provided with a 106mm American M40 recoilless rifle mounted over the troop compartment to give them some anti-tank capability. Unlike more recent vehicles, the Spz 12-3 has no amphibious capability and can ford only to a depth of 2ft 4in (0.7m); also, it does not have an NBC system. Many trial versions were developed: these included a multiple rocket-launcher, a 90mm tank-destroyer (rather like the *Jagdpanzer Kanone*) and a tank-destroyer with a turret-mounted 90mm gun. Specialised versions in service with the German Army today include a 120mm mortar carrier, command and radio vehicles, and a fire-control vehicle. The *Jagdpanzer Rakete* (Jpz 3-3) is a tank-destroyer armed with a launcher for the French SS-11 ATGW. This model has a crew of three: commander, driver and missile controller. Recently trials have been carried out with HS-30s fitted with the American TOW and French/German Milan anti-tank missile systems. As the HS-30s are withdrawn from infantry battalions they may well be refitted with one of the above anti-tank missile systems and issued to Territorial units to increase their anti-tank capabilities.

Above: The SPZ 12-3 APC has been in service with the German Army since the late 1950s.

Right: A JPZ 3-3 tank-destroyer launches a French SS-11 ATGW. Production of the SPZ 12-3 range of AFVs was undertaken in both Britain and Germany; the prototype was a Swiss-designed SP anti-aircraft syztem.

JAGDPANZER KANONE/RAKETE TANK DESTROYER

Jpz. 4-5, Jpz. Rakete
Crew: 4.
Armament: One 90mm gun; one 7.62mm MG3 machine-gun co-axial with main armament; one 7.62mm MG3 anti-aircraft machine-gun, eight smoke dischargers.
Armour: 10mm–50mm (0.39–1.96in).
Dimensions: Length (including armament) 28ft 9in (8.75m); length (hull) 20ft 6in (6.238m); width 9ft 9in (2.98m); height (without anti-aircraft machine-gun) 6ft 10in (2.085m).
Weight: Combat 60,627lbs (27,500kg).
Ground pressure: 10.67lb/in² (0.75kg/cm²).
Engine: Daimler-Benz Model MB 837 Aa eight-cylinder water-cooled diesel developing 500hp at 2,200rpm.
Performance: Road speed 43.5mph (70km/h); range 249 miles (400km); vertical obstacle 2ft 6in (0.75m); trench 6ft 7in (2m); gradient 60 per cent.
History: Entered service with the German Army in 1965 and with the Belgian Army in 1975. Production now complete, but see text.

The *Jagdpanzer Kanone* (Jpz.4-5 for short) is a member of a range of vehicles developed for the German Army from the late 1950s, the other two members of the family which reached production being the *Jagdpanzer Rakete* and the *Marder* MICV. The first prototypes were completed in 1960 by Hanomag and Henschel of Germany, and MOWAG of Switzerland. These were followed by further prototypes from the two German companies before the design was finally approved for production. Production began in 1965: 375 were built by Henschel and a similar number by Hanomag, production being completed in 1967. The primary role of the *Jagdpanzer Kanone* is to hunt and destroy enemy tanks. It relies on its low silhouette and speed for its survival – it has a very high road and cross-country speed, and can be driven at the same speed backwards and forwards. The hull of the vehicle is of all-welded steel construction with the maximum armour thickness of 2in (50mm) being concentrated at the front. The fighting compartment is at the front of the hull, with the engine and transmission at the rear. The suspension is of the torsion-bar type, and consists of six road wheels with the idler at the front and drive sprocket at the rear. There are three track-return rollers on each side. The crew of four consists of the commander, gunner, loader and driver. The 90mm gun is mounted in the front of the hull and is slightly offset to the right. It has a traverse of 15° left and 15°

right, and can be elevated from −8° to +15°, both elevation and traverse being manual. A 7.62mm MG3 is mounted co-axially to the right of the main armament, and there is a similar weapon on the commander's hatch for anti-aircraft defence. Eight smoke dischargers are mounted on the roof of the hull, firing forwards. These would be used to cover the withdrawal of the vehicle. The 90mm gun has a maximum effective range of 2,187 yards (2,000m), and a maximum rate of fire of 12 rounds per minute can be achieved. A total of 51 rounds of 90mm and 4,000 rounds of 7.62mm ammunition is carried. An infra-red searchlight is mounted over the main armament, and this moves in elevation and traverse with the gun. The Jpz.4-5 is fitted with an NBC system, and can ford streams to a depth of 4ft 7in (1.4m) without preparation. A wading kit is also available. This can be fitted

quickly, and allows the vehicle to ford to a depth of 6ft 11in (2.1m). The Belgian Army has 80 Jpz.4-5s of a slightly different design, these being assembled in Belgium from components supplied by Germany. The Belgian vehicles use *Marder*-type suspension and a *Marder* transmission, as well as a Belgian-designed fire-control system which incorporates a laser range-finder. The German MG3 machine-guns are replaced by FN MAG 58 weapons of Belgian design and construction. The *Jagdpanzer Rakete* has an almost identical hull to the *Jagdpanzer Kanone* and has been designed to operate with the latter vehicle in order to give long-range anti-tank support. It has two launchers for French SS-11 anti-tank missiles, a total of 14 missiles (minimum range of 547 yards or 500m and maximum range of 3,280 yards or 3,000m) being carried. A total of 370 was built for the German Army

LEOPARD I MAIN BATTLE TANK

Leopard 1, ARV, AEV, AVLB and variants
Crew: 4.
Armament: One 105mm gun; one 7.62mm machine-gun co-axial with main armament; one 7.62mm machine-gun on roof; four smoke dischargers on each side of the turret.
Armour: 10mm–70mm (0.39–2.76in).
Dimensions: Length (including main armament) 31ft 4in (9.543m); length (hull) 23ft 3in (7.09m); width 10ft 8in (3.25m); height 8ft 8in (2.64m).
Weight: Combat 88,185lbs (40,000kg).
Ground pressure: 12.23lb/in² (0.86kg/cm²).
Engine: MTU MB 838 Ca.M500 10-cylinder multi-fuel engine developing 830hp at 2,200rpm.
Performance: Road speed 40mph (65km/h); range 373 miles (600km); vertical obstacle 3ft 9in (1.15m); trench 9ft 10in (3m); gradient 60 per cent.
History: Entered service with the German Army in 1965. In service with Australia, Belgium, Canada, Denmark, Germany, Italy, the Netherlands and Norway. Still in production.

Without doubt, the Leopard MBT built by Germany has been one of the most successful tanks to be developed since World War II, although when the German Army was re-formed it was equipped with American M47 medium tanks. At one time it was hoped that Germany and France would produce a common tank, but like so many programmes of this type nothing came of it. Prototypes of a new German tank were built by two German consortiums, known as Group A and Group B. At an early stage, however, it was decided to drop the Group B series and continue only with that of Group A. In 1963 it was decided to place this tank in production and the production contract was awarded to the Krauss-Maffei company of Munich, who are well known for their railway locomotives. The first production Leopard was completed in September 1965, and by late 1976 orders had been placed for almost 6,000 Leopards of all types, and the Leopard has been adopted by many NATO countries. It is also being built under licence in Italy by Oto Melara, and it may well be built in Turkey in the near future. The Leopard tank

has a crew of four, with the driver in the front of the hull on the right and the other three crew members in the turret. The engine and transmission are at the rear of the hull: the complete Leopard engine can be taken out in well under 30 minutes, which is a great advantage in battle conditions. The main armament of the Leopard is the 105mm L7 series gun manufactured at the Royal Ordnance Factory in Nottingham, England. A 7.62mm MG3 machine-gun is mounted co-axially with the main armament and there is a similar machine-gun on the roof of the tank for anti-aircraft defence. Four smoke dischargers are mounted each side of the turret. Sixty rounds of 105mm and 5,500 rounds of machine-

gun ammunition are carried. Standard equipment on the Leopard includes night-vision equipment, an NBC system and a crew heater. The vehicle can ford to a maximum depth of 7ft 5in (2.25m) without preparation or 13ft 2in (4m) with the aid of a schnorkel. Since the Leopard entered service it has been constantly updated and the most recent modifications include a stabilisation system for the main armament, thermal sleeve for the gun barrel, new tracks and passive rather than infra-red vision equipment for the driver and commander. The latest model is the Leopard 1A3, which has a new turret of spaced armour and other modifications. The Leopard chassis has been the

between 1967 and 1968. In addition this model has a bow-mounted machine-gun as well as a roof-mounted machine-gun and eight smoke dischargers. All of the *Jagdpanzer Raketen* will be rebuilt over the next five years with the Franco-German HOT (High-subsonic Optically-guided Tube-launched) missile system. This missile has a number of advantages over the SS-11 missile, including a minimum range of 82 yards (75m), a maximum range of 4,374 yards (4,000m) and simpler loading procedures. It is also much more accurate, and the aimer merely has to keep the target in his sight, which has a magnification of ×7, in order to achieve a hit. Although the *Jagdpanzer Kanone* was designed over 10 years ago, the manufacturers have recently proposed that the vehicle could be rearmed with a 105mm gun in place of the 90mm gun, which would extend the vehicle's operational life in the 1980s.

Below and left: The Jagdpanzer Rakete was designed to give long-range anti-tank support to the Jagdpanzer Kanone; 370 were built in 1967-68. Originally mounting two launchers for its 14 French SS-11 missiles, all Raketen are being rebuilt to carry the Franco-German HOT missile; lighter, easier to load, and with an effective range of 4,000m compared to the 3,000m of the SS-11.

Right: A Jagdpanzer Kanone (Jpz. 4-5), the first post-war German self-propelled gun, on exercise. The 750 Jpz. 4-5s built for the Federal Republic in 1965-67 mount the 90mm gun of the US M47 Patton tank, but their operational life may be extended by rearming with a 105mm gun. The 80 Kanone of the Belgian Army are of improved design, incorporating a laser range-finder.

basis for a whole family of variants sharing many common components, some of them (eg the *Gepard*) being manufactured by Krauss-Maffei and others by the MaK company of Kiel. The first variant to enter service was the Leopard armoured recovery vehicle (ARV). This has been designed to recover disabled vehicles and is fitted with a wide range of equipment including a dozer blade either for dozing operations or for stabilising the vehicle when the crane is being used. The latter is used to change tank engines and other similar components, and can lift a maximum of 19.68 tons (20,000kg). A winch is also provided, and this has a maximum pull of 63.97 tons (65,000kg). The Armoured Engineer Vehicle is almost identical with the ARV, but the dozer blade can be fitted with special teeth to rip up roadways and an auger is also carried for boring holes in the ground. The bridgelayer model is known as the *Biber* (Beaver): this carries a bridge 72ft 2in (22m) in length, which can be used to span a gap up to 65ft 8in (20m) in width. The *Gepard* anti-aircraft tank has twin 35mm guns and is now in production for Germany, Belgium and the Netherlands. The Germans have fitted the complete turret of the AMX-30 155mm GCT self-propelled gun to a Leopard chassis, but this has yet to be adopted. A driver training model without the gun turret is used by Belgium and the Netherlands. Currently undergoing trials are two special versions of the Leopard which will be used to prepare river crossing points. Another Leopard chassis has been fitted with a six-barrelled long-range rocket-launcher. This was being developed with Italy and Great Britain, although the latter country withdrew from the project a few years ago.

Left: The Leopard IA3, latest model of the Federal Republic's MBT, has an improved turret of spaced armour.

Right: A Leopard I in heavy going. In service since 1965, the AFV has been constantly updated, including new tracks recently.

MARDER MECHANISED INFANTRY COMBAT VEHICLE

Marder, Marder SAM, TAM and variants
Crew: 3 plus 7.
Armament: One 20mm Rh.202 cannon; one 7.62mm machine-gun co-axial with 20mm cannon; one 7.62mm machine-gun in remote mount; six smoke dischargers.
Armour: Classified.
Dimensions: Length 22ft 3in (6.79m); width 10ft 8in (3.24m); height 9ft 8in (2.95m).
Weight: Combat 62,169lbs (28,200kg).
Ground pressure: 11.3lb/in² (0.8kg/cm²).
Engine: MTU MB 833 Ea-500 six-cylinder diesel developing 600hp at 2,200rpm.
Performance: Road speed 46.6mph (75km/h); range 323 miles (520km); vertical obstacle 3ft 3in (1m); trench 8ft 2in (2.5m); gradient 60 per cent.
History: Entered service with German Army in 1971 and still in production.

In the late 1950s the German Army started to draw up plans for a whole range of vehicles in the 20-ton class. This range was to have included a MICV, tank-destroyer SP gun, tank-destroyer rocket vehicle, mortar carrier, reconnaissance tank, radar vehicle and rocket carrier. Priority was given to the tank-destroyers, however, and these entered service in the 1960s as the *Jagdpanzer Rakete* (rocket) and *Jagdpanzer Kanone* (gun). Prototypes of the MICV were built in Germany and Switzerland in the early 1960s, but these were not considered satisfactory and further prototypes were built until a satisfactory design was finally accepted in the late 1960s. The first production *Marder* (Marten) MICVs were completed in 1971, there being two production lines, one at the Atlas Mak plant at Kiel and the other at Rheinstahl's plant at Kassel. The *Marder* was the first MICV to enter service with any of the NATO armies and even today it is the best vehicle of its type in service in the west. The hull of the *Marder* is of all-welded steel and the front part gives protection against attack from weapons up to 20mm in calibre, whilst the sides and rear are immune to attack from weapons up to 12.7mm in calibre. The driver is seated at the front on the left, with the commander to his rear and the engine to his right. The power-operated turret is in the centre of the hull and the personnel compartment is at the rear. The turret has a 20mm Rheinmetall Rh.202 cannon, with an elevation of +65° and a depression of −17°; a 7.62mm MG3 machine-gun is mounted co-axially with the main armament. An infra-red searchlight is mounted on the left side of the turret and this moves in elevation with the main armament. In the roof of the troop compartment is another 7.62mm MG3 machine-gun, which can be aimed and fired from within the vehicle. Elevation limits are from −15° to +60°, and traverse is limited to 180°. A total of 1,250 rounds of 20mm and 5,000 rounds of 7.62mm ammu-

nition is carried. On each side of the personnel compartment are two spherical firing-ports with a periscope above each, allowing the infantry to aim and fire their 7.62mm G3 rifles with safety from within the vehicle. Over the top of the troop compartment are four circular roof hatches. The usual method of entry and exit for the infantry is via a large hydraulically operated ramp in the hull rear. An interesting feature of the troop seating arrangements is that they can quickly be converted into bunks so that some of the infantry can sleep in the vehicle. The *Marder* is provided with night driving equipment and a complete NBC system. The standard *Marder* can ford streams to a depth of 4ft 11in (1.5m) without preparation. A schnorkel can quickly be fitted, however, enabling the *Marder* to ford streams to a maximum depth of 8ft 2in (2.5m). An amphibious kit is also being developed. It can quickly be adapted for use as a cargo carrier or ambulance. The full designation of the *Marder* in the German Army is *Schützenpanzer, Neu,*

Marder. It has replaced the HS-30 in most front line units. An anti-aircraft version is now entering production for the German Army. This has a modified *Marder* chassis and mounts the French/German Roland 2 surface-to-air missile system. Two missiles are in the ready-to-launch position, with another eight missiles inside the hull. Roland 2 is an all-weather system and is also being used by the French Army, which mounts it on a modified AMX-30 tank chassis. Thyssen Henschel (formerly Rheinstahl) has recently completed the prototype of the TAM medium battle tank. This consists of a modified *Marder* chassis with a new turret, mounting a 105mm gun. It has a crew of three and is aimed at the export market. Further improvements to the *Marder* are being considered, including the installation of a new fully stabilised turret, which would allow the gunner to aim and fire the 20mm cannon on the move, and the installation of an anti-tank missile such as the French/German Milan.

Above and below: A Marder with the Euromissile 'Roland 2' all-weather anti-aircraft missile system, with an effective range of more than 6,000m. Two missiles are carried in ready-to-launch position, with eight more stored in the hull. The French Army is mounting its 'Roland' systems on the modified chassis of the AMX-30 main battle tank.

Above: The Marder is the standard MICV of the West German Army. It has a turret-mounted 20mm cannon and co-axial 7.62mm machine-gun with six smoke dischargers, and another 7.62mm gun in a remote-controlled mount at the hull rear. Production of the Marder was undertaken by Atlas MaK of Kiel and Rheinstahl (now Thyssen Henschel) of Kassel.

SPÄHPANZER LUCHS RECONNAISSANCE VEHICLE

Crew: 4.
Armament: One 20mm cannon; one 7.62mm machine-gun; eight smoke dischargers.
Armour: Classified.
Dimensions: Length 25ft 5in (7.743m); width 9ft 9in (2.98m); height 9ft 6in (2.905m).
Weight: Combat 42,990lbs (19,500kg).
Engine: Daimler-Benz Model OM 403 VA 10-cylinder multi-fuel engine developing 390hp at 2,500rpm when running on diesel fuel.
Performance: Road speed 56mph (90km/h); water speed 6.2mph (10km/h); range 497 miles (800km); vertical obstacle 2ft (0.6m); trench 6ft 6in (1.9m); gradient 60 per cent.
History: Entered service with the German Army in 1975. Not yet exported.

Right: The Luchs ('Lynx') is the latest in a line of German 8x8 armoured cars dating back to the 1920s. The German Army ordered 408 of these vehicles from Thyssen Henschel for delivery in 1975-1978.

The *Luchs* (Lynx) is the latest in a long line of German 8×8 armoured cars which can be traced back to the late 1920s. In the early 1960s the German Army laid the foundations for a whole new family of vehicles which would have included an 8×8 armoured car, 4×4 and 6×6 armoured amphibious load carriers, and 4×4, 6×6 and 8×8 trucks, some of which were to have been amphibious. All of these would share many common components such as axles, engines, transmissions and so on, to simplify logistics and training, wherever possible. Well tried commercial components were to be used to keep costs to a minimum. By 1976, however, only the *Luchs* was in service with the German Army. Prototypes were built by two companies, Daimler-Benz and a consortium of five other companies. In 1973 Rheinstahl (now Thyssen Henschel) of Kassel was awarded a contract to build 408 vehicles, the first of these being completed in May 1975, with final deliveries being made to the German Army in 1978. The *Luchs* is the replacement for the French Hotchkiss Spz. 11-2 vehicle which has now been in service with the German Army for 20 years. The hull of the *Luchs* is of all-welded steel construction with the driver in the front on the left side, commander and gunner in the turret (commander on the left and gunner on the right) and the second driver, who also operates the radios, to the rear of the turret, facing the rear. The power pack, which contains the engine, fully automatic transmission, air and oil filters, is mounted at the rear of the hull to the right of the radio operator. It can be removed from the *Luchs* as a complete unit to facilitate replacement in the field. It can also be run outside the vehicle for test purposes. The engine will run on a variety of fuels including diesel and petrol. When using the latter it develops 300hp at 2,500rpm. All eight wheels are powered, and steering can be done with the front four wheels, rear four wheels, or all eight wheels if required. The *Luchs* is armed with a 20mm Rheinmetall Rh.202 cannon, which is also mounted in the *Marder* MICV and used by the German Air Force in the anti-aircraft role. The turret has a traverse of 360° and the gun has an elevation of +80° and a depression of −15°. A 7.62mm MG3 machine gun is mounted on the turret roof for anti-aircraft defence and there are also four smoke dischargers on each side of the turret.

The *Luchs* is fully amphibious, being propelled in the water by two steerable propellers at the rear of the hull. A trim vane is hydraulically erected at the front of the hull before the vehicle enters the water. Standard equipment includes an NBC system, air conditioning and night driving lights. A white light/infra-red searchlight is mounted on the left side of the turret and moves in elevation with the main armament. Bullet proof fuel tanks are fitted, and the engine compartment is provided with an automatic fire extinguishing system. The primary role of the *Luchs* is that of reconnaissance. The type is not heavily armed as it has to obtain its information on enemy positions and movements by stealth. Should the vehicle run into any unexpected trouble the rear driver can quickly take over control as the vehicle can be driven the same speed in both directions.

Left and above: The Spähpanzer Luchs has now replaced the Hotchkiss Spz. 11-2 as the standard reconnaissance vehicle of the German Army. Armament consists of a turret-mounted 20mm Rh.202 cannon (also mounted in the Marder MICV), a 7.62mm machine-gun for anti-aircraft defence and eight smoke dischargers. The Luchs has a crew of four: commander, gunner and two drivers. One driver sits at the front, the other at the rear; the latter operates the radio and can also drive the vehicle in reverse at top speed if required. It is fully amphibious, driven in the water by two propellors. An NBC system is fitted, as is a full range of night vision equipment, including an infra-red searchlight left of the cannon.

LEOPARD II MAIN BATTLE TANK

Crew: 4.

Armament: One 120mm gun; one 7.62mm MG3 machine-gun co-axial with main armament; one 40mm grenade-launcher in turret roof; four or eight smoke dischargers on each side of turret (see text).

Armour: Classified.

Dimensions: Length (including main armament) 31ft 11in (9.74m); length (hull) 25ft 4in (7.73m); width 11ft 7in (3.54m); height 8ft 2in (2.49m).

Weight: Combat 111,332lbs (50,500kg).

Ground pressure: 11.8lb/in² (0.83kg/cm²).

Engine: MTU MB 873 Ka-500 12-cylinder water-cooled multi-fuel engine developing 1,500hp at 2,600rpm.

Performance: Road speed 42mph (68km/h); vertical obstacle 3ft 9in (1.15m); trench 9ft 10in (3m); gradient 60 per cent.

History: Prototypes completed 1973–74. Not yet in service with the German Army.

The development of the Leopard 2 MBT can be traced back to a project started in the 1960s. At this time the Germans and the Americans were still working on the MBT-70 programme, so this project had a very low priority. Once the MBT-70 was cancelled in January 1970, the Germans pushed ahead with the Leopard 2, and 17 prototypes were completed by 1974. These prototypes were built by the manufacturers of the Leopard 1, Krauss-Maffei of Munich, with the assistance of many other German companies. Without doubt, the Leopard 2 is one of the most advanced tanks in the world and the Germans have succeeded in designing a tank with high success in all three areas of tank design: mobility, firepower and armour protection. In the past most tanks have only been able to achieve two of these objectives at once. A good example is the British Chieftain, which has an excellent gun and good armour, but poor mobility; the French AMX-30 is at the other end of the scale and has good mobility, an adequate gun but rather thin armour. The layout of the Leopard 2 is conventional, with the driver at the front, turret with commander, gunner and loader in the centre, and the engine and transmission at the rear. The engine was in fact originally developed for the MBT-70. The complete powerpack can be removed in about 15 minutes for repair or replacement. At first it was widely believed that the Leopard 2's armour was of the spaced type, but late in 1976 it was revealed that it used the British-developed Chobham armour. This gives superior protection against attack from all known projectiles. It is of the laminate type, and consist of layers of steel and ceramics. The suspension system is of the torsion-bar type with dampers. It has seven road wheels, with the drive sprocket at the rear and the idler at the front, and there are four track-return rollers. The first prototypes were armed with a 105mm gun of the smooth-bore type, developed by Rheinmetall, but later prototypes had the 120mm smooth-bore gun, and this is the one which will probably be standardised. The 120mm gun fires two basic types of fin-stabilised ammunition (in which small fins unfold from the rear of the round just after it has left the barrel), and this means that the barrel does not need to be rifled. The anti-tank round is of the Armour-Piercing Discarding Sabot type, and has an effective range of well over 2,405 yards (2,200m); at this range it will penetrate a standard NATO heavy tank target. The second round is also fin-stabilised and is designed for use against field fortifications and other battlefield targets. The cartridge case is semi-combustible and only the cartridge stub, which is made of conventional steel, remains after the round has been fired. The job of the loader is eased by the use of the hydraulically-assisted loading mechanism. The gun has an elevation of +20° and a depression of −9°. A standard 7.62mm MG3 machine-gun is mounted co-axially with the main armament. Some prototypes had a 40mm grenade-launcher mounted in the roof to fire anti-personnel grenades, whilst other prototypes had a 7.62mm machine-gun on a standard mount, or a remote-controlled weapon which could be fired from within the turret. Forty rounds of 120mm and 3,000 rounds of 7.62mm ammunition are carried. Four smoke dischargers are mounted each side of the turret, although production

vehicles may well have eight on each side. A very advanced fire-control system is fitted, which includes a combined laser and stereoscopic rangefinder, and the gun is fully stabilised, enabling it to be laid and fired on the move with a high probability of the round hitting the target. Standard equipment includes infra-red and passive night-vision equipment, an NBC system and heaters for both the driver's and fighting compartments. The Leopard 2 can ford streams to a depth of 3ft 3in (1m) without preparation, and with the aid of a schnorkel can deep ford to a depth of

13ft 1in (4m). In 1976 a modified version of the tank was delivered to the United States for trials. This is designated the Leopard 2(AV), the letters standing for Austere Version. This has many modifications requested by the United States, including a redesigned turret fitted with the standard 105mm NATO rifled tank gun, a new fire-control system with a Hughes laser rangefinder, modified suspension and so on. It was thought by many that this would have been built in the United States in place of the XM1, but Chrysler won a contract for the latter in November 1976.

Above: One of the 1973-74 prototypes of the Leopard 2, mounting a Rheinmetall-developed 120mm smooth-bore gun. In May 1977 it was decided to put the Leopard 2 into production; it is expected that 1,800 will be built for the German Army by Krauss-Maffei of Munich in 1979-1980.

Right: A rear view of a Leopard 2 armed with a 120mm smooth-bore gun. This model is fitted with protective track skirts, and four smoke dischargers are mounted on the turret side. The Leopard 2 has a hull and turret of British-developed laminate armour which gives protection against all types of attack, including ATGWs. Secondary armament consists of a 7.62mm co-axial machine-gun, with a 40mm grenade launcher in the turret roof. The Leopard 2 can ford up to 1m, and wade up to 4m with schnorkel.

Above: The Leopard 2 (Austere Version) was developed to meet the requirements of the United States Army, with a new turret for the 105mm rifled tank gun used in the Leopard 1, a new fire-control system and many other modifications. The Leopard 2 (AV) was tested in the United States in 1976-77 but was not adopted by the US Army.

GEPARD SELF-PROPELLED AA GUN

Crew: 3.
Armament: Twin 35mm cannon; eight smoke dischargers.
Armour: 10mm–70mm (0.39–2.76in).
Dimensions: Length (guns forward) 25ft 3in (7.7m); length (guns rear) 23ft 10in (7.27m); width 10ft 8in (3.25m); height (with radar retracted) 10ft 1in (3.07m).
Weight: Combat 99,208lbs (45,000kg).
Ground pressure: 13.5lb/in² (0.95kg/cm²).
Engine: MTU MB 835 Ca.500 10-cylinder multi-fuel engine developing 830hp at 2,200rpm.
Performance: Road speed 40mph (65km/h); range 373 miles (600km); vertical obstacle 3ft 9in (1.15m); trench 9ft 10in (3m); gradient 60 per cent.
History: Entered service with the German Army in 1977. On order for Belgium and the Netherlands.

The American M42 twin 40mm self-propelled anti-aircraft gun has been the standard mobile anti-aircraft gun system of the German Army since the 1950s. It is only a clear-weather system, however, and must be considered obsolete by today's standards. In the 1960s the German Army issued a requirement for a new gun system with all-weather capability. In fact design work started as far back as 1955, and continued on and off for the next 10 years. Some prototypes were built, but none met the German Army requirement. To meet this requirement two different prototypes were built and tested, both on modified Leopard MBT chassis. The Rheinmetall model was armed with twin 30mm guns and was designated the ZLA, whilst the Contraves model was armed with twin 35mm cannon and designated the 5PZF-A. Both had an all-weather fire-control system. After extensive trials the German Army selected the 5PZF-A for further development and another six prototypes were built under the designation 5PZF-B. Later the Dutch Army became interested in the concept and ordered for trials a model called the 5PZF-C. This was an integrated search and tracking radar system developed by the Dutch company of *Hollandse Signaalapparaten*. The 5PZF-B is now in production for the armies of Germany (420) and Belgium (55), whilst the 5PZF-C is in production for the Dutch Army (100). The US Army has also tested the vehicle as it has a requirement for a system of this type. According to some reports, the total cost of a fully equipped *Gepard* is just under £1,000,000. The *Gepard* has a hull similar to that of the standard Leopard MBT, the major difference being the installation of a 95hp auxiliary engine, needed to cope with the additional amount of power required by all of the electrical equipment carried. The *Gepard* is armed with twin model KDA 35mm Oerlikon cannon, these having

an elevation of +85° and a depression of −5°, and a traverse of 360°. Elevation and traverse are powered, although manual controls are provided in case of a power failure. Each barrel is provided with muzzle-velocity measuring equipment, which continuously feeds muzzle-velocity data to the fire-control computer. A total of 680 rounds of ammunition is carried: of these 640 are for anti-aircraft use and 40 for anti-tank use, it taking the gunner only a few seconds to change from the anti-aircraft to anti-tank ammunition. The guns have a cyclic rate of fire of 550 rounds per barrel per minute, and the empty cartridge cases are automatically ejected from the turret. The gunner can select either single shots, bursts of 5 or 15 rounds, or continuous fire. The guns have an effective anti-aircraft range of 4,374 yards (4000m). The German version has four smoke dischargers mounted on each side of the turret, and the Dutch version has six. The *Gepard* (the Dutch call their model the CA 1) has been designed to protect mechanised units on the battlefield and as it is based on the well-tried Leopard tank chassis it can operate wherever the tanks operate. The search radar is mounted on the turret rear and can be retracted if required. The radar scanner rotates once every second and can pick up an aircraft at a range of 9.3 miles (15km). The aircraft then appears on the radar screen inside the turret and is at first identified as friend or foe. If it is an enemy aircraft the tracking radar, which is mounted on the front of the turret, takes over and tracks

the target. If required, the tracking radar can be traversed through 180° so that the scanner is facing inwards and therefore protected from shell splinters. The computer then slaves the guns onto the target and follows the aircraft. If the target enters the effective range of the guns, this is indicated to the crew and the vehicle opens fire. This avoids any waste of ammunition. Once the ammunition has been expended it takes between 20 and 30 minutes to reload the magazines from outside the vehicle. Optical sights are also provided. The guns can be aimed and fired whilst the tank is moving across country. Normally the tank would stop to fire as this would give a more stable firing platform. The *Gepard* is fitted with an NBC system, and can ford streams to a maximum depth of 7ft 5in (2.25m).

Above: The West German Gepard self-propelled all-weather anti-aircraft gun, with its turret traversed to the rear. Based on the Leopard tank hull, the Gepard 'flakpanzer' is said to cost little less than £1 million.

Below: A Gepard on test. Its twin 35mm AA cannon is an external Oerlikon-Contraves mounting have a range of 4,000m and a rate of fire of 550 rounds per barrel per minute. The guns can be aimed and fired on the move by a search-tracking radar computer system.

FUG M-1963 SCOUT CAR

Crew 5.
Armament: One 7.62mm SGMB machine-gun.
Armour: 10mm (0.39in) maximum.
Dimensions: Length 19ft (5.79m); width 7ft 9in (2.362m); height (without armament) 6ft 3in (1.91m).
Weight: 13,448lbs (6,100kg).
Engine: Csepel D-414.44 four-cylinder water-cooled diesel developing 100hp at 2,300rpm.
Performance: Road speed 54mph (87km/h); water speed 5.5mph (9km/h); range 310 miles (500km); vertical obstacle 1ft 8in (0.4m); trench 4ft 3in (1.3m); gradient 50 per cent.
History: Entered service with the Hungarian Army in 1963. Also used by Czechoslovakia, Poland and Romania.

The FUG (*Felderitö Uśzó Gėpkocsi*) M-1963 fulfils a similar role to the Russian BRDM-1 reconnaissance vehicle, and in some respects is similar in design to the Russian vehicle. The FUG M-1963 is also used by the Czech Army, which calls it the OT-65 (*Obrneny Transporter*). The vehicle has a hull of all-welded steel construction with a maximum thickness of only 4in (10mm). The driver is located at the front of the hull, the personnel compartment in the centre and the engine and transmission at the rear. The top of the personnel compartment is covered by two roof hatches and this is the only means of entry and exit for the crew. Firing-ports are provided in the hull sides and rear. The FUG is fully amphibious and is propelled in the water by two water-jets in the rear of the hull. A central tyre pressure-regulation system is fitted, allowing the driver to adjust the tyre pressures to suit the ground conditions. When crossing sand, for example, air is let out of the tyres, and when travelling on roads the pressure is increased. The M-1963 also has two belly wheels on each side of the hull, and these are lowered when crossing rough ground or trenches. Infra-red driving lights are fitted, and most models have an infra-red searchlight on the left side of the superstructure. The vehicle is normally armed with a pintle-mounted 7.62mm SGMB machine-gun with an elevation of +24° and a depression of −6°, traverse being limited to 90°. There is no protection at all for the person firing the weapon. Some 1,250 rounds of machine-gun ammunition are carried. There is a special model of the FUG to carry out the radio-logical-chemical reconnaissance role. This is provided with racks each side of the hull rear, these dispensing flags to mark safe lanes through contaminated areas so that other men and vehicles can follow. The Czechs have developed a model known as the OT-65A. This is a standard OT-65 fitted with a turret armed with 7.62mm machine-gun, and a 82mm T-21 Tarasnice recoilless rifle can be mounted on the right side of the turret if required. This can be fired from within the turret but can only be reloaded from outside. The machine-gun has an elevation of +20° and a depression of −10°. The turret is the same as that fitted to the OT-62B armoured personnel carrier. In 1966 a modified version of the FUG M-1963 was first seen, with a new turret mounting a 23mm cannon and a co-axial 7.62mm machine-gun. This served as the prototype for the FUG-70, first seen in 1970. This is now in service with the Hungarian and East Germany Armies. It has a different hull to the FUG-1963, with a door in each side of the hull. Armament consists of a turret-mounted Russian 14.5mm KPVT machine-gun and a co-axial 7.62mm PKT machine-gun. These weapons have an elevation of +30° and a depression of −5°, traverse being 360°. Some 2,000 rounds of 7.62mm and 500 rounds of 14.5mm ammunition are carried. This model does not have any belly wheels: this has not only allowed the vehicle to have side doors, but also permitted more room in the vehicle so that in addition to the crew of three, six infantrymen can be carried. This model is provided with an NBC system and a full range of night-vision equipment, and is fully amphibious. The FUG-70 is powered by a Raba-MAN six-cylinder diesel engine, which gives it a top road speed of 62mph (100km/h) and a water speed of 6mph (10km/h). There is also reported to be a command model of the FUG-70, without the turret.

Right and above right: The Hungarian FUG M-1963 scout car, in service since 1963, somewhat resembles the Russian BTR 40K (BRDM) reconnaissance vehicle. Like the BRDM it is fully amphibious, propelled at 9km/h by two rear-mounted hydro-jets, and has retractable belly-wheels which can be lowered for easier going over rough ground. One version of the FUG is specially equipped for radiological-chemical reconnaissance. It is armed with a single 7.62mm machine-gun in an unprotected mounting, but the FUG-70, seen in 1970, has a turret-mounted 14.5mm and a co-axial 7.62mm machine-gun.

Italy

The beginnings of the Italian use of armoured forces were dogged from the start with two drawbacks. One was a lack of adequate money, the other a misleading success in the use of light vehicles in the colonial actions in the North African possessions such as Libya, and later on Abyssinia. One can only be thankful that the same disease did not befall the British, who had every reason to be infected.

The shortage of funds led the Italians to follow the attractive but misleading path of building light armoured vehicles with minimal protection. The Carden-Loyd light carriers and two-man tanks looked a worthwhile proposition, as did the Vickers light tanks and the first Italian armoured units used these in small numbers. From them the first native designs were developed, still incorporating the fatal drawbacks of the originals. Indeed, by the start of World

War II the lighter series of tanks were using a suspension system almost identical with the Carden carriers, and suffering the speed restrictions that this involved.

In the North African colonies these light vehicles were quite useful, and since they never met any opposition worthy of the name they were also successful. It was therefore assumed that they would be equally good in actual war, although there were indications in the Spanish Civil War that all was not well; and that light armour and small guns were not necessarily as effective

against troops who had had a little training and were determined to fight. But by now the Italian designs were more or less fixed and the only changes were to be in quantities rather than quality.

The full realisation came in the first battles of the desert war in late 1941. These proved conclusively that the tank design had failed, and lack of armour, poor suspension, insufficient engine power and inadequate armament were no match for even quite elderly British tanks. But above all the crews lacked spirit: a real determination to fight would have made up for a lot, but the leadership was absent, and the armoured force wilted.

The poor showing of the Italian armoured troops is just one of the facets of that

unhappy army. Despite a brilliance in automobile design, the Italians somehow failed to carry it over to armaments, and tanks in particular. The virtues of sloped armour were never explored, nor were suspensions investigated to any great extent. One cannot cavil too much at the light armament since so many other countries were in the same position, but it demonstrated a failure to appreciate what a tank was meant to do in battle. Also, there were few variants apart from some self-propelled guns, which were rather hurried conversions using field guns and turretless tank chassis. The lack of money is quite evident.

The armoured divisions were reasonably well organised and intended to be used in support of infantry assaults, but were meant to act with some independence in so doing. The difficulty was the command and control of such a force, and there were insufficient radios for the running of a proper armoured tactical battle. The inevitable result was that the tactics were stereotyped and rather rigid and thus the greatest advantages of armoured forces, flexibility, was largely lost. Maintenance was sometimes lower than it should have been and the arrangements for recovering vehicle casualties were less than adequate. Nevertheless, despite these strictures, there were several occasions, particularly in the desert, when the Italian tank units fought bravely and with effect. The pity was that it did not happen more often.

When Italy joined NATO after the war she was re-equipped with US equipment such as the M47, of which there are still many in Italian service. These tanks gave a basis on which to build new armoured units and were followed in 1960 by M60s, which were built by Oto Melara. At the same time additional US vehicles were taken into use to give a complete range of support vehicles as the new armoured formations were brought up to strength. Unfortunately a lack of money has prevented the full realisation of all the plans, but there is now a steady re-equipment programme using Leopards built in Italy and strong representation in several NATO collaborative projects, particularly the UK, German and Italian self-propelled gun in 155mm calibre. Although still very dependant on elderly US equipment, the Italian army is highly effective and makes a substantial contribution to the NATO defences.

An Italian M14/41 tank in North Africa. Generally, the Italian tanks were no match for the Allied tanks of World War II.

LANCIA 1ZM ARMOURED CAR

Crew: 6.
Armament: Twin 8mm St Etienne Model 1907 machine-guns (see text).
Armour: 6mm (0.25in) maximum.
Dimensions: Length 18ft 9in (5.714m); width 6ft 4½in (1.937m); height 7ft 10½in (2.499m).
Weight: Combat 9,240lbs (4,192kg).
Engine: Four-cylinder water-cooled petrol engine developing 70bhp at 2,200rpm.
Performance: Road speed 37mph (60km/h); road range 270 miles (435km); gradient 16 per cent.
History: In service with the Italian Army from 1917 to 1941 (see text). Also used by Austria and Albania.

The Lancia was the standard armoured car of the Italian Army during World War I, having entered service in 1915. Twenty of the first model were built, these being armed with three 6.5mm machine-guns, two in the main turret and one in a smaller turret on top of the main turret. The second model, known as the Lancia 1 ZM, followed in 1917 and 110 of this model were built. The Lancia armoured car consisted of a standard Lancia light truck chassis fitted with a hull of armour plate with a maximum thickness of 0.24in (6mm), conversion work being carried out by the Ansaldo company. Seven firing ports were provided, three in each side of the hull and one in the rear, and entry doors were provided in each side of the hull. Main armament consisted of two French St Etienne 8mm machine-guns with an elevation of +35° and a depression of −15°. Some 15,600 rounds of machine-gun ammunition were carried. A third St Etienne could be mounted in the rear hull firing port. Four French Chauchat 8mm light machine-guns were also carried, and there were 4,800 rounds of ammunition for these weapons. After World War I the French St Etienne weapons were replaced by Italian FIAT 6.5mm machine-guns, which were water-cooled, whilst the Chauchat machine-guns were replaced by 8.5mm Model 91 carbines. In 1935 the water-cooled machine-guns were replaced by FIAT air-cooled machine-guns.

The pair of angled rails at the front of the hull was to assist the vehicle passing through wire obstacles. After World War I a few of these vehicles were issued to the Italian police for use in the internal security role. They were used by the Italians in China, Spain, East Africa and possibly Libya. They were finally phased out of service in 1941, and one is still in existence today at the Trieste War Museum. The first Italian armoured car was the Isotta-Fraschini of 1911 and some of these were used in the Italian-Turkish war. These were followed in 1912 by the FIAT armoured car, some of which were also used in Libya during the Italian-Turkish war. The Bianchi company of Milan also built at least two different armoured cars between 1912 and 1916, but neither of these was built in large numbers and the Lancia continued to be the Italian mainstay for many years.

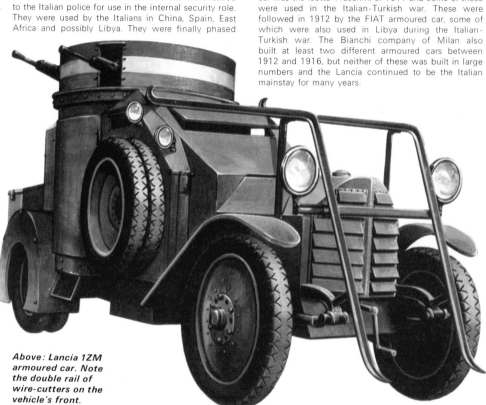

Above: Lancia 1ZM armoured car. Note the double rail of wire-cutters on the vehicle's front.

FIAT 3000 LIGHT TANK

Fiat 3000 Model 21, and Model 30 (3000B).
Crew: 2.
Armament: Twin SIA or FIAT Model 29 6.5mm machine-guns.
Armour: 6mm (0.24in) minimum, 16mm (0.63in) maximum.
Dimensions: Length (without tail) 11ft 9in (3.61m); length (with tail) 13ft 8in (4.17m); width 5ft 5in (1.64m); height 7ft (2.19m).
Weight: Combat 12,125lbs (5,500kg).
Engine: FIAT four-cylinder petrol engine developing 50hp at 1,700rpm.

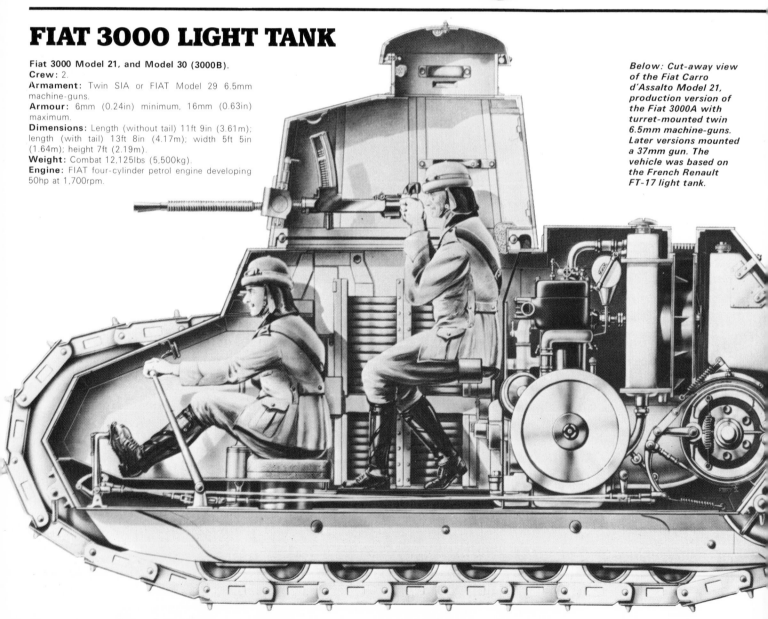

Below: Cut-away view of the Fiat Carro d'Assalto Model 21, production version of the Fiat 3000A with turret-mounted twin 6.5mm machine-guns. Later versions mounted a 37mm gun. The vehicle was based on the French Renault FT-17 light tank.

FIAT 2000 HEAVY TANK

Crew: 10.
Armament: One turret-mounted 65mm gun; seven FIAT 6.5mm machine-guns.
Armour: 20mm (0.79in) maximum; 15mm (0.59in) minimum.
Dimensions: Length 24ft 3in (7.4m); width 10ft 2in (3.1m); height 12ft 6in (3.8m).
Weight: Combat 88,185lbs (40,000kg).
Engine: Fiat A12 six-cylinder petrol engine developing 240hp.
Performance: Maximum road speed 3.7mph (6km/h); range 47 miles (75km); vertical obstacle 3ft 3in (1m); trench 9ft 10in (3m).
History: Entered service with Italian Army in 1919–20 and phased out of service in early 1930s.

Left: The Fiat 2000 heavy tank, mounting a 65mm gun and six 6.5mm machine-guns.

Whilst the Italian Army took an early interest in armoured cars, it was not until the appearance of Allied tanks on the battlefields of France in 1916 that Italy took any real interest in tracked armoured vehicles. In 1915, however, a Captain Luigi Cassali had designed a tank-type vehicle, a prototype of which was built by the Pavesi company, well known for its cross-country articulated vehicles. This vehicle had two turrets, each fitted with a single machine-gun, but after unsuccessful trials the project was dropped. It should be remembered that the conditions under which the Italian Army fought were not comparable with conditions on the Western Front, and many of the Italian actions were fought in terrain unsuitable for armoured operations. Italy did obtain a French Renault light tank and a Schneider medium tank for trials purposes, but as the French could not supply large numbers it was at first hoped that these types would be built in Italy. In the end, however, the Italians built an improved version of the Renault FT-17, the FIAT 3000, and built their own heavy tank, the FIAT 2000. Design work on the FIAT 2000 had in fact started in 1916 before the army even issued a requirement. The first two prototypes were completed at the end of 1918 but did not see any action. Most sources have stated

that these were followed by four further vehicles in 1920. These remained in service with the Italian Army until at least 1934, when they were finally phased out of service. In many respects the FIAT 2000 was an advanced vehicle, especially when one considers that the FIAT company had no experience of building tracked vehicles of this type. The driver was seated at the very front of the hull and had excellent vision: a periscope was provided for observation when in action, and a hatch could be opened up at the front when the vehicle was moving up to the front line. The engine was at the rear of the hull with the transmission at the front under the driver's position. Compared with those of other tanks of the period, the interior of the FIAT 2000 was quite roomy as most of the mechanical components were under the floor. Main armament consisted of a turret-mounted 65mm gun which could be traversed through 360°. The FIAT 2000 was in fact the first tank to mount such a heavy

armament in a turret, rather than in the front or side of the hull with limited traverse. In each side of the hull were three machine-guns, and there was a single machine-gun in the rear of the hull. These covered almost every angle of approach to the tank except the front, and most of this angle was in fact covered by the forward machine-guns on each side, which could be traversed through 100°. In the 1930s it is believed that some of the FIAT 2000s had their forward machine-guns replaced by 37mm guns. The suspension consisted of 10 road wheels, of which eight were grouped in pairs on bogie units, these being sprung on leaf springs. The other two road wheels were located between each end bogie and the idler or drive sprocket. Although the FIAT 2000 did not have the cross-country capability of the British tanks of this period, it was superior to the French Saint Chamond and Schneider tanks in this respect, and was also very well armed.

Performance: Road speed 15mph (24km/h); range 59 miles (95km); vertical obstacle 2ft (0.6m); trench 4ft 11in (1.5m); gradient 60 per cent.
History: Entered service with the Italian Army in 1923 and remained in service until 1943. Also exported to Albania, Ethiopia and Latvia.

In 1918 France supplied Italy with a Schneider tank and a few Renault FT-17 light tanks. Italy requested additional tanks but at that time France could not even meet her own requirements, let alone export orders. FIAT, assisted by Ansaldo and Breda, then started to design a vehicle similar to the FT-17 but using Italian

components. FIAT received an order for 1,400 tanks but this was reduced to 100 when World War I ended in 1918. The first prototype was completed in 1920 but it was not until 1923 that it entered service with the Italian Army. Compared with the French Renault FT-17, the Italian FIAT 3000 (or *Carro d'Assalto FIAT 3000 Model 21*) was lighter and much faster. First models were armed with turret-mounted twin 6.5mm machine-guns with an elevation of +24° and a depression of −17°, 2,000 rounds of machine gun ammunition being carried. In 1929 a FIAT 3000 was fitted with a 37mm gun in place of the machine-guns, and most surviving examples were rebuilt as the FIAT 3000 Model 30 (or FIAT 3000B). In addition to the

new armament the suspension was improved and a more powerful engine, which developed 63hp, was fitted. The 37mm gun was offset to the right and had an elevation of +20° and a depression of −10°, 68 rounds of 37mm ammunition being carried. Some FIAT 3000s were fitted with a radio for use in the command role, and trials versions included a 105mm self-propelled howitzer and another with twin 37mm guns. Until the arrival of the British Carden-Loyd Mark VI vehicles in 1929, the FIAT 3000 was the only tank the Italian Army had in quantity. The Italians used the tank in action in Abyssinia, Libya and in Italy itself. The type was last used in action in 1943, when some were encountered by the Allies in their invasion of Sicily.

Below: The Fiat Carro d'Assalto Model 30 (3000B), mounting a 37mm gun. Variants included a command vehicle and an experimental 105mm SP gun.

CARRO VELOCE CV 33 TANKETTE

Crew: 2.
Armament: Twin 8mm FIAT Model 18/35 machine-guns.
Armour: 15mm (0.6in) maximum; 5mm (0.2in) minimum.
Dimensions: Length 10ft 5in (3.16m); width 4ft 7in (1.4m); height 4ft 2in (1.28m).
Weight: Combat 7,571lbs (3,435kg).
Ground pressure: 7.1lb/in² (0.5kg/cm²).
Engine: SPA CV3 four-cylinder petrol engine developing 43bhp at 2,400rpm.
Performance: Road speed 26mph (42km/h); range 78 miles (125km); vertical obstacle 2ft 2in (0.65m); trench 4ft 9in (1.45m); gradient 100 per cent.
History: Entered service with the Italian Army in 1933 and phased out of service in 1943. Also used by Afghanistan, Albania, Austria, Bolivia, Brazil, Bulgaria, China, Germany (a few in 1943–44), Greece, Hungary, Iraq and Spain (civil war).

Side view of L3/33 tankette. This was in extensive service with the Italian Army during the initial campaigns in North Africa.

In 1929 the Italians purchased some British Carden-Loyd Mark VI tankettes and also obtained a licence to manufacture the type in Italy. Twenty-five of these vehicles were built in Italy under the designation CV 29, production being undertaken by Ansaldo with automotive components being supplied by FIAT. The CV 29 was armed with a 6.5mm water-cooled machine-gun, later replaced by an air-cooled weapon of the same calibre. Further development resulted in the CV 3, which was tested by the Italian Army in 1931–32, and with modifications this was placed in production as the *Carro Veloce* CV 33. The original production order was for some 1,300 vehicles, 1,100 armed with machine-guns and 200 (CV 33 Special) armed with a 37mm gun. In the end only 300 or so were built, and these were known as the Series I, production being undertaken by FIAT/Ansaldo. These were armed with a single 6.5mm machine-gun. The Series I was followed in production in 1935 by the Series II, and at a later date most Series I vehicles were brought up to Series II standard. Armament consisted of twin FIAT Model 18/35 machine-guns with an elevation of +15° and a depression of −12°, traverse being limited to 12° left and 12° right. A total of 3,200 rounds of machine-gun ammunition was carried. The hull of the CV 33 was of all-riveted/welded construction with a minimum thickness of 6.5mm (0.256in) and a maximum thickness of 13.5mm (0.53in). The commander/gunner was seated on the left of the hull and the driver on the right. The engine was mounted transversely at the rear of the hull, and power was transmitted to the gearbox in the forward part of the hull by a shaft. The suspension consisted of six small road wheels, with the drive sprocket at the front and the idler at the rear, although there was also an adjustable idler wheel to the rear of the sixth road wheel. There were no track-return rollers. Of the six road wheels, the four centre ones were mounted on two sprung bogies, two wheels to a bogie. There were a number of variants of the CV 33. The flamethrower was called the *Carro Lancia Fiamme* and had the machine-guns replaced by a flamethrower. Some 109 gallons (500 litres) of flame fuel were carried in a two-wheeled trailer towed behind the tankette.

Alternatively, a tank could be mounted on the rear of the hull, the tank holding 13 gallons (60 litres) of flame fuel. The maximum range of the flamethrower was about 110 yards (100m). The vehicle was used in North Africa. The radio model was called the *Carro Radio* and had a loop-type radio aerial on the rear of the hull. The command model was similar but had no armament. An armoured recovery vehicle known as the *Carro Veloce Recupero* was developed to the prototype stage but was not placed in production. This model was unarmed and was provided with a tow bar at the rear of the hull. The bridgelayer was known as the *Passerella* and towed a trailer on which was a bridge 23ft (7m) in length and in four components. The crew had to leave the tankette to assemble the bridge, but this took less than 10 minutes. The CV 33 could also tow a tracked trailer carrying ammunition and supplies, and some vehicles had an 8mm machine-gun over the roof of the fighting compartment for use in the anti-aircraft role. A few vehicles had their machine-guns replaced by the Swiss Solothurn s18–1000 20mm anti-tank gun, which

AUTOBLINDA AB 40 ARMOURED CAR

AB 40, AB 41, AB 42, AB 43, Camionetta 42 Sahariana (AS 42).
Crew: 4.
Armament: Twin 8mm turret-mounted machine-guns; one 8mm machine-gun in the rear of hull firing to the rear.
Armour: 9mm (0.35in) maximum.
Dimensions: Length 17ft 1in (5.2m); width 6ft 4in (1.93m); height 8ft (2.44m).
Weight: Combat 15,100lbs (6,850kg).
Engine: Six-cylinder inline petrol engine developing 80hp.
Performance: Road speed 47mph (76km/h); road range 250 miles (400km); vertical obstacle 1ft (0.3m); gradient 40 per cent.
History: Entered service with the Italian Army in 1940 and also used post-war.

In the 1930s the standard armoured car of the Italian Army was the Lancia IZ, which entered service in World War I. In the 1930s FIAT did produce some six-wheeled armoured cars for the Italian Army (the *Autoblinda* FIAT 611), but the type was too large for the reconnaissance role. In 1939 the prototype AB 39 armoured car was built, this being followed by the AB 40, which was accepted for service with the Italian Army. The AB 40 had a number of unusual features and had exceptional cross-country mobility. All four wheels were powered, both the front and rear wheels could be steered, and the type could be driven both backwards and forwards as there was a rear driving position. On each side of the hull was a spare wheel mounted on a spindle, this being allowed to rotate and so assist the vehicle in overcoming obstacles. Armament consisted of twin 8mm machine-guns in a turret with a traverse of 360°, and an 8mm machine gun was also mounted in the rear of the hull firing towards the rear. This had an elevation of +18° and a depression of −6°, traverse being 13° left and right. Some 4,008 rounds of machine-gun ammunition were carried. The AB 40 was followed in production by the AB 41, which had its turret-mounted machine-guns replaced by a 20mm cannon and a co-axial machine-gun. These weapons had an elevation of +20° and a depression of −12°, and 456 rounds of 20mm and 1,992 rounds of 8mm machine-gun ammunition were carried. The AB 41 was slightly heavier than the AB 40 and was powered by an 88hp engine. The last model to enter production was the AB 43, armed with a 47mm gun and a co-axial 8mm machine-gun, and as in the AB 42 the rear 8mm machine-gun was retained. Some 63 rounds of 47mm and 720 rounds of 8mm machine-gun ammunition were carried. This model was powered by a 110hp engine which gave it a top speed of 56mph (90km/h). There were two variants of the vehicle: the *Porta Munizione* had the turret removed and was used to carry ammunition, and for trials purposes a vehicle had its turret removed and replaced with a 47mm anti-tank gun. Production of all models amounted to about 550. Components of the AB 41 were also used in the *Camionetta 42 Sahariana* (AS 42) long-range reconnaissance vehicle which was widely used in North Africa. This was unarmoured but could be fitted with a wide range of armament installations including 20mm anti-aircraft cannon, 20mm anti-tank cannon, 37mm anti-tank gun and a 13.2mm machine-gun.

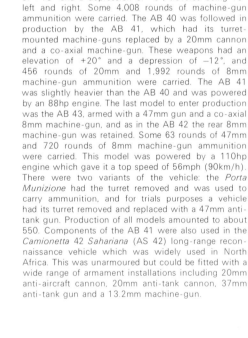

Left: AB 40 armoured car. These vehicles and the later AB 41 and AB 43 were assigned to the cavalry and reconnaissance units of Italian armoured and motorized divisions. They served in all the Italian Army's theatres of operation, including Russia. They were also used by the Army of the RSI, the pro-Axis force which the Germans built up from units of the Italian Army which remained loyal to them after the September 1943 armistice between Italy and the Allies. In the post-war years, armoured cars of this series were used by the Italian Police.

fired an armour-piercing round with a muzzle velocity of 2,460fps (750m/s). A Savoia-Marchetti SM82 aircraft was modified to carry a CV 33 recessed under its fuselage, but this was for experimental purposes only. In 1933–34 the CV 33 was followed in production by the CV 35. This had a redesigned hull of bolted construction, and was armed with a single Breda 13.2mm machine-gun. At least one CV 35 had its superstructure removed and a 47mm anti-tank gun mounted on the forward part of the hull, the vehicle being known as the *Semovente L 3 da 47/32*. The type did not enter service. The last model to enter service was the L 3/38, which had a new suspension. In 1937 FIAT/Ansaldo built a light tank based on a CV 33 chassis, the L3. This had a redesigned hull and a turret-mounted 20mm gun, but was not placed in production. In 1938 the designation of the CV 33 was changed to L-3-33, and the CV 35 became the L-3-35. About 2,500 of the CV 33/CV 35 were built both for the Italian Army and for export, although some of the latter were fitted with different armament. The CV 33 was used in the Spanish Civil War, where its short-comings soon became apparent

Above: The L3/33 (LF) Carro Lancia Fiamme. This flame-thrower variant of the tankette had a long-barrelled hooded flame-thrower replacing the machine-guns, with 500 litres of fuel towed in the wheeled trailer.

Right: Heavily-camouflaged L3/33 tankettes of the Italian Army travel through wooded country.

when it encountered the Russian tanks used by the Spanish Republican forces. It saw combat with the Italian Army in Albania, Ethiopia, France, North Africa, Russia and Yugoslavia. The tankette still formed a major part of the Italian armoured forces in North Africa when World War II started, but by that time the design was obsolete and the British had no trouble dealing with the vehicle as its armour was so thin.

CARRO ARMATO L6/40 LIGHT TANK

L6/40, and Semovente L40.
Crew: 2.
Armament: One Breda Model 35 20mm gun; one Breda Model 38 8mm machine-gun co-axial with main armament.
Armour: 30mm (1.26in) maximum; 6mm (0.24in) minimum.
Dimensions: Length 12ft 5in (3.78m); width 6ft 4in (1.92m); height 6ft 8in (2.03m).
Weight: 14,991lbs (6,800kg).
Ground pressure: 6.87lb/in² (0.61kg/cm²).
Engine: SPA 180 four-cylinder inline petrol engine developing 70hp.
Performance: Road speed 26mph (42km/h); road range 124 miles (200km); vertical obstacle 2ft 4in (0.7m); trench 5ft 7in (1.7m); gradient 60 per cent.
History: Entered service with the Italian Army in 1941 and used in small quantities by German Army in 1944. In service until the early 1950s.

The L 6/40 was developed from a series of 4.92ton (5,000kg) tracked vehicles developed by FIAT-Ansaldo mainly for the export market. The first prototypes were completed in 1936, one being armed with twin 8mm Breda machine-guns whilst another had a 37mm gun and a co-axial 8mm machine-gun. The Italian Army ordered 283 L 6/40s and these were

Right: The L6/40 light tank, with turret-mounted 20mm gun and co-axial 8mm machine-gun. More than 280 L6/40s were delivered in 1941-42, but it was not employed in significant quantity until 1942-43, when the tank was issued to the armoured groups of Italian cavalry divisions and to reconnaissance units. A number of these tanks were used by Italian forces on the Russian front—the heaviest tanks sent to that theatre by the Italian high command. The tank was also produced in small numbers as a flame-thrower, without the 20mm gun. This variant, which never entered service, was some 200kg heavier and carried 200 litres of flame fuel. A light assault and support vehicle was based on the chassis of the L6. This was designated the Semovente L40, and mounted a 47mm anti-tank gun.

delivered between 1941 and 1942. From the information available it would appear that a number of these were in fact completed as *Semovente* L40 47mm self-propelled anti-tank guns. The hull of the L 6/40 was of riveted construction with a minimum thickness of 0.24in (6mm) and a maximum thickness of 1.26in (30mm). The driver was seated at the front of the hull on the right; the turret was offset to the left, and the engine was located at the rear. The suspension consisted of two bogies each with two road wheels, with the drive sprocket at the front and the idler at the rear, and three track-return rollers were provided. The main armament consisted of a 20mm cannon with an elevation of +20° and a depression of −12°, and an

8mm machine-gun was mounted co-axial with the main armament. Some 296 rounds of 20mm and 1,560 rounds of 8mm machine gun ammunition were carried. The L 6/40 was designed to replace the CV 33 tankette, but it was already obsolete by the time it entered service with the Italian Army in 1941. It was used in Italy, North Africa and Russia. A flamethrower model was developed but this did not enter service. The command model was fitted with radios and had an open roof. The *Semovente* L40 was armed with a 47mm anti-tank gun mounted in the front of the superstructure to the left of the driver. This model had a crew of three, and 49 rounds of 47mm ammunition were carried.

CARRO ARMATO M 13/40 MEDIUM TANK

**M 13/40, M 14/41, M 15/42, P40 (P26), and
Semovente M42M, M42T.**
Crew: 4.
Armament: One 47mm gun; one 8mm machine-gun
co-axial with main armament; one 8mm anti-aircraft
machine-gun; twin 8mm machine-guns in hull front.
Armour: 42mm (1.65in) maximum; 6mm (0.24in)
minimum.
Dimensions: Length 16ft 2in (4.92m); width 7ft 3in
(2.2m); height 7ft 10in (2.38m).
Weight: Combat 30,865lbs (14,000kg).
Ground pressure: 13.2lb/in² (0.92kg/cm²).
Engine: SPA 8 TM40 eight-cylinder diesel developing
125hp.

*Right: A Carro Armato M 13/40 medium tank
(No. 1, 3 Ptn, 2 Coy, XI Bn) now preserved
as a memorial to Italians killed at El
Alamein. The tank mounted an effective high-
velocity 47mm gun, but inadequate armour
made it inferior to British infantry tanks
like the Matilda. Captured M 13/40s were
used by tank-starved Allied armoured units
for a short time in 1941.*

Performance: Road speed 20mph (32km/h) road
range 125 miles (200km); vertical obstacle 2ft 8in
(0.8m); trench 6ft 11in (2.1m); gradient 70 per cent.
History: Entered service with Italian Army in 1940
and phased out of service in 1942.

The Carro Armato M 11/39 was designed in 1936 with
the first prototype being completed the following year.
This used some suspension components of the L3
tankette. Armament consisted of twin turret-mounted
Breda 8mm machine-guns and a 37mm gun mounted
in the right side of the hull. The 37mm gun could be
traversed through 30° and had an elevation of +12°
and a depression of −8°, and 84 rounds of 37mm and
2,808 rounds of 8mm ammunition were carried. The

M 11/39, of which only 100 were built, weighed
10.83 tons (11,000kg) and had a crew of three, and
saw action in North Africa in 1940–41. It soon became
apparent that the main armament would have to be
mounted in a turret rather than in the hull front with a
limited traverse. The Americans came to the same
conclusion some years later with the Lee/Grant tank.
The chassis of the M 11/39 was retained on the new
vehicle, but the hull was redesigned. The first prototype of this M 13/40 was completed in 1940 with the first
production tanks being completed in the same year.
Main armament consisted of a turret-mounted 47mm
gun with an elevation of +20° and a depression of
−10°. An 8mm machine-gun was mounted co-axial
with the main armament and there was a similar

SEMOVENTE M41 SELF-PROPELLED ANTI-TANK GUN

90/53 M41, also Semovente 149 M13/40.
Crew: 4.
Armament: One 90mm gun.
Armour: 9mm (0.35in) minimum, 50mm (1.96in)
maximum.
Dimensions: Length (overall) 17ft 4in (5.282m);
width 7ft 4in (2.265m); height 7ft 5in (2.26m).
Weight: Combat 34,479lbs (17,000kg).
Ground pressure: 13.8lb/in² (0.97kg/cm²).
Engine: SPA 15 TM41 eight-cylinder diesel develop-
ing 125hp.
Performance: Road speed 22mph (35km/h); range
125 miles (200km); vertical obstacle 2ft 11in (0.889m);
trench 7ft (2.133m); gradient 50 per cent.
History: Entered service with the Italian Army in 1942.
Also used by the German Army.

The 90mm *Semovente*, or to give the vehicle its full
name the *Semovente da 90/53 su scafo di carro M41
(Modificato)*, was introduced into the Italian Army in
1942 to give it some mobile anti-tank capability. But
only 30 of the type were eventually built between
1942 and 1943 and these were used against the Allies
in Sicily. One of these weapons is still in existence
today at Aberdeen Proving Ground, Maryland, in the
United States. The 90mm *Semovente* consisted
basically of a modified M41 tank chassis with a 90mm
anti-aircraft gun (the *Canone de 90/53*, which was in
turn developed from a naval gun) mounted at the
rear of the hull. This was provided with a shield which
had a maximum thickness of 1.61in (41mm) at the
front and 0.35in (9mm) at the sides. There was very
limited overhead cover and no protection at all at the
rear. The crew of four consisted of the commander/
gunner, loader, radio operator and driver. The 90mm
gun had an elevation of +24° and depression of −5°,
traverse being 40° left and 40° right. The gun fired an
AP projectile weighing 22.2lbs (10kg) with a muzzle
velocity of 2,756 feet per second (840m/s), and this
would penetrate 5.5in (140mm) of armour at a range
of 500 yards (457m). Only six ready rounds were
carried and a further 26 rounds of ammunition were
carried in a tracked carrier which normally operated

with the gun. The carrier itself also towed a two-
wheeled ammunition trailer containing a further 40
rounds of ammunition. The *Semovente* 149 was an
M13/40 chassis with a 149mm Model 35 gun mounted
at the rear of the hull. This weapon was one of the best
artillery pieces in the Italian Army, and was widely
used in the towed role. The gun fired an HE shell to a
maximum range of 25,928 yards (23,700m). Combat
weight was 17.72 tons (18,000kg) and the type by a
250hp SPA engine which gave it a top road speed of
22mph (35km/h). Only one of these was built in 1943
by Ansaldo, and this is the vehicle now preserved at
Aberdeen Proving Ground in America.

The 90mm gun used in the Semovente M41 was
the Italian equivalent of the German 88mm anti-tank
gun. In fact, the Italian weapon had a slightly higher
muzzle velocity than the German weapon. Its main
drawback was its complete lack of rear or top armour
protection for the gun crew and this made them very
vulnerable to small arms fire and shell splinters. Some
24 of these weapons were used by the Italian 10°
Raggruppamento Semoventi in Sicily, these being
used German operation control. The 90mm gun was
also mounted on various 6×4 and 4×2 truck chassis,
including the Lancia 3 RO (4×2). This model had a
gun shield, gun platform and outriggers which could be
lowered to provide a stable firing platform.

*Above: The Semovente 90/53 M41 self-
propelled anti-tank gun was the heaviest
tracked artillery piece used by Italy in WWII
and was almost as effective as the German*
*88mm, but only 30 were built. The gun
carried only six ready rounds; in action in
Sicily it was accompanied by L6-40 light
tanks acting as ammunition carriers.*

weapon for the anti-aircraft role. Two 8mm machine-guns were mounted in the hull front on the right. Some 104 rounds of 47mm and 3,048 rounds of 8mm ammunition were carried. The hull was of bolted construction with a minimum thickness of 0.24in (6mm) and a maximum thickness of 1.65in (42mm). The driver and bow machine-gunner were seated in the front of the hull, and the loader and commander in the turret. The commander had to aim and fire the main armament in addition to his other duties. The suspension on each side consisted of four double-wheeled articulated bogies, mounted in two assemblies, each of the latter being carried on semi-elliptic springs. The drive sprocket was at the front and the idler at the rear, and there were three track-return rollers. The M 13/40

was used in North Africa in 1941 and was found to be very prone to breakdowns as it was not designed to operate in desert conditions. The M 13/40 was followed in production by the M14/41 which had a more powerful engine developing 145hp and fitted with filters to allow it to operate in the desert. The last model in the series was the M 15/42, which entered service in 1943. This had a slightly longer hull than the earlier models and was powered by an eight-cylinder petrol engine which developed 192hp, this giving the tank a top road speed of 25mph (40km/h). Other modifications included the re-siting of the hull escape door on the right of the hull, a longer gun barrel, power-operated turret traverse and heavier armour. Production of the tanks was undertaken by Ansaldo-Fossati and the

following quantities were built: M 13/40 799, M 14/41 1,103 and M 15/42 between 82 and 90. The M 13/40 and M 14/41 were the most important Italian tanks of World War II and were used in North Africa, Greece and Yugoslavia. Many were captured when they ran out of fuel and at least two Allied units, the British 6th Royal Tank Regiment and the Australian 6th Cavalry, were equipped with these tanks for a brief time when British tanks were in short supply in 1941. The Italians developed a variety of self-propelled artillery based on these chassis. There is a separate entry for the 90mm *Semovente* which also covers the *Semovente* 149. The *Semovente* M40, M41 and M42 were based respectively on the M13, M14 and M15 chassis. Armament consisted of a Model 35 75mm gun/howitzer with an elevation of +22° and a depression of −12°, traverse being 20° left and 18° right. There was also a command model with the main armament removed. This was armed with a hull-mounted 13.2mm machine-gun and an 8mm anti-aircraft machine-gun. The *Semovente* M42M (75/14) self-propelled gun was to have been based on the P40 tank chassis but as a result of delays less than 100 were built, and these were based on the M 15/42 chassis. Armament consisted of a 75mm gun with 42 rounds of ammunition. This was followed by the M42L which had a 105mm gun. When the Germans took over the Ansaldo works they built a model known as the M42T which had a 75mm gun. The M 13/40, M 14/41 and M 15/42 were to have been replaced by a new tank designated the P40 (or P26). Although design work on this tank started as early as 1940, it was not until 1942 that the first prototype was ready for trials. The delays were caused by changes in the main armament and the difficulty in finding a suitable engine for the tank. The tank entered production in 1943 but did not enter service with the Italian Army, although a few appear to have been used in the static defence role by the Germans in Italy. The P40 weighed 25.59 tons (26,000kg) and was armed with a 75mm gun and an 8mm co-axial machine-gun. The P40 was itself to have been followed by the P43, but this latter only reached the mock-up stage. The Italians also designed a tank called the *Carro Armato Celere Sahariano*, which had a Christie suspension and resembled the Crusader which the Italians encountered in North Africa, but this never entered production.

Left: US Army personnel inspect a captured M 13/40 tank. 1,960 M 13/40s were built.

FIAT/OTO MELARA 6616M ARMOURED CAR

Crew: 3.
Armament: One 20mm cannon; one 7.62mm machine-gun co-axial with main armament; one grenade-launcher in turret roof; six smoke dischargers.
Armour: 6mm–8mm (0.23–0.32in).
Dimensions: Length 17ft 2in (5.235m); width 8ft 2in (2.5m); height (to top of turret) 6ft 6in (1.98m).
Weight: Combat 16,314lbs (7,400kg).
Engine: Model 8062.22 six-cylinder inline liquid-cooled turbocharged diesel developing 147hp at 3,200rpm.
Performance: Maximum road speed 59mph (95km/h); water speed 2.8mph (4.5km/h); range 466 miles (750km); vertical obstacle 18in (0.45m); gradient 60 per cent.
History: Entered service with Italian Army and police in 1976–7.

When the Italian Army was reformed after World War II, most of its initial equipment came from Great Britain and the United States. In the early 1960s, the Italians obtained licences from the United States to build the M60A1 tank and the M113 armoured personnel carrier. A total of 200 M60A1s was built and the M113 is still being built by Oto Melara at La Spezia, some 4,000 having been delivered so far. The Fiat company of Turin, in association with Oto Melara, have designed a 4×4 armoured car with the designation Type 6616M, using many components of the Type 6614 armoured personnel carrier built by the same companies. An initial production batch of 50 armoured cars is being built, 30 for the police and 20 for the Italian Army. These will be subjected to extensive trials and if these are successful, further orders will be placed. The vehicle has been designed to undertake a variety of roles including reconnaissance, border patrol, convoy escort and airfield security. The hull of the Type 6616M is of all-welded steel construction with the driver

seated at the front on the right, with the commander and gunner in the turret. The engine, transmission and fuel tank are at the rear of the hull, these being separated from the crew compartment by a fireproof bulkhead. The main armament consists of a 20mm Rh.202 cannon, with a 7.62mm machine-gun mounted above it. The turret has full power traverse and elevation. The gun can be elevated at a speed of 25° a second from −5° to +35°. Traverse is a full 360° at a speed of 40° a second. The powered turret enables the gunner to lay the guns onto the target very quickly, and this factor is especially useful when tracking aircraft and helicopters. A 40mm smoke grenade-launcher is mounted in the roof of the commander's cupola, and there are three smoke dischargers on each side of the turret. If required, a 40mm automatic grenade-launcher or a TOW/Milan type anti-tank missile system can be mounted on the turret roof.

Empty cartridge cases from the 20mm gun are ejected externally so that the turret is not cluttered up with empty cartridge cases, this feature also reducing fumes in the turret. A total of 400 rounds of 20mm (250 being for ready use), 1,000 rounds of 7.62mm (300 for ready use) and 39 smoke grenades is carried. To reduce driver fatigue the steering is power-assisted, and the driver's seat can be adjusted so that he can drive in the head out position when not in action. The tyres are of the run-flat type, these enabling the vehicle to keep going even when its tyres have been damaged by small arms fire. The vehicle is fully amphibious, being propelled in the water by its wheels. Electric bilge pumps are fitted and some of the mechanical components can be pressurised to stop water entering them. Other equipment includes a winch for self-recovery operations, an NBC system, an air-conditioning system and a fire extinguishing system.

Right: The Fiat 6616M armoured car is now entering service with the Italian Army and Police. A multi-role vehicle, it is fully amphibious and incorporates an NBC system.

Japan

Japan started her armoured forces in the same way that she started all her sophisticated armaments: she bought foreign designs and copied them. Her first tanks were copies of Vickers models and were supplied in 1926. In fact the Japanese heavy industry had tried to build a tank in the early years of the 1920s, but on finding it more difficult than it looked, the Vickers Mark C was bought in small numbers to see them through. A few years later the home industry managed to get the design right, more by imitation than invention, and from then on the army was equipped with national models only.

From the very beginning the Japanese looked upon tanks as being supporting weapons for the infantry and other arms, and there was never, nor is there today, any tendency to try to use the armoured units as independent forces. Tanks were at all times tied to the slow-moving infantry and acted solely as supporting fire and morale raisers.

The Japanese high command realised that to carry out their projected strategy of Pacific domination the army had to be adapted to a policy of maritime aggression, and for armoured equipments this meant placing strict limits on the weight and bulk of individual items. All the tanks had the same general features of thin armour, relatively low power, and light guns. The early models were well supplied with machine-guns, in one case at least using sub-turrets, and in others by putting a machine-gun in the back face of the turret. None was really intended for any form of action other than assaulting purely infantry defensive positions. Tank to tank battles were the last thing that was likely to develop in the Pacific theatre, and in this respect the planners were quite right; indeed the number of times that one tank met another at all is remarkably small.

This rather restricted tactical outlook was sharply reflected in the quality and number of tanks produced in Japan, and the fact that there were few if any variants. To some extent this narrow range of vehicles was also due to Japanese industry not being well adjusted to the mass production of armoured vehicles. The largest heavy industry in the country was ship-building, there being no motor industry until after World War II, and ship-building is not a good basis on which to set up the making of armoured vehicles in anything but small quantities. As a result the Japanese Army relied on foreign manufacture for several years, and in so doing lost a good deal of time in which her designers could have been gaining experience.

Although the Japanese industrial capacity was mobilised for the war along with all other facilities in the country, there were overwhelming demands made upon it, and the factories could not keep pace. The predominantly infantry-type ground fighting did not require the large armoured formations that the Germans deployed, and

there was no real incentive to explore more effective types until quite late on in the war, when in any case it was already nearly too late to change. In the Malaya, Burma and East Indies campaigns one or two tanks among the leading infantry units had an effect upon the lightly armed opposition far out of proportion to their actual fighting ability. In the push southward through Malaya the Japanese used a few light tanks to clear roadblocks and defensive positions. Despite the fact that they were so thinly armoured that they were vulnerable even to anti-tank rifles, or possibly less powerful weapons, these tanks cleared practically everything before them and swept all the way

down the country to the Johore Straits, *en route* losing only two as actual battle casualties, though several broke down. Reliability was not one of the features of the pre-war Japanese tank force.

In the campaigns up and down the Pacific islands small forces of tanks were put ashore, and were generally successful locally, though their use was generally uninspired and timid. When the US Army equipped itself with the bazooka the effective use of tanks in jungle became very hazardous, and in the last year of the war very few were encountered.

After a long period in the Doldrums after the war, the Japanese Defence Forces were revived for the sole purpose of self-defence. The result of this policy has not been conducive to forming useful armoured

units, nor making any great efforts to equip them. For the most part the armoured troops operate in small formations in support of infantry and with little chance to train or exercise in a war setting. Most of the equipment is elderly US pattern and there are still Shermans in use, but there have also been some native designs, built by Mitsubishi. In addition to tanks there are APCs and support vehicles, and there have also been some interesting attempts at light armoured vehicles, particularly one or two for anti-tank warfare. For the most part, however, the atmosphere in Japan does not lend itself towards a recovery of any large armoured force, and it looks likely that it will not change for some time yet.

A column of Japanese Type 95 light tanks on the move. These were well suited to jungle warfare, but were obsolete by 1943.

MODEL 2592 (1932) OSAKA ARMOURED CAR

Crew: 3.
Armament: One machine-gun in hull front; one machine-gun in turret.
Armour: 11mm (0.43in) maximum.
Dimensions: Length 16ft 5in (5.003m); width 6ft 1in (1.854m); height 8ft 8in (2.641m).
Weight: 12,800lbs (5,805kg).
Engine: Four-cylinder water-cooled petrol engine developing 45hp.
Performance: Road speed 37mph (59.5km/h); range 150 miles (241km).
History: Entered service with Japanese Army in 1932 and used in early days of World War II.

The Japanese obtained an Austin armoured car shortly after the end of World War I, and this was tested in the early 1920s. It was not considered satisfactory, however, and so no further vehicles were obtained. It was not until 1928 that the Japanese automobile industry was established, and the first Japanese designed armoured cars followed shortly afterwards. The first Japanese-designed vehicle was in fact the ARM or *Sumida*, which was built by the Ishikawajima Motor Works and based on a standard commercial truck chassis with solid rubber tyres. Armament consisted of a single turret-mounted machine-gun. This was sent to Cheenan in China, where it was attached to the local garrison to protect Japanese interests. This was followed by the Model 2592 (1932 in Western years) *Osaka* armoured car. This was also based on a modified commercial chassis. When first introduced it also had solid rubber tyres, but these were later replaced by pneumatic tyres. The engine was at the front and the fighting compartment at the rear. This latter was of riveted construction with a maximum thickness of 0.3–0. 4in (8–11m). The radiator was provided with an armoured shutter. Armament consisted of a machine-gun in the turret, and another machine-gun in the front of the hull to the right of the driver. The *Osaka* had only limited mobility as it was powered on the

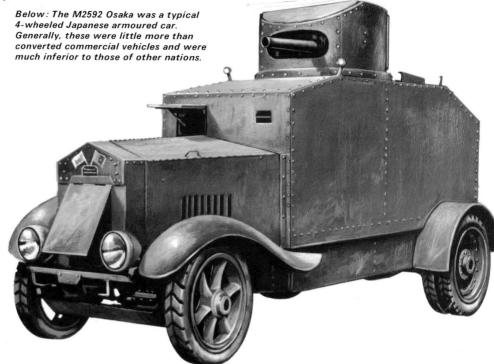

Below: The M2592 Osaka was a typical 4-wheeled Japanese armoured car. Generally, these were little more than converted commercial vehicles and were much inferior to those of other nations.

rear wheels only, that is it was a 4×2 vehicle. The Japanese Navy also used armoured cars, including the Crossley-Vickers Type 87, a British 1925 Indian pattern vehicle. When these entered service they had solid tyres, but these were replaced by pneumatic tyres later on. The Crossley had a hemispherical turret armed with two Vickers machine-guns (provision was made for mounting four machine-guns) and 3,500 rounds of ammunition were carried. The Type 87 was powered by a Crossley four-cylinder petrol engine which developed 50hp and gave the vehicle a top road speed of 40mph (64km/h).

TYPE 2593 (1933) SUMIDA ARMOURED CAR

Crew: 6.
Armament: One machine-gun.
Armour: 16mm (0.63in) maximum.
Dimensions: Length 21ft 6in (6.57m); width 6ft 3in (1.9m); height 9ft 8in (2.95m).
Weight: 15,432lbs (7,000kg).
Engine: Petrol engine developing 40hp.
Performance: Maximum road speed 37mph (60km/h); maximum rail speed 27mph (43km/h).
History: Entered service with Japanese Army in 1933 and still in use in early stages of World War II.

In the early 1930s the Japanese Corps of Railway Engineers designed a 6×4 vehicle for use on either roads or railways. According to current Japanese sources there were in fact two models, the Type 91 and the Type 95. American Intelligence reports of the war indicated only one type, the Type 2593 (or Model 93). This was a 6×4 vehicle with steering on the front wheels. Four jacks were provided to jack up the vehicle for wheel changes. The Type 93 had six flange-type railway wheels, and three solid rubber tyres were carried on each side of the hull. It took about 10 minutes to fit these solid tyres. The track of the wheels could be adjusted so that the vehicle could be run on railway lines of different gauges. Couplings and buffers were provided so that the vehicle could tow wagons and carriages for troops and supplies. The hull was of riveted construction with a maximum thickness of 0.63in (16mm). The engine was at the front of the hull, with the personnel compartment at the rear, the latter being provided with rifle and machine-gun ports. Armament consisted of a single turret-mounted machine-gun. The Type 93 was used operationally in China, where much of the country's roads were so poor, or non-existent, that the vehicle proved very useful. The Japanese Navy also had a six-wheeled armoured car called the Type 2592 (1932). This weighed 7 tons (7,112kg) and was powered by a six-cylinder petrol engine developing 85hp. Armament consisted of four machine-guns, one in the turret, one in each side of the hull and one in the front of the hull. The Type 2592 had a crew of four. An unusual feature of this armoured car was the set of the auxiliary wheels mounted to the rear of the front wheels, to prevent the vehicle from bellying when it was crossing rough country.

Right: Side view of the Type 2593 Sumida armoured car. The vehicle is shown in its normal road condition, with the special tyres by which it could be adapted to run on rails attached to the side of the hull.

Above: The Sumida was one of the most successful and widely-used Japanese armoured cars. This one is adapted for rails.

TYPE 89B MEDIUM TANK

Crew: 4.
Armament: One Type 90 57mm gun; one 6.5mm machine-gun in turret rear; one 6.5mm machine-gun in hull front.
Armour: 17mm (0.67in) maximum; 10mm (0.39in) minimum.
Dimensions: Length 14ft 1in (4.3m); width 7ft (2.15m); height 7ft 2in (2.2m).
Weight: Combat 25,353lbs (11,500kg).
Engine: Mitsubishi six-cylinder inline diesel developing 120hp at 1,800rpm.
Performance: Road speed 17mph (27km/h); range 100 miles (160km); vertical obstacle 3ft (0.914m); trench 6ft 7in (2m); gradient 60 per cent.
History: Entered service with the Japanese Army in 1934 and remained in service until at least 1943.

After the end of World War I, the Japanese purchased in Europe a number of tanks for experimental purposes, including a single British Mark IV (known as the Type 78 Heavy), a few British Whippets (known as the Type 79 Medium Mark A), and a small quantity of French Renault FT-17 light tanks (known as the Medium Type 79), these last remaining in service in China until 1940. These British and French World War I types were followed in the early 1920s by a single British Vickers Medium Mark C (or Type 89 Medium) and some French Renault NC1 (Type 89 Medium *ETSU* B), the latter being used in combat in China in 1932 but not proving very successful. The first tank of Japanese design and construction was the Type 87, or Experimental Tank Number 1, built in 1927 at the Osaka Arsenal. This tank had a crew of five and was powered by an eight-cylinder water-cooled petrol engine which developed 140hp, giving the tank a top speed of 12.5mph (20km/h). Armament consisted of a turret-mounted 57mm gun, a single 7.2mm machine-gun in a turret at the front of the hull, and another machine-gun in a similar turret at the rear of the hull. This was followed in 1929 by the Type 89 Experimental Tank Number 2. This weighed 9.84 tons (10,000kg) and was armed with a turret-mounted 37mm gun, a machine-gun in the turret rear and another machine-gun in the hull front. Its Daimler six-cylinder petrol engine gave it a top speed of 15mph (25km/h). This was then placed in production by Mitsubishi as the Type 89 medium tank. The type 89 was powered by a petrol engine, although later models had a diesel, the petrol-engined model then becoming known as the Type 89A. The Type 89B, sometimes called the Type 94 as it first appeared in 1934, replaced the Type 89A in production: the most significant improvement was the installation of a six-cylinder air-cooled diesel, which offered a number of advantages over the earlier petrol engines, including improved safety and easier starting in cold climates. Other changes included a new turret and a one-piece glacis plate rather than the two-piece glacis plate of the earlier model. Armament consisted of a turret-mounted Type 90 57mm gun, a Type 91 6.5mm machine-gun mounted in the rear of the turret and a similar weapon in the hull front on the left. Some 100 rounds of 57mm and 2,745 rounds of machine-gun ammunition were carried. The hull was of all-riveted construction with the driver at the front on the right and the bow machine-gunner to his left. The turret was in the centre of the hull and was provided with a cupola for the commander. The engine and transmission were at the rear of the hull. The suspension consisted of nine small wheels with the idler at the front and the drive sprocket at the rear. Four track-return rollers were fitted. An unditching tail was provided at the rear of the hull. The type 89 saw action in China from 1932, and was also employed in the early stages of World War II, some being used in the Philippines campaign. As has been mentioned, the first Japanese tank was the Type 87 Experimental Tank Number 1. This was heavy for the medium role, however as it weighed 11.8 tons (12,000kg), not much more than the weight of the fully developed Type 89B. Further development resulted in the Type 91 heavy tank, which was not completed until 1932. The Type 91 weighed 18 tons (18,290kg) and was powered by a six-cylinder BMW aircraft engine developing 224hp. This gave the tank a top road speed of 15mph (25km/h) and an operating range of about 100 miles (160km). Armament consisted of a 70mm turret-mounted gun with a machine-gun in the turret rear. There was also a machine-gun turret at the front of the hull and a similar turret at the rear. The Type 91 was followed by the Type 95 heavy tank, although it would appear that few of these were built. This had a turret with a 70mm gun and a machine-gun in the main turret rear, whilst the front turret had a 37mm gun and the rear turret a machine-gun. This tank had a combat weight of about 26 tons (26,417kg) and a crew of five. It was powered by a six-cylinder water-cooled inline diesel engine which developed 290hp at 1,600rpm, giving the tank a top speed of 14mph (22km/h). There were a number of further heavy tank projects, but none of these ever reached service. It is even believed that the Japanese were building a 98.4 ton (100,000kg) tank at one time. In fact the British, Americans and Germans all had designs for tanks of this type at one time or another, and some were even built, the German *Maus*, for example.

Above: The Japanese Type 89B medium tank, seen here in China where it was in extensive operational use, was the standard medium tank throughout the 1930s. The Japanese flags are for aerial recognition.

Below: A Type 89B tank as used in Manchuria. Note the special tail to assist in trench crossing. The tank entered service in 1934 and served into World War II.

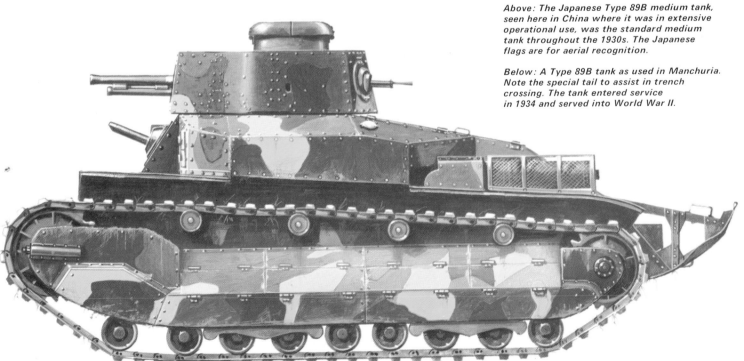

TYPE 95 HA-GO LIGHT TANK

Crew: 3.
Armament: One Type 94 37mm gun; Type 91 6.5mm machine-gun in hull front (see text).
Armour: 12mm (0.47in) maximum; 6mm (0.25in) minimum.
Dimensions: Length 14ft 4in (4.38m); width 6ft 9in (2,057m); height 7ft 2in (2.184m).
Weight: Combat 16,314lbs (7,400kg).
Ground pressure: 8.7lb/in² (0.61kg/cm²).
Engine: Mitsubishi Model NVD 6120 six-cylinder air-cooled diesel developing 120hp at 1,800rpm.
Performance: Road speed 28mph (45km/h); range 156 miles (250km); vertical obstacle 2ft 8in (0.812m); trench 6ft 7in (2m); gradient 60 per cent.
History: Entered service with Japanese Army in 1935 and remained in service until 1945.

In 1934 Mitsubishi Heavy Industries built the prototype of a new light tank, which was tested in both China and Japan, and followed by a second prototype the following year. This was standardised as the Type 95 light tank but was also known as the *HA-GO* (this being the Mitsubishi name) or the *KE-GO* (this being its official Japanese Army name). Although most sources state that Mitsubishi built the prototype, others claim that these were built at the Sagami Arsenal. The Type 95 was used by the cavalry and the infantry, and saw action in both China and throughout the World War II (or the Great East Asia War as the Japanese call it). Production amounted to about 1,250 tanks, most of which were built by Mitsubishi although numerous other companies and arsenals were also involved in component manufacture. When it was originally built the Type 95 compared well with other light tanks of that period, but by the early part of World War II it had become outdated, as indeed had most Japanese armoured vehicles. The Japanese used the Type 95 in small units or wasted them in the static defence role in many of the islands that they overran in the Pacific area. The hull of the tank was of riveted and welded construction varying in thickness from 0.35in (9mm) to 0.55in (14mm). The driver was seated at the front of the hull on the right, with the bow machine-gunner to his left. The commander, who also had to load, aim and fire the gun, was seated in the turret, which was offset to the left of the hull. The engine and transmission were at the rear of the hull, and the crew could reach the engine from within the hull. The inside of the tank was provided with a layer of asbestos padding in an effort to keep the temperature as low as possible, and this also gave the crew some protection against personal injury when the tank was travelling across very rough country. There was a space between the asbestos and the hull to allow air to circulate. The suspension was of the well-tried bellcrank type and consisted of four road wheels (two per bogie), with the drive sprocket at the front and the idler at the rear. There were two track-return rollers. Some of the Type 95s used in Manchuria had their suspensions modified as it was found that severe pitching occurred when the tank was crossing the local terrain, and these were redesignated the Type 35 (Special). Armament consisted of a turret-mounted 37mm tank gun which could fire both HE and AP rounds, and a Type 61 6.5mm machine-gun mounted

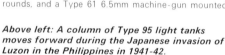

Above left: A column of Type 95 light tanks moves forward during the Japanese invasion of Luzon in the Philippines in 1941-42.

Left and Below: Top, front and rear views of the Type 95 HA-GO light tank. A wholly Japanese design, this tank had an air-cooled engine and high-mobility suspension and was well suited to the climate and terrain of Asia. A feature characteristic of Japanese tanks was separately located armament, with the machine-gun usually located at turret rear.

in the front of the hull with a traverse of 35° left and right. Later the Type 61 gun was replaced by a Type 97 7.7mm machine-gun and a similar weapon was mounted in the turret in the 5 o'clock position, this being operated by the commander/gunner. Later in the war the 37mm Type 94 tank gun was replaced by a Type 98 tank gun, which had a higher muzzle velocity. Some 119 rounds of 37mm and 2,970 rounds of machine-gun ammunition were carried. A number of tanks were also fitted with smoke dischargers on the sides of the hull, towards the rear. There were a number of variants of the Type 95 light tank, including an amphibious version for which there is a separate entry. In 1943 some Type 95s had their 37mm guns replaced by a 57mm gun as fitted to the Type 97 medium tank, and these vehicles then became the Type 3 light tank. The type 3 was followed by the Type 4 light tank in 1944: this was a Type 95 with the standard turret removed and replaced by the complete Type 97 medium tank turret with its 47mm gun. The Type 95 was to have been replaced by the Type 98 light tank, and prototypes of this were completed as early as 1938 by both Hino Motors and Mitsubishi Heavy Industries. This did not enter production until 1942, and only 100 seem to have been built (some sources state that 200 were built) before production was stopped in 1943. This model had a more powerful engine, which gave it a higher road speed, and thicker armour. Its suspension consisted of six road wheels with the drive sprocket at the front and the idler at the rear, there being three return rollers. The driver was seated at the front of the hull in the centre. Armament consisted of a 37mm Type 100 tank gun and two Type 97 7.7mm machine-guns. Other light tanks developed by Japan included the Improved Model 98 which had four road wheels, idler at the front and drive sprocket at the rear. No return rollers were fitted as the top of the track rested on the road wheels. Finally, there were the Type 2 (less than 30 built) and the Type 5, only one of which was built by Hino Motors before the end of the war.

Above: A column of Type 95 HA-GO light tanks, with the unusual feature that all the vehicles have had their main armament removed. Although the exact reason for this is not known, it is probably because the tanks are being used for some subsidiary purpose, such as carrying ammunition or supplies.

Below: Side view of a Type 95 tank, with bell-crank type suspension clearly visible. Note also the engine air-intake louvres, the front-sprocket drive, the rear machine-gun mounting, and the curved armour below the turret.

TYPE 97 CHI-HA MEDIUM TANK

Crew: 4.

Armament: One Type 90 57mm gun; one 7.7mm Type 97 machine-gun in turret rear; one 7.7mm Type 97 machine-gun in bow.

Armour: 25mm (0.98in) maximum; 8mm (0.3in) minimum.

Dimensions: Length 18ft 1in (5.516m); width 7ft 8in (2.33m); height 7ft 4in (2.23m).

Weight: Combat 33,069lbs (15,000kg).

Engine: Mitsubishi 12-cylinder air-cooled diesel developing 170hp at 2,000rpm.

Performance: Road speed 24mph (38km/h); range 130 miles (210km); vertical obstacle 2ft 6in (0.812m); trench 8ft 3in (2.514m); gradient 57 per cent.

History: Entered service with the Japanese Army in 1938 and continued in service until 1945. Also used by China after World War II.

The standard Japanese medium tank in the 1930s was the Type 89, but by 1936 it had become apparent that this would have to be replaced by a more modern vehicle. The General Staff Office and the Engineering Department could not agree on the best design, so two different prototypes were built. Osaka Arsenal built a prototype to the design of the General Staff, called the *CHI-NI*, whilst Mitsubishi built the model of the Engineering Department, called the *CHI-HA*. The *CHI-NI* weighed just under 9.84 tons (10,000kg) and was powered by a six-cylinder air-cooled diesel developing 135hp, which gave the tank a top speed of 18.5mph (30km/h). The *CHI-NI* had a three-man crew, and was armed with a 57mm Type 90 tank gun and a 6.5mm Type 91 machine-gun. The Mitsubishi design was much heavier and weighed 15 tons (15,241kg). It was powered by a Mitsubishi 12-

cylinder air-cooled diesel which developed 170hp and gave the tank a top road speed of 24mph (38km/h). Armament consisted of a 57mm gun and two 7.7mm machine-guns. The *CHI-HA* had a crew of four, of whom two were in the turret. Both of these prototypes were completed in 1937 and were subjected to comparative trials. Both tanks had good and bad points, however, and it was not until war broke out in China that it was decided to place the Mitsubishi tank in production as the Type 97 (*CHI-HA*) medium tank. Even today, many feel that the *CHI-NI* could have been developed into a first-class light tank. Most Type 97s were built by Mitsubishi, although other companies, including Hitachi, also built the tank. The hull was of riveted and welded construction. The driver was seated at the front of the hull on the right, with the bow machine-gunner to his left. The two-man turret was in the centre of the hull and offset to the right. The engine was at the rear of the hull, and power was transmitted to the gearbox in the front of the hull by a propeller-shaft which ran down the centreline of the hull. The suspension consisted of six dual rubber-tired road wheels, with the drive sprocket at the front and the idler at the rear. There were three track-return rollers, although the centre one supported the inside of the track only. The four central bogie wheels were paired and mounted on bellcranks resisted by armoured compression springs. Each end road wheel was independently bellcrank-mounted to the hull in a similar fashion. Armament consisted of a short-barrelled 57mm Model 97 tank gun, firing HE and AP rounds, a 7.7mm Model 97 machine-gun in the rear of the turret and a machine-gun of the same type in the bow of the tank. The main armament had an elevation of +11° and a depression of −9°, turret traverse being 360°. Two sets of trunnions allowed the gun to be traversed independently of the turret. The

inner vertical trunnions, set in a heavy steel bracket fitted to the cradle, permitted a 5° left and right traverse. Some 120 rounds (80 HE and 40 AP) of 57mm and 2,350 rounds of machine-gun ammunition were carried. The large provision of HE ammunition compared to other tanks of this period was because the Japanese believed that the role of the tank was to support the infantry rather than to destroy enemy armour. Compared with those of earlier Japanese tanks, the turret of the Type 97 was a great improvement: at last the tank commander could command the tank rather than operate the main armament. In later years, the large-diameter turret-ring fitted enabled the tank to be up-armed as more powerful weapons became available. As a result of combat experience gained against Soviet forces during the Nomonhan incident of 1939, it was decided that a gun with a higher muzzle velocity was required. A new turret was designed by Mitsubishi and when installed on the Type 97 it raised the tank's weight to 15.75 tons (16,000kg). These tanks were known as the Type 97 (Special). The gun fitted was the 47mm Type 1 (1941), which had a long barrel by Japanese standards and could fire both HE and AP rounds. The latter had a muzzle velocity of 2,700fps (823m/s) and would penetrate 2.76in (70mm) of armour at a range of 500 yards (457m). The breech-block was of the semi-automatic vertical sliding type. Some 104 rounds of 47mm and 2,575 rounds of machine-gun ammunition were carried. There were many variants of the Type 97 medium tank: flail type mineclearing tank, bulldozer tank, a variety of self-propelled guns (these are described in a separate entry), anti-aircraft tank with a 20mm gun, bridge laying tank and a number of different engineer and recovery models, to name a few. One of the most unusual models was the ram tank (*HO-K*), which had its turret removed and a steel

Below: One of the most successful Japanese tanks of World War II was the medium tank Type 97 CHI-HA. This tank was used in large numbers in the Asian and Pacific theatres until the end of the war. This illustration shows the vehicle as it appeared on service in Central Asia. It was used by China after WWII.

prow mounted at the front of the hull, developed for clearing a path through forests in Manchuria. The Type 97 medium tank was followed by the Type 1 medium tank, or *CHI-NE*. This weighed 17.2 tons (17,476kg) and its armour was increased to a maximum of 2in (50mm). It was powered by a Mitsubishi Type 100 12-cylinder air-cooled diesel which developed 240hp at 2,000rpm. Armament consisted of a Type 1 47mm gun and two Type 97 7.7mm machine-guns, one in the turret rear and one in the hull front. This was followed by the Type 3 (*CHI-NU*) medium tank in 1943. This had the same hull as the Type 1, but a new turret was fitted, increasing weight to 18.8 tons (19,100kg), which reduced top speed to 24mph (38km/h). Armament consisted of a 75mm Type 3 tank gun with a 7.7mm machine-gun in the hull front, there being no machine-gun in the turret rear. Production of the Type 3 commenced in 1944 but only some 50 or 60 examples were built. The Type 4 (*CHI-TO*) had a longer chassis and weighed 30 tons (30,480kg). This was armed with a turret-mounted 75mm gun and a bow-mounted 7.7mm machine-gun, and only a few of these were built. The final Japanese medium tank was the Type 5 (*CHI-RI*). This weighed 37 tons (37,594kg) and was armed with a turret-mounted 75mm gun and a bow-mounted 37mm gun. Its armour had a maximum thickness of 3in (75mm) and it was powered by a BMW aircraft engine developing 550hp at 1,500rpm. This gave the tank a top road speed of 28mph (45km/h). The suspension consisted of eight road wheels with the drive sprocket at the front and the idler at the rear, and there were three track-return rollers. This tank did not reach the production stage, however. If it had, it would have been a difficult tank for the Americans to destroy, although by the end of the war, the superior American M26 Pershing had been deployed to the Pacific area.

Above: Japanese medium tanks Type 97 CHI-HA drive down a road at Bukit Timah, Singapore. The radio frame aerial circumscribing the turret was a characteristic feature of Japanese tanks.

Left and right: Front and rear views of the Type 97 medium tank. The asymmetrical arrangement of its armour made the tank more difficult to build, but enhanced the effectiveness of its protection against small-arms fire.

Below: A Type 97 of the 3rd Company, 7th Tank Regiment, advances through jungle on the Bataan peninsula during the invasion of the Philippines, 1942. Smoke dischargers are mounted above the gun.

TYPE 97 (2597) TE-KE/KE-KE TANKETTE

Crew: 2.
Armament: One 37mm Type 94 gun (see text).
Armour: 12mm (0.47in) maximum.
Dimensions: Length 12ft 1in (3.682m); width 5ft 11in (1.803m); height 5ft 10in (1.773m).
Weight: Combat 10,469lbs (4,748kg).
Engine: Ikega four-cylinder inline air-cooled diesel developing 65hp at 2,300rpm.
Performance: Maximum road speed 26mph (42km/h); range 155 miles (250km); trench 5ft 7in (1.701m); gradient 60 per cent.
History: Entered service with the Japanese Army in 1938 and remained in service up to 1945.

The Type 97 tankette (or *Te-ke/Ke-ke*) was developed to replace the earlier Type 94 tankette which had proved rather unreliable in service. Two different prototypes of the Type 97 were built by the Tokyo Motor Industry (now known as Hino Motors), with engines supplied by Ikega. The first prototypes were completed in 1937. The initial model had the engine and driver at the front, with the turret at the rear, whilst the later model had the engine moved to the rear to facilitate communication between the driver and the gunner. After trials the second model was standardised as the Type 97 tankette, and this entered service with the Japanese Army in 1938. The Type 97 was the last tankette to be adopted by the Japanese Army as by the start of World War II this type of vehicle had become obsolete. Production of the vehicle continued well into the war, however, and the type was built in larger numbers than any other Japanese tankette. The vehicle had a hull of riveted construction, with the driver at the front of the vehicle on the left and the commander, who had to load, aim and fire the gun, in the turret located in the centre of the hull. The engine and transmission were at the rear. The suspension consisted of two bogies, each with two wheels, with the drive sprocket at the front and the idler at the rear, and there were two track-return rollers. Armament consisted of a 37mm gun with a total of 96 rounds of ammunition. Some models were armed with a single 7.7mm machine-gun in place of the 37mm gun. There were a number of variants of the Type 97 tankette including one with the turret removed, engine moved forward and a fully enclosed cargo area at the rear. This model was used for a wide variety of roles including those of ammunition carrier, observation post vehicle, barrage balloon mooring vehicle and self-propelled gun with a 37mm or 47mm anti-tank gun mounted at the rear of the hull.

Above right and right: Japanese Type 97 Tankette as examined by the British School of Tank Technology. In addition to commanding the tank the commander also had to operate the turret-mounted 37mm gun (or a 7·7mm MG).

TYPE 38 HO-RO 150mm SELF-PROPELLED HOWITZER

Crew: 5.
Armament: One 150mm howitzer.
Armour: 25mm (0.98in) maximum; 12mm (0.47in) minimum.
Dimensions: Length 18ft (5.486m); width 7ft 6in (2.286m); height 7ft 9in (2.362m).
Weight: 33,070lbs (15,000kg).
Engine: Twelve-cylinder air-cooled diesel developing 170hp.
Performance: Maximum road speed 25mph (40km/h); range 100 miles (160km); trench 8ft 3in 2.514m); gradient 57 per cent.
History: Entered service with the Japanese Army in 1942 and remained in service until 1945.

The Type 38 was developed to give a token of mobile fire support to the Japanese armoured divisions. It consisted of a Type 97 (1937) tank chassis with the turret removed and replaced by an open-topped superstructure of riveted construction. The front had a maximum thickness of 1in (25mm) and the sides were 0.47in (12mm) thick. In this was mounted a 150mm howitzer with a maximum elevation of +30°, traverse being very limited. The howitzer had a very short barrel and fired an HE projectile to a maximum range of 6,500 yards (5,943m). The Gun Tank Type 1 (or *HO-NI* I) was also based on a Type 97 tank and was armed with a 75mm Type 90 gun in an open-topped turret. The gun had an elevation of +25° and a depression of −5°, total traverse being 20°. The Gun Tank Type 2 (or *HO-I*) also had a 75mm howitzer, whilst the Gun Tank Type 3 (or *HO-NI* II) had a fully enclosed turret. The Japanese Navy also developed some self-propelled artillery, including a 200mm self-propelled howitzer on a *CHI-HA* chassis. Anti-aircraft artillery was not neglected and self-propelled models were

built in a variety of calibres (20mm, 75mm and 120mm) on different chassis. Even today no exact figures are available on Japanese armoured fighting vehicles built during World War II. Mitsubishi has stated that it accounted for some 4,650 AFVs (including 50 self-

propelled guns) and that this was 70 per cent of the total output of the Japanese factories during World War II. Most Japanese self-propelled artillery was built in such small numbers that they played a negligible part in most campaigns.

Left: Type 38 HO-RO self-propelled 150mm gun. This vehicle was based on the M.2597 medium tank chassis, having the turret replaced by an armoured shield and a special artillery mounting for the gun. It provided artillery fire support.

TYPE 94/TYPE 92 TANKETTE

Crew: 2.
Armament: One 6.5mm machine-gun.
Armour: 12mm (0.47in) maximum; 4mm (0.16in) minimum.
Dimensions: Length 10ft 1in (3.08m); width 5ft 4in (1.62m); height 5ft 4in (1.62m).
Weight: Combat 7,496lbs (3,400kg).
Engine: Four-cylinder air-cooled petrol engine developing 32hp at 2,500rpm.
Performance: Road speed 25mph (40km/h); range 130 miles (208km); vertical obstacle 1ft 8in (0.508m); trench 4ft 7in (1.4m); gradient 60 per cent.
History: Entered service in 1934 and still in service in 1943 at least.

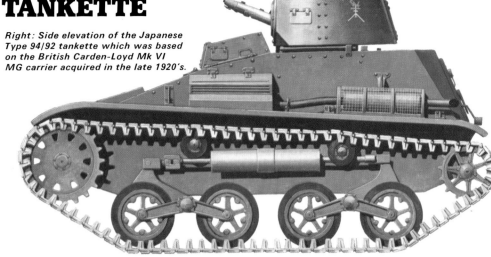

Right: Side elevation of the Japanese Type 94/92 tankette which was based on the British Carden-Loyd Mk VI MG carrier acquired in the late 1920's.

In the late 1920s the Japanese purchased six British Carden-Loyd Mark VI machine-gun carriers, and some time subsequently two Mark VIb carriers. As a result of trials with these vehicles the Japanese decided to develop a similar vehicle. The prototype was built in 1933–34 by the Tokyo Gas and Electric Industry (later to become Hino Motors) and after trials in both China and Japan it was standardised as the Type 94 tankette, although American sources have always referred to it as the Type 92 tankette. The hull of the tankette was of riveted construction, with the engine and driver at the front and the small turret at the rear of the hull. A large door was provided in the rear of the hull so that stores could be loaded quickly. Armament consisted of a single 6.5mm machine-gun in a turret with manual traverse. The suspension was designed by Tomio Hara and was similar to that used on most Japanese tanks. It consisted of four bogies (two on each side), these being suspended by bellcranks resisted by armoured compression springs placed horizontally one each side of the hull, externally. Each bogie had two small rubber-tired road wheels with the drive sprocket at the front and the idler at the rear, and there were two track-return rollers. When in service, the Type 94 was found to be very prone to throwing its tracks when it made a high speed turn. Further redesign work was carried out on the suspension and the small idler was replaced by a bigger idler, which was now on the ground. This increased the length of track on the ground, but it did not solve the basic problem. This model was powered by an air-cooled petrol engine which developed 35hp at 2,500rpm. Armament initially consisted of a single Type 91 6.5mm machine-gun, although in later models this was replaced by a single 7.7mm machine-gun. Some are reported to have been fitted with a 37mm gun. The primary role of the Type 94 was to carry supplies in the battlefield area, but it was often used in the reconnaissance role for which it was totally unsuited as its armour could be penetrated by ordinary rifle bullets. It was often used to tow a tracked ammunition trailer in a fashion similar to the British and French tankettes of this period. The Type 92 was replaced in service by the Type 97. Another interesting vehicle of this period was the so-called Type 92 combat car developed for the cavalry. The first prototype was completed by the Ishikawajima Motor Works in 1932, and after trials the vehicle was standardised as the Type 92 and was

used in China in the 1930s. The vehicle weighed 3.45 tons (3,500kg) and was powered by a six-cylinder air-cooled petrol engine. This gave it a top road speed of 25mph (40km/h) and an operational range of about 124 miles (200km). The Type 92s hull was of all-welded construction with some of its components riveted into position. The driver was seated at the front of the hull on the left, with the 12.7mm machine-gun and gunner to his right. This weapon could also be used against low-flying aircraft, although its lack of full traverse was a disadvantage. The commander's turret had a traverse of 360° and was armed with a 6.5mm machine-gun. The engine and transmission were at the rear of the hull. The suspension consisted of six small road wheels

with the drive sprocket at the front and the idler at the rear, there being three track-return rollers. Some Type 92s were later rebuilt with four larger road wheels and two return rollers as the earlier Type 92s' suspension had proved rather weak. There was also an amphibious model of the Type 92 combat car driven in the water by a propeller, but this was not adopted for service. The Type 92 was not built in very large numbers and was replaced by 1940

Below: A convoy of Type 94 Tankettes, these were also known as the Type 92 in Western sources. In 1936, each Japanese Infantry Division had a Tankette Company which had 6 Type 94's, for use in reconnaissance role.

TYPE 2 KA-MI AMPHIBIOUS TANK

Crew: 4–5.
Armament: On 37mm gun; one 7.7mm machine-gun co-axial with main armament; one 7.7mm machine-gun in bow of tank.
Armour: 13mm (0.51in) maximum; 9mm (0.35in) minimum.
Dimensions: Length 24ft 4in (7.416m); width 9ft 2in (2.794m); height 7ft 8in (2.336m).
Weight: Combat (with pontoons) 24,915lbs (11,300kg).
Engine: Six-cylinder air-cooled diesel developing 120hp.
Performance: Road speed 23mph (37km/h); water speed 6mph (9.6km/h); road range 124 miles (200km); water range 93 miles (150km); vertical obstacle 2ft 5in (0.736m); trench 6ft 7in (2.006m); gradient 50 per cent.
History: Entered service with the Japanese Marines in 1942 and remained in service until 1945.

The Japanese started experimenting with amphibious armoured vehicles as early as 1928, and up to 1940 most work was undertaken by the Japanese Army. Then the Japanese Navy took over the development of amphibious vehicles as these were to be used by the Marines. A whole series of vehicles was developed, including the *KA-MI-SHA* (Type 1), *KA-MI-SHA* (Type 2), *KA-CHI-SHA* (Type 3), *KA-TSU-SHA* (Type 4), *KA-TSU-SHA* II (also known as the Type 4) and finally the *TO-KU-SHA* (Type 5). The Type 2 used many components of the Type 95 light tank. The hull

was redesigned, and was of all-welded construction and fully sealed. Large pontoons were fitted front and rear to give the vehicle additional buoyancy. These were constructed of 0.12in (3mm) steel plate. The front pontoon was divided into eight compartments to minimise the effects of damage from shell fire. In the water the tank was propelled by two propellers driven by the main engine via transfer case. The Type 2 was steered in the water by two rudders, which were operated by the tank commander from his turret. Once ashore the pontoons were released by operating handwheels which controlled split-finger type pincerclamps. The tank was armed with a 37mm gun in a turret with a traverse of 360°, a 7.7mm machine-gun mounted co-axially with the main armament, and a

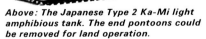

Above: The Japanese Type 2 Ka-Mi light amphibious tank. The end pontoons could be removed for land operation.

similar weapon in the bow of the tank on the left. Some 132 rounds of 37mm and 3,500 rounds of 7.7mm machine-gun ammunition were carried. These tanks were normally launched from ships or landing-craft offshore, and they would then head for the shore, cross the reef and, once ashore, discard their pontoons and head inland to their objectives. Some of the Japanese amphibious vehicles were designed to be carried on the decks of submarines whilst others could carry a naval torpedo on each side of the hull!

TYPE 60 SELF-PROPELLED RECOILLESS RIFLE

Crew: 3.
Armament: Two 106mm recoilless rifles; two .5in ranging machine-guns.
Armour: 15mm (0.59in) maximum.
Dimensions: Length 14ft 1in (4.3m); width 7ft 7in (2.23m); height 4ft 6in (1.38m).
Weight: 17,681lbs (8,020kg).
Ground pressure: 8.96lb/in² (0.63kg/cm²).
Engine: Komatsu T120 six-cylinder air-cooled diesel developing 120hp at 2,400rpm.
Performance: Maximum road speed 30mph (48km/h); range 80 miles (130km); vertical obstacle 1ft 9in (0.53m); trench 5ft 10in (1.78m); gradient 67 per cent.
History: Entered service with the Japanese Self-Defence Force (Army) in 1960 and still in service.

The Type 60 self-propelled recoilless rifle fulfils a role similar to that of the American M50 ONTOS (no longer in service) and the French Light Fighting Unit (tested by the French Army but not adopted). All three vehicles were developed in the 1950s. They are all lightly armoured and are designed to destroy enemy tanks with their recoilless rifles. For survival each vehicle relies on its small size and manoeuvrability. Design work on the Type 60 started in 1954 and prototypes were built by Komatsu (SS1) and Mitsubishi (SS2). These were tested in 1955 and had the distinction of being the first Japanese armoured fighting vehicles to be completed after the end of World War II. These were not considered satisfactory, so further prototypes were constructed, these being known as the SS3 and SS4. The latter was standardised as the Type 60 Self-Propelled Recoilless Rifle and production was undertaken by the Komatsu Manufacturing Company, which is today well known for its wide range of earth-moving equipment. The Type 60 has a hull of welded construction, with the driver at the front of the hull on the left. The armament is mounted to the right and rear of the driver's position. The engine is at the rear of the hull. Suspension is of the torsion-bar type and consists of five road wheels, with the drive sprocket at the front and the idler at the rear. There are three track-return rollers. The vehicle is armed with two 106mm recoilless rifles built by the Japan Steel Works. These have two positions, low and high. When in the low position, the guns' traverse is limited to 10° left and 10° right, and they can be elevated from −5° to +10°. When the mount is raised the guns have a traverse of 30° left and 30° right and can be elevated from −20° to +15°. On each of the recoilless rifles is a .5in ranging machine-gun. The commander, who also acts as the gunner, first aims the recoilless rifles at the target using a standard optical sight; once the weapons are lined up he fires a burst from the ranging machine-guns; if these strike the target he then knows that the weapons are correctly lined up, and can then fire the recoilless rifles. Only 10 rounds of High-Explosive

Above: The Type 60 self-propelled recoilless rifle with its twin 106mm weapons in travelling position. Built by the Komatsu Manufacturing Company—Japan's first post-war AFV entered service in 1960.

Right: The Type 60 SPRR. The main drawbacks of this type of anti-tank vehicle are that it cannot fire whilst on the move, and the backblast caused when the recoilless rifles are fired can be seen from some distance. This is a major tactical drawback and means that the SPRR can easily be detected and destroyed

Anti-Tank (or High Explosive when the vehicle is being used in the infantry support role) are carried. Once these have been fired the vehicle pulls back to the rear to be resupplied with further ammunition. The

vehicle can ford to a maximum depth of 2ft 8in (0.8m). It has no NBC equipment or night-vision equipment. Unlike most countries, the Japanese have yet to develop a missile-armed anti-tank vehicle.

Below: The Type 60 SPRR with its armament in the raised position. Mounted above each rifle is a .50in ranging machine gun. The commander gunner of the 3-man crew aims his rifles with an optical sight and confirms his accuracy with a burst of tracer from the machine-guns.

TYPE 61 MAIN BATTLE TANK

Type 61, Type 67 AVLB, Type 70 ARV and Type 67 AEV.
Crew: 4.
Armament: One 90mm gun; one .3in M1919A4 machine-gun co-axial with main armament; one .5in M2 anti-aircraft machine-gun.
Armour: 64mm (2.52in) maximum.
Dimensions: Length (overall) 26ft 10½in (8.19m); length (hull) 20ft 8in (6.3m); width 9ft 8in (2.95m); height (including commander's cupola) 10ft 4in (3.16m).
Weight: Combat 77,162lbs (35,000kg).
Ground pressure: 13.5lb/in² (0.95kg/cm²).
Engine: Mitsubishi Type 12 HM 21WT 12-cylinder diesel developing 600hp at 2,100rpm.
Performance: Road speed 28mph (45km/h); range 124 miles (200km); vertical obstacle 2ft 3in (0.685m); trench 8ft 2in (2.489m); gradient 60 per cent.
History: Entered service with Japanese Self-Defence Force (Army) in 1962 and still in service.

When the Japanese Self-Defence Force (Army) was re-formed after World War II, all of its initial equipment was of American origin, including the M24 Chaffee light tank (470 received) and the Sherman medium tank (360 received). The American tanks had one major drawback, however: they were designed for American crewmen rather than for the smaller Japanese. So design work on a new Japanese tank started as early as 1954, with the first prototypes being completed in 1957. Four different series of prototype tanks were built, these being the ST-A1, ST-A2, ST-A3 and finally the ST-A4. The last was finally selected for service as the Type 61 main battle tank, and production started at the Maruko works of Mitsubishi Heavy Industries. First production tanks were completed in 1962 and total production amounted to 500 tanks. Although the Type 74 main battle tank is now in service with the Japanese Army, the Type 61 will remain in service for some years yet. In appearance the Type 61 has a number of features of the American M47 medium tank, which the Japanese tested in small numbers in the early 1950s. The hull of the Type 61 is of all-welded construction, but the glacis plate can be removed for maintenance purposes. The driver is seated at the front of the hull on the right. The turret is cast, with the commander and gunner on the right and the loader on the left. A stowage box is mounted at the rear of the turret bustle. The engine and transmission are at the rear of the hull. The Japanese have always favoured diesel engines as these have a number of advantages over petrol engines, including low fuel consumption and much reduced fire hazard. The engine is air-cooled and turbocharged. The suspension is of

the torsion-bar type and consists of six road wheels, with the drive sprocket at the front and the idler at the rear. There are three track-return rollers. The Type 61 is armed with a 90mm gun built in Japan, and there is a .3in machine-gun mounted co-axially with the main armament. The gun is elevated and traversed hydraulically, with manual controls for use in an emergency. An M2 Browning machine-gun is mounted on the commander's cupola for anti-aircraft defence and this can be aimed and fired from within the cupola. The tank can ford to a depth of 3ft 3in (0.99m) without preparation, but there is no provision for the installation of a schnorkel for deep fording operations. Recently some tanks have been provided with both infra-red driving lights and an infra-red searchlight for night operations. Compared with other tanks of the early 1960s such as the Leopard and AMX-30, the Type 61 is undergunned, but it should be remembered that it was designed to meet Japanese rather than European requirements. The weight and size of the tank had to be kept within certain dimensions as the tank has to be able to be carried on Japanese railways, which pass through numerous narrow tunnels. There are three basic variants of the Type 61 MBT. The bridgelayer is called the Type 67 Armoured Vehicle Launched Bridge, and has a scissors-type bridge which unfolds over the forward part of the hull.

Above: The JSDF's Type 61 main battle tank has been in service since 1962. Although resembling the US M47 and mounting a similar 90mm gun, the Mitsubishi-built Type 61 is more compact, because of the smaller stature of Japanese crewmen, and features an air-cooled turbocharged diesel engine giving a maximum road speed of 45km/h. Variants include the Type 67 Armoured Engineer Vehicle and Type 70 Recovery Vehicle.

This model weighs 36.4 tons (37,000kg) and has a crew of three. Armament consists of a single .3in machine-gun. The recovery version is known as the Type 70 Armoured Recovery Vehicle. On this vehicle the turret is replaced by a small flat-sided superstructure. An 'A' frame is pivoted on this to lift tank components. A dozer blade is provided at the front of the hull. The ARV has a crew of four and a loaded weight of 34.45 tons (35,000kg). Armament consists of a .3in and a .5in machine-gun and an 81mm mortar. Finally there is an Armoured Engineer Vehicle known as the Type 67. This weighs 34.45 tons (35,000kg) and has a crew of four. All of these versions are still in service with the Japanese Self-Defence Force (Army).

Below: The Type 61 MBT. The 500 Type 61s built are likely to remain in service for some years, although they are now being supplemented by the Type 74.

TYPE 73 MECHANISED INFANTRY COMBAT VEHICLE

Crew: 2 plus 10.
Armament: One .5in machine-gun; one .3in machine-gun in ball mount; six smoke dischargers.
Armour: Classified.
Dimensions: Length 18ft 4in (5.6m); width 9ft 2in (2.8m); height 5ft 7in (1.71m).
Weight: Combat 30,865lbs (14,000kg).
Engine: Mitsubishi air-cooled diesel developing 300hp at 2,200rpm.
Performance: Maximum road speed 37mph (60km/h), vertical obstacle 2ft 2in (0.65m); trench 5ft 3in (1.6m); gradient 60 per cent.
History: Entered service with Japanese Self Defence Force (Army) in 1974

During World War II the Japanese did not develop any vehicles specifically for the APC role, although they did develop a wide range of tracked prime-movers to tow artillery or carry supplies. Large numbers of American half-tracks were obtained when the Japanese Self Defence Force was formed in the 1950s, and a few of these are still in service. The first Japanese-designed APC to enter service was the Type SU 60, which was built by Mitsubishi and entered service in 1960. It weighs just under 11.8 tons (12,000kg), has a crew of two (commander and driver) and can carry eight fully equipped infantrymen. Armament consists

of a .5in M2 machine-gun on the roof and a .3in M1919A4 machine-gun in a ball mount in the front of the hull, to the left of the driver. The latter is a very unusual feature in modern armoured vehicles, most countries having discarded hull-mounted machine-guns after 1945. The German *Jagdpanzer Rakete* and *Jagdpanzer Kanone* have similar hull machine-guns, but these supplement the main armament. There are two variants of the Type SU 60 APC, the SV 60 81mm mortar-carrier and the SX 4.2in mortar-carrier. In both vehicles the mortar is mounted in the rear of the hull. The Type SU 60 APC has no amphibious capability, but can ford to a maximum depth of 2ft 6in (0.76m) without preparation. In the late 1960s design work started on a new APC, and the first prototypes were completed in 1970. Two different prototypes, the SUB-1 and the SUB-2, were built. The first of these was armed with a low profile cupola with a .5in machine-gun mounted externally. This could be aimed and fired from within the vehicle, but the box magazine could not be replaced without the gunner leaving the turret. Three smoke dischargers were mounted on each side at the rear of the hull. The SUB-2 had a turret-mounted .5in machine-gun and three smoke dischargers mounted on each side of the turret. Both of these had a .3in machine-gun mounted in the left of the hull front. The SUB-1 was

selected for production as the Type 73 MICV and production is now being undertaken by Mitsubishi Heavy Industries. The vehicle has a hull of all-welded aluminium construction and carries 10 infantrymen as well as its crew of two. The driver is seated at the front of the hull on the right, with the bow machine-gunner to his left. The commander is to the rear of the gunner's and driver's position. The engine is on the left and the main armament on the right of the hull. The troop compartment is at the rear, and is provided with overhead roof hatches. There is a large ramp at the rear of the hull. The suspension is of the torsion-bar type and consists of five road wheels, with the drive sprocket at the front and the idler at the rear. The vehicle is fully amphibious and is propelled in the water by its tracks. An NBC system is fitted, as is infra-red night-vision equipment. Prototypes were provided with 'T' firing-ports, two in each side of the hull and one in the rear ramp. Although classed as an MICV by the Japanese, the Type 73 is not a true MICV. Most MICVs are today armed with at least a 20mm cannon to destroy other lightly armoured vehicles. The Type 73's firing-ports are also very primitive compared with the firing-ports and vision blocks fitted to such vehicles as the American XM723 and the German *Marder*. It may be that the Japanese intend to develop the Type 73 into a full MICV some time in the future.

Above: The Type 73 MICV, carrying 10 infantrymen, is now in service with the Japanese Self Defence Force (Army). It has a hull of all welded aluminium and is built by Mitsubishi Heavy Industries. It has a .50in Browning machine-gun mounted externally on the cupola and a .30in machine-gun mounted in the left front of the hull. The Type 73 is fully amphibious, and is propelled through the water by its tracks.

Left: One of the prototypes of the Type 73 MICV, designated the Model 2 or SUB-2. This was armed with a turret-mounted .50in machine-gun, with an infra-red searchlight on the left side of the turret. Three smoke dischargers were mounted each side of the turret. The Type 73 MICV cannot be compared to better-armed and more efficient types such as the Russian BMP-1 or the American XM723.

TYPE 74 MAIN BATTLE TANK

Crew: 4.
Armament: One 105mm L7 series gun; one 7.62mm machine-gun co-axial with the main armament; one .5in anti-aircraft machine-gun; six smoke dischargers.
Armour: Classified.
Dimensions: Length (gun forward) 29ft 10in (9.088); length (hull) 22ft 6in (6.85m); width 10ft 5in (3.18m); height (with anti-aircraft machine-gun) 8ft 10in (2.675m) at a ground clearance of 8in (0.2m).
Weight: Combat 83,776lbs (38,000kg).
Ground pressure: 12lb/in² (0.85kg/cm²).
Engine: Mitsubishi 10ZF Model 21 WT 10-cylinder air-cooled diesel developing 750bhp at 2,200rpm.
Performance: Maximum road speed 37mph (60km/h); range 310 miles (500km); vertical obstacle 3ft 3in (1m); trench 8ft 10in (2.7m); gradient 60 per cent.
History: Entered service with the Japanese Self-Defence Force (Army) in 1973 and still in production.

The Japanese realised in the early 1960s that the Type 61 would not meet its requirements for the 1980s, so in 1964 design work commenced on a new main battle tank. The first two prototypes, known as STB-1s, were completed at the Maruko works of Mitsubishi Heavy Industries in late 1969. Further prototypes, the STB-3 and the STB-6, were built before the type was considered ready for production. The vehicle entered production at the new tank plant run by Mitsubishi Heavy Industries at Sagamihara in 1973, and the first order was for 280 tanks. The Type 74 has not been exported as at the present time it is the policy of the Japanese government not to export arms of any type. The layout of the tank is conventional, with the driver at the front of the hull on the left and the other three crew members in the turret. The commander and gunner are on the right and the loader is on the left. The engine and transmission are at the rear of the hull. The suspension is of the hydro-pneumatic type and consists of five road wheels, with the drive sprocket at the rear and the idler at the front. There are no track-return rollers. The suspension can be adjusted by the driver to suit the type of ground being crossed. When crossing a rocky, broken area, for example, the suspension would be adjusted to give maximum ground clearance. This clearance can be adjusted from a minimum of 8in (.2m) to a maximum of 2ft 1½in (0.65m). It can also be used to give the tank a tactical advantage: when the tank is on a reverse slope, the suspension can be lowered at the front and increased at the rear so that the main armament is depressed further than normal. The only other tank in service with this type of suspension is the Swedish S tank, which has to have this type of suspension as the gun is fixed to the hull. This type of suspension was

also used on the American T95 and German/American MBT-70 tanks, but both these projects were cancelled. The Type 74 is armed with the British 105mm L7 series rifled tank gun, built under licence in Japan. A 7.62mm machine-gun is mounted co-axial with the main armament. The main gun has an elevation of +15° and a depression of −5°, and is fully stabilised on both the horizontal and vertical planes. The fire-control system includes a laser rangefinder and a ballistic computer, both of which are produced in Japan. Some 50 rounds of 105mm ammunition are carried. Prototypes had an automatic loader, but this would have cost too much to install in production

Below: The Type 74 MBT of the JSDF (Army) has several advanced features, including hydro-pneumatic suspension, a laser range-finder, night vision equipment and an NBC system. A schnorkel enables the tank to ford to a maximum depth of 3m. A dozer blade can be mounted at the front.

Above: A prototype Type 74 MBT with its hydro-pneumatic suspension lowered to give maximum ground clearance. The tank is armed with the British 105mm L7 rifled gun, now manufactured under licence by the Japan Steel Works. A co-axial 7.62mm machine-gun and .50in AA gun are also mounted.

tanks. A .5in M2 anti-aircraft machine-gun is mounted on the roof. On the prototypes this could be aimed and fired from within the turret, but this was also found to be too expensive for production vehicles. Three smoke dischargers are mounted on each side of the turret. The tank is provided with infra-red driving lights and there is also an infra-red searchlight to the left of the main armament. The Type 74 can ford to a maximum depth of 3ft 3in (1m) without preparation, although a schnorkel enabling it to ford to a depth of 9ft 10in (3m) can be fitted. All tanks are provided with an NBC system. Components of the Type 74 tank have also been used in the new Japanese 155mm self-propelled howitzer which should enter production in the near future. This is similar in appearance to the American 155mm M109A1 self-propelled howitzer, and is armed with a 155mm howitzer in a turret with a traverse of 360°. In designing the Type 74 MBT the Japanese have sought, and managed, to combine the best features of modern tank design within a weight limit of 37.6 tons (38,000kg).

DAF YP-408 ARMOURED PERSONNEL CARRIER

Crew: 2 plus 10.
Armament: One .5in (12.7mm) machine-gun; six smoke dischargers.
Armour: 8mm–15mm (0.32–0.59in).
Dimensions: Length 20ft 6in (6.23m); width 7ft 10in (2.4m); height (including machine-gun) 7ft 9in (2.37m).
Weight: Combat 26,456lbs (12,000kg).
Engine: DAF Model DS 575 six-cylinder inline turbocharged diesel developing 165hp at 2,400rpm.
Performance: Road speed 50mph (80km/h); range 311 miles (500km); vertical obstacle 2ft 4in (0.7m); trench 3ft 11in (1.2m); gradient 60 per cent.
History: Entered service with the Dutch Army in 1965 and used only by the Dutch Army.

In the 1950s the Dutch Army issued a requirement for a wheeled armoured personnel carrier, and it was natural that the DAF (Van Doorne *Automobiel Fabrieken*) company of Eindhoven should be awarded the contract. It was decided to base the vehicle on the DAF YA 328 (6×6) cargo truck, one of the standard trucks used by the Dutch Army. The mock-up was completed in 1957 with the first prototypes being completed the following year. Further development then took place, but it was six years before the first production vehicles were completed in 1964. A total of 750 was built by the time production was completed in 1968. The hull of the YP-408 is of all-welded steel construction and varies in thickness from 0.3in (8mm) to 0.6in (15mm). The engine is located at the front of the hull with the driver and commander/gunner to the rear. The driver is located to the left and the commander to the right. Both enter and leave the vehicle via roof hatches. The Browning .5in machine-gun can be traversed through a full 360°, elevation being from −8° to +70°, and the weapon is fed from a box on the left side. The commander's hatch is in two parts, opening vertically to his left and right to give some protection when he is using the machine-gun. The MG mounting was designed by DAF, and consists of a ball bearing with ring gear and pinion, and a gun cradle. The mount can be traversed through the full 360° with a hand wheel or the gunner's shoulder. If required, the mount can be locked in position, although when this is done the weapon can still be traversed 8°

left and right. Three smoke dischargers are mounted at the front of the engine on each side. The 10 infantry are seated at the rear of the hull, five down each side. The normal method of entry is via twin doors in the hull rear, each of these being provided with a single firing-port. Apart from these, however, there is no provision for the crew to use their small arms from

within the vehicle. There are six hatches in the roof, three down each side, and these open to the left and right. Although the YP-408 has eight road wheels,

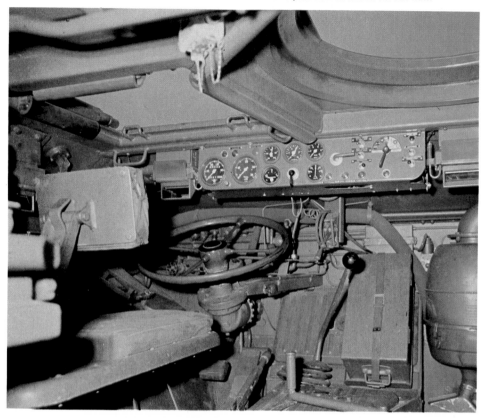

Below: Interior of the DAF YP-408 armoured personnel carrier, showing driver's position at the left front hull.

M39 PANSERWAGEN ARMOURED CAR

Crew: 6.
Armament: One 37mm gun; one 7.9mm machine-gun co-axial with main armament; one 7·9mm machine-gun in ball mount in front of hull; one 7.9mm machine-gun in rear of hull.
Armour: 12mm (0.47in) maximum.
Dimensions: Length 15ft 2in (4.63m); width 7ft 0½in (2.02m); height 7ft (2.014m).
Weight: Combat 13,228lbs (6,000kg).
Engine: Ford V-8 petrol engine developing 95hp.
Performance: Maximum road speed 37mph (60km/h); range 181 miles (300km).
History: Entered service with the Dutch Army in 1939. Subsequently used by the German Army.

After World War I some German Ehrhardt armoured cars were modified by Siderius for service with the Dutch police, and remained in service until the early 1930s. In 1932–33 the Dutch Motor Service Corps at Harlem designed and built four armoured cars known as the Buffalo type. Various other armoured and semi-armoured vehicles were built in the 1920s and 1930s, but none of these were produced in any great quantity. In the early 1930s the DAF company designed a truck called the TRADO, essentially a standard commercial truck modified for cross-country operations. The name TRADO originated from the designers, Van Der Trappen and Van Doorne. The Dutch Army asked DAF to undertake production of a British-designed armoured car in Holland, but DAF countered with the suggestion that a better vehicle could in fact be designed in Holland. In eight months DAF had completed design work and built the first prototype. The armoured car had a hull of all-welded construction, very well shaped to give maximum armour protection. The driver was seated at the front of the hull on the left, with the bow machine-gunner to his right. A door was provided in each side of the hull and the turret was mounted in the centre of the hull. The turret had a traverse of 360° and was provided with a one-piece hatch cover. The engine was mounted at the rear of the hull on the right with the rear gunner, who could also drive the vehicle backwards if required, on the left. The M39 had 6×4 drive, but there were two small wheels at the nose of the hull to increase the vehicle's cross-country capabilities. Main armament consisted of a turret-mounted 37mm gun with a 7.9mm machine-

gun mounted to its left; these weapons had an elevation of +23° and a depression of −9½°. Twelve production vehicles were built for the Dutch Army and these were issued to the 3rd Armoured Car Squadron (Cavalry) at the Hague. The vehicles were not used during the invasion of the Netherlands and were subsequently taken over by the Germans and used for the internal security role under the designation *Pz SpWg* L202(*h*). According to DAF, the British Army had started negotiations for the M39 to be built in Holland for the British Army. One of the more interesting

Above: The DAF Pantserwagen M39 entered service in 1939. They saw no action in the invasion of the Netherlands and were used by the Germans for internal security.

developments of the TRADO 6×4 truck was a model with the rear two wheels removed and replaced by circular saws! The Dutch relied to a great extent on their many canals for basic defensive purposes, and these vehicles would have been used to break up the ice if the canals had become frozen in winter.

only six of them are driven (the first, third and fourth pairs). Steering is power-assisted and is on the front four wheels. These have reinforced sidewalls and a bead spacer between the bead heels, enabling the vehicle to be driven at a reduced speed for 31 miles (50km) if one or more of the tires is punctured. An engine-driven air-compressor supplies air for the air-brake system and can also be used to inflate the tyres if required. The YP-408 has no amphibious capability although it can ford streams to a depth of 3ft 11in (1.2m) without preparation. (Before entering the water the driver operates a lever which closes off the crankcase ventilation so that water does not enter the engine.) Infra-red driving equipment can be installed and an infra-red searchlight can be mounted co-axially with the .5in machine-gun. No NBC system is installed. The basic YP-408 (this being the

DAF designation for the vehicle) is called the PWI-S(GR) by the Dutch Army, this standing for *Panzer Wagen Infanterie-Standard* (*Group*). There are a number of other versions in service. There are two command vehicles: the PWI-S(PC) platoon commander's vehicle and the PWCO company or battalion commander's vehicle. The ambulance model, which is unarmed, is called the PW-GWT: this has a crew of two and can carry two stretchers and four sitting patients. The PW-MT tows the French 120mm Brandt mortar: this has a crew of seven and carries 50 mortar bombs. Finally there is the PW-V, which is used to carry cargo, and this model has a crew of two. The Dutch Army also uses the American M113 and French AMX VCI APCs and has ordered some 800 of the new FMC Armoured Infantry Fighting Vehicle for delivery in 1977–78.

Below: Infantry dismount from the rear doors of a YP-408, which can carry ten men. From his roof hatch, the commander/gunner gives covering fire with a .50in machine-gun. All 750 YP-408s built in 1964-68 are in service with the Dutch Army.

Bottom: The commander's roof hatch on the YP-408 opens vertically to left and right, providing protection when he mans the machine-gun. Only the front and two rear pairs of the eight road wheels are driven; power-assisted steering is on the front four wheels. The vehicle has no NBC system and is not amphibious, although it can wade up to a depth of 1.2m.

TK-3 TANKETTE

TK-1, TK-2, TK-3, TKW, TKS-D and TKF.
Crew: 2.
Armament: One 7.92mm machine gun.
Armour: 8mm (0.31in) maximum.
Dimensions: Length 8ft 5½in (2.577m); width 5ft 10in (1.778m); height 4ft 3½in (1.307m).
Weight: 5,511lbs (2,500kg).
Engine: Ford Model A four-cylinder water-cooled diesel developing 40hp.
Performance: Maximum road speed 28mph (45km/h); road range 125 miles (201km); vertical obstacle 1ft 5in (0.431m); trench 4ft (1.219m); gradient 60 per cent.
History: Entered service with the Polish Army in 1932 and continued in service until German invasion when some of the vehicles were taken over by German Army.

In 1929 Poland purchased a British Carden Loyd Mark IV tankette and from this developed the TK-1 tankette. Further development resulted in the TK-2 and TK-3, the latter being placed in production for the Polish Army. Some 300 such vehicles were built in the early 1930s. In 1933 the TKS appeared: this had numerous improvements over the TK-3, including thicker armour (maximum now being 0.4in (10mm)), modified suspension and a different engine. The TKS entered service in 1934 and 390 were built. A turreted version, the TKW, was built but did not enter production. A similar fate befell the TKS-D, which was armed with a 37mm anti-tank gun in the front plate. The final model was the TKF, armed with a 7.9mm and a 9mm machine-gun, which could be used in the anti-aircraft role. By the late 1930s the Poles realised that their tankettes were quickly becoming obsolete. But as there was nothing to replace them at the time, steps were taken to increase the basic type's firepower. After trials with the Danish Madsen and the 20mm Swiss Solothurn weapons, the Poles eventually installed their own 20mm FK cannon. By the time war broke out, TK-3 and TKS tankettes had only just started to be fitted with these weapons. These tankettes stood no chance at all against the German armour and those that were not destroyed were taken over by the victors and used for carrying ammunition, or for internal security operations. These normally had their original armament removed and replaced by a French 8mm Hotchkiss M1914 machine-gun.

Above right: A German soldier poses with a Polish TK-3 tankette captured in 1939.

Right: A column of TK-1 tankettes assembled prior to maneouvres.

7TP LIGHT TANK

7TP, 7TP Improved, 10TP and 14TP.
Crew: 3.
Armament: One 37mm gun; one 7.92mm machine-gun co-axial with main armament.
Armour: 40mm (1.57in) maximum.
Dimensions: Length 15ft 1in (4.997m); width 7ft 11in (2.413m); height 7ft 0½in (2.159m).
Weight: 24,251lbs (11,000kg).
Engine: Saurer diesel developing 110hp.
Performance: Maximum road speed 20mph (32km/h); range 100 miles (160km); vertical obstacle 2ft (0.609m); trench 6ft (1.828m); gradient 60 per cent.
History: In service with the Polish Army from 1934 to 1939.

In the early 1930s Poland purchased between 40 and 50 Vickers 6ton tanks. Further development of this by the PKI resulted in the 7TP light tank, in production from 1934 to 1939. The first model had two turrets, each fitted with a single machine-gun, and weighed 8.86 tons (9,000kg). It was powered by a 110hp Saurer diesel. This was followed by the second model which had a Swedish turret armed with a Bofors 37mm gun and a co-axial 7.92mm machine-gun. As a result of difficulties in obtaining the turrets from Sweden this model was not built in large numbers. The final model (the 7TP Improved) had heavier armour, a redesigned turret with an overhanging rear, and stronger suspension. This did not enter production. The 7TP was to have been replaced by the 10TP, the first prototype of which was completed in 1937. This had a Christie type suspension and was powered by an American La France 210hp 12-cylinder engine. This gave the vehicle a top road speed of 31mph (50km/h). Like some of the American Christie tanks, the 10TP could also be run on its road wheels, top speed without its tracks being 44mph (70km/h). The 10TP had the same turret as the 7TP, but in addition had a hull-mounted machine-gun. The 14TP was a medium tank which also had Christie type suspension, although this model could run only on its tracks. The tank had a top road speed of 31mph (50km/h) and was powered by a German Maybach 12-cylinder engine. Combat weight was 13.78 tons (14,000kg). Like the 10TP, this never entered production. The Poles ordered two American Christie tanks in 1936, but as they never paid for them the tanks were never delivered and were taken over by the US Army. When the Germans invaded Poland in 1939 the Polish Army had 169 7TP tanks on strength as well as 50 Vickers 6ton tanks, 67 World War I Renault FT-17 light tanks, 53 French Renault R-35s (these were withdrawn to Romania and were not committed to action), some 700 TK/TKS tankettes and 100 assorted armoured cars. These were pitted against over 3,000 German tanks and most were soon destroyed or captured.

Above: The final model of the 7TP light tank, mounting the 37mm Bofors. The 7TP was developed from the Vickers 6-tonner.

MARMON-HERRINGTON MARK II ARMOURED CAR

Marks I-IV, VI-VIII.
Crew: 4.
Armament: One .303in turret-mounted machine-gun; one .303in machine-gun in left of hull (see text).
Armour: 12mm (0.47in) maximum.
Dimensions: Length 16ft (4.876m); width 6ft 6in (1.981m); height 7ft 3in to 7ft 11in (2.209m–2.413m) depending on armament installed.
Weight: Combat 13,228lbs (6,000kg).
Engine: Ford eight-cylinder petrol engine developing 95bhp.
Performance: Maximum road speed 50mph (80.4km/h); range 200 miles (322km).
History: Entered service with South African Army in 1940 and used until end of World War II. This and other marks have also been used by Great Britain, Greece, India, Rhodesia and other countries.

Above: The Marmon-Herrington Mk IV armoured car mounting a 2-pdr gun played a major part in the desert battles.

Below: The Marmon-Herrington Mk II was used in the Middle East from 1941 until the end of the Tunisian campaign.

In 1938 the South African Government placed an order for two armoured cars to be built in the country. After World War II broke out in Europe, it soon became apparent that the British could not even meet their own requirements, let alone South Africa's and other countries' requirements. The original South African order for two armoured cars was increased several times, and by late 1939 it stood at 266 vehicles. The first model was based on a standard Ford 4×2 3-ton truck chassis, whilst the second model had the American Marmon-Herrington conversion for 4×4 drive. The latter was selected for production after exhaustive trials although some of the 4×2 model were also built. In May 1940, the order for 266 armoured cars was increased yet again to 1,000, and these had to be delivered at the rate of 50 per week! To cope with this huge order many South African companies were called upon to provide assistance. The chassis came from Canada, most of the armament from Great Britain, the Marmon-Herrington 4×4 conversion kits from the United States, and armour from the South African Iron and Steel Industrial Corporation. Final assembly was carried out by the Ford Motor Company and the Dorman Long Company, although many other companies were also involved. The first model was known as the Mark I, but only 113 of these 4×2 models were built before they were followed by the Mark II, which had 4×4 drive. Early models had hulls of riveted construction although these soon gave way to hulls of welded construction. First deliveries of the Mark I were made to South African units in May 1940, with deliveries of the Mark II following in November 1940. As built, the Mark II was armed with a turret-mounted .303in water-cooled machine-gun with a similar weapon in the left of the hull. Many vehicles had these latter machine-guns removed and the position plated over, however. Mark IIs were used by the British Army from 1941, and these were armed with a turret-mounted .55in Boys anti-tank rifle, a Bren LMG to the left of the Boys, whilst on the roof was a Bren LMG and a Vickers .303in machine-gun. There were many local versions of the Mark II in North Africa, and some had their turrets removed and replaced by an Italian 20mm gun whilst others had a British 2pounder, German 37mm or Italian 47mm gun fitted in an effort to increase their firepower. Special variants of the Mark II included an RAF liaison vehicle, artillery observation post vehicle, command vehicle, Light Aid Detachment vehicle and ambulance. The Mark II was followed by the Mark III in May 1941. This was based on a Ford chassis with a wheelbase of 117in (2.971m) rather than the earlier 134in (3.4m) of the Mark II. This had a redesigned hull and turret of welded construction, but did not have the rear hull doors of the earlier model, the only means of entry and exit being the side doors and the turret. The Mark III also had many automotive improvements as a result of combat experience in North Africa. The Mark III's armament was similar to that of the Mark II, except a hull-mounted machine-gun was not fitted. The next model was the Mark IV. This had a new hull and turret of all-welded construction, with the engine at the rear rather than at the front as on previous models. Normal armament consisted of a turret-mounted 2pounder gun, a co-axial .3in machine-gun, a .3in or .5in machine-gun on the turret roof for anti-aircraft defence and a smoke discharger on the side of the turret. Late production models had a different Canadian chassis, and these were designated Mark IV (F). There is confusion about the Mark V, but some reports have stated that it was an improved Mark III, whilst others do not even mention a Mark V at all. The Mark VI was designed for operations in North Africa. It had 8×8 drive, and was powered by two Ford eight-cylinder petrol engines at the rear of the hull. The first prototype was armed with a 2pounder gun and a co-axial .3in Browning machine-gun, and two .3in machine-guns on the turret for anti-aircraft defence. The second prototype had a 6pounder gun and a co-axial 7.92mm Besa machine-gun, whilst a single .5in Browning machine-gun was mounted on

the roof for anti-aircraft defence. Large orders were placed for the Mark VI, but these were cancelled early in 1943 when it became apparent that the North African campaign would be over by the time they were ready for service. A similar fate befell the American 8×8 Boarhound armoured car which was developed to meet a similar requirement. The two prototypes of the Mark VI are still in existence today, one at the Royal Armoured Corps Museum at Bovington Camp in England and the other at the South African National War Museum. The Marks VII and VIII were also developed to prototype stage but were never placed

in production. The latter had a new hull and turret and was armed with a 2pounder gun and a co-axial machine-gun. The Marmon-Herrington armoured cars were first used in action by the South Africans against the Italians in East Africa. They were also widely used by British and South African units in North Africa and some even survive today in a few countries! Since World War II South Africa has used British armoured vehicles such as the Centurion, Saracen, Ferret and has also built over 1,200 of the Panhard AML armoured car under licence from France, these last being known as the Eland.

Left: A Marmon-Herrington Mk II armoured car of C Squadron, King's Dragoon Guards, dug in at Tobruk in September 1941. This is the early riveted-hull version of the South African Reconnaissance Car Mk II. From late 1940, until the Daimler became fully operational, Marmon-Herringtons were extensively used in the Western Desert by the King's Dragoon Guards and South African armoured units. The vehicles were built in South Africa; engine, transmission and suspension were imported from UK.

Soviet Union

French influence had always been strong in Russia, and the first armoured units were modelled on the French ones, being thereby tied to infantry formations in a purely supporting role with little freedom of action. However, some of the thinking of the Germans probably filtered through with the mutual co-operation arrangements of the 1920s and 1930s, because in 1930 a series of special tank brigades were formed and grouped into a mechanised corps. This corps was the equivalent of the later armoured and mechanised divisions in the Western armies, although the Soviet experiments hardly went as far in their tactical employment as did the later divisions. Nevertheless, they had their own artillery and infantry but still had to act in support of the slow-moving infantry forces. A preoccupation with cavalry led the Soviets to demand high speed from their tanks and their designers took the Christie suspension before anyone else recognised its value. At the same time the Soviets displayed a remarkable flair for producing highly effective tanks, a knack which they have retained to the present day. The BT-5 of 1933 still looks a modern design and displays all the virtues of sloped armour, good fire-power and high mobility which are fundamental in successful battle tanks.

The experiments with the mechanised corps were used as the basis for the armoured formations which fought through World War II, and from them also was deduced the primary lesson of all armoured warfare, that firepower counts above all else. Russia based her wartime tank units on the fewest possible varieties of tank, the backbone of the force being the T-34 in its various guises. This tank was, and still is, an object lesson in good design, and its appearance was a revelation to the German Army. At first its effectiveness was to some extent reduced by the then current Soviet habit of using tanks in cavalry charges. A mass of armoured vehicles was made to rush a position in the same way as a cavalry squadron,

and it was some time before it was discovered that it was often more profitable to stand off and shell the opposition into submission.

However the enthusiasm, drive and sheer grit of the Soviet armoured troops can never be denied. But communications have always been a problem, and even today there is doubt in some quarters as to whether every vehicle carries a radio, and this has led to the use of very simple and stereotyped tactics with little flexibility, wherein mass counts for more than manoeuvre. However, the mass is such that it over-matches the Western strength by a large margin and the niceties of

military finesse mean much less when one is holding most of the cards.

Although it has been fashionable for some years to claim that Soviet tanks are simple to the point of crudity, this is not true; they are also extremely well made, and use high grade materials. The Soviet high command looks on tanks as being the main striking force of the army, and it would seem that a great deal of money is poured into their manufacture and maintenance. They are backed up by substantial numbers of powerful self-propelled guns of a type which matches those of the tanks, but which are generally larger and more

powerful. In addition there is a full range of support vehicles and armoured supply columns.

Probably the greatest drawback that the Soviets face today is that they have not fought a war or even a full-scale campaign since 1945, and there can be few left now with any recollection of battle. The effect may not be significant, but it cannot entirely be ignored.

As shown in this still from a Soviet training film, Russia uses its armour en masse, *together with artillery and tactical air support.*

AUSTIN-PUTILOV HALF-TRACK ARMOURED CAR

Crew: 5.
Armament: Two 7.62mm Maxim machine-guns in separate turrets.
Armour: 8mm (0.31in) maximum; 5.5mm (0.22in) minimum.
Dimensions: Length 22ft 2in (6.75m); width 7ft 10in (2.40m); height 8ft 10in (2.70m).
Weight: 12,787lbs (5,800kg).
Ground pressure: Not known.
Power to weight ratio: 8.6hp/ton.
Engine: Austin four-cylinder water-cooled petrol engine developing 50hp.
Performance: Road speed 16mph (25km/h); range 50 miles (80km); vertical obstacle 1ft 3in (0.4m); trench 5ft 10in (1.9m); gradient 30 degrees.
History: In service with the Russian Army from 1916 to 1920.

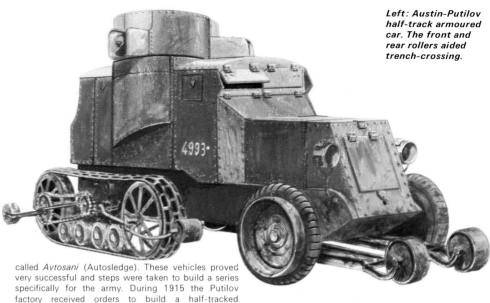

Left: Austin-Putilov half-track armoured car. The front and rear rollers aided trench-crossing.

The Putilov factory is one of the oldest completely Russian armament factories, founded in 1801 at Saint Petersburg (now Leningrad). In 1868 it became the property of the Russian industrialist G. Putilov; henceforth it was called the Putilov Factory (*Putilovsky Zavod*). During and after World War I it produced armoured cars; subsequently it began to produce half-track armoured cars and armoured trains. In 1922 the name of the factory was changed to *Krasny Putilov* (Red Putilov), and in December 1934 to the Kirov Machine and Metallurgical Plant, abbreviated to *Kirovsky Zavod*. During World War I, prior to the Revolution, the Putilov factory armoured many imported long chassis of Austin and Packard origin. In 1909, however, the personal chauffeur to the Tsar, and director of his garage in Tsarskoye Selo, Francis A. Kégresse, designed a light rubber track system for one of the Russo-Balt cars. The object of this design was to enable the vehicle to move across country and through snow. In 1913 this design was perfected at the Russo-Balt factory and applied to a small quantity of vehicles,

called *Avtosani* (Autosledge). These vehicles proved very successful and steps were taken to build a series specifically for the army. During 1915 the Putilov factory received orders to build a half-tracked armoured car utilising the Kégresse principle. The first trials with these vehicles were carried out in August 1916 and then later during the winter. As the result, 60 half-tracked armoured cars were ordered for the army. When delivered they received the designation Austin-Putilov Half-Track Armoured Car. Thirty of these vehicles were equipped with modified turrets designed by the Putilov factory. The layout of these turrets allowed the two machine-guns (provided with 6,000 rounds) to be aimed both at ground and air targets. In many official documents these half-tracked armoured

cars were referred to as 'Russian-type Tanks', and they were often used as such on the front. They remained in service from 1916 to 1920. Certain vehicles were provided with additional rollers, on special axles mounted at the front and rear of the hull, to help in the crossing of trenches. Under winter conditions it was possible to replace the front wheels by skis. After the Revolution, the Red Army adopted these vehicles and used them during the Civil War, the Allied Military Intervention and then later the Russo-Polish War.

KS LIGHT INFANTRY TANK

Crew: 2.
Armament: One 37mm gun; one 7.62mm machine-gun.
Armour: 16mm (0.63in) maximum; 8mm (0.31in) minimum.
Dimensions: Length (with tail) 16ft 5in (5m); length (without tail) 13ft 1in (4m); width 5ft 9in (1.75m); height 7ft 5in (2.25m).
Weight: Combat 15,432lbs (7,000kg).
Ground pressure: 5.68lb/in² (0.4kg/cm²).
Power to weight ratio: 4.86hp/ton.
Engine: One Fiat four-cylinder water-cooled petrol engine developing 33.5hp at 1,500rpm.
Performance: Road speed 5.3mph (8.5km/h); range 37.5 miles (60km); vertical obstacle 1ft 10in (0.6m); trench 5ft 11in (1.8m); gradient 38 degrees.
History: In service with the Russian Army from 1921 to 1941.

During the Russian Civil War the Soviets made their first attempts to provide the new Red Army with a serviceable tank. This was no easy task: at that time Russia had virtually no indigenous automobile and scarcely any established heavy industries. What scant facilities that had been developed by the Tsarist governments had been almost totally destroyed during the Civil War. Despite this, during September 1919 the Soviets established a special Military Industrial Council (*SVP*) to direct the native manufacture of heavy military technology, and this was headed by P. A. Bagdanov. During the spring of 1919 two small Renault FT tanks were captured by the Soviet 2nd Ukrainian Army from the White forces at Zakhvacheni. One of these was shipped back to the Krasny Sormovo Machine-Building Plant for investigation. The Military Industrial Council received a personal request from Lenin himself to undertake the production of a new Soviet light tank based on the captured Renault FT. This new light tank was intended purely for the accompaniment of infantry. It was, at that time, impossible for the Krasny Sormovo plant to manufacture the whole of the tank, so two other factories were drawn into the programme. The armour was to be produced by the Izhorskiy Factory in Petrograd and the power plant by AMO (later called ZIS and then ZIL). Production of the first tank began in February, and the armour was delivered to Sormovo in June, followed by the automotive components in July. Assembly of the tank was completed in August. The first preliminary trials showed up a number of faults in both design and manufacture, and these had to be corrected by September-October. By November 1920 the first completed tank, designated KS (Krasny

Sormovo), had been subjected to extensive military and automotive tests. On 1 December 1920, the Military Industrial Council was able to inform Lenin that the first Soviet tank had been successfully completed. On the same day Lenin sent a directive to the Military Industrial Council ordering the production of a further 14 such tanks, to be completed by the following spring. Delivery of the first tank was scheduled for 15 December and completion of the fifteenth tank between October 1919 and March 1920. The original vehicle was christened 'Comrade Lenin, the Freedom Fighter'. Subsequent vehicles were nicknamed 'Paris Commune', 'Red Fighter', 'Ilya Muromets', 'Proletariat', 'Tempest' and 'Victory'. These Sormovo tanks, which were also referred to as 'Russian Renaults', could be considered to be quite good for that time with respect to their combat characteristics and performance. The very first vehicles produced had either a machine-gun (with 3,000 rounds) or a 37mm gun (with 250 rounds) as their main armament, but subsequent vehicles had both – a substantial improvement over the original French tank which also had one or the other. As the Red Army captured more and more Renault tanks, they reworked them to the KS standard. KS tanks were used operationally against the Interventionist forces and

during the Russo-Polish War. Up until the time of their removal from service with the Red Army, they received several modifications and were finally handed over to the 'Ossoaviakhim', the Red Army's civilian para-military training organisation.

Below: The KS 'Russkiy-Renault' light tank of 1920 was modelled on the French Renault FT. The final production model, seen here, mounted a long-barrelled 37mm gun.

Right: An early KS tank with short-barrelled 37mm gun. Built by command of Lenin, the first production model bore his name.

MS LIGHT INFANTRY TANK

MS-1 and T-18*M*.
Crew: 2.
Armament: One 37mm Hotchkiss gun; one 7.62mm Fiodorov or Degtarov machine-gun.
Armour: 16mm (0.63in) maximum; 8mm (0.31in) minimum.
Dimensions: Length (with tail) 14ft 4in (4.38m); 11ft 6in (without tail) (3.50m); width 5ft 9in (1.76m); height 6ft 11in (2.12m).
Weight: Combat 12,125lbs (5,500kg) to 14,770lbs (6,700kg) depending on model.
Ground pressure: 4.76lb/in² (0.335kg/cm²).
Power to weight ratio: 6.00 to 6.36hp/ton depending on model.
Engine: One modified Fiat four-cylinder air-cooled petrol engine developing 35 to 40hp, depending on model.
Performance: Road speed 10.3mph (16.5km/h) to 13.8mph (22km/h) depending on model; range 37.5 miles (60km) to 41.3 miles (66km) depending on model; vertical obstacle 1ft 10in (0.6m); trench 4ft 3in (1.3m); gradient 40 degrees.
History: In service with the Russian Army from 1928 to 1942.

Right: The MS-1(T-18) light tank, the first tank of entirely Russian design, entered service in 1928.

Following the adoption of the KS tank, much experimental work was carried out to evolve a better light infantry accompanying tank. Towards the end of 1924, following the establishment of a special Tank Bureau on 6 May, the tactical-technical specifications were issued for a light tank: weight 2.95 tons (3,000kg), speed 7.5mph (12km/h), armament one 37mm gun or a machine-gun, armour 0.63in (16mm) and crew 2 men. During the spring of 1925 the Red Army staff reviewed the project and recommended that the weight be increased to 4.92 tons (5,000kg) and that both artillery and machine-gun armament be included. The first vehicle of this type to be completed successfully, in May 1927, was the five-ton T-16 tank. After

extensive tests changes were made to the engine, and the length of the tank increased to reduce the bad pitching effect. Work on improving the light tank was completed in November 1927, the final model being designated T-18. Without awaiting completion of design work and tests, on 6 July the Revolutionary Military Council accepted the T-18 as standard. It was officially designated Small Accompanying — One (*MS*-1). Production of the tank, which began in 1928, was entrusted to the Leningrad 'Bolshevik' plant which built the first batch of 30 utilising the resources of the *Ossoaviakhim* (the para-military training organisation) by May 1929. The *MS*-1 was the first Soviet tank to be placed in serial production. Some 960 were manufactured between 1928 and 1931, the tank being withdrawn from service in 1932 and relegated to the *Ossoaviakhim*. The tank had both artillery and machine-gun armament (with 109 and

2,016 rounds of ammunition respectively) and a special air-cooled engine. The use of rubber-tired bogies was a novelty. The designers had attempted to make the vehicle more compact and to reduce its weight, and for this reason the engine, which was built integral with the transmission, was mounted transversely at the rear of the hull. The improved layout made it possible to keep the tank weight down to 5.4 tons. Several improved models appeared, the final service model having a modified turret with overhang. By October-November 1929 a quantity of *MS*-1 tanks had been sent to the Special Far-Eastern Army and, on 20 November, units of this army used these tanks to put down the Chinese attempt to seize the Far-Eastern Railway. At the beginning of the Russo-German War, in mid-1941, some 200 *MS*-1 tanks were reworked into T-18*M*s mounting 45mm guns.

BA-27 ARMOURED CAR

BA-27, BA-27M, BA-20, BA-20*ZhD* and BA-20*M*.
Crew: 4.
Armament: One 37mm gun; one 7.62mm DT machine-gun.
Armour: 7mm (0.28in) maximum; 4mm (0.16in) minimum.
Dimensions: Length 15ft 2in (4.62m); width 5ft 11in (1.81m); height 8ft 3in (2.52m).
Weight: 9,921lbs (4,500kg).
Ground pressure: Not known.
Power to weight ratio: 8hp/ton.
Engine: Model AMO four-cylinder water-cooled inline petrol engine developing 36hp at 1,700rpm.
Performance: Road speed 30mph (48km/h); range 250 miles (400km); vertical obstacle negligible; trench negligible; gradient 30 degrees.
History: Served with the Russian Army in 1927.

In 1927 the Soviet Union introduced a new armoured car for the Red Army. This was the first armoured car to be adopted since the end of the Civil War. Designated *BA-27* (*Bronie-Automobil* 1927 *Goda*), the vehicle was a 4×2 type designed at the Izhorsk Factory. The initial series was built on the AMO F-15 four-wheeled long chassis, but later the slightly modified AMO-3 was utilised. These chassis were produced by the AMO Factory in Moscow, later renamed ZIL/ZIS. At that time the majority of the existing older types of armoured car began to be withdrawn from front-line units and relegated to instructional and police units (*OGPU* and *Osoaviakhim*). By the end of 1927 the Red Army had six armoured-car units equipped with *BA-27*s (totalling 54 cars). The *BA-27* remained the basic armoured car until 1931 when new models appeared under the Second Five-Year Plan. The BA-27 armoured car was intended to provide security for the infantry-support units (*NPP* groups) on the march. Its 37mm gun (provided with 40 rounds) was available to check the sudden emergence of enemy tank units. In Soviet doctrine this was envisaged as a lightly armoured, tank accompanying mobile weapon system. About 300 *BA-27* armoured-cars were produced in all. Some of these were issued to the 1st Mechanised Brigade during May 1930. They were used operationally by the Special Far Eastern Army during the battle for the Far-Eastern Railway and also for internal policing — particularly against the up-risings by peasant farmers on the collectives. The *BA-27*'s engine was located at the front under an armoured bonnet. All the armour was riveted and the turret was the same as that fitted to the MS tank. This turret mounted a 37mm gun, and a hull-mounted 7.62mm air-cooled DT tank machine-gun, with 2,016 rounds, was also provided. Solid rubber tires

were used, the rear pair of wheels being double-tired. Normally no radio equipment was fitted, but special commanders' models had a frame aerial around the turret. One fault with this vehicle was that the rear fuel tank obstructed the gun, but nevertheless the vehicle was very self-contained and could be manufactured very quickly and cheaply. In 1931 Repair Shop

(*Rembaza*) No 2 built an experimental series designated *BA-27M*. This was a six-wheeled vehicle with drive taken to the rear pair of axles. It utilised the armoured hull and turret of the *BA-27* on the chassis of the Ford-Tinken truck long imported from the United States of America. The vehicle weighed about 4.9 tons (5,000kg) and was powered by a 40hp water-cooled engine. When phased out, the *BA-27* was replaced by a whole series of armoured cars based on four-wheeled chassis. These were classified into both light and medium classes. The most notable of these was the *BA-20* series, which saw service right up until the Battle of Moscow. As with other Soviet armoured car types the *BA-20* was built both as a road vehicle and as a railway car (*BA-20ZhD*). An improved model was the *BA-20M*.

Left: Soviet BA-27 armoured car of 1927. This vehicle was extensively used for internal security — against "peasants' revolts" over the policy of collective farms.

T-26 LIGHT TANK

T-26, T-26/*TU**,* **T-26***s* **and variants.**
Crew: 3.
Armament: Various (see text).
Armour: Between 6mm (0.24in) and 25mm (0.98in) according to model.
Dimensions: Length between 15ft 2in (4.62m) and 16ft (4.88m); width between 8ft (2.44m) and 7ft 11in (2.41m); height between 7ft 8in (2.33m) and 6ft 10in (2.08m).
Weight: Between 17,637lbs (8,000kg) and 20,944lbs (9,500kg) according to model.
Ground pressure: Between 8.96lb/in² (0.55kg/cm²) and 9.96lb/in² (0.72kg/cm²) according to model.
Power to weight ratio: Between 11.4 and 9.6hp/ton.
Engine: Model T-26 four-cylinder air-cooled petrol engine developing 91hp at 2,200rpm.
Performance: Road speed between 17.5mph (28km/h) and 20mph (32km/h) according to model; range between 63 miles (100km) and 140 miles (225km) according to model; vertical obstacle 2ft 5in (0.79m); trench 5ft 10in (1.90m); gradient 40 degrees.
History: In service with the Russian Army from 1932 to 1945.

As was the case with many other Soviet tanks of the

early 1930s, the T-26 light tank was developed from a British model purchased from the Vickers-Armstrong company. In this instance the basic British model was the famous 6-ton twin-turreted tank. The Soviets developed it into their basic light infantry support tank to replace the obsolescent *MS* model, and it remained in mass production throughout the period between 1931 and 1940. Altogether, more than 12,000 of these vehicles, in a multiplicity of models, were manufactured. During 1930 a group of engineers in the Experimental Design Department (*OKMO*) at the Bolshevik factory in Leningrad, directed by N. V. Barikov and S. A. Ginzbury, manufactured 20 similar vehicles under the designations *TMM*-1 and *TMM*-2. Following comparison trials with Soviet-designed models (T-19 and T-20), on 13 February 1931 the Vickers design was accepted by the Revolutionary Military Council for adoption by the Red Army. After minor alterations by the engineer Zigelya, the vehicle was standardised as the T-26. The production vehicle was practically identical to the British original apart from a few alterations to the shape of the hull front and the shape of the two independently rotating machine-gun turrets. During the following year, mass production of the T-26 tank began at several factories, including the Kirov factory in Leningrad. Tanks of the original

series had two turrets in juxtaposition, and these could mount a multiplicity of armament combinations. For commanders a special version, fitted with radio and called the T-26*TU*, was developed. This had a hand-rail aerial circumscribing the hull. A companion version of this model, with one turret removed and the other mounting a new long-barrelled 37mm gun, was scheduled for adoption by the Red Army. Only a small number of these were produced, however, as a result of the decision to adopt a single-turreted model with larger turret. Mass production of this single-turreted model was carried out in 1933. Original models mounted the new 37mm gun, but eventually the tank received the new 45mm gun. During 1938 reports were received from General Blyukher, commander of the Special Far-Eastern Army, stating that the riveted T-26 tanks had proved ineffective against Japanese fire. It was therefore decided to adopt a new version with welded armour, designated T-26*s*. Some of the earlier models were retrofitted with the turret of this tank. Prior to the Russo-German War, the T-26 saw action in the two main battles with the Japanese in Manchuria, in Spain and in the Russo-Finnish War. During service with the Russian Army, the T-26 underwent many alterations and modifications, and several special-purpose vehicles were developed around its

T-27 TANKETTE

Crew: 2.
Armament: One 7.62mm DT machine-gun.
Armour: 4mm to 10mm (0.16in to 0.4in).
Dimensions: Length 8ft 6in (2.6m); width 6ft (1.83m); height 4ft 9in (1.44m).
Weight: 5,952lbs (2,700kg).
Ground pressure: 7.6lb/in² (0.54kg/cm²).
Power to weight ratio: 15hp/ton.
Engine: One GAZ-AA four-cylinder water-cooled petrol engine developing 40hp at 2,200rpm.
Performance: Road speed 26mph (42km/h); range 75 miles (120km); vertical obstacle 1ft 8in (0.5m); trench 4ft 4in (1.31m); gradient 40 degrees.
History: In service with Russian Army from 1931 to 1941.

One of the vehicles purchased by the Russians from the English Vickers-Armstrong company was the Carden-Loyd Mark VI machine-gun carrier. Together with the 6 ton (6,096kg) tank, this was one of the most widely used armoured vehicles during the 1930s. Soviet designers utilised this chassis to produce their own tankette model during 1931, which was adapted by the Red Army as the T-27. On 13 February 1931 the Revolutionary Military Council of the USSR

authorised the standardisation of this vehicle and ordered its mass production. This commenced shortly afterwards at the Bolshevik Factory in Leningrad and also at the Factory in Memory of S. Ordzhonikidz in Moscow. During 1931 348 of these tankettes were produced, in 1932 there were 1,693, and in 1933 it was planned to turn out 5,000. The allotment for 1933, however, was not completely fulfilled since the Red Army classiffied the vehicle as unsatisfactory and authorised a replacement in the form of the light amphibious tank (T-37). It was discovered that the T-27 would not even provide protection from rifle-calibre ammunition, and the crew conditions were virtually intolerable. Altogether, over the three years of its production, about 2,500 T-27s were built. The first series of T-27 differed little externally from the English original, but had a 7.62mm machine-gun with 2,250 rounds. Soon afterwards, however, the design was modified significantly – having a lengthened chassis, with one additional pair of bogie wheels, which to a certain extent improved the performance of the vehicle across country. Thicker armour was applied. In place of the original Ford engine the tankette was provided with the GAZ-AA car engine, together with its gearbox and transmission. During the first half of the 1930s the T-27 tankette was employed as a recon-

naissance vehicle for infantry and cavalry units. It was also the first ever armoured vehicle to be transported by air. This took place during the Red Army exercises of autumn 1935. The T-27 was used operationally for the first time during the defeat of renegade bands in the Karakumov district. Here it was used to support horse-cavalry and also acted as a command vehicle. The chassis of the T-27 was used to produce several special-purpose vehicles. One of these was a small tank-destroyer designed in 1931 and armed with a 37mm gun, of which two different prototypes were produced. When the T-27 was replaced in service by the T-37 amphibious tankette, it became used for instructing drivers both in the Army and in the *Ossoaviakhim*. Some vehicles were modified as special artillery support vehicles and were often used to tow 37mm and 45mm anti-tank guns. One of the principal failings of the T-27 was that the crew had to be composed of men of small stature, due to the restricted space inside the vehicle. Despite its drawbacks, the T-27 served the Red Army as a useful introduction to the technicalities and application of armoured fighting vehicles. It also provided basic experience in the production of small armoured vehicles which led to the development of the amphibious tankettes and light tanks.

chassis: these included self-propelled guns, flame-throwers, bridge-layers, smoke and chemical tanks, artillery tractors, remote-controlled tank mines, and many others.

Right: More than 12,000 light tanks of the T-26 series, based on the British Vickers Models A and B, were built in 1931-1940.

Below left: T-26B tanks pass infantry positions. Russo-Japanese conflict in Manchuria in 1938 revealed weaknesses in the T-26's riveted armour; the final production model, the T-26S, had armour of 10 to 25mm and was welded throughout.

Below: The T-26A-4V command version of the T-26 series, identifiable by its all-round 'handrail' frame radio aerial. Most T-26As had the twin turrets of the Vickers proto-type; the T-26B and later models had a single turret mounting a 45mm gun.

Above: The light tanks of the T-27 series were modified versions of the British Carden-Loyd machine-gun carrier. More than 4,000 of these tankettes were built in 1932-1941. During exercises in 1935, the T-27 became the first AFV to be transported by air, slung beneath the fuselage of the four-engine Tupolev TB-3 bomber.

Left: The many variants of the T-27 included a tank-destroyer mounting a 37mm gun and a prime mover for anti-tank guns.

T-37 LIGHT AMPHIBIOUS TANK

T-37, T-37A, T-37U and T-37TU.
Crew: 2.
Armament: One 7.62mm Degtarov machine-gun.
Armour: 9mm (0.35in) maximum; 4mm (0.16in) minimum.
Dimensions: Length 12ft 4in (3.75m); width 6ft 7in (2m); height 5ft 11in (1.82m).
Weight: Combat 7,055lbs (3,200kg).
Ground pressure: 7.5lb/in² (0.5kg/cm²).
Power to weight ratio: 12.5hp/ton.
Engine: One GAZ-AA four-cylinder water-cooled petrol engine developing 40hp at 3,000rpm.
Performance: Road speed 21.9mph (35km/h); water speed 2.5mph (4km/h); land range 116 miles (185km); vertical obstacle 1ft 7in (0.5m); trench 5ft 3in (1.6m); gradient 40 degrees.
History: Served with the Russian Army from 1934 to 1942.

During 1930 some examples of the Carden-Loyd Light Amphibious Tank (A4E11) were purchased from the British Vickers-Armstrong company. Soviet designers and engineers at Factory No 37 in memory of S. Ordzhonikidz in Moscow, directed by N.A. Astrov, developed a series of experimental vehicles of this type. The first of these, the T-33 (often referred to as MT-33), was completed in prototype form in 1932 and subjected to extensive tests. This tank was not accepted for mass production, however, because of the many limitations revealed during the trials. A subsequent vehicle of this type, the T-41, was then produced during 1932 and tested. This also failed to meet the requirements. These tanks, however, did serve as the basis for developing a further model, designated T-37. On 11 August 1933, following the successful completion of trials with the Red Army, the T-37 light amphibious tank was accepted for service. Production began at Factory No 37. Prior to this, however, improvement of the vehicle had been effected by another group of engineers under N. N. Koziryev, resulting in the variant designated T-37A. Since the original vehicle never entered service, however, the suffix A was dropped and the improved variant became referred to purely as the T-37. Mass production of the tank began towards the end of 1933 and continued

until the end of 1936 when the improved T-38 type was adopted. Altogether about 1,200 vehicles of this type were built in various models, successive production series incorporating various improvements. The most noticeable of these were the adoption of a turret having a cupola and the use of die-formed armour on the hull. Platoon and company commander's tanks, designated T-37U or T-37TU (TU standing for Command Tank) were provided with radio equipment and had the characteristic hand-rail aerial running round the hull. All vehicles were armed with one 7.62mm DT machine-gun, with 585 rounds, mounted in a rotary turret. T-37 tanks were issued to sub-units of armoured reconnaissance formations as well as organic tank battalions of infantry and cavalry units, where they replaced the obsolescent T-27 tankette in the reconnaissance role. During 1935 T-37 tanks were successfully transported by air, carried by TB-1 and TB-3 bombers. They were later deployed in this manner during the Soviet occupation of Bessarabia in

1940. Several trials were also carried out in which these tanks were launched into the water direct from their aircraft. In the course of production individual tanks underwent progressive alteration, and the chassis was also used to construct various experimental light self-propelled guns.

Above: The early model T-37 had a flush turret. Production began in 1933.

Right: A T-37A light amphibious tank, in Russian service from 1939 to 1942. Derived from the British Carden-Loyd A4E11, the T-37 replaced the T-27 tankette.

T-28 MEDIUM TANK

T-28, T-28 06 1938, T-28 06 1940, T-28M, IT-28 and T-29-5.
Crew: 6.
Armament: One 76.2mm gun; three DT machine-guns.
Armour: 20mm to 80mm (0.79in to 3.15in) depending on model.
Dimensions: Length 24ft 5in (7.44m); width 9ft 3in (2.81m); height 9ft 3in (2.82m).
Weight: 61,729lbs (28,000kg) to 70,547lbs (32,000 kg) depending on model.
Ground pressure: 10.25lb/in² (0.73kg/cm) to 10.95lb/in² (0.78kg/cm²) depending on model.
Power to weight ration: 18.1hp/ton to 15.9hp/ton depending on model.
Engine: One M-17L 12-cylinder water-cooled petrol engine developing 500hp at 1,450rpm.
Performance: Road speed 23mph (37km/h); range 140 miles (220km); vertical obstacle 3ft 5in (1.04m); trench 9ft 6in (2.9m); gradient 43 degrees.
History: Served with the Russian Army from 1933 to 1941.

Work on building a suitable type of medium tank was undertaken during the early 1930s. After trials with numerous prototypes in this tank class (including the T12, T24 and TG), which for a multiplicity of reasons proved unsuitable for mass production; in 1932 the Leningrad Kirov plant built a new prototype medium tank based on the general design of the British A6E1 16 ton (16,257kg) tank. A specimen of this vehicle was not purchased (being still secret at the time), but it is believed that much information was obtained in it through espionage. The first Soviet specification for a multi-turreted 16 ton medium tank, intended for breaking through strongly fortified defensive zones and for exploitation by mechanised brigades, was issued to the Kirov plant in 1931. The specification demanded a crew of five men, 20mm to 30mm (0.79in to 1.18in) armour, a 500hp engine and a maximum speed of 37mph (60km/h). The armament was to comprise one 45mm gun and a machine-gun in the main turret, and one machine-gun in each of the two forward subsidiary turrets. Some 7,938 rounds of machine-gun ammunition were to be carried. A prototype, which weighed 17.3 tons (17,575kg), was completed during 1932. After trials with the prototype

vehicle, it was requested that heavier armour be applied and that the main armament be increased to 76.2mm (with 70 rounds). A specification was then laid down for a 27.56ton (28,000kg) medium tank, designated T-28. The final model was accepted for adoption by the Red Army on 11 August 1933. All tanks of this type were provided with two-way radio equipment, having the characteristic frame aerial around the top of the main turret. They were also fitted with smoke-emitters. In later production vehicles a device was employed to stabilise the main turret. Designed by A. A. Prokofiev, this greatly improved accuracy of fire while on the move. The T-28 was noted for its quiet, smooth motion and abnormal capability for crossing trenches and other terrain obstacles. During 1938 this tank was subjected to extreme modification (now called T-28 06 1938). The existing armament (16.5 calibres long) was replaced by the 76.2mm L-10 gun of 26 calibres length. T-28 tanks were employed against the Japanese in 1939 and also during the Russo-Finnish War. In the course of this war, it was discovered that the armour was in-

adequate and, as the result, modification of the armour was carried out. This was achieved by 'screening' (*yekpanirovki*) suitable parts of the existing armour. The turret and hull frontal plates were increased from 50mm to 80mm (1.97in to 3.15in) the sides and rear to 40mm. Consequently, the weight of this new model (called T-28 06 1940 or T-28M) rose to 31.5 tons (32,000kg). Despite the increase in weight the speed was not significantly impaired. This up-armoured tank gained much acclaim during the break-through of the Mannerheim Line in 1940. Its mass production was terminated soon after the conclusion of hostilities between the USSR and Finland, when the type was replaced in production by the new T-34 medium tank. The chassis of the T-28 was used for several types of experimental self-propelled gun as well as special-purpose tanks (eg bridgelayer IT-28 and a mine-clearing tank). During 1934 the design bureau at the Kirov Factory developed a wheel/track variant of the T-28, called the T-29-5. Although this never passed beyond the prototype stage, it formed the first link in the eventual development of the T-34.

Left: The T-28, the Red Army's first medium tank, entered service in 1933. Its design owed much to the British A6E1.

BA-10 ARMOURED CAR

BA-10, BA-10ZhD and variants.
Crew: 4
Armament: One 45mm gun; one 7.62mm DT machine-gun co-axial with main armament; 7.62mm DT machine-gun in the hull (next to driver).
Armour: 15mm (0.59in) maximum; 6mm (0.24in) minimum.
Dimensions: Length 15ft 3in (4.65m); width 6ft 9in (2.07m); height 7ft 3in (2.21m).
Weight: 11,332lbs (5,140kg).
Ground pressure: 51.3lb/in² (3.15kg/cm²).
Power to weight ratio: 9.7hp/ton.
Engine: Model GAZ-M1 four-cylinder water-cooled inline petrol engine developing 50hp at 2,800rpm.
Performance: Road speed 34mph (55km/h); range 188 miles (300km); vertical obstacle negligible; trench negligible; gradient 20 degrees.
History: In service with the Russian Army from 1938 to 1943.

From 1931 onwards the Soviet automobile industry undertook the development of a series of six-wheeled armoured cars for the Red Army. The first of these was the BA-27M (see the section on the BA-27), followed in the same year by the BAD amphibian and the D-13. All of these vehicles, however, remained purely experimental. The first medium six-wheeled armoured car to be adopted by the Red Army was the BA-1, in 1932. This was a 6×4 vehicle built at the Izhorsk factory, and was also known as the BAI. It utilised the chassis of the imported Ford-Timken lorry from the USA. A small series was produced with varying armament and other minor differences, and later vehicles were built around the GAZ-AAA six-wheeled chassis. In 1933 the BA-3 was developed; also a 6×4 vehicle, it was produced by the Izhorsk factory. It was an improved BA-1 produced on the GAZ-AAA chassis, having a 45mm gun and co-axial machine-gun mounted in the turret of the T-26 light tank. Special tracks could be placed around the rear wheels to improve cross-country performance. The spare wheels were mounted on axles on the hull sides and revolved freely, serving as additional support when the vehicle was crossing obstacles. This feature, and the use of spare tracks, was continued on all these six-wheeled vehicles. The BA-3 was adopted by reconnaissance sub-units of the Red Army as standard equipment and remained in service until the beginning of World War II. In 1935 the Russians developed their first experimental amphibious vehicle, a 6×4 armoured car. This was the PB-4, which remained purely experimental. Also in 1935, the Izhorsk factory developed an improvement of the BA-3 vehicle, designated BA-6. Three versions of this vehicle were produced and adopted by the Red Army: the BA-6 (1935), the BA-6ZhD adapted to run along railway lines (1935), and the BA-6M (1936). All three of these vehicles took part in military operations from 1936 to 1939. During 1936 a modified version of the BA-6M appeared, designated BA-9. Built on the GAZ-AAA lorry chassis, it differed from its predecessors in weight and armament. Only a small series of these vehicles was made. Starting in that year production six-wheeled armoured cars were used by Republican troops in Spain. Altogether the Soviet Union sent out about 100 such vehicles. Soviet engineers also assisted in preparing the production of such vehicles in Spain itself, which took place between 1937–38. In 1938 the Red Army adopted the BA-10 model, which was a further improvement on the BA-9. The vehicle also originated in the design bureau of the Izhorsk factory. It was mass-produced from 1938 to 1941. Apart from the basic BA-10 model, in 1938 the BA-10ZhD railway variant appeared. The BA-10 became the standard equipment of reconnaissance units as well as of independent armoured brigades. It remained in service until 1943. Apart from Spain all the armoured cars taken into service saw action against the Japanese in Manchuria, during the Russo-Finnish War and in the initial period of the Russo-German War. In parallel with the medium six-wheeled armoured car series, the Russians developed several heavy six-wheeled armoured cars, including the famous BAZ amphibian, and culminating in the BA-11 (petrol) and BA-1LD (diesel) vehicles which also saw action during the Russo-German War. Many other six-wheeled variants were also produced, including armoured ambulances, ammunition carriers and troop carriers.

The BA-10 was a direct development from the BA-3 (shown here), through the BA-6, BA-6M, and the BA-9 armoured cars.

T-35 HEAVY TANK

T-35 and SU-14.
Crew: 11 (when provided with all turrets; some models had some of the turrets removed).
Armament: Basic model – One 76.2mm gun; two 45mm guns; six 7·62mm DT machine-guns; one P-40 AA machine-gun. (Some later models had a few of the subsidiary weapons removed).
Armour: 30mm (1.18in) maximum; 10mm (0.39in) minimum.
Dimensions: Length 31ft 10in (9.72m); width 10ft 6in (3.2m); height 11ft 3in (3.43m).
Weight: Combat 110,230lbs (50,000kg). (Some models were lighter.)
Ground pressure: 11.08lb/in² (0.78kg/cm²).
Power to weight ratio: 10hp/ton.
Engine: One Model M-17T V-12 12-cylinder water-cooled petrol engine developing 500hp at 2,200rpm.
Performance: Road speed 19mph (30km/h); range 94 miles (150km); vertical obstacle 4ft (1.2m); trench 11ft 6in (3.5m); gradient 20 degrees.
History: The T-35 heavy tank was approved for adoption by the Red Army on 11 August 1933. It remained in production until 1939.

At the beginning of the 1930s, when widespread investigation into the field of AFVs was being carried out in the Soviet Union, the Red Army staff intended vehicles of the heavy, multi-turreted type to act as a shock force when breaking through enemy defensive positions. This required the use of 'Bronenoster' (Ironclads) of immense dimensions and having extraordinary firepower. Based on the general philosophy of the British A-1 'Independent' tank (a specimen was never actually purchased), the 36.4 ton (37,000kg) prototype of the T-35 was manufactured. This vehicle had five turrets – a main one mounting a 76.2mm gun (with 90 rounds), two diagonally placed subsidiary turrets each mounting one 37mm gun (front and rear of the main turret) and two further small turrets each mounting one 7.62mm machine-gun and placed on the opposite diagonals to the 37mm turrets. To man this massive firepower the tank required a crew of 11 men. Subsequent production vehicles dispensed with some of these turrets, and a few had 45mm guns (with 113 rounds each) in place of the 37mm type. The final model had sloping welded armour. The T-35 was a typical member of the multi-turreted heavy tank family which prevailed in the 1920s and 1930s and considered to be a highly promising weapon. About the middle of the 1930s, however, the appearance of a multiplicity of anti-tank weapons made it necessary to up-armour the heavy tank. Because of the excessive weight increases involved, this could not be achieved with a multi-turreted design. Two experimental tanks – the SMK and the T-100 – were produced with only two turrets, but at the same time there appeared the experimental single-turreted KV tank, designed by Zh. Kotin. All three vehicles were tried out during the breakthrough of the Mannerheim Line (in Russo-Finnish War of 1939–40), and the KV proved the most successful. Even though the T-35 was outmoded at the beginning of the Russo-German War, it was retained in service until its final action during the Battle of Moscow (December 1941). The T-35 appeared in several variants and about 60 were produced and issued to the tank brigades of the High Command Reserve. Apart from changes to the armour layout and weapon availability, there were differences to the number of wheels and types of suspension. All vehicles were fitted with radio equipment and had the characteristic frame aerial around the top of the main turret. On this tank chassis several experimental self-propelled artillery mountings were developed, particularly the heavy SU-14 series, which had interchangeable armament. When finally phased out, towards the end of 1941, the armoured hulls of the later T-35 tanks were removed from their chassis and, after slight modification, attached to railway flatcars. In this manner they comprised armoured train units used throughout the entire war.

Above: The multi-turreted T-35 mounted a 76.2mm gun, two 45mm and six machine-guns.

Right: The T-35 heavy tank replaced the T-32 from 1933. A notable feature was radio, with a frame aerial on the main turret.

BT-7 FAST TANK

BT-7, BT-7A, BT-7M, BT-7U, BT-7TU and variants, plus **BT-1, BT-S** and **BT-5.**
Crew: 3..
Armament: One 45mm M1935 gun; one co-axial 7.62mm DT machine-gun. (Some vehicles had an additional 7.62mm DT machine-gun in turret rear and a P.40 machine-gun).
Armour: 22mm (0.87in) maximum; 10mm (0.39in) minimum.
Dimensions: Length 18ft 7in (5.66m); width 7ft 6in (2.29m); height 7ft 11in (2.42m).
Weight: 30,644lbs (13,900kg).
Ground pressure: 11.25lb/in² (0.79kg/cm²).
Power to weight ratio: 36hp/ton.
Engine: One Model M17T 12-cylinder water-cooled petrol engine developing 500hp at 1,650rpm.
Performance: Road speed on wheels 46mph (73km/h); road speed on tracks 33mph (53km/h); range on wheels 450 miles (730km); range on tracks 270 miles (430km); vertical obstacle 1ft 10in (0.55m); trench 6ft 7in (2m); gradient 32 degrees.
History: In service with the Russian Army from 1935 to 1945.

Next to the T-26 light infantry-accompanying tank, the *BT* fast tank was the most prolific AFV vehicle in the Red Army during the 1930s. The initials *BT* form an acronym for *Bistrokhodny Tank*, or Fast Tank. It was known among Soviet tankmen as the *Betka* (Beetle) or as the *Tri-Tankista* (Three Tanker — as the result of

its three-man crew). As distinct from most of the other Soviet vehicles at that time, which were based on British Vickers models, the *BT* tank was derived from an American design by J. W. Christie. This design was also later taken up by the British to develop their famous Cruiser tank range, the most famous member being the Crusader. The basic Christie vehicle was purchased by Soviet officials in America during 1930 and one vehicle was shipped back to Russia during that year and delivered to the Kharkhov Locomotive Works. After extensive tests of the Christie vehicle, on 23 May 1931 the Revolutionary Military Council of the USSR authorised the tank for Red Army use and requested its mass production. The drawings for the BT tank prototype were delivered to the *Komintern* Factory in Kharkhov during August 1931. On 3 September 1931, the first two prototypes, designated *BT-1*, left the factory gates and were delivered to the Red Army for trails. This first vehicle was provided with machine-gun armament only, and the Red Army test commission which investigated the tank requested that the production model be armed with an artillery weapon. In the meantime the *BT-2* model, still with machine-gun armament, was developed in limited quantities. After the production of a small number of vehicles, however, the *BT-2* tank received a 37mm Model 1930 tank gun mounted in the original machine-gun turret. During 1932 the Red Army requested that the *BT* tank be armed with a more powerful weapon, in the form of the 45mm gun. After various prototypes had been tested, the *BT-S* model was accepted. This

mounted a 45mm gun in a turret almost identical to that fitted to the T-26 light tank. A co-axial 7.62mm DT machine-gun was also installed. Commanders' vehicles, which received the suffix *U* or *TU* (*BT-5U* or *BT-5TU*), were provided with two-way radio equipment, which was mounted in the turret overhang, thereby displacing some of the 45mm ammunition. As in the case of the T-26 commander's model, the turret was fitted with the characteristic frame aerial. The *BT* tank was intended for large, independent long-range armoured and mechanised units (called *DD* groups). These were to act in the rear of enemy positions and take out nerve centres such as headquarters, supply bases, airfields, etc. Under such circumstances high speed was a great advantage. One of the basic attributes of the Christie design was the ability of the tank to run on either tracks or the road wheels. Track drive was used when moving across country or along poor roads, whilst wheel drive was used for long strategic road drives. The time taken to change from one mode to the other was put at between 10 and 15 minutes. This ability to run on wheels, however, was never actually exploited by the Red Army

Below: BT-7 tanks accompany infantry in an attack on Japanese units in the Khalkin-Gol area of Manchuria/Mongolia in 1939. The Russians deployed 3 divisions and 5 armoured brigades, commanded by General Zhukov (of WWII fame). Losses on both sides were reported to be very heavy.

STZ ARMOURED TRACTOR

STZ and versions (including Pioneer and ZIS-30/SU-57.
Crew: 2 (plus up to 8 passengers).
Armament: Basic vehicle one 7.62mm DT machine-gun. Various other weapons fitted or towed. Used as the basis for a number of self-propelled guns (see text).
Armour: 6mm to 16mm (0.24in to 0.63in).
Dimensions: Length (overall) 11ft 2in (3.4m); width 6ft (1.84m); height 4ft 7in (1.4m).
Weight: 2,205lbs (1,000kg).
Ground pressure: 8.5lb/in² (0.6kg/cm²).
Power to weight ratio: 51hp/ton.
Engine: GAZ-AA 6002-Z four-cylinder water-cooled petrol engine developing 50hp at 2,800rpm.
Performance: Road speed 25mph (40km/h); range 94 miles (150km); vertical obstacle 1ft 2in (0.36m); trench 4ft 7in (1.4m); gradient 30 degrees.
History: Served with the Russian Army from 1939 to 1945.

From the very beginning of the Red Army mechanisation programme, during the early 1930s, the Red Army placed great emphasis upon providing effective traction for artillery. A special tractor factory was established at Stalingrad called the Stalingrad Tractor Factory (STZ) in Memory of F. Dzierzhinski. This factory provided a whole range of artillery tractors of light, medium and heavy types. Initially these differed little from the types of tractors provided to agriculture. When the Red Army began to re-

introduce the large armoured and mechanised units during 1939, special fast tracked prime-movers began to appear for the artillery. There was considered a particular need at that time for a light, armoured tractor which could tow infantry-support artillery such as the 37mm and 45mm anti-tank guns, the 76mm infantry howitzer and various heavy mortars and light anti-aircraft guns. Such a tractor needed to be armoured so as to be able to operate with forward echelons of the mechanised corps. As the result engineers at the Stalingrad Tractor Factory produced a completely new vehicle designated the *Komsomolets*. The *Komsomolets* tractor was built in two basic versions: a gun tractor with seats for the crew at the rear, and an ammunition- and cargo-carrying version. Both had an armoured compartment at the front for the driver and machine-gunner. The machine-gunner sat alongside the driver and operated the 7.62mm DT machine-gun, ball mounted in the front plate of the compartment. The gun-tractor version had seats for six men at the rear, which could be folded down. The gun crew sat back to back over the engine at the rear. Mounted above the rear compartment was an aerial which could be folded down and also served as a frame for a large canvas hood. In the cargo-carrying version the rear seats were removed. An unarmoured version of the *Komsomolets*, known as the Pioneer tractor, was produced and this had a pressed mild-steel engine compartment at the front. The armoured *Komsomolets* performed very badly during the Finnish War, where the armour proved ineffective

against small-calibre fire. The very first self-propelled gun to be standardised by the Red Army (apart from a few earlier wheeled types) was based on this chassis. At the beginning of the Russo-German War the Soviets were desperately in need of a self-propelled anti-tank gun. The artillery designer V. Grabin, at Artillery Factory No 92 in Gorki, adapted the ultra-new 57mm M1941 anti-tank gun to be mounted on the *Komsomolets* vehicle. Called ZIS-30 (also known as *SU*-57), a small number of these were built and supplied to the Red Army towards the end of July 1941. They were used effectively during the Battle of Moscow in the following December and later during the Battle of Stalingrad and the Caucasus in mid-1942. Another self-propelled version, here mounting a 45mm gun, consisted of the basic tractor chassis with an armoured box-like superstructure built up from the hull at the rear. The 45mm gun was placed in a limited-traverse mounting at the front of the superstructure.

Right: A captured Russian STZ Komsomolets armoured tractor is inspected by German troops. Note the large canvas hood which was spread over the radio frame-aerial. The tractor was used in the forward battle area to tow infantry support weapons such as anti-tank guns, light anti-aircraft guns, field guns and heavy mortars. A version was also produced to act as an ammunition- and supply-carrier.

in military operations. When the tank was operated in the wheeled mode, the tracks were attached along the track guards, and engine power was transmitted to the rear pair of wheels. The two front road wheels could be turned to provide steering. In contrast to most other tanks, where two steering levers were employed, the *BT* was controlled by a steering wheel. As the result of large-scale exercises carried out by the Red Army during the early 1930s, it was realised that the long-range *DD* groups required some form of accompanying artillery to provide artillery fire-support during the attack. For this reason, special artillery support tanks, which received the suffix *A*, were developed. The first of these, the *BT-5A*, was introduced in 1935. It mounted a short-barrelled 76.2mm gun in a turret very similar to that used as the main one on the T-28 medium tank. As a result of combat experience, the Red Army requested that the *BT* be redesigned with welded armour and that the armour be sloped to increase its immunity. Thus there emerged the *BT-7* model a vast improvement over the previous models. Ammunition stowage comprised 188 45mm rounds and 2,142 7.62mm rounds. As in the case of the *BT-5*, a commander's model was developed, designated *BT-7U* or *BT-7TU*. The first series of this vehicle still retained the original cylindrical turret of the T-26 tank, however. In 1938, following experience against the Japanese in Manchuria, the new turret which had been designed for the T-26 light tank was also fitted to the *BT-7*. A commander's version of this model was also produced. To provide artillery fire-support the *BT-7A*

version was developed. This had the same turret as the *BT-5A*. Other alterations to the *BT-7* were the use of a more powerful engine and an improved transmission system. During 1938 the new V-2 diesel engine had been developed specifically for tank use, and this was installed in all subsequent *BT-7* tanks. To distinguish it from previous models, the vehicle was designated *BT-7M*; it has, however, also been referred to as the *BT-8*. This new engine developed 500hp at 1,800rpm, and being a diesel powerplant allowed the *DD* groups a much greater range of operation than had been possible previously. It also reduced the fire risk since diesel fuel is not so volatile as petrol. Several specialised and experimental vehicles were developed from the *BT* tank. During 1936 the experimental *BT-IS* (investigator tank) was developed. This had heavily sloped armour that shrouded the tracks. This vehicle contributed greatly to the eventual development of the T-34 tank. During 1937 several *BT* tanks were equipped with schnorkels, enabling them to deepford water obstacles. Such vehicles were designated *BT-5PH*. As the *BT-5* and *BT-7* models gained numerical significance in the Red Army, the older *BT* models were used to develop special-purpose vehicles such as the *BT* bridgelayer, smoke tank and chemical tank. *BT* tanks took part in operations during the Spanish Civil War. The *BT-7M*, in particular, also saw service during Zhukov's debut at the Khalkhin-Gol battles, at Lake Khasan and also during the Russo-Finnish War. All *BT* tanks saw service during the early operations of the Russo-German War.

Above: Front view of a late production model BT-7, with a conical turret and twin horn periscopes. Its gun is a modification of the standard Russian 45mm anti-tank gun, the M-1935, firing an AP round with a muzzle-velocity of 820m per second.

Below: Side view of a BT-7-I(V), the command version of the early BT-7. It has the cylindrical turret of the BT-5 command tank with all-round frame radio aerial. These models were used to control BT-7 fast tank units in action.

Right: Side view of a gun-crew carrier version of the STZ Komsomolets armoured tractor. Note the folding seats and the aerial frame which normally supported a canvas hood.

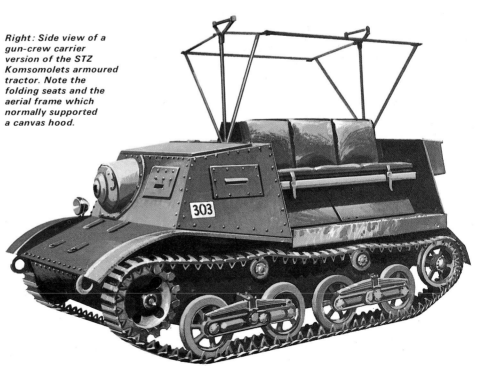

KV-1 HEAVY TANK

KV-1, KV-1s, KV-2, KV-3 and KV-85.
Crew: 5.
Armament: One 76.2mm gun (various types); three 7.62mm DT machine-guns. (Some vehicles had an additional machine-gun in the turret rear and a P-40 AA machine-gun.)
Armour: 100mm (3.94in) to 75mm (2.95in), varying with model.
Dimensions: Length 20ft 7in (6.273m); width 10ft 2in (3.098m); height 7ft 11in (2.413m). (Dimensions varied slightly according to models.)
Weight: 104,719lbs (47,500kg), varying slightly with model.
Ground pressure: 10.68lb/in² (0.75kg/cm²).
Power to weight ratio: 12.6hp/ton, varying with model.
Engine: One Model V-2-K 12-cylinder water-cooled diesel developing 600hp at 2,000rpm.
Performance: Road speed 22mph (35km/h); range 156 miles (250km); vertical obstacle 3ft 8in (1.2m); trench 8ft 6in (2.8m); gradient 36 degrees.
History: Served with the Russian Army from 1940 to 1945.

At the outbreak of World War II, the Russian Army was practically the only armed force in the world to be equipped with production heavy tanks. The first of these, the KV-1 (Klim Voroshilov) was designed by a group of engineers at the Kirov Factory in Leningrad, under the direction of Zh. Kotin. Work began in February 1939 and the State Defence Committee approved a mock-up in April. The completed tank was demonstrated to the Red Army staff in September. It was accepted as standard at the same time as the T-34 medium, on 19 December 1939. Production

began in February 1940 and in that year 243 vehicles of the type were produced. A platoon of these, meanwhile, was sent to Finland for combat tests, and in February 1940 the tanks took part in the breakthrough of the Finnish main position. Not one of them was destroyed, although companion multi-turreted models were knocked out. Subsequent production was undertaken at the Chelyabinsk Tractor Factory to where in September 1941, as a result of the imminent German threat to Leningrad, the Kirov factory was evacuated. By June 1941, however, when the Germans attacked, 636 had been built. In Chelyabinsk

the Kirov Factory was amalgamated with the Chelyabinsk Tractor Factory, and other industry transferred there, to form the immense complex called 'Tankograd'. This became the sole Soviet industrial establishment producing heavy tanks and heavy self-propelled guns for the remainder of the war. By the time of the Battle of Moscow, 1,364 KVs had been built; of course, many of these had been destroyed or captured in the meantime. Throughout the war, Tankograd supplied the Red Army with some 13,500 heavy tanks and self-propelled guns on this chassis. Alongside the KV-1 tank, which was armed with the same gun as

Below: Front, side and rear views of a KV-1A tank. This version had a turret with a rear-mounted 7.62mm DT machine-gun.

T-40 LIGHT AMPHIBIOUS TANK

T-40, T-40A and T-40S.
Crew: 2.
Armament: One 12.7mm DShK heavy machine-gun; one 7.62mm DT machine-gun.
Armour: 6mm to 13mm (0.24in to 0.51in).
Dimensions: Length (overall) 13ft 6in (4.43m); width 7ft 8in (2.51m); height 6ft 6in (2.12m).
Weight: 12,324lbs (5,590kg).
Ground pressure: 6.55lb/in² (0.5kg/cm²).
Power to weight ratio: 15.45hp/ton.
Engine: GAZ-202 six-cylinder water-cooled petrol engine developing 85hp at 3,600rpm.
Performance: Road speed 28mph (45km/h); range 220 miles (350km); vertical obstacle 2ft 2in (0.7m); trench 5ft 8in (1.85m); gradient 34 degrees.
History: In service with Russian Army from 1941 to 1946.

Following the adoption of the KV heavy and the T-34 medium tanks, the Red Army was supplied with a new light amphibious tank, designated T-40. This was intended as a replacement for the older T-37 and T-38 amphibious tanks. It was introduced into the Red Army to equip reconnaissance and armoured liaison units at the beginning of 1941. It is interesting that this tank was a complete departure from previous Soviet light tank designs, utilising independent torsion-bar suspension, welded armour throughout, and a new turret design. The turret and mantlet were very similar to those currently fitted to Swedish tanks, but no vehicles had ever been purchased by the Soviets from Sweden. It is thought that the Russians may have been influenced by investigation of captured Polish 7TP tanks, which they obtained during the occupation of eastern Poland in 1939; these tanks utilised Swedish Bofors gun mountings. The T-40 was armed with machine-guns only (one 12.7mm heavy machine-gun with 550 rounds and a

7.62mm machine-gun with 2,016 rounds) and was relatively thinly armoured. About the time of the introduction of the T-60 light tank, some T-40s were rearmed with the 20mm ShVAK-20 gun. As with previous light tank models, to simplify production, conventional automobile components were employed. The T-40A, introduced during late 1941, differed from the original tank in having the bow top faired away at the sides where originally it had been flat. The T-40A also had a trim vane which unfolded from the bow. During 1942 the T-40S was placed in limited production as a successor to the T-40 and T-40A. Since the thin armour on the previous models became a considerable handicap during operations, this new model had the armour increased on certain

parts of the hull and turret. With the increase in weight, however, the tank lost its amphibious capability, so the water-propulsion and water-steering devices were removed during production. The hull of this series of tank was very original, slightly resembling a boat, with a large squat front, and the turret mounted slightly to the rear on the left-hand side. Flotation tanks were built into the hull to assist buoyancy, and in the water the T-40 was driven by a single four-bladed propeller at the rear and steered by two rudders.

Below: Side view of a T-40 light amphibious tank used by Russian reconnaissance units in the armoured battles of 1941-42.

the T-34 (76mm), a special artillery fire-support version, the KV-2, was adopted. This had a massive box-shaped turret mounting a 152mm howitzer. Immediately after the start of production of the KV-1 and KV-2, the Kirov Factory received orders to design an even heavier tank with more powerful armament (107mm gun) and thicker armour. A prototype, designated KV-3, was built at the beginning of 1941 but the German attack interrupted plans for its mass production. During the period 1941—42, therefore, production of the KV-1 continued. The KV-2 was dropped as the result of its poor performance. Successive models of the KV-1 received thicker armour and some had castings in place of welded components. A new longer-barrelled gun was also introduced. Experience at the front showed that the KV was now becoming too slow, so a lighter, faster version, the KV-1s, was introduced during the second half of 1942. As the need arose for more powerful armament, an 85mm gun was adopted in autumn 1943 for a model designated KV-85. In subsequent attempts to improve the KV tank a whole range of experimental vehicles was produced, but eventually the tank was replaced by the new IS (Iosef Stalin) series with much better armament and a radical approach to armour protection.

Left: A KV-2 heavy tank, first used by the Red Army against the Mannerheim line defences in the Russo-Finnish War, 1940.

Left: A KV-1 production line at the Leningrad Defence Plant in October 1942. The plant worked throughout the 900-day siege.

Right: KV-1s built with funds donated by farmers in the Moscow area are presented to representatives of the Red Army by a group of the patriotic donors.

T-60 LIGHT TANK

T-60 and T-60A
Crew: 2.
Armament: One 20mm ShVAK cannon; one 7.62mm DT machine-gun.
Armour: 7mm to 20mm (0.28in to 0.79in).
Dimensions: Length (overall) 14ft 1in (4.3m); width 8ft 1in (2.46m); height 6ft 2in (1.89m).
Weight: 11,354lbs (5,150kg).
Ground pressure: 6.55lb/in² (0.46kg/cm²).
Power to weight ratio: 13.8hp/ton.
Engine: GAZ-202 six-cylinder water-cooled petrol engine developing 70hp at 2,800rpm.
Performance: Road speed 28mph (45km/h); range 382 miles (615km); vertical obstacle 1ft 9in (0.54m); trench 6ft 1in (1.85m); gradient 29 degrees.
History: In service with the Russian Army from 1941 to 1945.

In 1941 the T-60 light tank appeared as a replacement for the T-40 light amphibious tank. In this case, however, because of the need for much heavier armour, the tank was a purely land-based vehicle. Experience gained during the first months of the Russo-German War had shown that high mobility and an amphibious capability were not all that were needed in battle. Designers in Soviet tank factories therefore took steps to increase the armour and firepower on the light tank. As the result they developed the T-60 light tank with 20mm (0.79in) armour on the front. The greatest stumbling block, however, was the provision of more powerful armament. Soviet engineers attempted to mount a 37mm gun but, even with a reduced charge round, the turret ring was incapable of absorbing the recoil of this weapon. The Soviet armament designer B. Shpital'n was therefore given the task of developing a special high-powered weapon for the tank. He developed the rapid-firing 20mm ShVAK-20 gun. Despite the reduced calibre, the armour-piercing

Above: The T-60 light tank was used as a replacement for the T-40 and T-50 series in reconnaissance units from late 1941. Designed for operating in snow, it was well suited to winter fighting.

incendiary round of this gun possessed the same armour-penetration qualities as the original 37mm gun. It fired a heavy soft-core round incorporating a sub-calibre slug. In comparison with previous light-tank models, the hull front and turret had improved protection against heavy-calibre machine-gun rounds, and although cast armour had been adopted for the medium and heavy tank classes and for the turret of the T-50 light tank, both hull and turret of the T-60 were welded throughout. The T-60 entered production during November 1941 and over 6,000 were produced before the type was supplanted by the successor T-70 light tank. The vehicle was issued to reconnaissance

units and also to infantry units for direct infantry support. The turret was offset to the left, with the engine mounted alongside it on the right and the driver was placed centrally in the front. An improved model of the T-60 was produced in late 1941/early 1942, and this was designated T-60A. It had increased armour, but the main external difference lay in the wheels. The T-60 had spoked road-wheels and rollers whilst those on the T-60A were pressed solid. When eventually replaced by the more powerful T-70 light tank, the T-60 chassis were employed as mountings for M-8 and M-13 (Katyusha) rocket-launchers, and also as artillery tractors for 57mm anti-tank guns.

179

T-34/85 MEDIUM TANK

A-20, T-32, T-34 and T-34/85.
Crew: 5.
Armament: One 85mm M1944 Z1S S53 L/51 gun; two 7.62mm DT machine-guns.
Armour: 18mm to 60mm (0.71in to 2.36in).
Dimensions: Length (including gun) 24ft 7in (7.5m); width 9ft 7in (2.92m); height 7ft 10in (2.39m).
Weight: 70,547lbs (32,000kg).
Ground pressure: 11.2lb/in² (0.8kg/cm²).
Power to weight ratio: 15.9hp/ton.
Engine: One V-2-34 12-cylinder water-cooled diesel developing 500hp at 1,800rpm.
Performance: Road speed 31mph (50km/h); range 186 miles (300km); vertical obstacle 2ft 7in (0.79m); trench 8ft 2in (2.49m); gradient 30 degrees.
History: In service with the Russian Army from 1940. Still used by many countries today.

During 1936 the young engineer M. I. Koshkin was transferred to the Komintern Factory in Kharkov as chief designer. The design bureau of the factory had been concerned with the continued modernisation of the BT wheel/track tank. At the beginning of 1937 this factory was assigned the task of designing a new medium tank, also a wheel/track design, designated A-20. The design of this tank was completed in November of that year. The 17.7 ton (18,000kg) A-20, armed with a 45mm gun, was the first of the so-called 'Shellproof Tanks', having greatly inclined armour, a characteristic feature of the later T-34 tank. The chassis was similar to that used on the BT tank but with certain automotive changes. A further version, mounting a 76.2mm gun, was developed and designated A-30. In the meantime, Koshkin had come to the conclusion that to produce the new medium tank as a wheel/track vehicle was erroneous. The Red Army had seldom ever used the BT tank in the wheeled mode, and to incorporate this facility required complication of design and severe weight penalties. He therefore proposed the development of a purely tracked variant, designated A-32 (later T-32). The Main Military Council of the USSR accepted this proposal and authorised the construction of a prototype. They had not, however, yet dismissed the wheel/track project and awaited comparison trials at a later date. Prototypes of the A-20 and T-32 tanks were completed at Kharkov at the beginning of 1939, and during that year were exhibited to the

Armoured Directorate. The Directorate recommended an increase in armour on the T-32 and the adoption of more powerful armament. The group under Koshkin achieved this, the final variant being called T-34. Due to the serious international situation, on 19 December 1939, before the completion of a prototype, the Main Military Council accepted the T-34 project for equipping the armoured units of the Red Army. Towards the end of January 1940, the first production models of the T-34, designated T-34 06 1940, were released from the Komintern Factory. At the beginning of February two of these underwent a trial march, under the personal supervision of Koshkin. This followed the route Kharkov-Moscow-Smolensk-Kiev-Kharkov. In Moscow the tank was presented before the High Command in Red Square. In the meantime, Koshkin had developed pneumonia and went to hospital, where he died on 26 September 1940. During June 1940, the manufacturing drawings were completed and the tank entered mass production. Since Koshkin had been taken ill, his assistant A. A. Morozov had taken over the final design. The T-34 (called *Prinadlezhit-Chetverki* or 'Thirty-Four' by the troops) was noted for its excellently shaped armour, which considerably increased its resistance to shell penetration. The armament, a

7.62mm long-barrelled high-velocity gun, was also an innovation for tanks of this class. The use of the new 500hp V-2 diesel engine (already in service on the BT-7M tank) reduced the fire risk and greatly increased the operational range of the tank. The modified Christie suspension permitted high speeds, even on rough terrain, and the wide tracks reduced the ground pressure to a minimum. The overall design of the tank facilitated rapid mass production and lent itself to simple maintenance and repair in the field. In general, Koshkin's T-34 was Russia's equivalent to Mitchell's Spitfire. The analogy is almost too true: both designers died through their efforts to provide their nations with a war-winning weapon. By the end of 1940 115 T-34s had been produced. Some were dispatched to Finland for combat tests but arrived too late to participate in operations. By June 1941, when the Germans attacked, a total of 1,225 had been produced. By the Battle of Moscow, 1,853 had been delivered to units, but of course many of these had since been destroyed. The T-34 made its combat debut on 22 June 1941, in the vicinity of Grodno (Belorussia). It was a complete surprise to the German Army, who learned to treat this tank with the greatest respect. The question was raised of manufacturing a copy of it in Germany, but this

Below: Soviet T-34/85 medium tanks support infantry in an attack on the Third Ukrainian Front near Odessa in 1944.

T-70 LIGHT TANK

proved impracticable. As the result, the Germans developed their famous Panther tank, whose general design was greatly influenced by that of the T-34. With the evacuation of the Soviet tank industry to the east, subsequent production of the T-34 was carried out at the *Uralmashzavod* (Ural Machine-Building Plant) in the Urals, as well as a number of subsidiary plants. The T-34 tank was originally armed with the 76.2mm Model 1939 L-11 gun mounted in a welded turret of rolled plate. In order to accelerate production, a new cast turret was soon introduced. During mid-1941 a new Model 40 F-34 gun was adopted. This had a longer barrel and higher muzzle velocity. A multiplicity of minor and major changes were made to the T-34 during production, but the most significant took place in autumn 1943, when the 85mm 215 S-53 or D-5T gun, with 55 rounds, was adopted. Some 2,394 rounds of 7.62mm ammunition were also carried. This new tank was called T-34/85 and was approved for mass production on 15 December 1943. By the end of the year 283 had been built, and in the following year a further 11,000 were produced. The T-34/85 remained in production until the mid-1950s, when the T-54 was adopted. It served with other armies as late as the mid-1960s.

Left: The T-34/76B medium tank, a heavier and more powerful version of the T-34/76A, the Red Army's main tank of WWII. The 76B had a turret of rolled plate, its armour welded on earlier models but later cast.

T-70 and T-70A.
Crew: 2.
Armament: One 45mm L/46 gun; one 7.62mm DT machine-gun.
Armour: 0.39in (10mm) minimum; 2.36in (60mm) maximum.
Dimensions: Length 15ft 3in (5m); width 7ft 8in (2.52m); height 6ft 9in (2.22m).
Weight: 21,958lbs (9,960kg).
Ground pressure: 9.53lb/in² (0.67kg/cm²).
Power to weight ratio: 14.29hp/ton.
Engine: Two ZIS-202 six-cylinder water-cooled petrol engines each developing 70hp at 2,800rpm.
Performance: Road speed 32mph (51km/h); range 279 miles (446km); vertical obstacle 2ft 2in (0.71m); trench 9ft 6in (3.12m); gradient 34 degrees.
History: In service with the Red Army from 1942 to 1948.

During late January 1942 the T-70 light tank began to replace the T-60 model in Russian service. Despite the fact that it had been shown that the light tank was not an effective vehicle, it was cheaper and easier to mass produce and this meant that units could receive tanks where they would otherwise have none. With the tremendous losses suffered by the Soviet tank parks during the first six months of the war (put at over 18,000 vehicles) and the fact that most of the Soviet tank industry had to be transferred to the central regions of the USSR, thereby delaying production, any

tank production was imperative. As the war progressed however, the production of medium and heavy tanks soon reached the desired level and the final light tank model to enter service remained the T-70. The T-70 light tank was mass produced at the Gorki Automobile Works. It replaced the T-60 in light tank units. The T-70 had the same chassis as the T-60 (with the drive taken to the front, instead of the rear), slightly reinforced to take the extra weight, but mounted a 45mm gun (with 70 rounds) and co-axial 7.62mm DT machine-gun (with 945 rounds) in a new welded turret. The hull armour was also modified to give a cleaner outline and better protection, and the driver was provided with an armoured visor. The engine power was doubled by providing two engines of the type used in the T-60. During mid-1943 the T-70A was produced. This was an improved version with increased armour and slightly more powerful engines. The turret, which was more heavily armoured, had a squared-off rear, as distinct from the rounded type of the T-70. Production of the T-70 and T-70A light tanks was discontinued in the autumn of 1943 as the result of increased medium tank output. Altogether, 8,226 of the T-70 light tank were turned out. In 1944 the surviving chassis were modified (an extra bogie wheel on each side) and converted to self-propelled gun mountings. Towards the end of 1943 a further development of the T-70A was produced, resulting in the T-80 light tank. This appeared to be identical to the former, but had heavier armour. This vehicle, however, never entered large-scale production.

Above: Front and rear views of a T-34/76B. The radio aerial and stowage boxes on the track covers show this to be a company commander's tank—often the only one in a company with radio. Like later T-34/76As, the 76B mounted the longer L/40 76.2mm gun. The T-34/85 of late 1943 mounted an 85mm.

Bottom: A T-70A light tank, showing the squared off rear turret armour that distinguished it from the T-70. The better-armoured T-80 was based on the T-70A, but the increasing availability of US half-tracks on Lend-Lease meant that few Russian light tanks were built after 1944.

Below: Side view of a T-70; 8,226 T-70 type light tanks were built in 1941-43. From 1944, T-70 chassis were modified for conversion to SP gun mountings.

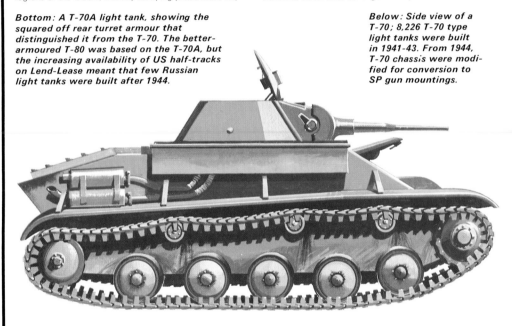

BA-64 ARMOURED CAR

BA-64, BA-64B, BA-64ZhD, BA-64DShK and other variants.
Crew: 2.
Armament: Usually one 7.62mm DT machine-gun.
Armour: Between 6 and 10mm (0.24in to 0.39in).
Dimensions: Length 12ft (3.66m); width 5ft (1.53m); height 6ft 3in (1.9m).
Weight: 5,291lbs (2,400kg).
Power to weight ratio: 22.9hp/ton.
Engine: Model GAZ-MM four-cylinder water-cooled inline petrol engine developing 54hp at 2,800rpm.
Performance: Road speed 50mph (80km/h); range 375 miles (600km); verticle obstacle negligible; trench negligible; gradient 30 degree.
History: In service with Russian Army from 1942 to 1956. Still used by some countries today.

Left: The BA-64 armoured car entered Red Army service in 1942 as a reconnaissance and liaison vehicle. A half-track variant could be fitted with skis for winter duty.

This light two-man armoured car was adopted for service during 1942 as a reconnaissance vehicle for commanders and staff officers, and as a liaison vehicle for all reconnaissance units in all troop arms. It was designed by a group of engineers under the direction of V. Grachov at the GAZ Factory in Moscow, and was based on the chassis of the GAZ-64 light cross-country car. The general layout of the armour, which was heavily faceted, was greatly influenced by the design incorporated in the German light four-wheeled Horch armoured car series. For ease of production, however, the Soviets (in opposition to the Germans) retained the engine at the front, as they always did in all their production armoured cars right up until the late 1960s, when the rear-engined BRDM was introduced. Even then, this was a result of Czech and Hungarian developments along these lines. Several variants of the *BA-64* were built, including a multiplicity of prototypes. Among others were the *BA-64B* with a widened wheel track and special bullet-proof 'run-flat' tyres; the *BA-64 ZhD* (a version adapted to run along railway lines as scout for armoured trains); the *BA-64DShK*, a conventional *BA-64* armed with the 12.7mm DShK heavy machine-gun (the normal variant was armed with a 7.62mm machine-gun with 1,260 or 1,071 rounds, depending on whether or not a radio was fitted); and an armoured command vehicle, fitted out with map-boards, long-range radio, etc. One interesting variant was a half-

track which, like the Putilovs of World War I, could be fitted with snow skis for winter operation. In wartime production models, a number of changes were introduced by various units. The vehicle was fitted with the 14.5mm PTRS Model 1941 anti-tank rifle, and others with captured German 20mm guns. Mass production of the *BA-64* was terminated at GAZ following the conclusion of the war. There never really was any profuse production, because greater emphasis was always placed on turning out tanks and self-propelled guns. Indeed, the production of wheeled vehicles in general (jeeps and trucks) was run on low priority, the Russians relying for these on

US vehicles provided under the Lend-Lease arrangement. Under this agreement they also received a fair number of US half-track armoured cars. Following World War II the Russians replaced the *BA-64* by the *BTR-40*, which is really a small wheeled armoured personnel carrier. *BA-64* armoured cars were then provided to the Korean and Chinese Communists. During the 1950s the East Germans built a modernised version of the *BA-64*, designated the *SK-1*. This was based on the Robur Garant 30K long chassis and was very similar externally to the *BA-64*. This armoured car was issued to the German Democratic Republic Police Force as well as the special border police.

SU-76 LIGHT SELF-PROPELLED GUN

SU-76, SU-76M and variants.
Crew: 4 (Commander, gunner, loader, driver.).
Armament: One 76.2mm Model 1942 (215-3) gun.
Armour: 35mm (1.38in) maximum; 10mm (0.39in) minimum.
Dimensions: Length (including gun) 16ft 5in (5m); width 8ft 11in (2.74m); height 7ft 3in (2.20m).
Weight: combat 24,692lbs (11,200kg).
Ground pressure: 8.09lb/in² (0.57kg/cm²).
Power to weight ratio: 12.5hp/ton.
Engine: Two GAZ-202 six-cylinder water-cooled petrol engines each developing 70hp at 3,400rpm.
Performance: Road speed 28mph (44km/h); range 166 miles (265km); vertical obstacle 2ft (0.6m); trench 6ft 7in (2m); gradient 28 degrees.
History: In service with the Russian Army from 1943 to after end of World War II.

The Russian offensive operations of 1942, although still carried out on a relatively small scale, were characterised by a growth in the advance rate of the Red Army. This brought to light the need for increasing the mobility of artillery. Offensive units — infantry

as much as armour — required supporting fire, not only during the breakthrough of defences but also during the course of further operations conducted in the rear of the enemy defences. With the increases in tank production then being achieved by Soviet industry it now became possible to begin the production of self-propelled artillery. In particular, Factory Number 38 received orders to produce prototypes of a light semi-armoured 76.2mm self-propelled gun intended for destroying enemy armour. The chassis of the T-70 light tank was selected and somewhat modified, having a lengthened hull and track system with six road wheels per side. The armament of the vehicle, an adaptation of the 76.2mm Model 1942 (215-3) gun was designed by General V. Grabin. Some 60 rounds of ammunition were provided. Factory and proving ground trials of this new self-propelled gun, then referred to as the *SU-12*, continued until autumn 1942. In December the high command accepted the vehicle for adoption by the Red Army, under the designation *SU-76*. A companion model, the *OSU-76*, was rejected. Production of the *SU-76* began shortly afterwards at Factory Number 38. Like the prototype, the

first series of *SU-76* had two engines mounted one on each side of the vehicle. Successive vehicles, however, had them mounted in tandem. On delivery to the front it was soon discovered that the type was subject to breakdown. As the result, the necessary modifications were undertaken by a group directed by N. Astrov at the beginning of 1943. In May 1943 trials were begun with a new modified variant, designated *SU-76M*, and in June this vehicle entered series production. Since, at the same time, Russia discontinued production of the earlier *SU-76* model, the *SU-76M* subsequently became referred to purely as the *SU-76*. Apart from continual modification of the basic *SU-76* vehicle, experiments were carried out in order to provide other types of self-propelled guns based on its chassis. As a result, during 1943 the *SU-76B* model appeared. This was entirely armoured, but never passed the prototype stage, however. In 1944 the *SU-74* model, also entirely armoured, was developed. This mounted the 57mm Model 1943 (215-2) anti-tank gun. In 1945 the prototype *SU-85A* and *SU-85B* were developed, both provided with 85mm guns and an improved chassis. None of these latter vehicles were standardised. Both the *SU-76* and *SU-76M* chassis were utilised to develop the ZSU-37 single-barrelled self-propelled 37mm anti-aircraft gun, which entered limited serial production. Initial production of the *SU-76* began towards the end of 1942 at Factory Number 38. Later both the GAZ and Number 37 factories shared in production also. During 1942 26 *SU-76*s were produced, and in 1943 a further 1,928 (of which some were *SU-76*s and some *SU-76M*s). In 1944 7,155 *SU-76M* vehicles were built and in 1945 more than 3,562. Altogether, throughout World War II more than 12,600 self-propelled guns on this chassis were produced.

Left: The SU-76 self-propelled gun entered service in 1943. A lightly-armoured tank-destroyer and infantry support weapon, it mounted a modified 76.2mm Model 1942 gun on a modification of the T-70 tank chassis. More than 12,600 self-propelled guns of the SU-76 series were built before the end of World War II.

ISU-122/152 SELF-PROPELLED GUN

SU -122, *SU*-152, ISU-122*BM*, ISU-152*BM*, ISU-122/152.

Crew: 5.

Armament: (ISU-122) either 122mm A-19*s* or 122mm D-25*s* gun; (ISU-152) 152mm ML-20 gun/howitzer.

Armour: 20mm to 110mm (0.79in to 4.33in).

Dimensions: Length (overall) between 29ft 4in (8.93m) and 36ft 10in (11.23m) depending on armament; width 11ft (3.36m); height 8ft. 10in (2.68m).

Weight: Between 90,830lbs (41,200kg) and 92,152lbs (41,800kg) depending on armament.

Ground pressure: From 11.6lb/in² (0.82kg/cm²) to 11.8lb/in² (0.83kg/cm²) depending on armament.

Power to weight ratio: Between 13.56 and 12.64 hp/ton depending on armament.

Engine: Model V-2 IS 12-cylinder water-cooled diesel developing 520hp at 2,200rpm.

Performance: Road speed 23mph (37km/h); range 150 miles (240km); verticle obstacle 3ft 5in (1.03m); trench 8ft 10in (2.7m); gradient 36 degrees.

History: In service with Russian Army from 1943, and still in service with some countries today.

During the course of the Battle for Stalingrad, the Soviet Army began the preparations for carrying out a decisive attack. Taking into account the fact that,

Right: The SU-152 SP gun, a 152mm howitzer mounted on a KV-1 tank chassis, made a successful combat debut at Kursk in July 1943.

during the course of such an attack, it would have to neutralise strong enemy fortifications and new models of German heavy tanks and self-propelled guns, on 4 January 1943 the *GKO* (State Defence Committee) submitted the following directive: that in the course of 25 days an experimental model of a self-propelled artillery mounting, armed with a 152mm M1937 gun/howitzer, should be designed and built on the chassis of the KV-Is tank. The group of designers under the direction of L. S. Troyanov, together with the engineering staff of the Chelyabinsk-Kirov combine (Tankograd), completed this task and on 7 February a prototype vehicle, designated *SU-152*, was completed on the chassis of the KV-Is heavy tank. As the result of a further directive from the *GKO*, dated 14 February 1943, the new *SU-152* heavy self-propelled artillery mounting was accepted for adoption by the Red Army. By 1 March 1943 the first series of 35 vehicles of this type had been completed. During July of that year, one *SU-152* regiment was deployed in the Kursk salient where it destroyed 12 Tiger tanks and 7 Ferdinand heavy self-propelled guns. Following this battle, the *SU-152* was christened *Zveroboi* or Conquering Beast. The *SU-152* mounted the same 152mm Model 1937 corps gun/howitzer as was fitted to the KV-2 heavy tank. It remained the only standardised self-propelled mounting based on

the heavy tank chassis until 1944, when the ISU-122 was built. The 152mm gun/howitzer mounting was interchangeable with the 122mm Model 1931-7 gun to form the *SU-122*. This latter vehicle was introduced to destroy German heavy tanks at long range. Only 35 *SU-122*s were produced during 1943, however, and these were not widely used; production ceased when the Stalin tank appeared. With the appearance of the Stalin tank during autumn 1943, Soviet industry began to provide the Red Army with the new ISU-152 and ISU-122, which were almost identical to the earlier vehicles, but now based on the IS heavy tank chassis as opposed to the KV. Two variants of the ISU-122 were taken into service – one mounting the 122mm A-19 gun, the other (designated ISU-122*s*) mounting the 122mm D-25*s* gun. The ISU-152 mounted the ML-20*s* gun/howitzer. On these new *SU*s the crew compartment was made higher and more rectangular, with the armour on the sides less sloped. The old circular KV hatches were replaced by tank and *SU*-100 cupolas. The hatches were fitted with the new standard periscope. Some 2,510 ISU-122s were produced during 1944; all of these mounted the A-19 gun, with 40 rounds. Further production vehicles utilised the D-25*s* gun (distinguishable by its muzzle-brake). The ISU-152 fired a 48.5kg (107lb) armour-piercing shot or on a 43kg (94.8lb) high-explosive shell. Despite a slow rate of fire, the ISU-152 was intended to engage armour with AP shot at quite long ranges. The effectiveness of the ISU-152 was greatly hampered by carrying only 20 rounds of ammunition. Unlike most other Soviet SPGs a machine-gun was mounted on

the right-hand side of the ISU's superstructure. Several prototypes based on the ISU-122 and ISU-152 were also produced over the period 1943–44, including the ISU-122*BM* and ISU-152*BM*, utilising the powerful *BL* series of guns. These were intended to defeat possible new German super-heavy tanks such as the *Maus* and E-100, both of which were known to the Soviets through their intelligence network. About 4,400 *SU*-152, *SU*-122, ISU-152 and ISU-122 vehicles were built.

IS-2 HEAVY TANK

IS-1, IS-2 and IS-3.

Crew: 4.

Armament: One 122mm M1943 (D-25) L/43 tank gun; one 12.7mm M1938 DShK machine-gun; one 7.62mm DT or DTM machine-gun.

Armour: 132mm (5.2in) maximum; 19mm (0.75in) minimum.

Dimensions: Length (including gun) 32ft 9in (10.74m); width 10ft 6in (3.44m); height 8ft 11in (2.93m).

Weight: 101,963lbs (46,250kg).

Ground pressure: 11.25lb/in² (0.79kg/cm²).

Power to weight ratio: 11.3hp/ton.

Engine: One Model V-2 IS 12-cylinder water-cooled diesel developing 520hp at 2,000rpm.

Performance: Road speed 23mph (37km/h); range 94 miles (150km); vertical obstacle 3ft 3in (1m); trench 8ft 2in (2.86m); gradient 36 degrees.

History: In service with the Russian Army from 1943 to late 1970s.

In August 1942 the Soviet high command was well aware of the fact that Germany was developing new heavy tanks with more powerful armament and thicker armour. Work on a new heavy tank was therefore begun. Based on the experience gained

so far in the design of experimental KV models (KV-3 and KV-13), in 1943 the design bureau investigated a new project designated IS (Iosef Stalin). Early in autumn 1943 the first three prototypes of the IS-1 (also called IS-85 because of its 85mm gun) were completed. After demonstration before the special commission from the Main Defence Commissariat and the completion of general factory trials, the IS design was approved. Directions were given to begin mass-production in October 1943. The new tank, weighing little more than the KV (and for that matter, the German Panther medium tank) had thicker, better shaped armour which provided excellent protection. In addition, the weight was kept low by the use of more compact component design. The tank had a new cast turret mounting an 85mm gun specially designed by General F. Petrov (the same turret as fitted to the KV-85 as an expedient). Soon after the start of production of the IS-1 tank, the need arose for a more powerfully armed vehicle. At that time the 85mm gun was being used in the T-34 medium (T-34/85) and it was considered inappropriate that a heavy tank should have the same armament. A few prototypes were therefore fitted with a new 100m gun (IS-100), but were not accepted for production. This was because another group, under General Petrov,

had within two weeks conceived a scheme for mounting a 122mm gun (with 28 rounds). Towards the end of October 1943 factory and proving ground tests were concluded for the IS tank fitted with this weapon. On 31 October the tank was accepted as standard and designated IS-2. By the end of the year the Kirov Factory had produced 102 IS-2 tanks. The IS tank was used for the first time during February 1944 at Korsun Shevkenskovsky. During this battle General Kotin personally observed the performance of the IS-2 tank and gained vital information as to its performance and short-comings. After producing several other experimental vehicles of this type, work on a further improvement to the armour layout led, towards the end of 1944, to the new IS-3 model. The design of this tank, carried out by a group under N. Dukhov, was conceived around the armour philosophy of the T-34. Armour plate of even greater thickness and better ballistic shape was heavily inclined to give maximum protection. In contrast to its predecessors, the IS-3 hull was made of rolled plate and the turret was carapace-shaped. Despite all these improvements, the overall weight of the new tank still did not exceed that of the contemporary German medium tank. The final model of this heavy tank, T-10, was the tenth model to be produced. The prefix 'IS' was discontinued as a result of the general de-Stalinisation policy adopted in the Soviet Union during the mid-1950s.

Left: The heavy tanks of the IS (Josef Stalin) series appeared in 1943-45. The IS-3 may not have seen action in WWII, but it significantly influenced post-war design.

SU-85 MEDIUM SELF-PROPELLED GUN

Crew: 4.
Armament: One 85mm Model 1943 (D-5S) gun; two 7.62mm PPS sub-machine guns.
Armour: 45mm (1.77in) maximum; 20mm (0.79in) minimum.
Dimensions: Length (including gun) 26ft 9in (8.15m); width 9ft 10in (3.00m); height 8ft 4in (2.45m).
Weight: Combat 65,256lbs (29,600kg).
Ground pressure: 9.94lb/in² (0.7kg/cm²).
Power to weight ratio: 16.8hp/ton.
Engine: Model V-2-34 12-cylinder water-cooled diesel developing 500hp at 1,800rpm.
Performance: Road speed 31mph (50km/h); range 250 miles (400km); vertical obstacle 2ft 6in (0.75m); trench 8ft 2in (2.5m).
History: In service with the Russian Army from 1943 to 1945.

In 1943, with the deployment by Germany of the 'new Panther and Tiger tanks, much haste was made by Soviet designers to produce a countermeasure. The medium tank of the time, T-34, was armed only with the 76.2mm gun and the two standard self-propelled guns — the SU-76 and SU-122, were not sufficiently powerfully armed to defeat these new vehicles. Towards the end of 1943 the 'Uralmashzvod' tank combine, then building T-34 tanks, released its first batch of SU-85 tank destroyers. This vehicle was intended to support medium tanks and thence engage any enemy tanks encountered. Design of the SU-85 was undertaken by the design bureau headed by L. I. Gorlits and General F. F. Petrov, following a resolution passed by the State Defence Committee. The designers were given the task of producing, within the shortest possible time, qualitatively new models of

self-propelled mountings possessing high mobility, excellent armour-piercing capabilities, flexibility of fire, rapidity of aim, high rate of fire, and satisfying the requirements for rapid production and low unit cost. In order to save time, the chassis of the SU-122 self-propelled howitzer together with parts of the barrel of the 85mm anti-aircraft gun and its projectile, were selected. All of the latter were already in series production and had been thoroughly proved in battle. The use of these simplified production work, repairs, spare-part and logistic supplies, and alleviated the training of personnel in both combat and maintenance sub-units. The development of the armament was undertaken by the group under General Petrov. In order to produce the gun, which was later designated the 85mm Model 1943 (D-5) gun, Soviet engineers utilised the existing 85mm Model 1939 anti-aircraft gun. Work on adapting the SU-122 chassis (itself a derivative of the T-34 medium tank) was concluded by the group of designers at Uralmashzavod in Sverdlovsk and the Kirov Factory in Chelyabinsk, directed by L. Troyanov. L. Gorlits became the chief designer of the new vehicle. Instead of a rotating turret of the T-34, a casemate was mounted on the chassis, and in this was placed a special mounting for the 85mm gun. In order to reduce the effort involved in elevation a spring-equilibriator was introduced; it was attached to the cradle of the gun and fixed to the chassis. For indirect fire a panoramic telescope was fitted, and for direct fire a TSh-15 telescopic sight. After three months of intensive work, the prototypes of the SU-85 were completed. In August 1943 these were subjected to driving and firing tests. The vehicle proved to have good manoeuvrability and mobility and could attain a road speed of 31mph (50km/h).

Its ammunition stowage comprised 48 rounds. On 7 August 1943, the SU-85 self-propelled artillery mounting was accepted as standard by the Soviet High Command and entered serial production at Uralmashzavod. The design bureau at this combine, headed by L. Lulievim, set up a special group of engineers which, collaborating with factory technologists, prepared the production drawings. Much attention was paid to improving the technical design, to decreasing unit cost, and to simplifying production of the armament. The design group under N. Turin produced a machine for casting gun barrels centrifugally, which resulted in an eightfold increase in output. Every effort was made to speed up production, which was accomplished within one month. As the result 150 vehicles had been produced as early as the end of August, and by the end of the year over 750 had been delivered to units of the Red Army. Individual series of the SU-85 differed in certain details and equipment. Later vehicles were provided with a special cupola for the commander. The SU-85 was employed in action during the second half of 1943, during the forcing of the River Dniepr and the battle for the Ukraine. During the final stages of the war it was replaced by the new SU-100 armoured gun as a result of the up-gunning of the T-34 tank to 85mm.

Right: The SU-85 medium self-propelled gun was produced in 1943. A modification of the 85mm Model 1939 A.A. gun mounted on a T-34 tank chassis, it was developed quickly: ordered early in 1943, more than 750 entered combat by the year's end.

SU-100 MEDIUM SELF-PROPELLED GUN

Crew: 4.
Armament: One 100mm Model 1944 (D-10S) gun; two 7.62mm PPS sub-machine guns.
Armour: 20mm to 54mm (0.79in to 2.13in).
Dimensions: Length (including gun) 31ft (9.45m); width 9ft 10in (3m); height 7ft 4in (2.25m).
Weight: Combat 69,665lbs (31,600kg).
Ground pressure: 11.6lb/in² (0.82kg/cm²).
Power to weight ratio: 16hp/ton.
Engine: Model V-2-34 12-cylinder water-cooled diesel developing 500hp at 1,800rpm.
Performance: Road speed 30mph (48km/h); range 200 miles (320km); vertical obstacle 2ft 1in (0.64m); trench 9ft 10in (3m); gradient 30 degrees.
History: Entered service with Russian Army in 1944 and still used by many armies today, including Albania, Algeria, Bulgaria, Communist China, Cuba, Czechoslovakia, East Germany, Egypt, Iraq, Mongolia, Morocco, North Korea, North Yemen, Romania, Soviet Union, Syria and Yugoslavia.

With the application of the 85mm gun to the T-34 medium tank, to form the T-34/85, it became necessary to increase the firepower of the medium self-propelled mounting on this chassis. The current SU-85 could no longer be considered as an effective supporting vehicle for the medium tank. During 1944, the Soviets began to replace the SU-85 by the new, more powerful SU-100 self-propelled gun. This was very similar to its predecessor, but mounted a new gun — the 100mm Model 1944 (D-10S) designed

by the group under General F. F. Petrov. Production of the SU-100 began at Uralmashzavod during September 1944, and by the end of the year about 500 had been delivered to units of the Red Army. Up until the end of the war over 1,800 of these vehicles were produced. The SU-100 proved to be an effective means of destroying German heavy tanks and tank destroyers — such as the Panther, Tiger, Ferdinand, Jagdpanther and Jagdtiger. It played a very important role during the final phases of World War II. The 100mm gun on this vehicle was adapted from the prewar naval 100/56 high-velocity dual-purpose gun. As on the SU-85, the gun was mounted at the front of an heavily-sloped fixed armoured superstructure and was laid with a tank-gun periscope. Unlike the T-34 tank, on which the SU-100 was based, the driver of the SU-100 was separated from the other crew members by armour plate and, as a result, an internal communication system was necessary. As was the

case with the SU-85, no secondary armament was carried. The 100mm gun had a performance greatly increased over that of the 85mm gun, firing a 16kg (35.3lb) HE shell to a range of 19,200m (21,000 yards), or a 19.5kg (43lb) armour-piercing round. Some 34 rounds of 100mm ammunition were carried. In addition to its distinctively long gun, the SU-100 could be distinguished from its predecessor by the new shape of mantlet and the circular cupola which was attached to the right-hand side of the superstructure top. The SU-100 remained the standard support gun for armoured and mechanised divisions until their reorganisation in 1957, when it was replaced by the ISU-122 based on the IS heavy tank chassis. With their guns removed, both the SU-85 and the SU-100 were employed for a long time after the war as both armoured command and armoured recovery vehicles. In these forms the apertures left by the guns' removal were covered by armour plate.

Below: The SU-100 self-propelled gun began to replace the SU-85 in 1944. Its 100mm gun derived from the naval 100/56 high-velocity DP rifle and mounted on a T-34 tank chassis proved extremely effective. The illustration clearly shows the external fuel tanks fitted to increase the vehicle's radius of action—an obvious combat hazard. The SU-100 was the standard support gun for Soviet armoured and mechanised divisions until replaced by the ISU-122 in 1957.

Right: Front, rear and top views of the SU-100. Although obsolescent, the SU-100 remains in service with many armies of the Communist bloc and Arab nations. In the Yom Kippur War of 1973 the Egyptian and Syrian armies deployed SU-100 battalions with each armoured, mechanised and infantry division. The Israelis are said to have captured many SU-100s, but it has been suggested that the Russian gun has been confused with Israel's French-derived 155mm self-propelled L-33 howitzer.

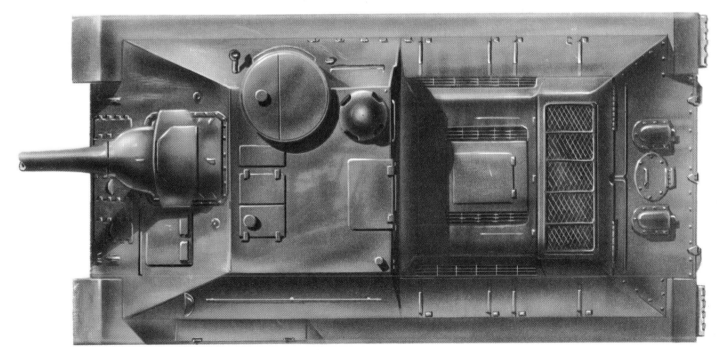

T-54/T-55 MAIN BATTLE TANK

T-54/T-55, ARV, bridgelayer, and mine-clearance tank.
Crew: 4.
Armament: One 100mm gun; one 7.62mm SGMT machine-gun co-axial with main armament; one 7.62mm SGMT machine-gun in bow of tank; one 12.7mm DShk anti-aircraft machine-gun.
Armour: 170mm (6.7in) maximum.
Dimensions: Length (including armament) 29ft 6in (9m); length (hull) 21ft 2in (6.45m); width 10ft 9in (3.27m); height (without anti-aircraft armament) 7ft 10in (2.4m).
Weight: Combat 79,366lbs (36,000kg).
Ground pressure: 11.52lb/in² (0.81kg/cm²).
Engine: Model V-54 12-cylinder air-cooled diesel developing 520hp at 2,000rpm.
Performance: Maximum road speed 30mph (48km/h); range 249 miles (400km); vertical obstacle 2ft 8in (0.8m); trench 8ft 10in (2.7m); gradient 60 per cent.
History: Entered service with the Russian Army in 1950. Also used by Albania, Algeria, Afghanistan, Angola, Bangladesh, Bulgaria, Communist China, Cuba, Cyprus, Czechoslovakia, East Germany, Egypt, Finland, Hungary, India, Iraq, Israel, Libya, Morocco, North Korea, Vietnam, North Yemen, Pakistan, Peru, PLA, Poland, Romania, Somalia, South Yemen, Sudan, Syria, Uganda and Yugoslavia. (Note: data refer to T-54.)

The first prototype of the T-54 was completed in 1947. This was a logical development of the T-44 tank developed towards the end of World War II. The latter tank was in turn a development of the T-34 which is considered by many to be the best medium tank of the war. The T-54 has also been built in China as the T-59 as well as in Czechoslovakia and Poland. No accurate production figures of the T-54/T-55 have been released but it is likely that between 60,000 and 70,000 of all models of the T-54 and T-55 have been built. The hull of the T-54 is of all-welded construction and the turret is cast, with the top then welded into position. The driver is seated at the front of the hull on the right, with the other three crew members in the turret. The commander and gunner are on the left with the loader on the right. Two hatches are provided. The engine and transmission are at the rear of the hull, separated from the fighting compartment by a bulkhead. The suspension consists of five road wheels per side, with the drive sprocket at the front and the idler at the rear. There are no return rollers as the top of the track rests on the tops of the road wheels. The suspension is of the well-tried torsion-bar type. Main armament consists of a 100mm D-10T rifled tank gun firing APHE, HEAT or HE rounds. The gun is capable of an elevation of ×17° and a depression of −4°. The latter is one of the major drawbacks of the tank compared with Western tanks. A 7.62mm SGMT machine-gun is mounted co-axially with the main armament, and there is a similar weapon in the front of the hull, operated by the driver. A 12.7mm DShK machine-gun is mounted on the loader's hatch for use in the anti-aircraft role. Some 34 rounds of 100mm, 500 rounds of 12.7mm and 3,000 rounds of 7.62mm ammunition are carried. Most T-54 and T-55 tanks have a full range of night-vision equipment of the infra-red type, including driving lights, commander's searchlight and searchlight to the right of the main armament. Additional fuel tanks can be fitted to the rear of the hull to increase the operating range of the tank. The tank can also lay its own smoke-screen in a similar fashion to the PT-76 by injecting vaporised diesel fuel into the exhaust system on either side of the tank. The tank can

ford to a maximum depth of 4ft 7in (1.4m) without preparation, and with the aid of a schnorkel it can ford to a depth of 18ft (5.486m). Most tanks can be fitted with a dozer blade on the front of the hull. When first introduced, the T-54 did not have an NBC system. Late production models have one installed, however, as do T-55s. There are at least five models of the T-54 differing in minor detail: the T-54 (early), T-54, T-54A, T-54B and T-54C. In 1960 there appeared the T-55, with many improvements over the

T-54 including a more powerful 580hp engine, increased main armament ammunition stowage (43 rounds), fully stabilized main armament, no anti-aircraft machine-gun (this was subsequently fitted to most T-55s). The T-55A followed in 1963: this had no bow machine-gun and the co-axial 7.62mm SGMT was replaced by a PKT machine-gun. The basic T-54/T-55 has been adopted for a wide range of roles. There are at least four different armoured recovery vehicles, these being known as the T-54-T, T-54A

Above: A column of Russian T-54 MBTs advances through woods. It is estimated that more than 60,000 T-54/T-55s were built. The T-54 is also built in China.

Below: An Egyptian T-54 tank which took part in the Yom Kippur War of 1973. The T-54 has seen action in many parts of the world, including Angola, China, Vietnam and North Africa. India has used the Russian T-54/T-55, while Pakistan used the Chinese-built tanks of the series.

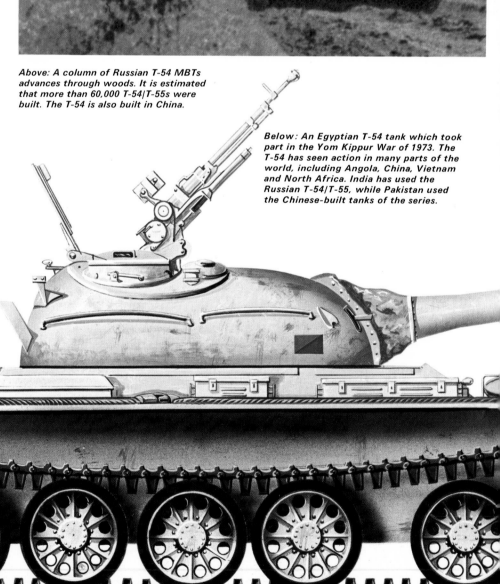

ARV, T-54B ARV and the T-54C ARV. The most common model is the T-54-T which has a spade at the rear, a platform for carrying spare tank components and a jib crane. A schnorkel can be mounted for deep fording operations. Two basic types of mine-clearing tank are in service, one being of the plough type and the other of the roller type. (There are a number of different types of the latter.) More recently the Russians have developed a mine-clearing system similar to that of the British Giant Viper system, which fires an explosive line into the minefield; the line is then detonated, with luck clearing the mines. Three types of bridgelayer are in service. The first of these to enter service was the MTU-54/MTU-55, which carries a bridge 40ft 4in (12.3m) in length. The M1967 has a bridge whose ends fold up when the vehicle is moving. When opened out this bridge can span a gap of up to 65ft 7in (20m). The Czechs have developed a model called the MT-55, which has a scissors type bridge which can be used to span gaps of up to 55ft 9in (17m).

Components of the T-54 are also used in the ZSU-57-2 twin 57mm anti-aircraft tank, the ATS-59 tracked tractor and the PTS amphibian. Further development of the tank has resulted in the T-62 main battle tank. The T-54 has been used in combat by North Vietnam, Pakistan, India, Egypt, Syria, Iraq, Angola, Algeria, Libya and Somalia, and has proved to be a reliable tank in service. It is much simpler to handle than comparable Western tanks, but it is outranged by such tanks as the Leopard and M60.

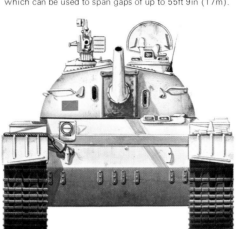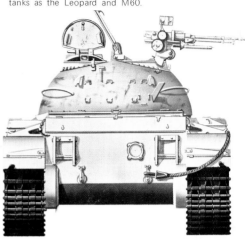

Right: Front and rear views of a T-54 MBT of the Egyptian Army as used in the 1967 Middle East campaign. The T-54 was a development of the T-44 which in turn was a development of the T-34 tank of World War II. The T-54 has proved to be a very reliable tank and simple to operate and maintain; these are very important features as most of the Russian army is composed of conscripts. The main drawbacks of the T-54 are its lack of depression (only − 4°) of the main gun, which means that the tank cannot take up an effective fire position on a reverse slope. An unusual feature of the T-54 was the 7.62mm machine gun which was fixed in the front of the hull and operated by the driver who was provided with a firing button on the top of one of his steering levers, this was not provided on the later T-55 main battle tank.

Above: A T-55 emerges from a river. The Soviets place great emphasis on river-crossing capability; all Russian tanks can be quickly fitted with a schnorkel to enable them to ford to a depth of 5.486m.
Left: The T-54 MBT was followed by the T-55 in 1960. Improvements on the earlier model included a more powerful 580hp engine, modified transmission, fully-stabilized main armament and increased ammunition capacity. The first T-55s did not mount a 12.7mm DShk anti-aircraft machine-gun but most have now been thus equipped, as have the more recent T-62 tanks. The T-55 has an NBC system and a full range of infra-red night vision equipment. Most of the tanks in this series are capable of having a dozer blade mounted on the front of the hull. Variants include 3 bridgelayers.

BTR-152 ARMOURED PERSONNEL CARRIER

BTR-152, BTR-152VI, BTR-152V2, BTR-152V3, BTR-152K, BTR-152U, BTR-152A
Crew: 2 plus 17.
Armament: One 7.62mm SGMB machine-gun.
Armour: 6mm–135mm (0.23–5.40in).
Dimensions: Length 22ft 5in (6.83m); width 7ft 7in (2.32m); height (without armament) 6ft 9in (2.05m).
Weight: Combat 19,731lbs (8,950kg).
Engine: ZIL-123 six-cylinder inline water-cooled petrol engine developing 110hp at 2,900rpm.
Performance: Road speed 46.6mph (75km/h); range 404 miles (650km); vertical obstacle 2ft (0.6m); trench 2ft 3in (0.69m); gradient 50 per cent.
History: Entered service with Russian Army in 1950. In service with Afghanistan, Albania, Algeria, Bulgaria, Cambodia, Ceylon, China, Congo, Cuba, Cyprus, East Germany, Egypt, Guinea, Hungary, India, Indonesia, Iran, Iraq, Israel, Mongolia, North Korea, North Yemen, PLO, Poland, Romania, Somalia, Soviet Union, Sudan, Syria, Tanzania, Uganda and Yugoslavia. Built in China as the Type 56 APC. Production completed in early 1960s.

The BTR-152 was developed shortly after the end of World War II to meet a Russian requirement for an armoured personnel carrier, and entered service in 1950. It has been replaced in most front line Russian motor rifle divisions by the BTR-60P series of 8×8 vehicles but is, however, still used in large numbers

Right: The BTR-152K was introduced in 1961 and is basically the BTR-152V3 with full overhead armour protection for the troop compartment at the rear of the hull. Now replaced in most Soviet front-line Motor Rifle Divisions by the newer BTR-60 APC, it is still used by many countries that have received Soviet aid since 1950.

outside Russia. The hull is of all-welded construction, varying in thickness from 0.24in (6mm) on the hull top to 0.51in (13mm) on the hull front. The engine and transmission are at the front of the vehicle, the latter having five forward and one reverse gears and a two-speed transfer case, with the driver and commander in the centre and personnel compartment at the rear. The driver and commander are each provided with a bullet-proof windscreen which can be covered by an armoured hatch, complete with an integral vision device, when required. They each have a side door, and the top of this can be folded down if required. The infantry are seated on bench-type seats that run across the hull or on a bench-type seat down each side of the hull, and normally enter and leave the vehicle via twin doors in the hull rear. Firing-ports are provided in the

sides of the hull. The BTR-152 is normally armed with a 7.62mm SGMB machine-gun on a single mount in the forward part of the troop compartment, but some vehicles have been fitted with either a 12.7mm DShK or 14.5mm KPV machine-gun. A 7.62mm SGMB weapon can be mounted on each side of the hull if required, and a total of 1,250 rounds of 7.62mm ammunition is carried. The first BTR-152s to enter service were based on the standard 6×6 ZIL-151 chassis, but most subsequent vehicles used the ZIL-157 6×6 chassis. The second model to enter service was the BTR-152V1. This has a winch mounted at the front and a tyre pressure-regulation system with external air lines which can easily be recognised. The next model was the BTR-152V2. This does not have a winch and is fitted with internal air lines for the tyre pressure-

T-10 HEAVY TANK

Crew: 4.
Armament: One 122mm gun; one 14.5mm machine-gun co-axial with main armament; one 14.5mm anti-aircraft machine-gun.
Armour: 20mm–250mm (0.79–10.08in).
Dimensions: Length (gun forward) 34ft 9in (10.6m); length (hull) 23ft 1in (7.04m); width 11ft 8in (3.566m); height 8ft (2.43m) without anti-aircraft machine-gun.
Weight: Combat 114,640lbs (52,000kg).
Ground pressure: 11.09lb/in² (0.78kg/cm²).
Engine: V-2-IS(V2K), 12-cylinder water-cooled diesel developing 700hp at 2,000rpm.
Performance: Road speed 26mph (42km/h); range 155 miles (250km); vertical obstacle 2ft 11in (0.9m); trench 9ft 10in (3m); gradient 60 per cent.
History: Entered service in 1957. In service with Bulgaria, Czechoslovakia, East Germany, Egypt, Hungary, Poland, Romania, Soviet Union, Syria and Vietnam. Production completed in early 1960s. (Note: data above relate to T-10M)

The standard Russian heavy tanks during the closing years of World War II were the IS series. The IS-4 entered service in small numbers in 1946–7 and further development resulted in the IS-5, IS-6, IS-7, IS-8, IS-9 and finally the IS-10. The last was placed in production in 1956 as the T-10. The tank has the same engine as the IS-3, but a more powerful gun and much

improved armour layout. Today T-10 do not form a part of the normal equipment of Russian tank regiments or divisions, but are instead formed into special battalions and attached to divisions as required. The T-10 has a crew of four (commander, gunner, loader and driver). The driver is seated at the front of the vehicle with the other three crew members in the turret, the commander being on the left. The engine and transmission are at the rear of the hull. The suspension consists of seven road wheels (the IS series have six) with the idler at the front and the drive sprocket at the rear; there are three track-return rollers on each side. The first model to enter service was the T-10. This is armed with a 122mm gun and 12.7mm DShK anti-aircraft and co-axial machine-guns. The 122mm gun has an elevation of +17° and a depression of −3°, and a total of 30 rounds of 122mm ammunition of the separate loading type is carried, as well as 1,000 rounds of 12.7mm machine-gun ammunition. The T-10 fires two types of ammunition, an HE projectile which weighs 60lbs (27.3kg) and an APHE projectile which weighs 55lbs (25kg); both have a muzzle velocity of 2,904ft/s (885m/s). The APHE round will penetrate 7.3in (185mm) of armour at a range of 1,092 yards (1,000m). The 122mm gun has a maximum range of 18,154 yards (16,600m) with the gun at its maximum elevation, and its effective range in the anti-tank role is between 1,312 and 2,187 yards (1,200–2,000m). The T-10M is a

further development of the T-10 and this has a number of major improvements to increase its combat effectiveness. The 12.7mm machine-guns have been replaced by 14.5mm KPVT (co-axial) and KPV (anti-aircraft) machine-guns. The double baffle muzzle-brake on the T-10 has been replaced by a multi-baffle muzzle-brake, but the fume extractor has been retained. The main armament is now stabilised in both planes, eg elevation and traverse. In addition to the HE and APHE rounds the 122mm gun can fire a HEAT round with a muzzle velocity of 2,953ft/s (900m/s), which will penetrate 15.75in (400mm) of armour. The basic T-10 is provided with infra-red driving lights, but in addition the T-10M has an infra-red searchlight on the commander's cupola; there is another infra-red searchlight mounted to the right of the main armament, and this moves in elevation with the main armament. The T-10 can ford to a depth of 3ft 11in (1.2m) without preparation, but the T-10M can be provided with a schnorkel for deep fording operations. The T-10M is also provided with an NBC system and many have been fitted with a large stowage box of sheet metal welded to the turret rear. Additional fuel tanks can be fitted at the rear of the hull to increase the operating range of the tank. The T-10 has been used by Egypt and Syria in the 1973 Middle East campaign. It is normally used to provide long-range anti-tank support to the T-55/T-62 tanks. It would also be used to spearhead a breakthrough on a vital sector, where its firepower and armour would prove most useful. The T-10 does have a number of drawbacks. First, it is slightly slower than the T-62 and T-55 MBTs, which could mean that an advance has to slow down to allow the T-10s to keep place. Second, as with most Russian tanks, the T-10's gun has a very limited depression, making it difficult to fire from reverse slopes. And third, its ammunition is of the separate loading type (eg projectile and separate cartridge case), which takes a little longer to load and therefore reduces the tank's rate of fire to three or four rounds per minute. On the bonus side the T-10 has excellent armour, and this makes it the most difficult of all current Russian tanks to destroy on the battlefield.

Left: Rear view of a T-10M tank, lacking the usual stowage box on the rear of the turret. The T-10 was designed as the replacement for the IS-3 heavy tank and entered service with the Russian Army in 1957. The T-10M is armed with a 122mm gun with a co-axial 14.5mm KPVT machine-gun. A KPV (anti-aircraft) 14.5mm machine-gun is mounted on the turret roof. The T-10M is provided with a full range of night vision equipment, including infra-red driving lights and two infra-red searchlights.

regulation system. The fourth model, the BTR-152V3, has a front-mounted winch, internal air lines and infra-red driving lights. By the late 1950s the design of the BTR-152 was becoming a little dated, so in 1961 the BTR-152K was introduced. This is similar to the BTR-152V3 but has full overhead armour for the troop compartment. The BTR-152U is a special command vehicle which has a much higher roof so that the command staff can work standing up; a generator is normally carried as additional radios are fitted. There is also an anti-aircraft model of the BTR-152 known as the BTR-152A. This is armed with two 14.5mm KPV heavy machine-guns, mounted in a manually-operated turret with a traverse of 360°, elevation being from −5° to plus 80°. These guns have a cyclic rate of fire of 600 rounds per barrel per minute, but the practical rate of fire is 150 rounds per minute. The guns' effective range in the anti-aircraft role is 1,531 yards (1,400m), or 2,187 yards (2,000m) in the ground role. The Egyptians have fitted some of their BTR-152 vehicles with four 12.7mm Czech machine-guns for use in the anti-aircraft role. The basic BTR-152 is also used as a cargo carrier and as a prime mover for light artillery and 160mm mortars. The standard vehicle is not fitted with an NBC system, although the BTR-152K may possibly have such a system. It has no amphibious capability although it can ford streams to a depth of 2ft 7in (0.8m).

Right: BTR-152 APCs with T-54 tanks in support take part in the "Yug" army exercises held in June 1971. The basic BTR-152 carries 17 infantrymen, but has an open roof and is thus most vulnerable to overhead shell-bursts. Some models have infra-red night vision equipment. It is also used as a supply-carrier and prime mover.

ZSU-57-2 SELF-PROPELLED ANTI-AIRCRAFT GUN

Crew: 6.
Armament: Twin 57mm S-68 guns.
Armour: 15mm (0.59in) maximum.
Dimensions: Length (guns forward) 27ft 10in (8.48m); length (hull) 20ft 5in (6.22m); width 10ft 9in (3.27m); height 9ft (2.75m).
Weight: Combat 61,949lbs (28,100kg).
Ground pressure: 8.96lb/in² (0.63kg/cm²).
Engine: Model V-54 12-cylinder water-cooled diesel developing 520hp at 2,000rpm.
Performance: Road speed 30mph (48km/h); range 249 miles (400km); vertical obstacle 2ft 8in (0.8m); trench 8ft 10in (2.7m); gradient 60 per cent.
History: Entered service with Russian Army in 1955–6. In service with Bulgaria, Czechoslovakia, East Germany, Egypt, Finland, Hungary, Iran, Iraq, North Korea, Poland, Romania, Soviet Union, Syria, Vietnam and Yugoslavia. Production of the ZSU-57-2 was completed in the mid 1960s.

The ZSU-57-2 was introduced into the Soviet Army in the mid-1950s to provide mobile anti-aircraft defence to armoured forces. In the Russian Army it was normally attached to tank regiments in batteries of eight weapons. It is based on a modified T-54 MBT chassis but is both lighter (its maximum armour thickness is 0.56in or 15mm) and slightly shorter (it has one less road wheel than the T-54). The armament consists of twin S-68 57mm guns mounted in a large open-topped turret with a traverse of 360°. The guns have a maximum elevation of +85° and a depression of −5°, elevation and traverse both being powered, with manual controls provided for emergency use. The guns used are an adaptation of the S-60 57mm single towed gun which is also used by the Russian and many other armies around the world. The guns have an effective range in the anti-aircraft role of 4,374 yards (4,000m), or 3,280 yards (3,000m) when being used in the ground-to-ground role. The guns have a practical rate of fire of 70 rounds per minute per barrel. A total of 316 rounds of ammunition is carried. These are in clips of four rounds and are fed into each magazine by the two loaders. The empty cartridge cases and clips are deposited onto a conveyer belt which takes them to the rear of the turret, where they fall through an opening into the large wire cage on the turret rear. The ZSU-57-2 fires both High Explosive (projectile weight being 6.1lbs or 2.8kg) and Armour-Piercing rounds (projectile weight being 6.8lbs or 3.1kg), with a muzzle velocity of 3,281ft/s (1,000m/s). The latter will penetrate just over 4in (106mm) of armour at a range of 547 yards (500m). This makes it a highly effective weapon against most armoured vehicles on the battlefield. With the introduction of fast, low-flying aircraft, the effectiveness of the ZSU-57-2 as an AA system has diminished in recent years, and it has been

replaced in many Russian units by the ZSU-23-4 weapon. In particular it is not fitted with radar and has to rely on its optical sights. It is therefore limited to clear weather operations. It would, however, be possible for the ZSU-57-2 to receive information over the radio on the approach of enemy aircraft and this would enable it to line its guns roughly in the general direction of the aircraft before they appeared. The driver is seated in the front of the hull on the left side, whilst the other five crew members are seated in the turret. On the left side of the turret are the loader, gunner and fuze setter, whilst on the right side are the vehicle commander and the second loader. The vehicle is provided with infra-red driving lights, but is not fitted with an NBC system and has no amphibious capability. It can ford to a maximum depth of 4ft 7in (1.4m) without preparation. Like most Russian tanks, the ZSU-57-2's operating range can be extended by the fitting of additional fuel drums on the rear of the hull.

Below: The ZSU-57-2 SP anti-aircraft gun entered Red Army service in 1955-56. It is limited to clear-weather operations because no radar system is provided. It carries 316 rounds of ammunition in clips of four for its twin 57mm S-68 guns. The ZSU-57-2 has been replaced in many units by the newer ZSU-23-4, which is much more effective against fast, low-flying aircraft.

PT-76 LIGHT AMPHIBIOUS TANK

Crew: 3.
Armament: One 76.2mm gun; one 7.62mm machine gun co-axial with main armament.
Armour: 14mm (0.55in) maximum.
Dimensions: Length (gun forwards) 25ft (7.625m); length (hull) 22ft 8in (6.91m); width 10ft 4in (3.14m); height 7ft 2in (2.195m).
Weight: Combat 30,865lbs (14,000kg).
Ground pressure: 6.8lb/in² (0.48kg/cm²).
Power to weight ratio: 17.1hp/t.
Performance: Road speed 27.34mph (44km/h); water speed 6.2mph (10km/h); range 162 miles (260km); vertical obstacle 3ft 8in (1.1m); trench 9ft 2in (2.8m); gradient 60 per cent.
History: Entered service in 1952. In service with Afghanistan, Angola, Bulgaria, China, Congo, Cuba, Czechoslovakia, East Germany, Egypt, Finland, Hungary, India, Indonesia, Iraq, Israel, Laos, North Korea, Pakistan, Poland, Soviet Union, Syria and Yugoslavia. Production completed in early 1960s.

The Russians have been using amphibious tanks since the early 1920s. The PT-76 (*Plavaushiy Tank*) is based on the *Pinguin* cross-country vehicle. Since it entered service with the Russian Army in 1952, it has been exported to many countries and has seen combat in Africa, the Middle East and the Far East. It has a hull of all-welded steel construction. The driver is seated at the front of the hull, with the commander and gunner in the turret, and the engine and transmission at the rear of the hull. The PT-76 is armed with a 76.2mm gun, this having an elevation of +30° and a depression of −4°. A 7.62mm SGMT machine-gun is mounted co-axially with the main armament. Forty rounds of 76.2mm and 1,000 rounds of 7.62mm ammunition are carried. The most outstanding feature of the PT-76 is its amphibious capability. It is propelled in the water by two water-jets, one in each side of the hull, with their exits in the hull rear. Before entering the water a trim vane is erected at the front of the hull and the driver's centre periscope is raised so that he can see over the top of the trim vane. The PT-76 has been built in large numbers and its basic chassis has been used for a whole family of armoured vehicles including the BTR-50 armoured personnel carrier, ASU-85 air-portable anti-tank gun, ZSU-23-4 self-propelled anti-aircraft gun, SA-6 'Gainful' anti-aircraft missile system, BMP-1 MICV, 'Frog' 2, 3, 4 and 5 tactical missile systems,

GSP amphibious ferry, SP-74 122mm SPG and GTT vehicle to name just a few. A modified version has been built in China as the Type 60. This has a similar hull to the PT-76 but has a new turret mounting an 85mm gun and a co-axial 7.62mm machine-gun; there is also a 12.7mm anti-aircraft machine-gun on the roof. Although well over 20 years old, the PT-76 is still a very useful vehicle in the reconnaissance role. Its replacement in the Soviet Army is believed to be the new BMD light tank/fire-support vehicle.

Right and below right: Rear and side views of the PT-76 light amphibious tank, in Soviet service since 1952. It was the first amphibious tank to use hydro-jet propulsion: water is drawn into vents in the tank's belly, pressurised by pumps powered from the engine and expelled through two rear-mounted vents. While swimming, at a maximum 10km/h, the tank is steered by opening and closing 'clam-shell' covers over the hydro-jet vents. On 3 March 1969, four US M-48s destroyed two VietCong PT-76s in an engagement near Ben Het.

Left: PT-76s make a river crossing, with schnorkel tubes erect at the rear of their turrets. When swimming, the driver's periscope is raised so that he can see over the frontal trim vane, as seen here.

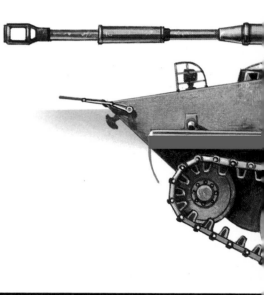

BRDM-1 RECONNAISSANCE VEHICLE

BRDM-1, BRDM-1 (Snapper), BRDM-1 (Swatter), BRDM-1 (Sagger), BRDM-U, BRDM-1 rkh
Crew: 5.
Armament: One 7.62mm or one 12.7mm machine-gun.
Armour: 10mm (0.39in) maximum.

Dimensions: Length 18ft 8in (5.7m); width 7ft 4in (2.225m); height (without armament) 6ft 3in (1.9m).
Weight: Combat 12,346lbs (5,600kg).
Engine: GAZ-40P six-cylinder inline water-cooled petrol engine developing 90hp at 3,400rpm.
Performance: Road speed 49.7mph (80km/h); water speed 5.6mph (9km/h); range 310 miles (500km); vertical obstacle 1ft 7in (0.47m); trench (with belly wheels lowered) 4ft (1.22m); gradient 60 per cent.

History: Entered service with the Russian Army in 1959. In service with Albania, Bulgaria, Congo, Cuba, East Germany, Egypt, Israel, Poland, Soviet Union, Syria and Uganda. Production completed in the 1960s.

The standard reconnaissance vehicles in the Russian Army in the early 1950s were the old World War II BA-64 armoured car and the BTR-40, which appeared in 1948. Both of these had two major drawbacks: first they lacked amphibious capability, and second their cross-country performance left a lot to be desired. In the late 1950s they were replaced by the BRDM-1 vehicle, also called the BTR-40P for some time. The BRDM-1 has a hull of all-welded steel which provides the crew with protection from small arms fire. The engine and transmission are at the front and the personnel compartment at the rear. All four wheels are powered and a central tyre pressure-regulation system is provided. There are also two belly wheels on each side, lowered by the driver when crossing rough country. The vehicle is fully amphibious and is propelled in the water by a single water-jet in the rear of the hull. Infra-red driving lights are normally provided and some vehicles have an infra-red searchlight mounted on the roof. Armament normally consists of

Left: The BRDM-1, armed with six 'Sagger' wire-guided anti-tank missiles. Other BRDM systems mount three 'Snapper' missiles or four 'Swatter' missiles.

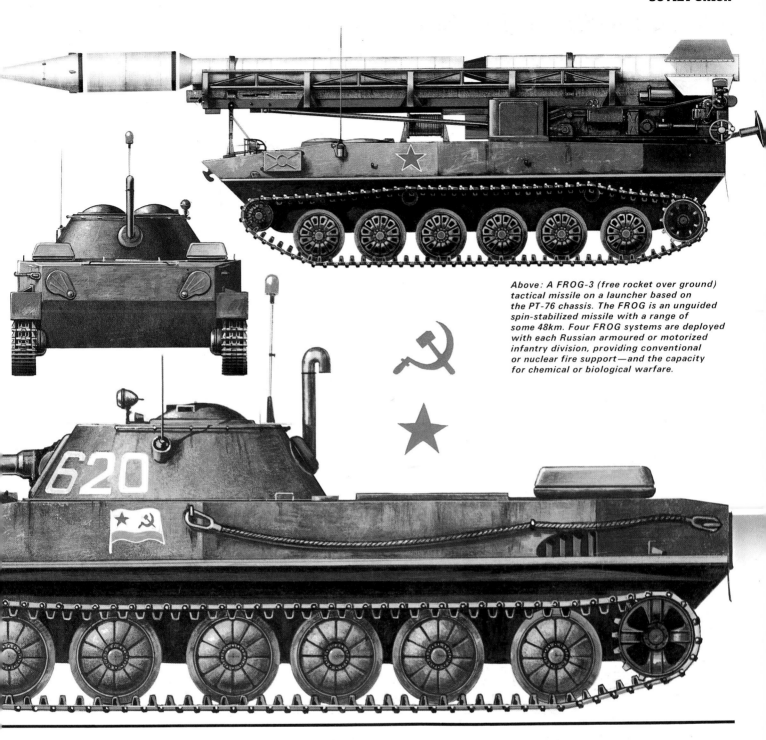

Above: A FROG-3 (free rocket over ground) tactical missile on a launcher based on the PT-76 chassis. The FROG is an unguided spin-stabilized missile with a range of some 48km. Four FROG systems are deployed with each Russian armoured or motorized infantry division, providing conventional or nuclear fire support—and the capacity for chemical or biological warfare.

a 12.7mm DShK or a 7.62mm SGMB machine-gun on a simple pintle mount without a shield. The BRDM-U is a command model with additional radios, whilst the BRDM-1 rkh is used to mark clear lanes through NBC contaminated areas. There are three anti-tank missile variants in service. The BRDM-1 (Snapper) has three 'Snapper' missiles, which have a maximum effective range of 2,187 yards (2,000m), whilst the BRDM-1 (Swatter) has four missiles with a maximum range of 2,734 yards (2,500m) although it has been reported that there is also a missile with a range of 3,827 yards (3,500m). The most common model in service is the BRDM-1 (Sagger). This has a total of six 'Sagger' missiles, which have a maximum range of 2,734 yards (2,500m), and a warhead which will penetrate 15.75in (400mm) of armour at that range. The BRDM-1 vehicles are being replaced by the BRDM-2 range.

Right: A BRDM series vehicle firing a 'Sagger' ATGW. The 'Sagger', carrying an 11.34kg HEAT (high explosive anti-tank) warhead to a maximum 3,000m, was first extensively used in the Yom Kippur War of 1973. It can be fired either from a vehicle or from an infantry position. From the 1973 combat, where the latter method was more usual, an authority on armoured warfare has deduced that—given manoeuvrability and a high-velocity gun—the tank is still capable of holding its own against an opponent with considerable ATGW strength.

191

BTR-60 ARMOURED PERSONNEL CARRIER

BTR-60P, BTR-60PK, BTR-60PB, BTR-60PU, BTR-60PB (FAC)
Crew: 2 plus 14.
Armament: One 14.5mm KPVT machine-gun; one 7.62mm PKT machine-gun co-axial with KPVT machine-gun.
Armour: 14mm (0.55in).
Dimensions: Length 24ft 10in (7.56m); width 9ft 3in (2.825m); height (with turret) 7ft 7in (2.31m).
Weight: Combat 22,707lbs (10,300kg).
Engines: Two GAZ-49B six-cylinder inline petrol engines developing 90hp at 3,400rpm each.
Performance: Road speed 49.7mph (80km/h); water speed 6.2mph (10km/h); range 311 miles (500km); vertical obstacle 1ft 4in (0.4m); trench 6ft 7in (2m); gradient 60 per cent.
History: Entered service in 1961. In service with Afghanistan, Algeria, Angola, Bulgaria, Cuba, East Germany, Egypt, Hungary, Iran, Iraq, Israel, Libya, Mongolia, North Korea, Poland, Romania, Soviet Union, Syria, Yugoslavia and Vietnam. Production is believed to have been completed in the early 1970s. (Note: data relate to BTR-60PB)

The BTR-60P series was introduced in 1960-1 as the replacement for the older BTR-152 armoured personnel carrier as the latter was based on a standard truck chassis and was therefore limited in cross-country performance. The BTR-60 is used mainly in the motor rifle divisions as the tank divisions have the tracked BMP-1 MICVs. The advantage of the wheeled BTR-60 is that it has a higher road speed than a tracked vehicle and therefore has greater strategic, rather than tactical, mobility. The designation BTR-60P is broken down as follows – BTR is *Bronetransporter* (armoured personnel carrier), 60 is the abbreviation for the year of introduction, and P is for *Plavayushchiy* (amphibious). The P is also used in other Soviet vehicle designations, such as the PT-76 tank. It has a total of eight road wheels and all of these are powered (eg, 8×8), the front four being used for steering, which is power-assisted to reduce driver fatigue. A central tyre pressure-regulation system is provided so that the ground pressure can be adjusted by the driver to suit the conditions over which the vehicle is travelling. The BTR-60P has excellent amphibious characteristics and is powered in the water by a single water-jet at the rear of the hull. The vehicle is in fact used by the Russian marines as well as the

Army. Standard equipment includes infra-red equipment and electric bilge pumps, and some vehicles have a winch mounted internally at the front of the vehicle to assist in self-recovery operations. The first model to enter service was the BTR-60P. This, like all later vehicles, has the driver and commander at the very front of the hull. Its roof, however, is open and the infantry are seated on bench seats running across the width of the hull. They are very vulnerable to shell splinters and have to wear NBC suits when in an NBC environment. Small doors are provided in each side of the hull, as are firing-ports. This model is normally

armed with a 12.7mm DShK and up to three 7.62mm SGMB or PKT machine-guns on pintle mounts. The next model to enter service was the BTR-60PK, which had a fully enclosed troop compartment provided with an NBC system, normal means of entry and exit being through hatches in the roof. The BTR-60PK also has firing-ports in the sides of the hull, and is normally armed with a single DShK machine-gun and two 7.62mm SGMB or PKT machine-guns. Like the earlier BTR-60P, the BTR-60PK's machine-guns are not provided with a shield and the gunners are therefore very vulnerable to small arms fire. The latest model to

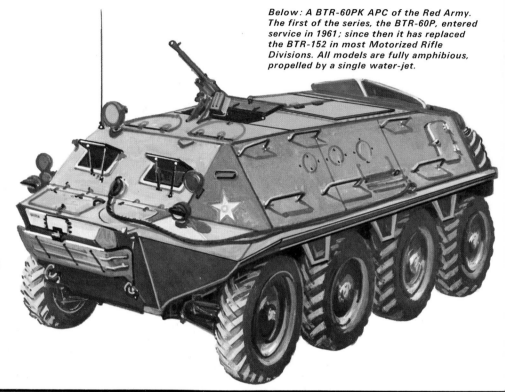

Below: A BTR-60PK APC of the Red Army. The first of the series, the BTR-60P, entered service in 1961; since then it has replaced the BTR-152 in most Motorized Rifle Divisions. All models are fully amphibious, propelled by a single water-jet.

ASU-85 SELF-PROPELLED ANTI-TANK GUN

Crew: 4.
Armament: One 85mm gun; one 7.62mm PKT machine-gun co-axial with main armament.
Armour: 10mm–40mm (0.39–1.57in).
Dimensions: Length (with armament) 27ft 10in (8.49m); length (hull) 19ft 8in (6m); width 9ft 2in (2.8m); height 7ft 11in (2.1m).
Weight: Combat 30,865lbs (14,000kg).
Ground pressure: 6.25lb/in² (0.44kg/cm²).
Engine: Model V-6 six-cylinder inline water-cooled diesel developing 240hp at 1,800rpm.
Performance: Road speed 27.3mph (44km/h); range 162 miles (260km); vertical obstacle 3ft 8in (1.1m); trench 9ft 2in (2.8m); gradient 70 per cent.
History: Entered service with the Russian Army in 1961. In service with East Germany, Poland and the Soviet Union. Production completed about 1964.

Until the introduction of the ASU-85 in 1961, the only self-propelled anti-tank weapons in the Russian airborne units were ASU-57s. These have two drawbacks. First they have very thin armour and no overhead protection at all, and secondly their 57mm gun is not adequate against tanks. Each Russian airborne regiment has a battery of nine ASU-57s, whilst each airborne division has a battalion of 18 ASU-85s. The ASU-85 (ASU is the abbreviation for *Aviadezantnaya Samochodnaya Ustanovka*, and the 85 refers to the size of the main armament) is normally transported in the Autonov An-12 'Cub' transport aircraft and can be air-dropped. For air-dropping the vehicle is mounted on a platform to which are attached a number of parachutes. Just before the platform reaches the ground a number of retro-rockets are fired to reduce the platform's velocity so that no damage occurs. The ASU-85 has a hull of all-welded steel construction which varies in thickness from 0.4in (10mm) on the hull roof to 1.57in (40mm) on the glacis and mantlet. The fighting compartment is at the front, with the engine and transmission at the rear. Many components of the ASU-85 are taken from the PT-76 amphibious light tank family. The crew consists of commander, gunner, loader and driver, the last being seated at the front of the vehicle on the right side. The ASU-85 has torsion-bar suspension and a total of six road wheels with the idler at the

front and the drive sprocket at the rear, but does not have any track-return rollers. The 85mm gun is provided with a double baffle muzzle-brake and a fume extractor, and is mounted slightly offset to the vehicle's left; traverse is a total of 12° and elevation from −4° to +15°. A 7.62mm PKT machine-gun is mounted co-axially with the main armament. A total of 40 rounds of 85mm ammunition is carried, including HE, APHE and HVAP. The AP projectile weighs 20.9lbs (9.5kg) and has a muzzle velocity of 2,598ft/s (792m/s), the APHE projectile weighs 20.5lbs (9.3kg) and also has a muzzle velocity of 2,598ft/s, and the HVAP projectile weighs 11.02lbs (5kg) and has a muzzle velocity of 3,379ft/s (1,030m/s). The APHE round will penetrate 4in (102mm) of armour at a range of 1,093 yards (1,000m) whilst the HVAP round will penetrate 5.12in (130mm) of armour at a similar range. The ASU-85 is believed to be fitted with an NBC system. Infra-red

driving lights are fitted and there is an infra-red searchlight over the main armament and another in front of the commander's hatch, the last controllable from within the vehicle. The vehicle does not have any amphibious capability, although it can ford to a depth of 3ft 8in (1.1m) without preparation. Two fuel drums can be attached to the rear of the hull to increase operational range.

Right: An ASU-85 SP anti-tank gun is unloaded from an aircraft of the Soviet Air Force. The ASU-85 is normally issued on the scale of 18 per airborne division.

Below: An ASU-85 of a Russian airborne division on winter exercises. The ASU-85 has a full range of night vision equipment and is believed to have an NBC system.

enter service is the BTR-60PB. This is almost identical to the earlier BTR-60PK but has the same turret as that fitted to the BRDM-2 (4×4) reconnaissance vehicle. This is armed with a 14.5mm KPVT heavy machine-gun and a co-axial 7.62mm PKT machine-gun, these having an elevation of +30° and a depression of −5°, traverse being 360°. A total of 500 rounds of 14.5mm and 2,000 rounds of 7.62mm ammunition is carried. The KPVT machine-gun is widely used in the Russian Army in various machines including the ZPU-1, ZPU-2 and ZPU-4 anti-aircraft weapons, twin-mounted on the

BTR-40 and BTR-152 vehicles, mounted co-axially in the T-10M tank, mounted on the T-10M tank in the anti-aircraft role, as well as on the OT-64, BRDM-2 and FUG-70 reconnaissance vehicles. It has a cyclic rate of fire of 600 rounds per minute and an effective range in the ground role of 2,187 yards (2,000m). It fires an armour-piercing incendiary round weighing 64.4gr with a muzzle velocity of 3,281ft/s (1,000m/s). This will penetrate 1.26in (32mm) of armour at a range of 547 yards (500m). Finally there are two specialised models of the BTR-60P. The first is the BTR-60PU

command vehicle, which has additional radios; second is the BTR-60PB forward air-control vehicle. This is unarmed and is fitted with a generator to cope with the the additional communications equipment installed.

Below: Russian Marines disembark from BTR-60P APCs during exercises. The BTR-60P can carry 14 men and, like most Soviet vehicles of its type, has a central tyre-pressure regulation system.

T-62 MAIN BATTLE TANK

Crew: 4.
Armament: One 115mm U-5TS gun; one 7.62mm PKT machine-gun co-axial with main armament; one 12.7mm DShK anti-aircraft machine-gun (optional).
Armour: 20mm–170mm (0.79–6.80in).
Dimensions: Length (overall) 32ft (9.77m); length (hull) 22ft (6.715m); width 11ft (3.35m); height (without anti-aircraft machine-gun) 7ft 10in (2.4m).
Weight: Combat 80,468lbs (36,500kg).
Ground pressure: 10.24lb/in^2 (0.72kg/cm^2)
Engine: Model V-2-62 12-cylinder water-cooled diesel engine developing 700hp at 2,200rpm.
Performance: Road speed 31mph (50km/h); range (without additional fuel tanks) 310 miles (500km); vertical obstacle 2ft 8in (0.8m); trench 9ft 2in (2.8m); gradient 60 per cent.
History: Entered service with the Russian Army in 1963. In service with Afghanistan, Bulgaria, Czechoslovakia, East Germany, Hungary, India, Iraq, Israel, Libya, Poland, Romania, Soviet Union and Syria. Still being built.

The T-62 was developed in the late 1950s as the successor to the earlier T-54/T-55 series, and was first seen in public in May 1965. In appearance it is very similar to the earlier T-54. It does, however, have a longer and wider hull, a new turret and main armament, and can easily be distinguished from the T-54 as the latter has a distinct gap between its first and second road wheels, whereas the T-62's road wheels are more evenly spaced, and the T-62's gun is provided with a bore evacuator. The hull of the T-62 is of all-welded construction with the glacis plate being 4in (100mm) thick. The turret is of cast armour, and this varies in thickness from 6.7in (170mm) at the front to 2.4in (60mm) at the rear. The driver is seated at the front of the hull on the left side, with the other three crew members in the turret, the commander and gunner on the left and the loader on the right. The engine and transmission are at the rear of the hull. The suspension is of the well tried torsion-bar type, and consists of five road wheels with the idler at the front and the drive sprocket at the rear. The U-5TS gun is of the smoothbore type, and has an elevation of +17° and a depression of −4°. A 7.62mm PKT machine-gun is mounted co-axially with the main armament. When the T-62 first entered service it did not have an anti-aircraft machine-gun, but in the last few years many T-62s have been provided with the standard 12.7mm DShK weapon which is mounted on the loader's cupola, T-62s thus fitted being designated T-62A. Three types of ammunition are carried – High Explosive, Fin-Stabilised Armour-Piercing Discarding Sabot (FSAPDS) and High Explosive Anti-Tank (HEAT). The FSAPDS round has a muzzle velocity of 5,512ft/s (1,680m/s) and an effective range of 1,749 yards (1,600m). When this round is fired the sabot (the disposable 'slipper' around the projectile) drops off after the round has left the barrel and the fins of the

Below: Front view of a T-62, showing infra-red night vision equipment including a searchlight to the left of the gun and another in front of the commander's hatch.

projectile unfold to stabilise the round in flight. According to Israeli reports, this round will penetrate 11.8in (300mm) of armour at a range of 1,094 yards (1,000m). The 115mm round is manually loaded but once the gun has been fired the gun automatically returns to a set angle at which the empty cartridge case is ejected from the breech, after which it moves onto a chute and is then thrown out through a small hatch in the turret rear. It would appear that this is a somewhat unreliable system. The tank has an average rate of fire of four rounds per minute, and a stabiliser is provided to stabilise the gun in both elevation and traverse. A total of 40 rounds of 115mm and 3,500 rounds of 7.62mm ammunition is carried. The T-62 is provided with an NBC system, infra-red driving lights, infra-red searchlight on the commander's cupola and an infra-red searchlight to the right of the main armament, moving in elevation with the main armament, to allow the T-62 to engage targets at night. The tank

can ford streams to a depth of 4ft 7in (1.4m) without preparation. A 'schnorkel' can be erected on the loader's hatch, held in the upright position by stays. When fitted with this device the tank can ford to a maximum depth of 18 feet (5.486m). When not required the schnorkel is carried on the rear of the tank in sections. Like the T-55, the T-62 can lay its own smoke screen, this being achieved by injecting vaporised diesel fuel into the exhaust pipes on each side of the hull. Additional fuel tanks can be mounted at the rear of the hull in order to increase the operating range of the tank, these being jettisoned by the driver before the tank goes into action. The T-62 has been used in combat by the Egyptian and Syrian forces. Although not so sophisticated as western tanks, the T-62 has proved itself a rugged and reliable vehicle. It is estimated that over 15,000 T-62 tanks have been built by Russia, although it does not appear that the tank has been built in any of the Warsaw Pact countries, as

Above: T-62 tanks fitted with schnorkels, giving them the ability to wade to a depth of 5.486m. The drums on the hull rear contain additional fuel to extend the tank's operational range.

Above: A Russian T-62 tank advances fully closed up. Like most other contemporary Soviet AFVs, the T-62 is fully sealed and can operate in complete safety for at least 24 hours in a nuclear, bacteriological or chemical warfare zone.

were the earlier T-54/T-55 tanks. Although the Russians now have a new tank designated the T-64/T-72 in service, production of the T-62 is believed to be continuing, and the type will remain in service with the Russians for many years yet.

Above: The T-62 entered service with the Red Army in 1963. Since then it has replaced the T-54 in most front-line units. The T-62 is extensively used by Arab forces in the Middle East, where many have been captured by Israel.

Below: A T-62 used during the invasion of Czechoslovakia. The white band on the turret was an identification sign carried by most Soviet AFVs at that time.

195

ZSU-23-4 SELF-PROPELLED ANTI-AIRCRAFT GUN

Crew: 4.
Armament: Four 23mm Zu-23 cannon.
Armour: 15mm (0.59in) maximum.
Dimensions: Length 20ft 8in (6.3m); width 9ft 8in (2.95m); height (with radar retracted) 7ft 5in (2.25m).
Weight: Combat 30,865lbs (14,000kg).
Ground pressure: 6.82lb/sq² (0.48kg/cm²).
Engine: Model V-6 six-cylinder in-line water-cooled diesel developing 240hp at 1800rpm.
Performance: Road speed 27.34mph (44km/h); range 162 miles (260km); vertical obstacle 3ft 7in (1.1m); trench 9ft 2in (2.8m); gradient 60 per cent.
History: Entered service with the Russian Army in 1964. In service with Bulgaria, Czechoslovakia, East Germany, Egypt, Finland, Hungary, India, Iraq, Iran, Poland, Soviet Union, South Yemen and Syria. Believed still to be in production.

With the introduction of accurate surface-to-air missiles such as the SA-2 and Bloodhound in the late

1950s, aircraft have been forced to fly at tree-top height to avoid detection. The standard Russian self-propelled anti-aircraft gun system in the 1950s was the ZSU-57-2, but as this could not be used to counter the new threat, a new self-propelled weapon was developed. This was the ZSU-23-4, or *Shilka* as the Russians call it, first seen in public in 1965. The vehicle is based on components of the PT-76 light tank. The hull and turret are of all-welded steel construction with a maximum armour thickness of 0.6in (15mm). The suspension system is of the torsion-bar type and consists of six road wheels, with the idler at the front and the drive sprocket at the rear. The driver is seated at the front of the hull on the left side with the turret in the centre and the engine and transmission at the rear. Unlike the PT-76, the ZSU-23-4 is not amphibious, although it can ford to a depth of 3ft 6in (1.07m). It is provided with an NBC system and infra-red night-vision equipment. It is armed with four 23mm Zu-23 guns in a power-operated turret having a tra-

verse of 360°. The guns can be elevated from −7° to +80°. The guns are gas-operated and water-cooled. Each gun has a cyclic rate of fire of 800 to 1,000 rounds per minute, although in practice each barrel normally fires in bursts of 50 rounds to conserve ammunition. A total of 2,000 rounds of ammunition is carried, 500 rounds for each barrel. Two types of ammunition are used: Armour-Piercing Incendiary and High Explosive Incendiary, both of these having a muzzle velocity of 3,182ft/s (970m/s). The guns have a maximum effective range in the anti-aircraft role of 2,734 yards (2,500m). The vehicle normally halts to open fire, this giving a more stable firing platform, although if required the ZSU-23-4 can fire on the move. A radar scanner called 'Gun Dish' is mounted on the rear of the turret and this can be folded down behind the turret rear if required. This radar has two roles: it can first

Left: Side view of a Russian ZSU-23-4 'Shilka' self-propelled anti-aircraft gun, with its radar scanner, folded down when not in use, operational.

BRDM-2 AMPHIBIOUS RECONNAISSANCE VEHICLE

BRDM-2, BRDM-2U, BRDM-2 rkh, BRDM-2 (Sagger), BRDM-2 (SA-9).
Crew: 4.
Armament: One 14.5mm KPVT machine-gun; one 7.62mm PKT machine-gun co-axial with main armament.
Armour: 10mm (0.39in) maximum.
Dimensions: Length 18ft 10in (5.75m); width 7ft 9in (2.35m); height 7ft 7in (2.31m).
Weight: Combat 15,432lbs (7,000kg).
Engine: GAZ-41 eight-cylinder petrol engine developing 140hp.
Performance: Road speed 62mph (100km/h); water speed 6.2mph (10km/h); range 466 miles (750km); vertical obstacle 16in (0.4m); trench crossing (with belly wheels in position) 4ft 1in (1.25m); gradient 60 per cent.
History: Entered service with the Russian Army in 1964–65. In service with Angola, Bulgaria, East Germany, Egypt, Israel, Mali, Poland, Romania, Soviet Union, Syria and Yugoslavia.

The BRDM-2 (formerly known as the BTR-40PB) was developed as the replacement for the earlier BRDM-1 in the early 1960s, and was first seen in public in 1966. The main improvements over the earlier vehicle are a fully enclosed turret, higher road and water speed, and a greater operating range, all of which are essential to a reconnaissance vehicle. The BRDM-2 has a hull of all-welded steel armour which has a maximum thickness of 0.4in (10mm). The driver and commander are seated at the front of the hull, each being provided

with a bullet-proof windscreen which can be covered by a steel hatch if required. The only method of entry and exit is via two roof hatches over the commander's and driver's positions. The turret, which is unusual in that it has no roof hatch cover, is mounted on the top of the hull, and is identical to that used on the BTR-60PB and OT-64C armoured personnel carriers. This turret contains a 14.5mm KPVT and 7.62mm PKT machine-gun, both of which are capable of an elevation of +30° and a depression of −5°. Five hundred rounds of 14.5mm and 2,000 rounds of 7.62mm ammunition are carried. The BRDM-2 is also provided

with powered belly wheels which are lowered when crossing rough country, a front-mounted winch, an NBC system, infra-red driving lights, an infra-red searchlight on the roof which can be controlled from within the vehicle by the commander, and finally the standard tyre pressure-regulation system. The BRDM-2 is fully amphibious, being propelled in the water by a single water-jet in the rear of the hull. There are four basic versions of the BRDM-2. The first of these is the BRDM-2 command vehicle (designated BRDM-2U). This has no turret and is fitted with additional radios and a generator. The BRDM-2 rkh is used to mark clear

locate enemy aircraft at a maximum range of 12.4 miles (20km), and second track the aircraft and slave the guns onto the aircraft. The radar operates in the J band (formerly the Ku band). The ZSU-23-4 was first used in action by the Syrian and Egyptian forces in the 1973 Middle East campaign. According to most reports, the weapon shot down more Israeli aircraft than any other weapon system, including the SA-6 and SA-7 missiles. In the Warsaw Pact the ZSU-23-4 is issued on the scale of four per motor rifle regiment and eight per tank regiment. At divisional level there is an anti-aircraft regiment with four batteries each of six ZSU-23-4s. A typical Soviet army group could have a total of 128 such weapons deployed along its front. Without doubt the ZSU-23-4 is the most effective mobile anti-aircraft gun system of its type at present deployed in the world, although the German *Gepard* should prove a superior system and the Americans are also developing a rapid-fire anti-aircraft system.

Right: The 'Shilka' at action readiness. Developed in the early 1960s to combat aircraft flying low to evade surface-to-air missiles, the ZSU-23-4's 'Gun Dish' radar can detect aircraft at 20km, track the target and direct fire on to it. It is probably the best AA weapon in service.

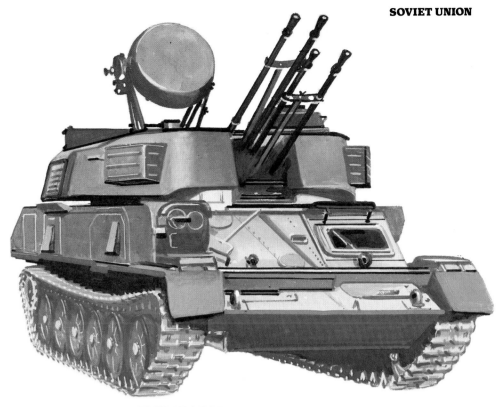

Above: The ZSU-23-4 can fire its four 23mm cannon at a cyclic rate of 800 to 1,000 rounds per minute, but since only 2,000 rounds are carried, firing is normally in 50-round bursts. Spent cases are automatically ejected.

Left: A 'Shilka' of the East German Army. Since entering Russian service in 1964, the ZSU-23-4 has equipped armies of the Eastern bloc and Arab and Asian nations. A few were reported operational in Vietnam.

lanes through an NBC contaminated area. The BRDM-2 (Sagger) was first encountered in the 1973 Middle East campaign, and has no turret. A total of six 'Sagger' missiles is carried in the ready-to-launch position, these being raised from within the vehicle complete with overhead armour, a further eight missiles being carried in reserve. These missiles can be launched from within the vehicle itself, or up to 87 yards (80m) away from the vehicle with the aid of a separation cable and control unit. If the BRDM-2 (Sagger) is disabled, the missiles can be removed from the launchers and fired from a normal ground mount. The AT-3 'Sagger' is wire-guided, and has a minimum range of 547 yards (500m) and a maximum range of

3,280 yards (3,000m). The missile itself weighs 24.25lbs (11kg), is 32in (815mm) in length and has a HEAT warhead which will penetrate 15.75in (400mm) of armour. According to an American report, it takes the Sagger 27 seconds to reach its maximum range of 3,280 yards and its average velocity is 394ft/s (120m/s). Also it has a 60 per cent chance of hitting a stationary tank at its maximum range. The latest model to appear is the BRDM-2 anti-aircraft vehicle. This entered service with the Russian Army in 1972 and the following year some were supplied to Syria and Egypt

in time to be used in the 1973 Middle East campaign. It consists of a BRDM-2 with its turret replaced by a new turret fitted with two SAMs on each side, although recently some have been seen with just one missile each side. The system has been given the NATO code name of SA-9 'Gaskin'. According to most reports these are in fact a modified version of the SA-7 'Grail' missile with an improved warhead. This missile is believed to have an effective horizontal range of about 3,827 yards (3,500m) and a maximum altitude of 4,921 feet (1,500m).

Left: Side view of the Russian 100km/h BRDM-2 reconnaissance vehicle, which replaced the BRDM-1 from 1964-65. Fully amphibious, swimming at 10km/h with a single rear-mounted hydro-jet, the vehicle also has powered belly-wheels which are lowered when crossing rough terrain. Its turret-mounted 14.5mm machine-gun is supplemented by a 7.62mm.
Right: BRDM-2s of the Red Army. Variants of this scout car include the BRDM-2 rkh, specially equipped to find safe paths through nuclear-biological contaminated areas; the turret-less BRDM-2U command vehicle; the BRDM-2 (Sagger), mounting six wire-guided missiles in ready-to-launch position; and an AA variant with SAMs.

BMP-1 MECHANISED INFANTRY COMBAT VEHICLE

Crew: 3 plus 8.
Armament: One 73mm gun; one 7.62mm PKT machine-gun co-axial with main armament; one launcher rail for 'Sagger' ATGW.
Armour: 14mm (0.55in) maximum.
Dimensions: Length 20ft 8in (6.3m); width 10ft (3.05m); height 6ft (1.83m).
Weight: Combat 26,456lbs (12,000kg).
Ground pressure: 8.1lb/in² (0.57kg/cm²).
Power/weight ratio: 22.4hp/t.
Engine: One Model V-6 six-cylinder inline water-cooled diesel developing 280hp at 2,000rpm.
Performance: Road speed 36mph (60km/h); water speed 5mph (8km/h); range 310 miles (500km); vertical obstacle 3ft 7in (1.1m); trench 6ft 6in (1.98m); gradient 60 per cent.
History: Entered service in 1967. In service with Czechoslovakia, East Germany, Egypt, Iraq, Libya, Poland, Soviet Union, Syria.

The Soviet BMP-1 has the distinction of being the first Mechanised Infantry Combat Vehicle (MICV) to enter service in the world. Previously, armies used the Armoured Personnel Carrier or APC (eg, the American M113) to transport infantry across the battlefield. On reaching their objective they dismounted from the vehicle and fought on foot. The MICV has the added advantage that the crew can use their weapons from within the hull, since the vehicle is provided with firing-ports in both the hull sides and rear. In addition the MICV is normally provided with a more powerful armament installation than the standard APC, so that it can deal with light armoured vehicles as well as infantry. Since the BMP-1 entered service with the Russian Army in 1967, it has been exported to a number of countries, and has since been used in combat by the Egyptian and Syrian Armies during the 1973 Middle East campaigns. The hull is of all-welded construction. The driver is seated at the front of the hull on the left, with the vehicle commander to his rear, the engine being mounted to the right of the driver. The turret is in the centre of the vehicle, with the personnel compartment at the rear. The eight infantry are seated in the

Right: An SA-7 'Grail' surface-to-air missile is launched from a Russian BM P-1 MICV. The BMP-1 is fully amphibious, swimming by aid of its tracks at a maximum 8km/h.

rear of the vehicle and enter and leave via the twin doors in the hull rear; these doors contain additional fuel. In addition there are four roof hatches over the troop compartment. The turret of the BMP-1 is also fitted to the new BMD vehicle (*qv*). This turret is armed with a 73mm gun of the smooth-bore type, and is fed from a magazine holding 30 rounds of ammunition. The gun fires a fin-stabilised HEAT or HE round

with a maximum effective range of 1,640 yards (1,500m). The turret can be traversed through 360° and the gun elevated from −5° to +20°. A 7.62mm PKT machine-gun is mounted co-axially with the main armament and a total of 1,000 rounds of 7.62mm ammunition is carried. A launcher rail for the AT-3 'Sagger' ATGW is mounted over the 73mm gun. This missile has a maximum range of 3,280 yards (3,000m);

BMD LIGHT TANK FIRE SUPPORT VEHICLE

Crew: 3 plus 6.
Armament: One 73mm gun; one 7.62mm PKT machine-gun co-axial with main armament; one 7.62mm PKT machine-gun in each side of hull; one launcher rail for 'Sagger' ATGW.
Armour: Not available.
Dimensions: Length 17ft 4in (5.3m); width 8ft 8in (2.65m); height 6ft 1in (1.85m).
Weight: Combat 19,842lbs (9,000kg).
Performance: Road speed 34mph (55km/h); water speed 3.7mph (6km/h); vertical obstacle 2ft (0.6m); trench 6ft 7in (2m); gradient 60 per cent.
History: Entered service with the Russian Army in 1971–72 and expected to enter service with other members of the Warsaw Pact in the near future.
(Note: the above data are provisional.)

The BMD, or M1970 as it was first known, was first seen in public in November 1973, when it was shown in the markings of a Russian air-borne unit. This is a new vehicle rather than a development of an existing design, although its turret is identical with that mounted on the BMP-1 MICV. The role of the BMD (the letters stand for *Boyevaya Mashina Desantnaya*) is believed to be twofold: first to provide mobile fire support for Russian airborne units, which up to now have lacked it; and second to act as an infantry carrier to allow the airborne units to strike at targets some way from their landing zones. Up to now, the only armoured vehicles used by Russian airborne units have been the ASU-57 and ASU-85 self-propelled anti-tank guns. It is very probable that the vehicle is also the replacement for the PT-76 amphibious light tank, which has now been in service for over 20 years. The BMD is air-portable and can be dropped by parachute. The hull is of all-welded construction, but it is not known if this is of steel or aluminium. The driver is seated in the centre of the hull at the front, with the turret behind him and the personnel compartment at the rear. The suspension has five road wheels, with the idler at the front and the drive sprocket at the rear, and there are four track-return rollers. The BMD is armed with a 73mm gun which is fed from a magazine holding about 28 rounds. Elevation of the gun is +20° and depression −5°,

traverse being 360°. There is also a 7.62mm PKT machine-gun mounted co-axially with the main armament. A similar machine-gun is located in each side of the hull firing forwards, and these two guns are believed to be operated by the driver. A launcher rail for the 'Sagger' ATGW is mounted over the main armament. The BMD is fully amphibious and is propelled in the water by two water-jets at the rear of the hull; before entering the water a trim vane is erected at the front of the hull. Night-vision equipment is provided, and the BMD most probably has an NBC system. The vehicle has a crew of three: commander, gunner and driver. When seen in Moscow six infantry-

Below: The BMD light tank fire support vehicle entered service with Russian airborne units in 1971-72. Its turret is identical to that of the BMP-1, with a 73mm gun, co-axial 7.62mm machine-gun and a launcher rail for 'Sagger' ATGWs.

men were seated in the personnel compartment at the rear, in two rows of three across the vehicle. It would appear that there is insufficient room inside the rear of the hull for the engine, transmission and all six men. It does appear, however, that it is possible for the infantrymen to move from the rear of the hull to the front part, as there are periscopes in the sides of the hull. In addition there are two hatches, one on each side, to the rear of the driver's position. There is no provision for the infantry to use their weapons from within the hull. For its size and weight, the BMD is a unique vehicle and there is no other vehicle in service anywhere in the world with which it can be compared.

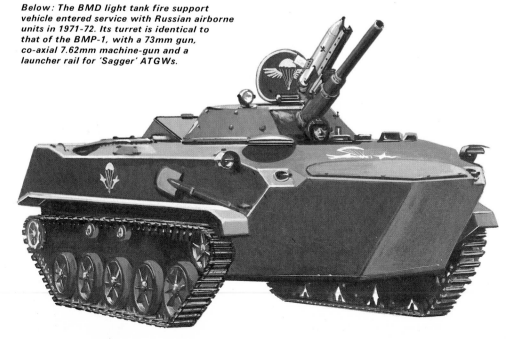

a total of five missiles is carried on the BMP-1. In addition to the AKMS rifles and the light machine-gun of the infantry, an SA-7 'Grail' surface-to-air missile (SAM) is also carried for use against low-flying aircraft. The BMP-1 is fully amphibious, being propelled in the water by its tracks. As with most modern vehicles, an NBC system is provided to allow the BMP-1 to operate in a nuclear, biological or chemical contaminated environment. A full range of night-vision equipment is provided, including infra-red driving lights and infra-red searchlights for both the commander and gunner. The BMP-1 has been designed to operate as part of the tank/infantry team with the T-62 MBT. If required, though, it can operate on its own as it is the most powerfully armed MICV in service anywhere in the world. There is, however, much discussion within the Soviet Army on the actual role of the BMP-1 on the battlefield of the future.

Right: Infantry advance in front of their BMP-1 MICVs. The vehicles seen here do not have 'Sagger' ATGWs mounted over the 73mm gun. The BMP-1 has a full range of night vision equipment and an NBC system.

Below: A BMP-1 of the Polish Army. The firing ports in the sides of the troop compartment are visible.

SA-8 MOBILE ANTI-AIRCRAFT MISSILE SYSTEM

SA-8 and other surface-to-air missile systems (including SA-4, SA-6, SA-7, SA-9)

The Soviet Union has developed a complete range of mobile surface-to-air missiles (SAMs) to complement their ZSU-23-4 and ZSU-57-2 self-propelled anti-aircraft gun systems. The SA-4 'Ganef' was first seen in public in 1964 and can engage aircraft up to a maximum ceiling of 80,000ft (24,400m) and a slant range of 43.4 miles (70km). Two SA-4 missiles are carried on a chassis based on the GMZ tracked mine-layer. The SA-6 'Gainful' was first seen in public during a parade in Moscow during November 1967. Its chassis is based on the PT-76 light tank, although it is not amphibious. Three missiles are carried and these are elevated before launching. The SA-6 is used by most members of the Warsaw Pact and was used successfully by Syria and Egypt in the 1973 Middle East campaign, in which it proved very effective. It forced Israeli aircraft to fly at very low altitude, where they could be engaged by the deadly ZSU-23-4 self-propelled anti-aircraft gun. The SA-6 does not have its own fire-control system as this is provided by another vehicle on a similar chassis. The latter vehicle carries the 'Straight Flush' (NATO codename) system, comprising two radars, one for target-tracking and the other for target-acquisition. Long-range target detection is carried out by the standard Flat Face' radar system, which is mounted on a normal 6×6 truck chassis. The SA-9 'Gaskin' was first used in the 1973 Middle East campaign by Egypt and Syria. It consists of a standard BRDM-2 4×4 amphibious reconnaissance vehicle with its turret removed and replaced by a new turret mounting four missiles in their launcher tubes, two on each side of the turret. Most reports have stated that these missiles are an improved version of the SA-7 'Grail' shoulder-launched missile, the SA-9 having a heavier and more effective warhead and longer range. This is a clear-weather system only, as the missiles home onto the heat of the aircraft engines. The SA-8 'Gecko' was first seen in the November 1975 Moscow display. Its chassis has six road wheels and has not been seen before, and may well have amphibious capability. Four missiles, two on each side, are carried in the ready-to-launch position, and additional missiles may be carried inside

the hull. Full details of this system are still not available, although it is known that it does have both surveillance and tracking radars and is thought to have a TV tracking system as well. Other Soviet SAMs are the SA-1 'Guild', SA-2 'Guideline', SA-3 'Goa', SA-5 'Gammon', SA-7 'Grail' and the new SA-10, of which very little is known.

Below: The SA-8 'Gecko' anti-aircraft missile system was first seen in November 1975. It is thought the Gecko has a similar role to the British Rapier and Franco-German Roland systems. Four missiles are carried in the ready-to-launch position.

T-64 MAIN BATTLE TANK

Crew: 3.
Armament: One 122mm (or 125mm) gun; 7.62mm PKT machine-gun co-axial with main armament; one 12.7mm DShK anti-aircraft machine-gun.
Armour: Not available.
Dimensions: Length (including armament) 33ft 1in (10.1m); length (hull) 24ft 3in (7.4m); width 10ft 10in (3.3m); height 8ft 1in (2.46m).
Weight: Combat 88,185lbs (40,000kg).
Engine: Water-cooled diesel developing 1,000hp.
Performance: Road speed 37mph (60km/h); range 311 miles (500km); vertical obstacle 2ft 8in (0.8m); trench 9ft 2in (2.8m); gradient 60 per cent.
History: Entered service with the Russian Army in 1974, and expected to enter service with members of the Warsaw Pact in the next few years.
(Note: the above data are provisional.)

The development of an armoured fighting vehicle as complex as an MBT is a long process, and in peacetime it can take anything up to 10 years to design a tank, test it and then place a modified version in production. In the West, the whole development cycle is generally made public at a very early stage. The Russians do just the opposite, and it is very difficult in the West to follow the complete development programme of any armoured vehicle. It does appear that the T-64 (or T-72 as it is called in Great Britain) was in fact preceded by a tank known as the M1970, which had a new chassis but was armed with the same 115mm smooth-bore gun as the standard T-62 MBT. The T-64 is armed with a 122mm or 125mm gun, which is smooth for most of its length but rifled towards the breech end (eg, the part nearest the turret). The gun is fed from an automatic loader which holds about 30 rounds of ammunition. Most sources state that the empty cartridge cases are ejected out of the hatch in the turret rear in a manner similar to that used on the T-62 MBT, but other sources have stated that the gun uses a combustible cartridge case. The use of an automatic loader has enabled the crew to be reduced to three men: commander, gunner and driver. The driver is seated at the front of the hull in the centre, with the other two crew members in the turret, the gunner on the left and the commander on the right. A 7.62mm PKT machine-gun is mounted co-axially with the main armament, and there is a 12.7mm DShK machine-gun on the roof for anti-aircraft defence. The suspension is different from that used on the previous T-54/T-62 series of tanks and consists of six road wheels with the idler at the front, drive sprocket at the rear and three track-return rollers. Standard equipment includes an NBC system, night-vision equipment and smoke generators. A schnorkel can be fitted for deep fording operations, and additional fuel tanks can be mounted at the rear to increase operating range. It is also thought that AT-3 'Sagger' ATGW or SA-7 'Grail' SAMs can be mounted on the rear of the turret.

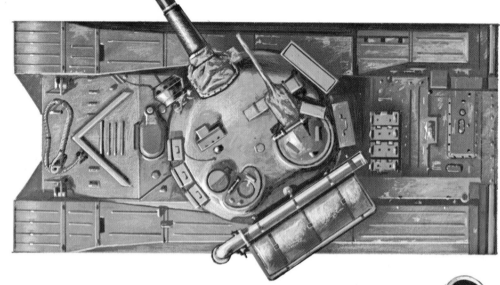

Above right: Top view of the Russian T-64/T-72 MBT introduced in 1974, a considerable improvement on the older T-54/T-55 and T-62 models. It is reported that several thousands of these tanks are now in service as part of the modernization and build-up of conventional weapons of countries of the Warsaw Pact in Eastern Europe.

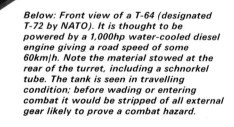

Below: Front view of a T-64 (designated T-72 by NATO). It is thought to be powered by a 1,000hp water-cooled diesel engine giving a road speed of some 60km/h. Note the material stowed at the rear of the turret, including a schnorkel tube. The tank is seen in travelling condition; before wading or entering combat it would be stripped of all external gear likely to prove a combat hazard.

M/39-40 ARMOURED CAR

Crew: 6.
Armament: One 20mm cannon; one 8mm machine-gun co-axial with 20mm cannon; one 8mm machine-gun in ball mount in front of hull; and one 8mm machine-gun in rear of hull.
Armour: 18mm (0.71in) maximum.
Dimensions: Length 16ft 9in (5.104m); width 7ft 6½in (2.29m); height 7ft 3in (2.209m).
Weight: 17,196lbs (7,800kg).
Engine: Volvo six-cylinder petrol engine developing 135hp.
Performance: Road speed 44mph (71km/h).
History: Entered service with the Swedish Army in 1939 and remained in service until early 1950s.

The first armoured cars were built in Sweden by the Tidaholms company in 1926, but these were little more than truck chassis fitted with armoured bodies. In 1929 the *Pansarbil* fm/29 was developed. This had 4×4 drive and was fully armoured. Fully loaded the fm/29 weighed 7.87 tons (8,000kg) and its armament consisted of a 37mm gun in the front, an 8mm machine-gun in the turret and an 8mm machine-gun in the rear. Another version had the 37mm gun replaced by an 8mm machine-gun. The vehicle was powered by an 85hp engine which gave it a maximum road speed of 37mph (60km/h). Various other armoured wheeled vehicles were built in the 1930s, including the *Pansarbil* m/31 which was used by the Swedish Army. This was a standard truck chassis fitted with armour plate and armed with a 20mm cannon (or a 37mm gun which was provided with a shield) and up to two 8mm machine-guns, one of these being mounted to the right of the driver. The Landsverk company also built armoured cars as well as tanks and in 1938 built a 4×4 armoured car called the Lynx. The Lynx had a well shaped hull and was adopted for service as the m/39. Later models had a modified

Right: A Lynx armoured car, in Swedish service from 1939 to the 1950s. It had a turret-mounted 20mm cannon and co-axial 8mm machine-gun, with two more 8mm guns in ball mounts at the front and rear of the hull.

turret with a radio mounted in its rear, and were known by the designation m/40. When built they had solid tires, but later these were replaced by pneumatic ones. Armament consisted of a turret-mounted 20mm cannon with a co-axial 8mm machine-gun, similar machine-guns being mounted to the right of the driver and in the rear of the hull. Landsverk also built a whole series of six-wheeled armoured cars known as the L180, L181 and L182, exported to a number of countries including Eire, Finland, Hungary (which also

built the type under licence) and the Netherlands (the L180 being known there as the M36, and the L182 as the M38). These were 6×2 vehicles and had limited cross-country mobility. Armament varied, but consisted normally of a turret-mounted 20mm cannon with a co-axial machine-gun and another machine-gun mounted to the right of the driver. Some of the Irish vehicles are still in existence, although their original Swedish chassis, engines and wheels were replaced by standard Leyland chassis.

LANDSVERK L-30 LIGHT TANK

Crew: 3.
Armament: One 37mm gun; one 8mm machine-gun co-axial with main armament.
Armour: 14mm (0.55in) maximum.
Dimensions: Length 17ft 0¾in (5.2m); width 8ft 0½in (2.45m); height (on tracks) 7ft 4½in (2.24m); height (on wheels) 8ft 1½in (2.475m).
Weight: 25,353lbs (11,500kg).
Engine: Maybach petrol engine developing 200hp.
Performance: Maximum speed (on tracks) 22mph (35km/h); maximum speed (on wheels) 46mph (75km/h).
History: On trial from 1931. Did not enter production.

In the 1920s and 1930s many countries built armoured vehicles which could run on both tracks or wheels. The wheels gave such vehicles a high road speed, enabling them to be deployed quickly to that part of the front

where they were required, and the tracks gave them a cross-country performance superior to that of conventional armoured cars. Some wheel/track vehicles, such as the American Christie T-3, carried the tracks on top of the hull when the tank was travelling on its wheels. This had the disadvantage, however, that the tracks took something like 30 minutes to fit back on the tank. The first armoured vehicle to be designed by Landsverk was the L-5. This was a wheel/track vehicle, but although work on the prototype started in 1929, it was never completed. In 1930–31 the company built a wheel/track vehicle known as the L-30, this being built at the same time as the L-10 light tank. The hull of the L-30 was of all-welded construction, with the driver seated at the front of the hull on the left, the two-man turret located in the centre and the engine and transmission installed at the rear. Armament consisted of a turret-mounted 37mm gun and a machine-

gun mounted co-axially to the left of the main armament. The vehicle was tested by the Swedish Army under the designation *Stridsvagn* fm/31, but was not adopted. The vehicle is still in existence today at the Swedish Armour Museum. The L-30 was followed by the L-80 wheel/track light tank. This had a crew of two and weighed only 6.4 tons (6,500kg). This was tested in 1933–34, but as it attracted little interest Landsverk halted development of this type of vehicle and concentrated on more conventional vehicles.

Below: One of the Landsverk-designed L-5/L-30/L-80 light tanks of the 1930s. The tracks were already fitted to the vehicle rather than carried on the hull top; this would have resulted in better combat performance. Although tested, these tanks never entered production.

STRIDSVAGN Strv. m/40 LIGHT TANK

Crew: 3.
Armament: One 37mm gun; two 8mm machine-guns co-axial with main armament.
Armour: 24mm (0.94in) maximum.
Dimensions: Length 16ft 1in (4.901m); width 6ft 11in (2.108m); height 6ft 10in (2.082m).
Weight: 20,944lbs (9,500kg).
Engine: Scania-Vabis six-cylinder water-cooled petrol engine developing 142hp (see text).
Performance: Road speed 30mph (48km/h); vertical obstacle 2ft (0.609m); trench 5ft 6in (1.676m); gradient 60 per cent.
History: Entered service with Swedish Army in 1940 and phased out of service in 1950s. Some were then exported to Dominica and these remained in service until recently.

The first Swedish tank was completed in 1921 and was known as the *Stridsvagn* m/21. Ten of these were built, and they weighed 9.55 tons (9,700kg), were armed with twin 6.5mm machine-guns (female) or one 37mm gun (male) and were powered by 55hp Daimler engines giving them a road speed of 13mph (21km/h). They were designed by the German tank designer Joseph Vollmer, who had also designed the German A7V, K-*Wagen* and LKI/LKII tanks. In appearance the m/21 owed a lot to the last German design. In 1929 these were fitted with more powerful 85hp engines and then became known under the designation m/21-29. Sweden also purchased some British Carden-Loyd carriers and French Renault NC 27 light tanks. In the late 1920s the Landsverk company was formed, and this concern developed a number of tracked and tracked/wheeled vehicles. Their first tracked vehicle was the L-5, and this was followed by the L-10 (some of which were purchased by the Swedish Army as the m/31), L-30 (wheel/track), L-80 (wheel/track), L-60 (a type not adopted by Swedish Army, but of which some were sold to Eire and others were built under licence in Hungary), L-100 and L-101. Further development of the L-60 resulted in the Strv m/38, which was built for the Swedish Army. This weighed 8.37 tons (8,500kg), had a crew of three and was armed with a 37mm gun and an 8mm machine-gun. The m/38 was followed by the similar m/39, which had a twin rather than a single 8mm machine-gun, but

retained the 37mm gun. The first tank to be built in large numbers for the Swedish Army was the Strv m/40. The first production model was known as the Strv m/40L, and had a 142hp engine. This was followed by the Strv m/40K, which had heavier armour, which increased weight to 10.73 tons (10,900kg), and was powered by a 160hp engine. In 1944 the Strv m/42 entered service. This had a longer chassis than the earlier m/40, and had six rather than four road wheels. It had a crew of four, and was armed with a 75mm gun and twin 8mm co-axial machine-guns. There was also a 8mm machine-gun mounted in the front of the hull. Combat weight was 22.14 tons (22,500kg) and top road speed 28mph (45km/h). Between 1956 and 1958 these were rebuilt with a revised turret armed with a new 75mm gun, and were designated Strv 74H or 74V. These are now being replaced by the Ikv 91 light tank/tank destroyer. There was also a 105mm self-propelled gun called the m/43, which used a hull similar to that of the m/42.

Below: An Strv m/40L light tank (also known as the Strv 33) produced in 1941 for the Swedish Army. Mounting a 37mm gun, it was an improvement on the m/38 tank of 1935. On the m/40L the front glacis ventilator was removed and a door was provided in the centre of the glacis.

155mm BANDKANON 1A SELF-PROPELLED GUN

Self-propelled gun
Crew: 6.
Armament: One 155mm gun; one 7.62mm anti-aircraft machine-gun.
Armour: 20mm (0.79in) maximum.
Dimensions: Length (overall) 36ft 1in (11m); length (hull) 21ft 6in (6.55m); width 11ft 1in (3.37m); height (with anti-aircraft MG) 12ft 8in (3.85m).
Weight: Combat 116,850lbs (53,000kg).
Ground pressure: 12lb/in² (0.85kg/cm²).
Engines: One Rolls-Royce K.60 diesel developing 240hp at 3,750rpm, and one Boeing Model 502/10MA gas turbine developing 300shp at 38,000rpm.
Performance: Road speed 17mph (28km/h); range 143 miles (230km); vertical obstacle 3ft 2in (0.95m); trench 6ft 7in (2m); gradient 60 per cent.
History: Entered service with Swedish Army in 1963, production being completed 1964. Still in service.

The *Bandkanon* 1A, or VK-155 as it is also known, is one of the heaviest self-propelled guns in service anywhere in the world. The prototype was built by the famous Bofors Ordnance Company in 1960, but the type was not produced in large numbers, staying in production for only two years. The VK-155 shares many automotive components with the S-Tank, for example the power pack, which was also designed and built by Bofors. The driver is seated in the front part of the hull whilst the other five crew members (commander, gun-layer, radio operator, loader and anti-aircraft gunner) are seated in the large turret. The 155mm gun has an elevation of +40° and a depression of −3°, and traverse is 15° left and 15° right. Elevation and traverse are both powered, but manual controls are provided for use in an emergency. The gun is fed from a magazine which holds 14 rounds in two layers of seven rounds, allowing the weapon to achieve a high rate of fire – a complete magazine in one minute. Once the magazine is empty a full magazine is brought up by a truck and loaded in place of the empty magazine, which takes about two minutes. The 155mm gun fires its HE round to a maximum range of 23,410 yards (25,600m). As soon as the weapon has fired the required number of rounds it would normally move to a new fire position before the enemy could pinpoint its exact position and return fire. A 7.62mm machine-gun is mounted on the left side of the turret, and can be used against both ground and air targets. The chassis

has six road wheels, with the drive sprocket at the front. The suspension, which is of the hydro-pneumatic type, is locked in position when the gun is fired, thus providing a more stable firing platform. Although a unique gun, the VK-155 has a number of drawbacks. It is very heavy, rather slow and difficult to move across some bridges and roads. It is not possible to change types of ammunition quickly. For example, a forward observer may ask for five rounds of HE on a target, followed by smoke rounds. But unless the magazine has a smoke round it at that time it would not be able to comply. Moreover, unlike most other Swedish AFVs, for example the S-Tank, the Pbv.302

APC and the Ikv.91 tank destroyer, the VK-155 has no amphibious capability at all. Sweden is not going to build any more self-propelled guns of this type, and instead has designed a new towed weapon, the 155mm FH77, now in production at Bofors.

Right: A view of the 155mm Bandkanon 1A SPG, showing the gun's unusual automatic reloading system and 14-round magazine.

Below: Side view of the 155mm Bandkanon 1A which can fire its full 14-round magazine in 60 seconds, ranging up to 25,600m.

STRIDSVAGN Strv. m/41 LIGHT TANK

Strv 41 SI and SII, Strv m/43 SPG, and Pbv 301.
Crew: 3.
Armament: One 37mm gun; one 8mm machine-gun co-axial with main armament; one 8mm machine-gun in hull front.
Armour: 25mm (1in) maximum.
Dimensions: Length 15ft (4.572m); width 7ft (2.133m); height 7ft 8in (2.336m).
Weight: Combat 23,148lbs (10,500kg).
Engine: Scania-Vabis six-cylinder water-cooled petrol engine developing 145 or 160hp.
Performance: Road speed 26mph (45km/h); range 125 miles (201km); vertical obstacle 2ft 7in (0.787m); trench 6ft 2in (1.879m); gradient 60 per cent.

History: Entered service with the Swedish Army in 1942 and phased out of service in 1950s (see text).

Shortly before World War II, the Swedish Jungner company assembled 50 Czech AN-IV-S (or TNHS) light tanks for the Swedish Army, these being designated Strv m/37. The m/37 weighed 4.43 tons (4,500kg), had a crew of two and was armed with twin 8mm machine-guns. Its 80hp engine gave it a top road speed of 37mph (60km/h). The Swedish Army then placed an order for the Czech TNHP tank, but World War II broke out before these could be delivered. Sweden was able to obtain a licence to build the type in Sweden, however, and 238 were built by Scania Vabis between 1942 and 1944. Two

basic models were built, the SI with a 145hp engine, and the SII with a more powerful 160hp engine. There was also a self-propelled gun model built in 1944, this being known as the *Stormartillerivagn m/43*. The m/43 SPG had a crew of four and was armed with a 105mm gun in a ball-type mount in the front of the superstructure. Loaded weight was 11.8 tons (12,000kg), and a 140hp engine gave the weapon a top road speed of 27mph (43km/h). The m/41 served in the Swedish Army until the 1950s when they were withdrawn from service and rebuilt by Hägglund and Söner to become the *Pansarbandvagn 301* armoured personnel carrier. These were the first full tracked APCs of the Swedish Army but have now been replaced by the Pbv 302 APC.

Above: Side view of the Strv m/42 light tank which entered Swedish service in 1944. In the late 1950s m/42s were rebuilt as the Strv 74H or 74V, which differed in the number of rounds carried for the new 75mm gun and in what type of gearbox was installed.

Right: The m/41 light tank, a licence-built version of the Czechoslovakian-designed TNHP light tank with an improved engine. The m/41s served until the 1950s, when they were rebuilt as Pbv 301 armoured personnel carriers mounting a 20mm cannon. The Pbv 301 was phased out of service with the Swedish Army in 1971.

STRIDSVAGN (S) 103 MAIN BATTLE TANK

Crew: 3.
Armament: One 105mm gun; one 7.62mm machine-gun on commander's cupola; two 7.62mm machine-guns on hull top; eight smoke dischargers.
Armour: Classified.
Dimensions: Length (including armament) 32ft 2in (9.8m); length (hull) 27ft 7in (8.4m); width 11ft 10in (3.6m); height (overall) 8ft 2½in (2.5m).
Weight: Combat 85,980lbs (39,000kg).
Ground pressure: 12.8lb/in² (0.9kg/cm²).
Engines: Rolls-Royce K.60 multi-fuel engine developing 240bhp at 3,650rpm; Boeing 553 gas turbine developing 490shp at 38,000rpm.
Performance: Maximum road speed 31mph (50km/h); water speed 6mph (3.7km/h); range 242 miles (390km); vertical obstacle 2ft 11in (0.9m); trench 7ft 7in (2.3m); gradient 60 per cent.
History: Entered service with the Swedish Army in 1966 and still in service.

Of all the tanks in service today, the 'S' tank is perhaps the most unusual and controversial. Its design dates back to the 1950s and is based on an original idea by Sven Berge of the Swedish Army Ordnance department. The main battle tank of the Swedish Army in the 1960s was to have been a tank called the KPV, armed with a 150mm smooth-bore gun. Two prototypes of this tank were completed by Landsverk, but these were never fitted with their turrets and armament. These, and a number of other tanks including a Sherman and an Ikv-103 assault gun, were then used to test the basic S tank concept. In 1958 Bofors was awarded a full development contract and the first two prototype S tanks were completed in 1961. These were powered by a gas turbine engine and an eight-cylinder petrol engine. Apart from the 105mm gun they had five 7.62mm machine-guns: one on the commander's cupola and two in a box on each side of the hull firing forwards. Their suspension was also different from later models. These were followed by a pre-production batch of 10 tanks. First production tanks were completed in 1966, and 300 were eventually built, the last of them being completed in 1971. The other MBT of the Swedish Army is the British Centurion, of which 350 are in service. These are to be rebuilt in the near future. The S tank (or to give it the correct name, the *Stridsvagen 103*), has a crew of three (commander, driver/gunner and radio operator). The driver is seated on the left, with the radio operator behind him, facing the rear. The commander is on the right of the hull. The radio operator can drive the tank backwards if required, and the commander also has an accelerator and brake pedal. The tank is armed with a 105mm rifled tank gun which is fixed to the hull rather than mounted in a turret as in conventional tanks. This has not only enabled the overall height of the tank to be reduced, but has also allowed an automatic loader to be installed. The 105mm gun is a longer version of the famous British L7 series gun and is made in Sweden. The gun is fed from a magazine which holds 50 rounds of ammunition of five types: Armour-Piercing Discarding Sabot, High-Explosive Squash-Head, Smoke and High Explosive.

The empty cartridge cases are automatically ejected through a hatch in the rear of the hull. The tank can fire between 10 and 15 aimed rounds per minute. Some of the prototypes were fitted with a .5in ranging machine-gun, but production models have an optical range-finder, and a laser rangefinder has now been developed. Two 7.62mm machine-guns are mounted in a box on the left of the hull, firing forwards, and there is a single 7.62mm machine-gun on the commander's cupola. The latter can be aimed and fired from within the vehicle. Some 2,750 rounds of 7.62mm machine-gun ammunition are carried. Eight smoke dischargers are provided, and some S tanks have been fitted with Bofors Lyran flare launchers so that they can engage targets at night. The suspension is of the hydro-pneumatic type, and consists of four road wheels (these are the same as those fitted to the Centurion tank), with the drive sprocket at the front and the idler at the rear, there being two track-return rollers. The gun is laid in elevation by the driver, who can adjust the suspension so that the gun can be elevated to +12° and depressed to −10°. It is aimed in traverse by slewing the tank in its tracks. When the gun is fired, the suspension is locked so as to provide a more stable firing platform. Another unusual feature of the tank is its powerpack, which is mounted in the forward part of the hull. This consists of two engines, a diesel and gas turbine. The diesel is the Rolls-Royce K.60, which is also used in the British FV432 APC and FV433 Abbot self-propelled gun, whilst the gas turbine is of American design but built in Belgium by FN. For normal operations the diesel is used, but in combat, or crossing very rough country, the gas turbine is also used. The first production models of the S tank (these were designated Strv.103As) were not

Above: This head on view of the Bofors S tank clearly shows the 105mm gun which is fixed in the front of the hull. On the right side of the hull can be seen the two 7.62mm machine guns which, like the main armament, are operated by the driver/gunner. This tank, and the British Centurion, are the mainstays of the Swedish armoured forces. A new MBT is now being developed.

fitted with flotation screens, but these are standard on the Strv.103Bs, and all earlier tanks have now been refitted with them. The screen is carried collapsed around the top of the hull and takes about 15 minutes to erect. The tank is propelled in the water by its tracks. There are many lakes and rivers in sweden too deep for schnorkel crossing, so the only practical solution was the fitting of the flotation screen. The tank is provided with infra-red driving lights but does not have an infra-red searchlight. A dozer blade is mounted at the front of the hull for the preparation of fire positions. The S tank has a very low silhouette compared with other main battle tanks, and its glacis plate is well sloped, giving the maximum amount of protection available. The S tank has been tested by a number of other countries including Great Britain and the United States, but no other country has yet produced a similar vehicle, although the Germans were reported several years ago to have constructed a tank like the S tank armed with twin 105mm guns. There are no variants of the S tank although components of the tank are used in the VK 155 self-propelled gun built by Bofors a few years ago, as well as the Bofors 40mm self-propelled anti-aircraft gun, development of which was stopped some years ago.

Above: A camouflaged S tank on exercise. The design for a turretless tank with its main armament mounted on the centre line of the hull was initiated in 1956; the S tank entered service just ten years later.

Left: Strv. 103Bs in support of infantry. The main armament, automatically loaded from a 50-round magazine, is a longer-tubed Swedish modification of the British 105mm gun. Spent shells are automatically ejected at the rear of the hull.

Right: This view of the S tank clearly shows the dozer blade mounted under the hull front. It is lowered and locked into position before use in clearing away obstacles or digging a firing position.

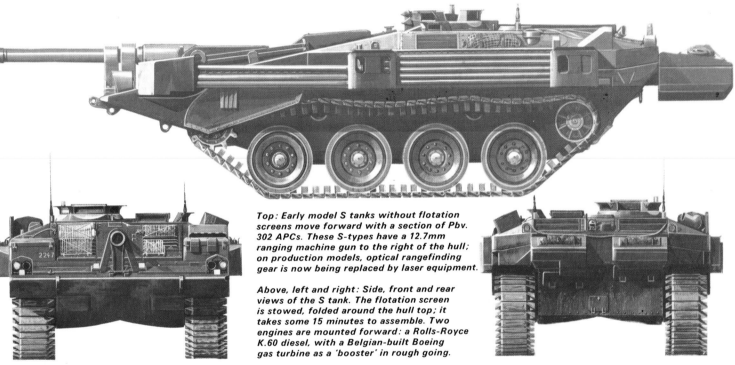

Top: Early model S tanks without flotation screens move forward with a section of Pbv. 302 APCs. These S-types have a 12.7mm ranging machine gun to the right of the hull; on production models, optical rangefinding gear is now being replaced by laser equipment.

Above, left and right: Side, front and rear views of the S tank. The flotation screen is stowed, folded around the hull top; it takes some 15 minutes to assemble. Two engines are mounted forward: a Rolls-Royce K.60 diesel, with a Belgian-built Boeing gas turbine as a 'booster' in rough going.

PANSERBANDVAGN Pbv.302 APC

Crew: 2 plus 10.
Armament: One 20mm cannon.
Armour: 20mm (0.79in) maximum.
Dimensions: Length 17ft 7in (5.35m); width 9ft 5in (2.86m); height 8ft 2in (2.5m).
Weight: Combat 29,760lbs (13,500kg).
Ground pressure: 8.5lb/in² (0.6kg/cm²).
Engine: Volvo-Penta Model THD 100B six-cylinder turbocharged diesel developing 280bhp at 2,200rpm.
Performance: Road speed 41mph (66km/h); water speed 5mph (8km/h); range 186 miles (300km); vertical obstacle 2ft (0.61m); trench 5ft 11in (1.8m); gradient 60 per cent.
History: Entered service with Swedish Army in 1966, and still in service.

The Pbv.301 was the first tracked APC to be used by the Swedish Army. The vehicle was essentially the chassis of the Czech-derived m/41 light tank (built in the early part of World War II) fitted with a new hull designed by Hägglund. In 1961, the Swedish Army issued a requirement for a new APC and the firm of Hägglund and Soner of Örnsköldsvik was awarded a contract to design and build prototypes. The first of these was completed in 1963, with first production vehicles following in 1966; production continued until 1971. The Pbv.302 (*Pansarbandvagn* 302) operates in conjunction with the S-Tank as part of the tank/infantry team. The Pbv.302 has a hull of all-welded steel construction sufficient to protect the crew from small arms fire. The driver is seated at the front of the vehicle, in the centre, with the gunner on his left and the commander on his right. The infantry are seated at the rear of the hull and enter and leave the vehicle via twin doors in the rear of the hull. Over the troop compartment are two double hatches, one on each side. These enable the crew to use their small arms from within the vehicle. The vehicle is armed with a turret-mounted 20mm cannon, which has an elevation of +50° and a depression of –10°, traverse being a full 360°. A total of 505 rounds of HE and AP ammunition is carried. In addition, smoke dischargers are fitted. Like most modern APCs the Pbv.302 is fully amphibious, being propelled in the water by its tracks. A trim vane is erected at the front of the hull before the vehicle enters the water (to stop water splashing over the front of the hull). Bilge pumps are also provided. The Volvo engine is mounted in the forward part of the hull under the driver's position, and is coupled to the clutch, gearbox, steering clutch, drive shaft, steering brake and thence to the final drive and drive sprocket. The suspension is of the torsion-bar type and consists of five road wheels with the idler at the rear and the drive sprocket at the front. The Pbv.302 can be quickly adapted for use as an ambulance, cargo carrier or recovery vehicle. Specialised versions of the vehicle have also been developed; these include an armoured command vehicle with additional radios, an armoured

observation post vehicle with a new turret incorporating an optical rangefinder for measuring target ranges, and an armoured fire direction post vehicle with additional radios, a fire control computer and a ranging section of seven men. The Pbv.302 is also the basis for a whole family of vehicles for the Swedish Army, including the Ikv.91 tank-destroyer, Bgbv.82 armoured recovery vehicle and Brobv.941 bridgelaying vehicle. This has enabled the Swedish Army to deploy a range of vehicles which share many common components, thus facilitating training and stores support.

Above: The Pbv.302 is the standard APC of the Swedish Army. Designed and built by Hägglund and Söner, it was in production in 1966-71. It is fully amphibious, propelled in the water by its tracks at 8km/h. Before swimming, a trim vane is erected at the bow to stop water splashing into the hull. The Pbv.302 has a crew of 2 and can carry 10 fully-equipped infantrymen. Infra-red driving lights are fitted, but the vehicle has no NBC system.

Above: Side and front views of the Pbv.302 APC. Armament consists of a turret-mounted Type 804 20mm cannon with a cyclic rate of fire of 500 rounds per minute, for which 505 rounds of HE and AP ammunition are carried. The cannon has an elevation of +50° and a depression of –10°. A x8 magnification sight is fitted for engaging ground targets; there is also an AA sight.

Left: An important feature of the Pbv.302 is that double hatches over the roof of the fighting compartment allow its occupants to fire their small-arms from within the vehicle with some degree of protection from return fire. Variants include a command vehicle (Stripbv.3021), observation vehicle (Epbv.3022), and a fire control vehicle with computer and extra radios.

Pz 68 MAIN BATTLE TANK

Pz 58, Pz 61, Pz 68, Pz 68 AA2, ARV, SPG and bridgelayer.
Crew: 4.
Armament: One 105mm gun; one 7.5mm machine-gun co-axial with main armament; one 7.5mm anti-aircraft machine-gun; three smoke dischargers on each side of turret.
Armour: 60mm (2.36in) maximum.
Dimensions: Length (including main armament) 31ft 1½in (9.49m); length (hull only) 22ft 8in (6.9m); width 10ft 3½in (3.14m); height (overall) 9ft (2.75m).
Weight: Combat 87,523lbs (39,700kg).
Ground Pressure: 12.23lb/in² (0.86kg/cm²).
Engine: MTU MB 837 eight-cylinder diesel developing 704hp at 2,200rpm.
Performance: Maximum road speed 34mph (55km/h); road range 186 miles (300km); vertical obstacle 2ft 6in (0.75m); trench 8ft 6in (2.6m); gradient 60 per cent.
History: Entered service with the Swiss Army in 1971 and still in service.

Shortly after the end of World War I, the Swiss purchased two Renault FT-17 light tanks for trials. These were followed in 1934 by four British Carden-Loyd tankettes. Just before World War II, Switzerland ordered some Czech CTH light tanks, to be assembled in Switzerland and fitted with Swiss armament and engines. By the time Czechoslovakia was overrun by the Germans only 24 tanks were in service with the Swiss Army under the designation Pz 39. In 1944 the Swiss built the prototype of a self-propelled anti-tank gun called the NKI, this being followed in 1945 by the NKII assault gun. Neither of these vehicles entered production. Between 1947 and 1952 158 *Jagdpanzer 38 (t)* anti-tank guns were obtained from Czechoslovakia, and these remained in service until quite recently. Other post-war purchases included 200 AMX-13 light tanks and 300 Centurion MBTs, all of which are still in service today. In the early 1950s design work started on a Swiss main battle tank, and the first prototype, the Pz 58, was completed in 1958. Main armament consisted of a Swiss 90mm gun. The second prototype was completed the following year, and this was armed with a British 20pounder gun. Between 1960 and 1961 a further 10 pre-production tanks were built, and these were armed with the British 105mm L7 tank gun. These tanks were known under the designation Pz 61, and 150 examples were built between 1964 and 1966 at the Federal Engineering Works at Thun. The main armament consisted of a 105mm gun built under licence in Switzerland; a 20mm Oerlikon cannon was mounted to the left of the main armament and a 7.5mm machine-gun was fitted on the loader's hatch for anti-aircraft defence. In most Western tanks the latter machine-gun is on the commander's hatch, but the Swiss decided, quite rightly, that the role of the commander is to command, not to operate machine-

Above: A Swiss Entpannungspanzer 65 ARV changing an engine on another ARV. The vehicle on the right uses its hydraulically operated dozer blade as stabilizer.

guns! Some 52 rounds of 105mm, 240 rounds of 20mm and 3,000 rounds of 7.5mm ammunition are carried. Between 1971 and 1973 170 of an improved model, the Pz 68, were built. The Pz 68 has an improved fire-control system and the main armament is stabilised in both the horizontal and vertical planes. The tank also has a slightly more powerful engine and a modified gearbox. The hull of the Pz 68 is of cast construction, as is the turret. The driver is seated in the front of the hull and the other three crew members in the turret, the commander and gunner on the right and the loader on the left. The engine, which is imported from Germany, is at the rear of the hull, as is the Swiss transmission. The suspension consists of six road wheels, with the drive sprocket at the rear and the idler at the front. There are three return rollers. Each of the road wheels is independently located and sprung by layers of Belleville washers. The Germans had a similar system towards the end of World War II, but the Pz 61/Pz 68 is the first tank with this suspension to be built in quantity. The main armament is a 105mm gun with an elevation of +21° and a depression of −10°; a 7.5mm machine-gun is mounted co-axially with the main armament and there is a similar machine-gun on the loader's hatch for anti-aircraft defence. Some 52 rounds of 105mm and 7,500 rounds of 7.5mm ammunition are carried. The tank is provided with an NBC system and infra-red driving lights, but

no infra-red searchlight is provided to enable the tank to engage targets at night. The Pz 68 can ford streams to a maximum depth of 3ft 8in (1.1m). Currently undergoing development is the Pz 68 AA2, of which 110 are to be built for the Swiss Army over the next few years. This has many improvements over the earlier model including a thermal sleeve for the main armament, and improved NBC and FC systems. There are a number of variants of the Pz 61 and Pz 68 in service with the Swiss Army. The armoured recovery vehicle is known as the *Entpannungspanzer* 65 and weighs 38.38 tons (39,000kg). This is provided with a dozer blade at the front of the hull, an 'A' frame which can lift a maximum of 14.76 tons (15,000kg) and two winches. The main winch has a capacity of 24.6 tons (25,000kg) and the secondary winch has a capacity of 0.49 tons (500kg). This model has a crew of five and is armed with a single 7.5mm machine-gun and smoke dischargers. The bridgelayer is known as the *Brückenpanzer* 68: this is provided with a one-piece aluminium bridge 59ft 10in (18.23m) in length taking about two minutes to lay and five minutes to retract. A prototype of a self-propelled gun called the *Panzer-Kanone* 68 was built in the early 1970s. This is essentially a Pz 68 chassis fitted with a new turret mounting a 155mm Swiss gun, which has a range of 18.6 miles (30km). A 7.5mm machine-gun is mounted on the roof for anti-aircraft defence and smoke dischargers are also provided.

Below: A Pz 61 battle tank of the Swiss Army. In 1964-66, 170 of these were built at the Federal Engineering Works, Thun. The improved Pz 68 AA2 is now in production.

United States of America

In World War I the United States Army received a good deal of equipment from the French, and with it came some of the tactical thinking. Thus, in the early 1920s the American army followed very much the same approach to armoured warfare as did the French and British; there were light tanks for reconnaissance and heavy, slow moving tanks for immediate infantry support in the assault. The light tanks were versions of the French Renault, the heavy tanks were Mark VIII rhomboids. These ideas persisted throughout the lean years of the 1920s and early 1930s with only one ray of light breaking through. The cavalry in their manoeuvres with the light tanks soon discovered that the ideal armoured force was a combined arms team with elements from all arms. They were given little encouragement in this philosophy, but the notion took root and flowered later.

American observers came to watch the British armoured experiments in the late 1920s and early 1930s, and took away the idea of the independent armoured force acting in support of, but not tied to, the infantry formations. However, little was done actually to implement these ideas, and despite the obvious need for greater mobility and higher power-weight ratios in all armoured vehicles, the teachings of Christie were completely ignored, and he was forced to offer his inventions outside the USA. Reluctantly, a few new designs were drawn up in the late 1930s, but the firm intention not to get involved in a European conflict prevented anything being done to build any new vehicles.

The urgent need to rearm was only clearly seen in 1940 and, without further revision, some unsuitable designs were put into production. Even then the full impact of the German use of armour was not appreciated, until General Chaffee began to point it out in clear and positive terms. He was the man who put the US armoured force on the right footing to go to war, and the lesson he rammed home was that of the combined arms team. He was justified in Tunisia and later in Sicily, where the value of firepower and mobility were also amply demonstrated. The pity was that the protection afforded by the US tanks was only just adequate, and later in the war it was less than adequate.

But the great lesson that the US taught the world in World War II was that successful tanks are ones that are easy to maintain and are reliable in action. The M4 Sherman may have lacked many battle qualities, but it was very straightforward and relatively simple for its crew to manage. Training was uncomplicated, a big factor in war, and what it lost in effectiveness was more than made up in sheer numbers. It has survived until the present

day, largely because of these features.

Korea repeated the need for firepower and mobility, but gave the latter a new dimension by emphasising the requirement for armour to be able to operate in all types of terrain, and this has been seen in the later US tank designs where agility and cross-country mobility have been given much attention. Vietnam came as a complete antithesis to the teachings of Korea, and was seen as an infantry jungle war and nothing else. The war had been going for three or four years before it was seen how effective armour could be when it was properly used, and from then on there was an increasing employment of light armoured forces, though in a slightly different way from that in Europe. Armoured personnel carriers with extra protection and extra armament were highly effective against the VietCong, who were unable to make any great impression on them with their simple weapons. By using tracks and paths well away from recognised routes the armoured columns were able to outflank the opposition and brush away any ambushes hurriedly laid on the approach march. It was not the traditional way to use an armoured force but it was an effective and sensible way, and it used all the old principles of the employment of combined arms teams, together with surprise, mobility and shock.

The current US armoured force is modelled much on the lines of the remainder of NATO. The forces committed to NATO are heavily armoured with substantial numbers of tanks (slightly elderly tanks at the moment), backed up with a comprehensive support organisation, and all operating as fully integrated combined arms teams at all levels. There is almost complete mechanisation throughout the formations, and the firepower of the whole force is considerable, with the ultimate provision of tactical nuclear weapons.

An allied Sherman tank being unloaded from an American LCT (Landing Craft Tank) on to a Rhino ferry during the invasion of Europe.

MARK VIII (LIBERTY) INTERNATIONAL HEAVY TANK

Heavy (Infantry) tank ('Liberty Tank', also known as the 'International').
Crew: 10–12.
Armament: Two 6pounder QF guns of naval origin in sponson mounts, one per side; up to seven Browning .3in machine-guns in armoured mounts.
Armour: 6mm to 16mm.
Dimensions: Length 34ft 2in (10.4m); width 12ft 6in (3.81m); height 10ft 3in (3.12m).
Weight: Combat 37–44 tons (37,594–44,707kg).
Ground Pressure: approximately 5.2lb/in² 0.37 kg/cm².
Power to weight ratio: Approximately 9hp/ton.
Engine: Liberty V-12 water-cooled inline aircraft engine developing 338hp at 1,400rpm.
Performance: Road speed 6.5mph (10.4km/h); road range 50 miles (80km); vertical obstacle 4ft 3in (1.3m); trench 14ft (4.3m); gradient climbing ability stated to be 'good'.
History: Entered service with US Army in 1920. Never used in action, but surplus US Army vehicles used by Canada for training in 1940.

In 1916 General John J. Pershing detailed an officer to plan a Tank Corps for the US Army. This officer, Major James Drain, was sent to London where he discussed his task with Lieutenant-Colonel Albert Stern, who had been appointed Secretary to the Royal Naval Air Service Landships Committee. (It is interesting to note the tri-service flavour of this pioneer committee!) A provisional order for 600 Mark VI tanks was placed, but in September 1917 Major Drain recommended that the British Mark VIII, then in the design stage, be substituted. In those early days the attractions of Allied standardisation were apparent and a proposal was made to use British expertise combined with American production capability. A draft tripartite agreement was submitted to Winston Churchill, then Minister of Munitions, on 11 November 1917. The agreement provided, *inter alia*, for a programme to design and build a new tank incorporating British experience and American resources, and to assemble the tank in a new factory in France. Churchill approved the proposal in December and early in 1918 the Anglo-American Tank Treaty was signed in London by Arthur Balfour, the British Foreign Secretary, and Walter Page, the United States Ambassador. Design of the tank was undertaken by the Mechanical Warfare Supply Department of the Ministry of Munitions, Lieutenant G. J. Rackham being responsible for the design drawings. The British contribution was to be the armour plate, structural members, track shoes and rollers, and armament. The United States was to provide the automotive components, whilst France would provide the facilities for the new assembly plant, which would be built with construction equipment from the United Kingdom. The first design conference held by the Allied Tank Commission took place in France on 4 December 1917 and

it was anticipated that initial production would be about 300 tanks per month, later increasing to 1,200 per month. The high ideals expressed by the Anglo-American Tank Treaty were unfortunately overtaken by events. The German offensive of March 1918 exacted a heavy toll of British *matériel*, and the failure of the American aircraft programme prevented the diversion of Liberty engines to tank production. Thus by the time of the Armistice in November 1918 only 100 sets of components had been produced in Great Britain, whilst the United States had completed enough parts for half of the initial production of 2,950. The French withdrew from the project a week after the Armistice and British involvement had to all intents and purposes lapsed after the losses in March 1918, so it was left to the United States to assemble 100 tanks at Rock Island Arsenal in 1919 from parts purchased from Britain. These tanks served the US Army until 1932, when they were withdrawn and stored. In 1940 about 90 were provided at scrap value to Canada, where they formed the basis of General Worthington's Tank Corps. The Mark VIII had the familiar lozenge shape of the tanks of World War I and was intended from the outset to be capable of crossing a 14ft (4.3m) trench. The hull was of rivet face-hardened armour, .875in (22.2225mm) thick on the front and sides but somewhat less elsewhere on the vehicle. Incorporated for the first time was a bulkhead to seal off the engine room at the rear from the fighting compartment. This latter was provided with a positive overpressure to expel fumes, and reduced heat and noise as well as the risk of fire, and was the first real attempt to apply 'Human Factors Engineering' to a tank. Unfortunately it was still necessary for an engineer-mechanic to travel in the engine compartment and his discomfort was doubtless heightened by this innovation. The Mark VIII used a steering system devised by Major W. G. Wilson in probably the first practical application of the geared steering system, in which power is divided between tracks, rather than merely disconnected, when steering. Engine cooling was a problem in the Mark VIII, and this deficiency meant that the tank could not sustain its maximum speed for long periods, much to the relief of the mechanic in the engine room. As late as 1929 attempts were being made to improve the engine cooling. Although it never saw action, the Mark VIII is significant as the first collaborative venture. But for the Armistice, production of the Mark VIII in 1919 would have outstripped all other Allied tank production to date.

Below: The only surviving British-built Mk VIII tank, now on permanent display at the Royal Armoured Corps Tank Museum, Bovington Camp, Wareham, Dorset.

Below: Side and top views of the Mk VIII tank, which had a crew of 10-12 men and was armed with two 6-pounder QF naval guns and up to seven Browning .30in machine-guns Each US-manufactured tank cost $85,000 to build in 1918-1919.

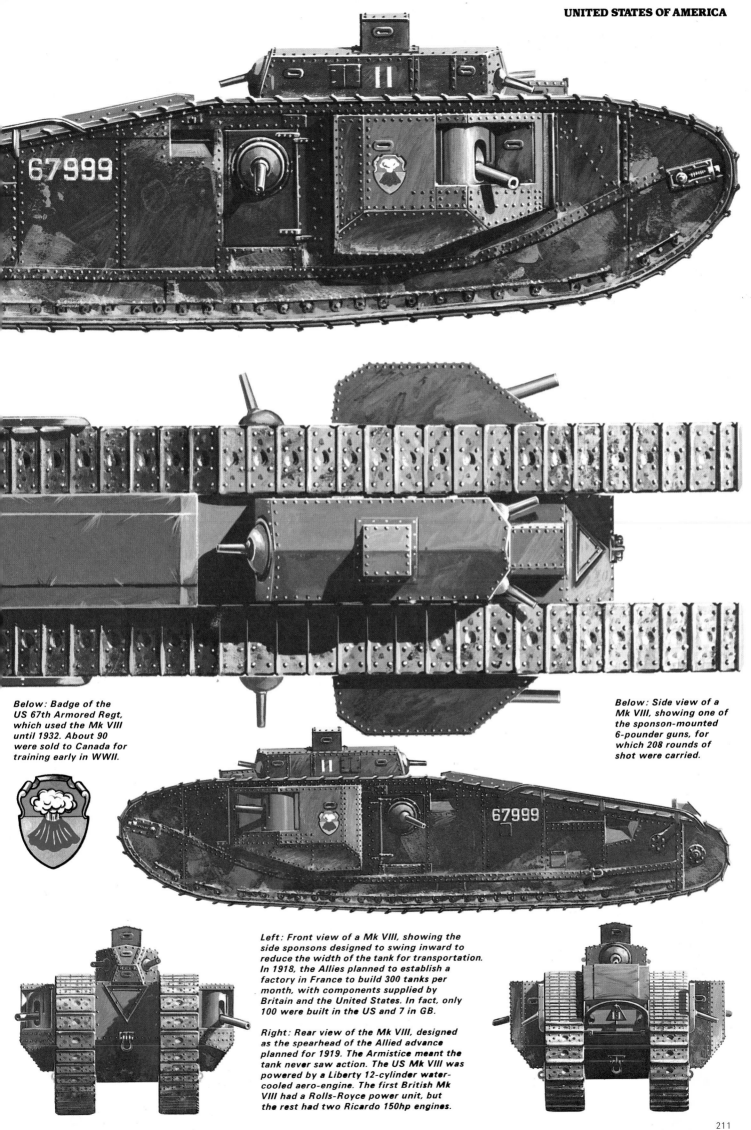

Below: Badge of the US 67th Armored Regt, which used the Mk VIII until 1932. About 90 were sold to Canada for training early in WWII.

Below: Side view of a Mk VIII, showing one of the sponson-mounted 6-pounder guns, for which 208 rounds of shot were carried.

Left: Front view of a Mk VIII, showing the side sponsons designed to swing inward to reduce the width of the tank for transportation. In 1918, the Allies planned to establish a factory in France to build 300 tanks per month, with components supplied by Britain and the United States. In fact, only 100 were built in the US and 7 in GB.

Right: Rear view of the Mk VIII, designed as the spearhead of the Allied advance planned for 1919. The Armistice meant the tank never saw action. The US Mk VIII was powered by a Liberty 12-cylinder water-cooled aero-engine. The first British Mk VIII had a Rolls-Royce power unit, but the rest had two Ricardo 150hp engines.

211

T3 CHRISTIE MEDIUM TANK

M1919, M1921, M1928, T3 M1931, Combat Car T1, T3E1 and BT-1.

Crew: 3.

Armament: One 37mm gun; one .3in machine-gun mounted co-axial with main armament; one .3in machine-gun in each side of turret; one .3in machine-gun in hull.

Armour: 16mm (0.625in) maximum; 12.7mm (.5in) minimum.

Dimensions: Length 19ft 1in (5.82m); width 8ft 1in (2.46m); height 7ft 7in (2.31m).

Weight: Combat 24,200lbs (10,977kg).

Ground pressure: 9.96lb/in² (0.7kg/cm²).

Power to weight ratio: 31.3hp/ton.

Engine: Ordnance Liberty 12-cylinder water-cooled petrol engine developing 338hp at 1,400rpm.

Performance: Road speed (wheels) 46mph (74km/h); road speed (tracks) 27mph (43km/h); vertical obstacle 3ft (0.9m); trench 8ft 3in (2.5m); gradient 42 per cent.

History: Small number used by US Army in 1930s. Christie's emphasis on speed differed from US Army's preference for reliability and official interest waned accordingly. Precursor of British Cruiser and Soviet T-34 series.

Although J. Walter Christie gave his name to a form of suspension which greatly influenced tank development in the 1930s and 1940s, his first designs gave little indication of such promise. An enterprising engineer, he had first set up a company to motorise horse-drawn fire engines and proceeded from there to motorise gun carriages for the US Army. He was attracted by the possibilities of the newly-publicised tank, and produced a design of his own which was tested by the US Army as the M1919. While his self-propelled gun carriages had been successful, the tank was hastily conceived and constructed and did not perform well as it was seriously underpowered. In its favour it must be pointed out that the M1919 showed considerable ingenuity and originality, drawing little from the first designs produced in Europe. Although it did not feature all-round traverse of its armament, the gun was mounted in a barbette which allowed good visibility, and the trackwork incorporated a form of springing. Christie's next design, the M1921, remedied some of the shortcomings of the M1919 and resembled even more the conventional modern turreted tank despite the fact that it still did not have a traversing turret. Nonetheless, Christie's bread and butter came from his self-propelled artillery designs, of which there were several in the early 1920s. He also investigated amphibious tanks with a certain degree of success but was unable to interest the US authorities in his designs. The breakthrough came in 1928 when the first 'Christie Tank' appeared. The classic Christie suspension con-

sisted of four big road wheels mounted on large coil springs and tracks consisting of large plates. The tracks could be removed, allowing the vehicle to run on its road wheels. Extremely high speeds were achieved on roads, a figure of 70mph (113km/h) being quoted, and even on rough terrain a speed of 30mph (48km/h) was claimed. A demonstration of the M1928 to the US Army resulted in an order for five examples to be known as the T3 Medium Tank, and Christie set up the US Wheel and Tracklayer Corporation to produce these. The T3, or M1931, was constructed of face-hardened armour of .5in (12.7mm) thickness and had four large, rubber-tired road wheels of 27in (68.6cm) diameter on each side. These were mounted on swinging arms and supported by long coil springs in compression, which allowed a wheel travel of 16in (40.65cm). Thus each wheel could be raised until the tire was level with the hull floor, and this feature allowed the suspension to conform with very uneven terrain. The tracks were steel plates approximately 10in² (645cm²), and a disadvantage of Christie's system was the large angular movement required of such large track plates, resulting in heavy wear. Another disadvantage was the reduction in available space in the hull because the suspension springs were enclosed by the side plates. Two men could remove the tracks in 30 minutes to

prepare the vehicle for road running – in this mode the two front wheels could be steered and the two middle pairs were raised. The engine was essentially the Liberty engine of the Mark VIII tank. Even in its standard state, the T3 was overpowered. With the Liberty engine 'tweaked' by Christie to develop 387hp, the power was excessive and resulted in an intolerably high oil consumption. The hull was well shaped ballistically, with the coil springs for the front wheels anchored at a common mounting inside the pointed nose of the hull – another Christie characteristic. The turret mounted a short-barrelled 37mm gun with 360° traverse and was advanced for its time, presenting few shot traps. The US Wheel and Tracklayer Corporation built nine examples of the M1931 design, of which five were the T3 (in fact three of these were for the cavalry and were designated Combat Car T1 to conform with the 1920 National Defense Act), two were for the Polish Army and were taken into US Army service as the T3E1, and two were sold to the Soviet Union, where they became BT-1s and led to the development of the T-34. Christie was a volatile character and was apt to offend his customers by continually improving his design, thus delaying delivery. This tendency to apply his own interpretation to contracts, and to refine his product at the client's

Above right: Front view of the Christie T3.

Right: Front, side, top and rear views of a Christie T3 'Tornado' of the US 67th Infantry (Tanks) Regiment.

expense and delay meant that when in 1932 the US Army required a further five T3 tanks the contract was let to the American La France and Foamite Company, and Christie built no further vehicles for the US Army. Christie's inventive and impetuous approach is well illustrated by the fact that in 1930, in the middle of developing his M1931, he was proposing to the US Army a plan to modernise its Renault M1918 light tanks by converting them to steam propulsion. His idea, using Christie suspension and rubber tracks, envisaged a road speed of some 85mph (137km/h). Nothing further was heard of this project. In 1936 one example of the M1931 was bought and tested by the British Army. While the vehicle performed satisfactorily it did not conform with current British thinking. It was instead used as the basis of the A13E2 cruiser tank. Poland, despite having defaulted on her contract for two M1931s, copied Christie's design in the 10TP and 14TP tanks. Christie's preoccupation with speed led to both his success and his failure. On the one hand his suspension allowed improved mobility and was exploited by both Britain and the Soviet Union; on the other hand the poor reliability did not impress the US Army, and the renowned reliability of the M3 and M4 series tanks was probably of more value in World War II than high speed and minimal protection.

Above right: T3 'Hurricane'. The T3s were used largely in a tactical training role while in service in the 1930s.

Below: The three T3s that went into service with the US 67th Regiment: the 'Tornado', the 'Hurricane' and the 'Cyclone'.

Left: Side view of the 'Tornado' with its tracks in the stowed position, showing the chain drive from the sprocket to the rear road wheel. Several countries, notably the USSR, experimented with wheeled/tracked vehicles in the inter-war years.

M3 LIGHT TANK

M3, M3A1, M3A2 and M3A3.
Crew: 4.
Armament: One 37mm M5 or M6 gun; one .3in M1919A4 machine-gun co-axial with main armament; two .3in machine-guns in hull sponsons; one .3in machine-gun on turret roof.
Armour: 44.5mm (1.75in) maximum; 10mm (0.375in) minimum.
Dimensions: Length 14ft 10½in (4.53m); width 7ft 4in (2.23m); height 8ft 3in (2.51m).
Weight: Combat 27,400lbs (12,428kg).
Ground pressure: 10.5lb/in² (0.74kg/cm²).
Power to weight ratio: 20.4hp/ton.
Engine: Continental W-670 seven-cylinder air-cooled radial petrol engine developing 250hp at 2,400rpm.
Performance: Road speed 36mph (58km/h); cross-country speed 20mph (32km/h); road range 70 miles (112km); vertical obstacle 2ft (0.6m); trench 6ft (1.8m); fording depth 3ft (0.9m); gradient 60 per cent.
History: Entered service with US Army in 1941. Also widely used by British and other Allied armies during World War II.

The standard US light tank in June 1940 was the M2A4, standardised in 1939 and the culmination of a development which began with the M2A1 in 1935. The M2A4 weighed some 12 tons (12,193kg), had a 37mm turret-mounted gun and was constructed from riveted armour plate. Increasing the thickness of the armour of the M2A4 called for the use of a trailing idler in the suspension system. This, with improved protection from aircraft attack, led to the standardisation of the type as the M3 light tank in July 1940. The Continental seven-cylinder radial engine of 250hp had been inherited from the M2A4, but in 1941 shortages of this engine meant that the Guiberson T-1020 diesel engine was authorised for 500 M3 light tanks. Additional fuel capacity in the form of two external fuel tanks, which could be jettisoned, was provided as a result of battle experience in British hands in North Africa. The M3 was produced in quantity by the American Car and Foundry Company, 5,811 having been built by August 1942. The M3A1 light tank incorporated an improved turret of welded homogeneous plate (as opposed to the earlier brittle, face-hardened armour) with power traverse, a gyrostabiliser to permit more accurate firing of the 37mm gun on the move, and a turret basket. The M3A1 was standardised

in August 1941 and used the hull of the M3, which was still constructed from riveted plate. A pilot with both hull and turret formed of welded armour, the M3A1E1, led eventually to the M5 light tank. The next model, the M3A2, was also to be of welded construction but similar to the M3A1 in all other respects. The M3A2 was not built, but American Car and Foundry produced 4,621 of the M3A1, of which 211 were diesel-engined. The M3A3 was a much more comprehensive redesign and included changes in the turret, hull and sponsons, and it was considered worthwhile to continue producing the M3A3 even after the production line for its successor, the M5, was established. Some 3,427 M3A3s were built. There were several experimental models of the M3 series, mostly involving different automotive installations. In British service the M3 provided a much-needed addition to the tank strength in the Western Desert in 1941 and 1942. It subsequently appeared in all theatres of World War II, but is chiefly remembered for its service in the Desert, with the empire forces in Burma, in the capture of Antwerp, and with the American forces in the Pacific. It was undergunned and poorly armoured but mobile and reliable, and was affectionately known as the 'Honey' by

Left: The M2 light tank which led to the development of the M3. A particular comparison point is the rear idlerwheel, which is at the top on the M2 and at the bottom on the M3 (see below).

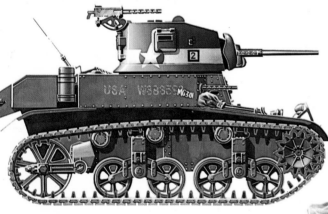

Left: An M3AI of the United StatesMarine Corps on Guadalcanal Island in the Solomons; September 1942.

Bottom: Side and rear views of a Stuart Mk I light tank of the 8th (King's Royal Irish) Hussars, at the battle of Sidi Rezegh; November 1941.

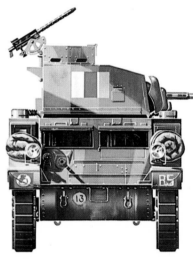

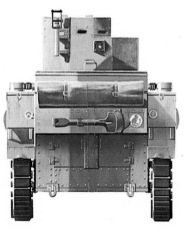

M1 COMBAT CAR

British cavalry regiments. Indeed, many units preferred it to the Daimler armoured car in the reconnaissance role. The M3 was the most widely used light tank of World War II and was built in larger numbers than its two successors, the M5 and M24. A total of 13,859 had been produced by October 1943, even though the type had been declared obsolete in July of that year. Although it was fast and had good ground-crossing ability for the 'cavalry' scouting role for which it was intended, the M3 had little scope for development or adaptation. The hull was too narrow, effectively limiting the size of the main armament to below the required 75mm, and it was too high and angular, offering a high silhouette and many shot traps. It did lead directly to the M5 light tank, however, and its history continued under that heading.

Below and below left: Front and top views of a Stuart Mk I of the 8th (King's Royal Irish) Hussars. This regiment formed part of the 4th Armoured Brigade, 7th Armoured Division, which had the famous "Desert Rat" as its divisional formation sign.

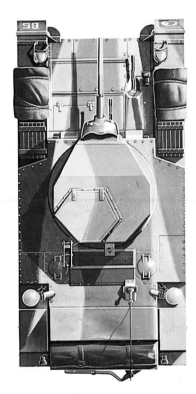

Crew: 4.
Armament: One .5in M2 machine-gun and one .3in M1919A4 machine-gun in turret; one .3in machine-gun in hull.
Armour: 6mm to 16mm.
Dimensions: Length 13ft 7in (4.14m); width 7ft 10in (2.39m); height 7ft 9in (2.36m).
Weight: Combat 19,400lbs (8,799kg).
Ground pressure: 8.23lb/in^2 (0.58kg/cm^2).
Power to weight ratio: 28.9hp/ton.
Engine: Continental 'Star 8' W670 seven-cylinder air-cooled radial petrol engine developing 250hp at 2,400rpm.
Performance: Road speed 45mph (72km/h); cross-country speed 15–25mph (25–40km/h); road range 150 miles (240km); fording depth 4ft 4in (1.32m); gradient 62 per cent.
History: Entered service with US Cavalry in 1937 and declared obsolete in 1942.

Although the 1920s were lean years for armour in the United States, the experiments conducted in Britain with an integrated armoured force led Lieutenant-Colonel Adna R. Chaffee to organise an *ad hoc* collection of units in 1929. This 'Mechanized Force' embraced practically every motor vehicle in the US Army at the time and was somewhat short-lived, but it paved the way for the establishment on a more regular basis of a cadre around which a mechanised cavalry regiment could be formed. The only infantry participation consisted of truck-mounted infantrymen; however, under the terms of the 1920 National Defense Act, the infantry were the only arm permitted to use tanks. To satisfy General Douglas MacArthur's requirement that the new mechanised cavalry should have their own tanks, the term 'Combat Car' was used to describe a tank when used by the cavalry. The T1 combat car was essentially identical to the T3 medium tank, the only difference being in the armament. In order that the 'Combat Car' distinction should not appear to be an obvious circumvention of the 1920 Act, the cavalry had agreed that 'Military Characteristics' for combat cars should specify an armament of one .5in and one .3in machine-gun in separate turrets, and so the T1 was thus equipped. Only four vehicles were made and these were scrapped in 1936, ending their days as targets. Like the T1, the T2 combat car was convertible. That is to say, it was capable of running either on tracks or, with the tracks removed, on road wheels. This feature was felt to give greater flexibility by permitting higher speeds on roads and is covered in more detail in the description of the T3 medium tank. Rock Island Arsenal produced one example of the T2 in 1931.

The designation T3 was applied temporarily to a modified T1E1 light tank and also to a proposed modification of the T2 combat car. The T4 and T5 combat cars were developed concurrently. The convertible T4 combat car was a continuation of the Christie line of evolution, while the T5 was developed in parallel with the T2 light tank. A suspension using vertical volute springs supporting pairs of bogie wheels had first been used on the T3 light tractor in 1933, and this suspension was used on the T5 combat car. The T2 light tank, on the other hand, was equipped with a Vickers-type leaf spring system, but tests in April 1934 showed the vertical volute spring system to be superior and this was accordingly adopted in the T2 light tank. In 1934, a service test of the T4 and T5 resulted in deadlock between the War Department and the using arm, the cavalry. The War Department

preferred the T5, which proved to be highly manoeuvrable. The cavalry, on the other hand, favoured the T4, which was a more stable gun platform and had superior ditch-crossing ability. The view of the War Department prevailed, and as a result the US Army adopted the vertical volute spring suspension. This feature was adopted on the recommendations of staff officers (some of whom had little or no experience of either of the competing suspensions), and the vertical volute suspension remained a feature of American tanks until the introduction of the M24 and M26 at the end of World War II. In November 1934 the prototype T5 combat car had been driven the 900 miles (1,450km) from Rock Island Arsenal to Washington at an average speed of 30mph. (48kp/h). Setting out on 14 November, Captain T. K. Nixon and Mr Joseph Proske arrived in Washington on 17 November having broken all existing records for non-convertible tracked vehicles. No doubt this feat of reliability had some bearing on the War Department selection of the T5 for standardisation as the M1 combat car, after which quantity production ensued. An improved transmission was introduced in the M1A1 and by the end of 1938 the 7th Cavalry Brigade had a total of 112 of the M1 and M1A1. The original design had one major drawback: a propeller shaft bisecting the fighting compartment. This feature was eliminated in the M2, of which 292 were ordered under the Protective Mobilization Plan of 1940. The trailing idler, which so characterised the suspensions of the M3 and M5 light tanks, was introduced in the M2. By this time, the Armoured Force had been organised and there was no further need to indulge in subtle discrimination between tanks and combat cars, so all the M2s became M1A1 light tanks, while the M1s became M1A2 light tanks. The pioneer combat cars continued to serve the US Army as training vehicles until December 1942, by which time maintenance problems. and the fact that they were no longer a reasonable substitute for the Light Tank M3, caused the Ordnance Committee to declare all former combat cars obsolete. Some 147 were scrapped. The designation T6 was reserved for a projected convertible combat car, but at 27,000lbs (12,247kg) it was apparent that it would be too heavy and the project was abandoned without a prototype being built. In 1937 Rock Island Arsenal built one example of the convertible T7 combat car, using the hull and automotive components of the M1. Despite what was probably the first use of pneumatic tires on a tracked vehicle, by this stage the convertible feature was a lost cause and the project was dropped. The little combat cars were the vehicles with which the US Army developed its armoured tactics and as such contributed to the establishment of modern concepts and doctrines in the army by the time it went to war. In 1937 a German colonel remarked that the M1 was in his opinion 'equal to the best in Europe', and although even by 1939 standards combat cars were critically under-gunned, their mobility was excellent. Indeed the basic chassis remained in production as the M5 Light Tank until June 1944, and the use of the vertical volute spring suspension was the most distinctive feature of American light and medium tanks until the final year of the war.

Below: The M1 'Combat Car' travelling at speed over rough ground. These light tanks were used by the US 7th Cavalry Brigade (Mechanized). They were called 'combat cars' to circumvent the 1920 National Defense Act, limiting tanks to infantry use.

M2 MEDIUM TANK

Crew: 6.
Armament: One 37mm M6 gun with a co-axial .3in M1919A4 machine-gun in turret; four .3in machine-guns, one at each corner of barbette superstructure; two .3in machine-guns in hull, firing forward in fixed mount.
Armour: 9.5mm to 32mm.
Dimensions: Length 17ft 8in (5.38m); width 8ft 7in (2.62m); height 9ft 4½in (2.86m).
Weight: Combat 47,040lbs (21,337kg).
Ground pressure: 11.67lb/in² (0.82kg/cm²).
Power to weight ratio: 19.05hp/ton.
Engine: Wright nine-cylinder air-cooled radial petrol engine, supercharged, developing 400hp at 2,400rpm.
Performance: Road speed 26mph (43km/h); cross-country speed 17mph (27km/h); road range 130 miles (209km); vertical obstacle 2ft (0.6m); trench 7ft 6in (3.54m); 25 per cent.
History: Obsolete before entering production and superseded by M3 medium tank. Never used in action.

Between the wars, US tanks were generally still hand-built by government arsenals, although the turret and some of the hull of the M2 were welded, which was an innovation. In spite of the fact that the M2 never saw action, it was the first tank to which production-line thinking was applied. In the rapidly changing situation in the summer of 1940, industry prepared itself for the production of 1,000 M2 medium tanks at Detroit Arsenal, which had still to be built. Events in Europe showed that the M2 would be obsolete before it could enter production, but the M3 medium tank, armed with a 75mm gun, was ordered into production in place of the M2. The M2 was of straightforward construction. The turret and parts of the hull were welded face-hardened armour, while the remainder was riveted. The suspension was derived from the M2 light tank and was of the familiar vertical volute spring type with rubber-tired bogie wheels. The tracks were rubber-padded for quietness and smooth

Right: The M2 medium tank was never used in combat but had a valuable training role.

running, although combined with the rubber bushings for the track pins this entailed a build-up of static electricity which made use of the radio difficult when the tank was on the move. As well as being the forerunner of the M3, the M2 formed the basis of several experimental variations, one of which, the T9 medium tractor, was standardised as the M4, served as a prime mover throughout World War II and remains in service with the Spanish Army today. Complaints about a lack of power led to the M2A1, in which the Wright

aircraft engine was supercharged to deliver another 50hp. The tracks were also widened and some armour increased. The Rock Island Arsenal produced some 94 M2A1 tanks, most of which were used for training until sufficient numbers of the M3 became available. The M2 was the only medium tank standardised whilst the 1920 National Defense Act remained in force and reflected the short-sighted and out-dated nature of this legislation. But it did have a significant contribution to the development of the M3.

M3 HALF-TRACK ARMOURED PERSONNEL CARRIER

Crew: 3 plus 10.
Armament: One .5in M2 or .3in M1919A4 machine-gun.
Armour: 7mm to 13mm.
Dimensions: Length 20ft 3in (6.17m); width 7ft 4in (2.22m); height 7ft 5in (2.26m).
Weight: Combat 20,000lbs (9,072kg).
Ground pressure: 11.3lb/in² (0.79kg/cm²).
Power to weight ratio: 16.5hp/ton.
Engine: White 160AX six-cylinder inline petrol engine developing 147hp at 3,000rpm.
Performance: Road speed 45mph (72km/h); road range 210 miles (312km); vertical obstacle 1ft (0.3m); fording depth 2ft 8in (0.8m); gradient 60 per cent.
History: Entered service with US Army in the summer of 1941. Also used by Britain, France, Soviet Union and the Netherlands. Still in service with the Israeli Defence Force.

Some 41,000 half-track vehicles were produced by the

United States during World War II, making this sort of vehicle one of the most prolific types of the period. Its development dates back to 1938, when a four-wheeled scout car was fitted with the tracked rear bogie of the T9 halftrack truck. This successful experiment was followed by the manufacture of the T7 halftrack personnel carrier by the White Motor Company and Rock Island Arsenal. A further development, the T14, formed the basis of the halftrack family which served so well in World War II. The T14 was intended primarily as a reconnaissance vehicle and prime mover, while the T8 version was conceived as a personnel carrier. A third version was intended to transport the 81mm mortar and its crew, ammunition and accessories. On 19 September 1940 the T14 was standardised as the Half Track Car M2, the T8 became the Half Track Personnel Carrier M3 and the mortar vehicle became the 81mm Mortar Carrier M4. The Autocar Company submitted the most favourable tender for the manu-

facture of halftracks, the initial contract calling for 424 M2 vehicles. Less than a week after this contract had been negotiated it became obvious that, in the numbers in which halftracks were needed, one manufacturer alone would be unable to meet the demand. The Diamond T Motor Car Company and the White Motor Company, both of whom had bid unsuccessfully for the original contract, were therefore included in the production plan. The probability of large quantities of similar vehicles being produced by different manufacturers highlighted the advantages of standardisation of components, and a committee was set up with the task of ensuring that all parts of the M2 and M3, whatever the manufacturer, should be completely interchangeable with the one exception of armour plate. In tactical terms the halftrack was basically equivalent to the British Bren Carrier, although it was of course larger and more powerful. It found many uses with all the Allied Armies in World War II

Left and right: An M3A1 half-track APC of the 60th Armored Infantry Battalion, 9th Armored Division, 3rd United States Army, which served in Europe in 1944-45. Total production of half-tracks during WWII was

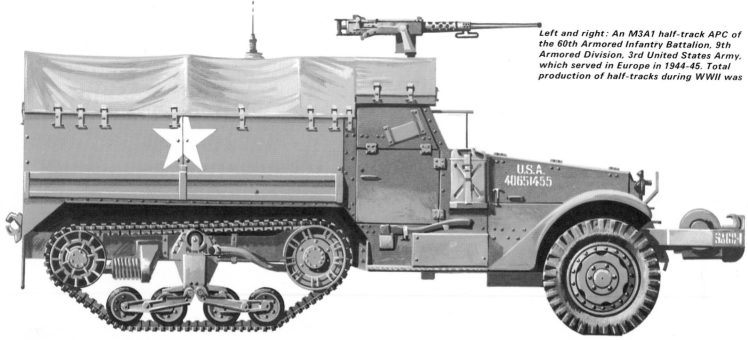

M3A1 RECONNAISSANCE VEHICLE

M3A1; M1; M2; M2A1; M3; M3A2 and variants.
Crew: 8.
Armament: Normally one .5in M2 and one .3in M1919A4 machine-gun on a skate mount around rear of hull.
Dimensions: Length 18ft 5in (5.62m); width 6ft 8in (2.03m); height 6ft 11in (2.11m).
Weight: Combat 12,400lbs (5,624kg).
Ground pressure: Estimated at 60lb/in² (4.22kg/cm²).
Power to weight ratio: 15.7hp/ton.
Engine: Hercules JXD six-cylinder water-cooled inline engine developing 87hp at 2,400rpm.
Performance: Road speed 55mph (88km/h); road range 250 miles (400km); vertical obstacle 1ft 2in (0.35m); fording depth 2ft 4in (0.71m); gradient 30 degrees.
History: Introduced into US Army as reconnaissance and command vehicle in 1939. This type of vehicle was not developed further but served as a basis for half-track development.

In 1936 the M2A1, with radio and other minor modifications, was standardised as the M3 scout car. This vehicle had four-wheel drive, 0.5in (12.7mm) armour and seating for eight men, and was capable of 62mph (100km/h) on roads. A skate ring on three sides of the open-topped crew compartment added to the flexibility of the machine-gun armament, and the M3 was adopted as a personnel carrier and reconnaissance vehicle in the 13th Cavalry Regiment of the mechanised 7th Cavalry Brigade in 1938. At that time the Chief of Cavalry recommended that all cavalry unit tables of establishment should be revised, substituting scout cars for all armoured cars, halftrack trucks and mortar carriers. The M3A1, standardised in 1939, was the definitive vehicle of the scout car series and introduced the distinctive front roller, designed to prevent the vehicle from digging its nose into ditches and other obstacles. It also featured a

wider body, new machine-gun mounts and revised crew seating and equipment stowage. It was Ordnance Department policy in 1939 that all combat vehicles should be diesel-engined. Accordingly a prototype of the M3A1 was fitted with a diesel engine and standardised as the M3A2. Although 100 were built, the diesel engine policy was never fully implemented and finally lapsed in March 1942. The vehicles were cannibalised for spares and the engines returned to store. Other experimental modifications included attempts to improve overhead cover, and the provision of a 37mm gun. The M3A1 was produced in quantity (20,918 were produced) and was one of the first vehicles made available under the Lend-Lease Act of 1941. Many were supplied to Britain and the Soviet Union, and there is a strong similarity between the M3A1 and the postwar Soviet *BTR*-40 personnel carrier. In the British Army the American scout cars were used as command vehicles, ambulances and personnel carriers, and in fact were seldom used for reconnaissance. Scout cars of the M3 series continue in service today with many armies of the Third World, including Brazil, Chile, Liberia, the Congo Republic and Spain. The M3A1 marked the end of wheeled reconnaissance

vehicles as such in the US Army, their role being divided between the jeep and the light tank. Nevertheless, other lines of development were investigated and a few are mentioned here. The T13 scout car was essentially similar to the M3. Marmon-Herrington produced 38 in mild steel plate for the National Guard in 1938. The T24 scout car featured an armoured body on a Willys 6×6 chassis, and was produced for the Tank Destroyer Command, and also used for the T14 37mm gun motor carriage. The T25 scout car was a commercial project by the Smart company to provide armour for a jeep. The Ordnance Department considered the vehicle too heavy and reported it unsatisfactory, but the project was reopened and various efforts made to improve the vehicle. As there was no way to avoid heavily overloading the suspension the project ended in September 1943. The T1 observation post tender was a small armoured vehicle with an open top and four-wheel drive, intended for artillery use. The T2 observation post tender was similar to the T1 but based on the Ford GAJ ⅜ton 4×4 truck chassis, which was also used for the T33 37mm gun motor carriage and the T44 57mm gun motor carriage.

Right: The M3A1 ASC was extensively used for reconnaissance duties early in WWII.

and formed the basis of several specialised variants. American developments totalled more than 50 types, whilst Britain and the Soviet Union each made their own modifications. The Israeli Army used halftracks extensively in both the 1967 and 1973 wars. Although the concept was pioneered by Kégresse in Russia before World War I, the American halftrack was an entirely original design by the Ordnance Department. Despite its widespread use the halftrack was essentially a compromise between fully tracked and wheeled vehicles, and although at its inception it may have combined the better features of both, by 1945 it was outdated. The US Army had also tried three-quarter tracked vehicles but felt that all vehicles combining wheels and tracks had too many disadvantages (the low reliability of tracks and the poor off-road mobility of wheels) and that it would be more effective to pursue separate development on the basis of fully tracked vehicles.

around 41,000 vehicles of all types. Many are still in service with Third World armies; the largest contemporary user is the Israeli Defence Force, which operates more than 1,000.

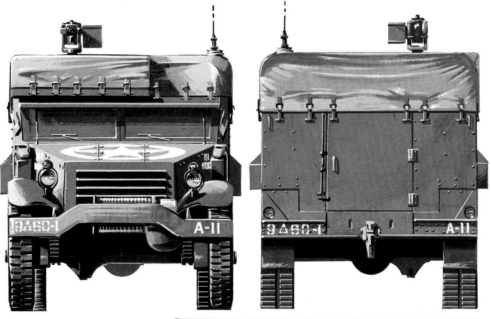

M3 GRANT/LEE MEDIUM TANK

M3, M3A1, M3A2, M3A3, M3A4, M3A5, and variants.
Crew: 6.
Armament: One 75mm M2 or M3 gun in hull sponson; one 37mm M5 or M6 gun in turret; one .3in M1919A4 machine-gun co-axial with turret gun; one .3in machine-gun in cupola on turret; two .3in machine-guns in bow.
Armour: 12mm to 37mm.
Dimensions: Length 18ft 6in (5.64m); width 8ft 11in (2.72m); height 10ft 3in (3.12m).
Weight: Combat 60,000lbs (27,216kg).
Ground pressure: 13.4lb/in² (0.94kg/cm²).
Power to weight ratio: 12.7hp/ton.
Engine: Wright Continental R-975-EC2 nine-cylinder air-cooled radial petrol engine developing 340hp at 2,400rpm.
Performance: Road speed 26mph (42km/h); cross-country speed 16mph (26km/h); road range 120 miles (193km); vertical obstacle 2ft (0.6m); trench 6ft 3in (1.9m); gradient 60 per cent.
History: Entered service with US Army and British Army in 1941. Also used by Canadian and Russian armies.

Battlefield experience reported from Europe in 1939 showed that the 37mm gun of the American M2 medium tank was not powerful enough for modern warfare, and accordingly the 75mm pack howitzer was experimentally mounted in the right-hand sponson of the Medium Tank T5 Phase III, a vehicle closely related to the M2. Such a vehicle would previously have been classed as a howitzer motor carriage. Meanwhile in the United States rearmament programme William S. Knudsen, president of the General Motors Corporation, had been co-opted to the National Defense Advisory Committee to co-ordinate the capabilities of industry to the needs of defence. In the summer of 1940 it became apparent from events in Europe that tanks would be required in large numbers, and would have to be better armed. The existing contract for 329 M2A4 light tanks was clearly insufficient and industry did not seem able to cope with the order for 1,500 M2 medium tanks which was then envisaged. In 1940 it was suggested that the M2 be improved by increasing its armour and adapting the 75mm M1897 gun (as the T7) to a sponson mounting in the hull. This new tank was designated the M3 medium tank by the Ordnance Committee on 11 July 1940, and on 28 August 1940 the contract for 1,000 M2A1 medium tanks, signed only 15 days

previously, was changed in favour of the M3. Up to this point, America's tank needs had been met largely by the heavy engineering industry, which was better suited to the production of railway equipment, or possibly small quantities of tanks, than to the series production of modern tanks. Knudsen, now a lieutenant-general, took the view that apart from the manufacturing and casting of armour, there was little difference between manufacturing a car and a tank. He therefore arranged with K. T. Keller, president of the Chrysler Corporation, for Chrysler to lease a 113-acre (45.73-hectare) site for a new tank factory. The site at Warren, Michigan was to become the government-owned, Chrysler-operated arsenal responsible for the production of some 25,000 armoured vehicles during World War II. The M3 was ordered into production from the drawing board and Chrysler, the American Locomotive Company (Alco) and the Baldwin Locomotive Works all produced pilot models by April 1941. Production began in August 1941 and continued until December 1942, by which time 6,258 vehicles of the M3 series had been built. Of this total

Chrysler built 3,352, Alco 685, Baldwin 1,220, Pressed Steel 501 and Pullman 500. These figures are quoted to illustrate what was basically the first application of motorcar mass-production techniques to tank production. During production it became necessary to make various modifications to overcome shortages and to improve the tank. The M3A1 used a cast hull produced by Alco, this hull having no side doors for reasons of strength. A welded hull, stronger than the riveted hull of the M3, was used to save weight in the M3A2, of which Baldwin built 12. Baldwin also built 322 of the M3A3 which used two General Motors 6-71 diesel bus engines coupled together as an alternative to the Wright radial engine. Otherwise the M3A3 was identical to the M3A2. The M3, M3A1 and M3A2 could also be fitted with a Guiberson diesel engine in which case the designation became, for example, M3A1 (Diesel). To overcome a critical shortage of the Wright engine in 1941, Chrysler combined five standard car engines to provide a tank powerpack. This 'Eggbeater' engine required modifications to the hull and suspension, resulting in

Left: An M3 medium tank, fitted with a dummy lorry body as a disguise. While Germany rearmed during the 1930s, the US Army began development of a new series of tanks. A new specification for a medium tank was laid down and, following trials of numerous prototypes, the M3 medium was evolved. This tank was notable in that it had an anti-tank gun mounted in its revolving turret and an HE-firing weapon in the hull. These tanks, known as the Grant or Lee according to type, were used by the British in the Western Desert.

Right and below right: Front and side views of an M3 Grant medium tank in British service. A peculiar feature of this tank, in addition to its unusual armament layout, is the use of the tractor-type suspension system (generally referred to as the 'scissors'), which was also applied to most US tanks until the latter part of World War II. Early production vehicles were made up of castings and flat plates riveted together, but later the hulls and turrets were entirely cast. The M3 was also used by Canada and Russia.

Left: In this view of the M3 Grant medium tank the most noticeable feature is the multiplicity of weapons with which the vehicle was armed, arranged in three tiers. The tank commander could operate the .30in Browning machine-gun in the independently-rotating cast cupola, while the turret gunner could engage armour with the 37mm anti-tank gun or infantry with his .30in machine-gun. The 75mm weapon provided HE fire.

the M3A4. The hull was riveted as in the M3, and 109 were built. The M3A5 resulted from the installation of the twin GM diesels of the M3A3 in the riveted hull of the M3, and Baldwin built 591 of these. In British service the M3 was known as the Grant (after General Ulysses S. Grant) and the Lee (after General Robert E. Lee). A British Tank Commission had arrived in June 1940 with the intention of ordering British-designed tanks from American firms. But as at that time the defeat of the British appeared imminent, the National Defense Advisory Committee refused to allow tanks to be produced to British designs. As a result of this refusal the M3 was chosen as being the next best choice. Those purchased by the British Tank Commission from Pullman and Pressed Steel had a British-designed turret and were known as Grant I. The name Lee was given to the standard M3 (Lee I), M3A1 (Lee II), M3A3 (Lee IV), M3A3 (diesel) (Lee V), and M3A4 (Lee VI), while the M3A5 was known as the Grant II, these tanks being supplied under the terms of the 1941 Lend-Lease Act. The Grant I had its first impact at the battle of Gazala on 27 May 1942, the

first time the 8th Army had managed to achieve any degree of parity with the 75mm gun of the PzKpfw IV, although it was some time before problems associated with fuses for the HE shell could be resolved. By October 1942 a further 350 M3s had been supplied and these tanks made a significant contribution to the success at El Alamein in November of that year. Some M3s were shipped to the UK for training units, but the majority were used in North Africa and the Middle East. As the M4 medium tank entered service in 1942, the M3 was gradually replaced and sent to the Far East where it replaced the Matilda, Valentine and Stuart. By April 1943 the M4 was in full production and the M3 was finally declared obsolete on 16 March 1944. Despite this the M3 lived on in the form of variants such as the M7 'Priest' and the M31 Tank Recovery Vehicle. The chassis was also used for many experimental variations, including: Mine Exploder T1, Tank Recovery Vehicle T2 (M31), 155mm Gun Motor Carriage T6 (M12), Shop Tractor T10 (Canal Defense Light, or searchlight tank), Cargo Carrier T14, Heavy Tractor T16, 3in Gun

Motor Carriage T24, 105mm Howitzer Motor Carriage T25, 75mm Gun Motor Carriage T26, 105mm Howitzer Motor Carriage T32 (M7 'Priest'), 40mm Gun Motor Carriage T36, 3in Gun Motor Carriage T40 (M9), 25pounder Gun Motor Carriage T51, Flamethrower Vehicles (several were made, using the E3 and M5R2 flame guns). Vehicles of the M3 series supplied to the British Army were also modified for various purposes, for example as recovery vehicles, command vehicles, mineclearing vehicles, and as a canal defence light.

Below: An M3 Grant tank negotiates very difficult terrain. Although a fairly successful tank, giving a good account of itself with the 8th Army in the Western Desert, the Grant had several weak features. The use of two separate weapons to fire high-explosive and anti-tank ammunition, and the cramped quarters provided for the crew of six—the latter especially important in desert conditions —were the most significant.

M4 SHERMAN MEDIUM TANK

Crew: 5.
Armament: One 75mm M3 gun; one .3in M1919A4 machine-gun co-axial with main armament; one .3in M1919A4 machine-gun in ball mount in bow; one .5in M2 machine-gun on turret roof; one 2in M3 smoke mortar in turret roof.
Armour: 0.6in (15mm) minimum; 3.94in (100mm) maximum.
Dimensions: Length 20ft 7in (6.27m); width 8ft 11in (2.67m); height 11ft 1in (3.37m).
Weight: Combat 69,565lbs (31,554kg).
Ground pressure: 14.3lb/in² (1kg/cm²).
Power to weight ratio: 16.9hp/ton.
Engine: Ford GAA V-8 water-cooled inline petrol engine developing 500hp at 2,600rpm.
Performance: Road speed 26mph (42km/h); road range 100 miles (160km); vertical obstacle 2ft (0.61m); trench 7ft 6in (2.29m); fording depth 3ft (0.91m); gradient 60 per cent.
History: Entered service in 1942 and saw extensive service with US Army and most Allied armies during

and after World War II. The most prolific medium tank of World War II, and widely adapted to other uses. Also used in action in Korea and Middle East and still in service with some armies.
(Note Data relate to a typical M4A3.)

On 29th August 1940, the day following the decision to produce the M3 medium tank in place of the M2A1, work began on a new medium tank which would mount the 75mm gun in a turret with a full 360° traverse. The new tank was designated the T6 medium tank, and its design was based on the use of components of the M3 as far as possible. Elimination of the sponson mount would reduce the hull space enclosed by armour, and thus reduce weight or permit a greater thickness of armour. The T6 was standardised in September 1941 as the M4 medium tank, but in all its many models it was more widely and popularly known as the 'Sherman', after General William Sherman. As adopted, the Sherman weighed about 30 tons (30,482kg) and was armed with the 75mm

M2 gun. The turret was a one-piece rounded casting, 3in (76.2mm) thick at the front, and power operated. A gyrostabiliser controlled the gun in elevation. The lower hull was welded, while the construction of the upper hull provided a certain degree of identification of the various models. The M4 had a welded upper hull, while the M4A1 had a cast, rounded upper hull. Both were approximately 2in (50.8mm) thick. Variations between the major models in the M4 series were mainly due to different engine installations, apart from the difference in hull construction in the case of the M4 and M4A1. Production of the Sherman was authorised to replace the M3 as soon as possible.

Below: The M4A3E8 Sherman mounting a 105mm howitzer with which it gave close support to the medium tank formations of the US Army, replacing the M8 75mm SPG. Later models had horizontal volute suspension systems (HVSS), which gave the vehicle's crew a smoother ride.

Above: Front view of an M4A3E8. Its insignia denote, from left to right, 7th Army, 191st Tank Battalion, A Company, Tank No. 12. Note the camouflage paint on the tank's hull.

Below: Rear view of the M4A3E8, with insignia rearranged. The tank commander's .50in M2 machine-gun has been dismounted from the turret bracket and is stowed away at the rear of the turret.

Right: A posed picture of a US Army Sherman with infantry 'fighting' from the rear of the tank. In practice, it was rare for infantry to fight from the tank; they usually followed the vehicle, using it as a shield. The main Allied exception to this method was that of the Red Army, which formulated the concept of 'tank-riding battalions', often formed from partizan groups, on the Eastern Front.

Facilities involved included the Chrysler-operated Detroit Arsenal, the Fisher Body Division of GMC, the Ford Motor Company, Pacific Car and Foundry, Federal Machine and Welder Company, Lima Locomotive Works and the Montreal Locomotive Works, and 49,230 Shermans of all variants were produced. Product improvement was a continuous process throughout, and indeed after production had ceased. The most significant improvements centred on armament, stowage of ammunition and suspension. The gun conceived for the T6 medium tank prototype was the 75mm T6 gun but, as was mentioned in the description of the variants of the M3 medium tank, the T6 gun was a disappointment. The next model, the T7, was better and became the 75mm M2 gun in May 1941, but was still relatively short-barrelled and had a muzzle velocity of only 1,850fps (564mps). Early models of the Sherman had the M2 gun, but even in September 1940 the Armored Force had requested a higher muzzle velocity, and this request was met in the 75mm T8 gun, adopted in June 1941 as the M3.

This gun fired armour-piercing shot at a muzzle velocity of 2,030fps (619mps) and was also more suited to tank use. The longer barrel was better balanced for installation in a gyrostabiliser mount and rotation of the breech to allow the block to open horizontally permitted greater depression of the gun in a turret mount. Although the 75mm gun was accepted as the standard weapon, the Ordnance Department felt that more penetrating power would be required, and despite the absence of any expressed desire or direction from the using arm, investigated more powerful weapons. The 3in gun of the M6 heavy tank was not ideal, but adapting the 75mm breech to the 3in barrel produced a most satisfactory weapon. At first known as the 3in T13 gun but later as the 76mm T1 gun, this weapon was mounted on the Sherman in a project which began in August 1942. The project, although promising, found no support and was dropped in November of the same year. Later the T23 medium tank turret, with the 76mm gun, was mounted on the Sherman. The improvement was so marked that

the Armored Board admitted to a requirement for 76mm guns to supplant 75mm guns when the extra firepower was needed. This was a face-saving gesture to allow production to begin after the earlier refusal. The fact that by July 1944 over 2,000 76mm gun tanks had been produced illustrates just how much the extra firepower was needed — and this after vehicles armed with the 76mm gun had been declared obsolete in May 1943! By this time the Ordnance Department was thinking in terms of the 90mm gun. Another innovation in armament concerned the 105mm howitzer. In April 1941 the Aberdeen Proving Ground had suggested that the Sherman would conveniently mount the 105mm howitzer, but it was not until late 1942 that two M4A4s were modified for this purpose. Further tests were carried out on a similarly modified vehicle, the M4E5, and the howitzer in the M52 mount was adopted as a standard item. These vehicles were used in headquarter companies to provide fire support and some 4,680 were built on the M4 and M4A3 hulls. Early models of the Sherman had a somewhat un-

continued on page 223 ▶

Below: Side view of the M4A3E8, known to the Americans as the 'Easy Eight' because of its HVSS suspension. The vehicle is shown as it appeared on ceremonial parade with the United States Occupation Forces in Munich, in June 1945.

ADAM   36114493

Below: Rare view of Red Army Shermans before Kharkov in 1943. Note the fuel drums at the hull rear.

M4 SHERMAN MEDIUM TANK continued

▶ fortunate reputation for 'brewing up' when hit by anti-tank fire. To overcome this fault attempts were made to protect the ammunition stowed in the tank. Stowage racks were provided in the lower hull and those for 75mm and 76mm ammunition were surrounded by water jackets, while the semi-fixed howitzer ammunition was protected by armour plate. The suffix 'wet' was added to nomenclature in May 1945 to distinguish those tanks with water jacket stowage. To improve the ride and stability, and at the same time reduce the specific ground pressure of the Sherman, experiments were made with different suspensions and tracks. The original and highly characteristic vertical volute spring suspension of the Sherman series originated with the M2 medium tank, as did the 16in (0.41m) track, but both were more suited to a 20ton (20,321kg) vehicle than the 30-plus tons of the M4. Eventually a new horizontal volute spring suspension and 23in (0.58m) track were perfected and incorporated in production. The suffix 'HVSS' was often added

Right: The Sherman Crab 'flail tank' was developed by the British to clear a path through minefields and was used by the 79th Armoured Division in 1944-45. When the drum at the front of the tank rotated at speed, the flailing chains detonated any mines in the vehicle's path. Chains were used because they were not easily damaged or destroyed by exploding mines.

LVT AMPHIBIOUS LOAD CARRIER SERIES

Landing Vehicle Tracked Mark 4 Water Buffalo, M1935, M1940, LVT1, LVT(A)1, LVT2, LVT(A)2, LVT3, LVT(A)4 and LVT(A)5.
Crew: 3.
Armament: One .3in M1919A4 machine-gun in ball mount in bow; one or two .5in M2 and one or two .3in M1919A4 machine-guns in cargo compartment.
Dimensions: Length 26ft 2in (7.97m); width 10ft 8in (3.25m); height 10ft 1in (3.07m) excluding external armament.
Weight: Combat 36,398lbs (16,510kg) including 9,000lbs (4,082kg) payload.
Ground pressure: 8.4lb/in² (0.59kg/cm²).
Power to weight ratio: 15.4hp/ton net.
Engine: Continental W670-9A seven-cylinder air-cooled radial petrol engine developing 250hp at 2,400rpm.
Performance: Road speed 17mph (27km/h); waterborne speed 6mph (10km/h); road range 150 miles (240km); waterborne range 75 miles (120km); vertical obstacle 3ft 2in (0.98m); trench 5ft (1.52m); gradient 60 per cent.
History: First LVT entered service in 1942 and was used in logistic role at Guadalcanal. Provided to British Army during World War II and supplied postwar to France, Italy and Spain among others. Used in Korea and Indochina. Replaced by LVTP5 series and later by LVTP7.

A vehicle with truly high mobility had long been an unfulfilled military requirement. Such a vehicle would be amphibious without special preparations, yet its performance on land would not be affected by its amphibious capability. The small hull volume and high weight of tanks usually precluded the attainment of this aim, although successful trials were carried out between World Wars I and II with the original 'lozenge' tanks, with various of Christie's designs and with Straussler's flotation devices in the United Kingdom. The Florida Everglades gave rise to a vehicle which went a long way to providing that mobility. The inhabitants of the Everglades used a variety of boats, airscrew-propelled 'skimmers' and adapted vehicles to traverse the swamps. Most of the land vehicles adapted for this purpose relied on wheels, but in 1935 Donald Roebling unveiled a design which owed its success to the use of tracks rather than wheels. These tracks had 'grousers' so shaped as to propel the vehicle in water. Buoyancy was provided by the hull volume, while the use of duralumin made possible a lighter construction. This vehicle was intended primarily for use in flood relief operations and for the rescue of crashed airmen, but its military potential was seen by the US Navy. A later model, the M1940, incorporated all the experience gained with the M1935. The M1940 received considerable publicity which led to tests by the US Marine Corps. Like the M1935, the M1940 was built of duralumin, a somewhat unknown quantity as far as military vehicles were concerned. Some 200 of a steel version with a 120hp engine replacing the 95hp powerplant of the M1940 were ordered by 1941 by the US Navy under the designation Landing Vehicle, Tracked, Mark 1. Roebling's vehicle had become known as the Alligator after other inhabitants of the Everglades and this name came to be widely used for the early amphibians. The designation was commonly abbreviated to LVT1 and in all, 1,225 were produced. The LVT1 had a rigid suspension with a rear-mounted engine and was unarmoured. Quite soon the need arose for armour protection and at the same time some offensive capability was desirable. By the addition of armour plating and the turret of the M3 light tank, the Landing Vehicle, Tracked (Armored), Mk 1 or LVT(A)1 was formed. To a large extent the quick manufacture of prototypes and production of the vehicle was due to the foresight of the Borg-Warner company, which had been brought into LVT production, and 509 of the LVT(A)1 were built. The LVT1 was mainly used for the ship-to-shore transport of cargo. The LVT2 or Water Buffalo or 1943 introduced the 'torsilastic' suspension, in which the road wheel arms were held on shafts mounted concentrically inside rubber-filled tubes. This use of rubber in torsion is unusual, although a more modern refinement is to combine it with a torsion-bar suspension. The tracks of the LVT2 used a cast aluminium W-shaped grouser as standard, bolted on to the track links. The LVT(A)2 was an armoured form of the LVT2 and was intended purely as an armoured cargo carrier, without armament. It was taken into British use as the Amphibian, Tracked, 2 ton, General Service. The LVT1 and LVT2 models all had rear engines, the LVT2 using the engine and transmission of the M3 light tank. A total of 3,413 of both the LVT2 and LVT(A)2 models was produced. Improvements to the basic LVT2 by the Borg-Warner company in 1943 resulted in the so-called 'Model B', also known as the T11. This had a ramp, allowing more use to be made of the cargo space. From the T11

Below: The LVT2 'Water Buffalo'. This model has two .50in Browning machine-guns in open mounts.

to designations to indicate the newer suspension. The Sherman proved to be extremely adaptable and improvements were made continuously during production, so that there was little similarity between the original M4 and the final production M4A3, with its improved armour, engine, armament and suspension. The type also lent itself to the production of many variants and most authorities list over 50 significant American experimental models. At least one of these is apparently still classified after 30 years. Tanks and other vehicles of the M4 series were supplied to many countries during and after World War II, and more Shermans were manufactured than any other single tank. Critics pointed out its deficiencies compared with the Panther, for example, but it made up for these shortcomings in reliability, endurance and sheer weight of numbers. Thirty-six years after its introduction the Sherman lives on in many armies around the world and has appeared in almost every armoured conflict since 1945.

Right: The Sherman DD (Duplex Drive) was developed for the Normandy landings in 1944. The floatation screen was lowered before the tank entered the water, where it was driven along by two propellers at the rear of the hull, powered from the main engine. These tanks were satisfactory in calm weather, but were too easily swamped in rough seas.

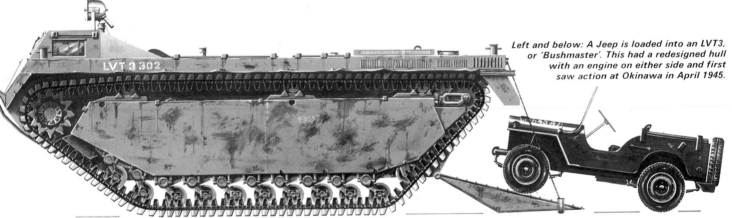

Left and below: A Jeep is loaded into an LVT3, or 'Bushmaster'. This had a redesigned hull with an engine on either side and first saw action at Okinawa in April 1945.

was developed the Model D, which in mid-1943 was standardised as the LVT3. The major change in the LVT3, which made possible the rear ramp, was the moving of the engine forward. The LVT3 used automotive components of the M5A1 light tank as opposed to the use of M3 assemblies in the LVT2. A total of 2,962 LVT2s was manufactured. In October 1942 the Army Ordnance Committee had agreed that the US Navy should be the sole source for all amphibious craft, but Ordnance designations were allocated to two LVTs. The LVT1 was taken into the US Army inventory as the T33 Amphibian Tractor, while the Borg-Warner Model D was given the nomenclature T11 Amphibian Tractor. With the implementation of the October 1942 decision that the US Navy should be responsible for all LVTs the Army designations were dropped but the name 'Amtrac', a contraction of 'Amphibian Tractor', remained in popular use throughout the war. In August 1943 the Food Machinery Corporation successfully modified the LVT2 to incorporate a front engine and rear ramp, the vehicle being designated LVT4. Some 8,438 LVT4s were built, making this type the most widely built of the wartime LVTs, and the data at the beginning of this entry refer to the LVT4. An armoured version was also developed and this, the LVT(A)4, mounted the turret and howitzer of the M8 75mm howitzer motor carriage. This was, incidentally, the third vehicle to use this turret. In all, 1,890 of the LVT(A)4 were built and another version designated LVT(A)5 differed only in that stabilisation and power traverse were provided. Some 269 were built. Originally unarmoured, the LVT4 was later provided with armoured crew compartments and bolt-on armour around the cargo compartment. A typical 9,000lb payload for the LVT4 might consist of 30 troops, or a jeep, or an anti-tank gun. It was at Guadalcanal in August 1942 that LVTs were first used operationally. In this case they were used in a logistic role for the ship-to-shore transfer of ammunition, men and supplies. The first tactical use of the LVT came in November 1943 at Tarawa in the Pacific, and after that LVTs were instrumental in the Scheldt estuary assault and the crossing of the Rhine, to name but two amphibious operations. Considerable effort was diverted into amphibious

vehicles. There were experimental modifications to the LVTs. In one, the LVT(A)1 mounted the E14-7R2 flamethrower in place of the 37mm gun, while the T44 4.5in and T54 7.2in rocket launchers were also designed for use with the LVT4. After the war many LVT3s were modified by the addition of overhead armour and a machine-gun cupola, to the LVT3C standard. In this form they continued in US Marine Corps service until replaced by the LVTP5 series. Other postwar developments included tracked landing craft capable of carrying medium or heavy tanks, as well as hydrofoil landing vehicles. Two generations later with the introduction to service of the LVTP7, the LVT4 remains in service in Taiwan and Thailand.

Below: The LVT(A)4 had the same turret-mounted 75mm howitzer as the M8 howitzer motor carriage and first saw action at Saipan in June 1944. It was used to give supporting fire during the crucial early stages of an amphibious assault.

M7 SELF-PROPELLED HOWITZER

M7, M7B1, M7B2, Sexton and T51.
Crew: 7.
Armament: One 105mm M2 howitzer; one .5in M2 anti-aircraft machine-gun.
Armour: 0.5in (12.7mm) minimum; 4.5in (114.3mm) maximum.
Dimensions: Length 19ft 9in (6.02m); width 9ft 5in (2.87m); height 9ft 7in (2.92m).
Weight: Combat 50,634lbs (22,967kg).
Ground pressure: 10.4lb/in² (0.73kg/cm²).
Power to weight ratio: 15hp/ton.
Engine: Continental R-975 series nine-cylinder air-cooled radial petrol engine developing 340hp at 2,400rpm.
Performance: Road speed 26mph (42km/h); cross-country speed 15mph (24km/h); road range 125 miles (200km); vertical obstacle 2ft (0.61m); trench 7ft 6in (2.29m); fording depth 4ft (1.22m); gradient 60 per cent.
History: Entered service in 1942 and widely used in World War II. Used postwar by many countries until recently and still in service in Brazil.

As a result of earlier American thinking about self-propelled artillery and attempts to mount the 75mm howitzer on the light tank chassis, work began in June 1941 on a self-propelled version of the 105mm field howitzer on the chassis of the M3 medium tank, then in quantity production. It was clear that this chassis, and that of the M4 which differed only slightly, would be the most suitable and easily available chassis for any development so two pilot models of the new vehicle were built, and designated the T32 105mm Howitzer Motor Carriage. The T32 consisted of the M1A2 field howitzer, in its standard field carriage mount, in an open-topped, high-sided superstructure built on the chassis of the M3 tank. Tests at Aberdeen Proving Ground showed that the T32 had promise and in fact the only major criticism was that the vehicle

lacked an anti-aircraft weapon. A ring mount for a .5in machine-gun was added to the front right-hand corner of the superstructure and when armoured, this mount took on the appearance of a pulpit, resulting in the nickname 'Priest' by which the vehicle was invariably known. Some 600 T32s were ordered in February 1942 and standardisation as the M7 105mm Howitzer Motor Carriage followed in April 1942. The Priest entered production at the American Locomotive Company (Alco), and was initially manufactured on the chassis of the M3 tank. When production of the M3 ended in December 1942, it was found that the hull of the M4A3 medium tank would be suitable for the Priest and production continued on this basis.

Priests with the M4A3 and the Ford GAA engine were designated M7B1. Later slight modifications to the upper hull superstructure resulted in a higher pulpit and the designation M7B2. The standard 105mm howitzer fired the high-explosive shell to a range of 12,000 yards (10,973m) and was provided with many other types of ammunition, including smoke and chemical projectiles. In British service the equivalent of the 105mm howitzer was the 25pounder gun, and a very similar conversion was made on the chassis of the M3, mounting the 25pounder and known as the 'Sexton'. It was found to be more convenient for Britain to retain the 25pounder while the United States kept the 105mm, as this released the 105mm

---

M8 LIGHT ARMOURED CAR

T21, T22, T23, T22E1, T23E1, T22E2, M8, M10 and many variants.
Crew: 4.
Armament: One 37mm M6 gun; one .3in M1919A4 machine-gun co-axial with main armament; one .5in M2 anti-aircraft machine-gun on turret roof.
Armour: 0.12in (3.17mm) minimum; 0.75in (19.05 mm) maximum.
Dimensions: Length 16ft 5in (5m); width 8ft 4in (2.54m); height 7ft 4in (2.23m).
Weight: Combat 17,000lbs (7,711kg).
Ground pressure: 13.6lb/in² (0.96kg/cm²) at 3in (7.62cm) penetration.
Power to weight ratio: 14.5hp/ton.
Engine: Hercules JXD six-cylinder water-cooled inline petrol engine developing 110hp at 3,000rpm.
Performance: Road speed 55mph (88km/h); road range 350 miles (560km); vertical obstacle 1ft (0.3m); fording depth 2ft (0.6m); gradient 60 per cent.
History: Entered US service in 1943 and was widely used by US Army and Allies during World War II. Postwar US Army doctrine preferred tracked vehicles, but the M8 still remains in service with many armies.

In late 1941 requirements were published for a light armoured car, to be armed with the 37mm gun. In fact the first requirements defined the vehicle as a wheeled gun motor carriage, and the first contender to emerge was a 6×4 vehicle produced by Studebaker. Originally known as the T43 37mm Gun Motor Carriage, in March 1942 the nomenclature was changed to T21 Light Armored Car. There were still differences of opinion over the relative merits of 4×4 and 6×6 wheel configurations, and it was decided to produce two new vehicles, each in 4×4 and 6×6 versions. At the same time the T21, with its 6×4 arrangement, was dropped. The new vehicles were designated the T22 and T23 armoured cars (although for a while they were described as 37mm Gun Motor Carriages) and were primarily conceived as tank destroyers. Even in early 1942 it was obvious that the 37mm gun had no part to play in the anti-tank battle, so the Gun Motor Carriage nomenclature may have been yet another ruse to obtain financial or political approval for armoured cars, in the same manner as the term 'Combat Car' had been used prior to 1940. The Ford Motor Company was responsible for the 6×6 T22 and the 4×4 T22E1, while the Fargo Company produced the 6×6 T23 and the 4×4 T23E1. The four-wheeled designs were discarded at an

early stage, and the hull of the T22 was redesigned. With improved stowage arrangements, modifications to the gun mount and the addition of sandshields, the T22E2 was standardised in June 1942 as the M8 Light Armored Car. The M8 had a one-piece welded hull with an average thickness of 0.75in (19.05mm) which provided structural strength, and the M6 37mm gun was mounted in an open-topped turret. The six wheels were mounted on beam axles, and semi-elliptic leaf springs allowed a fair degree of cross-country mobility. Some 8,523 were produced by the Ford Motor Company before production ended in late 1944. Most of the vehicles in the planned family of variants based on the M8 did not materialise. Of those which did, only one was standardised. A version for the transport of personnel, ammunition and cargo was designated T20; the command vehicle was designated T26 and the T30 was a version designed to fire 7in (178mm) rockets from 10 projectors with restricted traverse. Lastly there was an anti-aircraft version, the T69. It was realised that the functions of the T20 and T26 could be combined into one vehicle, and this was standardised as the M10 Armored Utility Car. To avoid

confusing this vehicle with the M10 3in Gun Motor Carriage the designation was later changed to M20, and Ford eventually produced 3,791 of this useful vehicle. The M20 was in effect the armoured equivalent of the jeep and assumed most of the functions previously performed by the M3 scout car. Development of medium armoured cars continued while the M8 was in production. Studebaker produced the T27, an eight-wheeled vehicle with six driven wheels. Despite good cross-country performance and a road speed of 61mph (98km/h) the T27 still only mounted the 37mm gun and did not offer a significant improvement over the M8. Development ended in July 1944. A second medium armoured car, the T28, was manufactured by Chevrolet and was a 6×6 vehicle. The T28 had independent suspension on all wheels, and the three axles were equally spaced. Although still armed with the 37mm gun, the T28 was judged suitable to replace the M8 and, with certain modifications, the M20 and was standardised in December 1944 as the M38. Reducing requirements for this type of vehicle meant that, despite its adoption as standard, no series production of the M38 took place.

Right: The US M8 light armoured car, called 'Greyhound' by the British, was developed by the Ford Motor Company. A total of 8,523 were built between 1942 and 1945.

Right: M7 on exercise in 1944. The 'pulpit' mounting of the .5in AA machine-gun gave it the nickname 'Priest'. A Canadian variant mounting a 25 pounder was called the 'Sexton'.

Left: The M7 105mm self-propelled howitzer was based on the US M3 Grant tank chassis, and later on the M4 Sherman.

ammunition for US use and standardised on the 25pounder within the 21st Army Group, so the Sexton was produced in quantity for the British and Commonwealth armies. A compromise, the T51 25pounder Gun Motor Carriage, was produced in July 1942 but discarded when it was found that no requirement for it existed. The Priest was the first significant self-propelled artillery weapon in the Allied inventory, and as early as March 1942 the British Tank Commission in the United States requested 5,500 for delivery by the end of 1943. Although the request was never met in full, production got under way rapidly and 90 were made available to the 8th Army in September 1942. At El Alamein in November, Priests of the 5th Regiment, Royal Horse Artillery engaged 88mm guns in dug-in emplacements to provide cover for British tanks. The American Locomotive Company built 3,314 M7s, while Pressed Steel built 826 (of which some 450 were M7B1s). The Federal Machine and Welder Company produced 127 of the M7B2, making a total of 4,267. In American service, the M7 was replaced by the M37 105mm Howitzer Motor Carriage based on the M24 light tank, while those Priests supplied to the United Kingdom served in Italy and Normandy. Most were displaced by Sextons and then converted to Observation Post vehicles and 'Kangaroo' armoured personnel carriers: the howitzer was removed and up to 20 infantrymen could be carried.

M10 TANK DESTROYER

Crew: 5.
Armament: One 3in M7 gun; one .5in M2 anti-aircraft machine-gun.
Armour: 0.5in (12.7mm) minimum; 2in (50.8mm) maximum.
Dimensions: Length 19ft 7in (5.97m); width 10ft (3.05m); height 8ft 1½in (2.48m).
Weight: Combat 66,000lbs (29,937kg).
Ground pressure: 13.6lb/in² (0.95kg/cm²).
Power to weight ratio: 12.7hp/ton.
Engine: Two General Motors 6-71 six-cylinder water-cooled diesel engines developing a total of 375hp at 2,100rpm.
Performance: Road speed 30mph (48km/h); cross-country speed 20mph (32km/h); road range 200 miles (320km); vertical obstacle 2ft (0.61m); trench 7ft 6in (2.29m); gradient 60 per cent.
History: Entered service with US Army in 1942. Also widely used by British and Allied armies during World War II and continued in service postwar.

In June 1942 a modified T35E1 vehicle was adopted and designated the M10 3inch Gun Motor Carriage. The name 'Wolverine' was given to the M10 but was scarcely used. The M10 was a good fighting vehicle, with a relatively low silhouette and good ballistic protection from its sloped armour. Bosses were provided on vulnerable surfaces for the addition of extra armour but this feature does not appear to have been widely used. The M10 also had its disadvantages. The open-topped turret left the crew (and some ammunition) vulnerable to shell splinters and air attack, and the massive 3in gun both cramped and unbalanced the turret. It fired the capped armour-piercing shot to a maximum range of 16,000 yards (14,631m) at a muzzle velocity of 2,600fps (792mps) and would penetrate 4in (102mm) of face-hardened armour at 1,000 yards (914m). However, being developed from an anti-aircraft weapon, little thought

had been given to reducing the inboard length of the M7 gun and as a result the long and heavy barrel required a counterweight of 2,500lbs (1,134kg) to balance the turret for hand traverse. To make use of the M4A3 chassis the M10A1 was authorised, but apart from the Ford GAA engine there were no significant differences. A total of 6,346 M10s and M10A1s was built. Most of the M10A1s were retained in the United States or converted by the removal of the turret into M35 prime movers, in which role the acted as tractors for the 240mm howitzer and 8in gun matériel. In British service the armament was removed and the 17pounder gun substituted in many cases. This conversion was known as the 'Achilles' and was a much more effective vehicle. The Achilles continued in service with the Royal Artillery into the postwar period and was used by the Royal Danish Army until recently. The 3in gun could be traced back to at least 1918 and was, if not outdated, at least lacking in potential for further development. In September 1942 an investigation was begun to see whether the 90mm

anti-aircraft gun, then under development as a tank and anti-tank gun, might be fitted into the turret of the M10. The T7 90mm gun did not fit the M10 turret, so a new turret was designed and the M10 with the new turret designated the T71 90mm Gun Motor Carriage. However, it took almost two years for the 90mm gun to reach troops in the field while the lack of anti-tank power in the European theatre was causing grave concern. A quantity of 500 T71s was ordered in November 1943, 300 of which were taken direct from M10 production, and the T7 gun (which was the M1 anti-aircraft gun modified to fit the 3in gun mount) had been standardised in August 1943 as the M3 90mm gun. In June 1944 the T71 was standardised as the M36 90mm Gun Motor Carriage and production, which had begun with the 'Limited Procurement' order for 500, continued, the first vehicles arriving with troops in July 1944. The M36 used the same hull as the M10A1 but production difficulties led to a trial mounting of the M36 turret on the standard M4A3 tank hull.

Right: M10 tank destroyer of the Free French forces in North Africa. The US M10 mounted a 3in gun; it was more effective as the 'Achilles' with a British 17 pounder.

M24 CHAFFEE LIGHT TANK

T17, M8, M8A1, T24, M24, M37, M19, M41, T77, T9, T13, T22, T23, T33, T42, T9, T6E1 and T31.
Crew: 5, sometimes reduced to 4.
Armament: One 75mm M6 gun; one .3in M1919A4 machine-gun co-axial with main armament; one .3in M1919A4 machine-gun; one .5in M2 machine-gun; one 2in M3 smoke mortar.
Armour: 0.375in (10mm) minimum; 1.5in (38mm) maximum.
Dimensions: Length 18ft (5.49m); height 8ft 2in (2.77m); width 9ft 8in (2.95m).
Weight: Combat 40,500lbs (18,370kg).
Ground pressure: 11.3lb/in² (0.79kg/cm²).
Power to weight ratio: 12.2hp/ton.
Engines: Two Cadillac 44T24 V-8 water-cooled petrol engines each developing 110hp at 3,400rpm.
Performance: Road speed 34mph (54km/h); road range 100 miles (160km); vertical obstacle 3ft (0.91m); trench 8ft (2.44m); fording depth 3ft 4in (1.02m) unprepared and 6ft 6in (1.98m) prepared; gradient 60 per cent.
History: Entered US Army service in 1944. Supplied to many other countries including (in small numbers) UK, and still in wide use in 1977. Basis of original 'Lightweight Combat Team'.

Right: The M24 Chaffee entered US service in 1944. Many still serve in other armies.

Compared with the M5 light tank which it replaced, the M24 was a quantum advance. In two of the three attributes of armour — firepower and protection, the M24 surpassed all other light tanks of World War II, while its mobility was comparable with the exceptionally agile M5. Its 75mm gun was almost the equal to that of the Sherman and more powerful than the armament of most medium tanks in 1939. The vastly improved hull and turret shape increased protection by the elimination of shot traps, reduction of the silhouette and better sloping of the armour. Today it is normal to consider ease of maintenance as another attribute of the tank and the M24 was designed with accessibility of major assemblies in mind. Attempts to mount the 75mm gun in a light tank began at almost the same time as the project for a 75mm gun medium tank. The T17 75mm Howitzer Motor Carriage, based on the M1E3 Combat Car, was the first step in this direction, and later when requirement was shown to exist for a light tank with the firepower of the M4 Medium Tank, the M8 Howitzer Motor Carriage was modified accordingly. With the M3 75mm Gun, the combination was known as the M8A1, although this nomenclature was not formally assigned. This equipment showed that the M5 chassis could accept the firing stresses imposed by the 75mm gun, but the M8A1 version lacked the essential characteristics of a tank. Military characteristics defined for the new light tank were that the power train of the M5A1 should be retained; the suspension should be improved; the gross weight should not exceed 16 long tons (16,257kg), and that the armour should reach a maximum of 1in (25.4mm) thickness and be acutely angled to the horizontal. The M5A1 light tank was limited in the space available within the turret, a fact which precluded the installation of the 75mm gun. A T21 light tank was considered, but at 21.5 tons (21,845kg) this would have been too heavy. The T7 light tank was examined exhaustively by the Armored Force. It had been designed around the 57mm gun at

Right: M24 Chaffee light tank on firing practice. The versatile Chaffee was replaced in the United States Army in the 1950s by the M41 Walker Bulldog.

the request of the British Army and when the Armored Force asked for a 75mm gun, the resultant weight increase moved the T7 into the medium tank category. In fact standardisation as the M7 medium tank, with the 75mm gun, was approved but later cancelled to avoid the logistic disadvantages of having two standard medium tank types. The Cadillac Motor Division of the General Motors Corporation delivered pilot models of a vehicle to meet the stated requirements in October 1943. The T24, as it was designated, was found satisfactory and 1,000 were ordered before service tests had begun. In addition, pilots of the T24E1 with the power train of the M18 tank destroyer were also ordered, but this development was later cancelled. The T24 mounted the T13E1 75mm gun in a Concentric Recoil Mechanism T33 with a .3in machine-gun in the Combination Gun Mount T90. The gun was a lightweight weapon developed from the M5 aircraft gun, and although the standardised nomenclature M6 was assigned, this merely indicated tank use as opposed to airborne use. The twin Cadillac engines of

the T24 were mounted on rails for ease of maintenance — a feature of the T7 light tank — and were identical with those of the M5A1. Indeed, it was because the T24 shared the same power plant as the M5A1 that Cadillac was chosen to produce the T24 in quantity, although later American Car & Foundry and Massey-Harris were to be indluded in production. The torsion-bar suspension of the M18 tank destroyer was used in the T24. Although the invention of this suspension is often ascribed to German tank designers, the American patent on torsion bar suspension was granted in December 1935 to G. M. Barnes and W. E. Preston. (Later General Barnes was to lead the Ordnance Research and Development Service until 1946.) Five pairs of stamped disc wheels, 25in (63.5cm) in diameter and rubber-tired, were mounted on each side and a sprocket at the front drove the 16in (40.6cm) tracks. The hull of the T24 was of all welded construction, reaching a maximum thickness on frontal surfaces of 2.5in (63.5mm) although in less critical places the armour was thinner to conform to the

M22 LOCUST LIGHT TANK (AIRBORNE)

Crew: 3.
Armament: One 37mm M6 gun; one .3in M1919A4 co-axial machine-gun.
Armour: 9mm to 25mm.
Dimensions: Length 12ft 11in (3.32m); width 7ft 4in (2.23m); height 5ft 8in (1.74m).
Weight: Combat 17,024lbs (7,722kg).
Ground pressure: 7.21lb/in² (0.51kg/cm²).
Power to weight ratio: 21.3hp/ton.
Engine: Lycoming 0-435T six-cylinder horizontally-opposed petrol engine developing 162hp at 3,000rpm.
Performance: Road speed 40mph (64km/h); cross-country speed 27mph (43km/h); road range 135 miles (216km); vertical obstacle 1ft 4in (0.4m); trench 5ft 5in (1.65m); gradient 52 per cent; fording depth 3ft 6in (1.1m).
History: Entered service with US Army in 1944. Also used by the British and Egyptian Armies.

Having taken note of the development by both Germany and the Soviet Union of airborne capability, the US Army decided in February 1941 that it too should have such forces. In order that these forces

might have armoured support an airportable tank, weighing no more than 7½ tons (7,620kg), was proposed, and the General Motors Corporation, J. W. Christie and Marmon-Herrington were all invited to submit designs. The Marmon-Herrington proposal was selected, and in May 1941 one pilot model was ordered under the designation Light Tank T9 (Airborne). At the same time development of an aircraft capable of carrying the T9 was begun. The first T9 weighed 7.9 tons (8,027kg), but this increase was accepted by the Army Air Corps and also by the British Army who had by now become interested in the project. The vehicle had a welded hull and cast turret, and the familiar vertical volute spring suspension of contemporary American light tanks. In January 1942 two pilot models of the improved T9E1 were ordered. The shape of the turret was altered, power traverse and a gyrostabiliser were added, the front plate was modified and the two bow machine-guns were removed. Brackets were added to enable the tank to be slung beneath the C-54 cargo aircraft, and the T9E1 was tested in this form by the 28th Airborne Tank Battalion. For transport in this

way it was necessary to remove the turret, a feature which severely limited the surprise effect of delivering the tank by air. The Army Service Forces ordered 500 T9E1 tanks in April 1942 before service tests had begun. Problems in manufacture and continual amendments to the design meant that of the anticipated total order of 1,900, only 830 were delivered by February 1944, when production came to an end. The T9E1 received the designation M22 in August 1944, but was always better known by its popular name of 'Locust'. The Locust was supplied to the British Army in small numbers and it was in British service that it saw its only operational use. Some Locusts were used by the Airlanding Brigade of the 6th Airborne Division in the crossing of the Rhine in March 1945. For this operation the tanks were carried in the Hamilcar glider, which could also carry the British Tetrarch airborne tank. In general, tanks are considered to combine firepower, protection and mobility to produce a fighting machine, and in practice a shortcoming in one particular factor may be offset by a superiority in another. The unfortunate Locust possessed none of these vital attributes.

concept of the light tank. A large cover in the glacis plate could be removed for access to the controlled differential steering, and dual controls were provided for the driver and assistant driver. In July 1944 the T24 was standardised as the M24 Light Tank, popularly known as the 'Chaffee', and by June 1945 a total of 4,070 had been produced. In keeping with the idea of a Lightweight Combat Team, other vehicles using the M24 chassis were designed for specialist applications. A variety of gun and mortar motor carriages was developed, of which the T77 Multiple Gun Motor Carriage is one of the more interesting. A new turret mounting six .5in machine-guns was mounted on a basically standard M24 chassis and in a way this vehicle foreshadowed the modern six-barrelled Vulcan Air Defense System. Two armored utility vehicles, the T9 and T13, were designed and three cargo carriers also developed. The T22E1 and T23E1 were adaptations of the T22 and T23 which were based on the M5 light tank and described under that heading. The T33 Cargo Carrier was a later development which, with the substitution of the medium tank engine and torque converter transmission of the Hellcat, became the T42 Cargo Tractor. The T43 Cargo Tractor was a lighter version of the T42. A bulldozer kit, the T9, was developed and adopted as the M4 but was not widely used. Various aids to flotation were tried, as in the case of the Hellcat, but none were adopted for widespread use. Each of the Combat Team families was provided with a recovery vehicle, and the T6E1 Tank Recovery Vehicle was the model compatible with the M24 series. Although pilots were built, development was not pursued. In the concept stage of the M24 project, Army Ground Forces had hoped that the M24 would be capable of being carried by air. Even with the lighter Locust, air transport in the C-54 aircraft involved removing the turret and slinging the hull beneath the fuselage. The advent of the C-82 aircraft with its 10 ton (10,161kg) payload would, it was hoped, make it possible to transport the M24 in two loads but the amount of dismantling involved was prohibitive in time, labour and equipment. Furthermore, aircraft then under development would be able to carry M24-sized vehicles in a single load. After Word War II, Chaffees were employed by many armies and saw action in Korea and Indo-China. The versatile Chaffee also served as the basis for much experimentation. Turrets were exchanged with the French AMX-13 and at Aberdeen Proving Ground one M24 was fitted with the suspension of the German ¾-tracked 11.8 ton (12,000 kg) tractor. Although rolling resistance was less than the standard running gear below 15mph (24km/h), there was no advantage above this speed and the performance in mud was inferior. An automatically-loaded 76mm gun was produced in a working mock-up for the M24, but this project proceeded no further. The T31 Antipersonnel Device used banks of antipersonnel mines on each side of the hull, to repel close-in infantry, and an experimental cupola mounted two .5in machine-guns to increase the firepower at the commander's disposal. Many Chaffees remain in service with armies throughout the world, including those of Iraq, Pakistan and Uruguay. The Norwegian Army has modified the M24 as a tank destroyer with a French 90mm high/low pressure gun and this vehicle is known as the NM116.

Right: Front and rear views of the M24 Chaffee tank. By June 1945, more than 4,000 M24s had been built by the Cadillac Motor Company and Massey Harris.

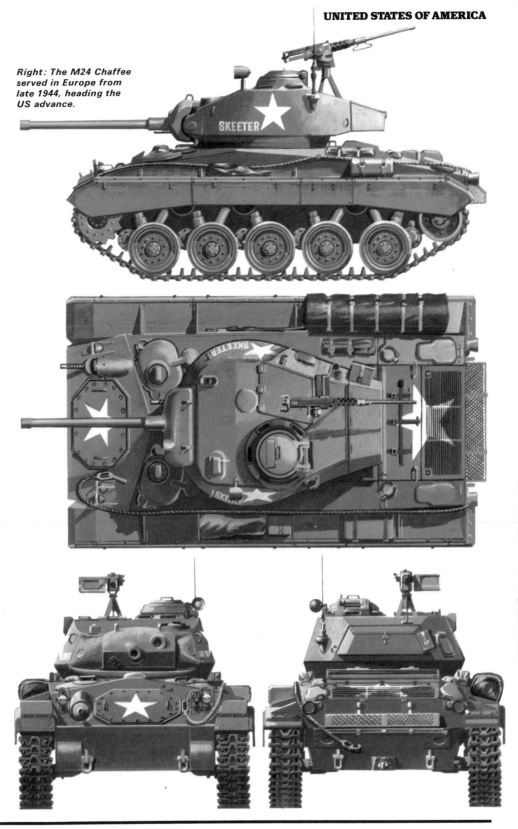

Right: The M24 Chaffee served in Europe from late 1944, heading the US advance.

Because the United States had not managed to develop an aircraft or glider capable of carrying the 'Locust' without the need to disassemble the tank, no advantage could be taken of the light weight. The 'Locust' had very thin armour, which could be defeated by the .5in AP round, and by the standards of 1945 it was underpowered and undergunned. An attempt was made in the T9E2 to provide more HE firepower in the form of a breechloading 81mm mortar, but this project, although successful, was dropped at the cessation of hostilities in 1945.

Right: The M22 Locust airborne tank was developed specifically for use by US airborne forces. Although 830 were built by Marmon-Herrington by February 1944, the tank was not used in large numbers. The British 6th Airborne Division used some Locusts during the crossing of the Rhine in March 1945. After the war, some were supplied to the Egyptian Army.

M18 HELLCAT TANK DESTROYER

T49, T67, T70, M18, T41, M39, T9, T65, T86, T87, T88.
Crew: 5.
Armament: One 76mm M1A1 gun; one .5in M2 anti-aircraft machine-gun.
Armour: 0.3in (7.9mm) minimum; 1in (25.4mm) maximum.
Dimensions: Length 21ft 10in (6.65m); width 9ft 5in (2.87m); height 8ft 5in (2.58m).
Weight: Combat 37,557lbs (17,036kg).
Ground pressure: 11.9lb/in² (0.84kg/cm²).
Power to weight ratio: 23.8hp/ton.
Engine: Continental R 975-C4 nine-cylinder air-cooled radial petrol engine developing 400hp at 2,400rpm.
Performance: Road speed 55mph (88km/h); road range 105 miles (168km); trench 6ft 2in (1.88m); vertical obstacle 3ft (0.91m); fording depth 4ft (1.22m); gradient 60 per cent.
History: Entered US Army service in 1944 and was first vehicle to use torsion-bar suspension. Withdrawn from US service soon after World War II but still in use in Latin America.

Today, few people would dispute that the tank is the prime anti-tank weapon. However, the principle of 'Shoot and scoot' has always had its proponents, and this attitude has usually been reflected in American tank destroyers. The original M6 37mm Gun Motor Carriage had only its mobility for protection, and even this mobility was limited by the wheeled chassis. More recently, the 'Ontos' vehicle, with six 106mm recoilless rifles, and the M56 'Scorpion' have shown that the small, light but heavily armed vehicle was still felt to have a role. In the early years of World War II there was considerable debate and indecision within the Tank Destroyer Force as to the best vehicle to defeat enemy armour. A series of experimental vehicles had tried wheels, tracks and halftrack chassis, with inconclusive results. In December 1941 came the recommendation that a new tank destroyer be developed, incorporating all the experience gained thus far. At that time the tank destroyer was seen as having thinner armour, but higher speed, than a tank, and normally with an open turret. Better vision was obtained at the expense of protection, which was thought to be en-

hanced by better mobility. The new vehicle was to have Christie suspension to achieve its high speed, and should weigh around 12 tons (12,193kg). The 37mm gun quickly passed from favour and the 57mm gun was selected to arm the new vehicle, now designated the T49 57mm Gun Motor Carriage. The suspension was changed to incorporate shorter helical springs and only slightly resembled Christie's design. The T49 achieved a speed of 50mph (80km/h), which was a promising start, and the second pilot model was fitted with the M3 75mm gun which also equipped the Sherman. This vehicle was the T67 75mm Gun Motor Carriage. Tests were successful and it was recommended that the T67 should be equipped with a standard tank engine to replace the twin Buick engines used in the T49 and T67. Torsion-bar suspension and the 76mm gun were also recommended. A consequence of the selection of the Continental radial engine was

that the drive sprocket was moved from the rear to the front of the vehicle. A stepless torque converter transmission was used with the Continental engine, the same as that of the Sherman. Six pilot models of what was really a new design were ordered under the designation T70 76mm Gun Motor Carriage. As the development process had moved so quickly and with such little difficulty, Army Service Forces were confident enough in the outcome to order 1,000 of the T70 in January 1943, and their foresight was rewarded. The T70, weighing 19 tons (19,305kg) instead of the originally expected 12 tons (12,193kg), was still capable of 55mph (89km/h) and the 76mm gun proved to be a most effective weapon. Elimination of the bow machine-gun of the T49 and T67 released a further crew member, and a slightly wider track improved the flotation on soft ground. In February 1944 the T70 was adopted as standard by the US Army

M26 PERSHING HEAVY TANK

T25, T26, T26E1, T26E2, T26E3, M26, M45, M46 and many variants.
Crew: 5.
Armament: One 90mm M3 gun; one .3in M1919A4 machine-gun co-axial with main armament; one .3in M1919A4 machine-gun in hull front, one .5in M2 machine-gun on turret roof.
Armour: 0.51in (13mm) minimum; 4in (102mm) maximum.
Dimensions: Length 28ft 5in (8.65m); width 11ft 6in (3.51m); height 9ft 1in (2.78m).
Weight: Combat 92,355lbs (41,891kg).
Ground pressure: 13.1lb/in² (0.92kg/cm²).
Power to weight ratio: 10.9hp/ton.
Engine: Ford GAF V-8 water-cooled petrol engine developing 500hp at 2,600rpm.
Performance: Road speed 30mph (48km/h); road range 100 miles (160km); vertical obstacle 3ft 10in (1.17m); trench 8ft (2.44m); fording depth 4ft (1.22m); gradient 60 per cent.
History: Although doubts existed as to the need for such a tank, the Pershing entered US service in 1945. Saw service in Korea and in the 1950s with many foreign armies. Development of the M60 main battle tank can be traced to the M26.

When the M26 heavy tank was introduced into service with the US Army in 1945, it marked the end of a line of development which began in 1938 with the M2 medium tank. By the same token it marked the birth of a line culminating in the M60 series, the main battle tank of the 1960s. The story of the M26 begins in 1942 when the Ordnance Department received the approval of the Services of Supply for its proposed development of the T20 medium tank. This tank was intended to be an improvement on the M4 series but Ordnance hoped to be able to use the vehicle for comparative tests of armaments, transmissions and suspensions. Thirteen different models of the T20, T22 and T23 medium tanks were developed and these variously tried different weapons — for example the 76mm gun; different transmissions — for example the 'gas-electric' transmission

is also used in the M6 heavy tank; and different suspensions — for example the early form of horizontal volute spring suspension of the Sherman. Development of two heavy tanks followed and these were designated T25 and T26. Both mounted the new T7 90mm gun and used the Ford GAN engine with electric transmissions. The T26 was given a higher priority, and in the T26E1 the Ford GAF engine drove the vehicle through a hydraulic torque converter in series with planetary reduction gearing. This transmission gave three forward ratios and one reverse and was known as the 'torquematic' transmission. Torsion-bar suspension with a 24in (61cm) track was fitted. The turret was cast, while the hull was fabricated from a combination of castings and rolled plate. At this point the feelings of the various interested parties began to emerge, and opinions differed widely. Early in 1943 the Armored Command had expressed the view that the war would be won or lost with the M4 medium tank, and as a result of this Ordnance embarked on several improvements to crew safety, mechanical reliability and combat efficiency in the Sherman. The Armored Command also objected to heavy tanks in general on the grounds of

weight and size, quoting an Army Regulation which limited the size of vehicles to the capacity of Corps of Engineers' bridges. (It was pointed out that the German Army was apparently not constrained by this limitation.) Army Ground Forces, however, wanted 1,000 of the T26 and 7,000 of the lighter T25, the T26 to be armed with the 76mm gun and the T25 with the 75mm gun. On the other hand the Armored Command wanted neither the T25 nor the T26 but did require the 90mm gun. The T26E2 mounted the 105mm howitzer in a mount which was interchangeable with the 90mm mount, and in the T26E3 Ordnance believed that the best compromise had been reached. Army Ground Forces preferred to delay any standardisation action until the Armored Board had indicated its satisfaction and approved the vehicle's battleworthiness, so the Secretary of War provided the necessary impetus by sending 20 tanks to the European Theatre of Operations. This 'Zebra Mission' proved the battleworthiness of the T26E3 in the hands of the 3rd and 9th Armored Divisions and standardisation and production then proceeded. It is interesting to note that in June 1944, the European Theatre had reported to

Right: The M26 Pershing heavy (reclassified as medium) tank entered US service in 1945.

Left: The US M18 tank destroyer, nicknamed 'Hellcat', entered service in 1944. Its high-velocity 76mm gun was capable of penetrating the armour of most heavy tanks.

Right: The 'Hellcat' was lightly-armoured, relying on its speed (88km/h on road) for survival. Although the US abandoned the concept, the M18 served other armies into the 1970s.

under the designation M18 76mm Gun Motor Carriage and the nickname 'Hellcat' given. With its high speed and light armour (an average of 0.5in thickness), the Hellcat could afford to change firing positions many times during an engagement and it was well liked by its crews. The Buick Motor Division of General Motors built a total of 2,507 before production ended in October 1944. After World War II American thinking on the anti-tank battle was reversed with the admission that tank could fight tank. Overnight there was no role for the specialist tank destroyer, and the M18 disappeared from tables of entitlement. However, M18s were supplied to many other countries after 1945. The chassis of the M18 was the first really new chassis produced during the war and, because of its speed, was developed for other purposes. In 1944 the T41 Armored Utility Vehicle was produced by replacing the M18 turret by an open-topped superstructure. Origin-

ally intended as a prime mover for the 3in anti-tank gun, the T41 was developed into the M39 Armored Utility Vehicle in 1945 and 640 were built as command and reconnaissance vehicles. A few M39s were still in use in the Korean War as prime movers for anti-tank guns. Other modifications included the T9 Armored Utility Vehicle and the T65 Flame Tank. Considerable effort went into giving the relatively light M18 an amphibious capability under the general heading of the 'Ritchie Project'. Wading kits were produced, and a variety of flotation devices were tried. The T86 76mm Gun Motor Carriage was the M18 with additional buoyancy compartments in a boat-like hull and a similar vehicle, the T87, mounted the 105mm howitzer. The T12 105mm howitzer was mounted in the open-topped turret of the M18 to form the T88 Howitzer Motor Carriage, and two other projects also affected the turret. In the first a form of bolt-on overhead

armour was provided for the crew and in the second the complete turret of the M36 tank destroyer was mounted on the M18 hull. The weight of this turret on the light hull of the M18 probably resulted in problems of stability when firing and would probably require a change in gear ratios in the transmission, but this development took place in 1945 and was shelved at the end of hostilities in Japan. In the early 1950s a project was begun to lengthen and widen the hull and at the same time improve the rigidity and waterborne characteristics. This project does not appear to have reached the prototype stage. Hellcats surplus to US Army requirements were supplied to several countries including Argentina, Austria, Venezuela and Yugoslavia. A few were also sent to the Soviet Union. Both the Netherlands and the post-war German Army also received the M39. The M18 was still in service in South Korea, Venezuela and Yugoslavia in 1976.

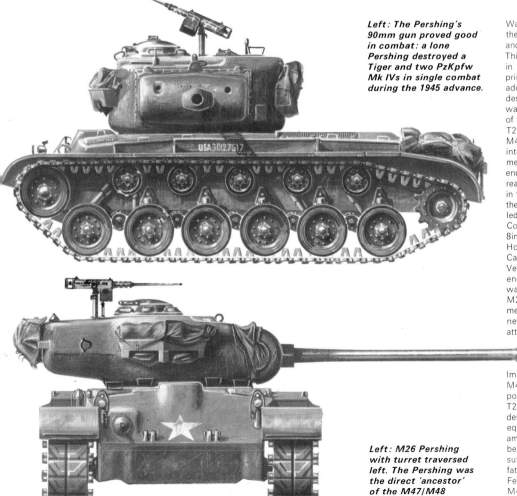

Left: The Pershing's 90mm gun proved good in combat: a lone Pershing destroyed a Tiger and two PzKpfw Mk IVs in single combat during the 1945 advance.

Left: M26 Pershing with turret traversed left. The Pershing was the direct 'ancestor' of the M47/M48 Patton and the M60 main battle tanks.

Washington that there was no requirement for either the 75mm or 76mm guns but that a mix of 90mm guns and 105mm howitzers in the ratio 1:3 was preferable. This was consistent with the perceived role of the tank in 1944 but conflicts with today's concept of the tank primarily as an anti-tank weapon. The T26E3 was adopted as standard in January 1945 under the designation M26 Heavy Tank, and the name 'Pershing' was given, after General John J. Pershing, the founder of the Tank Corps in World War I. At the same time the T26E2 with the 105mm howitzer was adopted as the M45 for the close-support role. The Pershing, although introduced as a heavy tank, was soon reclassified as a medium tank and production continued well past the end of World War II. Although too late to make any real contribution to that war, the M26 was widely used in the Korean War and later supplied to many armies in the Free World. As was usually the case, the Pershing led to a family of specialist vehicles. The 'Heavyweight Combat Team' was intended to consist of the T84 8in Howitzer Motor Carriage, the T92 240mm Howitzer Motor Carriage, the T93 8in Gun Motor Carriage, the T31 Cargo Carrier and the T12 Recovery Vehicle. A flamethrower tank, cargo tractor and combat engineer vehicle were also produced and consideration was also given to a mine resistant vehicle, based on the M26 chassis, to breach anti-tank minefields. It was mentioned earlier that the M26 marked the start of a new line of tanks, and these began with various attempts to increase the armament of the Pershing.

Improvements to the engine and gun resulted in the M46 Medium Tank, the first 'Patton', although the poor turret and cupola shape were retained. From the T26 series, further heavy tanks resulted under the designations T29, T30, T32 and T34. The T30 was equipped with a 155mm gun which fired semi-fixed ammunition, but development was dropped when it became apparent that such a vehicle would not be sufficiently effective relative to its weight. The same fate befell the T29, T32 and T34 for similar reasons. Few Pershings remain in service today but the many M47, M48 and M60 tanks throughout the world today owe their origins to the M26 and it is perhaps for this that the Pershing will be remembered.

M40 LONG TOM 155mm SELF-PROPELLED GUN

T6, M12, M30, T83, T89, M40, M43 and many variants.
Crew: 8 (including a gun detachment of 6).
Armament: 155mm M1A1 or M2 gun.
Armour: 0.47in (12mm).
Dimensions: Length 29ft 7in (9.02m); width 10ft 4in (3.15m); height 8ft 9in (2.67m).
Weight: Combat 80,020lbs (36,296kg).
Ground pressure: 12lb/in² (0.83kg/cm²).
Power to weight ratio: 9.5hp/ton.
Engine: Continental R-975 nine-cylinder radial air-cooled petrol engine developing 340hp at 2,400rpm.
Performance: Road speed 24mph (38km/h); cross-country speed 20mph (32km/h); road range 107 miles (171km); vertical obstacle 2ft 10in (0.86m); trench 7ft 9in (2.36m); fording depth 3ft (0.91m); gradient 60 per cent.
History: Entered service with US Army in 1945 and phased out in early 1950s. Also used by the British and French armies.

Early in the 1920s the US Ordnance Department evaluated several designs of self-propelled mounts for artillery. Each time the Field Artillery preferred towed guns. While a self-propelled gun could break down, a tractor could always be replaced by another tractor or even by horses. Early in 1941 the Ordnance Department had been giving serious consideration to self-propelled guns and had carried out experiments with guns up to 155mm calibre. It was shown that the chassis of the medium tank presently in use, the M3, was suitable for a 155mm gun mounting if a spade were used to transmit the shock of recoil to the ground. To circumvent the declared opposition of Army Ground Forces, the then Chief of Ordnance approached the Secretary of War directly and sought his approval for the T6 Gun Motor Carriage, as the vehicle was designated. The T6 mounted the M1918M1 155mm gun on a pedestal mount in the rear of the modified M3 chassis and was an impressive improvement over the towed piece both in mobility and also in the time taken to bring it into action. The T6 was found satisfactory and with the encouragement of the Secretary of War, Henry Stimson, was standardised as the M12 155mm Gun Motor Carriage in 1942. At the same time the T14 Cargo Carrier, a version of the T6 with ammunition stowage occupying the space used by the gun mount, was introduced as the M30. The M12 was sometimes known by the nickname 'King Kong'. Although the US Army now had self-propelled artillery in the inventory, the 100 built were used for training within the United

States and none were sent abroad. Opinion was evenly divided as to the merits of such weapons: while the Armored Board and the Ordnance Department were firmly convinced of the value of artillery which could keep pace with armoured advances, the Field Artillery Board also subscribing to this view, both Army Ground Forces and the Services of Supply opposed the idea. It was not until May 1944 that these two agencies changed their minds and the 74 M12s which remained were overhauled and sent to the European Theatre of Operations — three years after the first T6 appeared. Most of the M12s seem to have been used in the direct-fire role against fortifications in the drive through France but although this was hailed by the official Ordnance historian as a tactical innovation, such use is not the prime role of self-propelled artillery. More importantly, the M12 brought tactical mobility to counter-battery fire. Parallel with the reworking of the 74 M12s in May 1944, a project was begun to mount the new M1A1 155mm gun on a modified version of the M4A3 medium tank. This chassis, with horizontal volute spring suspension, had the engine moved forwar and a spade and platform at the rear and could mount either the 155mm gun or the 8in howitzer. These vehicles were designated the T83 155mm Gun Motor Carriage and the T89 8in Howitzer Motor Carriage and, as with the M12, a companion cargo carrier was built and designated T30. The T83 was eminently satisfactory and Limited Procurement of 304 (with an equal number of the T30) was authorised in July 1944. These vehicles were to use the hull of the M4A1. Limited Procurement was a subterfuge employed by the

Ordnance Department to procure equipment which it considered useful although Army Ground Forces had not approved. In the event, vehicles were produced in time to meet demands from both the European and Pacific theatres in July 1944. Standardisation of the T83 as the M40 came in March 1945, and the T89 became the M43. The T30 Cargo Carrier was not standardised although a modification, the T30E1, was developed with interchangeable racking for 240mm ammunition. Another variant of the M40 was the T94 Mortar Motor Carriage, mounting the T5E2 10in mortar on the chassis of the T83. The nickname 'Long Tom' given to the towed gun was often used for the M40 as well. Use of the M12 was confined to the US Army, but the M40 was supplied to allies, including the British and French armies. Probably the most important action in which the M40 featured was the capture of Cologne, although M40s were also used in Korea. It is interesting to note that the official Signal Corps photographs of the M40 at Cologne appear deliberately to conceal the suspension detail, although by that time photographs of the horizontal volute spring suspension on medium tanks had appeared.

Below: A 155mm M40 'Long Tom' self-propelled gun, with the spade in the lowered position.

M75 ARMOURED PERSONNEL CARRIER

Crew: 2 plus 10.
Armament: One .5in machine-gun on commander's cupola.
Armour: 9.5mm—25.4mm (0.37–1in).
Dimensions: Length 17ft (5.193m); width 9ft 4in (2.844m); height (overall) 10ft (3.041m).
Weight: Combat 41,500lbs (18,828kg).
Ground pressure: 8.1lb/in² (0.57kg/cm²).
Engine: Continental AO-895-4 six-cylinder air-cooled petrol engine developing 295bhp at 2,660rpm.
Performance: Road speed 44mph (71km/h); range 115 miles (185km); vertical obstacle 1ft 6in (0.457m); trench 5ft 6in (1.676m); gradient 60 per cent.
History: Entered service with United States Army in 1952. Now used only by the Belgian Army.

During World War II the standard American armoured personnel carrier was the M3 half-track. This had a number of limitations as it had no overhead armour protection and could not keep up with tanks across country. So in September 1945 the US Army issued a requirement for a full tracked carrier which would carry 12 men and could be used as an armoured personnel carrier, reconnaissance vehicle and command-post vehicle. It was also to be based on the chassis of the T43 cargo tractor. The following year development started under the designation T18, and the International Harvester company was awarded a contract to design and build four prototypes. Further development resulted in the T18E1 and later the T18E2. The basic T18 was unarmed, although later models were fitted with a variety of armament installations including remote-controlled machine-guns in single and twin mounts. The vehicle was authorised for production in 1951, and 1,729 production vehicles were built by International Harvester and FMC between 1952 and 1954. The M75 makes use of some of the

components of the M41 light tank developed in the same period. The M75 was used by the US Army for only a few years before it was replaced by the M59 APC. Although an improvement over the M44 utility vehicle, the M75 was very high, had no NBC system or amphibious capability and was very expensive to produce. Its cost was about $100,000, more than the M113A1 APC of today. The vehicle has a hull of all-welded steel construction, with the driver at the front on the left and the engine and transmission to his right. The personnel compartment is at the rear and the infantry enter and leave the vehicle via two doors in

the rear of the hull. There are also two roof hatches over the top of the troop compartment. Although some of the prototypes were fitted with some quite sophisticated armament systems, production vehicles have a single .5in Browning machine-gun on the commander's cupola, and 1,800 rounds of ammunition are carried for this. The M75 can ford streams to a maximum depth of 4ft (1.219m) without preparation, or 6ft 8in (2.032m) with the aid of a kit. Although a number of experimental models of different versions of the M75 were built, none of these were placed in production.

Right: The M75 armoured personnel carrier introduced in 1952 proved very expensive to build and was fairly swiftly replaced in US service by the M59 APC.

M41 WALKER BULLDOG LIGHT TANK

M41, M41A1, M41A2, M41A3
Crew: 4.
Armament: One 76mm gun; one .3in machine-gun co-axial with main armament; one .5in anti-aircraft machine-gun.
Armour: 12mm–38mm (0.47–1.50in).
Dimensions: Length (gun forward) 26ft 11in (8.212m); length (hull) 19ft 1in (5.819m); width 10ft 6in (3.198m); height (including .5in machine-gun 10ft 1in (3.075m).
Weight: Combat 51,800lbs (23,495kg).
Ground pressure: 10.24lb/in² (0.72kg/cm²).
Engine: Continental or Lycoming AOS-895-3 6-cylinder petrol engine developing 500bhp at 2,800rpm.
Performance: Road speed 45mph (72km/h); range 100 miles (161km); vertical obstacle 2ft 4in (0.711m); trench 6ft (1.828m); gradient 60 per cent.
History: Entered service with United States Army in 1951. No longer used by the United States but still in service with Argentina, Austria, Belgium, Bolivia, Brazil, Chile, Denmark, Ecuador, Ethiopia, Japan, Lebanon, New Zealand, Pakistan, the Philippines, Portugal, Saudi-Arabia, Spain, Taiwan, Thailand, Tunisia, Turkey and Vietnam.

The standard light tank in use with the United States Army at the end of World War II was the M24 Chaffee, which weighed 18 tons (18,289kg) and was armed with a 75mm gun. Shortly after the end of the war work started on a new light tank called the T37. The first prototype of this was completed in 1949 and was known as the T37 Phase I. This was followed by the T37 Phase II, which had a redesigned turret and different fire-control system. This model was then redesignated as the T41 and a slightly modified version of this, the T41E1, was standardised as the M41. The M41 was authorised for production in 1950 and was named the Little Bulldog, although the name was subsequently changed to the Walker Bulldog after General W. W. Walker, killed in an accident in Korea in 1951. Production of the M41 was undertaken by the Cadillac Car Division of the General Motors Corporation at the Cleveland Tank Plant, and first production models were completed in 1951. Further models of the M41 were the M41A1, M41A2 and the M41A3. These have a slightly different gun control system, whilst the M41A2 and M41A3 have a fuel-injection system for the engine. The M41 was one of the three main tanks developed for the US Army in the early 1950s, the others being the M47 medium and M103 heavy tanks. The M41 was the first member of a whole family of vehicles sharing many common components. The family included the M42 self-propelled anti-aircraft gun, the M44 and M52 self-propelled howitzers and the M75 armoured personnel carrier. In addition there were many trials versions in the 1950s. More recently M41s have been used by the United States Navy. Fitted with remote-control equipment, they are used as mobile targets for new air-to-ground missiles. The hull of the M41 is of all-welded steel construction, whilst the turret is of welded and cast construction. The driver is seated at the front of the hull on the left, with the other three crew members in the turret, the commander and gunner on the right and the loader on the left. The engine and transmission are at the rear of the hull, and are separated from the fighting compartment by a fireproof bulkhead. Like most American AFVs of that period, the M41 is provided with a hull escape hatch, thus enabling the crew to leave the vehicle with a better chance of survival than if they baled out via the turret or driver's hatch. The suspension is of the torsion-bar type and consists of five road wheels, with the drive sprocket at the rear and the idler at the front. There are three track-return rollers. The main armament of the M41 consists of a 76mm gun with an elevation of +19° and a depression of −9°, traverse being 360°. A .3in machine-gun is mounted to the left of the main armament and there is a .5in Browning machine-gun on the commander's cupola. Some 65 rounds of 76mm 2,175 rounds of .5in and 5,000 rounds of .3in ammunition are carried. The

barrel of the 76mm gun is provided with a bore evacuator and a 'T' type blast-deflector, the latter's function being to reduce the effects of blast and obscuration caused by the flow of propellant gases into the atmosphere. These gases otherwise raise a dust cloud and make aiming of the weapon more difficult. When developed the M41 was to have been fitted with an automatic loader (this was the T37 Phase III), but this was not installed in production vehicles. The M41 was also fitted with a 90mm gun for trials purposes, under the designation T49, but this did not progress beyond the prototype stage. The M41 can ford to a maximum depth of 3ft 4in (1.016m) without preparation or 8ft (2.44m) with the aid of a kit. Infra-red driving lights are provided, and some models have an infra-red searchlight for engaging targets at night. The M41 has been replaced by the M551 Sheridan in the United States Army, but is still used by many countries in most parts of the world. Until recently the American numbering system for their equipment operated as follows. When under development the vehicle had a T number (the M41 was the T37, for example) and if the type was then fitted with something like a new engine or new armament, the suffix E1 was added, this altering to E2 if yet another engine or other major item of equipment was

added. If this was found to be satisfactory, the type was then standardised for US Army issue and given an M number. The ONTOS, for example, was called the T165, then T165E1 and finally T165E2 before it was standardised as the M50. Once in service, the type keeps this designation until any major changes are made, such as the installation of a new engine, as happened with the M50, which thus became the M50A1. In some cases this can go on for a number of years, a good example being the M60, which started off as the M60, then became the M60A1, M60A2 and now the M60A3. More recently, during their development phase vehicles have been given an XM number, such as the XM1 tank, and when standardised they just drop the X: in the case of the XM1, this now becomes the M1. During the last war there was often confusion as there was an M3 tank, M3 howitzer, M3 sub-machine gun and so on!.

Below: An M41 Walker Bulldog light tank of the Danish Army. Introduced in 1951, the M41 has been replaced in US service by the M551 Sheridan, but it is still used by many countries and has proved to be a very reliable tank.

Right and above right: The M41 light tank was one of three main tank types developed for the US Army after the end of World War II: the other two were the M47 medium and the M103 heavy tanks. The M41 was to have been called the Little Bulldog but this was changed to Walker Bulldog to commemorate General W. W. Walker's death in a Jeep accident in Korea in 1951. The M41 mounted a 76mm gun, .30in co-axial machine-gun and a .50in AA machine-gun.

M47 MEDIUM TANK

M47, M102
Crew: 5.
Armament: One 90mm M36 gun; one .3in M1919-A4E1 machine-gun in bow; one .3in M1919A4E1 machine-gun co-axial with main armament; one .5in M2 machine-gun on commander's cupola.
Armour: 12.7mm–115mm (0.50in–4.60in).
Dimensions: Length (gun forward) 28ft 1in (8.508m); length (hull) 20ft 10¾in (6.362m); width 10ft 6in (3.51m); height (including anti-aircraft machine-gun) 11ft (3.352m).
Weight: Combat 101,775lbs (46,170kg).
Ground pressure: 13.3lb/in² (0.935kg/cm²).
Engine: Continental AV-1790-5B 12-cylinder air-cooled petrol engine developing 810bhp at 2,800rpm.
Performance: Road speed, 30mph (48km/h); range 80 miles (130km); vertical obstacle 3ft (0.914m); trench 8ft 6in (2.59m); gradient 60 per cent.

History: Entered service with the United States Army in 1952. Still used by Austria, Belgium, Brazil, Greece, Iran, Italy, Jordan, Pakistan, Saudi-Arabia, South Korea, Spain, Taiwan, Turkey and Yugoslavia. The M47 is no longer used by France, Germany or the United States.

After the end of World War II the M26 Pershing heavy tank was reclassified as a medium tank, and further development of the type resulted in the M46 medium tank. The M46 and M26 were the standard US medium tanks when the Korean War broke out in 1950. A new medium tank, the T42, was being developed, but this was not yet ready for production. To meet the urgent need to get an improved medium tank into production, a modified M26 tank chassis was fitted with the turret of the new T42 tank, armed with a new 90mm gun. This then became the M47 medium tank, also known as the Patton 1. Production started almost immediately at the Detroit Tank Arsenal and the American Locomotive Company, but the M47 did not see combat in Korea. The hull and the turret of the M47 are of all-cast construction. The driver is seated at the front of the hull on the left with the bow machine-gunner to his right. The commander and gunner are on the right of the turret, with the loader on the left. The engine and transmission are at the rear of the hull. The suspension is of the torsion-bar type and consists of six road wheels, with the drive sprocket at the rear and the idler at the front. There are three track-return rollers and a small tensioning wheel is located between the last road wheel and the drive sprocket. (When a tank is

Above right, front view of the basic M47 showing cylindrical blast deflector and no range-finder.

Left, side view of the M47 medium tank (90mm Gun Full Tracked Combat Tank, in official US Army jargon). The main armament was semi-automatic and controlled by either the gunner or commander, who had override controls. It took ten seconds to rotate the turret through 360°.

M103 HEAVY TANK

M103, M103A1, M103A2
Crew: 5.
Armament: One M58 120mm gun; one .3in M57 or M1919A4E1 machine-gun co-axial with main armament; one .5in M2 anti-aircraft machine-gun.
Armour: 12mm–178mm (0.47in–7.12in).
Dimensions: Length (gun forward) 37ft 1½in (11.315m); length (hull) 22ft 11in (6.984m); width 12ft 4in (3.758m); height 9ft 5½in (2.88m).
Weight: 125,000lbs (56,700kg).
Ground pressure: 12.85lb/in² (0.9kg/cm²).
Engine: Continental AV-1790-5B or 7C 12-cylinder air-cooled diesel developing 810hp at 2,800rpm.
Performance: Road speed 21mph (34km/h); range 80 miles (129km); vertical obstacle 3ft (0.914m); trench 7ft 6in (2.286m); gradient 60 per cent.
History: Entered service with the United States Army

in 1957/58. Last used by Marine Corps and phased out of service in 1972–73.

Towards the end of World War II the Americans had a number of heavy tanks under various stages of development, including the T28 (this was really an assault gun and weighed 90 tons (91,445kg), and was later redesignated the T95 Gun Motor Carriage), T29, T30, T32 and T34. None of these progressed beyond the prototype stage, however. After the war trials with these tanks continued, but it was eventually decided to start work on a new tank, the T43. Two prototypes of this were completed in 1948 and these were followed by four modified versions designated T43E1. The latter model was placed in production and 200 were built between 1952 and 1954 by Chrysler. The T43E1 was not standardised as the M103 until 1953. Many faults became apparent in service and the US Army promptly

declared the type unfit for front-line use. It was not until 1957–58 that the tank was considered fit for service as over 150 different modifications were required to each tank. The cost of a M103 in 1954 was just over $300,000, compared with the cost of a M60A1, 20 years later, of $297,000. The M103 was designed to fulfil a role similar to that of the British Conqueror heavy tank: engaging the Russian IS-3, and later the T-10, at long range. It was not surprising that the M103 had the same limitations as the Conqueror: on the battlefield it was underpowered and therefore lacked mobility. It had the same engine and transmission as the M47 tank, which weighed 10 tons (10,161kg) less. The M103 often broke down, and had a very short operational range. It was intended to fit auxiliary fuel tanks to the rear of the hull, but although tested these were not adopted. The M103 did not remain in front-line service with the United States Army for very long, and once the M60 was in production the older vehicle soon passed away. The M103A1 (development designation T43E2) was a rebuilt M103 with an improved fire-control system and a basket on the rear of the turret. The M103A2 (development designation M103A1E1) was basically an M103A1 with many improvements, including a new AVDS-1790-2AD diesel engine. Three prototypes were built in 1963 and these were followed by 153 conversions, all of which were for the Marine Corps, the last users of the M103 heavy tank. With the introduction of the M103 in service, a recovery vehicle also had to be developed as existing vehicles could not handle the heavy tank. This was designated M51 (development

Left, an M103 heavy tank of the US Army. The tank proved a most troublesome weapon—to its users! It often broke down, had a short operational range, was once declared unfit for front-line use and had to have over 150 modifications before it could enter service. Each M103 cost more than an M60A1, which entered service some 20 years later.

new its tracks tend to be fairly tight, but as these wear in service the tensioning wheel then takes up some of the slack.) The M47 has 86 track shoes per track when delivered. The main armament of the M47 consists of a 90mm gun with an elevation of +19° and a depression of −5°, traverse being 360°. Elevation and traverse are powered, although manual controls for use in an emergency are provided. A .3in machine-gun is mounted co-axially to the left of the main armament, and there is a similar weapon in the bow. The M47 was the last American tank to have a bow-mounted machine-gun. These have been dispensed with as they make an additional crew member necessary, and this space can be better used to carry additional fuel and ammunition. Some 71 rounds of

90mm, 440 rounds of .5in and 4,125 rounds of .3in ammunition are carried. The M47 has infra-red driving lights but no NBC system. The tank can ford streams to a maximum depth of 4ft (1.219m) without preparation. A special amphibious kit, designated T15, was developed for the M47, but this was not adopted. This kit consisted of large pontoons attached to the sides, front and rear of the hull, and the tank was propelled in the water by two propellers. As the M47 was replaced a few years after it entered service by the M48, few variants of the basic type were developed. The M102 was a special model developed for use by the engineers. This has its 90mm gun replaced by a short-barrelled 105mm howitzer. A dozer blade is mounted at the front of the hull and there is a jib for lifting purposes at the front and rear. A flame-thrower model called the T66 was developed, but this did not enter service. In the 1950s the M47 was issued to many NATO countries under the Military Assistance Program, and some of these still remain in service today. A number of countries, including Austria, France, Italy and Spain, have at various times rebuilt M47s to bring them up to modern standards. For example, in Italy Oto Melara rebuilt an M47 with a new engine and transmission, plus a new electrical system, and replaced the 90mm gun with the standard 105mm British L7 series weapon. This has been offered to a number of armies but has not so far been adopted. The Spanish Army is currently refitting some of its M47s with a new diesel engine and a modified transmission, and numerous other improvements have been incorporated. The M47 was soon replaced in the US Army by the M48, which is a direct development of the earlier M47. Although the M47 was designed almost 30 years ago, it will remain in service with some countries until the 1990s at least. Although under-gunned by today's standards, it is still a reliable and useful vehicle, despite the fact that it has an overly complicated fire-control system, which requires a well-trained gunner to get the best out of it.

Left: An M47 supporting infantry. The M47 was the first armoured fighting vehicle to be supplied to West German forces following the Soviet re-armament of East Germany.

---

designations being the T6 and later T6E1) and 200 of these were built by Chrysler, remaining in service until 1972–73. The M51 has a crew of four and weighs 54 tons (54,867kg), equipment fitted including a spade at the front and rear, a crane with a capacity of 30 tons (30,482kg) and a winch with a capacity of over 60 tons (60,963kg). The hull of the M103 is a homogeneous steel casting with the floor welded into position. The turret is also cast, but the floor of the bustle (that is the part underneath the turret rear) is welded into position. The hull is divided into three compartments, the driver's at the front, the fighting compartment in the centre and the engine and transmission at the rear. The suspension system is of the torsion-bar type and consists of seven road wheels, with the drive sprocket at the rear and the idler at the front, there being six track-return rollers. The main armament consists of a 120mm gun with an elevation of +15° and a depression

of −8°. A .3in machine-gun is mounted co-axially with the main armament and there is a Browning .5in machine-gun on the commander's cupola for use in the anti-aircraft role. Some 38 rounds of separate loading 120mm, 5,250 rounds of .3in and 1,000 rounds of .5in ammunition are carried. The main armament is not stabilised. The ammunition is of the separate loading type and the following types are available — Armour Piercing with Tracer, High Explosive, High Explosive with Tracer, Target Practice with Tracer, White Phosphorus and White Phosphorus with Tracer. The crew of five consists of commander, gunner, two loaders and the driver. The M103 is fitted with infra-red driving lights and most Marine tanks have an infra-red/white light searchlight over the main armament. The M103 can ford streams to a maximum depth of 4ft (1.219m). One would have thought that the M103 would be the last heavy tank

to be developed, but this was not so. Further tanks of this type were built, including the T54 (three different models), T57 (T32 chassis with a 120mm gun), T58 (T43 chassis with 155mm gun in an oscillating turret) and finally the T69 (T42 chassis with a 105mm gun), although none of these was ever adopted. Finally there were two heavy tanks, the T77 and T110, but details of these are still classified after 20 years. At one time there was even talk of an atomic heavy tank!

Below, top view of the M103, with turret reversed. The hull was divided into three compartments: driver's at the front, fighting compartment in the centre and engine and transmission at the rear. Main armament was a 120mm gun; other weapons were a .3in machine gun and a .5in A/A gun.

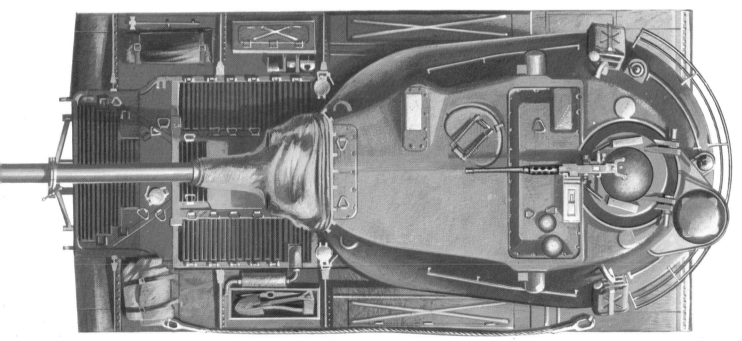

M48 MEDIUM TANK

M48, M48C, M48A1, M48A2, M48A2C, M48A3, M48A4, M48A5, M67, M67A1, M67A2, M48A VLB

Crew: 4.

Armament: One 90mm gun M41; one .3in M1919A-4E1 machine-gun co-axial with the main armament (some have a 7.62mm M73 MG); one .5in machine-gun in commander's cupola.

Armour: 12.7mm—120mm (0.50–4.80in).

Dimensions: Length (including main armament) 24ft 5in (7.442m); length (hull) 22ft 7in (6.882m); width 11ft 11in (3.631m); height (including cupola) 10ft 3in (3.124m).

Weight: Combat 104,000lbs (47,173kg).

Ground pressure: 11.80lb/in² (0.83kg/cm²).

Engine: Continental AVDS-1790-2A 12-cylinder air-cooled diesel developing 750hp at 2,400rpm.

Performance: Road speed 30mph (48km/h); range 288 miles (463km); vertical obstacle 3ft (0.915m); trench 8ft 6in (2.59m); gradient 60 per cent.

History: Entered service with the United States Army in 1953. Used by Germany, Greece, Israel, Jordan, Morocco, Norway, Pakistan, South Korea, Spain, Taiwan, Thailand, Turkey, United States and Vietnam.

Once the M47 was authorised for production, development started on a new medium tank as the M47 was only a stop-gap measure. So in October 1950 Detroit Arsenal started design work on a new medium tank armed with a 90mm gun. This design study was completed two months later and in December 1950 Chrysler was given a contract to complete the design work and build six prototypes under the designation T48. The first of these prototypes had to be completed by December 1951. In March 1951, before the prototypes were even completed, both the Ford company and the Fisher Body Division of the General Motors Corporation were given production orders for the T48, or M48 as it was to become known. Production started in 1952 and first deliveries were made to the US Army the following year. M48s were also built by Alco Products of Schenectady, New York, and production was finally completed by Chrysler at its Delaware plant in 1960. The M48 was followed by the M60, essentially an M48A3 with a 105mm gun and other detailed changes, production of this model being undertaken at the Detroit Tank Plant. The hull of the M48 is of cast armour construction, as is the turret. The driver is seated at the front of the hull with the other three crew members located in the turret, with the commander and gunner on the right and the loader on the left. The engine and transmission are at the rear of the hull, and are separated from the fighting compartment by a fireproof bulkhead. The suspension is of the torsion-bar type and consists of six road wheels, with the drive sprocket at the rear and the idler at the front. Depending on the model there are between three and five track-return rollers, and some models have a small track tensioning wheel between the sixth road wheel and the drive sprocket. The main armament consists of a 90mm gun with an elevation of +20° and a depression of −9°, traverse being 360°. A .3in M1919A4E1 machine-gun is mounted co-axially with the main armament, although most M48s in US

(except on the M48A1 which has a simple mount). This cupola can be traversed through 360°, and the machine-gun can be elevated from −10° to +60°. The amount of ammunition carried depends on the model, the M48A3 carrying 62 rounds of 90mm, 6,000 rounds of .3in and 630 rounds of .5in machine-gun ammunition. The M48 can be fitted with a dozer blade, if required, at the front of the hull. All M48s have infra-red driving lights and some an infra-red/white searchlight mounted over the main armament. The type can ford to a depth of 4ft (1.219m) without preparation or 8ft (2.438m) with the aid of a kit. Components of the M48 are also used in the M88 armoured recovery vehicle and the M53/M55 self-propelled weapons (the M55 is no longer in service). The first model to enter service was the M48, and this has a simple cupola for the commander, with the machine-gun mounted externally. The second model was the M48C, which was for training use only as it has a mild steel hull. The M48A1 was followed by the M48A2, which has many improvements including a fuel-injection system for the engine and larger capacity fuel tanks. The M48A2C was a slightly modified M48A2. The M48A3 was a significant improvement as this has a diesel engine, which increases the vehicle's operational range considerably, and a number of other modifications including a different fire-control system. The M48A4 was to have had the turrets taken from M60 tanks when they were refitted with a new turret with the 152mm Shillelagh Army service have a 7.62mm M73 machine-gun. There is also a .5in M2 machine-gun in the commander's cupola

missile system, but this plan was dropped so the M48A4 never entered service. The latest model is the M48A5, essentially an M48A1 or M48A2 with modifications including a new 105mm gun, new tracks, a 7.62mm M60D co-axial machine-gun and a similar weapon on the loader's hatch, plus many other detail modifications. Over 1,200 M48A5s are being converted, and deliveries have already started to the National Guard, as the new models will not be used by the Regular Army. Three flamethrower tanks were developed: the M67 (using an M48A1 chassis), the M67A1 (using an M48A2 chassis) and the M67A2 (using an M48A3 chassis). These were used by the Marines in Vietnam, but none are operational at the present time. Also in service is an M48 Armoured Vehicle-Launched Bridge. This has a scissors bridge which can be laid over gaps up to 60ft (18.288m) in width. There have been many trials versions of the M48 over the years. The Israeli Army has fitted many of its M48's with 105mm guns and a new low-profile commander's cupola, and this is now being adopted by the United States Army and is now being built in America. The M48 has been used in combat by Pakistan, Korea, the United States and Vietnam. When handled correctly the M48 is quite capable of taking on Russian tanks such as the T-54 and T-55, and the M48A5 with its 105mm gun should give a good account of itself against a Russian T-62. The Pakistanis lost almost 100 M48s in one action in the 1965 Indo-Pakistan campaign as a result mainly of bad tactics. Two years later the Israelis used their M48 very successfully in the Six-Day War.

Above: An M67 flame-thrower tank of the United States Marine Corps attacks VietCong positions in South Vietnam.

Below: The M48A5 is used only by American National Guard units. It is basically the M48A1/M48A2 with many improvements, notably replacement of the 90mm gun by the 105mm, which is also mounted in the US Army's M60 main battle tank.

M42 SELF-PROPELLED ANTI-AIRCRAFT GUN

Crew: 6.
Armament: Twin 40mm cannon; one .3in or 7.62mm machine-gun.
Armour: 9mm–25mm (0.35–0.99in).
Dimensions: Length (including guns) 20ft 10in (6.356m); length (hull) 19ft 1in (5.819m); width 10ft 7in (3.225m); height 9ft 4in (2.847m).
Weight: Combat 49,500lbs (22,452kg).
Ground pressure: 9.24lb/in² (0.65kg/cm²).
Engine: Continental (or Lycoming) six-cylinder air-cooled petrol engine developing 500bhp at 2,800rpm.
Performance: Road speed 45mph (72km/h); range 100 miles (161km); vertical obstacle 2ft 4in (0.711m); trench 6ft 4in (1.828 m); gradient 60 per cent.
History: Entered service with the United States Army in 1953. In service with Austria, Germany, Japan, Jordan, Lebanon, Vietnam (probably non-operational) and a few in the United States Army.

After the war only the M16 and M19 self-propelled anti-aircraft guns were retained in US Army service. With the outbreak of the Korean War in 1950, design work soon started on a new self-propelled anti-aircraft gun designated T141, using many components of a new family of armoured vehicles that eventually included the M14 light tank, and the M44 155mm and M52 105mm self-propelled guns. The T141 was authorised for production in 1952, and production continued until 1957. The T141 was to have been followed by another model designated T141E1, which would have the guns, and the T53, which would carry the fire-control equipment. This programme was subsequently cancelled and the M42 remained in service. The hull of the M42, or Duster as it is also known, is of all-welded steel armour varying in thickness from 0.35in (9mm) to 1in (25mm). The driver and radio operator are seated at the front of the vehicle with the other four crew members in the turret, which is in the centre of the hull. The engine and transmission are at the rear. The M42 has torsion-bar suspension and five road wheels, with the idler at the front and the drive sprocket at the rear, and there are three track-return rollers. The main armament consists of twin 40mm cannon mounted in an open-topped turret. These have powered elevation from −3° to +85°, and traverse through a full 360°. Manual controls are also provided, and with these the guns can be depressed a further 2°. Each barrel has a cyclic rate of fire of 120 rounds per minute. A total of 480 rounds of 40mm ammunition is carried. Types of ammunition available include Armour-Piercing Tracer and High Explosive Tracer. When the M42 first entered service, a standard .3in M1919A4 machine-gun and 1,750 rounds of ammunition were carried for local defence, but more recently this weapon has been replaced by a standard M60 7.62mm machine-gun. The M42 was used in Vietnam in some numbers, not for the air defence role, but for the defence of air bases and other vital targets from attack by VietCong ground units, in which capacity its high rate of fire proved very useful. It was realised at an early stage that the M42 had limited capabilities, however, and various projects were initiated to improve the basic vehicle, although these came to nothing. In the United States Army the M42 has been replaced to a large extent by the Vulcan Air Defense System, or the M163 as it is known. This is a standard M113A1 armoured personnel carrier fitted with a new powered turret mounting a six-barrel General Electric Gatling-type gun with two rates of fire, 1,000 or 3,000 rounds per minute. This is provided with a range-only and clear-weather radar system, and thus has no all-weather capability. The United States Army is at present testing an old XM701 MICV chassis fitted with two 25mm Philco-Ford cannon and an advanced fire-control system. The Americans have also tested the German *Gepard* twin 35mm anti-aircraft system, and there is a possibility that this may be built under licence in the United States. The Rockwell company has suggested that an M109 self-propelled gun chassis could be fitted with a redesigned turret to accept the 30mm General Electric cannon as used on the Fairchild Republic A-10 attack aircraft. This would be coupled to an advanced fire-control system. If built it would be one of the most deadly anti-aircraft gun systems ever developed. It is only in recent years that the US Army has become that interested in air defence gun systems, as it has relied on missiles such as the HAWK, Chaparral, Nike-Hercules and Redeye for the air defence of their units in the field since the Korean War. American aircraft lost over North Vietnam to anti-aircraft gun fire far exceeded those lost to missiles, however, and this trend was confirmed yet again by the Israeli Air Force in the 1973 Middle East war when the ZSU-23-4s used by Syria and Egypt accounted for many Israeli aircraft.

Left: An M42 self-propelled 40mm anti-aircraft gun system of the West German Army. Although developed in the 1950s and now obsolete, the M42 is still widely used.

M44 SELF-PROPELLED HOWITZER

M44, M44A1
Crew: 5.
Armament: One 155mm howitzer; one .5in machine-gun for anti-aircraft use.
Armour: 12.7mm (0.50in) maximum.
Dimensions: Length 20ft 2½in (6.159m); width 10ft 7½in (3.238m); height (overall) 10ft 2½in (3.111m).
Weight: Combat 62,500lbs (28,350kg).
Ground pressure: 9.38lb/in² (0.66kg/cm²).
Engine: Continental AOS-895-3 six-cylinder air-cooled petrol engine developing 500hp at 2,800rpm.
Performance: Road speed 35mph (56km/h); range 76 miles (122km); vertical obstacle 2ft 6in (0.762m); trench 6ft (1.828m); gradient 60 per cent.
History: Entered service with the United States Army in 1952. Still used by Greece, Italy, Japan, Spain and Turkey.

In 1947 there started development of a 155mm self-propelled howitzer designated the T99. It was then decided to use some of the components of a new light tank, the T41 (later to become the M41 Walker Bulldog), and with these components the T99 became the T99E1, which was then placed in production. A total of 250 T99E1s was built, but these vehicles had numerous deficiencies. After modification the type was placed in production again under the designation T194, and later the 250 T99E1s were rebuilt to the new standard. In 1953 the T194 was standardised as the M44. This was followed in 1956 by the M44A1, which has a fuel-injection system for the engine. Production of the M44 was undertaken by the Massey Harris company. The 105mm M52 self-propelled howitzer shares many components with the M44, but is no longer used by the United States Army. The M44 has been replaced in the British, German and United States Armies by the 155mm M109 self-propelled howitzer. The hull of the M44 is of all-welded construction with the engine and transmission at the front and the fighting compartment at the rear. The latter has no overhead protection, although steel hoops and a tarpaulin can be fitted if required. The suspension is of the torsion-bar type and consists of six road wheels, with the drive sprocket at the front and the sixth road wheel acting as the idler. There are four track-return rollers. A large spade is mounted at the rear of the hull and this is lowered before fire is opened. The 155mm howitzer has an elevation of +65° and a depression of −5°, traverse being 30° left and 30° right. A variety of ammunition can be fired, including High Explosive, Chemical, Nuclear, Smoke and Illuminating. A standard .5in Browning machine-gun is mounted for anti-aircraft defence on the right of the fighting compartment. Some 24 rounds of 155mm and 900 rounds of .5in ammunition are carried. The M44 can ford to a maximum depth of 3ft 6in (1,066m).

Right: An M44 155mm self-propelled howitzer in travelling order. Before firing, a large spade mounted at the rear of the gun is lowered to absorb the recoil.

M113 ARMOURED PERSONNEL CARRIER

M113, M113A1, M106, M132, M163 and variants
Crew: 2 plus 11.
Armament: One Browning .5in (12.7mm) machine-gun.
Armour: 12mm–38mm (0.47–1.58in).
Dimensions: Length 15ft 11in (4.863m); width 8ft 10in (2.686m); height 8ft 2in (2.5m).
Weight: Combat 24,600lbs (11,156kg).
Ground pressure: 7.82lb/in² (0.55kg/cm²).
Engine: General Motors Model 6V53 six-cylinder water-cooled diesel developing 215bhp at 2,800rpm.
Performance: Road speed 42mph (67.6km/h);

water speed 3.6mph (5.8km/h); range 300 miles (483km); vertical obstacle 2ft (0.61m); trench 5ft 6in (1.68m); gradient 60 per cent.
History: Entered service with the United States Army in 1960. Also used by Argentina, Australia, Bolivia, Brazil, Cambodia, Canada, Chile, Denmark, Ecuador, Ethiopia, Germany, Guatemala, Greece, Haiti, Iran, Israel, Italy, Laos, Lebanon, Libya, the Netherlands, New Zealand, Norway, Pakistan, Peru, the Philippines, Somalia, South Korea, Spain, Switzerland, Thailand, Turkey, Uruguay and Vietnam.

The M113A1 armoured personnel carrier is the most widely used APC in the world. It is built by FMC in the USA and by Oto Melara in Italy.

In the early 1950s the standard United States Army APC was the M75, followed in 1954 by the M59. Neither of these was satisfactory and in 1954 foundations were laid for a new series of vehicles. In 1956 prototypes of the T113 (aluminium hull) and T117 (steel hull) armoured personnel carriers were built. A modified version of the T113, the T113E1, was cleared for production in mid-1959 and production commenced at the FMC plant at San Jose, California in 1960. The vehicle is still in production today and so far over 60,000 have been built. It is also built in Italy by Oto Melara, which has produced a further 4,000 for the Italian Army and for export. In 1964 the M113 was replaced in production by the M113A1, identical with the earlier model but for a diesel rather than a petrol engine. The M113A1 has a larger radius of action than the earlier vehicle. The M113 has the distinction of being the first armoured fighting vehicle of aluminium construction to enter production. The driver is seated at the front of the hull on the left, with the engine to his right. The commander's hatch is in the centre of the roof and the personnel compartment is at the rear of the hull. The infantry enter and leave via a large ramp in the hull rear, although there is also a roof hatch over the troop compartment. The basic vehicle is normally armed with a pintle-mounted Browning .5in machine-gun, which has 2,000 rounds of ammunition. The M113 is fully amphibious and is propelled in the water by its tracks. Infra-red driving lights are fitted as standard. FMC has developed a wide variety of kits for the basic vehicle including an ambulance kit, NBC kit, heater kit, dozer-blade kit, various shields for machine-guns and so on. There are more variants of the M113 family than any other fighting vehicle in service today, and there is room here to mention only some of the more important models. The M577 is the command model, with a much higher roof and no armament. There are two mortar carriers, the M125 with an 81mm mortar, and the M106 with 107mm mortar. The flamethrower model is known as the M132A1, and is not used outside the United States Army. The M806A1 is the recovery model, and this is provided with a winch in the rear of the vehicle and spades at the rear. The anti-aircraft model is known as the Vulcan Air Defense System or M163; this is armed with a six-barrelled 20mm General Electric cannon. The M548 tracked cargo carrier is based on

M60 MAIN BATTLE TANK

M60, M60A1, M60A2, M60A3, M60 AVLB, M728 CEV
Crew: 4.
Armament: One 105mm gun; one 7.62mm machine-gun co-axial with main armament; one .5in anti-aircraft machine-gun in commander's cupola.
Armour: 12.7mm–120mm (0.50–4.80in).
Dimensions: Length (gun forward) 30ft 6in (9.309m); length (hull) 22ft 9½in (6.946m); width 11ft 11in (3.631m); height 10ft 8in (3.257m).
Weight: Combat 108,000lbs (48,987kg).
Ground pressure: 11.24lb/in² (0.79kg/cm²).
Engine: Continental AVDS-1790-2A 12-cylinder diesel developing 750bhp at 2,400rpm.
Performance: Road speed 30mph (48km/h); range 310 miles (500km); vertical obstacle 3ft (0.914m); trench 8ft 6in (2.59m); gradient 60 per cent.
History: The M60 entered service with the United States Army in 1960 and is also used by Austria, Ethiopia, Iran, Israel, Italy, Jordan, Saudi-Arabia, Somalia, South Korea, Turkey and the United States Marine Corps.

In the 1950s the standard tank of the United States Army was the M48. A new medium tank designated T95 was developed at this time, but although it had many advanced features it was not placed in production. It was then decided to develop the M48 tank further by improving its engine and firepower. In 1957 an M48 series tank was fitted with a new engine for trials purposes and this was followed by another three prototypes in 1958. Late in 1958 it was decided to arm the new tank with the British 105mm L7 series gun, to be built in the United States under the designation M68. In 1959 the first production order for the new tank, now called the M60, was placed with Chrysler, and the type entered production at Detroit Tank Arsenal in late 1959, with the first production tanks being completed the following year. The Detroit Arsenal is the only tank plant in use in the United States and is owned by the US Army but run by Chrysler. From late in 1962, the M60 was replaced in production by the M60A1, which has a number of improvements, the most important being the re-designed turret. The M60A1 has a turret and hull of all-cast construction. The driver is seated at the front of the hull with the other three crew members in the turret, commander and gunner on the right and the

loader on the left. The engine and transmission are at the rear, the latter having two reverse and two forward ranges. The M60 has torsion-bar suspension and six road wheels, with the idler at the front and the drive sprocket at the rear; there are four track-return rollers. The 105mm gun has an elevation of +20° and a depression of −10°, and traverse is 360°. Both elevation and traverse are powered. A 7.62mm M73 machine-gun is mounted co-axially with the main armament and there is a .5in M85 machine-gun in the commander's cupola. The latter can be aimed and fired from within the turret, and has an elevation of +60° and a depression of −15°. Some 63 rounds of 105mm, 900 rounds of .5in and 5,950 rounds of

Below: The M60A2 MBT is basically an M60 chassis with a new turret mounting a 152mm gun/launcher. This can launch a Shillelagh missile or fire conventional ammunition.

7.62mm ammunition are carried. Infra-red driving lights are fitted as standard and an infra-red/white light is mounted over the main armament. All M60s have an NBC system. The tank can also be fitted with a dozer blade on the front of the hull. The M60 can ford to a depth of 4ft (1.219m) without preparation or 8ft (2.438m) with the aid of a kit. For deep fording operations a schnorkel can be fitted, allowing the M60 to ford to a depth of 13ft 6in (4.114m). The M60A2 was developed in 1964–65 and consists of an M60 chassis with a new turret armed with the 152mm gun/launcher, which can fire a variety of ammunition with a combustible cartridge case or a Shillelagh missile. The M60A2 entered production in 1966, but

an M113 chassis, can carry 5 tons (5,080kg) of cargo and is fully amphibious. There are many models of the M548, including the M727, which carries three HAWK surface-to-air missiles, and the M730, which carries four Chaparral short-range surface-to-air missiles. Yet another version, the M752, carries the Lance tactical missile system, whilst the M688 carries two spare missiles. The British Aircraft Corporation has recently developed a model armed with eight Rapier SAMs in the ready-to-launch position, and this model is now in production for the Iranian Army. Many countries have adapted the basic M113 to their own requirements. For example, Australia has some vehicles with the

British Saladin armoured car turret and some with American Commando armoured car turrets; and currently undergoing trials is an M113 with the British Scorpion CVR(T) turret. The Germans and Dutch have modified the vehicle to carry the British Green Archer mortar-locating radar system. The Germans did not adopt the standard American M113 mortar carrier, but have fitted the 120mm Tampella mortar to many vehicles. The Germans also have various fire-control vehicles. The US Army uses the M113 to carry the TOW ATGW system. The M113 has been further developed by FMC into the Armoured Infantry Fighting Vehicle which is now in production for the

Above: A Chaparral short-range surface-to-air missile is launched from an M730. This vehicle is based on the M548 tracked cargo carrier and uses many components of the standard M113 APC.

Dutch Army. This has a turret-mounted 25mm cannon and a co-axial 7.62mm machine-gun, with firing-ports in the sides and rear of the hull. The Lynx, or M113½, reconnaissance vehicle uses many components of the M113 APC, and this model is used by both Canada and the Netherlands.

---

t was not until 1974 that the first M60A2 unit was formed as many problems were encountered with the whole Shillelagh/M60A2/Sheridan programme. The M60A2 is used only by the United States Army and just over 500 were built. The M60A2 also has a 7.62mm co-axial machine-gun and a .5in M85 anti-aircraft machine-gun. Thirteen Shillelagh missiles, and 33 rounds of conventional 152mm, 5,950 rounds of 7.62mm and 900 rounds of .5in ammunition are carried. A major improvement programme for the M60A1 is currently under way, and this is scheduled to be completed in a few years time. Tanks built with these modifications will be known as the M60A3. Not all of these modifications have been cleared for production yet, but the full list of improvements is as follows: a stabilisation system for the main armament, a laser rangefinder which is being developed by Hughes, new night-vision equipment, an improved

engine and air cleaners, new tracks, a modified cupola and a thermal sleeve for the main armament. There are two other variants of the M60 series, the M728 Combat Engineer Vehicle and the M60 Armoured Vehicle-Launched Bridge. The M728 has been designed for a variety of roles on the battlefield and is provided with a dozer blade, an 'A' frame for lifting obstacles and a 165mm demolition gun for use against field fortifications. It also has a 7.62mm co-axial machine-gun and a .5in anti-aircraft machine-gun. The M60 AVLB is almost identical to the M48 AVLB and has a scissors bridge which can be used to span gaps of up to 60ft (18.288m). Altogether some 4,000 M60 series MBTs have been built at the Detroit Tank

Plant. Initially production was running at only 30 tanks per month, but since 1973–74 production has been increasing and today about 100 tanks are being built each month and production should continue until the early 1980s, when the tank will be replaced in production by the XM1. Two hundred M60A1s were built in Italy by Oto Melara for the Italian Army. The M60 has proved to be a reliable tank in service and has been proved in combat by the Israeli Army, which has found it superior to the Russian T–54/T–62 tanks in the 1973 Middle East campaigns. The main disadvantage of the tank is its high silhouette, a tactical disadvantage exacerbated by the installation of the commander's cupola.

Right: M60A2 tanks on exercise in Germany. Since 1966, just over 500 M60A2s have been built for the US Army by Chrysler's Detroit Tank Arsenal.

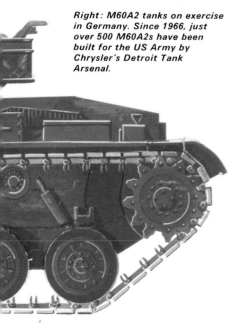

M50 ONTOS TANK DESTROYER

Crew: 3.
Armament: Six 106mm recoilless rifles; four .5in spotting rifles; one .3in machine-gun.
Armour: 16mm (0.63in) maximum.
Dimensions: Length 12ft 6¾in (3.828m); width overall 9ft 6¼in (2.9m); height 7ft (2.133m).
Weight: Combat 18,300lbs (8,300kg).
Ground pressure: 4.7lb/in² (0.33kg/cm²).
Engine: General Motors Corporation Model 302 water-cooled petrol engine developing 145bhp at 3,400rpm.
Performance: Road speed 30mph (48.28km/h); range 115 miles (70km); vertical obstacle 2ft 6in (0.762m); trench 4ft 6in (1.371m); gradient 60 per cent.
History: Entered service with the United States Marine Corps in 1956 and phased out of service from 1970.

In 1951 development started for the United States Army of a light and mobile tank destroyer known as the T165. Several different models were built and tested, and finally a modified version known as the T165E2 was authorised for production in 1955. A total of 297 was built for the United States Marine Corps before production was completed by Allis-Chalmers in 1957. In 1963, 294 M50s, or ONTOS as they are usually known, were fitted with a new engine and these became known as the M50A1s. They were used operationally in Vietnam and the Dominican Republic. The ONTOS withdrawn from service and scrapped from 1970. A whole series of vehicles was developed using a similar chassis, including a lightweight carrier, mortar carrier and anti-aircraft vehicle, but the US Army lost interest and the whole programme was cancelled. The ONTOS was armed with six 106mm M40A1C recoilless rifles mounted three on each side of the hull. Two of these could be dismounted for ground use as the weapon was almost identical to that

Right: An M50 ONTOS of the United States Marine Corps passes through a village en route from Da Nang to Chu Lai in 1966. Although originally designed as a tank-destroyer, the ONTOS was widely used in Vietnam in a fire support capacity.

Below: An M50 ONTOS moves through bush-country in Vietnam. It mounts six 106mm recoilless rifles, four .50in spotting rifles and a 30in anti-aircraft machine-gun The spotting rifles can be seen here, mounted above the 106mm rifles.

used by the infantry. The recoilless rifles had a traverse of 40° left and 40° right, with an elevation from −10° to +20°, both elevation and traverse being manual. Four .5in spotting rifles were also fitted. The basic idea was that the gunner lined up the recoilless rifles with the target and then fired a burst from the spotting rifles; if the weapons were correctly lined up the bullets would hit the target and the gunner would then know that the recoilless rifles were correctly aimed and so fire them individually, in pairs or all six together. The main drawback with this type of weapon was that once

the six weapons had been fired the crew had to leave the vehicle in order to reload them. Also, when the weapons were fired, the area to the rear of the ONTOS ended up like a sand storm thanks to the weapons' back-blast! Some 18 rounds of 106mm and 80 rounds of .5in spotting ammunition were carried. A .3in machine-gun was mounted on the top of the vehicle for local defence, and 1,000 rounds of ammunition were carried for this weapon. The ONTOS could ford streams to a depth of 2ft (0.609m) without preparation or 5ft (1.524m) with the aid of a special kit.

M551 SHERIDAN LIGHT TANK

Crew: 4.
Armament: One 152mm gun/missile launcher; one 7.62mm machine-gun co-axial with main armament; one .5in anti-aircraft machine-gun; four smoke dischargers on each side of turret.
Armour: Classified.
Dimensions: Length 20ft 8in (6.299m); width 9ft 3in (2.819m); height (overall) 9ft 8in (2.946m).
Weight: Combat 34,898lbs (15,830kg).
Ground pressure: 6.96lb/in² (0.49kg/cm²).
Engine: Detroit Diesel 6V53T six-cylinder diesel developing 300bhp at 2,800rpm.
Performance: Road speed 45mph (70km/h); water speed 3.6mph (5.8km/h); range 373 miles (600km); vertical obstacle 2ft 9in (0.838m); trench 8ft 4in (2.54m); gradient 60 per cent.
History: Entered service with United States Army in 1966 and still in service.

Above: M551 Sheridan light tanks of the US 4th Armoured Cavalry, 1st Infantry Division, carry out annual firing practice on ranges at Grafenwoehr, Germany.

In August 1959 the United States Army established a requirement for a 'new armoured vehicle with increased capabilities over any other weapon in its own inventory and that of any adversary'. The following year the Allison Division of General Motors was awarded a contract to design a vehicle called the Armored Reconnaissance Airborne Assault Vehicle (ARAAV) to meet the requirement. This was to carry out the reconnaissance and anti-tank roles, and would replace both the M41 light tank and the M56 90mm self-propelled anti-tank gun. The first prototype, designated XM551, was completed in 1962, and this was followed by a further 11 prototypes. Late in 1965 a production contract was awarded to Allison, and the first production vehicles were completed in 1966, these being known as the M551 or Sheridan. No sooner had production started than numerous deficiences began to appear in the vehicle, and as a result all the vehicles had to be stored as they came off the production line as they were unfit for service. Later the whole Sheridan/Shillelagh/M60A2 programme was to come before an Armed Services Investigating Sub-committee, to which a key witness said 'We have Sheridans coming out of our ears.' There were three main problem areas: first the automotive side of the vehicle, second the Shillelagh missile system and third the caseless ammunition. It took almost four years to solve all of these problems, and in 1968 the M551 was deployed to Vietnam where further deficiencies became apparent under combat conditions. Once these problems were resolved the M551 was issued to American units in the United States, Germany and South Korea. It was tested by a number of other armies, including that of Australia, but was not adopted by any of them. Production was

completed in 1970 after 1,700 vehicles had been built. The hull of the Sheridan is of all-aluminium construction whilst the turret is of welded steel. The driver is seated at the front of the hull and the other three crew members are in the turret, with the loader on the left and the gunner and commander on the right. The engine and transmission are at the rear of the hull. The suspension is of the torsion-bar type and consists of five road wheels, with the drive sprocket at the rear and the idler at the front. There are no track-return rollers. The most interesting feature of the Sheridan is its armament system. This consists of a 152mm gun/launcher which has an elevation of +19° and a depression of −8°, traverse being 360°. A 7.62mm machine-gun is mounted co-axially with the main armament, and there is a .5in Browning machine-gun on the commander's cupola. The latter cannot be aimed and fired from within the turret, and as a result of combat experience in Vietnam many vehicles have now been fitted with a shield for this weapon. The 152mm gun/launcher, later fitted to the M60A2 and MBT-70 tanks, can fire either a Shillelagh missile or a variety of conventional ammunition including HEAT-T-MP, WP and cannister, all of them having a combustible cartridge case. The problem in the early days was that this would not combust, and when the breech was opened after a round had been fired, it still had odd bits of cartridge case in it, some of which might be burning and could end up on the fighting compartment. The Shillelagh missile was developed

by the United States Army Missile Command and the Philco-Ford Corporation, and has a maximum range of about 3,281 yards (2,000m) The missile is controlled by the gunner, who simply has to' keep the cross-hairs of his sight on .the target to ensure a hit. This missile itself weighs 59lbs (26.7kg) and has a single-stage solid-propellant motor which has a burn time of 1.18 seconds. Once the missile leaves the gun/missile-launcher, four fins at the rear of the missile unfold and it is guided to the target by a two-way infra-red command link which eliminates the need for the gunner to estimate the lead and range of the target. A Sheridan normally carries eight missiles and 20 rounds of ammunition, but this mix can be adjusted as required. In addition, 1,000 rounds of .5in and 3,000 rounds of 7.62mm ammunition are carried. The Sheridan is provided with a flotation screen, and when erected this enables the vehicle to propel itself across rivers and streams by its tracks. Night-vision equipment is provided as is an NBC system. It was intended that the Sheridan would have been the basis for a whole range of vehicles including self-propelled guns, an anti-aircraft missile system, a cargo carrier, a mortar carrier and an MICV to name a few, but none of these ever left the drawing board. Recently a prototype of a Sheridan AVLB has been completed and this is currently being tested. As a result of the troubles with the whole M551/Shillelagh/M60A2 programme, the American Congress has kept all American tank programmes under very close attention.

Below: An M551 Sheridan fires an MGM-51C Shillelagh anti-tank missile, which delivers a 6.8kg hollow-charge warhead to a range of more than 4,000m.

M107 SELF-PROPELLED GUN

M107, M110, M110E2
Self-propelled gun
Crew: 5.
Armament: One 175mm gun.
Armour: 20mm (0.79in) maximum, estimated.
Dimensions: Length (including gun and spade in travelling position) 36ft 11in (11.256m); length (hull) 18ft 9in (5.72m); width 10ft 4in (3.149m); height (to top of barrel in travelling position) 12ft 1in (3.679m).
Weight: Combat 62,098lbs (28,168kg).
Ground pressure: 11.52lb/in² (0.81kg/cm²).
Engine: Detroit Diesel Model 8V71T eight-cylinder turbocharged diesel developing 405hp at 2,300rpm.
Performance: Road speed 35mph (56km/h); range 450 miles (725km); vertical obstacle 3ft 4in (1.016m); trench 7ft 9in (2.362m); gradient 60 per cent.
History: Entered service with the United States Army in 1963. Also used by Germany, Greece, Iran, Israel, Italy, the Netherlands, Spain, Turkey, and Vietnam (probably non-operational).

In 1956 the United States Army issued a requirement for a range of self-propelled artillery which would be air-transportable. The Pacific Car and Foundry Company of Washington were awarded the development contract and from 1958 built three different self-propelled weapons on the same chassis. These were the T235 (175mm gun), which became the M107, the T236 (203mm howitzer), which became the M110, and the T245 (155mm gun), which was subsequently dropped from the range. These prototypes were powered by a petrol engine, but it was soon decided to replace this by a diesel engine as this could give the vehicles a much greater range of action. When fitted with a diesel engine the T235 became the T235E1 and after further trials this was placed in production as the M107 in 1962, entering service

Right: An 8in/203mm M110 self-propelled howitzer fires an HE round during a demonstration at the Royal School of Artillery, Larkhill, Wiltshire. The M110 can also fire a tactical nuclear projectile.

with the army the following year. The M107 has in fact been built by three different companies at various times: FMC, Bowen-McLaughlin York and the Pacific Car and Foundry Company. It is not currently in production. The hull is of all-welded aluminium construction with the driver at the front on the left with the engine to his right. The gun is mounted towards the rear of the hull. The suspension is of the torsion-bar type and consists of five road wheels, with the fifth road wheel acting as the idler; the drive sprocket is at the front. Five crew are carried on the gun (driver, commander and three gun crew), the other eight crew members following in an M548 tracked vehicle (this is based on the M113 APC chassis), which also carries the ammunition, as only two ready rounds are carried on the M107 itself. The 175mm gun has an elevation of +65° and a depression of −2°, traverse being 30° left and 30° right. Elevation and traverse are both

powered, although there are manual controls for use in an emergency. The M107 fires an HE round to a maximum range of 35,870 yards (32,800m). A large hydraulically-operated spade is mounted at the rear of the hull and is lowered into position before the gun opens fire, and the suspension can also be locked when the gun is fired to provide a more stable firing platform. The gun can officially fire one round per minute, but a well trained crew can fire at least two rounds a minute. As the projectile is very heavy, an hydraulic hoist is provided to position the projectile on the ramming tray; the round is then pushed into the breech hydraulically before the charge is pushed home, the breechblock closed and the weapon is then fired. The M107 can ford streams to a maximum depth of 3ft 6in (1.066m) but has no amphibious capability. Infra-red driving lights are fitted as standard but the type does not have an NBC system. Three armoured recovery vehicles

M109 SELF-PROPELLED HOWITZER

Crew: 6.
Armament: One 155mm howitzer; one .5in (12.7mm) Browning anit-aircraft machine-gun.
Armour: 20mm (0.79in) maximum, estimated.
Dimensions: Length (including armament) 21ft 8in (6.612m); length (hull) 20ft 6in (6.256m); width 10ft 10in (3.295m); height (including anti-aircraft machine-gun) 10ft 10in (3.295m).
Weight: Combat 52,438lbs (23,786kg).
Ground pressure: 10.95lb/in² (0.77kg/cm²).
Engine: Detroit Diesel Model 8V71T eight-cylinder turbocharged diesel developing 405bhp at 2,300rpm.
Performance: Road speed 35mph (56km/h); range 242 miles (390km); vertical obstacle 1ft 9in (0.533m); trench 6ft (1.828m); gradient 60 per cent.
History: Entered service with the United States Army in 1963. Also used by Austria, Belgium, Canada, Denmark, Germany, Great Britain, Ethiopia, Iran, Israel, Italy, Libya, the Netherlands, Norway, Spain and Switzerland. Still in production.

In the 1950s the standard self-propelled artillery in the United States Army in the 105mm/155mm howitzer class were the M44 (155mm) and M52 (105mm), both of which used components of the M41 light tank. These weapons had a number of major drawbacks: first, their armament could only be traversed through a limited arc (on the M52 it was 120° and on the M44 it was only 60°); second, they were powered by petrol engines which gave them a very limited range of action, in the case of the M44 just 65 miles (120km). Also, whilst the M52 weighed only 24 tons (24,385kg), the M44 scaled 28tons (28,450kg), which meant it was difficult to transport by air. A programme was therefore started to develop a new range of self-propelled artillery to replace both the M44 and M52. Development of the larger calibre weapon started as early as 1953 with a vehicle designated T195, but it was not until 1961 that a modified vehicle, the T195E1, was ready for production as the M109. The reason for the long delay was that it was at first intended to use a 156mm weapon rather than a 155mm one, as well as components of the M113 APC. The first production models were completed in 1962, and some 3,000 examples have now been built, making the M109 the most widely used self-propelled howitzer in the world. It has a hull of all-welded aluminium construction, providing the crew with protection from small arms fire. The driver is seated

at the front of the hull on the left, with the engine to his right. The other five crew members are the commander, gunner and three ammunition members, all located in the turret at the rear of the hull. There is a large door in the rear of the hull for ammunition resupply purposes. Hatches are also provided in the sides and rear of the turret. There are two hatches in the roof of the turret, the commander's hatch being on the right. A .5in (12.7mm) Browning machine-gun is mounted on this for anti-aircraft defence. The suspension is of the torsion-bar type and consists of seven road wheels, with the drive sprocket at the front and the idler at the rear, and there are no track-return rollers. The 155mm howitzer has an elevation of +75° and a depression of −3°, and the turret can be traversed through 360°.

Elevation and traverse are powered, with manual controls for emergency use. The weapon can fire a variety of ammunition, including HE, tactical nuclear, illuminating, smoke and chemical rounds. A total of 28 rounds of separate-loading ammunition is carried, as well as 500 rounds of machine-gun ammunition. The latest model to enter service is the M109A1, identical with the M109 apart from its much longer barrel, which is provided with a fume extractor as well as a muzzle-brake. The fume extractor removes propellent gases from the barrel after a round has been fired and thus prevents fumes from entering the fighting compartment. The M109 fires a round to a maximum range of 16,076 yards (14,700m), whilst the M109A1 fires to a maximum range of 19,685 yards

Above: A M109 155mm self-propelled howitzer of the United States Marine Corps fires on VietCong position at Phu Bai, South Vietnam. Some 3,000 M109s have been built since 1962, making it the most widely used howitzer in the world.

were developed to the prototype stage using a similar chassis, these being the T119, T120 and T121. The T120 entered production as the M578 and this is the standard light ARV of the United States Army. The M110 8in (203mm) self-propelled howitzer has an identical hull and mount as the 175mm M107, and the 8in howitzer has the same elevation and traverse as the 175mm gun. The M110 is easily distinguishable from the M107 as the former has a much shorter and fatter barrel. The howitzer can fire both HE and tactical nuclear rounds to a maximum range of 18,372 yards (16,800m). Both the M110 and the M107 are now being replaced in service with the United States Army and Marines by the M110E2. This has a much longer barrel than the standard M110 and will be able to fire a variety of ammunition including HE, improved conventional munitions, chemical, dual-purpose, nuclear and rocket-assisted projectiles to a maximum range of 22,966 yards (21,000m), although the rocket-assisted projectiles will have a longer range than this. It has been estimated by the US Army that the total cost to convert all M107s and M110s to the new standard will be about $40,000,000, a great deal less than the cost of building a new vehicle. The M110E2 will be known as the M110A1 or as the M110A2 when fitted with a muzzle-brake. The installation of the muzzle-brake will enable it to fire an even better round. The M107/M110 is normally fielded in battalions of 12 guns. One of the problems with heavy artillery of this type is keeping the guns supplied with sufficient ammunition. As noted above the weapon is supported by an M548 tracked vehicle, and this in turn is kept supplied by 5- or 10-ton trucks. Another problem is that the M107 has a very high muzzle velocity which means that its barrel, like tank barrels, wears out after about 400 rounds have been fired. It takes about two hours to change the barrel on the M107 and spare barrels are held in reserve for just this purpose.

Right: An M107 175mm SP gun of the United States Marine Corps in action in Vietnam. The M107, built on the same chassis as the M110, fires a 91kg HE projectile to a range of 32,800m.

(18,000m). The M109 can ford streams to a maximum depth of 5ft (1.524m). A special amphibious kit has been developed for the vehicle but this is not widely used. It consists of nine inflatable airbags, normally carried by a truck. Four of these are fitted to each side of the hull and the last to the front of the hull. The vehicle is then propelled in the water by its tracks at a maximum speed of 4mph (6.4km/h). The M109 is provided with infra-red driving lights and some vehicles also have an NBC system. A number of armies have modified their M109s to suit their own special requirements. The Germans, for example, call their version the M109G as it has a number of modifications to the howitzer itself, as well as having smoke dischargers installed on the sides of the turret.

The Swiss call their version the Pz.Hb.66, whilst the Italians have modified a M109 to fire the new range of ammunition being developed for the 155mm FH70 towed howitzer. Early in 1972 the United States Army awarded a contract to Texas Instruments and Martin Marietta to design, develop and test a Cannon-Launched Guided Projectile (CLGP, or Copperhead as it is now called). As a result of trials carried out from 1974, a contract was awarded to Martin Marietta for full engineering development. The CLGP is basically a HEAT round with a laser seeker in the nose, some electronics, and control fins which unfold in flight. The basic idea is that the forward observer first sees an enemy tank which can be up to 12.5 miles (20km) away from the artillery. He gives the approximate

position of the tank to the fire-control centre, and one gun then fires a 155mm CLGP in the general direction of the tank. As soon as this is fired the forward observer illuminates the target with his laser designator and the CLGP then homes onto the target for a direct hit. This concept is being designed specifically for the M109A1, but it is also being studied by the United States Navy. It is considered to be one of the greatest advances in artillery in the last 50 years. The M108 105mm self-propelled howitzer is identical with the M109 apart from its armament and the fact that it does not have any spades at the rear of the hull. The M108 was in production for only a year as it was decided to concentrate on the M109. The M108 is used by Belgium, Brazil, Spain and the United States.

Below: An M109 155mm SP howitzer of the US Army. The M109 fires a wide variety of ammunition, including HE, tactical nuclear, smoke and chemical rounds.

Below: An M109 of the Royal Artillery with its gun at the maximum elevation of +75°. The 155mm gun can be depressed to −3° and traversed through a full 360°.

V-150 COMMANDO ARMOURED CAR/APC

V-100, V-150, V-200 and variants
Crew: 12
Armament: Varies according to mission requirements (see text).
Armour: Classified (estimated 12mm max.).
Dimensions: Length 20ft 8in (5.689m); width 7ft 5in (2.26m); height overall 8ft 4in (2.54m)
Weight: Combat 20,054lbs (9,550kg).
Engine: Chrysler eight-cylinder petrol or Cummins six-cylinder diesel developing 155hp.
Performance: Road speed 55mph (88km/h); water speed 3mph (4.8km/h); road range 600 miles (965km); vertical obstacle 2ft (0.609m); gradient 60 per cent.
History: Entered service in 1964 and used by over 20 countries including Bolivia, Ethiopia, Laos, Lebanon, Malaysia, Oman, Peru, Portugal, Saudi Arabia, Singapore, Somalia, Sudan, Tunisia, United States and Vietnam.

The US Army used armoured cars for both reconnaissance and liaison work very successfully during World War II, and by the end of the war had developed an excellent 6×6 armoured car, the M38. Although standardised, for some reason this was never placed in production, and after the war the Americans lost interest in armoured cars, although there were some paper projects at various times. In 1962 The Cadillac Gage company of Warren, Michigan, built a prototype of a 4×4 vehicle called the V-100, or Commando. Trials with this were successful, and the type entered production in 1964. The Commando was a private venture and was not built to any specific US Army requirement. The V-100 was followed by the slightly bigger V-200, and the latest model is the V-150. This last is essentially an improved V-100 with many modifications including stronger axles and a more powerful engine. So far well over 2,300 Commandos have been built, most of them for export. The Commando has been designed to fulfil a variety of roles including reconnaissance, armoured personnel carrier, mortar-carrier, command vehicle, ambulance, recovery vehicle, anti-tank vehicle and internal security vehicle, to name but a few. The Commando was widely used in Vietnam for both the convoy escort and airfield security roles, and many modifications have been carried out as a result of combat experience in Vietnam and elsewhere. The Commando is fully amphibious, being propelled in the water by its wheels. A winch can be mounted inside the front part of the hull for self-recovery if required. The vehicle has a hull of all-welded steel construction, which provides the crew with protection from small arms fire. The driver is seated at the front of the hull on the left, with the turret in the centre and the engine to the rear on the left of the hull. A two-piece door is provided in each side of the hull, and there is a further door to the right

Above: Cadillac Gage V-150 armoured car with turret-mounted cannon, 7.62mm co-axial and a 7.62mm AA machine-gun, smoke dischargers on turret sides, and a 7.62mm machine-gun mounted on the rear of the hull.

of the engine compartment; roof hatches are also provided. Firing-ports and vision-blocks are provided in the sides and rear of the hull, enabling the crew to fire their weapons from within the hull. The vehicle can be fitted with a wide variety of armament installations according to the role for which it is required. For example, the V-150 is currently being offered with a number of weapon options. There is a mortar-carrier armed with a 81mm mortar firing through the roof (this model does not have a turret). The reconnaissance vehicle has a turret-mounted Oerlikon cannon, this having an elevation of +60° and a depression of −8°, and a traverse of 360° (elevation and traverse are both powered); a 7.62mm machine-gun is mounted co-axially with the main armament and there is a similar weapon mounted on the roof for anti-aircraft defence; and four smoke dischargers are mounted each side of the turret. When in use as an armoured personnel carrier the Commando can carry 11 fully equipped troops in addition to the driver. The APC model is normally armed with turret-mounted twin 7.62mm machine-guns, or a turret with a single 7.62mm and a

single .5in machine-gun. For use in the anti-tank role the vehicle can be fitted with anti-tank missiles such as the Dragon or the Hughes TOW. A model has also been developed with a 90mm gun, a co-axial 7.62mm machine-gun and a similar anti-aircraft machine-gun; this model has a crew of four. When used for the command role, the vehicle has its turret removed and replaced by a pod which gives the crew more head room. For use in the internal security role a model complete with a water cannon is offered. The recovery vehicle is provided with a full range of equipment, including tools and an 'A' frame pivoted at the front of the hull. When erected this can be used to change engines and transmissions. The Commando is well suited for such roles as an internal security vehicle or an armoured personnel carrier, but really it is too large for use in the reconnaissance role. It was entered in the United States Armoured Reconnaissance Scout Vehicle Contest, but was not adopted. In 1974 the whole ARSV programme was cancelled after the US Army had spent some $40,000,000 on the project.

Below: Cadillac Gage V-150 armoured car running trials in the USA. More than 2,300 V-150 Commandos have been built, and the multi-role, fully-amphibious vehicle is in service with the forces of more than 20 countries.

LVTP-7 AMPHIBIOUS ASSAULT VEHICLE

LVTP-7, LVTC-7, LVTE-7, LVTH-7
Crew: 3 plus 25.
Armament: One M85 0.5in (12.7mm) machine-gun.
Armour: 7mm–30mm (0.28–1.18in).
Dimensions: Length 26ft 1in (7.943m); width, 10ft 9in (3.27m); height, 10ft 9in (3.27m).
Weight: Combat 52,150lbs (23,655kg).
Ground pressure: 8lb/in² (0.57kg/cm²).
Engine: Detroit Diesel Model 8V53T eight-cylinder turbocharged diesel developing 400bhp at 2,800rpm.
Performance: Road speed 39.5mph (63.37km/h); water speed 8.5mph (13.7km/h); range (road) 300 miles (482km); vertical obstacle 3ft (0.914m); trench 8ft (2.438m); gradient, 70 per cent.
History: Entered service with United States Marine Corps 1971. Also in service with Argentina, Italy, Spain and Thailand. No longer in production.

The standard amphibious assault carrier in service with the United States Marines in the 1950s was the LVTP-5 (Landing Vehicle Tracked Personnel-5). Although an improvement over earlier vehicles, the LVTP-5 proved very difficult to maintain service. So, in 1964, the Marines issued a requirement for a new LVTP and the FMC Corporation was selected to build 17 prototypes. The first of these was completed in 1967 under the designation of LVTPX-12. Trials were carried out in Alaska, Panama and various other Marine installations, and in 1970 FMC was awarded a production contract for 942 vehicles. The first production LVTP-7 was completed in August 1971 and production continued until September 1974. It has now completely replaced the older LVTP-5. The role of the LVTP-7 is to transport Marines from ships off shore to the beach, and if required, to carry them inland to their objective. The hull of the LVTP-7 is of all-welded aluminium construction and varies in thickness from 20 to 45mm. The engine and transmission are at the front of the hull and can be removed as a complete unit if required. The driver is seated at the front, on the left, with the commander to his rear. The LVTP-7 is armed with a turret-mounted M85 0.5in machine-gun. This is mounted on the right side and has an elevation of +60° and a depression of −15°; traverse is a full 360° and a total of 1,000 rounds of ammunition is carried. The personnel compartment is at the rear of the hull, where the 25 Marine are provided with bench type seats which can be quickly stowed so that the vehicle can be used as an ambulance or cargo carrier. The usual method of entry and exit is via a large ramp at the rear of the hull. Hatches are also provided over the troop compartment so that stores can be loaded when the vehicle is alongside a ship. The LVTP-7 is propelled in the water by two water-jets, one in each side of the hull towards the rear. These are driven by

propeller shafts from the transmission. Basically pumps draw water from above the track, and this is then discharged to the rear of the vehicle. Deflectors at the rear of each unit divert the water-jet stream for steering, stopping and reversing. There are two special versions of the LVTP-7 in service. The first of these is the LVTR-7. This is used to repair disabled vehicles, for which a wide range of equipment is carried, including an hydraulic crane and winch. The second model is the LVTC-7, a special command model with additional radios and other equipment. Two other models, the LVTE-7 (Engineer) and LVTH-7 (Howitzer) were not placed in production.

Above: LVTP-7 assault vehicle of the 2nd Marine Division, USMC, on a desert exercise in California. The LVTP-7 has an all-welded aluminium hull and is fully amphibious, propelled by two water-jets at a maximum 13.7km/h.

Below: Men of the 1st Bn, 8th Marine Rgt, 2nd Division, dismount from an LVTP-7 amphibious assault vehicle during exercises at Fort Stuart, Georgia. Main armament of the LVTP-7 is a turret-mounted 12.7mm machine-gun.

XM1 ABRAMS MAIN BATTLE TANK

Crew: 4.
Armament: One 105mm M68 gun; one 7.62mm machine-gun co-axial with main armament; one .5in machine-gun on commander's cupola; one 7.62mm machine-gun on loader's hatch (see text).
Armour: Classified.
Dimensions: Length (hull) 25ft 7in (7.797m); width 11ft 8in (3.555m); height (to top of turret) 7ft 8½in (2.438m).
Weight: Combat 116,000lbs (52,616kg).
Engine: Avco Lycoming AGT-T 1500 HP-C turbine developing 1,500hp.
Performance: Road speed 45mph (72.4km/h); range 300 miles (482km); vertical obstacle 3ft 6in (1.066m); trench 9ft (2.743m); gradient 60 per cent.
History: Will enter production in 1979 for the United States Army.
(Note: Above data relate to prototype tanks, and production tanks may differ.)

On August 1 1963 the American and German governments signed an agreement to develop jointly a tank called the MBT-70. Each country formed a development team and work soon started on the new tank. The first prototypes were completed in 1967. The MBT-70 had many advanced features including a crew of three (commander, gunner and driver) all seated in the turret, this being possible as an automatic loader was provided for the main armament. The suspension could be adjusted to suit the tactical situation and the type's 1,500hp engine gave it a top road speed of 44mph (71km/h). Standard equipment included an NBC system, night-vision equipment and a schnorkel for deep fording operations. Prototypes were armed with a 152mm Shillelagh gun/missile launcher and a co-axial 7.62mm machine-gun. In addition a 20mm cannon was provided for anti-aircraft defence and smoke dischargers were mounted on either side of the turret. The programme then started to run into trouble, for not only did the cost of the tank start to rise, but the Americans and Germans could not agree on the main armament, the Americans

wanting the Shillelagh system and the Germans a 120mm gun. In the end the whole programme was cancelled in January 1970, and the Germans went on to develop the Leopard 2. The Americans then pushed on with the development of the so-called 'Austere' MBT-70, the XM803, but this was cancelled by the Congress in late 1971. The US Army then started from scratch again and drew up a new set of requirements for a tank for the 1980s. In June 1973 contracts were awarded to both the Chrysler Corporation (which builds the M60 series) and the Detroit Diesel Allison Division of the General Motors Corporation (which built the MBT-70) to build prototypes of a new tank designated XM1, and later

named the Abrams tank. These tanks were handed over to the US Army for trials in February 1976. In November 1976 it was announced after a four-month delay that the Chrysler tank would be placed in production. Production will commence at the Lima Army Modification Centre at Lima in 1979 at the rate of 10 tanks per month, increasing to 30 tanks per month the following year. When production of the M60 is completed at Detroit Tank Arsenal early in the 1980s, this will also become available for production of the XM1. The United States Army has a requirement for 3,312 XM1s and the total cost of the programme will be $4,900,000,000. The first 300 or so tanks will have the standard 105mm rifled gun as fitted to the current

XM723 MECHANISED INFANTRY COMBAT VEHICLE

Crew: 2 plus 9.
Armament: One 20mm cannon; one 7.62mm machine-gun co-axial with main armament.
Armour: Classified.
Dimensions: Length 20ft 5in (6.223m); width 10ft 6in (3.2m); height 9ft 1in (2.768m).
Weight: Combat 43,000lbs (19,504kg).
Ground pressure: 6.82lb/in² (0.48kg/cm²).
Engine: Cummins VTA-903 water-cooled turbocharged diesel developing 450hp at 2,600rpm.
Performance: Road speed 45mph (72km/h); water speed 5mph (8km/h); range 300 miles (483km); vertical obstacle 3ft (0.914m); trench 8ft 4in (2.54m); gradient 60 per cent.
History: Should enter service with the United States Army in 1980.

The United States Army has had a requirement for an MICV for well over 10 years. The first American MICV was the XM701, developed in the early 1960s on the M107/M110 self-propelled gun chassis. This proved unsatisfactory during trials. The Americans then tried to modify the current M113 to meet the MICV role: a variety of different models was built and tested, but again these vehicles failed to meet the army requirement. One of these was developed further as a private venture by FMC into the Armoured Infantry Fighting Vehicle, however, and this is now in production for the Dutch Army. As a result of a competition held in 1972, the FMC Corporation, which still builds the M113A1, was awarded a contract to design an MICV designated the XM723. Prototypes are now being tested, and the vehicle should enter low-scale production in 1978–79 and enter service with the US Army in 1980. Some problems have been encountered during these trials, especially with the transmission and suspension, and the original tracks have been replaced by tracks similar to those fitted to the LVTP-7 amphibious assault vehicle. It is, however, common for problems of one sort or another to be encountered during tests, and it is for this reason that the vehicles are subjected to very rigorous trials in varying conditions. If the faults are not discovered until the vehicle is in service, they delay the whole programme and result in a costly refit schedule. The XM723 will replace some, but not all, of the current M113 APCs, as the latter are more than adequate for many roles on the battlefield. The XM723 will have three major advances over the existing M113 APC. First, the MICV will have greater mobility and better cross-country speed, enabling it to keep up with the XM1 MBT when acting as part of the tank/infantry

team. (According to FMC, if the M113 takes 10 hours to cross a stretch of country, then the MICV will accomplish this in five hours or less.) Second, it has much greater firepower. Third, it has superior armour protection. The tank provides long-range firepower whilst the MICV provides firepower against softer, close in targets. The XM723's infantry also assist the tank by locating and destroying enemy anti-tank weapons. The hull of the XM723 is of all-welded aluminium construction with an appliqué layer of steel armour welded to the hull front, upper sides and rear for added protection. The hull sides also have a thin layer of steel armour, the space between the aluminium and steel being filled with foam to increase the buoyancy of the vehicle. The driver is seated at the front of the vehicle on the left, with the engine to his right and the vehicle commander to his rear. The turret is in the centre of the hull and the personnel compartment is at the rear. Personnel entry is effected through a large power-operated ramp in the hull rear. First prototypes carried 12 men; driver, gunner and 10 men. During trials it was found that this left little space for additional equipment, however, so only nine infantrymen are now carried. Prototypes and early production vehicles will be armed with a turret-

mounted dual-feed 20mm cannon and a co-axial 7.62mm machine-gun. These have an elevation of +60° and a depression of −9°, traverse being a full 360°. A stabilisation system is provided, allowing the gunner to lay and fire the armament on the move across country. From 1980 it is expected that the 20mm cannon will be replaced by a new 25mm weapon now being developed by Philco-Ford. There are six firing-ports, two in each side of the hull and two in the rear. In addition to the infantry's rifles and M60 machine-gun, the vehicle carries four Light Anti-Tank Weapons and three Dragon ATGWs. The vehicle is fully amphibious and is propelled in the water by its tracks. An NBC system is installed, as is a full range of night-vision equipment. The XM723 should be in service in substantial numbers by the early 1980s, some 15 years after the Russians first fielded their BMP-1.

Below: Rear view of a prototype XM723 MICV developed by FMC. The firing ports in the sides and rear can be clearly seen.
Right: XM723 with a turret-mounted 20mm cannon and co-axial 7.62mm machine-gun. Production vehicles will have 25mm cannon and two TOW ATGWs.

Far left: Chrysler XM1 MBT with a 105mm gun. Production tanks will have a 120mm gun of British or German design.
Left: Rear view of the XM1 showing the armoured skirts that protect the tank's suspension. The XM1 has a maximum road speed of 72.4km/h.

M60A1, but it has yet to be decided what later production tanks will have. Contenders are the German 120mm smooth-bore gun and the British 120mm rifled gun. To complicate matters even further, the XM1 may well use parts of the German Leopard 2(AV), which was specially developed for the United States under a memorandum of understanding signed in December 1974. The XM1 has a hull and turret of the new British Chobham Armour, which is claimed to make the tank immune to attack from both missiles and tank guns. Its crew consists of four, the driver at the front, the commander and gunner on the right of the turret, and the loader on the left. The main armament consists of a standard 105mm

gun developed in Britain and produced under licence in the United States and a 7.62mm machine-gun is mounted co-axially with the main armament. A .5in machine-gun is mounted at the commander's station and a 7.62mm machine-gun at the loader's station. No details of the exact quantities of ammunition carried have been released yet. The main armament can be aimed and fired on the move. The gunner first selects the target, and then uses the laser rangefinder to get its range and then depresses the firing switch. The computer makes the calculations and adjustments required to ensure a hit. The fuel tanks are separated from the crew compartment by armoured bulkheads and sliding doors are provided for the ammunition

stowage areas. The suspension is of the torsion-bar type with rotary shock absorbers. The tank can travel across country at a speed of 35mph (56km/h) and accelerate from 0 to 20mph (0 to 32km/h) in six seconds, and this will make the XM1 a difficult tank to engage on the battlefield. The XM1 is powered by a turbine developed Avco-Lycoming, running on a variety of fuels including petrol, diesel and jet fuel. All the driver has to do is adjust a dial in his compartment. according to the manufacturers, the engine will not require an overhaul until the tank has travelled between 12,000 to 18,000 miles (19,312 to 28,968km), a great advance over existing tank engines. This engine is coupled to an Allison X 1100 transmission with four forward and two reverse gears. Great emphasis has been placed on reliability and maintenance, and it is claimed that the complete engine can be removed for replacement in under 30 minutes. It is not often realised that there are hundreds of sub-contractors to a major programme such as a tank. On the Chrysler XM1 there are eight major subcontractors: the government for the armament, Avco Lycoming for the engine, Cadillac Gage for the turret drive and the stabilisation system, the Control Data Corporation for the ballistic computer, the Detroit Diesel Allison Division of General Motors for the transmission and final drive, the Hughes Aircraft Company for the laser rangefinder, the Kollmorgen Corporation for the gunner's auxiliary sight and the Singer Kearfott Division for the line-of-sight data link. The XM1 is provided with an NBC system and a full range of night-vision equipment for the commander, gunner and driver. When the XM1 enters service as the M1 in 1980, the US Army should at last have the tank it has been wanting for 20 years.

Index

KHARTOUM.

M47 = 45.5 TONNES.
M48 = 46.5 " "

Picture Credits

The publishers would like to thank the following photographers, collections and organisations who supplied photographs for this book. Photographs have been credited by page number. Some references have, for reasons of space, been abbreviated as follows:

British Aerospace Corporation: BAC
John Milsom collection: JM
Imperial War Museum, London: IWM
Ministry of Defence, London: MOD
Educational and Television Films Ltd: E and TV Films
United States Marine Corps: USMC

End papers: Novosti. **Pages 10-11:** C. Foss collection. **12-13:** IWM. **17-18:** IWM. **19-20:** JM. **21-22:** IWM. **23:** JM. **24:** top, IWM; bottom, JM. **25:** top, JM; bottom, IWM. **26:** top, IWM; bottom: C. Foss collection. **27:** IWM. **28:** JM. **29-30:** IWM. **32-33:** JM. **35:** top, JM; bottom, IWM. **36:** IWM. **37-40:** JM. **41:** RAC Tank Museum. **43:** J. MacClancy collection. **44:** Finnish Army. **45:** IWM. **46:** JM. **47:** BAC. **48:** top, C. Foss; bottom, Photographers International. **49:** top, Australian Army; centre, Swedish Army; bottom, C. Foss. **51:** MOD. **53:** top, Alvis; bottom, MOD. **54-57:** Vickers. **58:** top, Rolls-Royce; bottom: MOD. **59-60:** MOD. **61:** left, MOD; right, Rolls-Royce. **62:** JM. **63:** top, JM; bottom, IWM. **64-67:** JM. **69:** ECPA. **70:** IWM. **71:** JM. **72:** IWM. **73-79:** JM. **80-81:** IWM. **82:** top, IWM; centre and bottom, JM. **83:** JM. **84:** IWM. **86-87:** JM. **88:** left, ECPA; right, Creusot-Loire. **89:** Aerospatiale. **90:** top, ECPA; bottom, Creusot-Loire. **91:** top, C. Foss collection; bottom, Hotchkiss Company. **92:** Netherlands Army. **93:** Panhard et Levassor. **94:** C. Foss collection. **96:** C. Foss. **97:** Panhard et Levassor. **98:** J. MacClancy collection. **101-102:** JM. **103:** Bundesarchiv. **104:** JM. **107:** top left, IWM; top right, JM; bottom, JM. **108:** IWM. **109:** JM. **111:** JM. **112:** IWM. **113:** A. Collins Collection. **114:** Novosti. **115:** A. Collins Collection. **117:** top, JM; bottom, C. Foss collection. **118:** JM. **119:** Bundesarchiv. **121-125:** JM. **126:** Suddeutsch. **127-131:** JM. **133:** top, JM; bottom, C. Foss collection. **134-136:** C. Foss collection. **137:** Thyssen Henschel. **138:** C. Foss collection. **139:** Krauss-Mafei. **140:** C. Foss collection. **141:** JM. **142-144:** FIAT. **145:** top, FIAT; bottom, JM. **146:** FIAT. **147:** top, JM; centre, IWM; bottom, FIAT. **149:** top, IWM; bottom, FIAT. **150-151:** Fujifotos. **152-153:** JM. **154:** Fujifotos. **155:** JM. **157:** Fujifotos; **159:** Fujifotos. **160-163:** C. Foss collection. **164-165:** DAF. **166:** top, IWM; bottom JM. **167:** IWM. **168-169:**

Novosti. **170:** JM. **172:** Novosti. **173:** top, Novosti; bottom, JM. **174-175:** JM. **176:** Novosti. **177:** JM. **178-180:** Novosti. **181-182:** JM. **185:** JM. **186-187:** Salamander Books/E and TV Films. **189:** APN. **190:** Salamander Books. **191:** Salamander Books/E and TV Films. **192:** Novosti. **193:** top, Novosti; bottom, Salamander Books/E and TV Films. **194:** top, Salamander Books/E and TV Films; bottom, JM. **195:** Novosti. **197:** left, Charles Kennedy; right, Salamander Books/E and TV Films; bottom, JM. **198:** Salamander Books. **199:** Salamander Books/E and TV Films. **201:** JM. **202:** top, JM; bottom, Swedish Army. **203:** left, JM; right, C. Foss collection; bottom Swedish Army. **207:** C. Foss collection. **208-209:** J. G. Moore collection. **210:** JM. **212-215:** JM. **216:** IWM. **217-219:** JM. **220:** US Army. **221:** Novosti. **222-225:** IWM. **226:** JM. **227:** US Army. **228:** top, US Army; bottom, IWM. **230:** top, JM; bottom, US Army. **231:** Danish Army. **232-233:** US Army. **234:** top, USMC; bottom, US Army. **235:** top, West German Army; bottom, JM. **237:** top, Aeronutronic Ford Corp; bottom, C. Foss collection. **238:** USMC. **239:** top, US Army; bottom, Aeronutronic Ford Corp. **240:** top, MOD; bottom, USMC. **241:** top, USMC; bottom, MOD. **242:** Cadillac Gage. **243:** USMC. **244:** top, Chrysler; bottom, Ford Motor Co. **245:** top, Chrysler; bottom, Ford Motor Co.

Artwork Credits

Copyright in the artwork on pages mentioned below in the property of Profile Publications Ltd, whom the publishers thank for permission to reproduce it:

Page 25; 16 (bottom and centre right); 20-21; 22-23; 27; 28-29; 30-31; 32-33; 34-35; 40-41; 44 (top); 45 (top and centre); 46 (bottom); 47 (bottom); 50; 52-53; 54-55; 60; 65; 68 (bottom); 70; 72; 75 (bottom); 77; 78-79; 81; 82-83; 85; 104 (right); 105; 106-107; 108; 109 (bottom); 110-111; 112-113; 114-115; 116-117; 118; 122-123; 124-125; 128; 129 (top and bottom); 130; 135; 146; 148 (top); 153; 154-155; 156-157; 167; 177 (top); 178 (top); 179 (centre); 180; 181 (left); 183; 184-185; 186; 187 (top) 190; 194-195 (bottom); 196 (top); 199 (top); 205; 206; 212-213; 214-215; 216-217; 218-219; 220-221; 222-223; 224; 227; 229; 231; 232-233; 236-237.

Copyright in the artwork on pages mentioned below is the property of James Leech, whom the publishers thank for permission to reproduce it:
Pages 36-37; 42-43; 88-89; 102-103; 120-121; 210-211.